Rethinking Unjust Enrichment

Rethinking Unjust Enrichment

History, Sociology, Doctrine, and Theory

Edited by
WARREN SWAIN AND SAGI PEARI

OXFORD
UNIVERSITY PRESS

Great Clarendon Street, Oxford, OX2 6DP,
United Kingdom

Oxford University Press is a department of the University of Oxford.
It furthers the University's objective of excellence in research, scholarship,
and education by publishing worldwide. Oxford is a registered trade mark of
Oxford University Press in the UK and in certain other countries

© The many contributors 2023

The moral rights of the authors have been asserted

First Edition published in 2023

All rights reserved. No part of this publication may be reproduced, stored in
a retrieval system, or transmitted, in any form or by any means, without the
prior permission in writing of Oxford University Press, or as expressly permitted
by law, by licence or under terms agreed with the appropriate reprographics
rights organization. Enquiries concerning reproduction outside the scope of the
above should be sent to the Rights Department, Oxford University Press, at the
address above

You must not circulate this work in any other form
and you must impose this same condition on any acquirer

Public sector information reproduced under Open Government Licence v3.0
(http://www.nationalarchives.gov.uk/doc/open-government-licence/open-government-licence.htm)

Published in the United States of America by Oxford University Press
198 Madison Avenue, New York, NY 10016, United States of America

British Library Cataloguing in Publication Data

Data available

Library of Congress Control Number: 2023944916

ISBN 978–0–19–287414–6

DOI: 10.1093/oso/9780192874146.001.0001

Printed and bound in the UK by
Clays Ltd, Elcograf S.p.A.

Links to third party websites are provided by Oxford in good faith and
for information only. Oxford disclaims any responsibility for the materials
contained in any third party website referenced in this work.

Foreword

Rethinking Unjust Enrichment is a collection of engaging, stimulating, and provocative essays on the 'law of unjust enrichment'. The unifying theme is to challenge and question unjust enrichment orthodoxy from numerous perspectives and by scholars from across the globe. In the life of the law, development, refinement, and sometimes radical realignment require such questions to be asked. The largest questions being asked in this book concern the content of the concept of unjust enrichment and the extent to which it can be treated as a 'universal idea' or 'overarching principle'. The views expressed by the contributing scholars range from those who seek to qualify or refine the existing structure and content of unjust enrichment to those who suggest radical restructuring or even abolition of unjust enrichment. The unique nature of this book is that it gathers a wide range of critical opinion with the goal of invigorating a constructive dialogue on the future development of this category of law.

One of the most significant lessons of this book is that answers to any questions about the structure of unjust enrichment will depend upon the reason the question is being asked. As the structure of this book powerfully shows, the nature or structure of 'unjust enrichment' may depend upon whether the question is asked from the perspective of history, sociology, theory, or doctrine—perspectives which are not rigid alternatives. Importantly, in many respects, the law of unjust enrichment, like all other areas of public and private law, is a story of levels of generality.

It is sometimes necessary to think about an area of law at a very high level of generality. This is most obvious when an area of law has historically been treated broadly or where broad sociological impact is being considered. So too with doctrine. A high level of generality can also be required by the approach taken to issues such as limitation periods, conflict of laws, or even procedural questions such as service of process outside a jurisdiction. At that high level of generality there might be dispute about the boundaries of a category of unjust enrichment: for instance, should a claim for restitution of a wrongful payment be treated in the same way as a claim for restitution of a mistaken payment or in the same way as compensation for a tort? On the other hand, at this high level of generality no reasonable court is likely to treat a claim for restitution of the value of a chattel as being analogous to a claim to enforce a contract, or to obtain monetary relief for a tort, rather than being analogous to a claim for restitution of the value of a payment made by mistake. The importance of the high level of generality is that it allows these questions to be asked in a coherent manner.

On the other hand, doctrine and theory will both sometimes require attention to be directed to lower levels of generality, particularly when issues arise such as whether analogies should be drawn in deciding how a particular type of claim should develop. Then, smaller differences between each type of claim can become more important when deciding whether an analogy can be drawn. The danger of what the editors of this excellent book describe as the 'seductive' principle of unjust enrichment is that the development of particular claims might occur by reference to principles formulated at a high level of generality. Errors will occur if relevant differences are overlooked. For instance, even in an apparently simple case where a claimant seeks restitution following a mistaken transfer of a chattel to a defendant, at the low levels of generality relevant to developing the law, the 'enrichment' of a defendant will be a different concept, requiring the application of different rules, depending upon whether a claimant seeks restitution in the form of: (1) the return of the physical chattel; (2) the creation of a trust over rights held by the defendant to the chattel; or (3) the return of the value of the defendant's rights to the chattel. The same can be said of whether an enrichment is 'at the expense of' a plaintiff or whether an enrichment is 'unjust' or 'unjustified'.

Ultimately, the level of generality at which a claim falls to be characterized will depend on the question being asked. Many of the chapters in this book do not dispute the very existence of this area of law as might have been done when the *Restatement of the Law of Restitution* was published in 1937 or even when Goff and Jones published *The Law of Restitution* in 1966. The focus is generally upon the proper arrangement of the category and its utility. Perhaps the most important question is: what should be the content of this area of law as a subject to be taught to the next generation? In this respect, as this book admirably demonstrates, the high priests and the heretics may disagree at almost every level but, for the moment, disagreement about orthodoxy requires unjust enrichment to be taught, and sceptical essays to consider the subject, at a high level of generality that includes a vast range of disparate claims. Only in that way can category errors or false analogies be highlighted. With that approach, the editors have produced a book that will be a great success in encouraging the rethinking of unjust enrichment.

JJ Edelman
High Court of Australia
Canberra
21 April 2023

Acknowledgements

We are grateful to Caitlin White and Adam Lim (both from the UWA marketing team) and Simrin Panag (JD student, UWA) for assisting with the organization of three online symposiums that took place during September 2022. The University of Auckland provided the much-needed financial support. Rachel Atkinson (WA) was the one who created the website for the project. Christian Poland (University of Auckland) did a wonderful job with the editing of the chapters. The team at Oxford University Press has contributed much to this project: Kim, Matthew, Radhika, and Shenbagarajan. Special thanks go to the commentators of the chapters, whose involvement has improved the overall quality of the collection: Professors Elise Bant, Kit Barker, Hanoch Dagan, Rachel and Tim Leow, Caprice Roberts, Zoë Sinel, and Lionel Smith. Last, but not least, we would like to thank our families: Michelle, Donna, and Mali (Sagi Peari) and Jordan (Warren Swain) for their kindness, patience, and continuous support.

Contents

Table of Cases   xi
Table of Legislation   xxiii
List of Contributors   xxvii

Introduction   1
   Warren Swain and Sagi Peari

I. HISTORY

1. Contract and Unjust Enrichment: Lessons from History?   11
   Warren Swain

2. A Tale of Transplantation: The Historical Evolution of the Law of Unjust Enrichment in China   29
   Siyi Lin

3. Law of Unjust Enrichment in India: Historical Evolution and Contemporary Challenges   55
   Arpita Gupta

II. SOCIOLOGY

4. Academics and Legal Change: Birks, Savigny, and the Law of Unjust Enrichment   77
   Sagi Peari

5. Restitution in the United States   101
   Emily Sherwin

6. What was the Problem with 'Palm Tree Justice'? Language, Justice, Equity, and Enrichment   117
   Nolan Sharkey

III. THEORY

7. *Faute de Mieux*   143
   Robert Stevens

8. Restitution, Corrective Justice, and Mistakes   163
   James Penner

9. Agreement and Restitutionary Liability for Mistaken Payments 181
    Peter Chau and Lusina Ho

10. Law of Unjust Enrichment or Law of Unjust De-Enrichment? 201
    Lutz-Christian Wolff

11. The Way Forward 219
    Peter Jaffey

12. Doctrinal Design in Unjust Enrichment: On the Relation
    of Claims for Restitution and General Private Law 237
    Nils Jansen

IV. DOCTRINE

13. Monism versus Pluralism in Unjust Enrichment 253
    Mindy Chen-Wishart and Emma Hughes

14. Unjust Enrichment: Looking for a Role 275
    Steve Hedley

15. Embracing Private Law's Miscellany? Unjustified Enrichment
    and the Civilian Category of Quasi-Contracts 317
    Pablo Letelier

16. Challenges for Canadian Unjust Enrichment 333
    Mitchell McInnes

Conclusion 353
    Sagi Peari and Warren Swain

Index 355

Table of Cases

UNITED KINGDOM

Abou-Rahmah v Abacha [2006] EWCA Civ 1492; [2007] 1 All ER (Comm) 827 ..... 262n.62
Aiken v Short (1856) 1 H & N 210; 156 ER 1180 .... 149n.18
Al Nehayan v Kent [2018] EWHC 333 (Comm); [2018] 1 CLC 216 .... 265n.88
Alec Lobb (Garages) v Total Oil [1983] 1 WLR 87 (Ch) 270n.132
Alf Vaughan & Co Ltd v Royscot Trust plc [1999] 1 All ER (Comm) 856 .... 266n.93
Allcard v Skinner (1887) 36 Ch D 145 (CA) 267, 268n.116
Aluminium Industrie Vaassen BV v Romalpa Aluminium Ltd
    [1976] 1 WLR 676 (CA).. 98n.205
Associated Japanese Bank (International) Ltd v Crédit du Nord SA
    [1989] 1 WLR 255 (QB).. 263n.64
Attorney-General v R [2003] UKPC 22; [2003] EMLR 24 .... 266n.91, 266n.99

Bank of England v Vagliano Brothers [1891] App Cas 145 .... 62n.48
Bank of India v Riat [2014] EWHC 1775 (Ch) 266n.98
Bank of Montréal v Stuart [1911] AC 120 (PC)...................... 268n.118, 268n.121
Banque Financière de la Cité v Parc (Battersea) Ltd [1999] 1 AC 221 (HL)..........77n.2,
                                                                                                            226n.19, 340n.43, 348n.88
Barclays Bank plc v O'Brien [1994] 1 AC 180 (HL) 254n.4, 255n.10, 271n.141
Barclays Bank plc v Quincecare Ltd [1992] 4 All ER 363 (QB) 128n.55
Barnes & Co v Toye (1884) 13 QBD 410 (QB)..................................... 18n.57
Barton v Armstrong [1976] AC 104 (PC) 266n.101
Barton v Gwyn-Jones [2019] EWCA Civ 1999; [2020] 2 All ER (Comm) 652 ...... 158n.42
Barton v Hodgkinson (1739) LI MS Misc 133 f 33; LI MS Hill 25 f 1;
    LI MS Hill 29 f 225 .... 16n.40
Barton v Morris [2023] UKSC 3; [2023] 2 WLR 269 .... 158–59, 158n.42
Bell v Lever Bros Ltd [1932] AC 161 (HL)................................... 264n.79
Benedetti v Sawiris [2013] UKSC 50; [2014] AC 938............ 157–58, 157n.40, 340n.43
Bilbie v Lumley (1802) 2 East 469; 102 ER 448 .... 340n.42
Blacklocks v JB Developments (Godalming) Ltd [1982] Ch 183 (Ch)............. 176n.50
Boardman v Phipps [1967] 2 AC 46 (HL) 129n.59
Borrelli v Ting [2010] UKPC 21; [2010] Bus LR 1718 .... 266n.93
Boustany v Pigott (1995) 69 P & CR 298 (PC)....................... 270n.132, 270n.135
Boyse v Rossborough (1857) 6 HLC 2 (HL) 269n.128
BP Exploration Co (Libya) Ltd v Hunt (No 2) [1979] 1 WLR 783 (QB).......... 215n.93,
                                                                                                                           216n.98, 288n.53
BP Exploration Co (Libya) Ltd v Hunt (No 2) [1981] 1 WLR 232 (CA) 288n.54
Brewer Street Investments Ltd v Barclays Woollen Co Ltd [1954] 1 QB 428 (CA) 160n.45
Bridgman v Green (1755) 2 Ves Sen 627; 28 ER 399............ 254n.4, 258n.31, 267n.106
British Bank for Foreign Trade Ltd v Novinex Ltd [1949] 1 KB 623 (CA).......... 154n.28
Brown & Davis Ltd v Galbraith [1972] 1 WLR 997 (CA)....................... 151n.19
Burn v Miller (1813) 4 Taunt 745; 128 ER 523................................ 25n.114

Capital Insurance Co Ltd v Samsoondar [2020] UKPC 33; [2021] 2 All ER 1105 ... 263n.67
Carrington v Roots (1837) 2 M & W 248; 150 ER 748 .... 20n.84

Case v Barber (1680) Sir T Raym 450; 83 ER 235 .... 20n.82
Cavendish Square Holding BV v Makdessi [2015] UKSC 67; [2016] AC 1172 .... 13n.11
Chaplin v Leslie Frewin (Publishers) Ltd [1966] Ch 71 (CA) 19n.64, 19n.72
Chase Manhattan Bank NA v Israel-British Bank (London) Ltd
    [1981] Ch 105 (Ch) 226n.21, 233n.35
Chater v Beckett (1797) 7 TR 201; 101 ER 931 .... 20n.83
Cheese v Thomas [1994] 1 WLR 129 (CA) 255n.10, 268n.115
Chillingworth v Esche [1924] 1 Ch 97 (CA) 157n.39
CIBC Mortgages plc v Pitt [1994] 1 AC 200 (HL) 268n.122, 272n.147
Clark v Malpas (1862) 4 De GF & J 401; 45 ER 1238 .... 270n.134
Clark v Malpas (1862) 31 Beav 80; 54 ER 1067 .... 270n.134
Clark v Smith (1735) LI MS Misc 37 f 98 .... 23n.99
Clarke v Prus [1995] NPC 41 (Ch) 268n.117
CMOC Sales & Marketing Ltd v Person Unknown [2018] EWHC 2230 (Comm) 226n.21
Cobbe v Yeoman's Row Management Ltd [2008] UKHL 55; [2008] 1 WLR 1752 ... 157n.39
Cooke v Tombs (1794) 2 Anst 420; 145 ER 922 .... 20n.83
Cowan v Scargill [1985] Ch 270 (Ch) 128n.56
Cowern v Nield [1912] 2 KB 419 (KB) 319n.7
Crabb v Arun DC [1976] Ch 179 (CA) 286n.39
Craig (decd), Re [1971] Ch 95 (Ch) 268n.120, 269n.123
Crédit Lyonnais Bank Nederland NV v Burch [1997] 1 All ER 144 (CA) 268n.118,
                                                              268nn.120–21, 269n.125
Crosby v Wadsworth (1805) 6 East 602; 102 ER 1419 .... 20n.84
Cutter v Powell (1795) 6 TR 320; 101 ER 573 .... 24nn.106–7

Dargamo Holdings Ltd v Avonwick Holdings Ltd [2021] EWCA Civ 1149;
    [2022] 1 All ER (Comm) 1244 .... 255n.12, 293n.96
Darjan Estate Co plc v Hurley [2012] EWHC 189 (Ch); [2012] 1 WLR 1782 ...... 272n.147
Davis Contractors v Fareham UDC [1956] AC 696 (HL) 264n.80
Decker v Pope (1757) LI MS Misc 129 (unfold) 27n.123
Denny v Hancock (1870) LR 6 Ch App 1 (CA) 14n.22
Deutsche Morgan Grenfell Group plc v Inland Revenue Comrs
    [2006] UKHL 49; [2007] 1 AC 558 .... 262n.57, 263n.66, 264–65n.84
Dextra Bank & Trust Co Ltd v Bank of Jamaica [2001] UKPC 50;
    [2002] 1 All ER (Comm) 193 .... 187n.27, 197n.70, 197n.72, 264n.76
Dick Bentley Productions Ltd v Harold Smith (Motors) Ltd
    [1965] 1 WLR 623 (CA) 126n.39
Dimond v Lovell [2002] 1 AC 384 (HL) 20n.81
Dimskal Shipping Co SA v International Transport Workers Federation
    (The Evia Luck) (No 2) [1992] 2 AC 152 (HL) 265n.88, 266n.93, 266n.99
Doyle v White City Stadium Ltd [1935] 1 KB 110 (CA) 19n.64, 19n.72
DPP for Northern Ireland v Lynch [1975] AC 653 (HL) 265n.88
DSND Subsea Ltd v Petroleum Geo-Services ASA [2000] BLR 530 (QB) 266n.97
Dyer v Dyer (1788) 2 Cox 92; 30 ER 42 .... 153n.24

Earl of Aylesford v Morris (1873) LR 8 Ch App 484 .... 270n.131, 270n.139
Earle v Peale (1711) 1 Salk 386; 91 ER 336 .... 18n.52
Edgington v Fitzmaurice (1885) 29 Ch D 459 (CA) 262n.59
Edwards (decd), Re [2007] EWHC 1119 (Ch) 269n.128
Ellis v Hamlen (1810) 3 Taunt 52; 128 ER 21 .... 24n.112
Esben Finance Ltd v Wong Hou-Lianq Neil' (2023) 86 MLR 518 .... 292n.87
Evans v Llewellin (1787) 1 Cox 333; 29 ER 1191 .... 270n.134

TABLE OF CASES   xiii

Fibrosa Spolka Akcyjna v Fairbairn Lawson Combe Barbour Ltd
   [1943] AC 32 (HL) 63n.61, 68n.89, 70n.102, 351n.105
Foskett v McKeown [2001] 1 AC 102 (HL) 217n.108
Fry v Lane (1888) 40 Ch D 312 (Ch). 270n.134

Gibbon v Mitchell [1990] 1 WLR 1304 (Ch) 176n.54
Gray v Hill (1826) Ry & M 420; 171 ER 1070. .... 156n.37
Greenwood v Bennett [1973] 1 QB 195 (CA) 174n.43
Griffith v Brymer (1903) 19 TLR 434 (KB) 264n.75
Griffiths (decd), Re [2008] EWHC 118 (Ch); [2009] Ch 162 .... 263, 264n.77
Guardians of Pontypridd Union v Drew [1927] 1 KB 214 (CA) 19n.72
Guest v Guest [2022] UKSC 27; [2022] 3 WLR 911 .... 277n.2

Hammond v Osborn [2002] EWCA Civ 885 (CA). 268n.115, 268n.121
Harris v Oke (1759) LI MS Hill 6 f 217 .... 23n.104
Hart v O'Connor [1985] AC 1000 (PC) 258n.29, 261n.45, 261n.48
Hays v Warren (1733) W Kel 117; 25 ER 522. .... 16n.37
Hedley Byrne & Co Ltd v Heller & Partners Ltd [1964] AC 465 (HL) 160n.44
Hennessy v Craigmyle & Co Ltd [1986] ICR 461 (CA) 266n.98
Hubbard v Scott [2011] EWHC 2750 (Ch) 269n.128
Huguenin v Baseley (1807) 14 Ves Jun 273; 33 ER 526. .... 254n.4
Hulle v Heightman (1802) 2 East 145; 102 ER 324 .... 24n.110
Hunt v Silk (1804) 5 East 449; 102 ER 1142 .... 24n.110
Huyton SA v Peter Cremer GmbH & Co [1999] 1 Lloyd's Rep 620 (QB). 266n.92,
                                                                                                             266n.95, 266n.99

Imperial Bank of Canada v Bank of Hamilton [1903] AC 49 (PC) 262n.58
Inche Noriah v Shaik Allie Bin Omar [1929] AC 127 (PC) 267n.105
International Energy Group Ltd v Zurich Insurance plc UK Branch
   [2015] UKSC 33; [2016] AC 509. .... 277n.1
Investment Trust Companies v Revenue and Customs Comrs [2017] UKSC 29;
   [2018] AC 275. .... 64n.65, 207n.32, 207n.33, 210n.65, 215n.93,
                                                                                  226n.19, 293n.95, 321n.19, 340n.44
Investors Compensation Scheme Ltd v West Bromwich Building Society
   [1998] 1 WLR 896 (HL). 126n.41, 126n.43
Ive v Chester (1619) Cro Jac 560; 79 ER 480 .... 18n.55

James v Thomas H Kent & Co Ltd [1951] 1 KB 551 (CA) 22, 22n.94, 156n.35, 156n.36
Jennings v Cairns [2003] EWCA Civ 1935 .... 268n.115
Johnstone v Marks (1887) 19 QBD 509 (QB) 18n.56
Jones v Churcher [2009] EWHC 722 (QB) 262n.62

Kelly v Solari (1841) 9 M & W 54; 152 ER 24. ...... 89n.109, 233n.34, 262, 262n.58, 320n.10
Keteley's Case (1613) 1 Brownl 120; 123 ER 704. .... 19n.65
Kleinwort Benson Ltd v Lincoln CC [1999] 2 AC 349 (HL) 187n.27, 197n.70,
                                                                                     262n.56, 290n.71, 320n.11, 333n.2
Kolmar Group AG v Traxpo Enterprises PVT Ltd [2010] EWHC 113 (Comm);
   [2011] 1 All ER (Comm) 46. .... 266n.97
Krell v Henry [1903] 2 KB 740 (CA). 264n.75

Lady Hood of Avalon v Mackinnon [1909] 1 Ch 476 (Ch) 5n.25, 176n.52
Lampleigh v Brathwait (1615) Hobart 105; 80 ER 255 .... 62n.45

xiv TABLE OF CASES

Leroux v Brown (1852) 12 CB 801; 138 ER 1119. .... 20n.85
Lipkin Gorman v Karpnale Ltd [1991] 2 AC 548 (HL) 3n.9, 72n.112, 203n.14,
              204n.15, 223n.16, 224, 226n.19, 237n.3, 262n.62, 333n.1, 340n.43
London Trocadero (2015) LLP v Picturehouse Cinemas Ltd
    [2021] EWHC 2591 (Ch). 312n.184

Macklin v Dowsett [2004] EWCA Civ 904 .... 268n.115
Makarell v Bachelor (1596) Cro Eliz 583; 78 ER 826 .... 18n.55
Mannai Investments Co Ltd v Eagle Star Life Assurance Co Ltd
    [1997] AC 749 (HL) 126, 126n.44
Marine Trade SA v Pioneer Freight Futures Co Ltd BVI [2009] EWHC
    2656 (Comm); [2010] 1 Lloyd's Rep 631 .... 263n.66
Martin v Webb (1763) LI MS Misc 129 f 71. .... 23n.99
Masters of Tobacco Pipe Makers Co v Loader (1851) 16 QB 765 (QB) 26n.119
Matson v Wharam (1787) 2 TR 80; 100 ER 44 .... 20n.83
May and Butcher Ltd v R [1934] 2 KB 17 (KB) 157n.41
Menelaou v Bank of Cyprus UK Ltd [2015] UKSC 66; [2016] AC 176 .... 289n.62, 340n.43
Miller v Duell (1735) HLS MS 4062 .... 23n.99
Monarch Steamship Co Ltd v Karlshamns Oljefabriker (A/B)
    [1949] AC 196 (HL). 263n.65
Moses v Macferlan (1760) 2 Burr 1005; 97 ER 676 (KB) 27n.124, 64n.63,
                                                              93n.158, 102n.4, 340n.42
Mr Keck's Case 23
Mulloy v Backer (1804) 5 East 316; 102 ER 1091 .... 24n.111
Multiservice Bookbinding Ltd v Marden [1979] Ch 84 (Ch) 270n.137

Nash v Inman [1908] 2 KB 1 (CA) 18n.58, 18n.61, 19n.68
National Commercial Bank (Jamaica) Ltd v Hew [2003] UKPC 51;
    [2004] 2 LRC 396 .... 267n.113
Niersmans v Pesticcio [2004] EWCA Civ 372. .... 268n.115
Niru Battery Manufacturing Co v Milestone Trading Ltd [2002] EWHC
    1425 (Comm); [2002] 2 All ER (Comm) 705 .... 262n.62

O'Rorke v Bolingbroke (1877) 2 App Cas 814 (HL). 270n.139
Occidental Worldwide Investment Corp v Skibs A/S Avanti
    (The Siboen and the Sibotre) [1976] 1 Lloyd's Rep 293 (QB) 265n.86
Ogilvie v Littleboy (1897) 13 TLR 399 (CA); sub nom Ogilvie v Allen
    (1889) 15 TLR 294 (HL) 176n.51, 178, 308n.176
Orakpo v Manson Investments Ltd [1978] AC 95 (HL). 255n.14, 281n.18
Orwell v Mortoft (1505). 15n.31
Overseas Tankship (UK) Ltd v Morts Dock & Engineering Co Ltd
    (The Wagon Mound) [1961] AC 388 (PC) 342n.56
Overseas Tankship (UK) Ltd v The Miller Steamship Co Pty (The Wagon
    Mound (No 2)) [1967] AC 617 (PC) 342n.56

Pao On v Lau Yiu Long [1980] AC 614 (PC). 265n.86
Patel v Mirza [2016] UKSC 42; [2017] AC 467 .... 255n.12, 255n.14, 311n.181
Pepper v Burland (1791) Peake 139; 170 ER 107. .... 24n.105
Peters v Fleming (1840) 6 M & W 42; 151 ER 314. .... 59n.19, 70n.101, 261n.47
Photo Production Ltd v Securicor Transport Ltd [1980] AC 827 (HL) 13n.11
Pickering v Gunning (1627) Palm 528; 81 ER 1204 .... 18n.55, 19n.66
Pitt v Holt [2011] EWCA Civ 197; [2012] Ch 132. .... 263n.71

TABLE OF CASES xv

Pitt v Holt [2013] UKSC 26; [2013] 2 AC 108 .... 176–77, 176n.53, 177n.55, 197n.71, 198n.74, 262n.58, 263n.66, 263n.70, 264n.77, 264n.81, 265n.85, 294n.100, 308n.176
Planché v Colburn (1831) 5 C & P 58; 172 ER 876 .... 160n.45
Planché v Colburn (1831) 8 Bing 14; 131 ER 305 .... 25, 25n.116, 26n.120
Portman Building Society v Dusangh [2000] 2 All ER (Comm) 221 .... 269n.124, 270n.137
Powell v Braun [1954] 1 WLR 401 (CA) 155n.32
Prudential Assurance Co Ltd v Revenue and Customs Comrs [2018] UKSC 39;
    [2019] AC 929....................... 288n.52, 289n.63, 294n.99, 321n.19, 333n.4
Pulbrook v Lawes (1876) 1 QBD 284 (QB) 21–22, 21n.90
Pykeryng v Thurgoode (1532).. 15n.30

R (Child Poverty Action Group) v Secretary of State for Work and Pensions
    [2010] UKSC 54; [2011] 2 AC 15 .... 288n.51
R (Rowe) v Vale of White Horse DC [2003] EWHC 388 (Admin) 263n.68
R Leslie Ltd v Sheill [1914] 3 KB 607 (CA)................................... 260n.43
Randall v Randall [2004] EWHC 2258 (Ch).................................. 270n.138
RE Jones Ltd v Waring and Gillow Ltd [1926] AC 670 (HL) 262n.58
Reade v Lamb (1851) 6 Ex 130; 155 ER 483.................................... 20n.84
Retchford v Spurlinge (1591) 14n.28
Rhodes, Re (1890) 44 ChD 94 (CA) 19n.70
Richardson v Mellish (1824) 2 Bing 229; 130 ER 294 .... 337n.29
Roberts v Gray [1913] 1 KB 520 (CA) 19n.74
Royal Bank of Scotland plc v Etridge (No 2) [1998] 4 All ER 705 (CA) 255n.10
Royal Bank of Scotland plc v Etridge (No 2) [2001] UKHL 44;
    [2002] 2 AC 773 .... 254n.3, 256n.20, 258n.30, 267, 267n.103, 267n.113, 268n.119, 269n.127, 271–72, 271n.140, 271n.143, 272n.148
Ruxley Electronics and Construction Ltd v Forsyth [1996] AC 344 (HL).......... 209n.52

Salisbury v Yates (1724) LI MS Hill 8 f 208 .... 23n.103
Sapporo Breweries Ltd v Lupofresh Ltd [2013] EWCA Civ 948; [2013] CN 1213..... 265n.88
Sayre v Hughes (1868) LR 5 Eq 376 .... 153n.24
Scarisbrick v Parkinson (1869) 20 LT 175 (QB) 21n.92, 22
Scott v Pattison [1923] 2 KB 723 (KB) 22, 22n.93, 156n.35
Sempra Metals Ltd v IRC [2007] UKHL 34; [2008] 1 AC 561 .... 226n.19, 294n.99
Shogun Finance Ltd v Hudson [2003] UKHL 62; [2004] 1 AC 919 .... 176n.48
Simon v Metivier (1766) 1 Wm Bla 599; 96 ER 347 .... 21n.87
Sinclair v Brougham [1914] AC 398 (HL) 319n.6
Skandinaviska Enskilda Banken AB (Publ) v Conway [2019] UKPC 36;
    [2020] AC 1111.. 340n.43
Slade's Case (1602) 4 Co Rep 92b; 76 ER 1074................................. 15n.32
Smith v Hughes (1871) LR 6 QB 597 (QB)..................................... 14n.22
Souch v Strawbridge (1846) 2 CB 808; 135 ER 1161.......................... 21nn.87–88
Steam Saw Mills Co Ltd v Baring Bros and Co Ltd [1922] 1 Ch 244 (CA).......... 172n.36
Swynson Ltd v Lowick Rose LLP [2017] UKSC 32;
    [2018] AC 313.. 255n.12, 321n.19, 340n.44

Tamplin v James (1880) 15 Ch D 215 (CA) 14n.22
Taylor v Laird (1856) 25 LJ Ex 329 (Exch) 89n.110, 227n.22
Taylor v Motability Finance Ltd [2004] EWHC 2619 (Comm)................... 338n.35
Tecnimont Arabia Ltd v National Westminster Bank plc
    [2022] EWHC 1172 (Comm) 263n.67, 293n.95

xvi TABLE OF CASES

Test Claimants in the FII Group Litigation v Revenue and Customs Comrs
    [2012] UKSC 19; [2012] 2 AC 337 .... 255n.12
The Moorcock (1889) 14 PD 64 (CA).. 126n.40
The Port Caledonia and the Ann [1903] P 184 (Prob) 265n.89
The Six Carpenters' Case (1610) 8 Co Rep 146a; 77 ER 695 .... 15, 15n.34
Thomas v Brown (1876) 1 QBD 714 (QB).. 20n.86
Thurstan v Nottingham Permanent Benefit Building Society [1902] 1 Ch 1 (CA).... 19n.73
Times Travel (UK) Ltd v Pakistan International Airlines Corp [2021] UKSC 40;
    [2021] 3 WLR 727................ 266n.94, 266n.99, 266n.100, 266n.102, 270n.133
Trustee of the Property of FC Jones & Sons v Jones [1997] Ch 159 (CA)......... 217n.108
Twinsectra Ltd v Yardley [2002] UKHL 12; [2002] 2 AC 164 .... 125n.37

United Australia Ltd v Barclays Bank Ltd [1941] AC 1 (HL)..................... 335n.15
Universe Tankships Inc of Monrovia v International Transport Workers
    Federation (The Universe Sentinel) [1983] 1 AC 366 (HL) 265n.88, 266n.91, 266n.99

Valentini v Canali (1889) 24 QBD 166 (QB) 260n.39

Way v Latilla [1937] 3 All ER 759 (HL) 154n.29, 155, 156, 157–58
Weatherby v Banham (1832) 5 C & P 228; 172 ER 950........................... 184n.13
Weaver v Boroughs (1725) 1 Stra 648; 93 ER 757; LI MS Hill 12 (1) f 6 .... 23n.97
Westdeutsche Landesbank Girozentrale v Islington LBC
    [1996] AC 669 (HL) 139n.90, 262n.61, 321n.18
Whittingham v Hill (1618) Cro Jac 494; 79 ER 421 .... 18n.55
Whittingham v Murdy (1889) 60 LT 956 (QB) 19n.66, 19n.73
Whittington v Seale-Hayne (1900) 82 LT 49 (HC)......................... 152n.22, 153
William Lacey (Hounslow) Ltd v Davis [1957] 1 WLR 932 (QB)................ 158n.42
Williams v Wheeler (1860) 8 CB (NS); 141 ER 1181 .... 20n.85
Williams v Williams [2003] EWHC 742 (Ch)................................. 255n.11

Zurich Insurance Co plc v Hayward [2016] UKSC 48; [2017] AC 142 .... 262n.60

NATIONAL CASES

Australia

Australian Financial Services and Leasing Pty Ltd v Hills Industries Ltd
    [2014] HCA 14; (2014) 253 CLR 560 .... 149n.17
Birtchnell v Equity Trustees, Executors & Agency Co Ltd (1929) 42 CLR 384 ...... 129n.59
Brambles Holdings Ltd v Bathurst CC [2001] NSWCA 61; (2001) 53 NSWLR 153 .... 126n.42
Bridgewater v Leahy (1998) 194 CLR 457 .... 270n.138
Brunninghausen v Glavanics [1999] NSWCA 199;
    (1999) 46 NSWLR 538.. 134–37, 134n.80, 138
Bryant Bros v Thiele [1923] SASR 393 (SCFC).............................. 125n.32
Byrnes v Kendle [2011] HCA 26; (2011) 243 CLR 253......................... 126n.43
Codelfa Constructions Pty Ltd v State Rail Authority (NSW)
    (1982) 149 CLR 337 .... 126n.43
Commercial Bank of Australia Ltd v Amadio (1983) 151 CLR 447 .... 267n.104
Commissioner of Stamp Duties (Qld) v Jolliffe (1920) 28 CLR 178............. 127n.46
Crescendo Management Pty Ltd v Westpac Banking Corp
    (1988) 19 NSWLR 40 (NSWCA) 265n.88, 266n.93
David Securities Pty Ltd v Commonwealth Bank of Australia
    (1992) 175 CLR 353 .... 209n.45, 333n.1

TABLE OF CASES   xvii

Equuscorp Pty Ltd v Haxton [2012] HCA 7; (2012) 246 CLR 498 .... 5n.28
Farah Constructions Pty Ltd v Say-Dee Pty Ltd [2007] HCA 22; (2007) 230 CLR 89 ..... 5n.26
Hospital Products Ltd v United States Surgical Corp
    (1984) 156 CLR 41 .... 128n.47, 133, 133n.78
Hyhonie Holdings Pty Ltd v Leroy [2003] NSWSC 624........................ 125n.36
Jelekainen v Frikton [2007] QSC 98.. 125n.32
Lumbers v W Cook Builders Pty Ltd [2008] HCA 27; (2008) 232 CLR 635 ..... 22n.95, 149n.17
Mann v Paterson Constructions Pty Ltd [2019] HCA 32;
    (2019) 267 CLR 560 .... 5n.28, 312n.184, 338n.35, 341n.45
Pavey & Matthews Pty Ltd v Paul (1987) 162 CLR 221 .... 5n.28, 20n.81,
                                                                              157n.38, 158, 159, 290n.70, 340n.43
Roxborough v Rothmans of Pall Mall Australia Ltd [2001] HCA 68;
    (2001) 208 CLR 516 .... 5n.26
Starr v Starr [1935] SASR 263 (SC).. 125n.35
State Rail Authority of NSW v Heath Outdoor Pty Ltd (1986) 7 NSWLR 170 (CA) 125n.33
Thorne v Kennedy [2017] HCA 49; (2017) 263 CLR 85....................... 267n.104
Waltons Stores (Interstate) Ltd v Maher (1988) 164 CLR 387............. 160–61, 160n.43

Canada

100193 PEI Inc v Canada 2016 FCA 280 .... 348–49n.92
1242311 Alberta Ltd v Tricon Developments Inc 2020 ABQB 411 .... 343n.69
Air Canada v British Columbia [1989] 1 SCR 1161 .... 333n.2, 344n.74
Air Canada v British Columbia [1989] 2 SCR 1067 .... 337n.24
Air Canada v Liquor Control Board of Ontario [1997] 2 SCR 581..... 344n.74, 346–47n.87
Alberta Union of Provincial Employees v Alberta (Boulter Grievance)
    (2016) LAC (4th) 149.. 343n.64
Alberta v Elder Advocates of Alberta Society 2011 SCC 24;
    [2011] 2 SCR 261 .... 333n.5, 337–38n.32
Alterna Savings and Credit Union Ltd v Norman [2006] OJ No 485 (ONSC) 344n.71
Annapolis (County) v Kings Transit Authority 2012 NSSC 401.................. 343n.64
Atlantic Lottery Corp Inc v Babstock 2020 SCC 19 .... 334n.10, 335n.15, 335n.16,
                                                                                       337–38n.32, 341n.48
Attorney General of Canada v Gladstone 2005 SCC 21; [2005] 1 SCR 325 ..... 337–38n.32,
                                                                                                       341n.48, 341n.51
Attorney General of Nova Scotia v Walsh 2002 SCC 83; [2002] 4 SCR 325......... 337n.23
Balmoral Holdings Inc v Rogers Communications Inc 2021 BCSC 2330 .... 344n.73
Bank of Montreal v Asia Pacific International Inc 2018 ONSC 4215.............. 343n.69
Bank of Nova Scotia v Jorgensen [2008] OJ No 1490 (ONSC) 344n.71, 344n.73
Barafield Realty Ltd v Just Energy (BC) Limited Partnership
    2015 BCCA 421 .... 343n.67, 344n.72, 346–47n.87
Barclays Bank Ltd v WJ Simms Son & Cooke (Southern) Ltd
    [1980] 1 QB 677 (QB) 262n.55, 344n.74
Best v Hendry 2021 NLCA 43... 345n.78
Bhasin v Hrynew 2014 SCC 71; [2014] 3 SCR 494 .... 345n.81
Binichakis v Smitherman 2009 BCPC 131 .... 340n.42
BMP Global Distribution Inc v Bank of Nova Scotia 2009 SCC 15;
    [2009] 1 SCR 504 .... 337n.31, 343, 343n.65, 344n.71, 345–46
BNSF Railway Co v Teck Metals Ltd 2016 BCCA 350 .... 345n.77
British Columbia Hydro and Power Authority v BG Checo International Ltd
    [1993] 1 SCR 12 .... 344n.70
Canada (Attorney General) v Geophysical Services Inc 2022 NSCA 41 .... 341n.47

xviii   TABLE OF CASES

Canadian Imperial Bank of Commerce v Bloomforex Corp 2020 ONSC 69 .... 343n.69
Canadian Imperial Bank of Commerce v Desrochers 2020 ONSC 7629........... 345n.79
Canadian Pacific Air Lines Ltd v British Columbia [1989] 1 SCR 1133..... 333n.2, 344n.74
Cannon v Funds for Canada Foundation 2012 ONSC 399 .... 333n.5
Capilano Mobile Park v Squamish Indian Band 2016 BCCA 437 .... 346–47n.87
Catalyst Capital Group Inc v Dundee Kilmer Developments Limited
  Partnership 2020 ONCA 272 .... 340n.40
Central Guaranty Trust Co v Dixdale Mortgage Investment Corp
  [1994] OJ No 2949 (ONCA) 344n.74
Central Trust Co v Rafuse [1986] 2 SCR 147................................. 344n.70
Chao Yin Canada Group Inc v Xenova Property Development Ltd
  2021 BCSC 1445.. 333n.3
Chevallier Estate v Chevallier Geo-Con Ltd 2019 ABQB 190................... 344n.71
Chevron Canada Resources v Canada (Attorney General) 2022 ABCA 108 .... 345n.76
CIBC Trust Corp v Bayly 2005 BCSC 133 .... 344n.73
Cie Immobilière Viger Ltée v Lauréat Giguère Inc [1977] 2 SCR 67.............. 336n.21
Citadel General Assurance Co v Lloyds Bank Canada [1997] 3 SCR 805 ....334n.6,
                                                           337n.24, 346–47n.87
Consulate Ventures Inc v Amico Contracting & Engineering
  (1992) Inc 2011 ONCA 418... 343n.68
County of Carleton v City of Ottawa [1965] SCR 663 .... 346–47n.87
CropConnect Conference Inc v Bank of Montreal 2020 MBQB 186.............. 343n.69
Dantzer v CP Loewen Enterprises Ltd (cob Loewen Windows) 2004 ABQB 6,
  aff'd Dantzer v CP Loewen Enterprises Ltd (cob Loewen Windows)
  2005 ABCA 159 .... 346–47n.87
Deglman v Guaranty Trust Co of Canada [1954] SCR 725 .... 156n.37, 159, 161,
                                        290n.69, 334n.9, 343n.66, 346–47n.87, 350n.104
Dobson v Dobson (Litigation Guardian of) [1999] 2 SCR 753.................. 349n.101
Dyson Estate v Moser 2003 BCSC 1720...................................... 344n.73
Ermineskin Indian Band v Canada 2009 SCC 9; [2009] 1 SCR 222 ....337–38n.32, 341n.48
Eurig Estate, Re [1998] 2 SCR 565 .... 337n.24
Falcke v Scottish Imperial Insurance Co (1886) 34 ChD 234 (CA) 217n.111
Garland v Consumers' Gas Co Ltd 2004 SCC 25; [2004] 1 SCR 629.......... 6n.29, 337n.25,
                        337n.26, 337n.30, 338–40, 338n.33, 339n.36, 340n.42, 341, 342–44,
                        345–46, 345n.80, 346–47n.87, 348n.90, 350n.104, 351
Gold v Rosenberg [1997] 3 SCR 767... 337n.24
Gould v Gould Estate (Trustee of) 2009 BCSC 1528 .... 151n.19, 346–47n.87
Great Peace Shipping Ltd v Tsavliris Salvage (International) Ltd
  [2002] EWCA Civ 1407; [2003] QB 679 .... 263n.64
Greenwood v Bennett [1973] QB 195 (CA).................................. 306n.164
Gregory N Harney Law Corp (cob Shields Harney) v Angleland Holdings Inc
  2016 BCCA 262 .... 343n.68
Halpern v Halpern [2007] EWCA Civ 291; [2008] QB 195...................... 266n.96
Hercules Managements Ltd v Ernst & Young [1997] 2 SCR 165................. 349n.97
Hertz Corp v McLaren Collision Centre 2016 ONSC 1327........... 151n.19, 346–47n.87
Hopp v Lepp [1980] 2 SCR 192.. 350n.102
Horsley v MacLaren [1972] SCR 441.. 349n.96
Huang v Li 2020 BCSC 1727 .... 343n.69
i Trade Finance Inc v Bank of Montreal 2011 SCC 26; [2011] 2 SCR 360 .... 337–38n.32
Ileman v Rogers Communications Inc 2014 BCSC 1002....................... 345n.79
Ileman v Rogers Communications Inc 2015 BCCA 260 .... 345n.79
Imperial Loan Co Ltd v Stone [1892] 1 QB 599 (CA)................... 261n.45, 261n.48

Intermarket Cam Ltd v Weiss 2021 ONSC 4445.................................342n.59
International Longshore & Warehouse Union, Local 502 v Ford
    2016 BCCA 226 ....343n.67, 346–47n.87
Jedfro Investments (USA) Ltd v Jacyk 2007 SCC 55; [2007] 3 SCR 679........ 337–38n.32,
                                                          341n.48, 346–47n.87
Just v British Columbia [1989] 2 SCR 1228...................................349n.98
Kerr v Baranow 2011 SCC 10; [2011] 1 SCR 269 ....334nn.7–9, 337–38n.32,
                        341n.47, 342n.61, 343n.63, 346n.85, 346–47n.87, 348n.91
Kingstreet Investments Ltd v New Brunswick (Finance) 2007 SCC 1;
    [2007] 1 SCR 3 .... 207n.32, 214n.80, 337–38n.32, 342n.62, 348n.90
KLB v British Columbia 2003 SCC 51; [2003] 2 SCR 403 ....128n.55
Lac Minerals Ltd v International Corona Resources Ltd [1989] 2 SCR 574 ....334n.6
Levesque v New Brunswick 2010 NBQB 150 ....343n.68
Lloyds Bank plc v Independent Insurance Co Ltd [2000] QB 110 (CA) 262n.57
Low v Pfizer Canada Inc 2014 BCSC 1469....................................339n.36
Low v Pfizer Canada Inc 2015 BCCA 506 ....339n.36
MacLellan v Morash 2006 NSSC 101 ....340n.40
Manning v Algard Estate 2008 BCSC 1129; Pershad v Lachan 2015 ONSC 5290....342n.58
Maver v Greenheat Energy Corp 2012 BCSC 1139 ....343n.68
Montreal Tramways Co v Léveillé [1933] SCR 456.............................349n.101
Moore v Sweet 2018 SCC 52; [2018] 3 SCR 303 ......333–34nn.5–7, 337–38n.32, 341n.47,
                                                          345n.81, 346–47n.87
Mustapha v Culligan of Canada Ltd 2008 SCC 27; [2008] 2 SCR 114 ....349n.100
Nepean (Township) Hydro Electric Commission v Ontario Hydro
    [1982] 1 SCR 347 ....337n.24, 344n.74
Newbigging v Adam (1886) 34 ChD 582 (CA).................................152n.22
Newman v Beta Maritime Ltd 2018 BCSC 1442................ 343n.67, 343n.69, 345n.75
Nicholson v Brown Estate 2018 BCSC 141 ....345n.79
Nishi v Rascal Trucking Ltd 2013 SCC 33; [2013] 2 SCR 438 ....346–47n.87
NR Excavating & Services Ltd v Mand 2013 BCSC 723........................346–47n.87
Odhavji Estate v Woodhouse 2003 SCC 69; [2003] 3 SCR 263 ....349n.98
Ontario (Pension Board) v Hosack [2004] OJ No 1105 (ONSC) 344n.71
Pacific National Investments Ltd v Victoria (City) 2004 SCC 75;
    [2004] 3 SCR 575 ....337–38n.32, 339n.36, 341n.51
Palachik v Kiss [1983] 1 SCR 623 ....337n.24
Patel v Chief Medical Supplies Ltd 2019 ABQB 760.............................333n.3
Pattison Outdoor Advertising Ltd v Winchester Real Estate Investment
    Trust Ltd 2018 ONSC 4277 ....344n.71, 344n.73
Pearce v 4 Pillars Consulting Group Inc 2021 BCCA 198 ....333n.3
Perfect Auto Lease & Sales Inc (cob Pals Auto Wholesale) v Gagnier Trucking
    (Fingal) Ltd (cob Beaudry Bros) [2007] OJ No 5471 (ONSC) 344n.71
Peter v Beblow [1993] 1 SCR 980 ......334n.7, 334n.9, 337n.23, 346n.86, 348–49nn.91–92
Pettkus v Becker [1980] 2 SCR 834.......... 215n.92, 334n.9, 336nn.21–22, 338, 341n.50,
                                              343–44, 346–47n.87, 348n.91, 350n.104
Pinnacle Bank NA v 1317414 Ontario Inc (cob Jay-B Conversions)
    [2002] OJ No 281 (ONCA) 344n.71
Pro-Sys Consultants Ltd v Microsoft Corp 2013 SCC 57;
    [2013] 3 SCR 477 ....333n.5, 335n.13, 337–38n.32, 346–47n.87
Professional Institute of the Public Service of Canada v Attorney General
    of Canada 2012 SCC 71; [2012] 3 SCR 660 ....334n.7, 337–38n.32, 348–49n.92
R v Imperial Tobacco Canada Ltd 2011 SCC 42; [2011] 3 SCR 45 ....349n.97
R v Martel Building Ltd 2000 SCC 60; [2000] 2 SCR 860.......................349n.99

Radio 1540 Ltd v Muhammad 2018 ONSC 1377 ....343n.69
Rathwell v Rathwell [1978] 2 SCR 436 ....336n.21
Rawluk v Rawluk [1990] 1 SCR 70 ....334n.9
Reference Re: Goods and Services Tax [1992] 2 SCR 445 ....337n.23, 346–47n.87
Regional Municipality of Peel v Canada [1992] 3 SCR 762 ....337n.24, 340n.41,
   345n.82, 346–47n.87
Reibl v Hughes [1980] 2 SCR 880 ....350n.102
Robinson v Saskatoon (City) 2010 SKQB 98 ....337n.29
Rosenfeldt v Olson (1984) 16 DLR (4th) 103 (BCSC) 335n.14
Rosenfeldt v Olson (1986) 25 DLR (4th) 472 (BCCA) 335n.14
Royal Bank v The King [1931] 2 DLR 685 (MBKB) 344n.71
Rural Municipality of Storthoaks v Mobil Oil Canada Ltd [1976] 2 SCR 147 ....333n.1
Saadati v Moorhead 2017 SCC 28; [2017] 1 SCR 543 ....349n.100
Samji (Trustee of) v Whitmore 2017 BCSC 1917 ....343n.67
Sanderson v Campsall 2000 BCSC 583 ....151n.19, 346–47n.87
Serbian League of Canada v Stojanovich 2020 ONSC 105. . . . . 151n.19, 346–47n.87
Shamrock Fencing (1992) Ltd v Walker 2016 BCPC 244........................343n.68
Sivia v British Columbia (Superintendent of Motor Vehicles) 2016 BCCA 245 .....343n.67
Smith (Litigation Guardian of) v Croft [2015] OJ No 517 (ONSC) 342n.60
Sorochan v Sorochan [1986] 2 SCR 38...................................334n.9, 336n.22
Steele Industrial Supplies Inc v Elliott 2019 ONSC 3904 ....342n.58, 346–47n.87
Sun-Rype Products Ltd v Archer Daniels Midland Co 2013 SCC 58;
   [2013] 3 SCR 545 ....337–38n.32
Tappenden v Artus [1964] 2 QB 185 (CA)......................................151n.19
Van Camp v Chrome Horse Motorcycle Inc 2015 ABCA 83....................345n.76
Walsh v Quoddy Holdings Ltd 2006 NBQB 356 ....344n.71, 344n.73
Wong v Jang 2015 BCSC 1540..343n.67

Hong Kong

Globenet Droid Ltd v Hong Kong Hang Lung Electronic Co
   [2016] HKCU 1559; [2016] 3 HKLRD 863 ....203n.14

India

A Shanmugam v Ariya Kshatriya Rajakula Vamsathu Madalaya
   Nandhavana Paripalanai Sangam (2012) 6 SCC 430 ....66n.74
Akuate Internet Services v Star India Pvt Ltd (2013) SCC OnLine Del 3344 ....70n.100
Ananda Kishore Choudhury v Panchu Kapali AIR 1934 Cal 7.....................60n.32
Annamma v Ouseph Tressiamma AIR 1975 Ker 185..........................73n.116
Arulanandam Vethakannu Nadar v Bhagavathi Pillai Thankachi AIR 1972 Mad 207 .....61n.40
AV Palanivelu Mudaliar v Neelavathi Ammal AIR 1937 PC 50 ....63n.53, 63n.55
Balwantrao v Tulsa Pandharihath AIR 1937 Nag 225 ....59n.28
Banwarllal v Rajkishore Guru AIR 1946 Nag 21...............................59n.28
Bikram Chatterji v Union of India 68
Biraj Krishna v Purna Chandra AIR 1939 Cal 645..............................60n.33
Damodara Mudaliar v Secretary of State for India (1894) 18 Mad 88 ....62n.46, 62n.49
Fatima Khatoon Chowdrain v Mahomed Jan Chowdry (1868) 12 Moo Ind App 65 ...57n.11
Futteh Ali v Gunganath Roy (1881) 8 Cal 113.........................60, 60n.33, 60n.34
Grindlays Bank Ltd v Income Tax Officer 1980 AIR 656.........................66n.76
Heerachand v Saraswathy Ammal (2000) 3 CTC 694 ....59n.26
Indian Aluminium Co Ltd v Thane Municipal Corp AIR 1992 SC 53..............71n.107
Indian Council for Enviro-Legal Action v Union of India 2011 (8) SCC 161 ....73n.114

Indian Council for Enviro-Legal Action v Union of India
 (2011) 12 SCC 768 .... 67n.82, 68n.88
Indore Development Authority v Manoharlal (2020) 8 SCC 129 .... 66nn.73–75, 67n.81
Jagon Ram Marwari v Mahadeo Prosad Sahu (1909) ILR 36 Cal 768 ...... 59n.18, 70n.101
Jayagopal Patnaik v Chairman Puri Joint Water Works Committee AIR 1964 Ori 69..... 63n.57
Karim Khan Mahtab Khan v Jaikiran Gadadmal Marwadi AIR 1937 Ngp 390 ...... 59n.23
Kavita Trehan v Balsara Hygience Products Ltd AIR 1995 SC 441................ 67n.80
Lachmiram v Pahlad Singh AIR 1925 Ngp 33; Mahmood Ali v Chinki Shah
 AIR 1930 All 128.. 59n.22
M Vedachala Mudaliar v S Rangaraju Naidu AIR (1960) 1 Mad LJ 445............. 60n.33
Mafatlal Industries Ltd v Union of India (1997) 5 SCC 536................ 64n.67, 65n.70,
  70n.103, 71, 71nn.107–8, 71n.109
Modi Vanaspati Manufacturing Co v Katihar Jute Mills Pvt Ltd AIR
 1969 Cal 496 .... 73n.116
Mohori Bibee v Dharmodas Ghose (1903) 30 Cal 539 (PC) 58n.15
Mojiram v Sagarmal AIR 1920 NAG 119....................................... 59n.28
Mothooranath Chuttopadhya v Kristokumar Ghose (1879) ILR 4 Cal 369 .... 60n.36
MS Devoraj v SV Krishnamurthy AIR 1969 Mys 350 .... 63nn.57–58
Mulamchand v State of Madhya Pradesh AIR 1968 SC 1218 ...... 63n.60, 63n.62, 70n.102
Munni Bibi v Triloki Nath AIR 1932 All 332................................. 61n.41
Muppudathi Pillai v Krishnaswami Pillai (1959) 2 MLJ 225..................... 59n.29
Nandlal Singh v Ram Kirit Singh AIR 1950 Pat 212............................ 60n.33
Nilkanth v Chandrabhan AIR 1922 Ngp 247 .... 58n.17
P Subbiah Mooppanar v SS Venkatarama Ayyangar AIR 1955 Mad 265............ 59n.27
Padmawati v Harijan Sewak Sangh 154 (2008) DLT 411........................ 66n.78
Prosunno Kumar v Jamaluddin 1914 Cal 672................................. 60n.32
Rajani Kanta v Rama Hath 1915 Cal 310.................................... 60n.32
Rakurti Manikyam v Medidi Satyanarayana AIR 1972 AP 367 .... 63n.52
Ram Lal v Khiroda Mohini 1914 Cal 208.................................... 60n.32
Ram Pratap Kamalia Mills v State of Bihar AIR 1963 Pat 153.................... 63n.54
Ram Tuhul Singh v Biseswar Lall Sahoo (1875) LR 3 IA 131..................... 61n.39
Rambux Chittangeo v Modhoosoodun Paul Chawdhry
 (1867) 7 WR (India) 377 .... 57n.12, 69n.94
Ramchandra v Hari AIR 1936 Ngp 12 .... 59n.21
Rameshwar v State of Haryana (2018) 6 SCC 215............................. 68n.87
Ramkishen Singh v Dulichand (1881) ILR 7 Cal 648...................... 61, 61n.38
Sadasheo Balaji v Firm Hiralal Ramgopal AIR 1938 Ngp 65: 175 IC 149 .... 59n.20
Sales Tax Officer, Banaras v Kanhaiya Lal Mukundalal Saraf 1959 SCR 1350......... 64n.69
Saran v Narayan Das AIR 1971 All 43 .... 63n.56
Sham Charan Mal v Chowdhry Debya Singh Pahraj (1894) 21 Cal 872 .... 59n.24
Shankerlal v Motilal AIR 1957 Raj 267..................................... 60n.33
Shiv Shankar Dal Mills v State of Haryana AIR 1980 SC 1037 .....71nn.107–8, 72, 72n.111
South Eastern Coalfields Ltd v State of MP (2003) 8 SCC 648 .... 66nn.74–75, 66n.79
Sree Rajah Vatsavaya Venkata Simhadri Jagapatiraju Bahadur Garuand His
 Legal Representative v Sree Rajah Thyada Pusapati Rudra Sri Lakshmi
 Nrusimha Roopa Sadrusannamarad Dugaraju Dakshina Kavata Dugaraju
 Bahadur Garu (1915) 39 Mad 795 .... 60n.33
Sri Devora Shiba Prasad Singh v Maharaja Srish Chandra Nandi (1950) 52 BOMLR 17 .... 64n.66
State of Gujarat v Essar Oil Ltd (2012) 3 SCC 522.............................. 66n.78
State of Madhya Pradesh v Vyankatlal AIR 1985 SC 901....................... 71n.107
State of West Bengal v BK Mondal & Sons 1962 AIR 779 .... 62n.51, 63n.57, 63n.59,
  69n.90, 70n.98

Subramania Iyer v Vengappa Reddi (1909) 19 MLJ 750. . . . . 60n.30
Sudhangshu Kumar Roy v Banamali Roy AIR 1946 Cal 63. . . . . 60n.33
Tata Engineering of Locomotive Co Ltd v Municipal Corp AIR 1992 SC 645 . . . . . . 71n.107
United India Fire and General Insurance Co Ltd v Pelaniappa Transport
    Carriers AIR 1986 AP 32. . . . . 60n.31
Watkins v Dhunnoo Baboo (1881) ILR 7 Cal 140. . . . . 59n.24

New Zealand

Coleman v Myers [1977] 2 NZLR 225 (CA) 134–38, 134n.79, 136n.86

Singapore

BOM v BOK [2018] SGCA 83; [2019] 1 SLR 349 . . . . 254n.4
Pinkroccade Educational Services Pte Ltd, Re [2002] SGHC 186;
    [2002] 4 SLR 867. . . . . 177n.58

South Africa

Divisional Council of Aliwal North v De Wet (1890) 7 SC 232. . . . . 264n.78

United States

Banque Worms v BankAmerica International 570 NE 2d 189 (NY 1991). 109n.33
Boomer v Muir 24 P 2d 570 (Cal App 1933) 338n.35
Bright v Boyd 4 F Cas 127 (CCD Me 1841) 102n.7
Cahill v Hall 161 Mass 512; 37 NE 573 (1894). 151n.19
Cook County v Barrett 344 NE 2d 540 (Ill App 1975) 109n.33
Effinger v Hall 81 Va 94 (1885) 102n.8
Kansas v Nebraska 574 US 445 (2015) 110n.37
Marvin v Marvin 557 P 2d 106 (Cal 1976). 109n.33
Meinhard v Salmon 249 NY 458; 164 NE 545 (1928). 130n.64
Olwell v Nye & Nissen Co 173 P 2d 652 (Wash 1946) 106n.20, 109n.33
Paramount Film Distributing Corp v State of New York 285 NE 2d 695
    (NY 1972) 109n.33
Pilot Life Ins Co v Cudd 36 SE 2d 860 (SC 1945) 106n.21
Seegers v Sprague 236 NW 2d 227 (Wisc 1975) 109n.33
Ulmer v Farnsworth 15 A 65 (Me SC 1888). 339n.38
Whitney v Richardson 31 Vt 300 (1858) 102n.8

Table of Legislation

AUSTRLIA

Conveyancing Act 1919 (NSW)
   s 54(a)........................125n.34

CANADA

Quebec's Civil Code SQ 1991
   c 64, Art 1494 ....339n.39
Law Reform Act 1993 (SNB),
   ch L-1.2, s 2 ....350n.102

CHINA

Civil Code of the People's Republic of China (promulgated by the National People's Congress [NPC] on 28 May 2020, effective 1 January 2021)........29–30, 34–37, 41–42, 44–45, 46, 47, 48–52, 53–54
   Art 118...........................47
   Art 122.....................44–45, 47
   Arts 179–183......................35
   Art 179...........................35
   Art 180...........................35
   Art 181...........................35
   Art 182...........................35
   Art 183...........................35
   Arts 985–988...................44–45
   Art 985...........................46
   Art 986.......................47, 51–52
   Art 987.......................47, 51–52
   Art 988.......................47, 51–52
Contract Law of the People's Republic of China] (promulgated by the NPC on 15 March 1999, effective 1 October 1999, expired 1 January 2021)..............36n.57
Draft of Civil Code of Great Qing (Da Qing Min Lv Cao An, Qing's Draft Civil Code) 29–30, 31–32, 34, 35–36, 41–42, 43–44, 49–50
   Arts 273–285......................34
   Arts 929–944...................31–32
   Art 929.......................32, 35
   Art 930(2) 32–33
   Art 931.........................32–33
   Art 932.........................32–33
   Art 933.........................32–33
   Art 934.........................32–33
   Art 935.........................32–33
   Art 936.........................32–33
   Art 937.........................32–33
   Art 938...........................33
   Art 941...........................33
   Art 944...........................33
General Principles of Civil Law of the People's Republic of China (promulgated by the NPC on 12 April 1986, effective 1 January 1987 and repealed 1 January 2021)........36n.57, 39–43
   Ch V, s 2 39–40
   Art 92............39–40, 41–42, 44–45, 49–50, 52–53
   Opinion, Art 131 ....40, 44–45, 47, 49–50
Law of the People's Republic of China on Foreign-Related Economic Contracts (promulgated by the NPC on 21 March 1985, effective 1 July 1985, expired 1 October 1999) 36n.57
Law of the People's Republic of China on Technology Contracts (promulgated by the NPCSC on 23 June 1987, effective 1 November 1987, expired 1 October 1999)...............36n.57
Qing's Draft Civil Code and completed a draft civil code for the Republic of China (1925 Draft)...............34, 35–36
Economic Contract Law (13 December 1981).............36n.57
Property Rights Law of the People's Republic of China] (promulgated by the NPC on 16 March 2007, effective 1 October 2007, expired 1 January 2021).......36n.57

Tort Liability Law of the People's Republic of China (promulgated by the NPCSC on 26 December 2009, effective 1 July 2010, expired 1 January 2021........ 36n.57

EUROPEAN UNION

Regulation (EC) 593/2008 of the European Parliament and of the Council of 17 June 2008 on the Law Applicable to Contractual Obligations (Rome I) [2008] OJ L177/6 (EU) (Rome Regulation)..... 96n.183
Art 5...................... 95n.180
Art 7...................... 95n.180

FRANCE

French Code Civil...... 6, 317–18, 323–24, 325–26, 327, 329, 331–32
Preamble 326–27
Art 1300.............. 326–28, 330–31
Arts 1301–1301-5................. 328
Arts 1303–1303-4..... 326, 328, 329–30
Art 1301-2...................... 328
Art 1303................ 211n.66, 328
Art 1371....................... 323
Art 1372.................... 323n.26
Art 1376.................... 323n.26

GERMANY

Civil Code (Bürgerliches Gesetzbuch, BGB) 29–30, 32, 33, 43–44, 49–50, 78
s 38 .... 241n.20
ss 812–17....................... 93
ss 812–822................. 77n.3, 239
s 812 .... 32–33, 145
s 812(1)............ 211n.67, 217n.109, 239–42, 244n.34, 339n.39
s 813(2)....................... 33n.29
s 814 .... 33n.29, 203n.14
s 815 .... 33n.30
s 815 .... 33n.31
s 817 .... 33n.27
s 818 .... 33n.32
s 818 (3) 243
s 819 .... 33n.33
s 822 .... 33n.35

HUNGARY

Civil Code (1978)................... 38

INDIA

Code of Civil Procedure
s 144 65–68
Constitution of India
s 142(1)....................... 65–66
s 226 65–66
s 299 63
Directive Principles of State Policy of the Constitution of India
Preamble 71
Art 38........................... 71
Art 39........................... 71
Indian Contract Act 1872 ...... 55–56, 57, 65, 69, 70
Ch V..................... 6, 58, 65
s 23 62
ss 68–72......................... 58
s 68 .... 58, 59, 70
s 68 illustration (a) 58n.16
s 68 illustrations (b) 58n.16
s 69 .... 59–60, 61, 62
s 70 .... 60, 61, 62, 63, 70
s 72 .... 64–65, 70

NETHERLANDS

Dutch Civil Code
Book 6:212, para 1 206

RUSSIAN SOVIET FEDERATED SOCIALIST REPUBLIC

Civil Code (1964)
Art 473....................... 39n.76

UNITED KINGDOM

Common Law Procedure Act 1852 (15 & 16 Vict c 76) 26
Consumer Rights Act 2015
s 51 .... 154n.27
Family Law Reform Act 1969
s 1 .... 17n.48, 260n.41
Infants Relief Act 1874 (37 & 38 Vict c 62)..................... 18
Law Reform (Frustrated Contracts) Act 1943........................ 91

Mental Capacity Act 2005
   s 7 .... 261n.47
Minors' Contracts Act 1987
   s 4(1)......................... 19n.75
Misrepresentation Act 1967
   s 2(1)............... 152n.23, 258n.28
Personal Property Securities Act
   2009 (Cth)
   s 10 .... 98n.204
   s 12 .... 98n.204
Sale of Goods Act 1979
   s 8 154
   s 17 .... 98n.205
Sale of Goods Act 1893 (56 &
   57 Vict c 71)
   s 2 .... 18n.60, 19n.75
Statute of Frauds 1677 155–56
   s 4 20
Supply of Goods and Services Act 1982
   s 15 155
   s 15(1)........................... 154

UNITED STATES

ALI, Restatement of the Law of
   Contracts (1932) vol 2
   § 347 comment a.............. 103n.11
ALI, Restatement of the Law of
   Restitution: Quasi- Contracts
   and Constructive Trusts (1937)
   (Restatement (First)) 101–2, 112,
                            334–36
   § 1 .... 104n.13
   § 1 comment a 105n.15
   § 1 comment e 105n.16
ALI, Restatement (Second) of the
   Law of Contracts (1981) 109
   § 153......................... 108n.30
   § 208......................... 108n.30
ALI, Restatement (Third) of Restitution
   and Unjust Enrichment (2011)...... 71,
                       109–11, 114, 334n.11
   § 1 .... 111n.38
   § 1 comment b................ 112n.39
   § 1 comment d................ 292n.83
   § 1 Reporter's Note a........... 114n.54
   § 28 112
   § 28(1) 112n.40
   § 37 .... 110n.37
   § 39 .... 110n.37
Draft Civil Code of New York 55–56
Draft Contract Bill 1867
   ss 54–61 55–56
   s 61 55–56
Uniform Commercial Code
   § 2-302 .... 108n.30
Fundamental Principles of Civil
   Legislation of the USSR (1962) 38

List of Contributors

Professor Peter Chau, University of Hong Kong, Hong Kong
Professor Mindy Chen-Wishart, University of Oxford, UK
Professor Arpita Gupta, Jindal University, India
Professor Steve Hedley, University College Cork, Ireland
Professor Lusina Ho, University of Hong Kong, Hong Kong
Emma Hughes, UK
Professor Peter Jaffey, University of Leicester, UK
Professor Nils Jansen, University of Münster, Germany
Dr Pablo Letelier, University of Chile, Chile
Assistant Professor Siyi Lin, The Chinese University of Hong Kong, Hong Kong
Professor Mitchell McInnes, University of Alberta, Canada
Associate Professor Sagi Peari, University of Western Australia, Australia
Professor James Penner, Singapore National University, Singapore
Professor Nolan Sharkey, University of Western Australia, Australia
Professor Emily Sherwin, Cornell University, USA
Professor Robert Stevens, University of Oxford, UK
Professor Warren Swain, University of Auckland, New Zealand
Professor Lutz-Christian Wolff, The Chinese University of Hong Kong, Hong Kong

Introduction

Warren Swain and Sagi Peari

I. Motivation

At the end of Chapter 7, Professor Stevens makes the important observation that:

> One of the problems that has arisen because of the adoption of a uniform 'unjust enrichment' framework for thinking about this area of law is that the ordinary dialectic between those with different viewpoints in relation to it has been stifled. We have fallen into opposing camps who are not listening to one another.

This collection is primarily motivated by a desire to reinvigorate a dialogue between supporters of unjust enrichment and those who are more sceptical. Sceptics of unjust enrichment have certainly had their say before and some of those in this volume are critics of long-standing. Yet there is, up until now, no single collection of sceptical opinion. Several participants in the project expressed disappointment that advocates of unjust enrichment had failed to engage seriously with the critical commentary.[1] These chapters are offered in the spirit of constructive dialogue.

The chapters do not speak with a single voice. Some contributors are much more sceptical than others. A few acknowledge problems with unjust enrichment but would probably not see themselves as sceptics in any stronger sense. Others would concede that unjust enrichment may still have an important if diminished role. There is also significant disagreement over details and possible alternatives to unjust enrichment. More fundamentally these chapters reflect four different interrelated perspectives: (1) historical; (2) sociological; (3) doctrinal; and (4) conceptual. Perhaps it is inevitable in such circumstances that critics will view unjust enrichment and its alternatives from very different perspectives. This is not a reason to be defensive. Supporters of unjust enrichment are not entirely unified either.[2] Some adopt a position closer to civil law and see merit in the idea of failure

---

[1] This is not a fair criticism of all supporters of unjust enrichment. Lord Burrows is one notable exception: Andrew Burrows, *The Law of Restitution* (3rd edn, OUP 2011); Andrew Burrows, 'In Defence of Unjust Enrichment' (2019) 78 CLJ 521.

[2] Kit Barker, 'Responsibility for Gain: Unjust Factors or Absence of Legal Ground? Starting Points in Unjust Enrichment Law' in Charles Rickett and Ross Grantham (eds), *Structure and Justification in Private Law: Essays for Peter Birks* (Hart Publishing 2008) 47–74; Birke Häcker, 'Unjust Factors versus

of basis. Professor Birks came round to that view.[3] Others have stuck to the idea that the subject is best understood using unjust factors.[4] Supporters of unjust enrichment still agree on much more than they differ. There is not the same level of common ground amongst the sceptics. There are nevertheless some common themes. For example, several contributions, agree that long-established legal doctrine in the law of property and contract might provide better answers than unjust enrichment. One of the merits of seeing some leading critics together in one place is that these links and others are easier to see.

II. A Short History of Unjust Enrichment

During the twentieth century, the development of a unified legal doctrine based on the principle of unjust enrichment was a pivotal moment, or more accurately a series of moments, in the history of the common law. The early pioneers were American. Drawing on the work of the legal historian James Barr Ames, William Keener produced his *A Treatise on the Law of Quasi-Contracts* in 1893.[5] Twenty years later, Frederic Woodward, attempted to show that quasi-contract should be equated with unjust enrichment.[6] The *First Restatement of the Law of Restitution* in 1937 reflected these ideas. As observed by Professor Sherwin in Chapter 5, 'the law of unjust enrichment has followed a different path in the United States'. These developments still have significant implications today. American lawyers have adopted what Sherwin calls a 'big tent' approach in which restitution describes an assortment of claims in situations that are not confined to cases of unjust enrichment.

It took longer for most English lawyers to abandon the link between quasi-contract and implied contract. By 1966, when Goff and Jones published *The Law of Restitution*,[7] the subject had started to come of age. By the mid-1980s, Birks had created a sophisticated conceptual model which he refined over nearly two decades.[8] Those fortunate enough to have attended Birks's post-graduate seminars in Oxford could hardly fail to be caught up in the excitement of it all. As a scholar, Birks was unquestionably learned, charismatic, and persuasive. It is perhaps no great surprise that his ideas were appealing to those who studied with, or were supervised by, him. Unjust enrichment was equally attractive to appellant judges, with Lord Goff, as he had then become, a prominent supporter of unjust

Absence of Juristic Reason (*Causa*)' in Elise Bant, Kit Barker, and Simone Degeling (eds), *Research Handbook on Unjust Enrichment and Restitution* (Edward Elgar 2020) 290–313.

[3] Peter Birks, *Unjust Enrichment* (2nd edn, OUP 2005).
[4] Notably, Burrows, *The Law of Restitution* (n 1); Burrows, *In Defence of Unjust Enrichment* (n 1).
[5] William A Keener, *A Treatise on the Law of Quasi-Contracts* (Baker, Voorhis and Co 1893).
[6] FC Woodward, *The Law of Quasi-Contracts* (Little, Brown and Co 1913).
[7] Robert Goff and Gareth Jones, *The Law of Restitution* (Sweet & Maxwell 1966).
[8] Peter Birks, *An Introduction to the Law of Restitution* (OUP 1985); Birks, *Unjust Enrichment* (n 3).

enrichment.[9] No hyperbole is involved in the claim that the development of unjust enrichment involved a shake-up in all common law jurisdictions comparable both with major events like the rise of negligence and the emergence of the classical model of contract a century earlier.

An earlier remodelling of private law provides a useful point of contrast with the development of unjust enrichment. In the nineteenth century, contract law was reshaped around the idea of will, the bargain and agreement.[10] The notion that a contract is formed by agreement is an idea of great antiquity. It can be found in ancient legal systems[11] and also in England during the Middle Ages.[12] The pedigree of unjust enrichment is different. In Chapters 1 and 14, Professors Swain and Hedley show why they are unconvinced by a historical narrative based on unjust enrichment. Even if they are wrong, then unjust enrichment fits the pre-twentieth century authorities but it does so by accident rather than design. Unjust enrichment is not an idea that was articulated in the historical case law. At best, it can only be an anachronistic construct.

Something close to the idea of unjust enrichment is found in Justinian's *Digest*, his comprehensive fifth-century collection of Roman law.[13] But the importance of unjust enrichment to Roman lawyers should not be pressed too far. At most, by the time of Justinian, it could be used to explain some of the category that Romans knew as quasi-contract, which included *negotiorium gestio* and the *condictio indebiti*.[14] Ironically, one of the merits of Roman law from the perspective of modern advocates of unjust enrichment is that the principle was very general. As a result, it was easy for lawyers centuries later to draw on the idea of unjust enrichment unencumbered by detailed legal doctrine.

The principle of unjust enrichment is seductive. There is something attractive in the simple idea that it is wrong for one person to unjustly enrich themselves at the expense of another. As Professor Siyi demonstrates in Chapter 2, unjust enrichment is not only a western idea. It can be found in China long before civil law unjust enrichment was transplanted into Chinese law. One result of this history is that the legal sense of unjust enrichment has not always been adequately articulated. Those who support unjust enrichment are not arguing that any enrichment should be subject to a legal remedy. Indeed, they have tried hard to keep the general principle of Roman law within proper boundaries. It in part explains why the history

---

[9] *Lipkin Gorman v Karpnale Ltd* [1991] 2 AC 548 (HL).
[10] W Swain, *The Law of Contract 1670–1870* (CUP 2015) 172–200.
[11] Roman law had an obvious category of consensual contract but the idea of agreement can be found earlier still, eg in Ancient Mesopotamia: Raymond Westbrook, 'Introduction: The Character of Ancient Near Eastern Law' in Raymond Westbrook (ed), *A History of Ancient Near Eastern Law*, vol 1 (Brill 2003) 63–67.
[12] David Ibbetson, *A Historical Introduction to the Law of Obligations* (OUP 1999) 73–76.
[13] D 12.6.14; D 50.17.206.
[14] Birks himself conceded that unjust enrichment and quasi-contract Roman law are not entirely coextensive: Peter Birks, *The Roman Law of Obligations* (Eric Descheemaeker ed, OUP 2014) 259.

of unjust enrichment in the modern law has become bound up with the question of legal taxonomy which in turn exposes a tension between the static and the dynamic in legal evolution.[15] As a result, unjust enrichment has also become part of a wider narrative around the way that the law develops.

III. The Academic and the Practitioner

Professor Birks was acutely aware of the importance of the relationship between legal academics and practitioners. In a lecture delivered in 1997, he talked about 'the necessity of sharing between judge and jurist the task of interpretative development of the law'.[16] The relationship between judges and jurists is not constant across time or jurisdiction.[17] Lord Burrows has suggested that in England it has become more important over recent decades but has also argued that the value of 'practical legal scholarship' needs to be given proper acknowledgement.[18]

Interest in the idea of unjust enrichment from legal writers is nothing new. The neo-scholastic writers of the sixteenth century thought that the proper limits to the more general principle of Roman law could be found in the work of Aristotle and Aquinas.[19] In modern times, it is an area of the law where academic writing has proved particularly influential. It is difficult to think of many other examples in the last fifty years where jurists have played such an important role in shaping the law, although administrative law might have a strong claim. In Chapter 4, Professor Peari highlights parallels between the great German scholar Professor Friedrich Carl von Savigny and Professor Birks. Whilst he concludes that each produced explanations of unjust enrichment that in the end were not entirely satisfactory, the story of both men tells us something important about the value of academic lawyers as agents of change. There are also limits to this academic approach. Birks was fond of quoting the English civilian, Thomas Wood, who described English law as a 'heap of good learning'.[20] The idea that legal taxonomy has great value has significant supporters,[21] yet as Hedley demonstrates in Chapter 14, we should not

---

[15] This important point is not much commented on explicitly although it is implicit in some criticism of unjust enrichment: see Richard Sutton, 'Restitution and the Discourse of System' in Charles Rickett and Ross Grantham (eds), *Structure and Justification in Private Law: Essays for Peter Birks* (Hart Publishing 2008) 127–45.
[16] Peter Birks, 'The Academic and the Practitioner' (1998) 18 LS 397, 413.
[17] Neil Duxbury, *Jurists and Judges: An Essay on Influence* (Hart Publishing 2001).
[18] Lord Burrows, 'Judges and Academics, and the Endless Road to Unattainable Perfection' (2022) 55 Israel L Rev 50.
[19] James Gordley, *Foundations of Private Law: Property, Tort, Contract, Unjust Enrichment* (OUP 2006) 423–25.
[20] Thomas Wood, *An Institute of the Laws of England in their Natural Order*, vol 1 (1720) ii. Eg Peter Birks, 'This Heap of Good Learning: The Jurist in the Common Law Tradition' in Basil S Markesinis (ed), *The Clifford Chance Lectures, 2: Law Making, Law Finding and Law Shaping: The Diverse Influences* (OUP 1997) 113–38.
[21] eg Ewan McKendrick, 'Taxonomy: Does It Matter?' in David Johnston and Reinhard Zimmermann (eds), *Unjustified Enrichment: Key Issues in Comparative Perspective* (CUP 2002) 627–57.

be afraid to admit if a high-level taxonomical approach is sometimes found to be wanting.[22] Perhaps after all one of the main reasons for the continued success of the common law is its inherent pragmatism and refusal to be pushed into structural boxes.

Unjust enrichment has also generated a sizable theoretical literature.[23] One prominent modern theorist of private law, Professor Weinrib, regards unjust enrichment as fitting within his wider model of private law based on 'corrective justice'.[24] In Chapter 8, Professor Penner examines the way that corrective justice has been used to explain restitution of mistaken payments. He shows how Weinrib's treatment depends on treating all mistaken payments as conditional. Penner thinks that this only takes us so far because there are cases of mistaken payments which do not involve payments or transfers made upon a condition, and hence cannot be explained by corrective justice. A mistaken gift case like *Lady Hood of Avalon v Mackinnon* is a prominent example.[25]

IV. Unjust Enrichment as a Universal Idea

One of the most powerful features of unjust enrichment or in its more civilian form, unjustified enrichment, is that these ideas have almost universal appeal. What dissent there is may in part be explained by the personnel on appellant court benches. Unjust enrichment has, for example, enjoyed a somewhat chequered history in Australia. In *Farah Constructions Pty Ltd v Say-Dee Pty Ltd*, the High Court of Australia described unjust enrichment as 'unhistorical'.[26] For a period, the High Court favoured an alternative equitable principle of unconscionability.[27] The pendulum may now be swinging back in favour of unjust enrichment.[28] Equity should not necessarily be so easily discarded. Professor Sharkey in Chapter 6 observes that, 'The propagation of the idea of unjust enrichment has therefore been strongly linked to perceived deficiencies in the law of equity' but concludes that the idea that equity is subjective does not withstand close scrutiny.

---

[22] For a useful account of some of the problems of mapping private law, see Stephen Waddams, *Dimensions of Private Law: Categories and Concepts in Anglo-American Legal Reasoning* (CUP 2003).
[23] For a series of essays from this perspective, see Robert Chambers, Charles Mitchell, and James Penner (eds), *Philosophical Foundations of the Law of Unjust Enrichment* (OUP 2009).
[24] Ernest J Weinrib, *Corrective Justice* (OUP 2012) 185–229.
[25] *Lady Hood of Avalon v Mackinnon* [1909] 1 Ch 476 (Ch).
[26] *Farah Constructions Pty Ltd v Say-Dee Pty Ltd* [2007] HCA 22; (2007) 230 CLR 89 [154]. See also *Roxborough v Rothmans of Pall Mall Australia Ltd* [2001] HCA 68; (2001) 208 CLR 516 [136].
[27] For a discussion, see Warren Swain, 'Unjust Enrichment and the Role of Legal History in England and Australia' (2013) 36 UNSWLJ 1030.
[28] Initially, there was initially strong support for a principle of unjust enrichment in the High Court: *Pavey & Matthews Pty Ltd v Paul* (1987) 162 CLR 221. More recently, see *Equuscorp Pty Ltd v Haxton* [2012] HCA 7; (2012) 246 CLR 498 [29]–[30]; *Mann v Paterson Construction Pty Ltd* [2019] HCA 32; (2019) 267 CLR 560 [199]. For an astute analysis, see Kit Barker, 'Unjust Enrichment in Australia: What Is(n't) It? Implications for Legal Reasoning and Practice' (2020) 43 MULR 903.

Elsewhere the idea of unjust enrichment may seemingly be more secure, but it is not necessarily more settled. Chapter V of the Indian Contract Act of 1872 decisively broke away from the idea that liability was based on implied contract. But as Professor Gupta shows in Chapter 3, a number of questions about the proper scope of unjust enrichment remain unanswered. In Chapter 16, Professor McInnes describes Canadian law as 'unique' as he considers the implications of the decision of the Supreme Court in *Garland v Consumers' Gas Co Ltd* which held that unjust enrichment requires 'an absence of juristic reason'.[29] This civilian-inspired approach is not without problems. At the same time, McInnes sees more benefits of the unified unjust enrichment approach than some of the other contributors. It does at least, he argues, give lawyers and judges 'easy access to the many instances of restitutionary liability' than a more fragmented model with restitution falling under different juridical categories.

V. Alternatives to Unjust Enrichment

It is one thing to criticize unjust enrichment as a poor fit with the existing law, but it is an altogether more difficult proposition to put forward alternative explanations. Abandoning unjust enrichment altogether might have some costs. In Chapter 15 Dr Letelier considers recent reforms to the French Civil Code in relation to quasi-contract and considers some of the challenges of an approach that does not depend on a unified single principle.

Professor Stevens explores some of the problems with property, contract, and loss-based explanations for liability in Chapter 7. His alternative model has recently been published in monograph form.[30] Stevens is not the only sceptic to recognize that there are drawbacks to some replacement strategies for unjust enrichment. Professors Chau and Ho in Chapter 9 critically consider in detail two different attempts to explain the return of payments made by mistake as resting on some form of agreement. Other sceptics certainly see value in existing principles. Building on his earlier work, in Chapter 11 Professor Jaffey finds answers in property and 'imputed contract' claims that he describes as operating 'in the shadow of contract'. In defending this approach, he addresses some of the criticism of these alternatives to unjust enrichment.

Other sceptics would prefer a more radical realignment. In Chapter 10, Professor Wolff points out that even in civil law jurisdictions issues around the scope of liability remain unresolved. He argues that the emphasis on enrichment is the problem. He favours shifting to focus on de-enrichment which looks to the detrimental impact on the claimant of the transaction. A remedy, he argues, should

---

[29] *Garland v Consumers' Gas Co Ltd* 2004 SCC 25; [2004] 1 SCR 629.
[30] Robert Stevens, *The Laws of Restitution* (OUP 2023).

be limited to situations where the claimant suffers loss. Individual doctrines within unjust enrichment might also be ripe for reform. In Chapter 13, Professor Chen-Wishart and Ms Hughes explore the way in which many of the unjust factors have been explained by either defective consent of the claimant or unconscientious behaviour by the defendant. They concede that both are relevant considerations but favour a more pluralistic approach which considers the claimant's responsibility to act reasonably in making a transfer, the subject matter and fairness of the transfer, public policy and community standards, and making workable rules.

No doubt there will be much within this collection that supporters of unjust enrichment will disagree with. That is almost beside the point. In Chapter 12, Professor Jansen makes the point that 'mapping should not be confused with explaining'. His invitation for unjust enrichment lawyers not to abandon unjust enrichment but to look for 'interconnections' with other branches of the law is critical. Theoretical neatness should not come at the expense of transparency of doctrinal principle. If this book helps to reinvigorate debate, then it will have achieved its aim. There are no easy answers, which is something that the more thoughtful sceptics and supporters of unjust enrichment can agree on.

PART I
HISTORY

1
Contract and Unjust Enrichment

Lessons from History?

Warren Swain

I. Introduction

> But a Quasi-Contract is not a contract at all. The commonest sample of the class is the relation subsisting between two persons, one of whom has paid money to the other through mistake. The law, consulting the interests of morality, imposes an obligation on the receiver to refund, but the very nature of the transaction indicates that it is not a contract, inasmuch as the Convention, the most essential ingredient of Contract, is wanting.[1]

In his classic work, *Ancient Law*, Sir Henry Maine criticized his contemporaries for equating quasi-contracts with implied contracts, arguing that implied contracts 'are true contracts, which quasi-contracts are not'.[2] The mark of a 'true contract', he wrote, was an agreement or a 'convention'. Maine belonged to a generation who were influenced by the idea that contracts were formed by a meeting of wills.[3] Will theory would itself evolve into the bargain or classical theory of contract in the second half of the nineteenth century. Much of the modern criticism of the idea of quasi-contract and, more specifically, the use of implied contract as a justification for imposing a quasi-contract, is based on the same or similar implicit assumptions about the nature of contractual obligations, that would be familiar more than a century ago.[4]

There are good historical reasons why quasi-contract came to be viewed as a form of implied contract. Before the nineteenth century, private law was organized around the forms of action based on the original writs rather than by substantive categories. Forms of action were procedural tickets by which plaintiffs gained

---

[1] Sir Henry Sumner Maine, *Ancient Law: Its Connection with the Early History of Society, and Its Relation to Modern Ideas* (10th edn, John Murray 1912) 354.
[2] ibid.
[3] Warren Swain, *The Law of Contract 1670–1870* (CUP 2015) 172–230.
[4] Andrew Burrows, *The Law of Restitution* (3rd edn, OUP 2011) 28.

entry to the litigation process.[5] As a result, the search for unjust enrichment involves a process of reconstruction. A substantive principle of unjust enrichment has been said to exist in the actions of account, debt, and later, assumpsit. Because the actions of assumpsit (and indeed debt) were usually associated with the law of contract, lawyers were encouraged to think of these as actions based on implied contracts. A second explanation lay in the way that English legal writers found an intellectual justification in implied contract.[6] For supporters of unjust enrichment, the tendency to equate quasi-contract as a sort of contract, or even an implied contract, was an error which hid the true basis of these obligations.

There may be another more mundane reason why these cases were treated as instances of implied contract. A re-evaluation of the historical evidence reveals that unjust enrichment scholars may have underestimated the genuinely contractual character of some of these claims. This is not to suggest that the totality of modern unjust enrichment can, or ought to, be subsumed within the law of contract.[7] Rather, it is to argue that the mono-cultural unjust enrichment approach may be flawed from a historical perspective. To this more limited extent, Maine was right to be sceptical about equating implied contract with quasi-contract.[8] Rather, my argument is that there had been an over-eagerness to bring some consensual or even contractual obligations within unjust enrichment. If this alternative approach is correct, then it also helps to explain something quite important, why despite the success of the doctrine of unjust enrichment, nagging doubts have remained about the overarching principle and why it remains difficult to argue that there is a *unified* body of law in this area.

II. The Nature of Contracts

In his *Introduction to the Law of Restitution*, Birks was careful to distinguish between restitution and other types of liability: 'The obligation to make restitution of benefits received through mistake or oppression or for a consideration which happens to fail are manifestly not generated by contract or by tort.'[9] Less attention was devoted to unpacking what was meant by the phrase 'generated by contract'.[10] More

---

[5] FW Maitland, *The Forms of Action at Common Law: A Course of Lectures* (AH Chaytor and WJ Whittaker eds, CUP 1948) 4.

[6] Peter Birks and Grant McLeod, 'The Implied Contract Theory of Quasi-Contract: Civilian Opinion Current in the Century Before Blackstone' (1986) 6 OJLS 46.

[7] Some claims may belong within the law of property, see Professor Jaffey and Professor Hedley, Chapters 11 and 14 in this volume.

[8] This is not to discount the possibility that some role can usefully be played by quasi-contract, as opposed to unjust enrichment. These claims may be consent-based but not contractual: Dan Priel, 'In Defence of Quasi-Contract' (2012) 75 MLR 54.

[9] Peter Birks, *An Introduction to the Law of Restitution* (rev edn, OUP 1989) 38.

[10] Birks discussed both consent and promising as elements of contractual liability, whereas he stressed that a promise in the cases of unjust enrichment was fortuitous rather than essential: ibid 44–48.

than a decade later, in *Unjust Enrichment*, Birks went on to explain that contracts (a primary right) were an obligation 'caused' by consent with breach of contract as a wrong creating secondary rights and duties.[11] This approach fits with the classical, or bargain, model which presents the law of contract as a unified doctrine based on consent (irrespective of the subject matter of the contract) and by which contract law is presented as a series of abstract rules from offer and acceptance, through to terms, vitiation, breach, and remedies.[12] The classical model emphasizes one-off negotiated contracts (which are, in this sense, truly consensual). This description is unlikely to reflect the messy reality of contracting concluded on standard terms,[13] the process of relational contracting,[14] or the prominence of regulation.[15] These and other flaws at the very least suggest that this prominent model of contract law might not be a perfect default analysis.[16] It is a curious fact that supporters of unjust enrichment, who have been so keen to discard fictions, have clung so firmly to a model of contract law that would not be out of place in the legal treatises of the 1870s.[17]

Steve Hedley has said of the orthodox model of contract law: 'This is the "express contract" fallacy, the fallacy that contracts are intrinsically the product of the parties' wills, and so are unbridgeably divided from non-contractual liabilities.'[18] More sophisticated modern consensual models exist[19] but it is unnecessary to debate the competing rationales of contemporary contract law, given Hedley's insight is even more powerful when applied to the law of contract in earlier centuries. This is because whilst agreement has been central to the law of contract for centuries, its meaning has changed. The medieval action of covenant was based on agreement.[20] With the rise of the action of assumpsit in the sixteenth century, agreement

---

[11] Peter Birks, *Unjust Enrichment* (2nd edn, OUP 2005) 21. Birks explored this issue further in Peter Birks, 'Definition and Division: A Meditation on *Institutes* 3.13' in Peter Birks (ed), *The Classification of Obligations* (OUP 1997). For judicial recognition of the distinction in contract law, see: *Photo Production Ltd v Securicor Transport Ltd* [1980] AC 827 (HL) 848–49 (Lord Diplock); *Cavendish Square Holding BV v Makdessi* [2015] UKSC 67; [2016] AC 1172 [13]–[14] (Lord Neuberger and Lord Sumption SCJJ).

[12] On the tendency for abstraction, see Hugh Beale, 'Relational Values in English Contract Law' in David Campbell and others (eds), *Changing Concepts of Contract: Essays in Honour of Ian Macneil* (Palgrave Macmillan 2013) 116–37.

[13] See Margaret Jane Radin, *Boilerplate: The Fine Print, Vanishing Rights, and the Rule of Law* (Princeton UP 2014).

[14] See David Campbell, *Contractual Relations: A Contribution to the Critique of the Classical Law of Contract* (OUP 2022); Ian Macneil, *The Relational Theory of Contract: Selected Works of Ian Macneil* (David Campbell ed, Sweet & Maxwell 2001).

[15] See Hugh Collins, *Regulating Contracts* (OUP 1999).

[16] Other problems of substance, emphasis, and fit could be highlighted: Melvin A Eisenberg, 'Why There is No Law of Relational Contracts' (2000) 94 NWULR 805, 808–12.

[17] The classical law of contract may not even have reflected the law in practice in the 1870s and even less so later on: see PS Atiyah, *The Rise and Fall of Freedom of Contract* (OUP 1979).

[18] Steve Hedley, *Restitution: Its Division and Ordering* (Sweet & Maxwell 2001) 55. For Professor Hedley's discussion of contract, see Chapter 14 in this volume.

[19] See, eg, Randy E Barnett, 'A Consent Theory of Contract' (1986) 86 Colum L Rev 269. I am grateful to Professor Dagan for the reminder that there are versions of consent theory of contract such as this one that deserve serious consideration.

[20] David Ibbetson, *A Historical Introduction to the Law of Obligations* (OUP 1999) 22.

became prominent once again.[21] By the late nineteenth century, an agreement, as described by Blackburn J in *Smith v Hughes*,[22] was the central component of the bargain model of contract. In common with other aspects of contract doctrine, agreements were given a legal definition.[23] As a result, even in a case tried by a jury (although juries were in terminal decline from the late nineteenth century in contract cases),[24] agreement had a very particular definition.

Before the mid-nineteenth century, the existence of an agreement was determined by a very different process involving pleading, a jury, and evidence. Under the general issue (eg non-assumpsit) which raised a defence by way of broad denial, it was for a jury to determine whether the parties had entered into an agreement. This older concept of an agreement was not legally defined in the same way. It might be express or it might be unstated and formed out of the mutual assumptions of the parties. If we can get beyond the classical model of contract, then agreements of the second kind are just as contractual as the first. When looking at cases before the nineteenth century, there is no reason to impose a rigid, and more recent, definition of a contract. To do so is to be guilty of anachronism. This simple observation has obvious implications when determining whether a claim is properly characterized as based on unjust enrichment or contract.

III. The Contractual Character of Assumpsit

By the early sixteenth century, the action on the case began to replace the older actions of account and debt. One standard example involved a claim against a receiver of money,[25] who had promised to pay the money over but had failed to do so.[26] There were two objections: first, that the proper action was account and, secondly, that consideration for the defendant's promise to pay the creditor was absent because he received no benefit. Because no damages could be recovered in account, it was said that there was no overlap with an existing action.[27] Consideration was found in 'having the money in his hands for only a day, or an hour'.[28] The fact that

---

[21] ibid 135–40.
[22] *Smith v Hughes* (1871) LR 6 QB 597 (QB) 607. See also *Denny v Hancock* (1870) LR 6 Ch App 1 (CA); *Tamplin v James* (1880) 15 Ch D 215 (CA).
[23] The emergence of legal rules around remoteness of damage and a doctrine of contractual mistake are examples of the same phenomena.
[24] Michael Lobban, 'The Strange Life of the English Civil Jury, 1837–1914' in John W Cairns and Grant McLeod (eds), '*The Dearest Birth Right of the People of England*': *The Jury in the History of the Common Law* (Hart Publishing 2002) 186–92.
[25] Sir John Baker, *The Oxford History of the Laws of England, vol VI 1483–1558* (OUP 2003) 879–80.
[26] ibid 879.
[27] The argument against overlapping actions meant that a new action could not be brought when there was an established action that already existed on the same facts.
[28] *Retchford v Spurlinge* (1591) as cited in Sir John Baker, *Baker and Milsom Sources of English Legal History: Private Law to 1750* (2nd edn, OUP 2019) 535 (hereafter Baker, *Baker and Milsom*).

consideration was required, however artificially constructed (which itself is hardly unique), in the context of a receiver of money reflects the contractual character of the claim.[29]

From the mid-sixteenth century, the action on the case began to be used to recover money paid on a transaction that had failed. Coningsby J and Fitzjames CJ explained in *Pykeryng v Thurgoode* in 1532 that: 'If a man bails money to be handed over to another, and he does not hand it over, it is at the bailor's pleasure whether to bring debt, account, or an action on his case; for the actions are based on different points.'[30] Another development would have long-term consequences. By alleging a subsequent promise to pay an underlying debt, the indebitatus form of count met the objection in *Orwell v Mortoft* that, '[s]o it seems that debt lies. And where a general action lies, a special action on the case does not'.[31] After *Slade's Case*,[32] it was settled that assumpsit could be brought even though an action in debt was available on the same facts. The underlying indebtedness gave rise to an implied (fictitious) promise to pay. The underlying debt in *Slade's Case* was contractual, but the decision created the possibility of using an indebitatus count for non-contractual debts. This potential would come to be realized with the emergence of the action for money had and received.

Although debt was the standard contract action for a long period, as a claim for a certain (fixed) sum, it posed a problem for a plaintiff recovering the price for goods or labour which were not settled at the time of the original agreement. The actions of assumpsit for a *quantum meruit* (for work done) or *quantum valebant* (for goods sold and delivered) were able to achieve what debt could not and were commonplace by the late sixteenth century.[33] In *The Six Carpenters' Case*, Coke CJ explained:

> ... if I bring cloth to a tailor, to have a gown made, [and] the price [is] not agreed in certain before ... the putting of [the] cloth to the tailor to be made into a gown, is sufficient evidence to prove the said special contract, for the law implies it: and if the tailor over-values the making, or the necessaries to it, the jury may mitigate it ...[34]

---

[29] On artificiality of consideration in respect to reciprocity, see David J Ibbetson, 'Consideration and the Theory of Contract in Sixteenth Century Common Law' in John Barton (ed), *Towards a General Law of Contract* (Duncker & Humblot 1990) 74–83.
[30] *Pykeryng v Thurgoode* (1532) as cited in Baker, *Baker and Milsom* (n 28) 453.
[31] *Orwell v Mortoft* (1505) as cited in ibid 451.
[32] *Slade's Case* (1602) 4 Co Rep 92b; 76 ER 1074; David Ibbetson, 'Sixteenth Century Contract Law: *Slade's Case* in Context' (1984) 4 OJLS 295.
[33] See, eg, JH Baker, 'The Use of Assumpsit for Restitutionary Money Claims 1600–1800' in Eltjo JH Schrage (ed), *Unjust Enrichment: The Comparative Legal History of the Law of Restitution* (2nd edn, Duncker & Humblot 1999) 36 (hereafter Baker, 'Use of Assumpsit').
[34] *The Six Carpenters' Case* (1610) 8 Co Rep 146a, 147a; 77 ER 695, 697–98.

A few years later, *Sheppard's Abridgement* referred to an anonymous case which held that, '[i]f one bid me do work for him, and do not promise anything for it; in this case the law implieth the promise and I may sue for wages'.[35] To modern lawyers schooled in the classical law of contract, it is easy to read these passages as suggesting that the contract or promise was implied in law and was some sort of fiction. In fact, these are genuine contracts implied from the surrounding circumstances. When one person does work for another, there is an expectation that it will be paid for, even if no price is settled on at the time. It was not too difficult for a jury of the period having considered the surrounding circumstances to reach the conclusion that there was an agreement even if it was not expressly stated, in much the same way as juries (particularly special juries) were perfectly comfortable in taking account of mercantile customs and other assumptions that people might make in their interactions.[36]

The allegation of a request is a contractual characteristic which establishes the assumption that the work was to be paid for by the person doing the requesting. It is another version of contractual reciprocity like the doctrines of quid pro quo in debt or consideration in assumpsit and is redolent of exchange rather than unjust enrichment. In *Hayes v Warren*, Serjeant Strange argued that even in the absence of a request, 'the defendant had the benefit of the work and labour, which is the same thing, and equal to a request'.[37] The King's Bench accepted his argument to the limited extent that approval of the work after it had been carried out was sufficient even if the request was omitted. One manuscript report went further by suggesting that the receipt of a sufficient benefit was enough to justify the action even in the absence of a request but, on the facts, it was held that the benefit was insufficient.[38] This version was contradicted by another manuscript report as well as the printed report.[39] A request was emphasized in *Barton v Hodgkinson*.[40] The defendant had separated from his pregnant wife, who went to live with the plaintiff along with her child. She subsequently left the child with the plaintiff, who brought a *quantum meruit* for the cost of the child's maintenance. The King's Bench rejected the claim. Lee CJ accepted in principle that the receipt of a benefit was sufficient to support an action in the absence of a request but thought that on the facts there was no benefit to the father. The other members of the majority approached the issue more narrowly. Probyn J conceded that the father was bound to bring up a child but only when it was done in his own way and not by someone else. Chapple J argued that the obligation only lay between the father and child. Only Page J seems to have thought that a benefit without a request was sufficient. His explanation was closer

---

[35] Baker, 'Use of Assumpsit' (n 33) 37–38.
[36] On special juries, see James C Oldham, 'The Origins of the Special Jury' (1983) 50 U Chi L Rev 137.
[37] *Hays v Warren* (1733) W Kel 117, 119; 25 ER 522, 523 (capitalization omitted).
[38] HLS MS 4055 f 6 (Raymond CJ, Probyn J, Page J (more obliquely)).
[39] LI MS Hill 39 f 92 (Raymond CJ, Page J).
[40] (1739) LI MS Misc 133 f 33; LI MS Hill 25 f 1; LI MS Hill 29 f 225.

to an unjust enrichment analysis. The emphasis on the presence of a request, or ratification once a benefit was received, meant that most judges of the time stopped short of his approach. They were closer to a contractual rather than an unjust enrichment analysis. These decisions not so much show the abandonment of contract but rather a demonstration that by the eighteenth century lawyers were willing to probe the boundaries of what, by this time, were well-established contract remedies. Other aspects of contract doctrine are open to different interpretations as can be illustrated by the example of contractual incapacity.

IV. Incapacity: A Case of Contractual Liability?

There are several reasons for denying capacity to contract. During the Middle Ages, monks and friars were treated as civilly dead[41] and unable to contract.[42] At the same time, as wealthy land owners, monasteries could not have operated without an ability to contract.[43] The solution was to allow monks to contract on behalf of the religious house in the person of the abbot or prior on the grounds that the institution had received a benefit or profit in cases of loans of money[44] and the supply of goods.[45] The relationship was not, strictly speaking, agency, but it operated in a similar manner and it is difficult to see the outcome as anything other than contractual—a view which fitted with the statement of 1521: 'The spiritual corporation is a body of persons dead in law who have a head, namely the abbot.'[46]

In 1355, it was held that a nine-year-old was not bound in covenant.[47] Infancy by its nature was a widespread instance of incapacity which created significant practical problems given that until quite recently the age of majority was twenty-one.[48] Various ad hoc solutions were adopted. For example, articles of apprenticeship[49] could be resolved by local custom.[50] Limits on an infant's capacity can be justified

---

[41] Sir Frederick Pollock and Frederic William Maitland, *The History of English Law Before the Time of Edward I*, vol 1 (2nd edn, CUP 1905) 433-38. See Henry de Bracton, *On the Laws and Customs of England*, vol 4 (Samuel E Thorne tr ed, Harvard UP 1968) 310. For a more detailed discussion of this form of incapacity, see David Ibbetson, 'Unjust Enrichment in England before 1600' in Eltjo JH Schrage (ed), *Unjust Enrichment: The Comparative Legal History of the Law of Restitution* (2nd edn, Duncker & Humblot 1999) 142-43.
[42] (1329) 13 Ed III pl 23, f 46(a)-46(b).
[43] This was true of some monastic orders which owned large amounts of land which was not true of the friars: RW Southern, *The Penguin History of the Church: Western Society and the Church in the Middle Ages* (Penguin 1990) 289.
[44] (1333) 7 Ed III f 35, pl 35a-36a; (1442) 20 Hen VI f 21a-22b, pl 19.
[45] (1348) 22 Ed III f 8a-8b, pl 16; (1401) 2 Hen IV f 21a, pl 1.
[46] *King's College Cambridge v Hekker* (1521) as cited in JH Baker, *Year Books of Henry VIII: 12-14 Henry VIII, 1520-1523* (Selden Society 2002) 68, 71.
[47] (1355) 29 Edw III f 27a-27b, pl 29. An infant could not be bound in debt because an infant could not wage their law which was the method of proof in the action: (1433) 11 Hen VI f 40b-41a, pl 35.
[48] Family Law Reform Act 1969, s 1.
[49] (1443) YB 21 Hen VI f 31, pl 18.
[50] By the custom of London, a deed of apprenticeship was binding from the age of 14: (1481) 21 Edw IV f 6, pl 17.

by the potential for exploitation. This was reflected in the rule that there was no need to know that the other party was an infant[51] and the particularly strict rules which applied to loans with infants.[52] On the other hand, if contracts with infants were completely unenforceable then benefits would be received without any obligation on the part of the infant to pay for them.

In 1478, Serjeant Vavasour reportedly 'said privately to Littleton JCP that an infant was not chargeable upon any contract, except for his meat, drink, and necessary apparel'.[53] Following the emergence of an exception for necessaries,[54] the onus of proving that the goods were necessaries[55] fell on the supplier[56] who sold goods to a minor at their own risk.[57] By the late nineteenth century, this situation was contained in statute. In *Nash v Inman*, a Savile Row tailor brought an action for an unpaid bill on goods delivered to the infant.[58] The Infants Relief Act 1874 stated that all contracts for money lent or the supply of goods were void unless the contract was for necessaries.[59] Not long afterwards, the Sale of Goods Act 1893 defined necessaries as 'goods suitable to the condition in life of such infant or minor or other person, and to his actual requirements at the time of the sale and delivery'.[60] The plaintiff failed to discharge the onus of showing that the clothes were necessaries, with Buckley LJ describing the clothing as 'an extravagant and ridiculous style having regard to the position of the boy'.[61]

Necessaries are one aspect of a more general exception to an infant's incapacity. In 1431, it was argued that:

> ... when an infant within age has 'quid pro quo' he will be bound by the law; if an infant within age be at board (a tabler) with me and pay (me) a certain sum every week, or he buy clothing (vesture) for his body, he will be charged by an action of Debt, because he must of necessity have this.[62]

---

[51] In contrast, mental incapacity and intoxication require knowledge of those conditions on the part of the other party.
[52] Even loans for necessaries were unenforceable during infancy because of the risk that the infant might spend the loan on non-necessaries: *Earle v Peale* (1711) 1 Salk 386; 91 ER 336.
[53] (1478) YB 18 Edw IV f 2, pl 7.
[54] AWB Simpson, *A History of the Common Law of Contract* (OUP 1987) 540–41 observed that, 'It is not very clear how this happened.'
[55] For attempts to define necessaries, see: *Makarell v Bachelor* (1596) Cro Eliz 583; 78 ER 826; *Whittingham v Hill* (1618) Cro Jac 494; 79 ER 421; *Ive v Chester* (1619) Cro Jac 560; 79 ER 480; *Pickering v Gunning* (1627) Palm 528; 81 ER 1204.
[56] *Johnstone v Marks* (1887) 19 QBD 509 (QB).
[57] *Barnes & Co v Toye* (1884) 13 QBD 410 (QB).
[58] *Nash v Inman* [1908] 2 KB 1 (CA).
[59] Infants Relief Act 1874 (37 & 38 Vict c 62).
[60] Sale of Goods Act 1893 (56 & 57 Vict c 71) s 2.
[61] *Nash v Inman* (n 58) 11.
[62] (1431) YB 10 Hen VI f 14, pl 46.

In the 1440s, Newton CJ held that an infant would be liable in debt for rent if they had occupied and cultivated leased land.[63] There are more recent examples,[64] but principled distinctions are lacking: an infant is liable for rent,[65] yet they are not liable for their trading contracts.[66] Attempts to rationalize the authorities have resulted in little more than a list of exceptions to the incapacity rule.[67]

In *Nash v Inman*, Fletcher Moulton LJ rejected a contractual justification: 'the basis of the action is hardly contract. Its real foundation is an obligation which the law imposes on the infant to make a fair payment in respect of needs satisfied'.[68] Buckley LJ disagreed[69] and Cozens-Hardy MR did not address the point. In a decision on the supply of necessaries to someone suffering from mental incapacity, Cotton LJ said, 'I think that the expression "implied contract" is erroneous and very unfortunate'[70] and in Lindley LJ's view there was no 'real contract'.[71] Twentieth-century authorities point in both directions.[72] There is little difficulty in saying that there is an agreement in these cases. The assertion that there is a contract is more problematic. It means arguing that an infant can consent to some contracts (eg for necessaries) and not others. The same problem faces those who favour a rationale in unjust enrichment because there is no obvious reason why some benefits received by infants generate liability and not others. Other factors support a contractual analysis. If liability is not contractual, it is difficult to understand why an infant's contract is treated as voidable,[73] why an executory contract for necessaries is binding on a minor,[74] or most important of all, why an agreement by an infant becomes an enforceable contract on ratification once they reach their majority.[75]

Whilst exceptions to incapacity emerged early, the first serious attempts to explain these claims came in the nineteenth century at a time when the bargain model of contract was dominant. This is probably not a coincidence. Agreements by monks and friars were most obviously contractual. Historically, a good argument

---

[63] (1443) YB 21 Hen VI f 31, pl 18.
[64] *Doyle v White City Stadium Ltd* [1935] 1 KB 110 (CA); *Chaplin v Leslie Frewin (Publishers) Ltd* [1966] Ch 71 (CA).
[65] *Keteley's Case* (1613) 1 Brownl 120; 123 ER 704.
[66] *Whittingham v Hill* (n 55); *Pickering v Gunning* (n 55).
[67] For examples over a century apart, see Frederick Pollock, *Principles of Contract at Law and in Equity* (1st edn, Stevens and Sons 1876) 32–56; Edwin Peel, *Treitel: The Law of Contract* (14th edn, Sweet & Maxwell 2015) [12-001]–[12-051].
[68] *Nash v Inman* (n 61) 8.
[69] ibid 12.
[70] *Re Rhodes* (1890) 44 ChD 94 (CA) 105.
[71] ibid 107.
[72] Supporting a contractual analysis: *Doyle v White City Stadium Ltd* (n 64); *Chaplin v Leslie Frewin (Publishers) Ltd* (n 64). Rejecting a contractual analysis: *Guardians of Pontypridd Union v Drew* [1927] 1 KB 214 (CA) 220 (Scrutton LJ obiter).
[73] eg a contract to purchase freehold land: *Whittingham v Murdy* (1889) 60 LT 956 (QB); *Thurstan v Nottingham Permanent Benefit Building Society* [1902] 1 Ch 1 (CA) 13.
[74] *Roberts v Gray* [1913] 1 KB 520 (CA). In a case of this type there is no receipt of a benefit.
[75] The Infants Relief Act 1874 restricted the infant's liability to be sued but not to claim. This did not reflect the pre-1874 law or the current law, Minors' Contracts Act 1987, s 4(1).

can be made for treating agreements with infants as contractual. It was, after all, said that quid pro quo, which was a precondition of an action of debt in the absence of a deed, was required.[76] This element of reciprocity is an essential characteristic of claims in contract which is also reflected in the doctrine of consideration.[77] Once assumpsit was used in place of debt, a claim for a fixed sum in debt was replaced by a claim for damages. Damages in assumpsit were generally calculated on the value of the promised performance albeit that the amount remained a matter within jury discretion.[78] In claims for necessaries, a plaintiff was also required to aver that the sum was reasonable.[79] The fact that there is in effect a contract to pay a reasonable sum does not mean that the claim is non-contractual or based on unjust enrichment. The requirement of a reasonable sum is mirrored, albeit more informally, in the way that a jury might award less than the value of performance (the expectation measure) in a standard case.

V. Contracts and Formalities

For centuries, some contracts have required writing to be enforceable.[80] It has been held that liability, where the formality requirements are not met, rests on unjust enrichment.[81] Section 4 of the Statute of Frauds 1677 states that in those contracts to which the statute applies: 'Noe Action shall be brought ... unlesse the Agreement upon which Action shall be brought ... shall be in Writeing.' Not very long after the statute, it was explained that in the absence of writing there was no remedy.[82] By the eighteenth century, this statement had become a rather different proposition: that if statute applied and the agreement was not in writing, then the contract was void.[83] This view survived into the nineteenth century.[84]

In 1852, *Leroux v Brown* restated the older position that the contract was unenforceable rather than void.[85] A contract that was unenforceable for want of writing could certainly be raised by way of a defence.[86] This still left open the question of

---

[76] (1431) YB 10 Hen VI f 14, pl 46.
[77] Ibbetson, *A Historical Introduction to the Law of Obligations* (n 20) 80–87.
[78] David Ibbetson, 'The Assessment of Contractual Damages at Common Law in the Late Sixteenth Century' in Matthew Dyson and David Ibbetson (eds), *Law and Legal Process: Substantive Law and Procedure in English Legal History* (CUP 2013) 126, 127.
[79] Baker, 'Use of Assumpsit' (n 33) 39–40.
[80] As a result of the Statute of Frauds 1677 (29 Cha 2 c 3).
[81] *Pavey & Matthews Pty Ltd v Paul* (1987) 162 CLR 221; *Dimond v Lovell* [2002] 1 AC 384 (HL).
[82] *Case v Barber* (1680) Sir T Raym 450; 83 ER 235.
[83] *Chater v Beckett* (1797) 7 TR 201, 204; 101 ER 931, 933; *Matson v Wharam* (1787) 2 TR 80, 81; 100 ER 44, 44–45; *Cooke v Tombs* (1794) 2 Anst 420, 425; 145 ER 922, 924.
[84] *Carrington v Roots* (1837) 2 M & W 248, 255; 150 ER 748, 751; *Reade v Lamb* (1851) 6 Ex 130, 132; 155 ER 483, 484–85. But see *Crosby v Wadsworth* (1805) 6 East 602, 611; 102 ER 1419, 1423.
[85] *Leroux v Brown* (1852) 12 CB 801, 824; 138 ER 1119, 1129 (Jervis CJ). But see Willes J in *Williams v Wheeler* (1860) 8 CB (NS) 299, 316; 141 ER 1181, 1188.
[86] *Thomas v Brown* (1876) 1 QBD 714 (QB) 723.

whether there was liability for work done under an unenforceable contract and, if so, what was the basis of that liability. In *Souch v Strawbridge*, a contract to recover the costs incurred maintaining a child at the defendant's request was held by Tindal CJ to be 'equivalent to the proof that is ordinarily given in an action for goods sold and delivered, whence the law implies a promise on the defendant's part to pay for them'.[87] Where work had been done or the goods delivered despite the absence of writing there was no need to deny a claim, in Tindal CJ's view liability rested on an 'executed contract'.[88]

Some situations are more difficult to rationalize.[89] In *Pulbrook v Lawes*, it was agreed that, prior to the plaintiff taking a lease on the defendant's house, work would be carried out on the property by both parties.[90] The plaintiff spent money on the renovations but because the defendant failed to finish his share of the work the lease was never granted. Blackburn J held that the plaintiff should be compensated for the value of the work done. It might be said that the defendant was otherwise unjustly enriched at the expense of the plaintiff.[91] It might also be said that there was no fictious contract. There was a genuinely implied agreement that in the event the lease was not granted then the plaintiff would be paid for the work that they had done. This is quite distinct from the agreement to enter a lease which is unenforceable without writing. Both Blackburn and Lush JJ were influenced by the fact that had the plaintiff paid for the defendant to do the work (rather than doing it himself) he would have been able to recover the cost from the defendant and thought that it should not matter that he had actually done the work himself.

In *Scarisbrick v Parkinson*, the plaintiff was an apprentice clerk for the defendant for three years under an agreement to pay a salary of £20 per year.[92] In recovering the three years' salary, the plaintiff was not recovering under the contract of employment which was both unenforceable and an annual contract. That contract was only relevant to determine a reasonable salary. But it does not follow that such a claim need be based on unjust enrichment. This situation is analogous to *Pulbrook v Lawes* because the original contract whilst unenforceable provides the basis for setting the expectations of the parties which on the facts meant that the plaintiff would pay the defendant for the work they had done. It is not obvious why a *quantum meruit* in this situation cannot be based on a genuinely implied contract. Salter J makes the point explicit in *Scott v Pattison*, when an oral contract of

---

[87] *Souch v Strawbridge* (1846) 2 CB 808, 814; 135 ER 1161, 1164. See also the earlier remarks of Lord Mansfield: *Simon v Metivier* (1766) 1 Wm Bla 599, 600; 96 ER 347, 347.
[88] *Souch v Strawbridge*, ibid 815.
[89] For a different view of some of these authorities, see David Ibbetson, 'Implied Contracts and Restitution: History in the High Court of Australia' (1988) 8 OJLS 312, 320–23.
[90] *Pulbrook v Lawes* (1876) 1 QBD 284 (QB).
[91] Although there is still some difficulty in saying that the defendant received a benefit on the grounds that there was subjective devaluation: see Burrows, *The Law of Restitution* (n 4) 384.
[92] *Scarisbrick v Parkinson* (1869) 20 LT 175 (QB).

employment is unenforceable there is an 'implied contract' which 'is not enforcing the unenforceable contract'.[93]

Lord Denning would be critical of contractual reasoning. In *James v Thomas H Kent & Co Ltd*, he held that:

> It used to be said in the old days that in that case his action was on an implied contract and that was also said in *Scott v. Pattison*; but that is not a correct way of approach because, in none of these cases can you have an implied contract covering the same ground as an existing special contract. The proper ground of the claim is not in contract at all, but in restitution. It is money which, in justice, ought to be paid for services rendered.[94]

In response, it might be said that the express and implied contract are not covering the 'same ground'. In *Scott v Pattison*, the unenforceable contract was to pay a weekly wage. The *quantum meruit* was an implied agreement based on custom. Equally, in *Scarisbrick v Parkinson*, the unenforceable annual contract was a different creature from an implied agreement to pay for three years of work based on a *quantum meruit*. This is not to say that the unenforceable contract should not be a relevant factor in determining that what the parties had impliedly agreed was reasonable. It is not mere semantics to say that these are different agreements. The existence of an unenforceable express contract should not prevent one from been implied provided it does not cover identical ground.

VI. Contracts Which Have Failed or Are Unenforceable

The situation where a valid contract has been discharged by breach or frustration or is otherwise unenforceable is superficially more difficult to justify using a contractual analysis. An express contract undeniable already exists. To argue that there is a second contract appears to undermine the bargain. In contemporary law, there can only be a claim in unjust enrichment when the contract has been discharged and there is a 'total failure of consideration'.[95] Abstractions of this sort would have been incomprehensible to eighteenth-century pleaders. In his account of the trial

---

[93] *Scott v Pattison* [1923] 2 KB 723 (KB) 728.
[94] *James v Thomas H Kent & Co Ltd* [1951] 1 KB 551 (CA) 556 (fn omitted). Lord Denning had much earlier discussed these issues writing extrajudicially: AT Denning, '*Quantum Meruit* and the Statute of Frauds' (1925) 41 LQR 79.
[95] For a particularly broad engagement with these issues, see *Lumbers v W Cook Builders Pty Ltd* [2008] HCA 27; (2008) 232 CLR 635. The decision also emphasized the need for a request in a *quantum meruit* action. This aspect of the case has been criticized: Michael Bryan, '*Lumbers v W Cook Builders Pty Ltd (in liq)*: Restitution for Services and the Allocation of Contractual Risk' (2009) 33 MULR 320, 328–30.

court of the period, Henry Bathurst distinguished two situations.[96] In the first, a plaintiff brought a *quantum meruit* and the defendant showed on the evidence that a fixed sum was agreed. In *Weaver v Boroughs* (cited by Bathurst in the margin), a plaintiff declared on a special assumpsit for the hire of a horse so much per day and then a distinct separate indebitatus count for hire.[97] In rejecting the claim, Raymond CJ gave a further example: 'he put the case of a contract for goods at a certain price, where the plaintiff is never suffered to recover on *quantum meruit*, if he fails to prove the particular price agreed on'.[98] The claim failed because the plaintiff could not prove the count as laid.[99] The special contract was what the parties had expressly agreed. The *quantum meruit* plea was contradicted by the facts.

A second scenario described by Bathurst concerned a situation where 'if he prove a special Agreement and the Work done, but not pursuant to such Agreement, he shall recover upon the *Quantum meruit*, for otherwise he would not be able to recover at all'.[100] The example used was *Mr Keck's Case*: the plaintiff had failed to perform according to the terms of the contract but was allowed to bring a *quantum meruit* for the value of his labour although, in Bathurst's view, proof of the agreement meant that it 'might be proper to lessen the *Quantum* of the Damages'.[101] The only comment on the *quantum meruit* was that it was not based on a special contract.[102]

There are other instances of a *quantum meruit* succeeding where a plaintiff was excluded from recovering on the special contract because, for example, they had mis-performed.[103] It was more convenient to declare on both the special contract and *quantum meruit* in the same action rather than resort to *quantum meruit* having failed in an action on special contract. Lord Mansfield supported this new mode of pleading, but it was also resisted.[104] In *Pepper v Burland*, a Nisi Prius decision in 1791, Lord Kenyon held that 'as far as it [the contract] can be traced to

---

[96] Henry Bathurst, *An Introduction to the Law Relative to Trials at Nisi Prius* (W Strahan and M Woodfall 1767) 129. Subsequent editions were edited by the future King's Bench and Common Pleas judge, Francis Buller. For a different view, see Tariq A Baloch, *Unjust Enrichment and Contract* (Hart Publishing 2009) 131–32.
[97] *Weaver v Boroughs* (1725) 1 Stra 648; 93 ER 757; LI MS Hill 12 (1) f 6.
[98] ibid. This part of the judgment is omitted from the printed report.
[99] *Miller v Duell* (1735) HLS MS 4062, 90; *Clark v Smith* (1735) LI MS Misc 37 f 98; *Martin v Webb* (1763) LI MS Misc 129 f 71.
[100] Bathurst (n 96) 129.
[101] ibid 129–30.
[102] See David Ibbetson, 'Development at Common Law' in Elise Bant, Kit Barker, and Simone Degeling (eds), *Research Handbook on Unjust Enrichment and Restitution* (Edward Elgar 2020) 28, 31, who draws different conclusions from this decision.
[103] *Salisbury v Yates* (1724) LI MS Hill 8 f 208, discussed in Swain, *The Law of Contract 1670–1870* (n 3) 69; JL Barton, 'Contract and Quantum Meruit: The Antecedents of *Cutter v Powell*' (1987) 8 JLH 48, 58.
[104] *Harris v Oke* (1759) LI MS Hill 6 f 217. The discussion of this mode of pleading belongs within a wider debate which included the action of money had and received which was substantively completely different to *quantum meruit*: Warren Swain, '*Cutter v Powell* and the Pleading of Claims of Unjust Enrichment' (2003) 11 RLR 46, 51.

have been followed', then the sum that the plaintiff could recover was governed by the contract.[105] Where the work deviated from the contract so that 'it is impossible to trace the contract', then the plaintiff could recover on the *quantum meruit*. In these passages, Lord Kenyon made explicit reference to *the contract*. By these remarks, he may have been doing no more than restating the existing rule that *quantum meruit* could not succeed if it contradicted the existence of a special contract. It was different when a claim on the special contract was unavailable to the plaintiff. There is no risk of two contradictory pleas. No great hardship follows in this situation from saying that there was an implied agreement that the work done would be paid for.

Some of the dicta in the leading case of *Cutter v Powell* can be read as rejecting the idea that *quantum meruit* claims were contractual in character.[106] Lord Kenyon explained 'that where the parties have come to an express contract none can be implied has prevailed so long as to be reduced to an axiom in the law'.[107] Ashhurst J said: 'but she has no right to desert the agreement; for wherever there is an express contract the parties must be guided by it; and one party cannot relinquish or abide by it as may suit his advantage'.[108] The language used was undoubtedly less tied to the mechanics of pleading than earlier authorities. But it should not be made to carry too much weight. Neither Lord Kenyon nor Ashhurst J deny that a *quantum meruit* might be based on an implied contract. Nor does the decision preclude a claim on a *quantum meruit* just because the parties had entered into an express contract. Several examples of this exact situation were given during argument.[109] It is a different matter when a claim on the special contract was possible. In *Cutter v Powell* itself, the plaintiff could not prove the claim as laid so that the claim fell into Bathurst's first category. A particular wage was agreed and *quantum meruit* was not to be used as a way of ignoring that agreement.

A special (express) contract was no obstacle to bringing a *quantum meruit* if the contract was rescinded. For a period, the application of these types of claims was restricted because a narrow view of rescission took hold[110] alongside a new pleading rule which meant if a defendant failed to fully perform his side of the agreement, the plaintiff was required to count on the special contract for breach and was barred from the *quantum meruit*.[111] In *Ellis v Hamlen*, the plaintiff contracted with the defendant to build a house but the completed house did not meet the specifications laid down in the special contract.[112] Having declared

---

[105] *Pepper v Burland* (1791) Peake 139; 170 ER 107.
[106] *Cutter v Powell* (1795) 6 TR 320; 101 ER 573. There was a strong element of public policy in this decision, see Martin Dockray, '*Cutter v Powell*: A Trip Outside the Text' (2001) 117 LQR 664.
[107] *Cutter v Powell*, ibid 324; 576.
[108] ibid 325; 576.
[109] For this point, see Baloch (n 96) 133.
[110] *Hulle v Heightman* (1802) 2 East 145; 102 ER 324; *Hunt v Silk* (1804) 5 East 449; 102 ER 1142.
[111] *Mulloy v Backer* (1804) 5 East 316, 322; 102 ER 1091, 1094 (Lord Ellenborough). This only applied to *quantum meruit* and not, eg, an action for money paid.
[112] *Ellis v Hamlen* (1810) 3 Taunt 52; 128 ER 21.

on the special contract, the plaintiff found himself unable to recover because the evidence was that he had not performed in accordance with the agreement. He sought to recoup the value of his work upon a *quantum valebant* for work, labour, and materials. Mansfield CJ, in non-suiting the plaintiff, was hostile to the action:

> It is said he has the benefit of the houses, and therefore the Plaintiff is entitled to recover on a quantum valebant. To be sure it is hard that he should build houses and not be paid for them; but the difficulty is to know where to draw the line; for if the Defendant is obliged to pay in a case where there is one deviation from his contract, he may equally be obliged to pay for any thing, how far soever distant from what the contract stipulated for.[113]

This approach was inconsistent with earlier authorities. It meant that even if no claim on the special contract was available, a *quantum meruit* or *quantum valebant* would not be allowed. Mansfield CJ seems to be groping towards the idea that the *quantum meruit* was subsidiary to the claim on the express contract. It does not follow that he was adopting an unjust enrichment analysis of the *quantum meruit*. His very narrow approach did not survive long. In *Burn v Miller*, a similar case three years later, a *quantum meruit* was successful.[114] It was said, 'there are many contracts made with relation to time, upon which, although the works are not finished when the time is expired, the work and labour or other beneficial matter may nevertheless be recovered for'.[115] It was emphasized that the defendant stood by while he saw the work done. In the words of the judgment, there was an action of assumpsit on 'implied promises' which can be interpreted as a *genuine* implied contract. In *Planché v Colburn*, Tindal CJ took an equally generous view:

> ... when a special contract is in existence and open, the Plaintiff cannot sue on a quantum meruit: part of the question here, therefore, was, whether the contract did exist or not. It distinctly appeared that the work was finally abandoned; and the jury found that no new contract had been entered into. Under these circumstances the Plaintiff ought not to lose the fruit of his labour ...[116]

---

[113] ibid 53; 22.
[114] *Burn v Miller* (1813) 4 Taunt 745; 128 ER 523.
[115] ibid 748; 525.
[116] *Planché v Colburn* (1831) 8 Bing 14, 16; 131 ER 305, 306. For the detail on this decision, see Charles Mitchell and Charlotte Mitchell, '*Planché v Colburn* (1831)' in Charles Mitchell and Paul Mitchell (eds), *Landmark Cases in the Law of Restitution* (Hart Publishing 2006).

VII. *Quantum Meruit*: Pleading and Substance

One of the important effects of the Common Law Procedure Act 1852 was to remove the necessity of stating a form of action in a summons on a civil claim.[117] Most of the cases discussed here predate that statute. Ibbetson has observed that '[a]n understanding of the old pleading forms may be useful to avoid misinterpreting old cases … but when the ghosts of the past start clanking their chains threateningly it is not always the most prudent response to ask to join in their dance'.[118] As might be expected, anyone looking for a principle of unjust enrichment in these decisions without resorting to anachronism will be disappointed. Where it was necessary for technical reasons to classify these claims, contractual rules applied.[119] The reason that it is not possible to recover on a *quantum meruit* in some situations where there is a special contract is not because unjust enrichment is subsidiary to contract. When these claims fail it is not because they are too different on the same facts, but rather because they are too similar. The *quantum meruit* is as much based on a contract as the claim on the special contract. One type of contract is created by express agreement. When bringing a claim on a special contract, the plaintiff was required to set out the promise and the consideration including what the parties agreed. In contrast, the declaration in *quantum meruit* alleged that the plaintiff had performed work at the defendant's request who had promised to pay him so much as he deserved. The second type of contract arises by genuine implication which is the very reason that judges were unwilling to allow a contract of this type to contradict the express contract. There is no need to force these decisions into an unjust enrichment framework.[120] The same can be said about the authorities on incapacity and unenforceability due to formalities. It is difficult to see liability here as anything other than consensual and, indeed, contractual. Perhaps these decisions are no more than a survival in modern times of an older version of the law of contract which was more pragmatic and therefore difficult to fit into a more rigid intellectual framework based on classical contract law, or more recently on taxonomical exactitude.

If the analysis here is correct, then the obvious question is why someone like Maine began to feel jittery about treating these cases as contractual. An explanation can be found in Sir William Evans's commentary on his translation of Pothier's *Treatise on Obligations*. Pothier's work would be the foundational text for those who viewed a contract as a product of a meeting of wills. Evans

---

[117] Common Law Procedure Act 1852 (15 & 16 Vict c 76).
[118] Ibbetson, 'Implied Contracts and Restitution: History in the High Court of Australia' (n 89) 313.
[119] eg in relation to the Statute of Limitations 1623 (8 Jac 1 c 16): *Masters of Tobacco Pipe Makers Co v Loader* (1851) 16 QB 765 (QB).
[120] Burrows has conceded that *Planché v Colburn* (n 116) is not a case on restitution: see Burrows, *The Law of Restitution* (n 4) 346, fn 31.

wrote: 'Quasi-contracts which with us would be treated by implication as actual contracts. They differ from contracts, as not being founded upon actual consent... Such are the cases of receiving money which ought to be refunded.'[121] The reason that the contract justification for these claims was questioned and then treated as fictitious was the result of the way that an unduly narrow doctrine of contract law came to operate. Under an approach to contract that emphasizes an express agreement, these authorities fit less happily within contract law. But that does not mean that they cannot properly be regarded as contractual, which was the way that earlier generations of lawyers viewed them. The second reason why contractual reasoning was sidelined is quite different. It reflects the primacy of the action for money had and received. There is significant disagreement on the true basis of this action amongst legal historians.[122] But no one would claim that this action fits very easily into a contractual framework. This was as true in the eighteenth century as it is now. The same could be said about the action for money paid—as long ago as the 1750s, it was accepted that no request was required.[123] There is no need to apply the same non-contractual reasoning to the *quantum meruit*.

Legal history has been used to argue for all kinds of positions in modern debates about the value of unjust enrichment. On one level, it is surprising that a decision like *Moses v Macferlan*, which after all is more than 250 years old, should be relevant.[124] It would be odd for a legal historian to dismiss the value of legal history but if history is to be used, then care needs to be taken not to use a selective version of history and that means at least considering the contractual character of some of these claims. Other claims may have other explanations, and this may include unjust enrichment in some cases.[125] In turn, this raises further questions not only about whether some legal historians have been too willing to accept a cohesive unjust enrichment analysis of the historical case law but whether some of the modern unjust enrichment territory might properly be ceded back to contract law.

---

[121] R Pothier, *A Treatise on the Law of Obligations or Contracts*, vol 1 (William Evans tr, A Strahan 1806) 85.
[122] Warren Swain, '*Moses v Macferlan* (1760)' in Charles Mitchell and Paul Mitchell (eds), *Landmark Cases in the Law of Restitution* (Hart Publishing 2006) 19, 26–27; Ibbetson, 'Development at Common Law' (n 102) 34.
[123] *Decker v Pope* (1757) LI MS Misc 129 (unfold).
[124] *Moses v Macferlan* (1760) 2 Burr 1005; 97 ER 676.
[125] There are some types of claims that are impossible to fit with contractual reasoning beyond money had and received. Eg mistaken improvements cannot be explained as consensual: Andrew Burrows, 'In Defence of Unjust Enrichment' (2019) 78 CLJ 521, 534–35.

2
A Tale of Transplantation
The Historical Evolution of the Law of Unjust Enrichment in China

Siyi Lin

I. Introduction

Unjust enrichment is not an indigenous concept in the China's legal system. The concept of unjust enrichment was transplanted into China in 1911 for the first time when Qing dynasty officials produced the first draft of a modern civil code in Chinese history, *Da Qing Min Lv Cao An* (The Draft of the Civil Law of Great Qing), modelled after the German Civil Code.[1] However, the notion that no one ought to be enriched without justification can be traced back to the ancient Chinese codes. The law of unjust enrichment in China has not received much attention from lawmakers, academia, or legal practitioners compared with contract law or tort law,[2] whereas this area is among the most debated private law topics in many other jurisdictions.[3] Two legal rules constituted the entire Chinese law of unjust enrichment over the past decades, which failed to provide comprehensive regulation of unjust enrichment.[4] In May 2020, China finally promulgated its first ever comprehensive civil code. The Chinese Civil Code of the People's Republic of China (Chinese Civil Code)—devotes one specific chapter to unjust enrichment.[5] That chapter has generated a wave of discussion in academia and is considered to represent significant progress for the Chinese law of unjust enrichment.[6] However, the chapter contains

---

[1] See Section II.B.
[2] Siyi Lin, *The Law of Unjust Enrichment in China: Necessary or Not?* (Springer 2022) ch 1 (hereafter Lin, *Unjust Enrichment in China*).
[3] Andrew Burrows, 'The English Law of Restitution: A Ten-Year Review' in Jason W Neyers, Mitchell McInnes, and Stephen GA Pitel (eds), *Understanding Unjust Enrichment* (Hart Publishing 2004) 14.
[4] See Section II.D.3.
[5] Zhonghua Renmin Gongheguo Minfa Dian (中华人民共和国民法典) [Civil Code of the People's Republic of China] (promulgated by the National People's Congress [NPC] on 28 May 2020, effective 1 January 2021).
[6] Examples of articles discussing the law of unjust enrichment after the promulgation of the Chinese Civil Code are: Zhicheng Wu and William Swadling, 'Unjustified Enrichment in the Chinese Civil Code: Questions From the Common Law' (2021) 29 Asia Pacific Law Review 402 (hereafter Wu and Swadling, 'Unjustified Enrichment'); Shuxing Liu (刘书星), 'The Position of Claims in Unjust Enrichment in the Chinese Civil Code and Relevant Litigation Issues' (《民法典》不当得利请求权的定位及相关诉讼问题) (2020) 19 Journal of Law Application 26; Ziqiang Chen (陈自强), 'Liability

only four articles, which are neither detailed nor sufficiently comprehensive to address various problems existing in the field of unjust enrichment. Whether it will make a difference in theory and practice requires an in-depth analysis. This chapter seeks to evaluate the current status of the law of unjust enrichment by embarking on a journey through time and exploring the historical evolution of unjust enrichment from its beginnings in China to its modern form.

Apart from this section, the ensuing discussion in this chapter proceeds in four parts. Section II traces the origin of unjust enrichment since the times of ancient China and explores the historical evolution of the Chinese law of unjust enrichment chronologically to lay a foundation for understanding this area of law. Section III examines the current law of unjust enrichment in China and evaluates whether the Chinese Civil Code makes a successful attempt to improve the law of unjust enrichment. Section IV summarizes the observations from the historical review and Section V concludes.

II. Historical Development

A. Ancient China

In ancient China, kings and emperors used law as a tool to rule the country and to mould people to the ruler's will.[7] Each dynasty promulgated its representative legal code, which usually continued those of the preceding dynasty but revised and adjusted in content, structure, and style.[8] Traditional Chinese law focused on the protection of hierarchical social order and state interests.[9] There was no concept of civil law, including unjust enrichment. However, legal rules could be found scattered in the codes of different dynasties targeting individuals who had obtained benefits in the absence of any justification. As early as the Warring States period, *Fa Jing* (Canon of Laws), the first legal code in imperial China, declared that a person who retained lost property would be sentenced to death.[10] In the Tang dynasty, *Tang Lv Shu Yi* (Annotation of Tang Code) stated that anyone claiming a slave or property of others as their own should be whipped forty times as if they had

---

System of Restitution for Unjust Enrichment in Chinese Civil Code' (民法典不当得利返还责任体系之展开) (2021) 43(4) Chinese Journal of Law 91.

[7] Jinfan Zhang, *The Tradition and Modern Transition of Chinese Law* (Zhang Lixin and others trs, Springer 2014) 271 (hereafter Zhang, *Tradition and Modern Transition*).

[8] Huixing Liang, *The Draft Civil Code of the People's Republic of China* (Martinus Nijhoff 2010)XI (hereafter Liang, *Draft Civil Code*); Demei Zhang (张德美), *Exploration and Choice: A Study of the Legal Transplantation in Late Qing Dynasty* (探索与抉择—晚清法律移植研究) (Tsinghua University Press 2003) 85.

[9] Jianfu Chen, *Chinese Law: Context and Transformation* (rev edn, Brill Nijhoff 2015) 328 (hereafter Chen, *Chinese Law*).

[10] Mi Zhou (周密), *History of Criminal Law in China* (中国刑法史) (Qunzhong Press 1985)181.

committed a crime.[11] Codes in the Ming and Qing dynasties also contained rules requiring the return of lost property.[12]

Law in imperial China contained no distinction between civil and criminal law, which was overwhelmingly penal in emphasis and was limited to being a compilation of ethical customs.[13] Matters of a civil nature were largely ignored, with merely limited treatment given in a criminal format.[14] This explains why rulers imposed criminal punishments on individuals who became enriched without justification. The purpose of such rules was not to protect individual property rights but to regulate ancient Chinese society. The rules stripping people of enrichment obtained without justification indicate that ancient Chinese ethics viewed the receipt of a windfall gain as morally unacceptable.[15]

B. Late Qing Dynasty

Unjust enrichment received its earliest description in China when the Qing government drafted the first civil code of China—the Draft of Civil Code of Great Qing (*Da Qing Min Lv Cao An*, Qing's Draft Civil Code).[16] In the late Qing dynasty (1644–1911), under the pressure of domestic and foreign demands, the Qing government initiated a modernization of China's legal system in 1902 and began the process of adopting foreign law.[17] Drafting the Qing's Draft Civil Code formally began in 1908.[18] Given the rising political tensions at the time, the Qing government ordered a speeding up of the drafting process and the code was completed within three years.[19] The Qing's Draft Civil Code was finally completed in September 1911, representing China's earliest effort to codify civil law.[20]

---

[11] Wuji Zhangsun (长孙无忌), *Annotation of the Tang Code* (唐律疏议) (The Commercial Press 1993) 381. *Tang Lv Shu Yi* is the penal law code of the Tang Dynasty (618–907) annotated by Zhangsun Wuji and other officials and the annotations had equal legal effect to the legal provisions: Zhang, *Tradition and Modern Transition* (n 7) 279.

[12] Xiaofeng Huai (怀效锋) (ed), *Statute Laws of the Ming Dynasty* (大明律) (Law Press China 1999) 82; Rongzheng Zhang (张荣铮) (ed), *The Law of Qing Dynasty* (大清律例) (Tianjin Ancient Works Publishing House 1999) 271.

[13] Falian Zhang, *A Comparative Study of Chinese and Western Legal Language and Culture* (Peking UP 2021) 182.

[14] Derk Bodde, 'Basic Concepts of Chinese Law: The Genesis and Evolution of Legal Thought in Traditional China' (1963) 107 Proceedings of the American Philosophical Society 375.

[15] See a similar discussion by the authors in Steve Gallagher, Lin Siyi, and Lutz-Christian Wolff, 'The History of a Mystery: The Evolution of the Law of Unjust Enrichment in Germany, England and China' (2020) 3 ICPELR 337, 362.

[16] Liang, *Draft Civil Code* (n 8) XIII.

[17] Hao Jiang, 'Chinese Tort Law: Tradition, Transplants and Some Difficulties' in Mauro Bussani and Anthony J Sebok (eds), *Comparative Tort Law: Global Perspectives* (Edward Elgar 2021) 404 (hereafter Jiang, 'Chinese Tort Law').

[18] Sheng Zhang (张生), 'Discussion of the Draft Civil Law in the Qing Dynasty' (《大清民律草案》摭遗) (2004) 3 Chinese Journal of Law 140 (hereafter Zhang, 'Discussion of Draft Civil Law').

[19] ibid 144.

[20] Yang Lixin (杨立新) (ed), *Draft of Civil Code of the Great Qing Dynasty and Draft Civil Law of the Republic of China* (大清民律草案民国民律草案) (Jilin People Press 2002) 6 (hereafter Yang, *Draft*

A Japanese jurist, Yoshimasa Matsuoka, was responsible for drafting the first three books of the code; that is, General Principles, Obligatory Rights, and Law of Rights *in Rem*, with the contents mainly borrowed from the German Civil Code and the Japanese Civil Code, containing civil law concepts that had never actually emerged in Chinese history.[21] The last two books, Family and Successions, were drafted by Chinese scholars mainly based on Chinese customs.[22] Book II Obligatory Rights of the Qing's Draft Civil Code contained one chapter devoted to unjust enrichment, consisting of sixteen articles (Arts 929 to 944).[23] Unjust enrichment was designated as a causative event creating obligatory rights alongside torts, contracts, and *negotiorum gestio*.[24]

Article 929 of the Qing's Draft Civil Code stated the general principle of unjust enrichment:

> A person obtaining benefits from another person's performance or in any other way without legal grounds, which results in another's loss, is bound to return the benefits. The duty also exists if the legal ground falls away subsequently or if a transfer fails to produce the result it was intended to produce in accordance with the contents of the legal act.
>
> Acknowledgement of the existence or non-existence of an obligation shall be deemed as performance.[25]

This provision was nearly identical to s 812 of the German Civil Code, following Germany's distinction between performance- and non-performance-based unjust enrichment.[26] In fact, the Qing's Draft Civil Code borrowed the whole chapter of unjust enrichment from the German Civil Code. Under the Qing's Draft Civil Code, the required elements for raising an unjust enrichment claim included: (1) the defendant's enrichment; (2) the plaintiff's loss; and (3) the unjustness of the enrichment. In addition to the absence of a legal basis, Art 933 of the Qing's Draft Civil Code imposed restitutionary liabilities where the defendant was in violation

---

Civil Code). Philip C Huang, *Code, Custom, and Legal Practice in China: The Qing and the Republic Compared* (Stanford UP 2001) 16 (hereafter Huang, *Code, Custom, and Legal Practice*).

[21] Liang, *Draft Civil Code* (n 8) XIII.
[22] James Gordley, Hao Jiang, and Arthur Taylor von Mehren, *An Introduction to the Comparative Study of Private Law: Readings, Cases, Materials* (2nd edn, CUP 2021) 48; Jiang, *Chinese Tort Law* (n 17) 404.
[23] Yang, *Draft Civil Code* (n 20) 121–23.
[24] ibid 121.
[25] ibid.
[26] An unofficial English translation is available at Langenscheidt Translation Service, 'German Civil Code' (Federal Ministry of Justice, 1 October 2013) <www.gesetze-im-internet.de/englisch_bgb/englisch_bgb.html> accessed 28 June 2023.

of the law and good customs by having received the benefit.[27] Article 930 stated that restitution of performance should also be rendered where the claimant had a defence that could be asserted to permanently exclude another's claim, but failed to invoke the defence and performed to satisfy the claim.[28] The Qing's Draft Civil Code also specified a series of defences against unjust enrichment claims. Articles 930(2) and 931 prevented restitution if the claimant paid an undue debt, knew the absence of an obligation to perform at the time of performance, the performance complied with a moral rather than a legal obligation, or the claimant paid to discharge a time-barred debt.[29] Article 932 further clarified that no restitution should be granted if a claimant performed to achieve certain results while knowing that the results would not occur at the outset or in bad faith deliberately preventing the results from occurring.[30] The underlying rationale was that the person ignoring their rights was not worthy of legal protection.

In terms of liabilities in unjust enrichment, Arts 934 and 935 governed restitutionary liabilities where an unauthorized disposition occurred.[31] Articles 936 and 937 replicated the 'three-step approach' to the measure of restitutionary liability in the German Civil Code.[32] The first step required the initial object of enrichment, any benefits associated with the enrichment, and any compensation received due to the reduction, damage, or embezzlement of the enrichment to be returned. Where it was impossible to return the initial object of enrichment in kind, the second step converted this into 'value received' and the enriched person was required to pay the value of the enrichment. Article 937 contained the third step concerning 'value remaining'. In most situations, the enriched person was only compelled to return the value remaining in their hands. However, mala fide defendants aware of the absence of a legal ground for receiving the enrichment (Art 938) or acting unlawfully or immorally by accepting the claimant's performance (Art 941) did not enjoy such an exemption of liability.[33] The distinction of liabilities assumed by mala fide and bona fide defendants was intended to protect innocent recipients. Article 944 further catered for the situation where an enriched person gratuitously passed the enrichment to a third party.[34] The third party would bear the liability to render restitution to the extent of the defendant's reduced obligation.[35]

---

[27] Yang, *Draft Civil Code* (n 20) 122. Article 933 of the Qing's Draft Civil Code was nearly identical to s 817 of the German Civil Code.
[28] ibid 121. This provision was similar to s 817 of the German Civil Code.
[29] ibid 121–22. Those defences are also provided in ss 813(2) and 814 of the German Civil Code.
[30] ibid 122. This provision was nearly the same as s 815 of the German Civil Code.
[31] ibid. These two provisions were replicas of s 816 of the German Civil Code.
[32] ibid. See s 818 of the German Civil Code. For a detailed account of the 'three-step approach' in the German Civil Code, see Gerhard Dannemann, *The German Law of Unjustified Enrichment and Restitution: A Comparative Introduction* (OUP 2009) 124.
[33] Yang, *Draft Civil Code* (n 20) 122–23. Similar contents can be found in s 819 of the German Civil Code.
[34] ibid 123.
[35] ibid. Section 822 of the German Civil Code imposes the same restitutionary duties on third parties.

This analysis of the Qing's Draft Civil Code reflects the fact that the concept of unjust enrichment was first transplanted into China by directly duplicating provisions concerning unjust enrichment in the German Civil Code. The transplantation occurred against a backdrop of almost no civil law having been developed in China and, due to time constraints, without any in-depth research of the history and operation of unjust enrichment in the legal system. The Qing's Draft Civil Code was never formally promulgated as the Qing Empire collapsed shortly after the draft was completed.[36] However, this first attempt to establish a separate modern civil code in Chinese legal history is still of significance.[37] The Qing's Draft Civil Code paved the way for future Chinese civil laws[38] and also laid the foundation for the evolution of the Chinese law of unjust enrichment.

C. The Kuomintang Era

The 1911 Revolution overthrew the Qing dynasty and gave birth to the Republic of China.[39] In spite of the political instability during this period, the Republican government did not stifle the efforts to establish a modern civil code.[40] By 1925, the Beiyang government (1912–28) drew upon the Qing's Draft Civil Code and completed a draft civil code for the Republic of China (1925 Draft).[41] The 1925 Draft also contained a sub-chapter on unjust enrichment consisting of thirteen provisions (Arts 273 to 285) and the contents remained largely the same as those in the Qing's Draft Civil Code.[42]

Immediately after the Nationalist government (1927–49) superseded the Beiyang government in 1928, it set up a Commission on Civil Codification and completed the Civil Law of the Republic of China (Republican Civil Code) in 1930.[43] This was the first formally enacted civil code in China's history.[44] The Republican Civil Code was based on the Qing's Draft Civil Code and the 1925

---

[36] Zhang, 'Discussion of Draft Civil Law' (n 18) 149–50.
[37] Lei Chen, 'The Historical Development of the Civil Law Tradition in China: A Private Law Perspective' (2010) 78 The Legal History Review 159, 168 (hereafter Chen, 'Historical Development').
[38] Xiuqing Li (李秀清), 'The New Trend of the Civil Law in Early 20th Century and the Republican Civil Code' (20世纪前期民法新潮流与《中华民国民法》) (2002) 1 Tribune of Political Science and Law 124, 126 (hereafter Li, 'New Trend'); Lei Chen, 'Continuity and Change: Some Reflections on the Chinese Civil Code' (2021) 29 Asia Pacific Law Review 287, 290 (hereafter Chen, 'Continuity and Change').
[39] Hanchao Lu, *The Birth of a Republic* (University of Washington Press 2010) 192–93.
[40] Chen, 'Historical Development' (n 37) 168.
[41] Limin Wang (王立民), 'The Compilation Process of the Chinese Civil Code over One Hundred Years and Insights' (中国百年民法典编纂历程与启示) (2020) 10 Law Science 160, 163 (hereafter Wang, 'Compilation Process').
[42] Yang, *Draft Civil Code* (n 20) 238–40.
[43] Roscoe Pound, 'The Chinese Civil Code in Action' (1955) 29 Tulane Law Review 277, 278 (hereafter Pound, 'Chinese Civil Code').
[44] Wang, 'Compilation Process' (n 41) 165.

Draft while also developed by drawing on western jurisdictions, mainly Germany, Japan, and Switzerland.[45] The legislators' key concern at that time was to modernize Chinese law while also adapting it to Chinese society.[46] The Republican Civil Code additionally recognized unjust enrichment as a cause of obligatory rights.[47] However, provisions concerning unjust enrichment in the Republican Civil Code were largely simplified in comparison to those in the Qing's Draft Civil Code and the 1925 Draft, of which the number of articles shrunk to five (Arts 179 to 183).[48]

Article 179 of the Republican Civil Code was a simplified version of Art 929 of the Qing's Draft Civil Code, providing the general principle of unjust enrichment. It stipulated that 'a person obtaining benefits without a legal ground and resulting in another's loss should return the benefits. The duty also exists if the legal ground later lapses.'[49] The dichotomy of performance- and non-performance-based unjust enrichment in the Qing's Draft Civil Code was discarded. Article 180 set out the defences against claims of unjust enrichment. Restitution should be barred where the claimant had performed to satisfy a moral obligation, discharged an undue debt, or knew that they were under no obligation to discharge a debt but still performed.[50] The Republican Civil Code also adopted the 'three-step approach' to the restitutionary liabilities of unjust enrichment. The primary remedy was restitution in kind; namely, to return the enrichment and also any other benefits associated with the enrichment, and if it was not possible to return the enrichment due to its nature or other reasons, the defendant should pay the value of the enrichment (Art 181).[51] A bona fide favoree unaware of a lack of legal basis was only liable to return what remained in hand. However, a mala fide favoree should return all benefits obtained at the time of receipt or to the extent that they remained in hand when the favoree knew there was a lack of legal basis, plus interest, and pay compensation if there were any damages to the obtained benefits (Art 182).[52] Article 183 addressed situations where a favoree gratuitously transferred the enrichment to a third party, stating that if the favoree's restitutionary liability was thus exempted, the third party should be liable for restitution to the extent that the favoree's liabilities were waived.[53]

Although the Republican Civil Code was based on the Qing's Draft Civil Code and the 1925 Draft, many 'otiose' provisions were eliminated to permit space for local custom.[54] The law of unjust enrichment was preserved, indicating that it

---

[45] George Keeton, 'The Progress of Law Reform in China' (1937) 20 19 Journal of Comparative Legislation and International Law 197, 208; Li, 'New Trend' (n 38) 135.
[46] Huang, *Code, Custom, and Legal Practice* (n 20) 53.
[47] Liu Yanhao (刘言浩), *The Formation and Development of the Law of Unjustified Enrichment* (不当得利法的形成与展开) (Law Press 2013)(hereafter Liu, *Formation and Development*) 203–04.
[48] ibid 204.
[49] ibid.
[50] ibid 207–08.
[51] ibid 208.
[52] ibid 209.
[53] ibid.
[54] Pound, 'Chinese Civil Code' (n 43) 278.

was perceived as being consistent with the Chinese custom that reaping without sowing was unjust. However, the simplification was a sign reflecting that the lawmakers considered the regulation of unjust enrichment in the Qing's Draft Civil Code and the 1925 Draft to be excessive.

D. The Law of Unjust Enrichment in the PRC Prior to the Chinese Civil Code

Since the inception of the People's Republic of China (PRC) in 1949, China has experienced massive economic, political, and social reconstruction. The Chinese Communist Party (CCP) denounced Kuomintang's entire legal system as early as February 1949 and began to establish its own legal system based on the Soviet Union's socialist system.[55] For over three decades, a Soviet-style planned economy and the PRC's Marxist ideology dominated the country, denying the legitimacy of private ownership and posing a serious hurdle for the development of civil law.[56] Nevertheless, against this political–economic backdrop, the CCP continuously endeavoured to draft a comprehensive civil code to fill the legal vacuum. Four rounds of civil law codification in the 1950s, 1960s, 1980s, and 1990s fashioned numerous drafts but failed outright to produce a civil law code, which was not actually promulgated until 2020. These failed attempts led to a piecemeal approach to enacting individual civil law statutes separately.[57] The following sections analyse the unjust enrichment provisions in those draft civil codes and the laws effective prior to the

---

[55] Tong Rou, 'The *General Principles of Civil Law of the PRC*: Its Birth, Characteristics, and Role' (1989) 52 Law and Contemporary Problems 151, 152; Henry R Zheng, 'China's New Civil Law' (1986) 34 American Journal of Comparative Law 669, 669–70 (hereafter Zheng, 'China's New Civil Law').

[56] Chen, *Chinese Law* (n 9) 457; Hao Jiang, 'The Making of a Civil Code in China: Promises and Perils of a New Civil Law' (2021) 95 Tulane Law Review 777, 784.

[57] The PRC enacted the General Principles of Civil Law in 1986, the Contract Law in 1999 replacing three separate contract law statutes, the Property Rights Law in 2007, and the Tort Liability Law in 2009. Zhonghua Renmin Gongheguo Minfa Tongze (中华人民共和国民法通则) [General Principles of Civil Law of the People's Republic of China] (promulgated by the NPC on 12 April 1986, effective 1 January 1987 and repealed 1 January 2021); Zhonghua Renmin Gongheguo Jinji Hetong Fa (中华人民共和国经济合同法) [Economic Contract Law of the People's Republic of China] (promulgated by the Standing Committee of National People's Congress [NPCSC] on 13 December 1981, effective 1 July 1982, expired 1 October 1999); Zhonghua Renmin Gongheguo Shewai Jinji Hetong Fa (中华人民共和国涉外经济合同法) [Law of the People's Republic of China on Foreign-Related Economic Contracts] (promulgated by the NPC on 21 March 1985, effective 1 July 1985, expired 1 October 1999); Zhonghua Renmin Gongheguo Jishu Hetong Fa (中华人民共和国技术合同法) [Law of the People's Republic of China on Technology Contracts] (promulgated by the NPCSC on 23 June 1987, effective 1 November 1987, expired 1 October 1999); Zhonghua Renmin Gongheguo Hetong Fa (中华人民共和国合同法) [Contract Law of the People's Republic of China] (promulgated by the NPC on 15 March 1999, effective 1 October 1999, expired 1 January 2021); Zhonghua Renmin Gongheguo Wuquan Fa (中华人民共和国物权法) [Property Rights Law of the People's Republic of China] (promulgated by the NPC on 16 March 2007, effective 1 October 2007, expired 1 January 2021); Zhonghua Renmin Gongheguo Qinquan Zeren Fa (中华人民共和国侵权责任法) [Tort Liability Law of the People's Republic of China] (promulgated by the NPCSC on 26 December 2009, effective 1 July 2010, expired 1 January 2021).

enactment of the Chinese Civil Code and thus present a roadmap of the evolution of this area of law in the PRC.

1. Draft civil codes in the 1950s and 1960s

The first attempt to develop a civil code began in 1954, during which three versions of the 'Law of Obligations' were created, modelled after those of the Soviet Union.[58] The centrally planned economy of the PRC did not permit much attention to be paid to the law of obligations.[59] Unjust enrichment was recognized as a cause of debt in all these drafts alongside tort, contract, and planning legislation.[60] In general, all the drafts required benefits obtained without a legal basis and causing another's loss to be returned but with each defining unjust enrichment differently. In the first version, only if an enrichment was not obtained by the favoree's positive conduct would it be recognized as unjust enrichment.[61] The second version provided that unjust enrichment occurred if such enrichment was acquired due to the negligence of the aggrieved party rather than the favoree's intent without a legal basis.[62] The third version stated that enrichment was unjust if it was not obtained by the favoree deliberately or negligently and was not supported by a legal or contractual basis.[63]

The changing definitions of what constituted unjust enrichment indicate that the draftsmen were puzzled by what unjust enrichment actually entailed and who were even uncertain about the meaning of a legal basis as the third version emphasized that an enrichment was unjust if it lacked both a legal and contractual basis. The first draft excluded situations where the defendant acquired the enrichment by their positive conduct. The second draft required that the enrichment should be as a result of the aggrieved party's negligence. The third version required that the enrichment should not be obtained due to the defendant's intention or negligence. The draftsmen probably held the view that where a defendant acquired benefits deliberately or by their positive conduct lacking a legal justification, they should be liable in tort rather than unjust enrichment. It can be inferred from the continuous adjustments that they were uncertain about how to distinguish unjust enrichment liability from tort liability.[64] In addition to the liability to return the unjust enrichment, all these three drafts held the favoree liable for compensating the claimant's loss caused by unjust enrichment.[65] Again, the imposition of

---

[58] Chen, *Chinese Law* (n 9) 459–60; Mo Zhang, *Chinese Contract Law: Theory and Practice* (Martinus Nijhoff 2006) 30 (hereafter Zhang, *Chinese Contract Law*).
[59] Liu, *Formation and Development* (n 47) 211.
[60] Qinhua He (何勤华), Xiuqing Li (李秀清), and Yi Chen (陈颐) (eds), *An Overview of the Drafts of Civil Codes in the New China*, vol I (新中国民法典草案总览：上卷) (Law Press China 2003) 179–80, 204, 247.
[61] ibid 179.
[62] ibid 204.
[63] ibid 247.
[64] ibid 250.
[65] ibid 180, 204, 247.

compensatory liability reflects the draftsmen's confusion as to the distinction between unjust enrichment and tort.

The first effort to draft a comprehensive civil code came to an abrupt end in 1958 when political campaigns (namely, the anti-Rightist Movement and the Great Leap Forward) overwhelmed the role of law in society.[66] The process of codifying the civil law was not resumed until 1962.[67] As the Sino-Soviet alliance went sour, the second attempt to codify the civil law constituted an intentional effort to move away from the impact of the Soviet model and pursue a civil code with Chinese characteristics.[68] The drafts issued during that time rejected foreign legislative experience, including 'conventional' civil law concepts such as 'right', 'obligation', and 'legal person'.[69] It is therefore unsurprising that provisions on unjust enrichment were also missing.[70]

2. Draft civil codes in the 1970s and 1980s

The third round of civil law codification began in the late 1970s following the adoption of the well-known 'open door' policy and economic reforms.[71] Four drafts of a civil code were produced between 1979 and 1982, based on the 1962 Fundamental Principles of Civil Legislation of the USSR, the 1964 Civil Code of the Russian Soviet Federated Socialist Republic, and the revised Hungarian Civil Code of 1978, which were all in the German tradition.[72] A single provision on unjust enrichment was contained in all four drafts. The first and second drafts had identical unjust enrichment provisions, which were placed in the chapters concerning special regulations of 'liability for damages' and 'liability for torts' respectively, stating:

> Where a person obtains benefits without a legitimate basis and resulting in another person's damages, the person should return the benefits to the aggrieved person or turn over the benefits to the state. The benefits should still be returned where there was a legal basis at the time of acquisition while the legal basis lapses later (such as a revoked legal act). The enriched person unaware of the lack of legal basis bears no obligation to return if the obtained benefits do not exist anymore.[73]

---

[66] Zheng, 'China's New Civil Law' (n 55) 670.
[67] Chen, *Chinese Law* (n 9) 460.
[68] Liang Huixing (梁慧星), 'Reception of Foreign Civil Laws in China' (中国对外国民法的继受) (2002) 26 Shangdong University Law Review 1, 5; Chen, 'Historical Development' (n 37) 174.
[69] Chen, ibid.
[70] Liu, *Formation and Development* (n 47) 216.
[71] ibid.
[72] Chen, *Chinese Law* (n 9) 461.
[73] Qinhua He (何勤华), Xiuqing Li (李秀清), and Yi Chen (陈颐) (eds), *An Overview of the Drafts of Civil Codes in the New China*, vol II (新中国民法典草案总览：下卷) (Law Press China 2003) (hereafter He, Li, and Chen, *An Overview II*) 430, 484; see also Guangyu Fu (傅广宇), '"Chinese Civil Code" and Unjustified Enrichment: Retrospect and Prospect' ('中国民法典'与不当得利：回顾与前瞻) (2019) 1 ECUPL Journal 116, 119 (hereafter Fu, 'Chinese Civil Code').

In the third and fourth drafts, the unjust enrichment provisions were set in the chapter entitled 'Civil Liability (Special Regulations)', of which the content remained roughly the same as the provisions in the first and second drafts.[74] One slight difference was that the third and fourth drafts clarified that only where the aggrieved person could not be identified, should the benefits obtained unjustly be turned over to the state.

During this period, Chinese jurists started to research unjust enrichment.[75] In these four drafts, unjust enrichment was considered as an event triggering liability for damages, liability for torts, or other kinds of civil liabilities rather than obligatory rights. The requirement to confiscate benefits obtained unjustly, on the one hand, showed the state's intervention in civil affairs and the impact of socialist ideology on civil law.[76] On the other hand, it implied that unjust enrichment was deemed as condemnable or even 'illegal' to a certain extent. Unjust enrichment was characterized as 'quasi-tortious' at this stage.[77]

The third round of civil codification was suspended because at that time economic reform had just begun and the economic and social relations regulated by the civil code were in upheaval.[78] The lawmakers began to pursue a more pragmatic 'piecemeal approach'; namely, to enact separate civil law statutes first dealing with legal issues in contract law, property law, family law, etc.[79] Under the 'piecemeal approach', a large number of individual statutes concerning civil matters were enacted in quick succession, including the General Principles of Civil Law of the People's Republic of China (GPCL) drafted on the basis of the fourth draft of the civil law produced in 1982.[80]

3. The GPCL and the Draft Civil Code in the 1990s

In 1986, the GPCL was adopted. For over thirty years, the GPCL acted as an all-embracing mini civil code, framing the general principles of civil law and broadly

---

[74] He, Li, and Chen, *An Overview II* (n 73) 556, 618.
[75] Liu, *Formation and Development* (n 47) 217.
[76] The confiscation requirement also existed in the law of unjust enrichment in Art 473 of the Civil Code of the Russian Soviet Federated Socialist Republic. See Whitmore Gray and Raymond Stults, *Civil Code of the Russian Soviet Federated Socialist Republic: An English Translation* (University of Michigan Law School 1965) 124. See also Jidong Chen (陈吉栋), 'General Clauses of Unjust Enrichment in the General Principles of Civil Code' (论《民法总则》不当得利一般条款的设置模式) (2017) 25 Journal of SJTU (Philosophy and Social Science) 59, 65 (hereafter Chen, 'General Clauses').
[77] Fu, 'Chinese Civil Code' (n 73) 120.
[78] Zhang, *Chinese Contract Law* (n 58) 111.
[79] Hui Zheng, 'General Part' in Yanshi Bu (ed), *Chinese Civil Law* (Hart Publishing 2013) 1; Hao Ran (冉昊) and Lihong Du (杜丽红), 'The Way to Rule of Law in New China: A Review of Civil Law in the Past 56 Years' (新中国法治历程：民法56年) (2005) 4 Journal of Nanjing University (Philosophy, Humanities and Social Sciences) 66, 68.
[80] Hanbin Wang (王汉斌), 'An Illustration to the Draft of the GPCL—On the Fourth Session of the Sixth National People's Congress' (关于《中华人民共和国民法通则（草案）》的说明—1986年4月2日在第六届全国人民代表大会第四次会议上) (The National People's Congress of China, 2 April 1986) <www.npc.gov.cn/zgrdw/huiyi/lfzt/swmsgxflsyf/2010-08/18/content_1588304.htm> accessed 3 August 2022. See also n 57.

covering subjects including contract, property, and tort.[81] The GPCL contained one provision stating the general principle of unjust enrichment, namely Art 92, which was located in Section 2 'Obligatory Rights' of Chapter V 'Civil Rights'. It stipulated: 'If one acquires unjust benefits without a legitimate basis, resulting in another person's loss, the unjust benefits shall be returned to the person suffering a loss.' The constituent elements of unjust enrichment under the provision remained largely the same as those in the drafts produced during the third effort to enact a civil code.[82] One difference was that the GPCL replaced the constituent element 'resulting in another person's damage' with 'resulting in another person's loss'. Moreover, the GPCL did not require any benefits obtained without a legal basis to be handed over to the state, even if the aggrieved party could not be identified.

Compared with the previous draft civil codes labelling unjust enrichment as a cause generating tort or other civil liabilities, the GPCL seemed to recognize unjust enrichment as a cause triggering a right for recovery rather than a liability. However, the phrase 'without a legitimate basis', still implied the condemnable nature of unjust enrichment. In 1988, the Supreme People's Court (SPC) issued a judicial opinion to facilitate the effective implementation of the GPCL (entitled 'Opinions on the GPCL').[83] Article 131 of the Opinions on the GPCL specified the scope of restitution for unjust enrichment, stating that 'the returned unjust benefits shall include the initial object and any benefits arising from the initial object, and other benefits obtained by using the enrichment obtained unjustly shall be confiscated by the state after deducting the expenses of labour services and management fees'. The confiscation requirement was an embodiment of the impact of the law of the former Soviet Union.[84] Article 92 of the GPCL and Art 131 of the Opinions on the GPCL constituted the totality of the law of unjust enrichment implemented in China for decades. The Chinese law of unjust enrichment at that time having the most simplified and abstract status since the Qing dynasty.

With only one general principle, the law of unjust enrichment could not answer the question of whether there was a basis for enrichment, which was instead decided by other branches of the law. In many unjust enrichment cases, other branches of the law could apply to reverse the transfer of benefits.[85] Therefore, it appears that the Chinese law of unjust enrichment acted more as a 'catch-all

---

[81] Chen, 'Continuity and Change' (n 38) 291.
[82] See Section II.D.2.
[83] Zuigao Renmin Fayuan Guanyu Guanche Zhixing Zhonghua Renmin Gongheguo Minfa Tongze Ruogan Wenti De Yijian (Shixing) (最高人民法院关于贯彻执行《中华人民共和国民法通则》若干问题的意见（试行）) [Opinions of the SPC on Several Issues Concerning the Implementation of the General Principles of Civil Law of the People's Republic of China (For Trial Implementation)] (promulgated by the SPC on 26 January 1988, effective the same date, expired 1 January 2021).
[84] See n 76.
[85] For a detailed analysis of the relationship between the Chinese law of unjust enrichment and other areas of private law and how other branches of law reverse benefits without a legal basis, see Lin, *Unjust Enrichment in China* (n 2) ch 4.

provision', which played a negative and residual role in correcting the transfers of benefits without a legal basis.

In 1998, the work to draft a civil code was again resumed after the 1993 Constitutional Amendments historically replaced the planned economy with the idea of developing a 'socialist market economy'.[86] The working plan of this round of civil law codification consisted of three steps, including enacting a uniform contract law by 1999, a property law in four to five years, and a comprehensive civil code by 2010.[87] A draft civil code was produced in 2002, which adopted Art 92 of the GPCL in its entirety.[88] The 2002 draft civil code was heavily criticized as it was prepared under extreme time pressure and was merely a collection of existing laws at the time.[89] As a result, the legislators moved back to the piecemeal approach and the fourth round of civil law codification ended.[90]

The Chinese law of unjust enrichment was stabilized by the implementation of the GPCL. The rules of unjust enrichment at that stage were so parsimoniously formulated that they express nothing more than a general prohibition of enrichment obtained without a legal basis. One scholar participating in drafting the GPCL pointed out that the adoption of the unjust enrichment principle was to comply with socialist morality.[91] It is unsurprising that these scarce and abstract statutory regulations failed to give proper guidance for addressing unjust enrichment scenarios in judicial practice and were subject to stern criticism from Chinese scholars and practitioners. The most frequently discussed problems existing in the law of unjust enrichment at that stage were as follows.

First, Art 92 of the GPCL simply stated that benefits obtained without a legal basis should be returned. However, not all types of benefit can be returned in kind. If enrichment takes the form of tangible property, the property may be damaged through no fault of the defendant or the defendant may have spent the money received without realizing that they were not entitled to the money. The situation was even more controversial if the obtained benefit lay in the receipt of a service. The oversimplified Chinese law of unjust enrichment at that stage did not adopt the 'three-step approach' to the measure of restitutionary liability in the Qing's Draft Civil Code[92] or the Republican Civil Code[93] or even clarify what to do if the defendant was unable to provide restitution in kind. Chinese scholars generally

---

[86] Xianchu Zhang, 'The New Round of Civil Law Codification in China' (2016) 1 University of Bologna Law Review 106, 113; Chen, *Chinese Law* (n 9) 462.
[87] Guangxin Zhu (朱广新), 'Codification of Civil Law: United Recodification of Civil Special Law' (民法典编纂：民事部门法典的统一再法典化) (2018) 6 Journal of Comparative Law 169, 174.
[88] Fu, 'Chinese Civil Code' (n 73) 120.
[89] Siyi Lin, 'Looking Back and Thinking Forward: The Current Round of Civil Law Codification in China' (2019) 52 International Lawyer 439, 451.
[90] ibid.
[91] Angran Gu (顾昂然) and others, *Seminars on the General Principles of Civil Law of the People's Republic of China* (中华人民共和国民法通则讲座) (China Legal Publishing House 2000) 183.
[92] See Section II.B.
[93] See Section II.C.

agreed that the defendant should be obliged to repay the monetary value of the benefit if it was impossible to return the enrichment in kind.[94] However, no guidance was provided regarding how to determine the value of the enrichment when the return of the very substance of the enrichment was impossible.[95]

Secondly, Art 92 of the GPCL granted restitutionary claims in a variety of circumstances, allowing claimants to seek the return of whatever had been obtained by the defendant without a legal basis, regardless of the state of mind of the claimant. From the perspective of fairness, it seems inappropriate for a legal system to grant restitution to a claimant who first enriched a defendant in spite of having been aware of the absence of an obligation to perform. The rules on this point were excessively concise and did not exclude restitutionary claims in such situations.[96]

Thirdly, Art 92 of the GPCL did not consider the defendant's participation, acquiescence, or knowledge of obtaining the enrichment.[97] The indiscrimination imposition of strict liability could lead to unfairness to defendants, especially where the enrichment could not be returned in kind. For example, if a claimant cleaned a defendant's shoes without any obligation, the defendant may in bad faith have induced the claimant to clean their shoes and passively accepted the claimant's service although they had an opportunity to reject that service or even if they had no knowledge of the fact that the claimant had cleaned their shoes. In that regard, Art 92 could force an innocent defendant who had no opportunity to reject the services to pay for what they had never in fact requested. Even if the claimant provided the service knowing that the defendant had not requested it, but claimed for payment, the defendant still bore liability for returning the value of the service. Such an imposition of liability infringed the freedom of an innocent defendant to choose how to distribute their resources, which potentially violated the principle of fairness.

In addition, among the constitutive elements of an unjust enrichment claim, the element 'without a legitimate basis' referred to a negative fact. The problem was how to prove something that did not existent. Did it mean that to establish a claim in unjust enrichment the claimant has to examine the entire corpus of legal rules

---

[94] Lixin Yang (杨立新), *General Introduction to Obligatory Law* (债法总论) (Law Press China 2011) 152; Xiuping Pan (潘修平) and others (eds), *Law of Obligation: Theory, Rule, Case* (债权法：原理·规则·案例) (Tsinghua UP 2006) 152 (hereafter Pan and others, *Law of Obligation*).

[95] This lack of guidance on the return of unjust enrichment is also discussed in Chen, 'General Clauses' (n 76) 65.

[96] This issue is discussed in: Yunhua Pan (潘运华), 'Rethinking the Scope of Return of Unjust Enrichment: Starting From the Functionality of Unjust Enrichment' (对不当得利返还范围的再思考—从不当得利制度的机能说起) (2012) 4 Tianjing Legal Science 25 (hereafter Pan, 'Rethinking Scope'); Chen, 'General Clauses' (n 76) 64–65.

[97] Whether the favoree's state of mind should make a difference to their restitutionary liability under an unjust enrichment claim is discussed in Jie Zhu (祝杰), 'A Brief Analysis of Restitution of Unjust Enrichment' (不当得利中返还利益浅析) (2003) 9 Contemporary Law Review 34, 36; Wenjie Zhao (赵文杰), 'A Discussion of the Return of Value in Unjust Enrichment and Statutory Discharge: Focusing on the Latter Part of Articles 58 and 57 of the Contract Law' (论不当得利与法定解除中的价值偿还：以《合同法》第58条和第97条后段为中心) (2015) Peking University Law Journal 1171, 1177; Pan, 'Rethinking Scope' (n 96); Chen, 'General Clauses' (n 76) 66.

to ensure that there was no legal basis for the enrichment? Is it more practical to require the defendant to prove their legal basis? Chinese scholars hold different views regarding how to prove a lack of legal basis for enrichment and which party bears the burden of proof.[98] The lack of any guidance in the law resulted in judges diverging in how they allocated the burden of proof in practice, even in the same types of unjust enrichment cases.[99] That divergence led to inconsistency and unpredictability in the Chinese legal system and needed to be eliminated.

Finally, another unfathomable problem concerned multiple liabilities.[100] The same set of facts could simultaneously give rise to a claim for unjust enrichment and other claims. If a party obtained an asset without a legal basis, the owner could seek return of the asset based on their proprietary right. If the asset were transferred under a void or rescinded contract, the claimant could also raise a contractual claim. The law did not stipulate the relationship between the claim for unjust enrichment and other claims; an issue of significance in judicial practice for deciding whether the court will allow a claimant to bring an unjust enrichment action when other branches of law also govern the case, for which no answer was provided.

E. Summary

This evolutionary roadmap shows that the Chinese law of unjust enrichment is a product of legal transplantation. Unjust enrichment first appeared when the Qing government rushed to formulate the Qing's Draft Civil Code modelled after the German Civil Code and the second-hand experience of Japan.[101] Against this

---

[98] Chinese scholars differ on this question and can be primarily divided into three perspectives: (1) burden on the defendants; (2) burden on the plaintiffs; and (3) distribution of the burden depending on the categorizations of unjust enrichment, ie performance-based unjust enrichment and non-performance-based unjust enrichment. For the first perspective, see Weijian Tang (汤维建), *The Theoretical Position of Civil Evidence Legislation* (民事证据立法的理论立场) (Peking UP 2008) 510; Wei Jiang (江伟), *Draft of China's Law on Evidence (Proposed Draft) and Legislative Reasons* (中国证据法草案(建议稿)及立法理由书) (Renmin UP 2004) 286. For the second view, see Liu, *Formation and Development* (n 47) 438–46; Dongdong Zhou (周冬冬), 'The Distribution of Burden of Proof in Unjust Enrichment' (不当得利的证明责任分配) (2010) 6 People's Judicature 83; Jian Yang (杨剑) and Yumei Dou (窦玉梅), 'Discussion on the Proof of the Negative Elements: Based on the Categorical Theory of Legal Elements' (论消极要件事实的证明—以法律要件分类说为基础) (2007) 7 Journal of Law Application 54. For the third view, see Yuqian Bi (毕玉谦), *Analysis of Practical Problems in Civil Cases* (民事案例实务问题解析) (People's Court Press 2009) 442–43; Jiangli Zhang (张江莉), 'Proof of "Without a Legal Basis" in Unjust Enrichment' (不当得利中'无法律原因'之证明) (2010) 28 Tribune of Political Science and Law 165.

[99] Lin, *Unjust Enrichment in China* (n 2) 126–27.

[100] For further discussion of this issue, see Jiangbo Zeng (曾江波) and Shaobo Wang (王少波), 'Claim Right on Unjust Enrichment and Claim Right on Property: Centering on the Patterns of Property Right Transfer' (论不当得利请求权与物上请求权—以物权变动模式为中心) (2005) 7 Peking University Law Review 230, 245–47; Xuejun Hong (洪学军) and Long Zhang (张龙), 'On the Concurrence Concerning the Right of Claim of Restitution of Unjust Enrichment and Other Rights of Claim' (不当得利返还请求权与其它请求权的竞合研究) (2003) 5 Modern Law Science 42.

[101] ibid.

backdrop, the law of unjust enrichment was transplanted into China without an adequate understanding or a profound theoretical or practical basis. Since then, the Chinese law of unjust enrichment had been preserved in most draft civil codes. This reflects the fact that the notion of unjust enrichment is in accordance with the deep-rooted ethical idea in Chinese culture against profiting from other people's work. Although in general the Chinese law of unjust enrichment has constantly followed the German-style 'absence of basis' approach, it was heavily impacted by Soviet law after the establishment of the PRC. Throughout history, the provisions concerning unjust enrichment have been continuously simplified until only one provision remained. The continuous simplification of unjust enrichment rules and adjustments to the constituent elements of unjust enrichment reveal the legislators' confusion and lack of deep understanding of this subject. This can be taken as evidence that the legislators were unsure about the concept, goals, and functions of the law of unjust enrichment when formulating this law.

III. The Law of Unjust Enrichment in the Chinese Civil Code

A. Constituent Elements of Unjust Enrichment Claims

The compendious law of unjust enrichment consisting of Art 92 of the GPCL and Art 131 of the Opinions on the GPCL was implemented in China for over three decades.[102] Unfairness and inconsistencies in judicial practice arising from the application of the law of unjust enrichment at that stage drew the attention of Chinese scholars and were subject to a barrage of criticisms for a long period.[103] In response to such strong criticism, the Chinese Civil Code specifically devotes one chapter to unjust enrichment (Chapter 29) which contains four articles (Arts 985 to 988). Chapter 29 is located in Part III, 'Quasi-Contracts' in Book III 'Contracts', along with the other chapter titled '*Negotiorum Gestio*'. The Chinese Civil Code contains a total of five provisions concerning unjust enrichment. Article 122 of the Chinese Civil Code provides the general principle of unjust enrichment, stating

---

[102] On 15 March 2017, the NPC issued the General Provisions of Civil Law of the People's Republic of China [General Provisions], which set out basic principles commonly applicable to different branches of civil law and was later incorporated into the Chinese Civil Code as Book I 'General Provisions'. The General Provisions only had one provision concerning unjust enrichment, ie Art 122, which later became Art 122 of the Chinese Civil Code. Therefore, this chapter only concerns provisions on unjust enrichment in the Chinese Civil Code and does not discuss the General Provisions.

[103] Scholars express their dissatisfaction of the Chinese law of unjust enrichment at this stage in a number of books and articles. Examples include: Zhengxin Huo (霍政欣), 'The Establishment and Improvement of the Chinese Law of Unjust Enrichment—A Comparative Law Perspective' (中国不当得利制度的构建与完善—以比较法为视角) (2006) 2 Seeking Truth 87; Chao Tang (唐超), 'The Structure of the German Law of Unjust Enrichment and the Perfection of the Chinese Law of Unjust Enrichment' (德国不当得利法的构造与中国不当得利法的完善) (2013) 1 Beihang Law Review 128; Pan, 'Rethinking Scope' (n 96).

'Where a party is unjustly enriched without a legal basis, the person who so suffers a loss shall have the right to require the enrichee to return the enrichment.' The other four provisions address specific issues of unjust enrichment, including defences to unjust enrichment claims, restitutionary liabilities assumed by bona fide and mala fide defendants, and the third party's restitutionary liability. Under the Chinese Civil Code, four elements are required to constitute a claim for unjust enrichment: (1) the defendant's enrichment; (2) the plaintiff's loss; (3) the absence of a legal basis for receiving the enrichment; and (4) no available defences.

1. Enrichment

When assessing unjust enrichment, the first question to be answered is whether the defendant is enriched by what they have received. Possible benefits that can constitute an enrichment include money and property, the provision of services, and the discharge of an obligation that the defendant would otherwise be under.[104] It is generally agreed that these benefits can either be 'positive' in the sense that they increase the wealth of the defendant, for example money, or 'negative' in the sense that they save necessary expenditure by the defendant, such as the rendering of services.[105] However, the Chinese Civil Code is still silent regarding what enrichment is in fact. The lack of any further explanation results in disputes over various issues, including whether the use of value of money, the pure possession of property without obtaining ownership, or a service rendered without request should be regarded as enrichment.

2. Loss

According to Art 122 of the Chinese Civil Code, only the person suffering a loss due to the defendant's enrichment is entitled to claim for return of any benefits obtained unjustly. In the analysis of an unjust enrichment claim, the plaintiff's loss is often taken for granted and thus only receives a fleeting mention because one person's gain is frequently correlated to loss by another. It is generally agreed that there must be a causal link between the plaintiff's loss and the defendant's gain, which provides justification for why it is the plaintiff who has the right to claim restitution.[106] The requirement of a causal link is usually satisfied if the enrichment and the loss result in the same set of facts.[107]

---

[104] Wei Huang (黄薇) (ed), *An Interpretation of the Book on Contract in the Civil Code of the People's Republic of China*, vol II (中华人民共和国民法典合同编释义(下册)) (China Legal Publishing House 2020) (hereafter Huang, *An Interpretation*) 1575.

[105] Xinwen Liu (刘心稳), *General Introduction of Obligatory Law* (债法总论) (China University of Political Science and Law Press 2009) 123 (hereafter Liu, *General Introduction*); Lixin Yang (杨立新), *Debts and Contract Law* (债与合同法) (Law Press China 2012) 109–10.

[106] Huang, *An Interpretation* (n 104) 1576; Pan and others, *Law of Obligation* (n 94) 82.

[107] Xiuping Ji (季修平), *Research on Protection of Proprietary Rights in Civil Law* (物权之民法保护制度研究) (China Legal Publishing House 2006) 265–66.

3. The absence of basis

The element 'without a legal basis' means that the defendant has no contractual or any other legal basis to obtain the enrichment.[108] Typical examples of benefits transferred without a legal basis include mistaken payment and performance rendered under a void or revoked contract. This element seems to be straightforward. However, the law of unjust enrichment per se does not answer the question of whether a legal basis for receiving an enrichment is lacking because the legal basis is provided by another area of law. 'Absence of legal basis' can be described as no other law providing any justification for receiving the enrichment.

As mentioned, several lacunas surround this core element of an unjust enrichment claim.[109] The Chinese Civil Code does not specify whether 'absence of legal basis' includes situations where a defendant receives an enrichment with a legal basis *ab initio* but the legal basis subsequently lapses. For instance, a plaintiff may transfer a benefit in order to perform a contract which is later terminated. Does the plaintiff's claim for restitution of benefits transferred under the terminated contract count as a claim for unjust enrichment? The answer to this question determines whether an unjust enrichment claim is 'concurrent' or 'subsidiary' where the same set of facts give rise to both an unjust enrichment claim and other claims. Moreover, 'absence of legal basis' refers to a negative fact and there has been no guidance on how to prove something which does not exist.[110] For many years, these issues have been subject to vigorous debate by Chinese academics, but the Chinese Civil Code still does not touch upon these issues.

4. Defences

If a plaintiff successfully establishes the constituent elements in the previous three sections, they prima facie make out an unjust enrichment case, though subject to any defences available to the defendant. Article 985 of the Chinese Civil Code sets out three defences against performance-based unjust enrichment claims, stating:

> Where an enrichee obtains an unjust benefit without a legal basis, the aggrieved party is entitled to claim restitution of the obtained benefit by the enrichee, except under any of the following circumstances:
>
> (1) performance made to satisfy a moral obligation;
> (2) discharge of undue debts; and
> (3) discharge of debts knowing there is no such an obligation.

---

[108] Liu, *General Introduction* (n 105) 123; Huang, *An Interpretation* (n 104) 1578.
[109] See Section II.D.3.
[110] ibid.

Article 986 provides an additional defence to all types of unjust enrichment claims; that is, the defendant's disenrichment. However, only a bona fide enrichee who did not know and could not have known that the obtained enrichment lacked a legal basis can be exempted from restitutionary liabilities if the obtained enrichment no longer exists.[111]

B. Remedies of Unjust Enrichment

Article 122 of the Chinese Civil Code grants the aggrieved party a right to claim for return of benefits obtained unjustly. As mentioned earlier, Art 986 confines the restitutionary liability of a bona fide enrichee to that which is still in existence.[112] According to Art 987, where a mala fide enrichee knew or should have known that the obtained enrichment lacked a legal basis, the aggrieved party is entitled to claim restitution of the enrichment no matter whether the enrichment still exists. Moreover, the aggrieved party has the right to claim compensation for loss, if any. Article 988 further stipulates that if the enrichee has transferred the obtained benefit to a third party gratuitously, the aggrieved party can require the third party to bear restitutionary liability to the corresponding extent.

Previously, Art 131 of the Opinions on the GPLC specified the scope of return of unjust enrichment, including the initial object received and any benefits generated from the initial object with those benefits being taken over by the state after deducting labour costs.[113] However, when the Chinese Civil Code came into effect, the Opinions of the GPCL was simultaneously repealed.[114] As a result, no currently effective legal provision clarifies the scope of return under an unjust enrichment claim.

C. The Nature of the Law of Unjust Enrichment

Article 118 of the Chinese Civil Code recognizes unjust enrichment as an independent cause generating obligatory rights, literally a 'causative reason of obligations' as follows:

---

[111] Chinese Civil Code, Arts 986–87.
[112] See Section III.A.4.
[113] See Section II.D.3.
[114] Zuigao Renmin Fayuan Guanyu Feizhi Bufen Sifa Jieshi Ji Xiangguan Guifanxing Wenjian De Jueding (最高人民法院关于废止部分司法解释及相关规范性文件的决定) [Decision of the Supreme People's Court on the Repeal of Some Judicial Interpretations and Relevant Regulatory Documents] (promulgated by the SPC on 29 December 2020, effective 1 January 2021).

An obligatory right is the right-holder's right to claim against a particular duty-bearer to conduct or not to conduct a particular act, triggered by contract, tort, *negotiorum gestio*, unjust enrichment, and miscellaneous other events provided by law.

Accordingly, unjust enrichment is a distinct head of obligation, as with contract and tort. Nevertheless, as noted, the unjust enrichment chapter is located in Book III 'Contracts' of the Chinese Civil Code, under the heading of 'Quasi-Contracts'. The other chapter under this heading covers *negotiorum gestio*. This is the first time that the concept of 'quasi-contracts' appears in Chinese law,[115] which seems to imply that unjust enrichment and *negotiorum gestio* are two sub-species of contract. However, the Chinese Civil Code provides no explanation of the meaning of 'quasi-contracts'. What are the similarities between quasi-contracts and contracts? Are unjust enrichment and *negotiorum gestio* the only two types of quasi-contracts? These questions remain unanswered. The term 'quasi-contracts' has triggered heated discussion.[116]

In fact, the sub-chapter on 'quasi-contracts' was created for reasons of pragmatism. The Chinese Civil Code consists of seven books: General Provisions, Property Rights, Contracts, Personality Rights, Marriage & Family, Succession, and Tort Liabilities. The lack of a book concerning general provisions of the law of obligations leaves no room for the rules of unjust enrichment and *negotiorum gestio*, which are thus placed in Book III 'Contracts'.[117] The obligations generated by unjust enrichment and *negotiorum gestio* arise out of the operation of law rather than the parties' consensus and have nothing to do with any contract.[118] The draftsmen also acknowledged that although unjust enrichment, *negotiorum gestio*, and contract are all part of the law of obligations, provisions on unjust enrichment and *negotiorum gestio* should be differentiated from contract law.[119] As a product of the structure of the Chinese Civil Code, the inclusion of unjust enrichment in the book on contracts and the use of the heading 'quasi-contract' is misleading and easily causes confusion over the nature of claims for restitution in unjust enrichment.

---

[115] Fei Anling (费安玲), 'Elements of Roman Law in the Interpretation of Quasi-Contracts in the Civil Code of the PRC' (我国民法典中准合同解释之罗马法因素) (2021) 5 Journal of Comparative Law 66, 67 (hereafter Fei, 'Elements of Roman Law').

[116] See ibid; Fu, 'Chinese Civil Code' (n 73) 131; Wu and Swadling, 'Unjustified Enrichment' (n 6) 403–06.

[117] Yongjun Li (李永军), 'On the Outer Limit of the Concept of "Quasi Contract"' ("准合同"概念之外延考—对我国《民法典》第985条的理论与实证分析) (2022) 5 Political Science and Law 80, 85; Fei, 'Elements of Roman Law' (n 115) 68.

[118] Wu and Swadling, 'Unjustified Enrichment' (n 6) 403.

[119] Chen Wang (王晨), 'Explanations on the Draft of the Chinese Civil Code of the People's Republic of China' (关于《中华人民共和国民法典（草案）的说明》) (The National People's Congress of China, 22 May 2020) <www.npc.gov.cn/npc/c30834/202005/50c0b507ad32464aba87c2ea65bea00d.shtml> accessed 29 December 2022.

This historical review reflects the fact that the Chinese law of unjust enrichment has been constantly simplified throughout history. Although the Chinese Civil Code now includes a chapter on unjust enrichment, which represents China's first attempt to improve this area of law, whether this attempt will be successful remains to be seen.

IV. Evaluation of the Chinese Law of Unjust Enrichment

A. The Shifts of Nature of Unjust Enrichment under Political Impacts

This historical review reflects that the law of unjust enrichment is not an inherent aspect of Chinese law, but rather an import from abroad. When the law of unjust enrichment first appeared in Qing's Draft Civil Code, the whole chapter was borrowed wholesale from the German Civil Code. After the Kuomingtang government took power, the law of unjust enrichment in the 1925 Draft and the Republican Civil Law was simplified to a large extent as the provisions concerning unjust enrichment were deemed to be 'otiose'. Nevertheless, by and large, the law of unjust enrichment in the late Qing dynasty and the Kuomintang era followed the civilian approach and unjust enrichment was regarded as an event triggering an obligatory right for restitution. Since the establishment of the PRC, the country's whole legal system, including the law of unjust enrichment, has been heavily impacted by the former Soviet Union's decidedly socialist legal system[120] with the provisions on unjust enrichment being further abridged. Unjust enrichment was no longer recognized as a cause of rights, but instead as a cause of liabilities or obligations.[121] In some drafts at this stage, a recipient of unjust enrichment was not only liable for restitution but also for compensation for the loss suffered by the claimant.[122] The recipient was also required to turn over any benefits received unjustly to the state if the aggrieved person could not be identified.[123] The shift from a cause of obligatory rights to liabilities, the imposition of compensatory liabilities, and the confiscation of unjust enrichment all indicated the condemnable nature of unjust enrichment, emphasizing the illegality of unjust enrichment. As such, the legislators were confused about the distinction between unjust enrichment and tort. The first few drafts of the civil code required that to constitute unjust enrichment, the defendant should not be at fault, acting deliberately to acquire the benefits.[124] These requirements were abandoned in the drafts produced in the 1970s and 1980s

---

[120] See Section II.D.
[121] ibid.
[122] See Section II.D.1.
[123] See Section II.D.2.
[124] See Section II.D.1.

which managed to reduce the impact of Soviet law.[125] In the GPCL promulgated in 1986, unjust enrichment was recognized as a cause of an obligatory right. However, Art 92 of the GPCL defined unjust enrichment as a benefit obtained without a 'legitimate' basis and required the benefit to be returned, which was more akin to compulsory liability. The confiscation requirement was still preserved in Art 131 of the Opinions on the GPCL while the scope was limited to benefits acquired by using unjust enrichment and deducting labour and management costs. This implied condemnable nature shows that the Chinese law of unjust enrichment in the GPCL had not yet thoroughly been ridden of the impact of the law of the former Soviet Union.

After deepening research on private law, the Chinese Civil Code promulgated in 2020 finally swept away the impact of the former Soviet Union. The core element of unjust enrichment shifted from 'without a legitimate basis' to 'without a legal basis'.[126] The consequence of unjust enrichment now is granting the aggrieved party a right to claim for restitution rather than imposing a direct liability to return on the enrichee.[127] This change removes the layer of illegitimacy from unjust enrichment. The requirement to confiscate other benefits acquired from unjust enrichment was also abandoned. The nature of unjust enrichment formally shifts from a cause of liability to a cause of obligatory rights.[128]

These shifts in the nature of unjust enrichment reflect that the Chinese law of unjust enrichment seems to be more indicative of a legal transplantation process over the years, led and heavily impacted by changes in the political context of Chinese society. When importing and drafting the doctrine of unjust enrichment, the draftsmen did not have a clear understanding of the nature of unjust enrichment or why the law even needed to be incorporated into the Chinese legal system.

B. The Uncertainty in the Function of the Law of Unjust Enrichment

This historical analysis shows that either the import of, or significant change to, the law of unjust enrichment happened without adequate research on, or an understanding of, the notion of unjust enrichment.[129] This notion was preserved in the legal system either because it accorded with traditional Chinese social values or under the impact of other jurisdictions. The repeated shifts in the nature of unjust enrichment and the confusion surrounding the distinction between unjust enrichment and tort illustrate that the most fundamental question—that is, the function

---

[125] See Section II.D.2.
[126] See Section III.A.3.
[127] See Section III.B.
[128] See Section III.C.
[129] See Section II.

of the law of unjust enrichment—has not yet been explicitly answered. In other words, why do we need an independent law of unjust enrichment in China's legal system? Before the Chinese Civil Code was enacted, there was only one general principle constituting the whole Chinese law of unjust enrichment, which functioned more like a final resort to avoid a situation where an enrichment obtained without a legal basis was not required to be returned to the person suffering the loss. However, under the Chinese Civil Code, unjust enrichment is formally recognized as a cause of an obligatory right alongside contract and tort. A set of specific rules has been added to regulate restitution of unjust enrichment and it thus seems that the law of unjust enrichment no longer acts only as a 'catch-all'" provision. However, by simply replicating the provisions from the Republican Civil Code, the fundamental question remains answered. Before a clear answer is found, it is hard, if not impossible, to successfully develop a set of sound rules of unjust enrichment.

C. Doctrinal Uncertainty

The newly added provisions in the Chinese Civil Code resolve several problematic issues existing in the previous Chinese law of unjust enrichment. Three out of the four articles in the unjust enrichment chapter concern defences. Article 985 excludes the defendant's liability where the claimant was under certain non-enforceable obligations to enrich the defendant, either a moral obligation or an undue one, or knowingly discharged a non-existent debt. Articles 986 and 987 make a distinction between liabilities assumed by bona fide and mala fide favorees, providing a defence only available to bona fide favorees. The exclusion of a bona fide favoree's restitutionary liability to the extent that the enrichment is no longer existent allocates the risk of loss of the enrichment to the claimant, avoiding the imposition of an excess burden of restitution on bona fide favorees. These defences avoid the injustice that may be caused by imposing restitutionary liabilities on innocent defendants or where the claimant is blameworthy, which is an improvement to the Chinese law of unjust enrichment.

Nonetheless, the Chinese Civil Code leaves other problems untouched. Issues such as the lack of guidance on determining the monetary value of an enrichment, proving the absence of legal basis, and the relationships between unjust enrichment claims and other claims are still unexplained.[130] In addition, the Chinese Civil Code generates new problems for the law of unjust enrichment. First, as discussed earlier,[131] the use of the heading 'quasi-contract' due to lack of space in the structure of the Chinese Civil Code is problematic and causes confusion. Secondly,

---

[130] The issues existing in the previous Chinese law of unjust enrichment are discussed in Section II.D.3.
[131] See Section III.C.

after the revocation of the Opinions on the GPCL, neither the Chinese Civil Code nor the judicial interpretations of the Chinese Civil Code clarify the scope of restitution.[132] The precise scope of benefits that should be returned under an unjust enrichment claim remains unspecified. Moreover, Art 986 of the Chinese Civil Code excludes bona fide favorees' restitutionary liability for unjust enrichment if the received benefits no longer exist. However, the law is silent on how to determine whether or not the benefits still exist. What if the favoree has used the money received to purchase an asset? It is uncertain whether the favoree should be deemed as no longer enriched or instead be required to return the purchased asset. Lastly, Art 988 of the Chinese Civil Code makes it clear that the aggrieved party is entitled to claim against a third party for restitution if the favoree has transferred the acquired benefit gratuitously, regardless of the favoree's state of mind. If the favoree was bona fide, they bear no restitutionary obligation pursuant to Art 986 as the enrichment should be deemed as non-existent. However, where the favoree knew or should have known of the absence of any legal basis for them to be enriched, even if the favoree has transferred the benefits to a third party gratuitously, they are still liable for restitution according to Art 987. As a result, under a textual interpretation of Art 988, the claimant may be entitled to undeserved double recovery from both the favoree and the third party.[133]

The legislator does not account for why they did not attempt to improve the law of unjust enrichment to a greater extent. By comparing the current situation with the unjust enrichment doctrines throughout Chinese history, it can be seen that the provisions in the Chinese Civil Code are nearly identical to the law of unjust enrichment in the Republican Civil Code, with a few simplifications. The legislator may have acquired these legislative ideas from China's historical draft civil codes and borrowed the provisions directly instead of drafting the rules based on the most up-to-date research on unjust enrichment by Chinese scholars and the comprehensive analysis of issues found in the application of the Chinese law unjust enrichment over the past decades. It is thus hard to regard the Chinese Civil Code as a successful attempt to perfect the law of unjust enrichment.

D. A Branch of Law with No Self-Development

In the late Qing dynasty, the import of the law of unjust enrichment from Germany into China took place without a solid understanding of this area of law due to the underdeveloped status of private law at that time.[134] Since then, the provisions on

---

[132] See n 114.
[133] Wu and Swadling, 'Unjustified Enrichment' (n 6) 418.
[134] See Section II.B.

unjust enrichment have been constantly simplified in China. After the inception of the PRC, there was a sudden change in the Chinese law of unjust enrichment, which drew experience from the former Soviet Union.[135] The main reason why this significant change occurred was the impact of the political environment then in existence. When the PRC was first established, academic research on unjust enrichment and the legislators' understanding of this area of law were still insufficient. Finally, when the Chinese Civil Code was promulgated in 2020, the previous law of unjust enrichment consisting of Art 92 of the GPCL and its judicial interpretation had been implemented in China for more than three decades, and academic research in this area of law had further advanced. Nevertheless, the newly added chapter on unjust enrichment in the Chinese Civil Code was not formulated based on a comprehensive analysis of the nature and function of unjust enrichment in the Chinese legal system or the issues existing in applying the Chinese unjust enrichment rules in judicial practice over the past decades. As discussed previously, the current unjust enrichment doctrines resemble a duplicate of those in the Republican Civil Code.[136] As a result, the Chinese Civil Code only partly resolves the issues existing in the previous Chinese law of unjust enrichment and does not respond to other the problems raised and discussed by Chinese scholars and practitioners over time.

The history of the Chinese law of unjust enrichment shows that from the perspective of statutes, the development of this area of law is not driven by the increasingly deepening research on unjust enrichment and private law by Chinese scholars. The pivotal changes in the evolving Chinese law of unjust enrichment occurred mostly to meet political needs at the time. In other words, since its import into China, the law of unjust enrichment has not developed in the context of Chinese law. The absence of self-development explains why a number of remaining issues exist in the current Chinese law of unjust enrichment.

V. Conclusion

This historical review demonstrates that the import and development of the law of unjust enrichment in China had been driven and heavily affected by politics. At different stages, the law of unjust enrichment was formulated without an adequate understanding and proper research on the subject. The law of unjust enrichment has been preserved in the Chinese legal system because it is consistent with Chinese ethics. There had been and still is no agreed answer as to the function of the law of unjust enrichment in China. To a certain extent, this

---

[135] See Section II.D.
[136] See Section IV.C.

explains why the Chinese law of unjust enrichment has not been considered an important part of the legal system and has had scant attention from the legislator and scholars. The lack of an answer to that question also illustrates that the 2020 attempt to perfect the law of unjust enrichment in the Chinese Civil Code cannot be successful.

3
Law of Unjust Enrichment in India
Historical Evolution and Contemporary Challenges

Arpita Gupta

I. Introduction

The shift in the inquiry from empirical to normative signals the emergence of a new field of study in its own right. As the youngest branch of private law, there are parts of the law of unjust enrichment that are still unclear. In many jurisdictions, including India, the nature of inquiry regarding this field of law has firmly transitioned from questions regarding the existence of the field to questions such as what ought to be the normative basis of the field. The unjust enrichment law in India did not witness the general uncertainty experienced in other common law jurisdictions. This was primarily due to the codification of parts of the law through the enactment of the Indian Contract Act in the nineteenth century.

The codification saga of the Indian Contract Act was a long-drawn-out process. In addition to there being divergent viewpoints on the merits of codification and on the questions of substantive aspects of the law due to a variety of factors, including conflict with some of the pre-existing personal laws of contract,[1] the Indian Legislative Council for a long period failed to enact the drafts submitted by the Third Law Commission. Owing to prolonged disagreements between the Law Commission and the Secretary of State, on the one side, and the Indian government, on the other side, the Third Law Commission resigned in 1870.[2] Two years after the Commission's resignation, a modified draft of the code was finally enacted in 1872. Parts of the enacted law departed from the Commission's draft in significant ways. For instance, some provisions such as those on specific relief were removed and some provisions were redrafted on the basis of new sources such as the draft Civil Code of New York.[3] Also, with respect to the provisions on unjust enrichment there were departures from the draft code (ss 54–61, Draft Contract Bill 1867), such as the number of sections being reduced from eight to five, and

---

[1] MP Jain, 'The Law of Contract Before Its Codification' (1972) J Indian Law Institute 178, 200.
[2] Gail Pearson, 'The Resignation of the Third Indian Law Commission: Who Makes Law?' (2020) 41 Adel L Rev 575.
[3] RN Gooderson, 'English Contract Problems in Indian Code and Case Law' (1958) 16 CLJ 67.

the ambit of the section on 'money had and received' (s 61, Draft Contract Bill 1867) being widened to include *things delivered* by mistake or under coercion.[4]

This chapter analyses the evolution of the law of unjust enrichment in India and its salient features in juxtaposition with English law in particular. Section II delineates the historical evolution of the law of unjust enrichment in India and its codification and divergence from English common law in the nineteenth century. Section III outlines the scope of the law of unjust enrichment in India, discussing the statutory provisions in the Indian Contract Law and the relevant case law. Section IV tackles the law of unjust enrichment beyond the Indian Contract Act, focusing on such themes as (1) protracted litigation and (2) breach of public trust. Section V analyses salient features of the unjust enrichment law in the country, contextualizing them in their relevant local and global contexts. Section VI concludes by identifying some of the major issues of concern in the current state of the law that need further deliberation.

II. Origins of the Law of Unjust Enrichment Law in India

The introduction and diffusion of English common law in India with the establishment of the Mayor's Courts in the towns of Madras, Bombay, and Calcutta through the charter of 1726, the Privy Council being designated as the highest court of appeal for the courts in India, and the subsequent transfer of power from the English East India Company to the British Crown, raises a strong presumption of the common law in India being closely modelled along the lines of English law. Although this presumption remains true to a large extent for private laws in India,[5] there have been significant points of divergence from English law, some necessitated by the context and some consciously introduced.[6]

An important feature of Indian law that resulted from legal experimentation by the British in its colonies in the nineteenth century was the codification of significant areas of the law including crime, contract, and what is now commonly referred to as 'unjust enrichment'.[7] Though the codified laws were primarily based on English law, these laws were interspersed with major instances of departures from English common law, the underlying rationale for which obviously went beyond the mere spirit of experimentation. This included the comparative ease of

---

[4] British Parliamentary Papers, 'East India Contract Law: Copies of Papers showing the present position of the Question of a Contract Law for India, And, of all Reports of the Indian Law Commissioners on the Subjects of Contracts' (1868) 63–64.

[5] Gooderson (n 3).

[6] Bijay Kisor Acharyya, *Codification in British India* (SK Banerji 1914).

[7] Sir Frederick Pollock, *The Law of Torts: A Treatise on the Principles of Obligations arising from Civil Wrongs in the Common Law: to which is added the Draft of a Code of Civil Wrongs prepared for the Government of India* (4th edn, Stevens and Sons 1895).

codification in an undemocratic context,[8] the need for developing effective tools of control to administer a subcontinent with a vast array of pre-existing legal sources, both indigenous and non-indigenous,[9] and the desire of those such as Sir James Fitzjames Stephen and Lord Thomas Macaulay, ardent supporters and effectuators of the codification project not only in the colonial periphery but also in the metropole with the hope of influencing the codification debate at home.[10]

A. Unjust Enrichment Law Before Codification

Prior to the enactment of the Indian Contract Act in 1872 which codified parts of the law of unjust enrichment, Indian judges and the Privy Council decided cases involving unjust enrichment in accordance with the precedents and the then prevalent rules of English common law.[11] Since the law of unjust enrichment as a legal category, distinct from the other more well-established areas of private law such as contract and tort, was still in the early stages of development, Indian judgments often mirrored the conflict of juristic opinion characterizing English law at the time.[12]

B. Unjust Enrichment Law After Codification

The codification of the law of unjust enrichment in India in the nineteenth century marked an important point of divergence between the unjust enrichment laws of the two jurisdictions. However, as was the case with other areas of law that were also codified, the break from English common law was not absolute and the common law principles and related case law have been relied upon by the courts in India (and the Privy Council) in both the pre-independence and post-independence periods, particularly to address the factual scenarios falling outside the purview of the statutory provisions, and at times even to interpret and supplement the statutory provisions.[13]

---

[8] Gunther A Weiss, 'The Enchantment of Codification in the Common-Law World' (2000) 25 Yale J Int'l Law 435; Lindsay Farmer, 'Reconstructing the English Codification Debate: The Criminal Law Commissioners, 1833–45' (2000) 18 L and Hist Rev 397.

[9] Elizabeth Kolsky, 'Codification and the Rule of Colonial Difference: Criminal Procedure in British India' (2005) 23 L and Hist Rev 631.

[10] John Roach, 'James Fitzjames Stephen (1829–94)' [1956] J Royal Asiatic Society of Great Britain and Ireland 1; George Otto Trevelyan, *The Life and Letters of Lord Macaulay* (Harper & Brothers 1876) 387.

[11] *Fatima Khatoon Chowdrain v Mahomed Jan Chowdry* (1868) 12 Moo Ind App 65 (notably, in this case the term 'unjust enrichment' was not used).

[12] *Rambux Chittangeo v Modhoosoodun Paul Chawdhry* (1867) 7 WR (India) 377.

[13] For an earlier exposition of the interaction between statute law and the common law, see PS Atiyah, 'Common Law and Statute Law' (1985) 48 MLR 1.

III. Scope of the Law of Unjust Enrichment: Indian Contract Act

Chapter V of the Indian Contract Act 1872 codifies parts of unjust enrichment law. The chapter is titled 'Of Certain Relations Resembling Those Created by Contract', the clear implication being that although it is part of the Indian Contract Act, it deals with situations lying beyond the ambit of contractual relationships.

Although Chapter V is obviously concerned with the relationships recognized by law that are primarily quasi-contractual in nature, the drafters steered clear of using the term 'quasi-contract'. The intent underlying this careful choice appears to be twofold: first, to avoid conceptual confusion with the law governing contractual relationships and, secondly, to bypass complications generally associated with legal fictions.[14] The five sections (ss 68–72) in the chapter provide for restitution with respect to a range of so-called quasi-contractual obligations that have traditionally been dealt with under English common law. As the following analysis will show, some aspects of the statutory provisions deliberately departed from English common law at the time.

A. Restitution for Providing Necessaries

According to s 68 of the Indian Contract Act 1872:

> If a person, incapable of entering into a contract, or any one whom he is legally bound to support, is supplied by another person with necessaries suited to his condition in life, the person who has furnished such supplies is entitled to be reimbursed from the property of such incapable person.

Additionally, the section provides two illustrations of supply of necessaries to a person of unsound mind and to the person's dependants. The section is applicable to those who do not possess capacity to contract, such as minors[15] and persons of unsound mind.[16] Unlike English law, there is no personal liability for a person incapable of contracting and a claim for the supply of necessaries stands only with respect to the estate of such person.[17] The term 'necessaries' has not been defined in the section, and the Indian courts have found it helpful to rely upon English case

---

[14] John Gwilliam, 'Legal Fictions—A Critical Analysis' (1978) 8 VUWLR 452; Kenneth Campbell, 'Fuller on Legal Fictions' (1983) 2 L and Phil 339.
[15] As per the Privy Council's decision in *Mohori Bibee v Dharmodas Ghose* (1903) 30 Cal 539 (PC), minors do not have capacity to contract, agreements of and with minors being void *ab initio* as opposed to the law in England where agreements by minors are voidable.
[16] Indian Contract Act 1872, s 68 illustrations (a) and (b).
[17] *Nilkanth v Chandrabhan* AIR 1922 Ngp 247.

law to expound the concept. In *Jagon Ram Marwari v Mahadeo Prosad Sahu*,[18] the Calcutta High Court found the following observation by Baron Parke helpful in determining the scope of the concept of necessaries:

> ... from the earliest time down to the present, the word necessaries was not confined, in its strict sense, to such articles as were necessary to the support of life, but extended to articles fit to maintain the particular person in the state, station, and degree in life in which he is ...[19]

Thus, depending upon the particular context, it has been held that the term necessaries in the context of s 68 can include essential education expenses,[20] house repairs,[21] payment of revenue arrears,[22] debt repayment,[23] and legal expenses.[24]

B. Restitution for Payment Due by Another

As per s 69 of the Indian Contract Act 1872, '[a] person who is interested in the payment of money which another is bound by law to pay, and who therefore, pays it, is entitled to be reimbursed by the other'.[25] Delineating the threefold requirement of the section, the court in *Heerachand v Saraswathy Ammal* held that '[t]here should be (1) a person interested in the payment of money, (2) the payment should be one which another is bound by law to pay, and (3) the person interested in the payment should actually pay it'.[26]

Further clarifying the law, the courts have held that the interest in question must be lawful[27] and the payment 'must be in order to avert some loss or to protect some interest which would otherwise be lost to the plaintiffs';[28] that is, the act of the plaintiff should have been intended as a safeguard against loss or to preserve the status quo of the said interest. In *Muppudathi Pillai v Krishnaswami Pillai*, the court held that having a legal proprietary interest is not a prerequisite for obtaining restitution under s 69.[29] Departing from the prevalent English common law, in

---

[18] *Jagon Ram Marwari v Mahadeo Prosad Sahu* (1909) ILR 36 Cal 768 [4].
[19] *Peters v Fleming* (1840) 6 M & W 42, 46–47; 151 ER 314, 315.
[20] *Sadasheo Balaji v Firm Hiralal Ramgopal* AIR 1938 Ngp 65, 68: 175 IC 149.
[21] *Ramchandra v Hari* AIR 1936 Ngp 12.
[22] *Lachmiram v Pahlad Singh* AIR 1925 Ngp 33; *Mahmood Ali v Chinki Shah* AIR 1930 All 128.
[23] *Karim Khan Mahtab Khan v Jaikiran Gadadmal Marwadi* AIR 1937 Ngp 390.
[24] *Watkins v Dhunnoo Baboo* (1881) ILR 7 Cal 140; *Sham Charan Mal v Chowdhry Debya Singh Pahraj* (1894) 21 Cal 872.
[25] ibid.
[26] *Heerachand v Saraswathy Ammal* (2000) 3 CTC 694 [37].
[27] *P Subbiah Mooppanar v SS Venkatarama Ayyangar* AIR 1955 Mad 265.
[28] *Mojiram v Sagarmal* AIR 1920 NAG 119; *Balwantrao v Tulsa Pandharihath* AIR 1937 Nag 225; *Banwarllal v Rajkishore Guru* AIR 1946 Nag 21.
[29] *Muppudathi Pillai v Krishnaswami Pillai* (1959) 2 MLJ 225.

Subramania Iyer v Vengappa Reddi, the court further expanded the meaning of the term 'interested' to include not only actual loss or detriment but also a 'reasonable apprehension of loss or inconvenience and even detriment assessable in money'.[30]

The ambit of the term 'interested' also includes a party making payment on behalf of another, such as an insurance company paying on behalf of the insured, and based upon the principle of subrogation can also claim restitution under this section.[31] Certainty on the question of subrogation has eluded the issue of contribution with respect to s 69. There has been a significant difference of judicial opinion on the question of applicability of s 69 (and s 70) to suits of contribution.

According to one viewpoint, based on the principles of equity, the plaintiff can claim reimbursement for a sum paid on behalf of the defendant that was in fact payable by both the plaintiff and the defendant.[32] Conversely, a second viewpoint favours preclusion of suits for contribution from the ambit of s 69.[33] Justifying this approach, the court in *Futteh Ali v Gunganath Roy* observed as follows:

> We very much doubt whether a suit for contribution, where both plaintiff and defendants were liable for the money paid by the plaintiff, falls within the scope of either Section 69 or Section 70 of the Contract Act, which seem rather to contemplate persons who not being themselves bound to pay the money or to do the act, do it under circumstances which give them a right to recover from the person who has allowed the payment to be made and has benefited by it.[34]

Based on the distinction between reimbursement and contribution, this view also found favour with the thirteenth Law Commission of India, proposing an amendment of s 69 to the effect of explicitly excluding from the purview of the section those bound by law to make the payment in question, such as those filing a contribution suit.[35]

Interpreting the phrase 'bound by law', the courts have held that the liability giving rise to the payment envisaged under this section not only refers to statutory liability but can also include other types of liability including contractual liability.[36] Also, the ambit of the section includes not only direct personal liability 'but all

---

[30] *Subramania Iyer v Vengappa Reddi* (1909) 19 MLJ 750 [1].
[31] *United India Fire and General Insurance Co Ltd v Pelaniappa Transport Carriers* AIR 1986 AP 32.
[32] *Ram Lal v Khiroda Mohini* 1914 Cal 208; *Prosunno Kumar v Jamaluddin* 1914 Cal 672; *Rajani Kanta v Rama Hath* 1915 Cal 310; *Ananda Kishore Choudhury v Panchu Kapali* AIR 1934 Cal 7.
[33] *Futteh Ali v Gunganath Roy* (1881) 8 Cal 113; *Sree Rajah Vatsavaya Venkata Simhadri Jagapatiraju Bahadur Garuand His Legal Representative v Sree Rajah Thyada Pusapati Rudra Sri Lakshmi Nrusimha Roopa Sadrusannamarad Dugaraju Dakshina Kavata Dugaraju Bahadur Garu* (1915) 39 Mad 795; *Biraj Krishna v Purna Chandra* AIR 1939 Cal 645; *Sudhangshu Kumar Roy v Banamali Roy* AIR 1946 Cal 63; *Nandlal Singh v Ram Kirit Singh* AIR 1950 Pat 212; *Shankerlal v Motilal* AIR 1957 Raj 267; *M Vedachala Mudaliar v S Rangaraju Naidu* AIR (1960) 1 Mad LJ 445.
[34] *Futteh Ali v Gunganath Roy* (n 33) [6].
[35] Law Commission of India, *Thirteenth Report: Contract Act 1972* (Ministry of Law 1958) 41.
[36] *Mothooranath Chuttopadhya v Kristokumar Ghose* (1879) ILR 4 Cal 369.

liabilities to payments for which owners of lands are indirectly liable, those liabilities being imposed upon the lands held by them'.[37]

Another requirement of the section is that the payment so made must be involuntary. Commenting on a payment made by the respondents owing to execution proceedings involving land purchased by the respondents, the court in *Ramkishen Singh v Dulichand* explained that:

> In this country, if the goods of a third person are seized by the Sheriff and are about to be sold as the goods of the defendant, and the true owner pays money to protect his goods and prevent the sale, he may bring an action to recover back the money he has so paid; it is the compulsion under which they are about to be sold that makes the payment involuntary.[38]

In *Ram Tuhul Singh v Biseswar Lall Sahoo*, the application of the section to provide restitution for a voluntary payment was expressly ruled out.[39] The section would also not benefit an individual who makes the payment for themselves rather than for the defendant,[40] a necessary corollary of which is the requirement on the part of the claimant to act in good faith.[41]

The third primary requirement of the section is actual payment on the part of the plaintiff. The phrase 'pays it' excludes from the ambit of s 69 scenarios involving a mere promise to pay without parting with any funds.[42]

C. Restitution for Performance of Non-Gratuitous Acts

According to s 70 of the Indian Contract Act 1872:[43]

> Where a person lawfully does anything for another person, or delivers anything to him, not intending to do so gratuitously, and such other person enjoys the benefit thereof, the latter is bound to make compensation to the former in respect of, or to restore, the thing so done or delivered.

---

[37] ibid [3].
[38] *Ramkishen Singh v Dulichand* (1881) ILR 7 Cal 648.
[39] *Ram Tuhul Singh v Biseswar Lall Sahoo* (1875) LR 3 IA 131.
[40] *Arulanandam Vethakannu Nadar v Bhagavathi Pillai Thankachi* AIR 1972 Mad 207.
[41] *Munni Bibi v Triloki Nath* AIR 1932 All 332.
[42] Sir Frederick Pollock and Sir Dinshaw Fardunji Mulla, *The Indian Contract Act* (P Yashod Vardhan, Chitra Narayan, and Vinod Kumar eds, 16th edn, LexisNexis 2021) (hereafter Pollock and Mulla, *Indian Contract Act*).
[43] Indian Contract Act 1872, s 70 entitled 'Obligation of person enjoying benefit of non-gratuitous act' (fn omitted).

Sections 69 and 70 of the Indian Contract Act are quintessential expressions of the classic doctrine of restitution for unjust enrichment.[44] The origins of the rule incorporated in s 70 can be traced back to Roman times and comparatively recently to the seventeenth-century English case of *Lampleigh v Brathwait*, where the court considered the two essential issues of request and implied assumpsit.[45] Although the English common law on *quantum meruit* claims for unjust enrichment formed the basis for s 70, the ambit of the section is much wider.

The distinction between English common law and s 70 was explained in *Damodara Mudaliar v Secretary of State for India*, one of the early judgments on s 70.[46] In this landmark judgment, the Madras High Court delineated the three essential elements for establishing a cause of action by an individual who does something for another under the section: 'The thing must be done lawfully; it must be done by a person not intending to act gratuitously; and the person for whom the act is done must enjoy the benefit of it.'[47]

The court also pointed out that the section was clearly much broader in comparison with English law, differing from it in at least two significant aspects: first, unlike English law, there were no explicit requirements of a relationship between the two parties of the nature of an implied contract and, secondly, performance of the said act under a necessity.[48] Elaborating on the absence of the requirement of necessity in the sense that where an act is done under an emergent situation or to preserve the concerned property, the court held that the ambit of the section 'may therefore be extended to cases into which no question of salvage enters'.[49] Recognizing the distinction between the two jurisdictions on this matter, in a very clear statement giving preference to Indian statute law over English common law, the court, referring to s 70, remarked that 'it is the law we have to apply and we ought not to be deterred from doing so, because the rule is not in harmony with English decisions'.[50]

Subsequent judgments have clarified the various nuances and aspects of the three elements mentioned earlier. The first element, where a person does something for another, is qualified by the term 'lawfully', thus excluding conduct that is unlawful in nature from benefiting from the section.[51] The courts have also relied upon s 23 of the Indian Contract Act 1872 to interpret the meaning of the term 'lawfully', observing that:

---

[44] Pollock and Mulla, *Indian Contract Act* (n 42).
[45] *Lampleigh v Brathwait* (1615) Hobart 105; 80 ER 255.
[46] *Damodara Mudaliar v Secretary of State for India* (1894) 18 Mad 88.
[47] ibid [4].
[48] *Bank of England v Vagliano Brothers* [1891] App Cas 145.
[49] *Damodara Mudaliar v Secretary of State for India* (n 46) [5].
[50] ibid [4].
[51] *State of West Bengal v BK Mondal & Sons* 1962 AIR 779.

... the doing or delivery of anything must not be 'forbidden by law' or 'of such a nature, that if permitted, it would defeat the provisions of any law or is fraudulent', or must not involve or imply 'injury to the person or property of another' or must not be that which may be regarded by the Court as 'immoral or opposed to public policy'.[52]

The second requirement of the section is that the underlying intention for performing the act in question should be non-gratuitous. Thus, voluntary acts are naturally excluded from the operation of the section.[53] Non-gratuitous acts imply acts having an element of self-interest[54] including those that are carried out with the expectation of remuneration, for instance, managing another person's estate[55] or carrying out repairs to a property[56] with the expectation of being reimbursed or paid.

The third essential requirement of the section is that the person for whom the act has been performed voluntarily accepts the benefit of the act.[57] This implies that the section will not be applicable in the event of the concerned act being forcibly imposed on the plaintiff.[58] Most importantly, for the section to be applicable, an individual should have had an opportunity to accept or refuse the benefit accruing from the act concerned. Settling a difference of opinion among the High Courts on this question, the Supreme Court in *State of West Bengal v BK Mondal* held that 'the person said to be made liable under s. 70 always has the option not to accept the thing or to return it. It is only where he voluntarily accepts the thing or enjoys the work done that the liability under s. 70 arises.'[59]

An important point of judicial discussion with respect to s 70 is its applicability to situations arising out of an invalid contract. In *Mulamchand v State of Madhya Pradesh*, the issue under consideration was whether s 70 could be invoked in a claim for a refund by a person whose contract was void due to technical requirements under art 299 of the Constitution of India being unfulfilled.[60] Agreeing with Lord Wright's observations in *Fibrosa Spolka Akcyjna v Fairbairn Lawson Combe Barbour Ltd*,[61] the court answered the question in the affirmative and stated that '[t]he juristic basis of the obligation in such a case is not founded upon any contract or tort but upon a third category of law, namely, quasi contract or restitution'.[62]

---

[52] *Rakurti Manikyam v Medidi Satyanarayana* AIR 1972 AP 367 [4].
[53] *AV Palanivelu Mudaliar v Neelavathi Ammal* AIR 1937 PC 50.
[54] *Ram Pratap Kamalia Mills v State of Bihar* AIR 1963 Pat 153.
[55] *AV Palanivelu Mudaliar v Neelavathi Ammal* (n 53).
[56] *Saran v Narayan Das* AIR 1971 All 43.
[57] *State of West Bengal v BK Mondal & Sons* (n 51); *Jayagopal Patnaik v Chairman Puri Joint Water Works Committee* AIR 1964 Ori 69; *MS Devoraj v SV Krishnamurthy* AIR 1969 Mys 350.
[58] *MS Devoraj v SV Krishnamurthy* (n 57).
[59] *State of West Bengal v BK Mondal & Sons* (n 51).
[60] *Mulamchand v State of Madhya Pradesh* AIR 1968 SC 1218.
[61] *Fibrosa Spolka Akcyjna v Fairbairn Lawson Combe Barbour Ltd* [1943] AC 32 (HL).
[62] *Mulamchand v State of Madhya Pradesh* (n 60).

D. Restitution for Payment/Delivery Made Under Mistake or Coercion

Section 72 of the Indian Contract Act imposes restitutionary liability on 'a person to whom money has been paid, or anything delivered, by mistake or under coercion' to repay/return the amount/item concerned. The section incorporates the traditional common law claim for money had and received that enabled a person to recover money (but not goods or services) that had been transferred/provided to another by mistake, under coercion, etc.[63] Such claims (for mistaken payment in particular) form the basis of the modern law of unjust enrichment[64] that aims to recompense the party unduly disadvantaged as a result of a 'normatively defective transfer'.[65]

As is apparent from the language of s 72, an obvious point of departure from the English law of the time was the provision of a restitutionary remedy for money paid as well as things delivered. Further, the term mistake in s 72 includes both mistakes of fact as well as mistakes of law.[66] Having so stated, it must also be noted that the Indian courts have heavily relied upon English jurisprudence in interpreting and applying the section. Acknowledging the law of restitution as forming the basis of the section and as a starting point of analysis of the concept of restitution, the Supreme Court in *Mafatlal Industries Ltd v Union of India*[67] quoted the three prerequisites of the law of restitution as stated by Goff and Jones, 'first, that the defendant has been enriched by the receipt of a benefit; secondly that he has been so enriched at the plaintiff's expense; and thirdly, that it would be unjust to allow him to retain the benefit'.[68] To understand the second prerequisite—the defendant being enriched 'at the expense of the plaintiff'—the court referred to Peter Birks's exposition of the phrase whereby he assigns two meanings to the phrase: first, the defendant's gain being caused by the plaintiff's loss and, secondly, the defendant gaining by causing a wrong to the plaintiff. This understanding of the phrase has informed the court's ruling on the question of unjust enrichment in cases involving tax refunds, a matter of significant relevance in the Indian context. Clarifying the law on the matter, and overruling its earlier decision in *Sales Tax Officer, Banaras v Kanhaiya Lal Mukundalal Saraf*,[69] the Supreme Court held that:

> The person claiming restitution should have suffered a 'loss or injury'. In my opinion, in cases where the assessee or the person claiming refund has passed on

---

[63] *Moses v Macferlan* [1760] 2 Burr 1005; 97 ER 676.
[64] Peter Birks, *Unjust Enrichment* (2nd edn, OUP 2005).
[65] *Investment Trust Companies v Revenue and Customs Comrs* [2017] UKSC 29; [2018] AC 275 [42].
[66] *Sri Devora Shiba Prasad Singh v Maharaja Srish Chandra Nandi* (1950) 52 BOMLR 17.
[67] *Mafatlal Industries Ltd v Union of India* (1997) 5 SCC 536 [9].
[68] Lord Goff and Gareth Jones, *The Law of Restitution* (3rd edn, Sweet & Maxwell 1986) (hereafter Goff and Jones, *The Law of Restitution*).
[69] *Sales Tax Officer, Banaras v Kanhaiya Lal Mukundalal Saraf* 1959 SCR 1350.

the incidence of tax to a third person, how can it be said that he has suffered a loss or injury? How is it possible to say that he has got ownership or title to the amount claimed, which he has already recouped from a third party? So, the very basic requirement for a claim of restitution under Section 72 of the Contract Act is that the person claiming restitution should plead and prove a loss or injury to him; in other words, he has not passed on the liability. If it is not so done, the action for restitution or refund, should fail.[70]

The court further observed that '[t]he very basis of the claim, though statutorily incorporated in Section 72 of the Contract Act, is equitable in nature' and '[i]f an assessee has passed on the tax to the consumer or a third party and sustained no loss or injury, grant of refund to him will result in a windfall to him', unjustly enriching such person.[71] The court refused to apply the doctrine of unjust enrichment to the state, holding that the 'State represents the people of the country. No one can speak of the people being unjustly enriched.'[72]

IV. Scope of the Law of Unjust Enrichment: Beyond the Indian Contract Act

Although most of the Indian case law discussing the law of unjust enrichment relates to the provisions of the Indian Contract Act examined previously, the unjust enrichment doctrine has also been discussed and applied with respect to cases concerning other areas of law. In such instances, courts often deliberate upon the doctrine of unjust enrichment in conjunction with the common law principle of restitution, placing considerable reliance on the common law jurisprudence on unjust enrichment in general and analysing developments in other common law jurisdictions. The following section discusses the application of the unjust enrichment doctrine to scenarios falling outside (and in some instances overlapping with) section V of the Indian Contract Act discussed earlier.

A. Protracted Litigation (s 144, Code of Civil Procedure and Beyond)

The courts in India have often invoked the unjust enrichment doctrine to provide restitution to a party who has been objectively placed in a position of loss as a result of the litigation process, particularly intentionally protracted litigation involving

---

[70] *Mafatlal Industries Ltd v Union of India* (n 67) [10].
[71] ibid [14].
[72] ibid [108].

multiple stays, injunctions, delayed hearings, execution proceedings, etc.[73] Courts have often observed that the power of restitution is an inherent power vested in them for meeting the ends of justice and that no one should be permitted to take undue advantage of the litigation process.[74] It has been held that though this power has been statutorily recognized through provisions such as s 144 of the Code of Civil Procedure, it is primarily based upon the fundamental principles of justice, equity, and fair play.[75]

This inherent power of the courts to do justice by providing restitution to the concerned party has been regarded as part of the extraordinary powers vested in the country's higher judiciary through constitutional provisions such as arts 226 and 142(1) of the Constitution of India. Commenting on the power of the High Courts to issue writs and to provide the remedy of restitution, the Supreme Court in *Grindlays Bank Ltd v Income Tax Officer* held that '[t]he interests of justice require that any undeserved or unfair advantage gained by a party invoking the jurisdiction of the court, by the mere circumstance that it has initiated a proceeding in the court, must be neutralized'.[76]

Section 144 of the Code of Civil Procedure 1908 explicitly recognizes the remedy of restitution in instances involving reversal, modification, or setting aside of a decree or an order to 'place the parties in the position which they would have occupied, but for such decree or such part thereof as has been varied or reversed'. The section is broadly worded, empowering the courts to order a range of remedies including 'payment of interest, damages, compensation and mesne profits' to the concerned party.[77] The courts have relied upon the common law jurisprudence on restitution and unjust enrichment to further expand the ambit of s 144, especially when a party engages in frivolous litigation and uses the processes of the court to gain an advantage against the other party.[78] For instance, commenting upon a litigant unjustly benefiting through interim orders, the courts have observed that 'if the concept of restitution is excluded from application to interim orders, then the litigant would stand to gain by swallowing the benefits yielding out of the interim order even though the battle has been lost at the end'.[79]

In addition to giving a broad interpretation to s 144 for providing restitution to the concerned party, in many instances the courts have ordered restitution in cases not strictly falling within the terms of the section. For instance, in *Kavita Trehan*

---

[73] *Indore Development Authority v Manoharlal* (2020) 8 SCC 129.
[74] *South Eastern Coalfields Ltd v State of MP* (2003) 8 SCC 648; *A Shanmugam v Ariya Kshatriya Rajakula Vamsathu Madalaya Nandhavana Paripalanai Sangam* (2012) 6 SCC 430; *Indore Development Authority v Manoharlal* (n 73).
[75] *South Eastern Coalfields Ltd v State of MP* (n 74); *Indore Development Authority v Manoharlal* (n 73).
[76] *Grindlays Bank Ltd v Income Tax Officer* 1980 AIR 656.
[77] ibid.
[78] *State of Gujarat v Essar Oil Ltd* (2012) 3 SCC 522; *Padmawati v Harijan Sewak Sangh* 154 (2008) DLT 411.
[79] *South Eastern Coalfields Ltd v State of MP* (n 74) [27].

v Balsara Hygience Products Ltd, while criticizing the impugned act of the court—that is, the interim order of the court of first instance in permitting the appellants to sell goods belonging to the respondent—the Supreme Court upheld the High Court's restitutionary order directing the appellants to furnish a security equivalent to the value of the goods sold aimed at restitution of the respondent's loss.[80] Clarifying the phrase 'act of the court' in this context, the Supreme Court has observed that:

> What attracts applicability of restitution is not the act of the court being wrongful or mistake or an error committed by the court; the test is whether, on account of an act of the party persuading the court to pass an order held at the end as not sustainable, resulting in one party gaining an advantage which it would not have otherwise earned, or the other party having suffered an impoverishment, restitution has to be made.[81]

This explanation throws important light on the question of the nature of an act leading to the unjust enrichment or unjust advantage of one party and a loss to the other party for which restitution can be ordered. Thus, the act of the court that can attract restitutionary relief can be an intentionally wrongful act, an erroneous act, an act done under the persuasion of one of the litigants, or an act resulting from routine legal procedures in general.

In the well-known case of *Indian Council for Enviro-Legal Action v Union of India* regarding pollution of the groundwater of a village because of a neighbouring industrial plant, the Supreme Court ruled in favour of the village directing the company to pay compensation.[82] However, even fifteen years after the final judgment, the company intentionally kept the litigation alive through interlocutory appeals to avoid paying the compensation. Criticizing the delaying tactics adopted by the company and taking upon itself the obligation 'to neutralize any unjust enrichment and undeserved gain made by any party by invoking the jurisdiction of the court', the court directed the company to pay the original amount awarded along with compound interest.[83] The rationale for awarding compound interest rather than simple interest was explained in terms of the principles of unjust enrichment and restitution that the court discussed with reference to s 144 of the Code of Civil Procedure along with English and US jurisprudence on the subject.

The expansive interpretation and application of the principles of unjust enrichment and restitution in India should be seen in the context of the Indian judicial system. The astronomical case pendency rates (particularly civil cases which

---

[80] *Kavita Trehan v Balsara Hygience Products Ltd* AIR 1995 SC 441.
[81] *Indore Development Authority v Manoharlal* (n 73) [332].
[82] *Indian Council for Enviro-Legal Action v Union of India* (2011) 12 SCC 768.
[83] ibid [223].

can take decades to adjudicate) and judicial delays that plague the Indian judicial system can be attributed in part to the outdated procedural laws of the country that provide ample scope for slowing down the administrative judicial systems through delaying tactics such as interlocutory orders, injunctions, and stays of execution.[84] Since attempts to reform procedural laws aimed at reducing judicial delays have so far failed, not least due to massive resistance from legal practitioners, the courts and the state[85] have taken to relying on other mechanisms, such as application of the restitutionary principle to a broad range of cases and establishing tribunals to address the long-standing issue of judicial delay.

B. Breach of Public Trust

In the Indian context, the unjust enrichment doctrine has also been invoked to provide restitution to those who are adversely affected due to a breach of public trust by public authorities/officials. In *Bikram Chatterji v Union of India*,[86] a case involving collusion between two governmental authorities and the builders of an apartment complex which allowed leaseholders who had defaulted in their payments to the authorities to sublease their land, the court ruled that the officials of the authorities in question were in blatant violation of the public trust doctrine as their actions had led to the unjust enrichment of the builder at the expense of the homeowners and the authorities.

In *Rameshwar v State of Haryana*,[87] another case involving collusion between state officials and builders/colonizers of the land under the process of acquisition, the court applied the principles of restitution and unjust enrichment as discussed in Indian and English cases such as *Indian Council for Enviro-Legal Action v Union of India*[88] and *Fibrosa Spolka Akcyjna v Fairbairn Lawson Combe Barbour Ltd* respectively.[89]

---

[84] Sumedha, 'The Clogged State of the Indian Judiciary' *The Hindu* (10 May 2022); Marc Galanter, 'India's Tort Deficit. Sketch for a Historical Portrait' in David M Engel and Michael McCann (eds), *Fault Lines: Tort Law as a Cultural Practice* (Stanford UP 2009); Marc Galanter, 'Affidavit in Support of the Union of India (Plaintiff) Submitted to the United States District Court, Southern District of New York, 1986 (In Re Union Carbide Corporation Gas Leak Disaster at Bhopal, India in 1984)' in Upendra Baxi and Paul Thomas (eds), *Valiant Victims and Lethal Litigation: The Bhopal Case* (Indian Law Institute 1990) 161–221.
[85] Marc Galanter, 'Law's Elusive Promise: Learning from Bhopal' in Michael Likosky (ed), *Transnational Legal Processes: Globalisation and Power Disparities* (Butterworths 2002) 172–85.
[86] Writ Petition (Civil) No 940 of 2017.
[87] *Rameshwar v State of Haryana* (2018) 6 SCC 215.
[88] *Indian Council for Enviro-Legal Action v Union of India* (n 82).
[89] *Fibrosa v Fairbairn* (n 61).

V. Salient Features of the Law of Unjust Enrichment in India

A. Quasi-Contract vs Implied Contract

Unlike the English experience, the Indian law of unjust enrichment has always been regarded as being firmly rooted in quasi-contract (to be more precise, 'certain relations resembling those created by contract') and not contract.[90] The English history of unjust enrichment is a history chequered with contestation over whether an action for money had and received was based on contract (implied) or quasi-contract, and whether the latter was part of the former.[91] In this historical debate spanning over two centuries, the initial balance of opinion was in favour of the action for money had and received being rooted in contract law (implied contract)[92] and it was only in the twentieth century that the consensus shifted towards recognizing it as being based neither on contract nor on tort, but on a third category of law—quasi-contract.[93] Conversely, in India this question was unambiguously settled in 1872 with the enactment of the Indian Contract Act. As discussed earlier, claims such as those for restitution of money had and received relate to 'certain relations resembling those created by contract', and not contract. In fact, even before the enactment of the Indian Contract Act, the courts in India had criticized the tendency of some English jurists to conflate quasi-contract with implied contract. Disregarding the prevalent juristic opinion in England at the time, in *Rambux Chittangeo v Modhoosoodun Paul Chawdhry*,[94] the High Court of Calcutta relied on, among other authorities, the following observations by Sir Henry Maine to declare the applicable law in the Indian context to be a clear distinction between true contracts (whether express or implied) and quasi-contracts:

> It has been usual with English critics to identify the quasi-contracts with implied contracts, but this is an error, for implied contracts are true contracts, which quasi-contracts are not. In implied contracts, acts and circumstances are the symbols of the same ingredients which are symbolized, in express contracts, by words; and whether a man employs one set of symbols or the other must be a matter of indifference so far as concerns the theory of agreement. But a Quasi-Contract is not a contract at all.[95]

---

[90] Although some High Courts did rely on English common law by applying the implied contract theory to interpret Part V of the Indian Contract Act, in the case of *State of West Bengal v BK Mondal & Sons* (n 51), the Supreme Court of India reiterated that it is not justified to rely upon English common law to interpret Indian statutes where the statutory provisions in question are clearly stated.
[91] Warren Swain, 'Unjust Enrichment and the Role of Legal History in England and Australia' (2013) 36 UNSWLJ 1030, 1034–36.
[92] 3 Bl Comm 162.
[93] Goff and Jones, *The Law of Restitution* (n 68).
[94] *Rambux Chittangeo v Modhoosoodun Paul Chawdhry* (n 12).
[95] Henry Sumner Maine, *Ancient Law: Its Connection with the Early History of Society, and Its Relation to Modern Ideas* (John Murray 1861) 343.

Departing from the prevailing juristic opinion in England at the time, the subsequent codification of the distinction between contract and quasi-contract[96] in India through enactment of the Indian Contract Act in whose drafting Sir Henry Maine played a pivotal role gives credence to the colonial legal laboratory theory of codification.[97]

B. Divergence/Convergence with Other Common Law Jurisdictions

The foregoing discussion on the implied vs quasi-contractual basis of the law of unjust enrichment, the nineteenth-century codification of parts of the law of unjust enrichment in India that deliberately departed from English common law, and the subsequent judicial pronouncements declaring that the provisions of Indian statutes should be read independently of English law unless necessitated by the context[98] demonstrate that historically there have indeed been deliberate points of departure from English law. Additionally, unlike other common law jurisdictions,[99] the 'unjust factor' is not the focus of Indian jurisprudence on the law of unjust enrichment.[100]

But these instances paint only a partial picture of the relationship between the unjust enrichment laws of India and other common law jurisdictions. A careful reading of Indian judgments shows that the law of unjust enrichment is not developing in isolation from other common law jurisdictions. There are also multiple points of convergence. For instance, as discussed in Section III, traditionally the Indian courts have placed considerable reliance on English jurisprudence while interpreting ss 68,[101] 70,[102] and 72[103] of the Indian Contract Act.

[96] Though terms such as restitution and unjust enrichment are now generally preferred over the term quasi-contract, there is value in continuing to use the term quasi-contract as the contract theory and doctrine can be helpful in developing the restitutionary theory, especially with respect to cases lying at the margin of consent-based liability. Dan Priel, 'In Defence of Quasi-Contract' (2012) 75 MLR 54.
[97] Assaf Likhovski, 'A Colonial Legal Laboratory? Jurisprudential Innovation in British India' (2021) 69 Am J Comp L 44.
[98] *State of West Bengal v BK Mondal & Sons* (n 51).
[99] Andrew Burrows, *A Restatement of the English Law of Unjust Enrichment* (OUP 2012) 44; Peter Birks, *An Introduction to the Law of Restitution* (rev edn, OUP 1989) 8.
[100] Only a few Indian judgments have referred to the question of the 'unjust factor'. In *Akuate Internet Services v Star India Pvt Ltd* (2013) SCC OnLine Del 3344, the Delhi High Court held that identifying the relevant 'unjust factor' is an essential element of the law of unjust enrichment in India. But this approach by the court has been criticized for relying on English law and disregarding the relevant Indian statutory provisions. See MP Ram Mohan and Mridul Godha, 'The Law of Restitution for Unjust Enrichment in India' [2020] LMCLQ 104, 112.
[101] *Jagon Ram Marwari v Mahadeo Prosad Sahu* (n 18), relying on *Peters v Fleming* (n 19) to understand the concept of necessaries under s 68 of the Indian Contract Act.
[102] *Mulamchand v State of Madhya Pradesh* (n 60), citing Lord Wright in *Fibrosa v Fairbairn* (n 61) to rule that s 70 of the Indian Contract Act was based neither on contract nor on tort, but on quasi-contract.
[103] *Mafatlal Industries Ltd v Union of India* (n 67) citing the three prerequisites of the law of restitution as stated by Goff and Jones, *The Law of Restitution* (n 68).

The Indian courts are now referring not only to English cases and authorities on restitution and unjust enrichment, but also relying upon legal developments in other jurisdictions such as the American Law Institute's *Restatement of the Law of Restitution*.[104] This reliance by the Indian courts on foreign jurisprudence on unjust enrichment has been criticized.[105] But, it is argued here that being aware of the legal developments in other jurisdictions is particularly relevant in today's globalized society. Codification should not lead to ossification and there are times when a decision needs to be made in the light of the local as well as the international context.

C. Application to Public Law

In the Indian context, the doctrine of unjust enrichment is relevant not only for private law, but also for public law.[106] This forms an important part of the country's administrative law and is particularly relevant for cases involving acts by public authorities such as an imposition of unauthorized indirect taxes (market fees, sales tax, customs duty, excise duty, etc).[107] While applying the doctrine of unjust enrichment in the context of tax refunds, the courts have also discussed the concept of economic justice as enshrined in arts 38 and 39 that are part of the Directive Principles of State Policy of the Constitution of India.[108]

Laying down the law that tax refunds can be made only to those who have not passed on the burden—as providing a tax refund to one who has already passed on the burden of an enhanced levy to others would amount to unjust enrichment—the Supreme Court in *Mafatlal Industries Ltd v Union of India* observed that:

> The Preamble and the aforesaid articles (viz art 38 and art 39) do demand that when a duty cannot be refunded to the real persons who have borne the burden, for one reason or the other reason, it is but appropriate that the said amounts are retained by the State for being used for public good.[109]

---

[104] Most recently American Law Institute, *Restatement (Third) of Restitution and Unjust Enrichment* (ALI 2011).
[105] Mohan and Godha, 'The Law of Restitution for Unjust Enrichment in India' (n 100).
[106] The dissolution of the public–private law divide in the Indian context is not a new phenomenon: Arpita Gupta, 'Mass Tort Jurisprudence and Critical Epistemologies of Risk: Dissolution of Public–Private Divide in the Indian Mass Tort Law' (2019) 40 Liverpool L Rev 227.
[107] *Shiv Shankar Dal Mills v State of Haryana* AIR 1980 SC 1037; *State of Madhya Pradesh v Vyankatlal* AIR 1985 SC 901; *Indian Aluminium Co Ltd v Thane Municipal Corp* AIR 1992 SC 53; *Tata Engineering of Locomotive Co Ltd v Municipal Corp* AIR 1992 SC 645; *Mafatlal Industries Ltd v Union of India* (n 67).
[108] *Shiv Shankar Dal Mills v State of Haryana* (n 107); *Mafatlal Industries Ltd v Union of India* (n 67).
[109] *Mafatlal Industries Ltd v Union of India* (n 67).

The Supreme Court of India has extended this line of reasoning to address the question of the theory of justice underlying the doctrine of unjust enrichment.[110] Espousing the notion of distributive justice, the Supreme Court of India in *Shiv Shankar Dal Mills v State of Haryana* held that:

> Distributive justice comprehends more than achieving lessening of inequalities by differential taxation, giving debt relief or distribution of property owned by one to many who have none by imposing ceiling on holdings, both agricultural and urban, or by direct regulation of contractual transactions, by forbidding certain transactions, and perhaps, by requiring others. It also means that those who have been deprived of their properties by unconscionable bargaining should be restored their property.[111]

VI. Conclusion

An early codification of the law of unjust enrichment provided a comparatively greater degree of clarity and stability to the field in India in comparison with other common law jurisdictions. However, the foregoing discussion on the relevant statutory provisions of the Indian Contract Act, among others, and the corresponding case law bring to the fore at least three important issues concerning the law itself and its application by the judiciary that warrants further scrutiny.

First, the definitional ambit of unjust enrichment in the Indian context is still relatively vague. The range of situations falling within the purview of unjust enrichment law in the country gives it an appearance of a residuary category, making it difficult to identify the core of the doctrine in the Indian context. The application of unjust enrichment by the Indian judiciary to a variety of situations, especially those falling outside the statutory provisions and their redress through the invocation of the inherent power of the judiciary, raises legitimate concerns about the judiciary having 'carte blanche'.[112] Often, the Indian judiciary has interpreted the term unjust to mean 'unfair'. The underlying rationale for the broad meaning assigned to the term unjust can perhaps be understood in the context of the activist nature of the Indian higher judiciary, whereby legal vacuums are often filled by judicial pronouncements based on considerations of justice.[113] Questions regarding

---

[110] Matthew Doyle, 'Corrective Justice and Unjust Enrichment' (2012) 62 UTLJ 229; Kit Barker, 'Theorising Unjust Enrichment: Being Realist(ic)?' (2006) 26 OJLS 609.
[111] *Shiv Shankar Dal Mills v State of Haryana* (n 107).
[112] *Lipkin Gorman v Karpnale Ltd* [1991] 2 AC 548 (HL) 578.
[113] The desirability or otherwise of judicial activism in India has long been a matter of debate. SP Sathe, 'Judicial Activism: The Indian Experience' (2001) 6 Washington U J Law Policy 29; Jamie Cassels, 'Judicial Activism and Public Interest Litigation in India: Attempting the Impossible?' (1989) 37 Am J Comp L 495.

CONCLUSION 73

the definitional parameters and the desirability or otherwise of judicial stewardship need to be reflected upon.

Secondly, this lack of definitional clarity has contributed to confusion with respect to the matters to which unjust enrichment doctrine should apply. For instance, in some cases the courts have failed to distinguish between restitution for unjust enrichment and restitution for wrongdoing.[114] Also, the practice of the courts in deciding matters of unjust enrichment without relying upon the relevant statutory provisions has been criticized.[115] Scholars have criticized instances where the courts have decided matters of unjust enrichment without relying upon the relevant statutory provisions.[116] An inquiry into whether the law of unjust enrichment is enshrined only in specific statutory provisions or whether there is a general theory of unjust enrichment would be helpful for addressing this concern.

Thirdly, the inapplicability of the doctrine of unjust enrichment to the state in certain circumstances needs to be reconsidered, particularly in the light of the jurisprudence on the role and responsibilities of public authorities. Given the wide-ranging impact of the decisions and actions of public authorities, the focus of the law in the first instance should be to ensure that they perform their duties with utmost due diligence, laying down guidelines to deter irresponsible conduct on their part. Even in instances where fair restitution to the specific individuals concerned is difficult, such as the unjust enrichment cases involving the imposition of indirect taxes subsequently regarded as unauthorized, for it to be justified for the state to deny claims for tax refunds, detailed guidelines on the way such funds can be spent by the state should be laid down.

Two plausible approaches to address these concerns are introducing the necessary amendments to Chapter V of the Indian Contract Act and a comprehensive exposition of the unjust enrichment law and related matters by the country's higher judiciary. Regardless of the approach adopted, a sustained engagement with the comparative discourse on unjust enrichment law will serve to provide a nuanced resolution concomitant with the relevant local and global contexts.

---

[114] *Indian Council for Enviro-Legal Action v Union of India* 2011 (8) SCC 161; Francesco Giglio, 'Restitution for Wrongs: A Comparative Analysis' [2001] Oxford U Comparative L Forum 6.
[115] Mohan and Godha, 'The Law of Restitution for Unjust Enrichment in India' (n 100).
[116] *Modi Vanaspati Manufacturing Co v Katihar Jute Mills Pvt Ltd* AIR 1969 Cal 496; *Annamma v Ouseph Tressiamma* AIR 1975 Ker 185.

PART II
SOCIOLOGY

4
Academics and Legal Change
Birks, Savigny, and the Law of Unjust Enrichment

*Sagi Peari**

I. Introduction

The practising lawyer who could merely do his job would be no more than a mechanic, useless in comparison with one endowed with the power of reasoning about the law and about its grounds and principles.[1]

The unjust enrichment formula in England consists of the following four components: (1) the defendant's enrichment; (2) the enrichment is at the expense of the claimant; (3) the enrichment is unjust; and (4) the unavailability of applicable defences to the defendant (*Formula 1*).[2] The unjust enrichment formula in Germany states the liability structure in the following terms: (1) a claimant's performance towards the defendant; (2) there is no legal basis for the defendant to retain the enrichment; and (3) the unavailability of applicable defences for the defendant (*Formula 2*).[3] In some countries the jurisprudence models itself on either German or the UK models. In other countries, the legislative provisions or the case law (or both) are influenced, or at least inspired by, one of the aforementioned models. Finally, some accounts are prone to a combination of the formulas,[4] offering a mixture of the two.

This chapter focuses on the legal academics who evidently played a decisive role in the creation of the two formulas: Professors Friedrich Carl von Savigny in Germany and Peter Birks in the UK. It places the contribution of these academics

---

[*] I am grateful for comments and discussion with Hanoch Dagan, Lusina Ho, James Penner, and Warren Swain.

[1] Peter Birks, 'Editor's Preface' in PBH Birks (ed), *What are Law Schools For?* (OUP 1996) v (hereafter Birks, *Law Schools*).

[2] See eg *Banque Financière de la Cité v Parc (Battersea) Ltd* [1999] 1 AC 221 (HL) 227, 234; Peter Birks, *An Introduction to the Law of Restitution* (OUP 1985) 21 (hereafter Birks, *Introduction*).

[3] German Civil Code, ss 812–22 (Bürgerliches Gesetzbuch, BGB); Gerhard Dannemann and Reiner Schulze (eds), *German Civil Code: Article-by-Article Commentary* (Nomos 2020).

[4] Peter Birks, *Unjust Enrichment* (1st edn, OUP 2003) 87–113 (hereafter Birks, *Unjust Enrichment*).

in the broader context of the role of legal academics in society and their role as agents of change. To what extent do legal academics impact legal change, and how does the birth of unjust enrichment fit within this framework?

It has been convincingly argued that Peter Birks was the forefather of the law of unjust enrichment in the UK. He was coined as 'the most influential English academic lawyer of his generation',[5] a scholar of 'immense' influence,[6] and as 'the dominant academic private lawyer of recent time'[7] whose work on unjust enrichment shaped the 'whole area of private law'.[8] Alan Rodger commented that '[e]veryone recognizes that he [Peter Birks] knew far more about unjust enrichment and its impact on other fields of private law than anyone else in the world'.[9] Birks's groundbreaking book *An Introduction to the Law of Restitution*[10] received 'near-universal approbation';[11] he was a figure who 'sparked an [unjust enrichment] revolution in England and Wales that has subsequently found its Robespierres among the English judiciary'.[12]

The same point applies to Savigny. It was his observations on unjust enrichment that led to the birth of unjust enrichment and provided the basis for its subsequent incorporation in the BGB provisions.[13] Reinhard Zimmermann and Jacques du Plessis commented that Savigny 'had the greatest impact on the adoption of a general enrichment action in the BGB'.[14] Dannemann has characterized Savigny's contribution to the German approach to unjust enrichment in similar terms.[15]

The chapter proceeds as follows: Section II discusses the role of legal academics in society and makes a case for their critical role in law reform. Section III focuses on the law of unjust enrichment. It presents the origins of the two formulas in the

---

[5] Andrew Burrows and Alan Rodger, 'Introduction' in Andrew Burrows and Alan Rodger (eds), *Mapping the Law: Essays in Memory of Peter Birks* (OUP 2006) 1 (hereafter Burrows and Rodger, 'Introduction').

[6] Michael Bryan, 'Peter Birks and Unjust Enrichment in Australia' (2004) 28 MULR 724, 725.

[7] Gerard McMeel, 'What Kind of Jurist Was Peter Birks?' (2011) 19 RLR 15, 15.

[8] Warren Swain, 'The Law of Obligations, the Common Law and Legal Change: A View from the Gutter' (2016) Inaugural Lecture, University of Auckland, 10 <https://ssrn.com/abstract=3830853> accessed 17 February 2023 (hereafter Swain, 'Gutter').

[9] Andrew Burrows and Alan Rodger, 'Addresses given at the Memorial Service for Peter Birks on 20 November 2004 in the University Church of St Mary the Virgin, Oxford' in Andrew Burrows and Alan Rodger (eds), *Mapping the Law: Essays in Memory of Peter Birks* (OUP 2006) xiv (hereafter Burrows and Rodger, 'Addresses').

[10] Birks, *Introduction* (n 2).

[11] McMeel (n 7) 26.

[12] Peter G Watts, '"Unjust Enrichment"—the Potion that Induces Well-Meaning Sloppiness of Thought' (2016) 69 CLP 289, 291.

[13] Reinhard Zimmermann, 'Unjustified Enrichment: The Modern Civilian Approach' (1995) 15 OJLS 403, 405 fn 9.

[14] Reinhard Zimmermann and Jacques du Plessis, 'Basic Features of the German Law of Unjustified Enrichment' (1994) 2 RLR 14, 15.

[15] Gerhard Dannemann, *The German Law of Unjustified Enrichment and Restitution: A Comparative Introduction* (OUP 2009) 8. See also Nils Jansen, 'Farewell to Unjustified Enrichment?' (2016) 20 Edin LR 123.

Savigny and Birks writings and situates those writings within the general literature on legal academics and legal change. Section IV offers some concluding remarks.

II. Legal Change and Academics

A. The World With and Without Legal Academics

Legal academics are essential to the development of legal doctrine as agents of change. In an important monograph published in 2016, titled *Divergent Paths: The Academy and the Judiciary*, then Judge Richard A Posner elaborates on the symbiotic relationships between the judiciary and legal academia.[16] Posner, a former leading law and economics scholar,[17] says that academia plays a central role in assisting the judiciary to map existing legal uncertainties and improve judicial performance.[18] As Posner puts it:

> So there is much to criticize in the judicial profession and therefore much room for improvement. But where is the improvement to come from? A possibility that appeals to me as a former law professor is the law schools. Law professors write a great deal about the judiciary...[19]

Posner talks about the judicial profession and improvement. He attributes a significant role in this process of improvement to legal scholars and their writings.[20] Many times, judicial decisions make explicit reference to academia by directly citing academic works.[21] Indeed, Posner was one of the most cited scholars in judicial decisions.[22] In other cases, the impact on the judicial decision-making process is indirect.[23]

Doctrinal analysis, which is not overly preoccupied with the decisions of the appellate courts, is the most helpful to judicial decision-making.[24] Through analysing and criticizing the courts' decisions and justifications, this analysis sets the scene for the law's improvement. This explains the significance of the practical experience of doctrinal academics and the need to enhance the practical aspects of legal education.[25] However, not every piece of scholarship is equally helpful. Echoing a

---

[16] Richard A Posner, *Divergent Paths: The Academy and the Judiciary* (Harvard UP 2016).
[17] See eg Richard A Posner, *Economic Analysis of Law* (Little Brown and Co 1973).
[18] Posner, *Divergent Paths* (n 16) 350.
[19] ibid xi.
[20] ibid 261–96.
[21] See eg Neil Duxbury, *Jurists and Judges: An Essay on Influence* (Hart Publishing 2001) 45.
[22] Fred R Shapiro, 'The Most-Cited Legal Scholars' (2000) 29 JLS 409, 424.
[23] Posner, *Divergent Paths* (n 16) 3–4. See also Duxbury, *Jurists and Judges* (n 21).
[24] Posner, *Divergent Paths* (n 16) 10, 266.
[25] ibid 42. See also Harry T Edwards, 'The Growing Disjunction Between Legal Education and the Legal Profession' (1992) 91 Mich L Rev 34, 78.

recent concern expressed by another former academic, Lord Burrows in the UK,[26] Posner suggests that interdisciplinary research provides little assistance for the judiciary.[27]

Posner sees legal academia and the judiciary in cross-beneficial terms. Judicial decisions provide academics with an invaluable source of legal scholarship. The work of academics, in turn, continuously refines and improves the work of the judiciary. Posner goes further by making a call for close collaborative research between academia and the judiciary.[28] Similarly, judges learn from academics in their continuing education programmes.[29] In the light of public concern about the somewhat static nature of the judiciary,[30] there is a call to advance these programmes.[31]

Furthermore, legal scholars bring the attention of the judiciary into comparative perspective. The presence of foreign legal academics in law schools and faculties facilitates this perspective.[32] These academics are 'agents of change' rather than 'irritants'.[33] Foreign academics challenge, shape, and refine domestic law. They illuminate the valuable first-hand comparative dimension of legal doctrine. Perhaps, disappointingly for Posner and Burrows, there is an indication that foreign scholars tend to depart from doctrinal studies towards interdisciplinary approaches to legal scholarship.[34]

While the impact of legal academia on legal change is greater in some countries than in others,[35] it is evident throughout the systems and jurisdictions. Consider the civil law systems. In those systems, scholars play a major role in the mandatory specialized education of judges.[36] They have a profound impact on the judicial decision-making process,[37] serving as the primary source for developing and interpreting law.[38] Academics are instrumental in all major legislative reforms.[39] As William Twining and others put it, 'it can certainly be said that academics play

---

[26] Lord Burrows, 'Judges and Academics, and the Endless Road to Unattainable Perfection: Lionel Cohen Lecture 2021, Jerusalem, 25 October 2021' (2022) 55 Israel L Rev 50, 55.
[27] Posner, *Divergent Paths* (n 16) 266, 284, 291. See also Richard A Posner, 'Legal Scholarship Today' (2002) 115 Harv L Rev 1314.
[28] Posner, *Divergent Paths* (n 16) 262.
[29] See eg Livingston Armytage, *Educating Judges: Towards Improving Justice—A Survey of Global Practice* (Brill 2015) 172–73, 189, 217–27.
[30] See eg Stacey Strong, 'How Legal Academics Can Participate in Judicial Education: A How-To Guide by Richard Posner' (2017) 66 J Leg Ed 421.
[31] ibid.
[32] See eg Mathias Siems, 'Foreign-Trained Legal Scholars in the UK: "Irritants" or "Change Agents"?' (2021) 41 LS 373, 373–74, 387.
[33] ibid.
[34] ibid 387.
[35] See eg Duxbury, *Jurists and Judges* (n 21).
[36] Charles H Koch, 'The Advantages of the Civil Law Judicial Design as the Model for Emerging Legal Systems' (2004) 11 Ind J Global Legal Stud 139.
[37] See eg Stefan Vogenauer, 'An Empire of Light? II: Learning and Lawmaking in Germany Today' (2006) 26 OJLS 627, 630–48.
[38] See eg RC van Caenegem, *Judges, Legislators and Professors: Chapters in European Legal History* (CUP 1987).
[39] Swain, 'Gutter' (n 8) 7.

a pre-eminent role in civil law countries. They exert an enormous influence on the law-making process, be it statutory or judicial.'[40] The overarching picture is clear: legal academia and the judiciary are symbiotic; they cannot exist without each other. This seems to be true for both common law and civil law.

This is not to say that the opposite argument cannot be made. In his thought-provoking chapter, published in 2011 and titled 'A World without Law Professors',[41] Mathias M Siems contemplates a world without legal academics. In theory, the law school's curriculum could be taught by practitioners,[42] which would indeed meet the aforementioned call for more practical, clinical dimensions of legal education.

As Siems suggests, practitioners are well equipped to assess and criticize the legal doctrine as it exists in practice.[43] They have the knowledge and the skills to comprehensively outline the legal doctrine and illustrate its operation in various factual and counterfactual scenarios.[44] Perhaps, they could do it better than academics. This point has some support in the lessons of history. At the time of the birth of the universities—in the twelfth century—practitioners oversaw legal education.[45] Even now, many law professors in countries such as Italy and the Netherlands simultaneously practice law.[46] The role of the practitioners in law schools remains central today.

Siems does acknowledge difficulty with what he calls 'deep research'.[47] However, this problem could be overcome by providing judges with competent research assistants,[48] and delegating the law subject to other faculties such as history, sociology, economics, and philosophy.[49] This would probably lead to a better quality of the 'law & x' research.[50] As Siems suggests: 'In a world without law professors this can be solved by shifting these [interdisciplinary] topics to other schools or faculties of the university.'[51] This makes sense: professionally trained philosophers, sociologists, historians, and economists seem to possess a better knowledge and skill for analysing legal doctrine. Their internal perspective has the depth and breadth to grasp the full scope of the issues at hand.

---

[40] William Twining and others, 'The Role of Academics in the Legal System' in Mark Tushnet and Peter Cane (eds), *The Oxford Handbook of Legal Studies* (OUP 2005) 936.
[41] Mathias M Siems, 'A World without Law Professors' in Mark Van Hoecke (ed), *Methodologies of Legal Research: Which Kind of Method for What Kind of Discipline?* (Hart Publishing 2011) 71.
[42] ibid 73.
[43] ibid 79.
[44] ibid 77.
[45] ibid 74.
[46] ibid 75.
[47] ibid 81. See also Geoffrey Samuel, 'What is the Role of a Legal Academic? A Response to Lord Burrows' (2022) Series 2, vol 3 Amicus Curiae 305, 305 (mentioning 'deep theory').
[48] Siems, 'A World without Law Professors' (n 41) 81.
[49] ibid 82.
[50] ibid 83.
[51] ibid 77.

B. The Autonomy of Law, Social Reality, and the Nature of Law

Siems' intellectual exercise hinges on the question of whether law is an *autonomous* discipline.[52] A positive answer to this question would be fatal to this exercise. Autonomy or even semi-autonomy of the law would be inconsistent with moving the research from the law faculties and delegating it to other disciplines. The lack of law's autonomy seems to be an implicit presumption in Siems' exercise.

Ernest J Weinrib's biting criticism against the law and economics analysis of private law is precisely to the point: 'the sole purpose of private law is to be private law'.[53] Focusing on private law, Weinrib says that it has a distinctive, independent value that should not be analysed through the foreign conceptual lens of disciplines such as economics, history, and so on.

Not surprisingly, Weinrib argues against the interdisciplinary law & x studies, and growing calls to deepen clinical legal education. Rather, Weinrib swims against the tide. In his article titled 'Can Law Survive Legal Education?', he favours the diametrically opposite position, arguing that legal education needs 'further theorizing'.[54] The distinctive autonomy of law would be at odds with the delegation of scholarly legal research to other faculties. Against Siems (and perhaps Posner), he would argue that the role of law schools is to enhance a deep conceptual understanding of the law's distinctive characteristics, an exercise that would be unsuitable for busy practitioners.

True, Weinrib's own writings are open to the same line of criticism. While rejecting the economic analysis of law, these writings are deeply informed by the Kantian philosophy of natural rights.[55] So, for Weinrib, private law *does* serve a purpose: to refine and improve itself towards the Kantian ideal of legal rights epitomizing equal freedom for all, within the multiplicity of state orders that secure those rights and approximate towards that ideal.[56] Weinrib would perhaps reply that Kantian philosophy makes a sharp distinction between legal and other philosophies. On a Kantian approach, the purpose of the law (or at least private law) is to reflect *legal philosophy*, rather than *other philosophy* or other disciplines. This explains the call for 'further theorizing' of the legal doctrine, uncovering its essentials for the benefit of law students, the judiciary, and the public. Grasping the deepest nature of law and its rationalization within the natural law philosophy

---

[52] See eg Brian H Bix, 'Law as an Autonomous Discipline' in Mark Tushnet and Peter Cane (eds), *The Oxford Handbook of Legal Studies* (OUP 2005); Dan Priel, 'Two Forms of Formalism' in Andrew Robertson and James Goudkamp (eds), *Form and Substance in the Law of Obligations* (Hart Publishing 2019). See also Hanoch Dagan, 'Law as an Academic Discipline' in Helge Dedek and Shauna Van Praagh (eds), *Stateless Law: Evolving Boundaries of a Discipline* (Ashgate Publishing 2015).
[53] Ernest J Weinrib, *The Idea of Private Law* (Harvard UP 1995) 8 (hereafter Weinrib, *The Idea*).
[54] Ernest J Weinrib, 'Can Law Survive Legal Education?' (2007) 60 Vand L Rev 401, 405.
[55] Weinrib, *The Idea* (n 53) ch 2; Ernest J Weinrib, 'Law as a Kantian Idea of Reason' (1987) 87 Colum L Rev 472.
[56] See Ernest J Weinrib, *Corrective Justice* (OUP 2012).

would enable us to contemplate on the way forward towards the plausible directions of legal reform led by *legal* academics.

Notwithstanding the question of the law's autonomy, Siems' intellectual exercise is difficult to reconcile as a matter of *social reality*. Prima facie, law professors are the best equipped with the knowledge and skills to comprehensively present and analyse the legal doctrine in a multi-layered way.[57] They have the time, education, and academic freedom to fully appreciate the depth and breadth of the doctrine. Contra to Siems, it is doubtful whether practitioners could successfully do this job. In order to do so, they would need to become de facto legal academics.

Legal reform and legal change are especially important. The lessons of history demonstrate the paradigmatic significance of legal academia on this front. Legal academics do not just teach law and publish scholarly outputs but often take active leadership in public service.[58] They work with the government, law reform, public policy commissions, and quasi-governmental bodies. Academics flesh out the doctrinal deficiencies of the present law and point to the important lessons of history. They deepen the conceptual understandings of the legal doctrine to adjust the law to meet the ever-changing social reality of complex commercial dealings, powerful actors, and technological innovations.[59]

In some cases, the scholarly inquiry would say that the law's adjustment and qualification is not enough; a full-blown revolution of the legal doctrine is required.[60] In other cases, this inquiry would resist the adjustment and change with a view that the old law is good enough to meet contemporary challenges.[61] Still, the point here is that legal academics appear to be the most suitable agents of legal change, or at least *the consideration* of that change. This claim is not about the internal normativity of law à la Weinrib, but rather about social reality.

Delegating the research role to other disciplines and practitioners may lose the focus of the scholarly inquiry and jeopardize the very heart of academics as agents of change. In this capacity, the obligation of legal academics is not solely towards the judiciary but rather towards the community at large: to improve the law, make it predictable, and align it with the conceptions of common sense, justice, and fairness of a particular community.[62] The law & x research may or may not contribute

---

[57] For a discussion along these lines, see Twining and others (n 40); Burrows (n 26) 55 (mentioning the significance of academics in the 'judicial development of principle' and bringing judges the 'big picture of the law').

[58] Twining and others (n 40) 923–26, 928–29.

[59] Donal Nolan, 'Offer and Acceptance in the Electronic Age' in Andrew Burrows and Edwin Peel (eds), *Contract Formation and Parties* (OUP 2010); Ernest J Weinrib, 'Back to the Future' in Helge Dedek and Shauna Van Praagh (eds), *Stateless Law: Evolving Boundaries of a Discipline* (Ashgate Publishing 2015) 33 (hereafter Weinrib, 'Future').

[60] Sagi Peari, *The Foundation of Choice of Law: Choice and Equality* (OUP 2018) 273–95 (hereafter Peari, *The Foundation*).

[61] cf Warren Swain, 'Change in the Common Law, Letting Our Illusions Die: Some Observations From History' (2017) New Zealand Institute of Judicial Studies <https://ssrn.com/abstract=3830851> accessed 17 February 2023 (hereafter Swain, 'Illusions').

[62] cf Samuel (n 47) 327.

to the study of law;[63] it may and may not be relevant for legal reform. At least the legal portion of those studies should be led by legal scholars who are most familiar with the movements and fluctuations of the legal doctrine and have a good sense of history.

The lessons of history demonstrate that these were legal academics who played a decisive role in legal reform, its consideration, the law's adjustment to social reality, and the impact of academic scholarship on the judiciary. Section III of this chapter further supports this point by focusing on the context of unjust enrichment and two prominent legal figures: Peter Birks (with a profound impact in the common law jurisdictions) and Friedrich Carl von Savigny (with a profound impact in the civil law tradition, and by extension China[64]). However, there is a rich array of other examples, such as the profound impact of legal scholars on the development of criminal law[65] and administrative law.[66]

The previous points about the autonomy of law and social reality bring me to a third, deeper point: the *nature of law*. What is the role of legal change within the leading branches of jurisprudence,[67] such as the natural law tradition, positivism, and socio-legal studies? The natural law tradition embraces legal change through the ability of legal change to create a desirable model of legal institutions and legal rights. This is the end that would stand at the core of legal reform led by natural law lawyers.[68] In other words, when it comes to law reform, natural law can supplant the role model for the legal rules to follow or at least aspire to it. Within this model, the role of academics is pre-eminent: they are the ones who work out the structure of the desired legal rules, setting the scene for reform.[69] A similar point applies to legal positivism. This branch of jurisprudence embraces legal change and the central role of legal academics within it. While legal positivism insists on a sharp distinction between what law *is* and what law *should be*, it does recognize the significance of reform. The fact that a social test serves to recognize the validity of the legal rules does not mean that legal academics should not lead the change to continuously improve the law through legal reform.[70]

However, the socio-legal theory is the branch of jurisprudence which deserves the most attention. In contrast to legal positivism and natural law,[71] it places legal

---

[63] Priel (n 52) 166–67.
[64] See eg Siyi Lin, Chapter 2 in this volume.
[65] Twining and others (n 40) 927.
[66] Warren Swain, 'Unjust Enrichment and the Role of Legal History in England and Australia' (2013) 36 UNSWLJ 1030, 1039 (hereafter Swain, 'Unjust Enrichment').
[67] See eg Brian Z Tamanaha, 'The Third Pillar of Jurisprudence: Social Legal Theory' (2015) 56 Wm & Mary L Rev 2235.
[68] See text to nn 52–56.
[69] See eg Weinrib, 'Future' (n 59).
[70] Jeremy Waldron, 'Kant's Legal Positivism' (1996) 109 Harv L Rev 1535; Arthur Ripstein, *Force and Freedom: Kant's Legal and Political Philosophy* (Harvard UP 2009) ch 6; Paul Torremans and James J Fawcett (eds), *Cheshire, North & Fawcett: Private International Law* (15th edn, OUP 2017) 30–31.
[71] Tamanaha (n 67) 2269–70.

change at the very forefront of its inquiry. This theory also deserves attention because, as we will see in Section III, both Birks and Savigny seem to belong to it.

C. The Socio-Legal Theory and Legal Scholars as Agents of Change

The socio-legal theory traces its intellectual foundations to the historical school of jurisprudence.[72] This school of jurisprudence views law as a social institution which reflects the morals, culture, religion, customs, economic circumstances, and other aspects of a particular community.[73] Savigny calls it 'spirit'.[74] The spirit is 'historical' in the sense that it is not attached to the universal morals of the natural law tradition.[75] Rather, the claim is about the law's evolution and growth through time. The variety of law is explained through the different spirits that each community may have.

Law is like language.[76] It continuously evolves and becomes more sophisticated to meet the requirements of social reality, the complexity of commerce, and technological progress. Thus, legal reform inevitably captures the needs of an ever-evolving community.[77] Law is grounded on the contingency and relativity of the social surroundings of a given community in a particular space and time. There is nothing further in legal normativity.[78] Similar to the legal positivists, social-legal theory rejects a rationalization of the law based on the universal values of the natural law tradition and instead favours a sharp division between law and morals, *is* and *ought*.

Of course, this dynamic movement creates a problem for law which is slow and lags behind society. Law cannot always be changing through legislation or by overruling legal precedents. Due to custom, legal change is rarely rapid.[79] It has been suggested that to change law requires passing the Rubicon of tipping points.[80] Some of the members of the historical school of jurisprudence have therefore attributed a central role to such phenomena as 'legal fictions' and 'equity'. These open-ended devices play a central role in the adjudication process by assisting

---

[72] ibid.
[73] ibid 7. See also Harold J Berman, 'The Historical Foundations of Law' (2005) 54 Emory LJ 13, 13–14.
[74] Friedrich Carl von Savigny, *Of the Vocation of Our Age for Legislation and Jurisprudence* (Abraham Hayward tr, Littlewood & Co 1831) 134 (hereafter Savigny, *Vocation*).
[75] ibid.
[76] ibid 27.
[77] Tamanaha (n 67) 2246.
[78] cf Joseph Raz, *The Authority of Law: Essays on Law and Morality* (2nd edn, OUP 2009) 104–05.
[79] Swain, 'Gutter' (n 8) 11–12; Swain, 'Illusions' (n 61) 6–9.
[80] Swain, 'Gutter' (n 8) 155.

judges in mitigating the ever-existing gap between the existing rules and advancing social reality.[81]

Viewing law as an exclusively social phenomenon places the historical school of jurisprudence within the burgeoning literature of socio-legal studies.[82] This is what bonds the historical school of jurisprudence with sociological literature.[83] A reference to the American Legal Realists' movement is especially attractive. Similar to the historical school, Legal Realists talk about the evolution of laws as linked to the needs and challenges of a particular community.[84] Critically, both perceive law as an exclusively social phenomenon. Only social facts, and not morality, determine the law.[85] Not surprisingly, some of the realists drew a parallel between the historical school of jurisprudence and Legal Realism in their writings.[86]

Furthermore, grounding the historical school of jurisprudence within the stances of socio-legal studies points to the even greater significance of legal academics as the agents of change. The writings of socio-legal scholars such as Eugen Ehrlich (Germany)[87] and Roscoe Pound (United States)[88] suggest that the significance of legal academics is not limited to reform and the consideration of it. More than that, their significance is relevant to the perception of law in the eyes of the community at a particular time and place. The daily adjudicative process and interpretation of the legal doctrine must reflect its understanding influenced by legal academics. It could be argued that legal academics are not just agents of change at the time of the reform, but also take on this role in the *daily activity* of the courts.

To explain this point, consider the nature of the judicial decision-making process from the standpoint of Legal Realism. Realists are famous for their rules scepticism, according to which the legal doctrine is inherently indeterminate.[89] The wide variety of opinions of the various interpretations, alongside the wide range and flexibility of potentially relevant applicable rules and doctrines, suggest that the actual law's practice represents an 'irreducible doctrinal indeterminacy'.[90] Both legislation and legal precedents of judicial decisions are inherently unpredictable.

---

[81] Henry Sumner Maine, *Ancient Law: Its Connection with the Early History of Society, and Its Relation to Modern Ideas* (John Murray 1920) 23, 29–35.

[82] See eg Neil Duxbury, 'A Century of Legal Studies' in Mark Tushnet and Peter Cane (eds), *The Oxford Handbook of Legal Studies* (OUP 2005) 950, 952; Richard Collier, '"We're All Socio-Legal Now?" Legal Education, Scholarship and the 'Global Knowledge Economy'—Reflections on the UK Experience' (2004) 26 Syd LR 503, 523–24.

[83] Tamanaha (n 67) 2254; Michael Oakeshott, 'The Concept of a Philosophical Jurisprudence: Essays and Reviews 1926–51' (Luke O'Sullivan ed, Imprint Academic 2007) 151.

[84] See eg Morris R Cohen, 'Legal Theories and Social Science' (1915) 25 Int'l J Ethics 469, 476.

[85] See eg Tamanaha (n 67).

[86] See eg Karl N Llewellyn, 'A Realistic Jurisprudence—The Next Step' (1930) 30 Colum L Rev 431, 454.

[87] Eugene Ehrlich, *Fundamental Principles of the Sociology of Law* (Walter Moll tr, Harvard UP 1936).

[88] Roscoe Pound, 'The Scope and Purpose of Sociological Jurisprudence' (1911) 24 Harv L Rev 591.

[89] Brian Leiter, *Naturalizing Jurisprudence: Essays on American Legal Realism and Naturalism in Legal Philosophy* (OUP 2007).

[90] Hanoch Dagan, 'The Real Legacy of American Legal Realism' (2018) 38 OJLS 123, 127.

However, this does not mean that the realists' vision of law collapses into indeterminacy. This is when the realists' vision of law as a social practice enters the picture, providing much-needed stability to the law. While the open texture of the legal rules, principles, concepts, and doctrines invites a broad range of interpretations, their particular vision within the conception and convention of the legal community is the one which limits the judiciary options.[91] As Hanoch Dagan put it:

> ... legal realism does not threaten the rule of law [legal certainty]; it only insists that the rule of law does not—because it cannot—depend on law's pedigreed sources [legislation and case law], but relies instead on the social practice of law.[92]

This point illustrates another key role of legal scholars in legal change. Through their writings and continued interaction with members of the profession, they frequently affect and shape the prevalent understanding in the legal community of the legislation and judicial decisions. As an inherent part of a legal community, their views may lead to convention change.[93] This suggests that legal scholars are not just agents of change when it comes to reform. Rather, they shape social practice, its spirit,[94] and the operation of the law.

Armed with these observations about the role of legal academics as agents of change, the next section uses the law of unjust enrichment as its litmus test. It explores the birth of this law within the works of its forefathers: Peter Birks and Friedrich Carl von Savigny.

III. The Unjust Enrichment Context: Birks and Savigny

A. Peter Birks

1. Legal academics, Roman law, and coherency

Peter Birks played a decisive role in the development of the law of unjust enrichment in the UK and the common law world. However, Birks also had strong views about the role of legal academics in society. In the opening quote in Section I, he refers to a practising lawyer as 'no more than a mechanic' which is sharply contrasted with an 'endowed' one who holds the 'power of reasoning'.[95] 'Endowed' is the word Birks uses to refer to legal academics.

---

[91] ibid 130–33.
[92] ibid 134.
[93] cf Hanoch Dagan, 'Two Genres of Interpretive Legal Theories' in Evan Fox-Decent and others (eds), *Understanding Private Law: Essays in Honour of Stephen A Smith* (2023) (forthcoming).
[94] Berman (n 73) 13.
[95] See n 1.

In contrast to the intellectual exercise of 'A World without Law Professors', Birks closely associated common law and its operation with *legal* academics. Academic freedom could only be achieved through means of academic work in law faculties, not through ad hoc governmental initiatives of research councils.[96] Legal academics underpin contemporary law practice due to the following three interrelated factors: (1) the shift towards the substantive nature of common law that has abandoned the traditional forms of action; (2) the growing volume of case law decisions; and (3) the requirements of judicial justification and reasoning.[97] Accordingly, the present legal social reality makes Siems' exercise unsustainable.

Birks, then, perceives legal academics as agents of change. They stand on the very frontline of shaping and continuously improving the law through scholarly articles, empirical studies, and comparative analysis.[98] Echoing Richard Posner's observations, Birks places critical doctrinal studies at the very heart of legal research:

> Traditional legal research and scholarship which criticizes, explains, corrects and *directs* legal doctrine is still and must remain the heart of the law schools' research.[99]

The impact of law professors on the judiciary is a critical one. Legal scholars collect, analyse, and rationalize the courts' decisions. They are mindful of the comparative perspective.[100] They are also the ones who set the direction for law reform.

One would think that Roman law served as a primary framework for Birks's intellectual aspiration. Birks admired[101] and published on Roman law.[102] Lord Burrows characterized this body of law as Birks's 'first love'.[103] Indeed, references to the sources of Roman law appear throughout Birks's work on unjust enrichment,[104] and his work on taxonomizing private law.[105] Thus, Birks mentioned the transformation of Gaius's twofold classification scheme of private law (comprised of contracts and wrongs) into a threefold scheme under Justinian's *Digest*, with its added residual category.[106] From this perspective, as Birks argues,[107] the unjust

---

[96] Birks, *Law Schools* (n 1) x.
[97] ibid vii. See also David Dyzenhaus 'What is a Democratic Culture of Justification?' in Murray Hunt, Hayler J Hooper, and Paul Yowell (eds), *Parliaments and Human Rights: Redressing the Democratic Deficit* (Hart Publishing 2015) 425.
[98] Birks, *Law Schools* (n 1) vii–viii.
[99] ibid ix (emphasis added).
[100] Burrows and Rodger, 'Introduction' (n 5) 1. See also Lionel Smith, 'Peter Birks and Comparative Law' (2013) 43 RDUS 193, 197.
[101] Burrows and Rodger, 'Introduction' (n 5) 1. See also Smith, 'Peter Birks and Comparative Law' (n 99) 198, 200.
[102] Justinian *Institutes* (Peter Birks and Grant McLeod trs, Cornell UP 1987).
[103] Burrows and Rodger, 'Addresses' (n 9) xii.
[104] Birks, *Unjust Enrichment* (n 4) 28; Birks, *Introduction* (n 2) 22–23.
[105] Birks, *Introduction* (n 2) 30.
[106] ibid 22–23, 28, 30; Smith, 'Peter Birks and Comparative Law' (n 99) 199. See also McMeel (n 7) 20–22.
[107] Birks, *Unjust Enrichment* (n 4) 28.

enrichment project can be seen as a natural extension of Roman law within the internal evolution of private law.

This reference to Roman law draws a direct parallel between Birks's scholarship and the historical school of jurisprudence. Recall, this school of jurisprudence is deeply mindful of historical processes; the gradual development and evolution of the legal doctrine in the light of societal challenges. Law is like language: it grows and matures alongside the sophistication and multi-layering of society. Indeed, one of the contemporary commentators has situated Birks precisely within this school of thought.[108]

The obvious difficulty with this line of reasoning lies with the doctrinal analysis used by Birks. Central cases such as *Kelly v Solari*[109] (which dealt with mistaken payments) and *Taylor v Laird*[110] (which dealt with the unrequested provision of services) were straightforward cases which relied on trivial factual scenarios that could have easily occurred in the Roman period. Prima facie, these cases do not represent a special challenge to the legal doctrine reflecting societal or technological changes. One would argue that Birks's scholarship epitomizes a much more direct challenge to Roman law, its vision of the legal process and classification schemes. It does not represent a gradual and natural evolution of its Roman predecessor.

In fact, Birks himself was brutally honest in acknowledging that Roman law was built around actions, not rights.[111] Within this structure, the Roman law's *Condictio* was an action of debt,[112] not a substantive right.[113] Along a similar line, Birks frankly admitted that 'the Romans never identified unjust enrichment as an independent category'.[114] This raises doubts as to whether Birks's work on Roman law could easily be 'flowed into his work on English Law'.[115]

Perhaps there was another stronger source of inspiration for Birks's thought: the notions of coherency, interconnectedness, internal rationality, and intelligibility of law, specifically private law. In the concluding remarks of his last work, Birks specified the following two advantages embedded in the recognition of an independent category of unjust enrichment: (1) making a large body of case law into an intelligible whole; and (2) contribution to a coherent understanding of private law and its categories.[116]

---

[108] See eg McMeel (n 7) 20.
[109] *Kelly v Solari* (1841) 9 M & W 54; 152 ER 24.
[110] *Taylor v Laird* (1856) 25 LJ Ex 329 (Exch).
[111] Birks, *Unjust Enrichment* (n 4) 115–16, 231.
[112] This chapter will say much more about the *Condictio* action in the context of Savigny's account of unjust enrichment (see Section III.B.2).
[113] Birks, *Unjust Enrichment* (n 4) 115.
[114] ibid 230.
[115] Burrows and Rodger, 'Addresses' (n 9) xii.
[116] Birks, *Unjust Enrichment* (n 4) 267; McMeel (n 7) 30.

These notions require an explanation. Birks believed in the internal coherency and intelligibility of private law and its categories.[117] Birks was concerned with not only the internal coherency of unjust enrichment, but of private law as a whole.[118] What Birks had in mind was 'fitting the cases into the *true structure of the law* ... which he had uncovered'.[119] A major portion of his scholarship was invested in this 'uncovering exercise'. Despite the multiplicity of titles, terms, legal principles, doctrines, rules, concepts, and fictions, private law and its categories are underpinned by a set of basic organizing principles. The internal unity and coherency of private law could be achieved through observation and analysis of the existing case law.[120] This is about the conceptualization and re-conceptualization of private law and filling it with rational unifying content.

The difficult cases would remain difficult. As Birks explains: 'Categories do not become incoherent or otherwise unsound merely because argument breaks out on their edges.'[121] Birks explicitly rejects the rules' scepticism of such Legal Realists as Jerome Frank.[122] For him, the operation of the legal doctrine is largely predictable, which explains the significance of uncovering the true structure of private law and its categories. The major effort made in discovering and rationalizing the new category of unjust enrichment is an essential step in this exercise.

Where are those ideas about internal rationality, coherency, and interrelatedness coming from? While they are not foreign to contemporary jurisprudence,[123] the ultimate source can perhaps be traced to the German natural law tradition of 'systematicity' in the eighteenth and nineteenth centuries.[124] It was precisely this tradition which forcefully put forward an argument about the internal unity and rationality of a wide range of legal rules, concepts, and doctrines.

This was a school of 'unifiers' which insisted on the internal coherency of an apparently disconnected thread of legal rules, placing them within a unifying conceptual framework of organizing principles. George Hegel, for example, criticized Roman law's divergence on actions related to contractual liability within this tradition which included various sub-categories of contract. Hegel thought that these could be unified through a single rational concept of contractual liability.[125] The essentials of the systematicity tradition are vividly evident in Birks's account of unjust enrichment and the argumentation mode used by him in the development of *Formula 1*.

---

[117] Birks, *Unjust Enrichment* (n 4) 9.
[118] ibid 40.
[119] Burrows and Rodger, 'Addresses' (n 9) xv (emphasis added).
[120] Birks, *Unjust Enrichment* (n 4) 35.
[121] ibid 10.
[122] ibid 4.
[123] See eg Ken Kress, 'Coherence and Formalism' (1993) 16 Harv J L & Pub Pol'y 639; Ernest J Weinrib, 'Legal Formalism: On the Immanent Rationality of Law' (1988) 97 Yale LJ 949.
[124] See eg James Q Whitman, *The Legacy of Roman Law in the German Romantic Era: Historical Vision and Legal Change* (Princeton UP 1990) 80.
[125] Georg Wilhelm Friedrich Hegel, *Philosophy of Right* (TM Knox tr, OUP 1967) [77].

2. Formula 1

Birks believed in his ability to reveal the 'skeleton' of the law of unjust enrichment.[126] *Formula 1* represents that skeleton.[127] He condemned the legal fictions of 'quasi-contract' and 'constructive trust' as something that abuses the legal doctrine.[128] These need to be 'rooted out'.[129]

Many common law rules, cases, and doctrines have been situated within the stances of *Formula 1*. The argument says that a careful conceptualization of those rules, cases, and doctrines rationalizes and coherently attributes them to the unjust enrichment formula. The same point applies to some legislative provisions, such as the UK's Law Reform (Frustrated Contracts) Act 1943.[130] Legislated in the context of contract frustration, this piece of legislation has been situated within the stances of *Formula 1*.[131] The law of unjust enrichment flows from the internal coherency of private law,[132] which for various reasons has overlooked this rationale category alongside the traditional categories of property, tort, equity, and contract. The unjust enrichment enterprise is about uncovering 'what is there already'.[133] This argument is not relevant only to the UK, but also to other common law jurisdictions, such as Australia.[134]

The conceptual and doctrinal difficulties with *Formula 1* are well known. Liability in private law is grounded in the idea of interference with the claimant's right. However, *Formula 1* does not state the right, nor does it provide a clue as to the nature of the interference.[135] The enrichment itself appears to be counterintuitive to the liberal ideals of advancing a human initiative and material happiness.[136] The idea of 'transfer of value', embedded in the 'enrichment' and 'at the expense' elements of the formula is vague. It is open to a serious objection pointing to many trivial scenarios when the transfer of value between the parties is clearly present in Birks's terms and yet it is equally clearly implausible to impose liability on the defendant.[137] The 'justice' element in the formula refers to specific factors such as mistake and undue influence.[138] This posits the question of whether the nature and doctrinal movements of those factors could be unified under the single framework

---

[126] Birks, *Introduction* (n 2) 4.
[127] ibid 7.
[128] ibid 4.
[129] ibid 7.
[130] Law Reform (Frustrated Contracts) Act 1943.
[131] Birks, *Introduction* (n 2) 222–42; Birks, *Unjust Enrichment* (n 4) 65.
[132] Birks, *Introduction* (n 2) 1, 21.
[133] ibid 27; Birks, *Unjust Enrichment* (n 4) 18.
[134] Birks, *Unjust Enrichment* (n 4) 18, 33, 233. See also Bryan (n 6).
[135] Jennifer M Nadler, 'What Right Does Unjust Enrichment Law Protect?' (2008) 28 OJLS 245.
[136] Watts (n 12) 291.
[137] See Lionel Smith, 'Restitution: A New Start?' in Peter Devonshire and Rohan Havelock (eds), *The Impact of Equity and Restitution in Commerce* (Hart Publishing 2019) 91, 98.
[138] Birks, *Introduction* (n 2) 20, 99.

of *Formula 1*. Many think that such an amalgamation is somewhat artificial; it mischaracterizes the unique nature of each one of the factors.

The justification difficulty goes further. Birks frequently deploys the case of mistaken payments.[139] In parts, the argument appears to run as follows: if other categories cannot explain mistaken payments, the law of unjust enrichment must exist.[140] As Birks puts it: 'This is crucial to independence of the law of unjust enrichment',[141] commenting that 'every case of unjust enrichment is materially identical to mistaken payment'.[142]

The convergence of the rights-based analysis into the Roman law rhetoric is difficult as well. Birks makes a sharp distinction between unjust enrichment and property rights. The former represents a situation when the property right ends as the ownership moves to the defendant. The unjust enrichment epitomizes a new right.[143] As Birks put it, 'The claim in unjust enrichment cannot be represented as a vindication [of property rights] in disguise.'[144] However, as we have seen, Roman law did not have the tradition of such a rights-based analysis. Roman law was not structured around the concepts of rights and duties, but rather through legal actions.[145]

In deriving a new body of law, Birks uses plenty of technical terms: 'free acceptance',[146] 'subjective devaluation',[147] 'inconvertible benefit',[148] 'interceptive subtraction',[149] 'transfer of value', 'second measure of restitution',[150] 'interceptive subtraction',[151] 'counter-restitution',[152] 'voluntary/participatory enrichment',[153] and 'disenrichment'.[154] This is an incomplete list. One can question whether those technicalities contribute to the rationality and coherency of private law and do not become fictions themselves. If the historical school of jurisprudence says that the fictions crystallize the gap between the legal doctrine and the evolving law,[155] establishing new ones does not advance legal change. It pushes it backwards.

Over the years, Peter Birks did not hesitate to change his mind with respect to several key aspects of *Formula 1*.[156] This applies to the adoption of the German

---

[139] ibid 10; Peter Birks, 'Annual Miegunyah Lecture: Equity, Conscience, and Unjust Enrichment' (1999) 23 MULR 1 (hereafter Birks, 'Equity'); Birks, *Unjust Enrichment* (n 4) 3, 6–9, 24, 45, 55.
[140] Birks, *Unjust Enrichment* (n 4).
[141] ibid 8.
[142] ibid 34.
[143] ibid 32–33.
[144] ibid 58.
[145] John Tarrant, 'Obligations as Property' (2011) 34 UNSWLJ 677.
[146] Birks, *Unjust Enrichment* (n 4) 104, 265. See also Birks, *Introduction* (n 2) 114–15.
[147] Birks, *Introduction* (n 2) 108–09.
[148] ibid 114.
[149] ibid 133.
[150] ibid 358.
[151] Birks, *Unjust Enrichment* (n 4) 66.
[152] Birks, *Introduction* (n 2) 106, 202.
[153] ibid 127.
[154] ibid 188.
[155] See text to nn 79–81.
[156] Burrows and Rodger, 'Addresses' (n 9) viii.

'no-basis' understanding of the 'unjust' element in the formula,[157] the treatment of the classical *Moses v Macferlan* case,[158] and the treatment of the restitution of wrongs.[159] What is interesting is that though Birks changed his mind, those changes have not generally been followed by Birks's academic followers and the judiciary,[160] who appear to remain loyal to the original version of the formula in 1985 (the publication of the *Introduction to Restitution*), not 2003 (the publication of *Unjust Enrichment*). It is Birks's 1985 understanding of the formula which navigates and guides the courts in the operation of the unjust enrichment doctrine on a daily basis. It is doubtful whether today many private or commercial law lawyers in the common law world are unfamiliar with this version of the formula.[161] This also suggests that revolutionaries are not always in control of the revolution.

B. Friedrich Carl von Savigny

1. The mixed foundations of Savigny's scholarship

Almost 150 years prior to Birks's *Introduction to Restitution*, in 1841 the renowned German jurist Friedrich Carl von Savigny in the fifth volume of his *System des heutigen Römischen Rechts* made some obscure observations about the nature of unjust enrichment.[162] Afterwards, those observations served as the foundation of the German approach to unjust enrichment adopted in ss 812–17 of the German BGB. If Birks was the intellectual father of *Formula 1*, Savigny was the father of *Formula 2*.[163]

The intellectual foundations of Savigny's scholarship are significant for this chapter. Many legal scholars consider him to be no less than the founder of the historical school of jurisprudence and a careful developer and adapter of Roman law.[164] At the same time, Savigny warmly embraces the systematicity notion of the German natural law tradition. Furthermore, in parts, he goes further by accepting the underpinnings of this tradition with respect to the very nature of law. The ensuing paragraphs illustrate the heterogeneous nature of Savigny's scholarship.

---

[157] Birks, *Unjust Enrichment* (n 4) 38–40, 112.
[158] *Moses v Macferlan* (1760) 2 Burr 1005; 97 ER 676. See Swain, 'Unjust Enrichment' (n 66) 1037.
[159] Birks, *Unjust Enrichment* (n 4) 12. See also Dannemann, *The German Law of Unjustified Enrichment and Restitution* (n 15) 1, fn 42.
[160] See eg Charles Mitchell, 'Current Issues in Unjust Enrichment: Failure of Basis, Contractual Rights to Enrichment, Mistake of Law and Limitation Defences' (2022) SSRN <https://ssrn.com/abstract=4022727> accessed 17 February 2023.
[161] Birks, 'Equity' (n 139) 1.
[162] Friedrich Carl von Savigny, *System des heutigen Römischen Rechts*, vol 5 (Berlin 1841) (hereafter Savigny, *System V*).
[163] See text to nn 13–15.
[164] Tamanaha (n 67) 2240 (characterizing Savigny as 'the nineteenth-century progenitor of historical jurisprudence'); Paul Vinogradoff, *Outlines of Historical Jurisprudence*, vol 1 (OUP 1920) 130–31; William Ewald, 'Comparative Jurisprudence (I): What Was It Like to Try a Rat?' (1995) 143 U Pa L Rev 1889, 2020.

Some scholars characterized Savigny's *The Vocation of Our Age for Legislation and Jurisprudence*[165] (*Vocation*) as 'the inaugural piece of historical jurisprudence'.[166] Indeed, this work presents the essentials of this school of jurisprudence: the significance of history and the Roman law sources used in the law's development, the slow evolution of the legal doctrine, and the equalization of the law and language.[167]

The *Vocation* has been frequently misunderstood by scholars as favouring case law, the judge-made approach to private law, at the expense of the legislation.[168] A close reading of this work disproves that reading: Savigny did not object to the legislation of private law as such. His problem was with the legislative trend of his time which he considered to be hasty and failed to take into consideration the organic growth of private law and its slow evolution through the Roman law sources.[169] This idea links legal reform to the slow development of the law and the attentive readings of historical sources as an essential element of this exercise.

The *Vocation* also presents a strong defence of the systematicity notion. Savigny views the Roman sources as a fruitful ground for analysing and conceptualization. He mentions such terms as 'systematicity', 'coherence of constituent parts', 'organic unity', 'organic whole', 'coherent whole', and 'totality of sources'.[170] Once again, the problem with the codification projects of his time was not the codification per se, but rather the lack of historical references to Roman law sources and their conceptualization under organizing principles.[171]

Furthermore, in parts Savigny's work provides the basis for the foundation of those organizing principles. Specifically, some scholars have noticed the natural rights, specifically Kantian, foundations of Savigny's thought.[172] Consider the following passage in *System 1*:

> Man stands in the midst of the outer world, and the most important element, to him in this surrounding of his, is the contact with those who are like him, by their nature and destination. If now in such contact free natures are to subsist beside one another mutually assisting, not hindering themselves, this is possible only through the recognition of an invisible boundary within which the existence and

---

[165] Savigny, *Vocation* (n 74).
[166] Tamanaha (n 67) 2245. See also Ehrlich (n 87) 443.
[167] See text to nn 72–81.
[168] See eg Karl A Mollnau, 'The Contributions of Savigny to the Theory of Legislation' (1989) 37 Am J Comp L 81.
[169] Savigny, *Vocation* (n 74) 132–39. See also Whitman (n 124) 126–29.
[170] Savigny, *Vocation* (n 74) 45–46, 125; Friedrich Carl von Savigny, *System of the Modern Roman Law*, vol 1 (William Holloway tr, Hyperion Press 1979)x, xix, 7–9, 212–13, 231–32 (hereafter Savigny, *System I*).
[171] See eg Savigny, *Vocation* (n 74) 49; Savigny, *System I* (n 170) 7, 14, 43. See also Peter Stein, *Roman Law in European History* (CUP 1999) 119.
[172] Mathias Reimann, 'Nineteenth Century German Legal Science' (1990) 31 BCL Rev 837, 891–92; Frantz Wieacker, *A History of Private Law in Europe* (Tony Weir tr, OUP 1995) 306, 315.

activity of each individual gains a secure, free space. The rule, by which those boundaries and that free space are determined, is the law.[173]

In this passage, Savigny adopts the basic stances of Kantian legal philosophy. The passage defines the law through the concept of equal freedom for all: the law's function is to enable the free activity of all members of society, as long as their actions do not interfere with the freedom of others.

Elsewhere, I illustrated the multi-layered nature of Savigny's scholarship through the example of conflict of laws.[174] This is an area of law that tackles the question of applicable law in cross-border situations. Savigny's *System VIII* accomplished a Copernican revolution and a paradigm change in this area.[175] While acknowledging that Roman law cannot assist with developing the conceptual account of the subject, Savigny insisted on the internal coherency and unity of the organizing principles of the conflict of laws doctrine.[176] He insisted on a unifying principle of parties' equal freedom as governing the legal aspects of cross-state private relationships. This principle has nothing to do with the historically popular (and sometimes contemporary) belief that the notion of applicable law should be grounded on the states' sovereign interests.[177]

However, Savigny's account of conflict of laws was not solely grounded on the Kantian notion of freedom. Another central element of this account was the notion of mandatory rules. With direct reference to the historical school of jurisprudence, Savigny argued that certain legal rules of the system are more important than others.[178] These cannot be an object to the application of the general organizing principle of equal freedom. Certain areas of private law, such as family law and some proprietary transactions, represent moral, cultural, and ethical interests of a particular nation that justify their exclusion from the ordinary conflict of laws process.[179] Today, this idea of mandatory rules is very much alive in Europe[180] and

---

[173] Savigny, *System I* (n 170) 269.
[174] I trust the reader will forgive this reference to conflict of laws literature. The reason is, of course, a sociological one: the author is very familiar with Savigny's writings in this area. Yet, I hope the discussion in the ensuing two paragraphs is to the point.
[175] Otto Kahn-Freund, 'General Problems of Private International Law' (1974) 143 Recueil des cours 139, 285; Hans Ulrich Jessurun d'Oliveira, 'The EU and a Metamorphosis of Private International Law' in James Fawcett (ed), *Reform and Development of Private International Law: Essays in Honour of Sir Peter North* (OUP 2002) 109, 111.
[176] Sagi Peari, 'Savigny's Theory of Choice-of-Law as a Principle of "Voluntary Submission"' (2014) 64 UTLJ 106.
[177] Peari, *The Foundation* (n 60) 37–39.
[178] Friedrich Carl von Savigny, *A Treatise on the Conflict of Laws, and the Limits of Their Operation in Respect of Place and Time* (William Guthrie tr, T & T Clark 1880) 76, 297–98 (hereafter Savigny, *System VIII*).
[179] Peari, *The Foundation* (n 60) 268–72.
[180] See eg Regulation (EC) 593/2008 of the European Parliament and of the Council of 17 June 2008 on the Law Applicable to Contractual Obligations (Rome I) [2008] OJ L177/6 (EU), arts 5, 7 (hereafter Rome Regulation).

is gaining force on the other side of the Atlantic.[181] It is acceptable that a nation can rule out certain areas which it considers to be critical to its internal values and perceptions from the ordinary conflict of laws rules. In contrast to Savigny's unfortunate examples,[182] the modern mandatory rules primarily revolve around protection of the weaker parties, such as consumers and employees.[183]

The previous example of conflict of laws marries them all: the historical school of jurisprudence, Roman law, the notion of systematicity, and Kant. As we will see in a moment, Savigny's account of unjust enrichment traces much of this complexity.

1. *Formula 2*

Formula 2 of the unjust enrichment category was born in the context of Savigny's discussion of the aforementioned Roman law concept of *Condictio*.[184] Within the framework of Roman law's legal actions (ie not substantive rights), *Condictio* represented an action that the claimant could undertake in order to recover certain personal property or money which was in the possession of the defendant.[185]

The discussion starts with the paradigmatic contract law case: a money loan contract.[186] Savigny considers it a primary example of the *Condictio*. He distinguishes between two scenarios: (A) a money loan contract; and (B) a contract under which a person possesses a sealed bag of money belonging to another person.[187] As Savigny explains, only Scenario B saves the owner's money from bankruptcy proceedings. The bag of money can be vindicated. This suggests a movement of ownership right in Scenario A, which moves hands at the time of the contract formation.[188] At the time of the contract formation, the ownership of the money ceases to be that of the creditor and becomes that of the debtor. Turning to the language of rights, specifically ownership rights, Savigny offers conceptual unity to the traditional *Condictio* action: the action is relevant in situations in which the claimant cannot trace their ownership right.[189] When the original ownership right is destroyed, the *Condictio* steps in. This is the organizing principle of all *Condictios*.

As Savigny explains, the claimant cannot vindicate their ownership right in many other scenarios beyond the money loan contract. These include situations

---

[181] Symeon C Symeonides, 'The Choice-of-Law Revolution Fifty Years After Currie: An End and a Beginning' [2015] U Ill L Rev 1847, 1852–62.

[182] Savigny's examples on the point of mandatory rules are devastating: he mentions the Prussian laws of that time which restricted the ability of Jews to purchase immovable property. Savigny did not see a problem with this provision, attributing it to the needs, culture, and preferences of a particular nation: Savigny, *System VIII* (n 178) 78, 167.

[183] See eg Rome Regulation (n 180).

[184] See text to nn 111–114.

[185] See eg Nikolaos A Davrados, 'Demystifying Enrichment Without Cause' (2018) 78 La L Rev 1223, 1227–31.

[186] Savigny, *System V* (n 162) 511.

[187] ibid 514, 518.

[188] ibid 514.

[189] ibid 515.

when the defendant consumes or destroys the claimant's property,[190] or when the defendant commits a wrongful action against the claimant's property,[191] the unrequested provision of services,[192] mistaken payments,[193] and terminated contracts.[194] In all these cases, Savigny explains, the property moves from the claimant to the defendant without a legal basis.[195] The *Condictio* action means a restoration of the previous state of affairs.[196]

The 'unjust enrichment' talk enters Savigny's discussion in a somewhat incidental, obiter dictum way. His discussion of unjust (meaning without basis) enrichment is a subtle one.[197] Savigny mentions the defendant's enrichment in the context of the claimant's property destruction,[198] and a case when the defendant sells the property to a third party.[199] The focus remains on the *Condictio* action as a unifying concept to capture scenarios when the owner of a property right transfers their right to the defendant without a legal basis.[200] Within this context, the unjust enrichment talk remains vague and appears similar to a means of *justification*, rather than a full-blown argument about the establishment of a new right.

In line with other works, Savigny's discussion on unjust enrichment refers to law's evolution and the internal coherency and unity of its doctrines, principles, concepts, and rules. While Savigny relies on Roman law sources, he acknowledges that his unification exercise does not directly rely on those sources.[201] Rather, following the historical school of jurisprudence, Savigny talks about the organic growth of the law and the significance of the quest embedded in searching for organizing principles and demonstrating the internal unity of apparently disconnected doctrinal threads.[202]

There are strong similarities between Savigny's and Birks's strategies. Both scholars embrace the concept of money at the very outset of their analysis. Both are somewhat ambivalent towards Roman law: while admiring this body of law, they acknowledge the innovative nature of their argument. Both scholars put the right-based analysis at the very heart of their account under which the unjust enrichment claim only becomes relevant when the claimant's ownership right ends. Both Birks and Savigny are devoted unifiers who evidently embrace the systematicity notion. While Birks's work provides an attentive reading of the case law and situates it

---

[190] ibid 514, 516.
[191] ibid 516, 518, 520.
[192] ibid 520.
[193] ibid 521.
[194] ibid 521.
[195] ibid 521, 525, 526.
[196] ibid 522.
[197] See also Nils Jansen, Chapter 12 in this volume.
[198] Savigny, *System V* (n 162) 518.
[199] ibid 523.
[200] ibid 526.
[201] ibid 512.
[202] ibid 511, 518, 521.

within *Formula 1*, Savigny follows a similar strategy by reviewing the Roman law's examples and unifying them through a common conceptual thread.

Similar to Birks, Savigny's account is not free from several interrelated difficulties. First, the very move from the Roman law's context of legal action towards the concept of rights is problematic. Savigny views the *Condictio* action as something that today we would see as part of the tort of conversion, secured transactions law, and tracing, not as a distinct form of action. Secondly, the nature of the claimant's right remains vague. We understand that the claimant does not have an ownership right in the money/goods. However, what is the nature of the claimant's right if it is not a property right? Thirdly, Savigny marries restitution of wrongs and unjust enrichment. The former seems to be based on the nature of the infringed right, as some unjust enrichment scholars have acknowledged.[203] Fourthly, reliance on bankruptcy/insolvency proceedings for the purposes of tracking the nature of rights between the claimant and the defendant is problematic. Those proceedings recognize the possible bifurcation between claimant–defendant rights and the rights of third parties, including defendants' creditors.[204] Put simply, the bankruptcy/insolvency dimension does not necessarily affect the normativity between the claimant and the defendant.

True, Savigny's observations about *Condictio* invoke some of the key topics of the contemporary private law theory about the very nature of contractual obligation, the significance of the property right within this obligation, contract law remedies, and the concept of money. When does the ownership of an object under a contract transaction move hands? If the parties do not make a stipulation on this point in the contract,[205] some would say that the transfer of ownership in a contract takes place at the time of contract formation.[206] Others would opt for the time of contract performance—the time of the delivery of the property to the transferee.[207] Furthermore, the concept of money complicates things, as some suggest that money has several dimensions including a proprietary one.[208] While Savigny's account raises those important questions, it is doubtful whether it grounds the law of unjust enrichment per se.

---

[203] See eg Andrew Burrows, *The Law of Restitution* (3rd edn, OUP 2011).

[204] See eg Personal Property Securities Act 2009 (Cth), ss 10, 12. See also Craig Wappett and Anthony Duggan, 'Rights in Collateral under the PPSA: Rebutting the Minimalist Approach' (2019) 30 JBFLP 169.

[205] Sale of Goods Act 1979, s 17. The personal property securities law could intervene in this allocation and revert the deal in some cases when, eg, the contract says that the creditor keeps ownership in the goods until discharge of the obligation by the debtor: see *Aluminium Industrie Vaassen BV v Romalpa Aluminium Ltd* [1976] 1 WLR 676 (CA).

[206] Peter Benson, *Justice in Transactions: A Theory of Contract Law* (Harvard UP 2019).

[207] Ernest J Weinrib, 'Punishment and Disgorgement as Contract Remedies' (2003) 78 Chi-Kent L Rev 55.

[208] David Fox, *Property Rights in Money* (OUP 2008); John Tarrant, *Legal and Equitable Property Rights* (Federation Press 2019).

IV. Conclusion

Legal academics have played and should continue to play a central role in legal change and legal reform. 'A World without Law Professors' is a utopian exercise as it is at odds with social practice and completely strips law of its autonomy as a distinctive discipline. Furthermore, it is inconsistent with our deepest thinking about the nature of law. Focusing on the school of jurisprudence, which embraces legal change at its deepest level, academics do not simply lead the reform, but shape law on a daily basis.

Taking the law of unjust enrichment as its litmus test, this chapter has explored the nature of legal change with respect to the work of two forefathers of unjust enrichment: Peter Birks and Friedrich Carl von Savigny. The findings here are mixed. Both Birks and Savigny were legal revolutionaries. It was important for them to use the rhetoric of development, organic growth, and historical consistency. Clearly, both scholars were devoted unifiers and allies of the systematicity notion. It does tell us something about legal change: legal academics are agents of change; the historical rhetoric mixed with the 'unifying' argument could well help in the advances of the revolution.

Yet, both formulas suffer from deficiencies. We may need another, third formula to capture the situations which used to be explained through the forms of actions. However, that is another story.

5
Restitution in the United States

*Emily Sherwin**

I. Introduction

The law of restitution and unjust enrichment has followed a different path in the United States than it has in most other common law jurisdictions. This is interesting because the law of restitution was an American invention. English courts and scholars, followed by courts and scholars throughout the common law world, adopted various versions of the idea and took it in new directions.

In the United States, restitution based on unjust enrichment flourished for a time in the early and middle twentieth century, then suffered setbacks, then more recently has recovered some ground. My main objective in this chapter is to trace the development of American law in the area. I will also offer some comparisons with approaches taken elsewhere.

II. Restitution in America

A. The First Restatement of Restitution

Restitution, so named, made its world debut as a legal topic in 1937, when the American Law Institute (ALI) published a volume entitled *Restatement of the Law of Restitution: Quasi-Contracts and Constructive Trusts*.[1] The ALI is an organization founded in 1923 to assist in the development and clarification of American law; its governing body is a council comprising judges, practitioners, and legal academics.[2] The specific motivation for the first round of ALI Restatements, published

---

* Thanks to Sagi Peari and Warren Swain for organizing a fascinating and logistically challenging series of discussions in connection with this volume, to Caprice Roberts for excellent commentary, to Kevin Clermont, Hanoch Dagan, James Penner, and Robert Stevens for astute comments on the conference draft, and to Lyndsey Clark for invaluable help with drafts.

[1] ALI, *Restatement of the Law of Restitution: Quasi-Contracts and Constructive Trusts* (1937) (hereafter *Restatement (First)*).

[2] Current council members are listed on the ALI website: ALI, 'Council Members' <www.ali.org/about-ali/governance/officers-council/list-council-members/> accessed 27 December 2022. The Institute also recognizes a set of ex officio members, including the Justices of the Supreme Court of the United States, the Chief Justice of each state court, law school deans, bar association representatives, and the like: *Restatement (First)* (n 1) viii.

in the 1920s and 1930s, was to preserve, precissify, and advance the common law. The worry was that, in the context of the fifty sovereign states that make up the United States, a multitude of judicial decisions, 'taken in connection with the growing complication of economic and other conditions of modern life', might lead to replacement of the common law by 'rigid legislative codes, unless a new factor promoting certainty and clarity can be found'.[3]

The ALI Reporters who oversaw the first Restatement of Restitution were Warren Seavey and Austin Scott, both professors at Harvard Law School. Seavey focused on quasi-contract; Scott, an expert in trust law, undertook the subtopic of constructive trusts. The surprising theme of the Restatement was that these two traditionally disparate topics—one built upon the ancient writ of assumpsit and the other drawing from remedies developed in equity, reflected a common principle that allowed judicially assisted recapture of unjust gains. Unjust enrichment played a role in Roman law, and Lord Mansfield had briefly linked assumpsit claims to something like unjust enrichment.[4] But the Restatement of Restitution was based on the much larger premise that unjust enrichment was a foundational principle of the common law, providing a third ground for private legal claims that was independent from the law of tort and the law of contract.[5]

Seavey and Scott did not single-handedly produce this insight. Andrew Kull tracks the earlier history of unjust enrichment in the United States in a meticulously researched article on the antecedents of the first Restatement of Restitution.[6] Simplifying greatly: in the mid-1800s, Justice Story, seemingly influenced by Roman sources as well as Lord Mansfield, hinted at the idea of unjust enrichment as a reason to give legal relief to a mistaken improver of land.[7] During the nineteenth century, a number of state court decisions echoed and expanded on Story's suggestion, but did not generalize to the existence of a new field of law.[8] Then in the

---

[3] *Restatement (First)* (n 1) ix. Over time, the ALI's objectives mutated somewhat: the current bylaws state that the organization aims 'to promote the clarification and simplification of the law and its better adaptation to social needs, to secure the better administration of justice, and to encourage and carry on scholarly and scientific legal work': ALI, 'Bylaws' (18 May 2016) [1.01].

[4] *Moses v Macferlan* (1760) 2 Burr 1005, 1013; 97 ER 676, 681.

[5] In an article published shortly after the completion of the first Restatement, Seavey and Scott explained that their work 'recognized the tripartite division of the law into contracts, torts and restitution... [T]he postulate of the law of contracts... is that a person is entitled to receive what another has promised him... The law of torts is based upon the premise that a person has a right not to be harmed by another... Beside these two postulates there is a third, sometimes overlapping the others, but different in its purpose. This third postulate... can be expressed thus: A person has a right to have restored to him a benefit gained at his expense by another, if the retention of the benefit by the other would be unjust': Warren A Seavey and Austin W Scott, 'Restitution' (1938) 54 LQR 29, 31–32 (hereafter Seavey and Scott, 'Restitution'). Seavey and Scott's description of unjust enrichment as a third postulate of the private law is not, of course, uncontested. To cite just one example, Nils Jansen's excellent contribution to this volume casts doubt on segregation of unjust enrichment as a category of law. See Nils Jansen, Chapter 12 in this volume.

[6] See Andrew Kull, 'James Barr Ames and the Early Modern History of Unjust Enrichment' (2005) 25 OJLS 297 (hereafter Kull, 'Ames').

[7] ibid 315, citing *Bright v Boyd* 4 F Cas 127 (CCD Me 1841).

[8] ibid 316, citing in particular *Whitney v Richardson* 31 Vt 300 (1858) and *Effinger v Hall* 81 Va 94 (1885).

1880s, still fifty years before publication of the Restatement of Restitution, James Barr Ames, a law professor and legal historian working at Harvard Law School, pursued the problem further in a set of law review articles focusing on the concept of unjust enrichment. Specifically, Ames observed that 'unjust enrichment' served as a common ground of recovery in both quasi-contract cases at law and equity cases involving the remedial device of constructive trust.[9]

Where, then, did 'Restitution' come from? Seavey and Scott conceived their task as 'restating' seemingly unrelated types of claim found in decided cases in a way that revealed a conceptual connection among them. As they put it in a joint article written shortly after publication of the Restatement:

... because of the way in which the English law developed, a group of situations having distinct unity has never been dealt with as a unit and because of this has never received adequate treatment.[10]

'Unjust enrichment' was the feature that justified legal relief in most or all of these cases, with or without a contract and independently of tortious wrongdoing. 'Restitution' was the term the Reporters chose to describe the new legal category they intended to present in their volume, working from disparate material involving unjust enrichment.[11]

At some point in the drafting process, 'Unjust Enrichment' was dropped from the Restatement's title, leaving only 'Restitution' followed by the sub-heading 'Quasi-Contracts and Constructive Trusts'. The reasons for the change are not clear

---

[9] See JB Ames, 'Purchase for Value Without Notice' (1887) 1 Harv L Rev 1, 3; JB Ames, 'The History of Assumpsit' (1888) 2 Harv L Rev 53, 64 — both described in Kull, 'Ames' (n 6) 302–05. Soon after Ames made the connection between quasi-contract and unjust enrichment, William Keener, a junior colleague of Ames, made a similar observation in a discussion of quasi-contract remedies William A Keener, 'Recovery of Money Paid Under Mistake of Fact' (1887) 1 Harv L Rev 211, 211, cited in Kull, 'Ames' (n 6) 305–07. Ames was likely familiar with both Roman and civil law doctrines referring to unjust enrichment, but his focus was on English and American doctrinal developments. On parallels in Roman law and civil law, see generally Helen Scott, 'Comparative Taxonomy: An Introduction' in Elise Bant, Kit Barker, and Simone Degeling (eds), *Research Handbook on Unjust Enrichment and Restitution* (Edward Elgar 2020) 147–60 (hereafter Scott, 'Taxonomy').

[10] Seavey and Scott, 'Restitution' (n 5) 29.

[11] At least, this is my interpretation. The term 'restitution' had already been used in the first *Restatement of Contracts* to describe *remedies* involving restoration of value: see ALI, *Restatement of the Law of Contracts* (1932) vol 2 § 347 comment a: 'Restitution is a remedy that is available in many kinds of cases, breach of contract being only one of these. In some cases it may be the only available remedy... In other cases it is an alternative remedy, as in the case of a tort whereby the defendant has been enriched at the plaintiff's expense'). In the case of Seavey and Scott's *Restatement of Restitution*, however, the eventual decision to delete 'Unjust Enrichment' from the volume's title indicates that 'restitution' described not just a type of remedy but a category of legal claims.

The term 'restitution' also appeared in a famous 1936 article by Lon Fuller and William Perdue on the 'reliance' interest in contract law: LL Fuller and William R Perdue, Jr, 'The Reliance Interest in Contract Damages' (1936) 46 Yale LJ 52, 53–54. Fuller and Perdue described three *interests* protected by contract law, one of which was the 'restitution' interest, based on the principle of unjust enrichment. Again, Seavey and Scott appear to have used the term restitution more broadly, to describe a category ground of legal relief.

and may have had to do with brevity more than conceptual nuance.[12] Unjust enrichment, however, continued to be the motivating idea, as evidenced in the first section of the volume:

> § 1. Unjust Enrichment
> A person who has been unjustly enriched at the expense of another is required to make restitution to the other.[13]

The examples of restitution provided in subsequent sections of the first Restatement were less novel than the idea itself. All were drawn from two sets of highly fictitious claims: 'quasi-contract' claims recognized by courts of law, and 'constructive trust' claims recognized by courts of equity. The important insight of the work was not the description of these claims, or the new term applied to them ('restitution'). Instead, the significance of the volume lies in the insight that both sets of claims pointed to the presence in law of a third fundamental category of relief. Claims between private actors include not only tort and contract claims, but also claims that are based on unjust enrichment and do not require proof of either a legally wrongful infliction of harm or a legally bargained contractual right.

The first Restatement embodied, at least implicitly, what Andrew Kull and others have called the American 'big tent' view of its subject matter.[14] Restitution is a fundamental category of legal claim, based on but not always perfectly aligned with the proposition that, in addition to enforcing the terms of valid contracts and giving relief against tortious harm, courts should act to prevent unjust enrichment of one party at the expense of another. Claims to restitution may arise in the context of a contractual relationship, a tortious wrong, a breach of duty, a mistake, or any other situation in which receipt of a benefit is legally unfounded.

Comments to the first section of the Restatement reflect this idea:

> A person is enriched if he has received a benefit ... A person is unjustly enriched if the retention of the benefit would be unjust ... Ordinarily, the measure of restitution is the amount of enrichment received ..., but ... if the loss suffered differs

---

[12] This is evident in various notes and drafts, including 1 ALI Proc 335 (1934); ALI, *Restatement of Restitution and Unjust Enrichment: Tentative Draft No 1* (1935); ALI, *Explanatory Notes on Restitution and Unjust Enrichment: Proposed Final Draft* (1936). Professor Kull reports that certain stenographic minutes of advisors' meetings, which might have shed light on decisions regarding the change in title, appear to have gone missing from the Harvard Law Library during a renovation: Andrew Kull, 'Three Restatements of Restitution' (2011) 68 Wash & Lee L Rev 867, 869 fn 6.

[13] *Restatement (First)* (n 1) § 1.

[14] This term appears in the introduction to a recent volume on restitution and unjust enrichment and also in ch 4 of the volume, which was authored by Andrew Kull. See Elise Bant, Kit Barker, and Simone Degeling, 'The Evolution of Unjust Enrichment Law: Theory and Practice' in Elise Bant, Kit Barker, and Simone Degeling (eds), *Research Handbook on Unjust Enrichment and Restitution* (Edward Elgar 2020); Andrew Kull, 'Restitution and Unjust Enrichment' in ibid. Who first used the term is not clear.

from the amount of benefit received, the measure of restitution may be more or less than the loss suffered or more or less than the enrichment.[15]

Further:

> The amount of recovery, however, is not invariably determined by the value of what has been received. In some cases the value of what is given is determinative...
>
> In other situations, a benefit has been received by the defendant but the plaintiff has not suffered a corresponding loss or, in some cases, any loss, but nevertheless the enrichment of the defendant would be unjust...
>
> On the other hand, a person who has been unjustly deprived of his property or its value or the value of his labor may be entitled to maintain an action for restitution against another although the other has not in fact been enriched thereby [as when the owner of property that was stolen claims restitution from someone who purchased the property in good faith from a thief].[16]

B. After the First Restatement

The Restatement of Restitution went unnoticed at first in the rest of the world, but it attracted immediate and enthusiastic interest in the United States. A number of law school casebooks on the previously non-existent subject of restitution appeared in the first fifteen years after publication of the Restatement.[17] Restitution also received significant scholarly attention, most prominently from two law professors then at the University of Michigan, John P Dawson and George Palmer.[18]

Courts, clearly influenced by the Restatement, decided innovative cases in the area.[19] Consider, for example, the famous case of the egg-washing machine. The

---

[15] *Restatement (First)* (n 1) § 1 comment a.
[16] Ibid, § 1 comment e.
[17] See eg Edward S Thurston, *Cases on Restitution* (West 1940); John W Wade, *Cases and Materials on Restitution* (Foundation 1958); John P Dawson and George E Palmer, *Cases on Restitution* (Bobbs-Merrill 1958).
[18] In addition to his casebook with Dawson, Palmer wrote a four-volume treatise, which was in progress through most of his teaching career and ultimately published in 1978: George E Palmer, *The Law of Restitution* (Little, Brown 1978). Dawson, who later moved to Harvard, wrote a number of articles, in part from a comparative perspective (relating restitution and unjust enrichment to Roman law and civil law) but also commenting on the role these subjects played in twentieth-century American law. Examples are John P Dawson, 'Erasable Enrichment in German Law' (1981) 61 BU L Rev 271; John P Dawson, 'Restitution Without Enrichment' (1981) 61 BU L Rev 563. He also delivered a widely followed series of lectures at Northwestern University Law School on the subject of unjust enrichment, which appear in John P Dawson, *Unjust Enrichment: A Comparative Analysis* (Little, Brown 1951) (hereafter Dawson, *Unjust Enrichment*).
[19] Most restitution cases in the United States are common law cases decided in the courts of the fifty states, although the federal courts also encounter restitution claims, particularly in the settings of bankruptcy proceedings and class actions.

proprietor of a company engaged in the business of selling eggs to the army during the Second World War helped himself to an egg-washing machine belonging to a former partner who had placed the machine in storage. The used machine was worth about $600 (judged by the owner's previous offer of sale). After quoting liberally from the Restatement, the court instead awarded restitution in the amount of $1,560, based on the costs the defendant saved by converting the plaintiff's machine rather than hiring workers to wash the eggs.[20]

The court's measure is not quite right: the defendant would likely have rented a machine rather than pay workers to wash eggs by the hour. But the restitutionary measure of costs saved is appropriate in the circumstances of a deliberate wrong. In any event, the point of the story is that American courts have not been too worried by uncertainties about the interaction of unjust enrichment with other wrongs, or questions about how to measure benefits and losses in different contexts.[21] They have endorsed the underlying concept of unjust enrichment and done their best to apply it in varying settings, without looking for perfect doctrinal symmetry.

Following the initial wave of interest, however, American attention to the law of restitution and unjust enrichment waned in the second half of the twentieth century. Part of the difficulty lay with the Restatement itself. After making the very significant claim that restitution was a distinct category of private law, based on unjust enrichment and separate from wrongful harm or contractual obligation, the volume clung rather closely to the examples of quasi-contract claims at law and constructive trust claims in equity. By mid-century, with equity courts in many states rapidly merging with courts of law and the quasi-contract fiction lapsing out of use, lawyers and judges no longer thought in these terms. Restitution and unjust enrichment were interesting ideas, but in order to be useful to practitioners and students, they needed to be expressed in modern language and set in the context of modern practice.

Perhaps more importantly, American views about the nature and aims of legal decision-making were changing. In the 1920s and 1930s when ALI began its Restatement project, American-style Legal Realism was rapidly gaining ground over more traditional forms of doctrinal reasoning about law, at least in academic circles.[22] Realism was a fairly broad category of legal thought: its adherents

---

[20] *Olwell v Nye & Nissen Co* 173 P 2d 652 (Wash 1946). The court was likely influenced by the fact that the defendant company been indicted for fraud in its sales of eggs and cheese to the army and navy). It may be worth noting that at 2023 prices, the sum awarded would be $23,816.88: Coin News, 'US Inflation Counter' <www.usinflationcalculator.com/> accessed 1 January 2023.

[21] Another classic early example of restitution based on unjust enrichment, with a different measure of enrichment, is *Pilot Life Ins Co v Cudd* 36 SE 2d 860 (SC 1945) (allowing an insurance company to recover money paid to the widow of a soldier who was presumed dead but later turned up alive).

[22] Some excellent sources on this subject are Hanoch Dagan, *Reconstructing American Legal Realism and Rethinking Private Law Theory* (OUP 2013); Brian Leiter, 'American Legal Realism' in Martin P Golding and William A Edmundson (eds), *The Blackwell Guide to the Philosophy of Law and Legal Theory* (Blackwell 2005). Interpretation of and reactions to 'American Legal Realism' vary widely. An interesting recent example of Dagan's commentary on Leiter's work is Hanoch Dagan, 'The Real Legacy of American Legal Realism' (2018) 38 OJLS 123.

followed a number of paths and not all of them were compatible. The most prominent versions of realism, however, converged on hostility towards 'mechanical jurisprudence' and scepticism about the effectiveness of seemingly determinate rules and other staples of traditional legal argument. Most realists endorsed the view that doctrine is inherently indeterminate and that rules do not and should not determine the outcome of legal disputes. In practice, they argued, judicial decisions inevitably are influenced, and usually are determined, by the particular facts presented and the judge's own understanding of the world.[23]

Not surprisingly, realists tended initially to be hostile to the ALI's project of restating the law.[24] Recording prevailing doctrine in carefully organized volumes made the rules of law more rigid and less responsive both to factual nuances and to background social and economic conditions. Leon Green called the project of restating tort law 'hopeless'.[25] Discussing the Contracts Restatement, Charles E Clark deplored '[t]he unreality resulting from attempting to divide up the law into small parts, each dogmatically stated apart from all other rules and apart from its actual operation in modern society'.[26] Edward Robinson chastised the ALI for supposing 'that it can help simple-minded lawyers by giving an artificial and arbitrary picture of the principles in terms of which human disputes are supposed to be settled'.[27]

Over time, however, realist hostility toward the ALI subsided. Realists such as Herman Oliphant, for example, proposed that legal doctrine could be enlisted in the realist project by altering doctrine in ways that turned the attention of judges from formulaic rules to the facts of particular cases.[28] Meanwhile, the ALI itself absorbed many aspects of the realist attitude towards law. Prominent realists joined the ranks of the ALI and contributed to the design and content of its Restatement projects.[29] A prime example of this collaboration was the incorporation of 'unconscionability'—a word with virtually no objective meaning—as an operative

---

[23] Leiter refers to this as the 'sociological' branch of American Legal Realism. Leiter, 'American Legal Realism' (n 22) 54, 55–56. An example is Herman Oliphant, 'A Return to Stare Decisis' (1928) 14 ABAJ 71 (hereafter Oliphant, 'Stare Decisis') (suggesting that decisions are responsive to social forces operating on judges).

[24] The complex relationship between 'American Legal Realism' and the ALI's Restatement projects in the 1900s is described at length in ALI's forthcoming centennial volume: Robert W Gordon, 'Restatement and Realists' in Andrew S Gold and Robert W Gordon (eds), The American Law Institute: A Centennial History (OUP 2023).

[25] Leon Green, 'The Duty Problem in Negligence Cases' (1928) 28 Colum L Rev 1014, 1014.

[26] Charles E Clark, 'The Restatement of the Law of Contracts' (1933) 42 Yale LJ 643, 659.

[27] Edward S Robinson, 'Law—An Unscientific Science' (1934) 44 Yale LJ 235, 260.

[28] Oliphant, 'Stare Decisis' (n 23) 75; Brian Leiter, 'Legal Realism & Legal Doctrine' (2015) 163 U Pa L Rev 1975, 1975–77 (hereafter Leiter, 'Legal Realism').

[29] A notable example is Charles Alan Wright, who was President of the ALI from 1993 to 2000 and an avowed realist. See Leiter, 'Legal Realism' (n 28) 1975–76. At least one of the advisors to the first Restatement of Restitution, Edwin W Patterson, appears to have been open to some of the realists' ideas: see Harry W Jones, 'Edwin Wilhite Patterson: Man and Ideas' (1957) 57 Colum L Rev 607, 612–16 (suggesting at 615, not too persuasively, that Patterson embraced a form of 'moderate Realism').

term in several sections of the *Restatement (Second) of the Law of Contracts*.[30] This was a significant move away from traditional ways of thinking about law and legal practice. Unconscionability is not a rule; it is an invitation to judges to engage in fact-specific judgement from case to case. Through mechanisms of this kind, the project of restating the law could easily coexist, at least by the time of the second cycle of Restatements, with many of the attitudes associated with American Legal Realism.

The Restatement of Restitution, however, was not much influenced by realism and therefore not likely to have broad appeal in an increasingly realist legal world. It began with the very broad principle of unjust enrichment, but the bulk of the work consisted of doctrinal provisions that closely tracked the decisional rules established in prior cases involving quasi-contract claims and constructive trusts. The Restatement's insight was an insight about the role these decisional rules played in the overall scheme of private law. This was an important jurisprudential point, but it was not one that advanced the realist programme.

If the Restatement of Restitution was not of particular interest to realists, it was even less interesting to participants in the next waves of theory that arose in the American legal academy. In the second half of the twentieth century, scholarly interest turned towards a variety of post-realist approaches to law such as critical legal studies, which assumes that law and judicial decisions are heavily weighted to serve the interests of dominant social groups, and 'law and economics', which analyses legal rules in terms of their effect on aggregate wealth.[31] Critical approaches see legal doctrine as a source of social manipulation; economic approaches explain legal doctrine in terms of its possibly beneficial but typically unintended effects on human behaviour. Neither of these approaches had much use for an explanation of the fundamental *legal* principle of unjust enrichment that underwrote the various claims described in the Restatement of Restitution or the role that principle plays in private law.

Critical legal studies, as well as more doctrine-friendly academic movements such as the legal process school, also tended to shift theoretical attention towards the public side of law, and particularly to federal rights, federal regulation of conduct, and the interaction between federal courts and other branches of the central government. The first-year curriculum of American law schools continues to cover the basics of property law, tort law, and contract law, but by the latter part of the twentieth century most law schools no longer offered courses in restitution. Bits of the law of restitution can be found in courses on remedies, but even remedies courses are no longer seen as a vital component of legal education. As a result,

---

[30] ALI, *Restatement (Second) of the Law of Contracts* (1981) § 153 (unilateral mistake), § 208 (unconscionable contract or term). Unconscionability appeared earlier in Karl Llewellyn's *Uniform Commercial Code*. See UCC § 2-302.

[31] An example is Saul Levmore, 'Explaining Restitution' (1985) 71 Va L Rev 65 (analysing restitution in terms of its economic effects).

terms such as 'subrogation', 'indemnity', 'estoppel', or even 'restitution' are likely to be mysterious to young American lawyers entering practice.[32]

C. The *Restatement (Third)* and Modern American Restitution

Although restitution now occupies a rather obscure corner of the academic and scholarly landscape in the United States, it remains a vital part of law and legal practice, at least for lawyers who know how to use it. Money is wired to the wrong party, taxes are discovered to be invalid after the tax bills are paid, subcontractors perform after contractors have defaulted, property is converted and used advantageously, public officials take bribes, and unmarried cohabitants part ways without having planned for this possibility.[33] By the second half of the twentieth century, the Restatement needed updating, in part because the transactional world had changed and in part because, apart from the central insight that unjust enrichment provided a ground of recovery separate from tort and contract, it was burdened by the history of quasi-contract and constructive trust.

The update, however, did not come quickly. A second series of ALI Restatements, some of them revisions of existing volumes and some covering new material, commenced in 1949 and continued into the 1980s. A new restitution project, which would have been the *Restatement (Second) of Restitution*, was commissioned in 1980, but later scrapped and superseded by a remedies project. The remedies project, in turn, was cancelled as a result of its inevitable overlap with the various substantive Restatement projects. Finally, in 1996, as the ALI's third set of Restatements was getting under way, the ALI voted to authorize the *Restatement (Third) of Restitution and Unjust Enrichment*.[34] (I will return in a moment to the matter of the title change.)

The *Restatement (Third) of Restitution and Unjust Enrichment* was an enormous project. Work began in earnest in 1998 and continued for fourteen years. The new Restatement was more than twice the size of the original: it filled two volumes and covered a great variety of legal problems, such as claims against common funds

---

[32] There are some signs of a revival of interest. One is a new restitution casebook by Andrew Kull and Ward Farnsworth (eds), *Restitution and Unjust Enrichment: Cases and Notes* (Wolters Kluwer 2018). Another is a remarkably well-executed 'Developments in the Law' project on unjust enrichment, conceived and carried out by the editors of the Harvard Law Review, which examines both the intellectual history of restitution and unjust enrichment and a variety of modern applications: 'Developments in the Law: Unjust Enrichment' (2020) 133 Harv L Rev 2062, 2084–100.
[33] See eg *Banque Worms v BankAmerica International* 570 NE 2d 189 (NY 1991) (international wire transfer); *Paramount Film Distributing Corp v State of New York* 285 NE 2d 695 (NY 1972) (invalid taxes); *Seegers v Sprague* 236 NW 2d 227 (Wisc 1975) (subcontractor claim); *Olwell v Nye & Nissen Co* (n 20) (conversion); *Cook County v Barrett* 344 NE 2d 540 (Ill App 1975) (bribed officials); *Marvin v Marvin* 557 P 2d 106 (Cal 1976) (cohabitants).
[34] ALI, *Restatement (Third) of Restitution and Unjust Enrichment* (2011) (hereafter *Restatement (Third)*).

resulting from class actions and claims between unmarried cohabitants, that had no counterparts in the world of 1937.

Despite its larger scope, the third Restatement is conceptually loyal to the first. It fully endorses the insight that restitution for unjust enrichment is a foundational category of private law, parallel to the law of tort and the law of contract. Its objective was to modernize this category of law and track its application in a variety of new settings that Seavey and Scott could not have anticipated when they first observed that unjust enrichment provided a link between the fictitious rules of quasi-contract and the fictitious rules of constructive trusts.[35]

By the ALI's own account, the second and third Restatement series leaned more towards law reform than the first series. A post on the ALI Advisor, an ALI-affiliated website, states that:

> In terms of substance, the First Restatements largely were restatements of the majority rule then applied by courts across the United States. ...
>
> The Second Restatements [and Third] were more reformist in character. They reflected changes in legal scholarship and the courts in the post-World War II era.[36]

The *Restatement (Third) of Restitution and Unjust Enrichment* was for the most part an exception to this pattern. It aimed to modernize, but not by revising the principles established in the first volume or altering the paths taken by courts. In almost all cases, the objectives of its reforms were to update the language and procedure associated with restitution and to describe and explain newer judicial applications of the ideas set out in the first Restatement as consistently as possible with the original concept.[37] The scope of the resulting volume was much larger and the details of its contents much more attuned to modern legal life, but the fundamental

---

[35] Many of the examples appearing in the third Restatement were products of, rather than omissions from, the first Restatement.

[36] H Mark Stichel, 'The Restatements—First, Second, Third ...' (*The ALI Adviser*, 12 August 2019) <www.thealiadviser.org/inside-the-ali-posts/the-restatements-first-second-third/> accessed 27 December 2022.

[37] An exception was s 39, a provision in which the normally cautious third Restatement authorized profit-based recovery for 'opportunistic' breaches of contract: *Restatement (Third)* (n 34) § 39. In *Kansas v Nebraska* 574 US 445 (2015), 475–76, a case involving this provision, Justice Scalia of the United States Supreme Court took the opportunity to rail against the Restatements generally for their reformist agenda: 'I write separately to note that modern Restatements—such as the Restatement (Third) of Restitution and Unjust Enrichment (2010) ... are of questionable value, and must be used with caution. The object of the original Restatements was "to present an orderly statement of the general common law." Restatement of Conflict of Laws, Introduction, p. viii (1934). Over time, the Restatements' authors have abandoned the mission of describing the law, and have chosen instead to set forth their aspirations for what the law ought to be. ... Restatement sections such as [section 39] should be given no weight whatever as to the current state of the law, and no more weight regarding what the law ought to be than the recommendations of any respected lawyer or scholar.'

idea—that restitution based on unjust enrichment plays a vital, definable, and defensible part in private law—was the same.

Apart from the many new contexts and examples covered in the volume, the Reporter, Andrew Kull, made two important changes. The first was to change the Restatement's name, making it the *Restatement (Third) of Restitution and Unjust Enrichment*. The original title, *Restatement of Restitution*, presented two difficulties, of different kinds. First, the title failed to capture the most distinctive feature of restitution, which was its connection to unjust enrichment and its independence, in many cases, from liability based on tort and contract. Secondly, restitution is not perfectly synonymous with unjust enrichment. As interpreted by American courts, restitution is not always based on injustice and enrichment at another's expense does not always lead to gain-based recovery. The 'big tent' approach that American courts had taken to the subject matter tolerated these discrepancies, but the title was imprecise. Kull's solution was not to eliminate non-conforming examples, but simply to fix the title, making the third Restatement a restatement of 'Restitution and Unjust Enrichment'.

The important change was not exactly a change but a clarification, which appeared in the Reporter's Notes to the first section of the third Restatement. The black-letter statement in the text appears very simple: 'A person who is unjustly enriched at the expense of another is subject to liability in restitution.'[38] The notes that follow address the complexities and imprecision associated with this statement:

> A significant tradition within English and American law refers to unjust enrichment as if it were something identifiable *a priori*, by the exercise of a moral judgment anterior to legal rules. This equitable conception of the law of restitution is crystallized by Lord Mansfield's famous statement in Moses v. Macferlan: 'In one word, the gist of this kind of action is, that the defendant, upon the circumstances of the case, is obliged by the ties of natural justice and equity to refund the money.'
>
> ...
>
> In reality, the law of restitution is very far from imposing liability for every instance of what might plausibly be called unjust enrichment.... '[U]njust enrichment' ... might seem to be a pervasive fact of human experience—given any prior standard ... by which people's relative entitlement might be measured.
>
> The concern of restitution is not, in fact, with unjust enrichment in any such broad sense, but with a narrower set of circumstances giving rise to what might more appropriately be called *unjustified enrichment*. Compared to the open-ended implications of the term 'unjust enrichment,' instances of unjustified enrichment are both predictable and objectively determined, because the justification in question is not moral but legal. Unjustified enrichment is enrichment

---

[38] *Restatement (Third)* (n 34) § 1.

that lacks an adequate legal basis; it results from a transaction that the law treats as ineffective to work a conclusive alteration in ownership rights.[39]

Unjust enrichment, then, is not an open-ended idea that courts should apply to particular facts as they see fit. Instead it is a *legal* concept—a doctrinal concept—to be applied in ways that conform to the expectations generated by legal decisions over time. Consistently with this advice, the Restatement itself contains more than 1,000 illustrations, all taken from decided cases.

There are occasional provisions in the third Restatement that appear to lapse into something like Legal Realism. One of these, which was debated at some length among advisors to the Restatement, is s 28, pertaining to claims between unmarried cohabitants following a break-up. If one cohabitant 'owns a specific asset to which the other has made substantial, uncompensated contributions in the form of property or services', the other may claim restitution 'as necessary to prevent unjust enrichment'.[40] The claim has moral appeal but no definition; the judge must assess after the fact what was just and unjust, and how much enrichment occurred, in a particular, fraught personal situation.[41] Provisions of this type, however, are not common. For the most part, the Restatement opts for guidance rather than case-by-case discretion, and backs up its guidance with concrete examples from decided cases.

III. American Restitution and the World

A. Restitution in England and the Commonwealth

Although American courts, scholars, and textbooks quickly engaged with the ideas of restitution and unjust enrichment after the publication of the first Restatement of Restitution in 1937, the rest of the world was not particularly interested. This changed in 1966 when the English scholars Robert Goff and Gareth Jones published the first edition of their treatise on restitution. Goff and Jones gave due credit for the idea of restitution to the American Restatement of Restitution, but their aim was to describe 'the English law of Restitution', a subject they described as 'all [English] claims ... which are founded on the principle of unjust enrichment'.[42]

---

[39] ibid § 1 comment b (citation omitted, emphasis in original).
[40] ibid § 28(1).
[41] For commentary on this section of the third Restatement and the controversy surrounding it at the time of its drafting, see eg Doug Rendleman, 'Restating Restitution: The Restatement Process and Its Critics' (2008) 65 Wash & Lee L Rev 933; Emily Sherwin, 'Love, Money, and Justice: Restitution Between Cohabitants' (2006) 77 U Colo L Rev 711.
[42] Robert Goff and Gareth H Jones, *The Law of Restitution* (Sweet & Maxwell 1966) preface v.

Goff and Jones's initial approach, like that of the American Restatement, was a doctrinal approach: 'Close study of the law of restitution reveals, as with contract and tort, a highly developed and reasonably systematic complex of rules.'[43] They also set out a general structure for the rules of restitution, stating that unjust enrichment (on which, in their view, all restitution claims were founded) 'presupposes three things: first, that the defendant has been enriched by the receipt of a benefit secondly, that he has been so enriched at the plaintiff's expense; and thirdly, that it would be unjust to allow him to retain the benefit'.[44] The volume proceeded to describe a large number of English decisions, covering a variety of topics, all of which could be explained in terms of the principle of unjust enrichment.

Although the insight of the first American Restatement of Restitution was fading from view in the United States, Goff and Jones's *The Law of Restitution* was a tremendous hit in England and, soon, throughout the Commonwealth. Six more editions appeared over time, followed by two more under the title *The Law of Unjust Enrichment*. English restitution as presented by Goff and Jones, however, was not quite the 'big tent' it had been in the United States; instead the authors worked carefully within the scope of the principle of unjust enrichment.

The work of Goff and Jones generated both a number of important judicial decisions and a very substantial body of scholarship on the subject of restitution and unjust enrichment.[45] Among the many scholars who responded to Goff and Jones's treatise was Peter Birks. Birks began with the general structure suggested by Goff and Jones and converted it to a precise and elaborate classification of necessary conditions for relief based on unjust enrichment. Birks's work in the area continued through several permutations, each gaining supporters in England and throughout the Commonwealth. Initially, he described 'unjust enrichment' as a set of causative events and 'restitution' as a legal response to unjust enrichment, with a relationship of 'perfect quadration' existing between the two.[46] Later, he concluded that the field of law under study should be called the law of 'unjust enrichment' rather than the law of 'restitution' and that restitution may follow from tort or contract or other causes as well as unjust enrichment.[47] In 2003, he decided that there was after all no

---

[43] ibid 13.
[44] ibid 14.
[45] The recently published *Research Handbook on Unjust Enrichment and Restitution* is just one example of the breadth of interest in the topic in Commonwealth countries: Elise Bant, Kit Barker, and Simone Degeling (eds), *Research Handbook on Unjust Enrichment and Restitution* (Edward Elgar 2020). Participants included scholars from Australia, Canada, England, Hong Kong, Israel, Singapore, South Africa, and the United States. Some other notable volumes (there are many) include Robert Chambers, Charles Mitchell, and James Penner (eds), *Philosophical Foundations of the Law of Unjust Enrichment* (OUP 2009); Hanoch Dagan, *The Law and Ethics of Restitution* (CUP 2004).
[46] Peter Birks, *An Introduction to the Law of Restitution* (OUP 1985) 17–18, 23–24, 26. Birks argued at the time that unjust enrichment can be parsed as: (1) enrichment that is (2) at the plaintiff's expense and (3) unjust (as defined by case law) and (4) there are no contrary considerations. Enrichment can be by 'subtraction' from the claimant or by a wrong done to the claimant.
[47] Peter Birks, 'Misnomer' in WR Cornish and others (eds), *Restitution: Past, Present and Future— Essays in Honour of Gareth Jones* (Hart Publishing 1998).

quadration between restitution and unjust enrichment.[48] Instead, he advocated a new approach, drawn loosely from civil law, which linked unjust enrichment to the absence of an adequate 'explanatory basis' for the enrichment at issue.[49]

Birks's tightly analytic approach to restitution and unjust enrichment, particularly as presented in his earlier work, inspired more scholarship along similar lines in England and throughout the Commonwealth.[50] It also inspired a wave of dissent, with opponents suggesting that too much attention to doctrinal symmetry may detract from sound normative reasoning.[51] In any event, it stands in sharp contrast to the American approach expressed in the Restatements, which placed reasoned doctrinal development above symmetry.[52]

Birks himself was keenly aware of the divergent paths taken in England and America, and did his best to set the Americans straight before the third Restatement was published. In 2003, during the drafting process of the Restatement, Birks (whose position at the time was that restitution was broader than unjust enrichment) sent a letter of advice. In it, he chastised the Reporter for selecting a title (*Restatement (Third) of Restitution and Unjust Enrichment*) that mixed remedial responses with substantive grounds for relief.[53] The Reporter, Andrew Kull, politely disregarded the advice and forged ahead with his 'big tent' title, which allowed courts to work creatively from precedent without worrying too much about maintaining an analytically definable doctrinal structure.[54]

B. Three Ways to Approach Restitution and Unjust Enrichment

The topic 'restitution and unjust enrichment' forms an interesting part of the common law because its existence was conceived rather suddenly as an explanation

---

[48] Peter Birks, *Unjust Enrichment* (OUP 2003) 4, 23 (now depicting private law in a four-by-four grid).
[49] ibid 14–127. The new scheme was updated in Peter Birks, *Unjust Enrichment* (2nd edn, OUP 2005) 129–42.
[50] Contributions to the literature are too numerous to list. One indication of the scope of interest is the establishment in 1993 of a *Restitution Law Review*, which continued in print with a board of eminent advisors until 2018. Another notable publication was an English Restatement assembled by Andrew Burrows and a group of advisors and published the year after publication of the third American Restatement: Andrew Burrows, *A Restatement of the English Law of Unjust Enrichment* (OUP 2012). Burrows and his advisors were less concerned with precise doctrinal symmetry than Birks, but their Restatement was, in Burrow's words, 'more conceptual, and less contextual' than the American Restatement, which 'contains a mass of detail with a compilation of all relevant cases from across the USA': at x.
[51] This is my interpretation of, for example, the lament in Robert Stevens, 'The Unjust Enrichment Disaster' (2018) 134 LQR 574.
[52] Helen Scott, in a chapter on taxonomy, comments that '[t]axonomy—the definition, arrangement and internal ordering of legal categories—was key to [Birks's] project. Birks believed fervently that the use of arbitrary categories in law ... was a kind of intellectual failure': Scott, 'Taxonomy' (n 9) 145.
[53] Peter BH Birks, 'A Letter to America: The New Restatement of Restitution' (2003) 3(2) Global Jurist Frontiers 2.
[54] Birks's 'Letter to America' is noted in *Restatement (Third)* (n 34) § 1 Reporter's Note a.

for diverse materials rather than developed over time within a rubric. The history of restitution and unjust enrichment over nearly a century from its invention in 1937 suggests that there are at least three general ways to approach the subject. One method—the method of the American Restatements in the area of restitution and unjust enrichment—was to define the governing concept in an open-ended way and then mine for specific applications in legal decisions. Another method—the method that reached its extreme in the work of Peter Birks—was to start with some doctrinal evidence and then engage in intense analysis of its structure and requirements to develop a precise definition of the subject matter. A third possibility, which occasionally showed itself in the third American Restatement, is a method associated with American Legal Realism: state the underlying objectives in broad terms and allow judges to fill in content in response to particular facts.

The analytic methodology employed by Birks has the advantage of encouraging judges to proceed systematically to a decision. Used in moderation, the system has many advantages. The difficulty is that legal doctrine is organic material, which does not always conform to symmetrical patterns or deductive logic. The disputes that engage it change over time and with context, and no analytic scheme can be made to fit all circumstances without a degree of artificiality that is probably not a good feature in legal decision-making.

Legal Realism encourages judges to respond to context: judges are both permitted and expected to react to the particular facts that gave rise to a claim. The drawback of realism is that it greatly weakens the basis for advance planning and discourages reliance on expected outcomes. There is a case to be made for a degree of realism in law, particularly in fields that are generally well established. Yet, in an area of law whose governing principle is 'unjust enrichment', doctrinal guidance is probably necessary to avoid random or subjective outcomes.

In comparison with doctrinal symmetry or Legal Realism, the somewhat unruly 'big tent' view that characterizes the American Restatement series in the area of restitution has much in its favour. The aim of this approach is to allow for refinement and improvement of the body of rules governing restitution without conferring full case-by-case discretion on courts as they apply the concept of unjust enrichment.[55] Doctrinal taxonomy is at most a marginal concern; instead, the focus in on explaining and rationalizing doctrine in ways that will provide guidance to courts and parties but also allow for further development. The preferred methodology is nicely captured by Kull's statement about 'unjustified enrichment'—unjust

---

[55] I do not believe that prior decisions 'constrain' decision-making, except insofar as they state determinate, authoritative rules for later decisions. On the other hand, given a judicial responsibility to reason as soundly as possible in the time given, to honour reasonable expectations, and to be evenhanded among parties, prior decisions can often guide later decision-making by assisting in natural reason. See eg Larry Alexander and Emily Sherwin, *Advanced Introduction to Legal Reasoning* (Edward Elgar 2021) 87–110.

enrichment 'is not a free-floating idea to be applied by courts in the Realist way, but a guide to rational development of doctrine to fit new legal problems'.

IV. Conclusion

John P Dawson, an eminent twentieth-century American historian and legal scholar, wrote and taught in the area of restitution and unjust enrichment at the height of its influence in the United States. In a series of published lectures, he traced the origins of unjust enrichment in Roman law and the parallels between American decisions and restitution in civil law and especially Germany. He acknowledged the somewhat frightening open-endedness of the American conception of unjust enrichment, but also resisted reductive approaches to the subject.

> The ideal of preventing enrichment through another's loss has a strong appeal to the sense of equal justice but it also has the delusive appearance of mathematical simplicity. ... It constantly tends to become a 'rule', to dictate solutions, to impose itself on the mind.[56]

Nonetheless, Dawson ended on a hopeful note:

> We have done much and can do more to fortify ourselves. If we know the forest is enchanted we have not too much to fear.[57]

---

[56] Dawson, *Unjust Enrichment* (n 18) 8.
[57] ibid 152.

6
What was the Problem with 'Palm Tree Justice'?
Language, Justice, Equity, and Enrichment

Nolan Sharkey

I. Introduction

Unjust enrichment arose as a twentieth-century phenomenon although it has roots apparently going back to the nineteenth century and draws significantly on case law back to the eighteenth century.[1] According to the proponents of unjust enrichment, it traces back to Roman law.[2] It has been considerably debated in the literature whether unjust enrichment is something new, a new way of summing up an underlying principle in the law, or the rediscovery of a principle that should have been in the law all along but had become distorted.[3] What is clear is that unjust enrichment has a deep relationship with the principles of equity. Whether this is by conceiving of it as a rationalization of equitable principles or something offering a functional alternative to equity.[4] The idea that it provides a rational basis for equity is predicated on the argument that equity otherwise lacks this rational nature in its own right. The argument for unjust enrichment as a superior functional alternative to equity is similarly predicated on an argument that equity lacks a rational or coherent basis.

II. The Critique of Equity

The propagation of the idea of unjust enrichment has therefore been strongly linked to perceived deficiencies in the law of equity.[5] Peter Birks, for example,

---

[1] See eg David Ibbetson, 'Development at Common Law' in Elise Bant, Kit Barker, and Simone Degeling (eds), *Research Handbook on Unjust Enrichment and Restitution* (Edward Elgar 2020).
[2] Andrew Kull, 'James Barr Ames and the Early Modern History of Unjust Enrichment' (2005) 25 OJLS 297.
[3] For an excellent review of the issue, see: Warren Swain, 'Unjust Enrichment and the Role of Legal History in England and Australia' (2013) 36 UNSWLJ 1030.
[4] cf Peter Devonshire and Rohan Havelock (eds), *The Impact of Equity and Restitution in Commerce* (Hart Publishing 2019).
[5] DG White, 'The Demise of Palm Tree Justice' (1969) 34 Sask L Rev 291.

thought that common law and equity should be integrated and not give different answers.[6] It follows logically that proponents of the equity critique accept that it has been used to fulfil a functional need but that it is a faulty instrument for this need.[7] Unjust enrichment is proposed as a non-faulty instrument to deal with this need, or as an overarching and coherent rationale for the remedies and institutions of equity in dealing with the need.

It is therefore instructive to consider what this need is. The need can be broadly conceptualized as the need for a corrective when the 'ordinary' or common law recognizes (or fails to recognize) rights and obligations in a way that is not just.[8] The court has long recognized this possibility and the place that this has been recognized is in the courts of equity. The idea goes beyond the Anglo world and has a heritage in appealing to the king when the court gives an unjust outcome. It is worth considering this issue further as it may be asked why the law cannot be 'just' from the outset. There are different aspects to this question. The first is that the creators of law cannot anticipate all different scenarios when making law. Law might be created anticipating certain situations, but life always throws up novelties and unexpected outcomes.

The second aspect follows the first and asks why the law cannot allow for flexibility in the first place. The answer to this is that rule of law calls for certainty in law and rights.[9] There are justice arguments for this and economic arguments for this. Justice being that people should know and anticipate their rights and responsibilities as a matter of fairness. Economically, the market depends upon people understanding how their rights work for its efficient functioning.[10]

It follows that there is a tension between rule of law and the idea of flexibility to create justice in all possible situations. This tension has caused a critique of equity in general as those from a business perspective in particular argue that the flexibility it allows is bad for the economy and that rights should fall as predicted regardless of ideas of inherent justice. It is also argued that this idea of 'inherent justice' is faulty and difficult to predict or understand. Nevertheless, there is general recognition of a need for a corrective when the law gets it wrong.[11]

One argument for the separation of the idea of equity from the common law is to try and balance this tension. The law comes first and is predictable. Only when things go wrong does one turn to the institutions of equity to try and find a just solution. This is not a fabricated division as some may suggest. Notably, equity comes

---

[6] See eg Peter Birks, 'Equity, Conscience, and Unjust Enrichment' (1999) 23 MULR 1; Peter Birks, 'Equity in the Modern Law: An Exercise in Taxonomy' (1996) 26 UWAL Rev 1.
[7] See also Irit Samet, *Equity: Conscience Goes to Market* (OUP 2018) 1–28.
[8] See eg Dennis Klimchuk, Irit Samet, and Henry E Smith (eds), *Philosophical Foundations of the Law of Equity* (OUP 2020).
[9] cf Samet (n 7) 16–28.
[10] Alastair Hudson, *Great Debates in Equity and Trusts* (Bloomsbury Publishing 2014).
[11] Alastair Hudson, 'Equity, Individualisation and Social Justice: Towards a New Law of the Home' in Alastair Hudson (ed), *New Perspectives on Property Law, Human Rights and the Home* (Cavendish 2004).

with real differences such as the equitable maxims that those who seek equity must come with clean hands. There is a system of protections and barriers in relation to equity that mean it really is not just another set of laws filed under a different heading.[12]

This separation is a good thing for balancing the tension between certainty and justice. This is not always recognized and there have been calls to simply consider the 'rules' of equity as part and parcel of the same law. It is true that some parts of the rules of equity have become so formalized and relied upon that they might arguably be better regarded as simply part of the (common) law.[13] This would be the case with the deliberately created trusts that are so prevalent in Australia. These trusts are simply an established legal institution available under the law in most people's views and use. They are not used as a corrective to seek justice but rather they are used commonly and with an expectation of predictability.[14]

When they are considered, calls for the formalization and fixing of the rights created under equity the same as any law are strong. Trusts are a common legal and financial arrangement; they should be treated as such for certainty and fairness. Very similar arguments are made in relation to fiduciary duties generally. People want the categories to be closed such that we know that a lawyer and a director have particular legal obligations, but we cannot have them spring from nowhere.

There is merit in these arguments, but when they are essentialized and applied to equity as a whole, they ignore that the world still has unanticipated possibilities in need of a corrective. Even within the field of trusts, it is clear that they retain a wide purpose for correcting legal rights and obligations in many non-anticipated situations. They are not simply institutions of finance and investment. There are many decisions where an injustice is corrected through the imposition of a trust. The same may be said about fiduciary duties.[15]

A superior position to these various arguments may be that equitable institutions that have taken life as common and formal legal structures should no longer be regarded as part of equity as such but instead as common law. This might be the case with many trust arrangements. When something has been codified, arguably this is already the case. For example, the inclusion of directors' equitable duties in company law[16]—even if there remains an issue of unresolved overlap in many cases. However, this formalization of equitable institutions does not mean all need for 'true' equity as a flexible system with its own constraints and rules of access has disappeared. The passing of time allows as many new novelties as it settles.

---

[12] Andrew Burrows, 'We Do This at Common Law But That in Equity' (2002) 22 OJLS 1.
[13] cf Jennifer Nadler, 'What is Distinctive about the Law of Equity?' (2021) 41 OJLS 854, 856–59.
[14] Douglas Laycock, 'The Triumph of Equity' (1993) 56(3) LCP 53.
[15] Marcia S Krieger, '"The Bankruptcy Court Is a Court of Equity": What Does That Mean?' (1999) 50 SCL Rev 275.
[16] GFK Santow, 'Codification of Directors' Duties' (1999) 73 ALJ 336.

The discomfort felt by some about having any flexibility in the predictable outcomes of law is part of the rationale for the superiority of unjust enrichment. However, at the outset it can be asserted that this is difficult to credit. One of the core concepts underlying unjust enrichment, and a necessary condition for it, is that someone has got something (been enriched), but that the outcome is unjust.[17] Clearly, the person must be enriched in accordance with (common) law. They have not been enriched by holding onto something that still belongs to another person and normal property law can correct the problem. There is only need for unjust enrichment when a person has been enriched under standard law.

Thus, at its core, unjust enrichment has a similar basis to equity. It seeks to correct things when the law has allowed someone to obtain legal rights in a way that might be wrong. Just, equitable, fair are all ideas aimed at the same goal. Given this similarity, it cannot be said that unjust enrichment is by definition superior to equity in its inherently similar function. To consider this issue, the critique of equity needs to be looked at in more depth. It can then be considered if unjust enrichment avoids these criticisms.

III. The Rise of Rationalism

As noted earlier in this chapter, the origin of equity is turning to the monarch when the law doesn't deliver justice.[18] The core idea being that the monarch could stand back and consider if, overall, things had worked out fairly. This ultimately became the equitable jurisdiction but in many ways retained the nature of someone standing back and seeing if justice has been done. Given the ideal of rule of law is not just about certainty in legal operations but also about placing the state under the law constitutionally, the discomfort associated with equitable jurisdiction has deep roots in western thinking.[19] If the king is not appropriate as the one who can stand back and measure justice, then who is? One answer in various places has been the Church. In times when right and wrong were considered as much in religious terms as in legal terms, the idea that the Church could be the Court of Conscience, would have seemed highly appropriate.[20]

However, the Reformation challenged the Church's moral authority in much of the west. Once the Reformation genie was out of the bottle, it was only a matter of time before the moral authority of any replacement reformed Church structures

---

[17] cf Steve Hedley, Chapter 14 in this volume.
[18] See also Mike Macnair, 'Equity and Conscience' (2007) 27 OJLS 659; Dennis R Klinck, *Conscience, Equity and the Court of Chancery in Early Modern England* (Ashgate 2010).
[19] Nolan Sharkey and Ian Murray, 'The Rule of Law and Leadership in Substitution and in Conflict: Social Psychological and Legal Perspectives on Chinese Tax Administration' (2015) 30 Australian Tax Forum 595.
[20] Sharon K Dobbins, 'Equity: The Court of Conscience or the King's Command, the Dialogues of St. German and Hobbes Compared' (1991) 9 JL & Relig 113.

also failed to measure up to new ideas of finding justice beyond the realm of Church authority. Luther's attack on the Catholic Church was the first step towards a secular west as the ideas it spawned moved from the Catholic Church to all Churches and religion as a whole and onto custom and tradition.[21] The Enlightenment spurned all these elements in favour of science, objectivity, individualism, Bentham, Locke, and the pursuit of happiness. While the Church remained important in the nineteenth century,[22] these ideas certainly penetrated countries that remained Catholic, such as France, and achieved new life there.

The scientific/rationalist critique is ultimately dismissive of anything that is seen as grounded in custom, hierarchy, tradition, religion, culture, and values. These are often viewed as inherently subjective and therefore unfair and spawning economic inefficiency.[23] This thought came to dominance in the twentieth century and impacted a vast array of academia and human thinking. There was a move in history academia, for example, against references to folklore and culture and towards scientific objectivity only.[24] The critique of religion and culture grew. Scientific method, measurement, and objective rational economics were the measure of all things.

Associated with this revolution of the mind in the west was a view that saw many non-western people as irrational and enmeshed in their inefficient and subjective cultures, customs, and values. This facilitated a view that was adopted in nineteenth-century imperialism that western countries were superior for their rational way of doing things and that this was in fact what caused their superiority. In turn, others were backward because of their irrational customs that dominated their lives.

This ideological position informs the mid-twentieth-century critique of equity. Nothing is more telling than its being epitomized as 'palm tree justice'.[25] The phrase that so quickly allowed people to see what the critique was, now looks problematic and vaguely racist. This phrase does, however, identify the problem with the 'secular' critique of equity. It shows how much it was informed by ideology and it is right to be suspicious of it for this reason alone.

While the scientific/objective position remains dominant, many areas have found fault with it. These problems rarely enter law due to its innate conservatism. However, they are real and need to be considered in relation to the critique of equity and the praise of unjust enrichment.

---

[21] The wider issue was the decline of the Church Courts in the Middle Ages, see eg RH Helmholz, *The Canon Law and Ecclesiastical Jurisdiction from 597 to the 1640s* (OUP 2004).
[22] See eg Frances Knight, *The Nineteenth-Century Church and English Society* (CUP 1995).
[23] Ruth W Grant, 'John Locke on Custom's Power and Reason's Authority' (2012) 74 Review of Politics 607.
[24] Mark Bevir, 'Objectivity in History' (1994) 33 History and Theory 328.
[25] White (n 5).

The core problem is that the idea that the utilitarian, secular ideology that has become dominant is somehow more objective and free of social values is false. There is simply no such thing as a human society free of values and social institutions. Utilitarian ideology is simply an ideology. It is a set of social values and is in no way a scientific, objective way of thinking. It may have changed society, but society remains as replete with values and social institutions as ever. This is not a reference to the multicultural world, however that simply adds to the complexity.[26]

Many developments in thinking and the world have challenged the idea of secular objectivity and rationality. The economic success of Confucian societies is a prime example. In the 1990s, western academia was still mystified by this success of what were regarded as irrational societies that broke the rules of success and yet succeeded.[27] However, the better position is that those rules were not the universal rules of objectivity that they were thought to be. Even the discipline of history has realized that its mid-twentieth-century obsession with objectivity was wrong and that there can be no such thing as objective history.

How does this impact the critique of equity as palm tree justice? The impact is that to call equity faulty due to its perceived basis in non-scientific, irrational principles is untenable. You cannot have a value-free society and you cannot have a value-free law. The law cannot be free of values and such a hypothetical law (even if possible) is not appropriate to a society that is not value-free in itself.

IV. Social Institutions

Few legal studies consider, in depth, what sits behind ideas such as conscionability and equity. These may be likened to ideas such as ethics and morality.[28] Some simply assume that these things exist and go no further while others see them as arbitrary and matters of individual outlook. Hence, the critique of equity. However, law is not the only thing that orders human society. The very nature of a society presupposes order, and all societies have order regardless of their own conceptualization of law. Of course, it may be argued persuasively that these rules and obligations are law. Thus, we have custom and customary law. However, what needs to be noted is that these rules of order precede formal laws of parliament and courts in time and the introduction of the latter does not bring about their general demise.[29] Of course, a statute that conflicts with a custom may impact it and change

---

[26] Milan Zafirovski, 'What is Really Rational Choice? Beyond the Utilitarian Concept of Rationality' (1999) 47(1) Current Sociology 47.

[27] Nolan Cormac Sharkey, 'Greater China and South East Asia: A Taxing problem?' in Nolan Cormac Sharkey (ed), *Taxation in ASEAN and China: Local Institutions, Regionalism, Global Systems and Economic Development* (Routledge 2012) 27.

[28] cf Samet (n 7) 28–65.

[29] cf Fernanda Pirie, *The Anthropology of Law* (OUP 2013).

it. However, a custom may also lead to a statute being viewed as wrong or unfair by people and a disregard of the law. Ultimately, many rules that order society do not spring from the laws of parliaments and courts. When one sees people queuing up at a shop counter, one may consider whether there is a law that requires them to do so.

Douglass North's seminal work has shown that human behaviour is significantly constrained by informal institutions that govern what is acceptable behaviour in various contexts.[30] These constraints are flexible and vary amongst different populations and over time. However, this variety and change in no way reduces the strength of these constraints which can be more powerful than formal constraints such as law. North's term 'social institutions' is a neutral term that acknowledges that human society is held together by rules and these rules are not all the product of government. The enforcement of the rules is social. People who do not comply with the rules are chastised or ostracized socially which provides a powerful incentive to behave in the expected manner. The more a society is regulated by social institutions, the more this is true. The more formal institutions such as law regulate behaviour, the less relevance there may be for social institutions but the two have a complex relationship of both mutual support and conflict depending on context.

The term 'social institutions' intersects with alternative ideas such as culture, values, ethics, and morality in their regulatory aspects. All these concepts refer to informal forces that shape human behaviour and society's expectations of human behaviour. It can be argued that there is little relevant distinction between these concepts. Of course, they are different in degree and extent but in terms of regulating human behaviour they are functionally similar. Social institutions, like ethics and morality, can be conceptualized in terms of duties. The duties that people have to do or not do certain things or to behave in a particular manner are ultimately what are relevant in all these areas. Thus, the term 'social duties' replaces concepts such as moral or ethical duty or behaviour and behaviour that is considered culturally appropriate.

Such social institutions can be far more elaborate than a requirement to queue. For example, business carried on by ethnic Chinese people in Australia, the UK, and New Zealand as well as in China and Southeast Asia may be heavily impacted by social rules supported by the relevant communities. These can be studied and documented and have an extensive and powerful impact. Elsewhere I have documented this and used accounting theory to show how all the elements of the accounting conceptualization of the world can be created through Chinese social institutions. These are assets, liabilities, entities, income, and expense. These institutions are tied to extended kinship and friendship networks and can be pervasive. The scope of these forms of business might be notable but they are not unique to

---

[30] Douglass C North, *Institutions, Institutional Change and Economic Performance* (CUP 1990).

Chinese social actors. They are very often a feature of family businesses (notably rural enterprise) in more strongly 'secular' groups and certain other social groupings can make more extended usage of these arrangements. Clearly, in a world of social diversity and cross-border mobility these issues are highly relevant, but they are not in any way the sole domain of such factors. Rather, they are the essential nature of human society.

When a social institutional duty exists, people in a society will generally regard a failure to comply with that duty as wrong. This is where right and wrong can exist in a way that is not determined by law. As noted earlier in this chapter, the law may align with the idea, or it may contradict it. In many cases, it may not consider the issue directly as it has not had to deal with it previously. For example, if something has not yet been before a court, it is possible to imagine where a queuing situation might result in serious enough consequences to result in a legal dispute. As noted earlier, the formal law cannot comprehensively cover all needs in terms of human behaviour. While society can informally enforce social duties to an extent, there will be instances where it has insufficient institutional strength to deal with those who disregard their duties and commit a wrong. This possibility may be enhanced where formal law exists and those who violate their duties assert they have no obligation to honour their social duties. They refuse to queue up and say there is no legal requirement for them to do so. In instances of major wrongs of this sort, it may be considered whether formal law can be used to pursue a just outcome. Here a just outcome is an honouring of the social obligation.

V. Why Not Rely on Formal Law Such as Contract?

The possibility of enforcing obligations that arise in contexts such as family arrangements raises significant problems. For example, this could be a farmer indicating to their adult child that they should work on the farm for years as one day it will all pass to them anyway or an elaborate Chinese business (guanxi) network as contemplated elsewhere and noted earlier in this chapter. What if the famer decides later that they do not wish to pass the farm onto their child or the person in the business network decides to redirect property that is legally theirs but is understood through the guanxi network to be in some way communal or at least covered by particular obligations. Can these obligations be enforced?

Possible ways that relevant legal principles may be employed to allow contractual enforcement of such social duties can be contemplated but ultimately significant controversies and uncertainties remain in these approaches. The key difficulties are in relation to the objective interpretation of contractual terms and in the contractual prerequisite that parties intended to be bound in court. Rules of evidence are also relevant.

With social arrangements, an essential part of any legal dispute concerning relations, rights, and obligations created, and available remedies will depend on the court's findings in relation to the original mutual intentions of the persons involved. In contract law, determining whether a contract was intended and what the intended terms of the contract were are the essence of many disputes. In many circumstances, intended contracts and terms, promises, or undertakings are also at the heart of any determination of whether a joint venture, partnership, or trust[31] exists.

How a court may determine intentions in relation to a social arrangement is therefore critical. Such a determination is also not likely to be easy to conclude. Written documentation encapsulating the essence of the overall arrangements is unlikely to exist and the documentation that does exist is likely to be incomplete at best and misleading at worst. A court must assess the nature of the various persons' intentions based on their statements and any available evidence of conduct.

There is scope at law to consider evidence of conduct and other available information to determine the nature of arrangements between people. For example, in determining whether a partnership exists, and its scope if it does, evidence of conduct can alter outcomes and find a partnership exists or that it differs from any written document. All the facts of the case should be considered, including the mode of dealing.[32] In contract law, other than when dealing with contracts wholly in writing[33] and land dealing subject to statutory control,[34] evidence of statements and conduct is clearly relevant in determining the existence of a contract, its terms, and variations to the contract. This is particularly so with oral or part contracts, which are likely to be relevant to this analysis.

When there is unclear documentation, the conduct of a person and relevant extrinsic evidence can be considered to determine the intention to create a trust.[35] It can also be relevant when the conduct of a person provides evidence of the intention to create or not to create a trust in the absence of a document or in contradiction of a document.[36] Finally, conduct and behaviour that is viewed as creating a trust will create a trust, even if the relevant person is unaware that a trust has been created.[37]

The statements in the previous paragraph relating to trusts and contract apply to arguments to support the finding of certain non-contractual, non-trust legal obligations as well. Outside trusts and established categories of fiduciary, the finding of a fiduciary duty or relationship is dependent on the finding of a non-fiduciary

---

[31] Clearly, contract existence is very important to trusts if contractarian theory is accepted. See John H Langbein, 'The Contractarian Basis of the Law of Trusts' (1995) 105 Yale LJ 625.
[32] *Bryant Bros v Thiele* [1923] SASR 393 (SCFC); *Jelekainen v Frikton* [2007] QSC 98.
[33] *State Rail Authority of NSW v Heath Outdoor Pty Ltd* (1986) 7 NSWLR 170 (CA).
[34] eg Conveyancing Act 1919 (NSW), s 54(a).
[35] *Starr v Starr* [1935] SASR 263 (SC).
[36] *Hyhonie Holdings Pty Ltd v Leroy* [2003] NSWSC 624.
[37] *Twinsectra Ltd v Yardley* [2002] UKHL 12; [2002] 2 AC 164, 171.

obligation. This obligation is essential to the establishment of a fiduciary duty.[38] Evidence of this non-fiduciary obligation will need to be sought again in various documents and conduct. Again, it will be unlikely that the non-fiduciary obligation will be documented completely, so inferences of intentions and obligations will have to be drawn from available evidence.

The aforementioned notes the importance of finding intentions from conduct, words, and documents. This raises issues about how these should be interpreted by the court. A distinction in law is that between determining objective intentions and determining subjective intentions. In relation to interpretation of contract, for example, it is clear that the court determines intention objectively. That is, the court considers how the words and conduct would be interpreted by a reasonable informed observer. Evidence of what a person actually subjectively meant is not relevant. The rationale for this is that if your words or actions mean one thing to you but another to your contracting partner, it is only fair that the court's interpretation of these is the reasonable or objectively correct interpretation. This objective interpretation is said to be that which an intelligent[39] or officious[40] bystander or reasonable person[41] would have of the words or conduct. The impact of this approach to interpretation is clearly illustrated in *Brambles Holdings v Bathurst CC* in which a contract was found to mean something different to the shared interpretation of the contracting parties.[42]

The objective approach ostensibly excludes reference to evidence of subjective intention. However, there is strong authority that reference to the full background and matrix of facts is allowable in finding objective interpretation.[43] This background may indicate that the objective interpretation that should be given to words or conduct can differ from an otherwise clear objective interpretation.[44] Thus, in accordance with Lord Hoffmann in *Mannai Investments Co Ltd v Eagle Star Life Assurance Co Ltd*, 'Mary' can objectively mean 'Jane'.[45] Such an objective interpretation may allow an interpretation that is closer to that subjectively intended by a party.

---

[38] Paul D Finn, *Fiduciary Obligations* (Law Book Co 1977) 233 [541]; Matthew Conaglen, *Fiduciary Loyalty: Protecting the Due Performance of Non-Fiduciary Duties* (Hart Publishing 2010) 59–76.
[39] *Dick Bentley Productions Ltd v Harold Smith (Motors) Ltd* [1965] 1 WLR 623 (CA).
[40] *The Moorcock* (1889) 14 PD 64 (CA).
[41] *Investors Compensation Scheme Ltd v West Bromwich Building Society* [1998] 1 WLR 896 (HL) 912–13.
[42] *Brambles Holdings Ltd v Bathurst CC* [2001] NSWCA 61; (2001) 53 NSWLR 153.
[43] Although there is continuing debate as to whether the approach taken in *Investors Compensation Scheme Ltd v West Bromwich Building Society* (n 41) is fully accepted in Australia. The issue of when the full matrix is allowed is contrasted with *Codelfa Constructions Pty Ltd v State Rail Authority (NSW)* (1982) 149 CLR 337. A more recent High Court consideration related to it can be found in *Byrnes v Kendle* [2011] HCA 26; (2011) 243 CLR 253.
[44] *Mannai Investments Co Ltd v Eagle Star Life Assurance Co Ltd* [1997] AC 749 (HL) 774–75.
[45] ibid.

In other areas, such as the formation of a trust, the law allows the court to consider subjective intention, thus other evidence showing specific intention is permitted.[46] Even though a partnership is established through contract, it is apparent from the discussion already presented that wider scope for determining actual intent exists.

Even though subjective intent may be considered in areas such as trust formation, the court must resort to reasonable and objective interpretation of the evidence of intent and conduct before it. It is submitted that the inquiry may often not differ greatly from that which takes place when an objective approach is considered. Of course, if clear statements of subjective intent exist in extrinsic materials and these contradict an existing and complete written document, the two approaches may yield different results. However, if there is no all-encompassing written document and intent needs to be inferred from mixed evidence of conduct and words, the two approaches may not yield noticeably different results. With both approaches, the court will need to determine what interpretation to give to the evidence in relation to the intentions of the relevant parties.

We have considered the notion of social duties and the difficulty of formally enforcing them in contract. It is pertinent to consider how these social institutions might relate to equity and whether they may lead to equitable support without being characterized as legal duties in their own right. In this way, of course, they may become legal duties, but the critical point is that they are not initially legal duties. It is infrequently asserted that law will support non-legal duties; however, what is being considered is whether this might not actually be the case in equity.

VI. Equity and Social Duties—Supporting Honourable Understandings

A. Fiduciary Loyalty

The key focus of the following inquiry is the recognition of non-legal duties in the area of fiduciary duty. Ultimately, what will be considered is whether a strong argument can be made for social duties giving rise to fiduciary duties without first finding that another legal institution—such as a partnership, trust, or contract—exists. Following this inquiry, the existence of other legal institutions and the impact they have in relation to the legal obligations created will be considered. In this consideration, again, fiduciary duty will be an integral part of the analysis. However, the initial consideration of the support of non-legal duties allows the analysis to ignore questions regarding intention to be bound by law and the

---

[46] *Commissioner of Stamp Duties (Qld) v Jolliffe* (1920) 28 CLR 178.

nature of such binding, which otherwise play a major role in any analysis of legal obligations.[47]

In his book *Fiduciary Loyalty*,[48] Conaglen has provided an extensive review of the nature of fiduciary duties. Other seminal and extensive scholarly studies are Finn's pioneering and extensively cited work *Fiduciary Obligations*[49] and the work of Scott,[50] Weinrib,[51] and Flannigan.[52] None of these works directly addresses the issue of fiduciary duties supporting non-legal obligations. However, it is submitted that it is implicit in Conaglen's work that he either believes that fiduciary duties do not support non-legal duties or fails to contemplate and consider such duties at all. The same cannot be said of Finn.

Conaglen argues extensively that fiduciary duties will only be found to support or protect non-fiduciary duties.[53] The essence of his argument is that fiduciary duties cannot stand alone and are necessarily prophylactic.[54] It is stated that they are the product of equitable doctrine stepping in to enforce loyalty to common law duties[55] when the general law surrounding these duties is insufficient to command the necessary loyalty in itself. In favour of his instrumentalist argument, Conaglen objects to the view that fiduciary duties are about morality. In support of this, he argues that a fiduciary duty may create a legal requirement for a person to act immorally when this effectively supports loyalty towards their non-fiduciary duty. Thus, he cites the well-known authority of *Cowan v Scargill*[56] that a trustee's duty may require immoral action in support of their duty to their beneficiary.[57]

Conaglen's view is that a fiduciary duty will only emerge to command loyalty to a non-fiduciary duty. It is implicit in his argument that he views these non-fiduciary duties as being other *legal* duties that require a greater level of loyalty than the common law or statute has provided for. Conaglen does not directly address the reason(s) why the original common law or statute could not have required such necessary greater levels of loyalty in themselves. It must be concluded that the reason why the non-equitable jurisdiction has failed to create these protections itself is that the original law either does not anticipate a particular disloyalty-related problem that has arisen or is unable to cater to all the possible instances of disloyalty.

---

[47] *Hospital Products Ltd v United States Surgical Corp* (1984) 156 CLR 41, 61–63.
[48] Conaglen (n 38).
[49] Finn, *Fiduciary Obligations* (n 38).
[50] Austin W Scott, 'The Fiduciary Principle' (1949) 37 Cal L Rev 539.
[51] Ernest J Weinrib, 'The Fiduciary Obligation' (1975) 25 UTLJ 1.
[52] Robert Flannigan, 'The Boundaries of Fiduciary Accountability' (2004) 83 Can Bar Rev 35.
[53] Conaglen (n 38) 59–76.
[54] ibid 61.
[55] ibid 60 cites as support *Barclays Bank plc v Quincecare Ltd* [1992] 4 All ER 363 (QB) 375; *KLB v British Columbia* 2003 SCC 51; [2003] 2 SCR 403 [48].
[56] *Cowan v Scargill* [1985] Ch 270 (Ch) 288.
[57] Conaglen (n 38) 107.

Conaglen's strong view that there must be a non-fiduciary *legal* duty leads him to take issue[58] with Finn's view that:

> The term 'duty' in the rule is used in no technical sense. It does not mean, for example, that the existence of a fiduciary relationship depends on it being shown that the undertaking given embodies duties of a *legally enforceable* character.[59]

Conaglen objects to this statement, as it indicates that no non-fiduciary *legal* duty is required. Conaglen proceeds to assert that Finn did not really mean the aforementioned statement in a strict sense and that it should be limited in context (or that it is wrong). He does this by quoting Finn's later statement in the same work, in which he argues that:

> [u]ntil the scope and ambit of the duties assumed by the fiduciary have been ascertained—until the subject matter over which the fiduciary obligations must extend has been defined—no question of conflict of duty and interest can arise. You must ascertain what the fiduciary has undertaken to do, before you can say that he has permitted his interests to conflict with his undertaking.[60]

The basis for Conaglen's use of the second quotation to assert that Finn did not mean exactly what he said in the first is that the second clearly indicates that Finn believes that a fiduciary duty must support another duty. In other words, it shows that Finn accepts that a fiduciary duty can only exist when a non-fiduciary duty exists. This is in clear agreement with Conaglen's view. However, it is contended that Finn's second quotation does not actually contradict his first in the manner that Conaglen believes. Rather, the second statement can be reconciled with the first if two factors are accepted. First, it must be accepted that duties exist that are not 'of a legally enforceable character'. Secondly, it must be accepted that at least some such duties are recognized in equity as meriting the prophylactic support of the fiduciary duty.

The acceptance of these two factors makes Finn's two statements completely consistent, so it is suggested that he was probably of this view when he wrote them. In contrast, Conaglen's objection to Finn's first quotation and his use of the second to disprove it indicate he believes that either there is no such thing as a non-legal (or social) duty, or such duties are never recognized and supported in equity.

---

[58] ibid 186.
[59] Finn, *Fiduciary Obligations* (n 38) 203 [471]. In his quotation of this passage, Conaglen excludes Finn's references to *Boardman v Phipps* [1967] 2 AC 46 (HL) 127 and *Birtchnell v Equity Trustees, Executors & Agency Co Ltd* (1929) 42 CLR 384, 408.
[60] Finn, *Fiduciary Obligations* (n 38) 233 [541].

B. Fiduciary Relationships and Morality

The potential recognition of social duties in the finding of fiduciary duties also requires a reconsideration of Conaglen's disagreement with the premise that fiduciary duties are fundamentally about morality and moral conduct. This premise of morality is argued in works by Rotman,[61] Cotterell,[62] and Fitzgibbon[63] and is cited in cases such as *Meinhard v Salmon*.[64] Conaglen cites and quotes Rotman's point that 'the fiduciary concept imposes law's highest ethical standards on a potentially infinite number of actors involved in a variety of circumstances'.[65] Conaglen proceeds to dismiss this view as being problematic, overly historically focused, and not '[providing] a sound basis on which to build a contemporary theory of fiduciary doctrine'.[66] He does not submit to Rotman's view that the fiduciary duty transmits 'ethical resolve to the field of human interaction'. Further, while Conaglen concedes that historically equity *may* have been more about morality and individualized justice, he strongly argues that this is certainly no longer the case.[67] He cites MacCormick's view that there is no more room for the non-universalistic application of rules in equity than there is in general law.[68]

Conaglen's strong objection to the morality or ethical argument must be reconsidered in view of the issue of non-legal duties. Such reconsideration may also allow some reconciliation between Conaglen's instrumental–prophylactic argument and those of Rotman, as has occurred with Finn. It has already been asked why a separate prophylactic legal doctrine is needed if all it does is support other legal doctrines. The only feasible answers (as I have suggested) are that either the original legal doctrine may not have anticipated the particular abuse taking place or the original doctrine could not deal with all the possibilities. The latter suggestion becomes difficult because the question arises as to why, if fiduciary doctrine can deal with it, the original doctrine cannot. The answer to this must be that the abuse cannot be anticipated as an abuse until it is seen. This effectively reconciles the latter suggestion to the first in that both suggestions are effectively about the original law being unable to anticipate wrongful conduct until it arises. Thus, there is a need for a more flexible and individualized mechanism to deal with unanticipated wrongs. As such, the prophylactic and separate role of the fiduciary duty arises.

---

[61] Leonard Ian Rotman, *Fiduciary Law* (Thomson Carswell 2005) 2–3.
[62] Roger Cotterrell, 'Trusting in Law: Legal and Moral Concepts of Trust' (1993) 46 CLP 75.
[63] Scott FitzGibbon, 'Fiduciary Relationships Are Not Contracts' (1999) 82 Marq L Rev 303.
[64] *Meinhard v Salmon* 249 NY 458; 164 NE 545 (1928).
[65] Conaglen (n 38) 109. Conaglen's citation is of Rotman (n 61) 244.
[66] Conaglen (n 38) 110.
[67] ibid 111.
[68] DN MacCormick, 'Formal Justice and the Form of Legal Arguments in Chaim Perelman (ed), *Etudes de Logique Juridique*, vol 6 (Bruylant 1976) 103, 111.

The presented analysis rationalizing and supporting *the need* for the Conaglen-asserted prophylactic role of fiduciary doctrine also raises problems for other aspects of Conaglen's arguments. First, it is suggested that this after-the-fact correction of wrongs is redolent of the individualized justice objected to by Conaglen himself. That is, Conaglen objects to the idea that equity is about individualized responses to wrongs because he submits that equity is as much about universal principles as general law. He quotes MacCormick:

> I cannot for the life of me understand how there can be such a thing as a good reason for deciding any single case which is not a good generic reason for deciding cases of the particular type of question.[69]

However, such a good reason does exist and it is the very reason that justifies Conaglen's own assertion that the role of fiduciary obligation is prophylactic. The law cannot establish the 'good generic reason' up front because it does not know what the wrong behaviour will be until it encounters it. Therefore, a flexible prophylactic doctrine is needed to cater to individualized cases as they arise.

Secondly, more fundamentally, the question that arises from the analysis is, what makes the behaviour wrong if the initial law has not and is not able to state specifically that it is wrong? This question clearly leads directly back to questions of ethics and morals and the suggestion made by Rotman that fiduciary doctrine is a way that law transmits an ethical perspective to the infinite interactions in human society. For, if something is wrong but is not illegal, it must be wrong according to a different standard. The only other standard is that of morals and ethics.

Of course, the Rotman statement taken at face value is too extreme. Clearly, fiduciary doctrine does not simply make morals, law. Thus, in some ways, it is completely understandable that Conaglen objects to it. However, this does not mean that morality and ethics have nothing to do with fiduciary doctrine. Part of the problem of any consideration of the issue is the difficulty associated with terms such as 'morality'. The concepts of 'ethics', 'morals', 'values', 'culture', and 'norms' and the distinctions between them are unclear.[70] What is clear is that a person's sense of what is right and wrong may be innate, based on personal thought and experience, socially imparted, or based on law and regulations.[71] To the extent that innate and personally formed views are held in common with other members of society, they are likely to overlap with those that are socially imparted. Debate about which of these positions are values, ethics, or morals is likely to be reduced to little more than a semantic debate. However, the key point is that persons in a society will

---

[69] ibid.
[70] The standard use in day-to-day language may differ considerably from that used in, say, sociology. Consider the definitions in Nicholas Abercrombie, Stephen Hill, and Bryan S Turner, *The Penguin Dictionary of Sociology* (5th edn, Penguin 2006).
[71] Noel Preston, 'The Ethical Challenge' in *Understanding Ethics* (2nd edn, Federation Press 2001).

have a shared understanding of what is right and wrong. This understanding creates social institutions that are capable of regulating human behaviour to a very significant degree.[72] A person who departs from the commonly conceived correct behaviour will be viewed as immoral or unethical.[73] Thus, the best way to conceive of the behaviour that is expected to generate a good outcome is within the paradigm of social institutions as noted earlier in this chapter. These will vary subtly according to social context and relevant group but are ultimately based on a shared understanding of the right way to act.[74]

What is essential in this discussion is that because social institutions constrain behaviour, they clearly create duties. Constraints on human behaviour, as conceptualized by North, may be restated as 'duties'. Duties to do certain things or act in a certain way or duties not to do certain things or act in a certain way. Alternatively put, ethics create duties or morality creates duties. Thus, duties that people are subjected to arise not only from law but also from society. The acceptance of this premise allows a reconciliation of Conaglen's instrumentalist–prophylactic conception of fiduciary duties with Finn's statement that no legally enforceable duty is required. It also allows reconciliation with the idea put forward by Rotman that the fiduciary duty transmits 'ethical resolve to the field of human interaction'. Conaglen no doubt objected to these propositions because he viewed them as contradicting his proposition. However, no contradiction occurs when it is accepted that a duty may arise from a non-legal origin. Rather, this awareness answers the question of the initial need for the prophylactic support role of fiduciary doctrine that is not adequately dealt with by Conaglen's analysis.

C. Evidence of the Support of Social Duties in Equity

Evidence of the fiduciary obligation being used to recognize non-legal duties is not difficult to find, at least historically. Considering the basic origin of the trust, it is clear that it is based on an equitable recognition of a non-legal duty rather than a common law duty. To quote Maitland:

> In the second half of the fourteenth century many causes were conspiring to induce the landholders of England to convey their lands to friends, who, while becoming the legal owners of those lands, would, nevertheless, be bound by an honourable understanding as to the uses to which their ownership should be put. ... The Chancellor began to hold himself out as willing to enforce these

---

[72] North (n 30) 3.
[73] Mark Granovetter, 'The Impact of Social Structure on Economic Outcomes' (2005) 19 J Economic Perspectives 33.
[74] This paragraph draws on an unpublished draft paper: Nolan Sharkey and Edmond Wong, 'Ethical Legal Practice: Cross Cultural Insights' (on file with the author).

honourable understandings, these 'uses, trusts or confidences' as they were called, to send to prison the trustee who would not keep faith.[75]

The nature of the duty created by these 'honourable understandings' that the chancellor belatedly enforced can only be ethical or moral. That is, in the terms of this chapter, they are social duties. There is nothing else to ground a concept of honourable behaviour or duty if it is not based on law.

Of course, this also indicates that the fiduciary duty does not necessarily simply support all non-legal duties. The fact that the chancellor only began to hold himself out at a certain stage indicates a choice to be made by the court of equity as to when it will support non-legal duties. When an individual case with facts dissimilar to previous cases comes before the court, it would appear unavoidable that some form of value judgement must be exercised by the court in deciding whether to support the non-legal duty. Both Finn[76] and Conaglen[77] note that courts make choices on whether fiduciary support is merited based on societal value, with Conaglen stating that the courts do not often acknowledge this.

In addition, as Conaglen correctly asserts, equity now very much has its own fixed legal precedent of universal rules to follow in relation to institutions such as the trust and fiduciary support. It is clear that the approach that courts now prefer to take in identifying fiduciary relationships is an incremental one that looks at parallels between the situation before the court and more established instances of fiduciary relationship. This is encapsulated by Mason J in *Hospital Products Ltd v United States Surgical Corp*:

> [When dealing with a non-established category of fiduciary relationship] it is important in the first instance to ascertain the characteristics which, according to tradition, identify a fiduciary relationship. As the courts have declined to define the concept, preferring instead to develop the law in a case by case approach, we have to distil the essence or the characteristics of the relationship from the illustrations which the judicial decisions provide. In so doing we must recognize that the categories of fiduciary relationships are not closed.[78]

For this reason, it is critical to consider more recent evidence of fiduciary duties arising to support non-legal duties and the types of duties supported for parallels to our context.

---

[75] Frederic William Maitland, *The Collected Papers of Frederic William Maitland: Downing Professor of the Laws of England*, vol 2 (CUP 1911) 492.
[76] Paul Desmond Finn, 'The Fiduciary Principle' in Timothy G Youdan (ed), *Equity, Fiduciaries and Trusts* (Carswell 1989) 25–26; Finn, *Fiduciary Obligations* (n 38) 171–2.
[77] Conaglen (n 38) 262–64.
[78] *Hospital Products Ltd v United States Surgical Corp* (n 47) 96 (citations omitted).

D. *Coleman v Myers*, *Brunninghausen v Glavanics*, and Family Duty

Two leading cases provide evidence of the foundation of fiduciary duties on essentially non-legal duties related to family: *Coleman v Myers*[79] and *Brunninghausen v Glavanics*.[80] The former is a New Zealand Court of Appeal case but its citation with approval in the latter case, as well as others, grants it substantial status in Australian law. It is noteworthy that the former is not mentioned in Conaglen's book at all, while the latter is only briefly cited without reference to these issues. Both these cases found fiduciary duties to exist. Both did so for a variety of reasons, but it is clear that in both of them the court believed that family loyalty and duties (ie non-legal or social duties) could be sufficient to found a fiduciary duty. It is worth extracting the relevant parts of the judgments that make this clear so that the other bases in the cases do not confuse this premise.

The following extracts are from Handley J's judgment in *Brunninghausen*:

> If a fiduciary duty exists here it must arise from the bare facts of the relationship. These include ... their close family association [and] the intervention of the mother-in-law to secure a family reconciliation....[81]
>
> In the present case there was a factual basis for some expectation on the part of the plaintiff. Mrs Lloyd had made known to both men her strong wish that they should settle their business differences so that harmony might be restored in the family. When the plaintiff accepted the defendant's last offer through Mr Abbott he said 'I'll agree to that for the sake of family harmony' and this was neither challenged nor denied.[82]
>
> The plaintiff had no idea of the real value of his shares to the defendant while the latter continued to operate the company, and made no attempt to find out. He would have had no reason to be unhappy if the company had continued to operate the business because he could not compare the true value of his shares with the value he received. In that event the transaction would probably have restored harmony in the family.[83]
>
> ... [T]he family relationship, and the initiative taken by Mrs Lloyd, created a situation in which the plaintiff was 'entitled to expect' that he would not be cheated ...[84]

---

[79] *Coleman v Myers* [1977] 2 NZLR 225 (CA).
[80] *Brunninghausen v Glavanics* [1999] NSWCA 199; (1999) 46 NSWLR 538.
[81] ibid [54].
[82] ibid [102] (citation omitted).
[83] ibid [103].
[84] ibid [104].

These extracts provide authority for the proposition that family relationships can found fiduciary duties when these family relationships result in a family member gaining the trust of other family members to look after their interests. In *Brunninghausen*, it is clear that the plaintiff placed trust in his brother-in-law to do the right thing based on both the close family relationship and the specific intervention of their shared mother-in-law, a family authority figure. It is submitted that because of these, the defendant was under a family duty to look after his brother-in-law's interests. The entitlement to expect not to be cheated referred to by Handley J in the extract is the equivalent of a duty not to cheat on the other party. This entitlement and duty do not refer to the ultimate legal duty. The judge is not saying that the plaintiff is entitled to expect that the court will step in and prevent cheating; rather, he is saying that there is a non-legal expectation and duty. It is this non-legal duty and expectation that the court enforced by the finding of a fiduciary duty.

However, it is important to consider the exact source of this family duty. It is proposed that the family relationship (brothers-in-law) in itself cannot be enough to found a family duty in general. First, in a general western context, this relationship is not considered that close. Secondly, it is doubtful whether a duty exists in business merely based on close family relationships. In contemporary Australia, some may say that it is wrong that an adult sibling (for example) does not act with loyalty to their sibling in a business matter. However, few would contend that such a duty really exists in contemporary morality merely because of the relationship. Serious family financial disputes involving siblings and even parents and children are far too common to sustain such a view. All facts being equal (and average), a person should not expect not to be cheated merely because they are dealing with a sibling let alone a sibling-in-law. Thus, having a technically close family relationship with a person is insufficient to found a family duty in an average Australian context. A 'technically close relationship' means that the relationship is close only because it is between brother, sister, father, mother, etc rather than any statement as to its actual emotional and co-dependent status.

Possibly, the actual substantive closeness of the relationship can provide the foundation of the duty. However, considering the facts of *Brunninghausen*, this is difficult to sustain. It is clear that the relationship that developed between the two brothers-in-law was poor and lacked trust. This was the source of their original dispute. Handley J states: 'The events of 1983 brought to an end the personal trust and confidential relationship between the two men.'[85] The year 1983 was several years before the ultimate dispute in question in the case. Thus, the two men had a nominally semi-close relationship and a substantively poor and untrusting relationship.

---

[85] ibid [9].

What, then, founds the expectation not to be cheated and duty not to cheat? By elimination, the answer to this must be found in the wider family–social context of the case. Notably, the involvement of the mutual mother-in-law and, it is submitted, her relative position of power or status in the family context. It is her involvement in settling the dispute with the two men that must make the difference. The loyalty and duty that they reasonably expected would be owed by each of them to the mother-in-law founds the duty. Her involvement and her position in the family meant that if either man cheated the other, this would be viewed as a transgression against the mother-in-law and the family in general. It is only by focusing on this element that the facts of *Brunninghausen* can be distinguished from numerous other disputes involving close relatives that have not been resolved by the finding of a fiduciary duty because there was no *meritus* underlying duty. The entire family context in this case creates the non-legal duty. The close relationship by itself is insufficient. Further, it is contended that the simple involvement of a parent or a parent-in-law may also not be enough. However, in a situation such as *Brunninghausen*, the duty and expectation arise when a relative such as a parent who objectively holds a position of power or status in a family such as to command the respect and trust of the main protagonists is involved.

The facts and outcome of *Coleman v Myers* support this analysis. In that case, the following extract from Cooke J is salient:

> In the particular circumstances of this case it seems to me obvious that each of the respondent directors did owe a fiduciary duty ... Broadly, the facts giving rise to the duty are the family character of this company; the positions of father and son in the company and the family; [and] their high degree of inside knowledge ... In more detail the facts include the following.
>
> From its early days the company had been very much a family one. For many years the second respondent had been its key figure. Inevitably and justifiably the shareholders must have come to repose confidence in him. The son was his natural successor. The very fact that he was his father's son must have been an advantage for him in dealing with shareholders. ...[86]
>
> The position of the second respondent has to be considered separately. That he was in a fiduciary position I have no doubt. Not only was there his role in the company and in the family and the fact that the proposed sale was to his son. As well he took an active part in the negotiations, first with his sisters and their representatives, later with the Cornwall Park trustees and the Colemans. ... His voice could well have been especially influential.[87]

From the judgment of Casey J:

---

[86] *Coleman v Myers* (n 79) 330.
[87] ibid 351.

I have no doubt that in this tightly-held family company, both directors owed a fiduciary duty to the appellants and to the other shareholders. It must have been clear to Mr AD Myers particularly that they were reposing trust and confidence in him, from their discussions and the inquiries they made. I have no doubt Sir Kenneth Myers was in everyone's eyes the head of the family group and its associated shareholders, whom they respected and trusted to look after their personal interests in the management of the company. ... In such a family situation the latter, as managing director, would inevitably have been expected to continue the care and prudence displayed by his father for the welfare of family and associates, notwithstanding the fact that he was bidding for their shares. ... Add to this special relationship their exclusive knowledge of facts and intentions affecting the shareholders in relation to the offer and there can be only one conclusion. These two directors clearly owed a fiduciary duty...[88]

The first extract from Cooke J's judgment clearly places the focus on the father's position within the family hierarchy as a leader to be both respected and trusted to look after the family's interests as a whole. This position of respect and trust is transposed to the son because he is his son and would be viewed as a natural successor to his father in the role. Casey J's judgment also emphasizes the father's position of leadership in the family and how this generated the other family members' trust. In addition, it is emphasized that the son was seen as the inheritor of the father's leadership position and the trust of the others. It is clear in these judgments that the court is placing fundamental emphasis on the family duty owed by both the father and the son in the context of this family situation and this duty is the one that is being enforced by the finding of a fiduciary duty.

E. Finding Enforceable Family Duties

The presented point is critical to understanding *Coleman v Myers*. The often-stated premise that it was a tightly held family company is insufficient to merit the outcome that eventuated alone. If 'tightly held family company' means simply that all or majority ownership of a company is in the hands of a group of relatives, it is doubtful that a fiduciary duty would be found. This would be analogous to the point made earlier that simply being relatives is not enough to found a duty.

For a 'family company' to lead to these duties, it has to be a family company in the sense that the entire formal legal ownership and control structure can be seen to be subsumed by an overriding non-legal familial structure with its own hierarchy of leadership, powers, obligations, and duties. In *Coleman v Myers*, the

[88] ibid 371.

business was such a family company and the wider family group members understood and trusted the family leadership structure and assumed that their 'correct interests' in accordance with this structure would be supported by the family structure and its duties on family members. When the leaders of the family sought to take advantage of the formal legal position to defeat the substantive family position for their own benefit, the court decided to support the family duties, by using fiduciary doctrine to formalize and protect it. In this way, it did what the chancellor did in the late fourteenth century when he supported the honourable understandings of the uses.[89]

As with the analysis of *Brunninghausen*, a key issue in *Coleman v Myers* is whether the non-legal familial structure of obligations and rights exists in the first place. It is proposed that, in contemporary western society, such a structure cannot be assumed from the basic nominal family relationships but must be shown to exist in the case at hand. It cannot be assumed because often it does not exist, despite a business or investment being in family hands. This inconsistency of incidence is no doubt why courts may be reluctant to find fiduciary duties simply based on familial duties. In addition, courts may find policy objections to supporting family hierarchies even when duties do exist. After all, the individualization of western society is intimately related to the growth of the state and formal law. Enforcing non-legal duties may be viewed as oppressive of individual rights. However, notwithstanding all this, the cases just reviewed show the law's ability to support non-legal duties arising from family.

The existence of these duties in mainstream contemporary society and business and their potential recognition at law is resultingly a difficult area. It has already been stated that family-related duties cannot be assumed simply from nominal family relationships. However, it is submitted that these nominal relationships would open the mind of a reasonable person to the possibility that the family hierarchy and duties may exist. It is suggested that the fact that the parties in *Brunninghausen* and *Coleman v Myers* were relatives was likely to have shaped the courts' acceptance of the existence of the non-legal hierarchy and duties. Thus, while the relationships alone did not result in them finding the duty (as such relationships are often not accompanied by the relevant duties), it is doubtful that they would have found the duty if the relationships did not exist. Ultimately, the courts found that non-legal duties did, in fact, exist. This is an objective conclusion related to social institutions and not a simple subjective moral judgement of the decision makers about right and wrong.

The legal fiduciary duties are founded upon social duties and these are objectively identified by the court. It is these social institutions that provide the objective basis of equity and are the reason that it does not amount to arbitrary justice. When

---

[89] Maitland (n 75) 492.

scholars such as Hudson and various courts attempted to argue that conscience is objectively determined, they were working on their strong understanding that right and wrong exist and are not something inherently individual and subjective. A full historical and sociological mind knows that this must be true. Those who believe that duties only come from formal law fail to appreciate what a lot of formal law is based upon or overestimate the role of law in society. The language and study of social institutions allows a strong theoretical- and evidenced-based way of substantiating the objectivity of conscience. Thus, Lord Browne-Wilkinson's strong restatement of conscience underpinning constructive trusts in *Westdeutsche Landesbank Girozentrale v Islington LBC*[90] can be appreciated as an objective rational approach far away from palm trees and irrational concepts.

There are, in addition, further ways of expressing and developing this idea that are noteworthy. Consideration of language and the great developments in the area of linguistics over the past fifty years is illuminating. Notably, it is abundantly clear that language and communication is never value- and ideology-free.[91] This applies to all language, speech, correspondence, text, and statute. There cannot be an objective, scientific meaning that is found only in the grammar. Certain language and actions that constitute communications are more so in evidence of this. For this reason, understanding what people meant and how they were understood and forcing them to keep to their obligations can never be a matter of simply looking at the objective meaning of words. Likewise, the establishment of economic efficiency is not about a hypothetical objective interpretation, it is about people being made to carry out their obligations as they have been understood by others around them and those involved. This might be seen as justice. The role of equity, whether it acknowledges it or not, is to engage in this wider interpretation of communication and its full context and circumstances. This includes social assumptions and values. This is where justice is to be found. Terms such as conscience have a strong place here. A contemporary linguistics paradigm would call this discourse analysis.

For justice and economic efficiency in the world of complex human communication, the law needs to have the facility to engage in a wider inquiry. However, as this is always a more 'messy' and nuanced business than simple words, it needs to be understood as 'special'. This impacts its position as precedent in the context of the rule of law. Does this make equity subjective? The answer must be no. The belief in objectivity in language is faulty to start with. However, equity does not enter into a rarefied world of palm tree justice. Rather it better inquires into the situation and the communications to understand the true nature of peoples' commitments and obligations. This is done in an objective manner. It is not the opening of the door to 'palm tree justice' and it is not making allowances for unreasonable people. It is

---

[90] *Westdeutsche Landesbank Girozentrale v Islington LBC* [1996] AC 669 (HL).
[91] Ron Scollon, Suzanne Wong Scollon, and Rodney H Jones, *Intercultural Communication: A Discourse Approach* (3rd edn, Wiley-Blackwell 2012).

best viewed as a form of critical discourse analysis even though the term did not exist for most of the existence of equity.

VII. Conclusion

Returning, then, to unjust enrichment, one must query how 'legal' enrichment can be found to be unjust in any other manner than that discussed in relation to equity. This chapter has looked at how the great appeal of unjust enrichment was purported to be its rational approach in the face of equity's irrational, subjective, and moral approach. Such an approach was thought to be unacceptable to the modern rational world that saw little place for things such as religion or morals in law and especially law dealing with economic matters. Unjust enrichment purported to resolve the issue by providing a rational objective approach to understanding (or replacing) equitable approaches. However, the critique of equity as subjective does not stand up. Equity's supporters have long argued that underlying concepts such as conscience are objective and not subjective. Using sociological approaches, this chapter has shown that this is indeed the case. Linguistics undeniably supports this proposition as well. It is only through a social value and discourse filter that language is given a rational interpretation. This is diametrically opposed to the idea that language is objective and rational and only ideas such as conscience make it irrational. Thus, the problem of palm tree justice may never have existed. However, it would be beneficial for equity to be more conscious of social institutions as a concept in order to better give reasons. Unjust enrichment's reliance on a concept such as unjust, interestingly means that it is in a very similar position to equity. It never solved a problem as the problem did not exist. However, if the problem did exist, unjust enrichment necessarily imported it in its own necessarily moral approach to determining something as unjust when it was legal.

PART III
THEORY

7
Faute de Mieux

Robert Stevens

I. Introduction

Why did the idea of 'unjust enrichment' prove so successful? This is a puzzle for those who consider that the judicial adoption in England of an omnibus 'unjust enrichment' framework, as dispositive of litigated cases, to have been a disaster.[1] This is especially so given that there is a large and long-standing body of work sceptical as to the utility of 'unjust enrichment'.[2] Indeed, it is unclear if there were a headcount of academics working in the area whether there would be a majority for or against.

Before turning to the main topic, the reasons why the product of the sceptics has not sold well in the market of ideas, it is worth reflecting on why 'unjust enrichment' found so many ready buyers.

First, it offered us a simple structure for understanding all, or almost all, of private law. Some authors claimed that the entire law of obligations could be divided into three compartments: contract, torts and other wrongs, and unjust enrichment.[3] This threefold division of 'events' seemed to map on to a threefold division of 'responses': making good expectations, compensating for losses, reversing gains. The third is presented as similar to, and as unified as, the other more familiar two.

Secondly, in his *Introduction to the Law of Restitution*, Peter Birks presented us with a straightforward method for understanding 'unjust enrichment'.[4] Instead of the pragmatic casuistic ordering of the American Restatements or *Goff & Jones*, a fourfold structure was proposed. Was the defendant enriched? Was the enrichment at the plaintiff's expense? Was the enrichment unjust? Is there a defence?

---

[1] See eg Robert Stevens, 'The Unjust Enrichment Disaster' (2018) 134 LQR 574; Robert Stevens, *The Laws of Restitution* (OUP 2023).
[2] Most prominent is that of Steve Hedley: Steve Hedley, 'Unjust Enrichment as the Basis of Restitution—An Overworked Concept' (1985) 5 LS 56; Steve Hedley, *Restitution: Its Division and Ordering* (Sweet & Maxwell 2001). See also Joachim Dietrich, *Restitution: A New Perspective* (Federation Press 1998); Ian Jackman, *The Varieties of Restitution* (2nd edn, Federation Press 2017); Peter Jaffey, *The Nature and Scope of Restitution* (Hart Publishing 2000); Peter G Watts, '"Unjust Enrichment"—the Potion that Induces Well-Meaning Sloppiness of Thought' (2016) 69 CLP 289; Charlie Webb, *Reason and Restitution: A Theory of Unjust Enrichment* (OUP 2016).
[3] See eg Warren A Seavey and Austin W Scott, 'Restitution' (1938) 54 LQR 29, 31; AS Burrows, 'Contract, Tort and Restitution—A Satisfactory Division or Not?' (1983) 99 LQR 217.
[4] Peter Birks, *An Introduction to the Law of Restitution* (rev edn, OUP 1989).

Birks sought to show how the apparent chaos of single instances could be reduced to these straightforward issues that corresponded with their meaning in everyday language.

For practitioners this proved attractive. This area of law is rarely covered in law degree programmes, and so it is natural to reach gratefully for a simple way of ordering the chaos and quickly making sense of it.

In part, this must be counted as a success. Although I may disagree with the current editors of *Goff & Jones* as to the nature, structure, and content of the subject, their approach, following Birks, is clear and understandable. As a result, I can always use their book to find the relevant legal materials on any issue I need an answer to. Even if my views as to what the law is and ought to be differ from theirs, I know where they will put the relevant statutes and cases. This means that I can find both them and the authors' discussion of the details.

For academics, it was seductive. The paradigm of what is thought of as academic research is that of the scientist, where the goal is to achieve discoveries and breakthroughs. In some areas of the legal academy something similar is achievable (a legal historian discovering a new source, for example) but not in long-established areas of private law that are not subject to external change. What was apparently offered was a new area, untilled by previous generations, and a way of understanding it.

Further, it provided a structure for assessing the law, and for calls for it to be changed in order to 'treat like cases alike'. This was particularly so in relation to rules originating in the equity jurisdiction, which often appear to differ from those at common law.

As a field, unjust enrichment was enticing not just because of its relative novelty, but also because Birks offered a way of discussing and assessing the law without needing to appeal to either the instrumental reasoning of 'law and economics', so fashionable in the 1980s, or to any commitment to or understanding of any other theory of justice. It was the archetype of lawyer's law. Judges could be criticized for failing to identify 'unjust factors' or for failing to draw the analogy between knowing receipt of trust property and the common law's action for money had and received, without the need to engage in any deep theory.

The product of the sceptics, inevitably, does not have these attractive features. We are generally offered diversity, with no overarching theory. Defenders of equity's distinctiveness often appeal to its history. But 'we've always done things this way' will, overtime and without more, always lose to a theory of how things ought to be. It takes a theory to beat a theory and the sceptics often either purported to be anti-theory, or to offer only a partial one.

Thirdly, it seemed to gain support from the loose comparative law monoglot English-speaking lawyers are capable of. Is it not true that legal systems of both the French and German traditions recognize a law of unjust enrichment?

Unfortunately, the French 'enrichissement sans cause' covers *much* less legal terrain than does the area that 'unjust enrichment' is claimed to explain within the common law. The French doctrine does not cover, for example, payments of money that are not due, supposedly the central case in the common law.

Although it is true that s 812 of the German Bürgerliches Gesetzbuch on its face presents us with a unified principle of unjustified enrichment, this too covers less ground than was encompassed by either *Goff & Jones* or the United States' Restatements. In 1934, aged twenty-nine, the Austrian, Walter Wilburg (who in my view is the most important and original thinker in the area that there has been) proposed a fourfold scheme for dividing up the general enrichment provision.[5] This has become generally accepted in Germany, Austria, and Switzerland. It is not, however, best understood as a clarification of the general provision, but its refutation.[6]

Fourthly, it is impossible to ignore the importance of individuals in the success of the idea. The proponents of the idea in England have been amongst the most important, able, and articulate academic lawyers of their generation(s). Robert Goff, appointed to the High Court in 1975, and a Law Lord in 1986, retiring in 1998. Gareth Jones, Downing Professor of the Laws of England from 1974 to 1998.

Most important for the subject, however, was probably Birks.[7] To those who never met Peter, it is difficult to convey his charisma and ability to inspire others. The Oxford BCL seminars on the subject he ran trained the best to think in a particular way, and to go forth and spread the gospel. Leading cases often feature, at least as junior counsel pulling the strings, those who are using his framework of ideas. He was also a clear and innovative writer, coining memorable labels for explanations of the doctrine that were then picked up by other authors and, sometimes, the courts: 'unjust factors'; 'subjective devaluation'; 'incontrovertible benefit'; 'interceptive subtraction'; 'proprietary base'; 'restitution for wrongs'. This putting of old wine into new, and (hopefully) better, bottles is a technique others have copied, usually with much less success.[8]

Birks had many important students but the two most significant were Andrew Burrows and James Edelman. Both have made the transition from academic life to the apex courts of their jurisdictions. Lord Burrows is more of a pragmatist than was Birks, writing more directly for practitioners, and being more reluctant

---

[5] Walter Wilburg, *Die Lehre von der ungerechtfertigten Bereicherung: nach österreichischem und deutschem Recht* (Leuschner & Lubensky 1934) 5, popularized by Ernst von Caemmerer, 'Bereicherung und unerlaubte Handlung' in Hans Dölle and Max Rheinstein (eds), *Festschrift für Ernst Rabel*, vol 1 (JCB Mohr 1954) 333: claims to reverse a performance rendered without legal ground (*Leistungskondiktion*), claims based upon the performance of another's obligation (*Rückgriffskondiktion*), claims based upon the interference with another's right (*Eingriffskondiktion*), claims by a bona fide possessor who has made unauthorized improvements of another's property (*Verwendungskondiktion*).

[6] cf Nils Jansen, Chapter 12 in this volume.

[7] See also Sagi Peari, Chapter 4 in this volume.

[8] I have been guilty of it, eg 'persistent rights' and 'substitutive damages'.

to emphasize any change of view. Justice Edelman made the move to the bench earlier, and has now been part of so many important decisions of the High Court that his role in the popularization of 'unjust enrichment' is a more minor part of his career. The importance of the group of proponents of 'unjust enrichment', and their connections, probably partially explains why 'unjust enrichment' has had more impact in England than in jurisdictions such as those of the United States.

Although those who have followed Birks often disagree with many of his claims at a micro level (most significantly, his late career abandonment of 'unjust factors' as an organizing idea), at a macro level there has been remarkable cohesion around the scope, structure, and nature of the subject. It is a feature of the academics working in this group that they have shown a deep knowledge of, and commitment to, the work of courts. Birks, for example, had an encyclopaedic knowledge of every case in the common law world. This has then created a feedback loop between the academics and the judges, personified by Burrows and Edelman. Their opponents, by contrast, have shown little agreement amongst themselves as to what the law should look like, and often discuss it at a theoretical level unhelpful for those wishing to have advice upon, or on how to decide, litigated cases. (This first section of the chapter is guilty of the same.) In the main, with the exception of Burrows's textbook,[9] the proponents of 'unjust enrichment' have often ignored the arguments of the sceptics, broadly starting from the assumption that there just is a law of 'unjust enrichment' that needs to be mapped out.

II. Three (Partial) Alternatives

A. The Options

It is impossible, without writing a book on the topic, to engage adequately with *all* of the alternative accounts to aspects of 'unjust enrichment' as an explanatory idea that have been proposed. Some authors of these account are therefore bound to be disappointed by what follows, for which I apologize.

The most common tactic has been to push 'the law of restitution' into other, more familiar, areas of law.[10] Here I shall discuss the three most common. First, attempts to explain the plaintiff's right to restitution of the mistaken payment of money, or other transfer of 'property', as based upon a pre-existing property right of the plaintiff.[11] Secondly, seeing the right to restitution of work done at another's request in terms of an expanded law of contract.[12] Thirdly, those which have seen

---

[9] Andrew Burrows, *The Law of Restitution* (3rd edn, OUP 2011) ch 2.
[10] See eg Hedley, *Restitution: Its Division and Ordering* (n 2) 224. See also Steve Hedley, Chapter 14 in this volume; Peter Jaffey, Chapter 11 in this volume.
[11] An example is Hedley, Chapter 14 in this volume, Section IV.B.
[12] ibid Section IV.C.

the solution in compensation for loss because of 'injurious reliance' or 'unjust sacrifice'. All three are problematic but contain elements of truth.

The central substantive claim is that these attempts to make do with *fewer* reasons for restitution, is exactly the wrong move. Restitution is, in fact, justified by a diverse variety of different reasons, which are neither reducible into other more familiar categories nor into one uber category of 'unjust enrichment'.

B. Property Theories

1. The problems

An early formulation of the idea that 'property law' could explain part of the area was propounded by Professor Stoljar. Stoljar had proposed that where a payment had been made by mistake, the payor had a right to restitution because he retained the right to what had been transferred.[13] Unfortunately, this is, on its face, obviously unsatisfactory as a proposition, as in most cases of mistaken payments of cash, the right is transferred not retained.

A more sophisticated 'property law' account is that of Professor Webb. His statement of his thesis is as follows:

> Where the law recognizes me as having an interest in determining the use and disposition of some item or advantage, it thereby recognizes a reason for restitution where that item or advantage is received by you without my consent.[14]

As a definition of 'property', this works reasonably well where the 'item or advantage' is a physical thing such as cash. My right has an object (here a thing) which can be received without my right having been transferred. Where my right has been transferred along with possession of the thing (as it usually will be in cases of mistaken payments of cash), we might say that the reason for my having the initial right with respect to the defendant can persist, even if the right itself is transferred for other reasons.[15] The transfer may be said to be occurring in order to protect third parties. Where my transfer is by mistake (or under duress or undue influence), my interest in choosing freely how and when to dispose of what is mine may be said to be vitiated. The reason which justified my initial entitlement with respect to the defendant thereby continues and justifies the obligation to make restitution.

As an explanation, this works best in relation to transfers of rights to things. Rights to things, which includes cash, are exigible against all others, including, before transfer, the transferee. It is therefore understandable how reasons that

---

[13] SJ Stoljar, *The Law of Quasi-Contract* (2nd edn, Law Book Co 1989), especially 5–10, 113, 250.
[14] Charlie Webb, *Reason and Restitution: A Theory of Unjust Enrichment* (OUP 2016) 85.
[15] The same thought is found in Peter Jaffey, Chapter 11 in this volume.

justified a prior duty to the plaintiff transferor that the defendant transferee owed could, after the transferor's mistaken transfer, generate a new duty to make restitution owed to the transferor.

However, 'property' on this account is intended to encompass all transferable rights (not all of which can sensibly be said to have as their object a separate 'item or advantage'). Where the anterior right that is transferred was not exigible against the transferee (as receivables are not), it is harder to understand how or why the reasons justifying a duty owed by someone else (the debtor) could be thought sufficient to justify the imposition of a duty upon the defendant. Without more, it is also difficult to understand how the payor's mistakenly causing the payee to acquire a right against someone else could justify the imposition of a duty upon the payee to him.

Further, and more fundamentally, payments do not require the payor to have lost, or the payee to have obtained, any 'property right', however loosely defined, at all. Two examples:

> P mistakenly thinks he owes D $100. P asks his brother, X to pay on P's behalf. X does so in cash.

Here it is X who has transferred his right to the cash to D but it is only P who has a claim against D.

Or:

> P mistakenly thinks he owes D $100. Sharing the same mistake, D requests that P pays the money to his sister Y, to whom he wishes to make a gift of the sum. P pays Y in cash.

Here it is Y who has received the right to the cash, but it is only D who is susceptible to a claim.

We could combine these examples, so that P loses no right and D acquires none, but the only claim would be between the parties to the payment: P and D. By focusing on any property right transfer, property theories give the wrong result: giving claims between the wrong parties, both as a matter of law and our intuitions as to what it should be. To whom each party is rendering the performance of payment is not determined by the parties (if any) between whom any right has been transferred. As a matter of practice, this issue most commonly arises in relation to bank transfers. The payor may have no right at all at the start of the story, as where an account is overdrawn and any further lending by the bank is at its discretion. Similarly, the payee may receive none, as where payment is made into an overdrawn account.[16]

---

[16] The claim by Peter Jaffey, ibid, that the bank's customer *must* initially have a 'property right' because there is a claim where a payment is made by the account holder by mistake, assumes the theory to be true and then distorts the law to make it accord with it.

A modern example of a court confusing who the correct parties to the action for restitution were, is the decision of the High Court of Australia in *Australian Financial Services and Leasing Pty Ltd v Hills Industries Ltd*.[17]

The plaintiff was a finance company and the defendant suppliers of commercial equipment. A group of companies controlled by a fraudster (the 'fraudulent group') created a number of false invoices purporting to show the purchase of equipment from the defendant. The plaintiff agreed to purchase the equipment from the fraudulent group, and to lease it back to them. It paid the defendant the amounts owing on the false invoices in order to buy the equipment from the fraudulent group. Upon receipt, the defendant, ignorant of the fraud, applied the payment in discharge of the fraudulent group's debts to them, and abandoned efforts to pursue enforcement proceedings against them or their directors. The defendant argued that this constituted a change of position providing a defence. The plaintiff contended that a mere book entry, which could be reversed, could not amount to a change of position, the debts discharged were valueless in any event, and that the prospects of recovery from the fraudulent group or its directors that had been foregone was of negligible value because of their inability to pay them.

The High Court accepted the somewhat speculative 'change of position' defence, but the result that the claim failed should have been reached at an earlier point in the analysis.

The plaintiff had made the payment in performance of their contract with the fraudulent group to buy the (non-existent) equipment. Although there had been a bank transfer between the plaintiff and defendant, the performance of the plaintiff had been rendered to their counterparty. The correct defendant in any claim for restitution of that performance was the fraudulent group at whose request and for whom the payment had been made. No claim in addition should have succeeded against the actual (solvent) defendants, who had received the payment as being made on behalf of the fraudulent group. The facts were materially identical to the classic *Aiken v Short*,[18] where the claim also failed. There were two transactions not one: the payment from the plaintiff to the fraudulent group and by the fraudulent group to the defendant. We should be suspicious of reasoning where the obviously correct result is only reached by applying a defence of change of position of extremely recent coinage. How would our predecessors, who did not have this weapon in their armoury, have reached the right answer? The High Court's expansive approach to that defence has the potential to distort the law where the defendant is the payee, and so the correct party to the action.

---

[17] *Australian Financial Services and Leasing Pty Ltd v Hills Industries Ltd* [2014] HCA 14; (2014) 253 CLR 560. Compare the High Court's earlier, and clearly correct, decision in *Lumbers v W Cook Builders Pty Ltd* [2008] HCA 27; (2008) 232 CLR 635.
[18] *Aiken v Short* (1856) 1 H & N 210; 156 ER 1180.

Finally, because it is a feature of Professor Webb's account that it is divorced from the plaintiff retaining any right to what has been received by the defendant, or any other connection between plaintiff and defendant, it leads to overinclusive results. For example:

> P mistakenly pays X $100 in cash. X delighted by what he believes to be a gift, uses the cash to pay Oxfam $100.

Because of the delivery with intent to pass title, X has acquired title to the cash. P has made no payment to Oxfam and, unless we resort to equity, there should be no claim, contrary to at least Professor Webb's version of the 'proprietary' thesis.

2. Importance

Although payments do not necessarily involve a 'property' transfer by the plaintiff to the defendant in any meaningful sense, they do differ from the provision of services in two significant ways. First, payments are actions that payor and payee necessarily do together, it being impossible to pay someone without either their personal acceptance or an acceptance by their agent for receipt (usually their bank). Secondly, payments are legal events. Without a system of rules, as in the game of Monopoly, 'payments' are meaningless. Cleaning shoes, repairing bridges, singing songs are all things that can be done without another's cooperation and without a legal system at all. Payments cannot be made without either.

That a payment is a legal event (as is the grant of an easement, a declaration of trust, or the alteration of a share register) is relevant to the law's willingness to reverse it where it has occurred without justification. The law requiring the reversal of a mistaken payment of money that was not due is much easier to justify than requiring the mistaken cleaning of another's windows to be paid for. This is so even if each may sometimes, but not always, leave another better off as a result. That something has *legally* happened between these parties that is without justification provides the law itself with a good reason for its correction.

This is the central insight of 'property theories' of restitution. They rightly draw a divide between claims for the reversal of payments and 'pure' services, claims for restitution of the latter requiring some further justificatory work. My cleaning your windows by mistake does not, without more, justify the law reversing what has happened. Nothing, legally, has happened that requires justification. That the law reverses a payment made by me, and accepted by you to which you were not entitled, is more readily understandable.

'Enrichment' theory wrongly supposes that the difference between the categories is constituted by whether the 'service' is enriching, some services not being enriching at all, whereas payments supposedly always are. Unfortunately, this is (at the least) doubly misleading. If I clean your windows thereby saving you an expense that you would otherwise have incurred, this should, without more, give rise to no claim.[19] By contrast, the homeowner's request that the work be done, or their 'free acceptance' may justify a claim, but this is wholly unrelated to whether or not they are enriched. If, at my request, you do work on *your* land that leaves me in no way better off, I must pay for the market value of the work, regardless of how much, if anything, I might have paid someone else to do the work. The request or free acceptance cannot establish that the defendant is thereby enriched. Birks's argument that the defendant who freely accepts or requests that work be done is thereby barred from denying that they are enriched, adopts a starting assumption (that services rendered are *ipso facto* always enriching, subject to the defendant objecting) that is unwarranted.

Enrichment proponents sometimes attempt to meet objections of this kind by arguing that 'enrichment' is a 'term of art'[20] or that it has an 'objective'[21] meaning, unrelated to the extent to which the defendant is, as a matter of fact, better off. This defensive move, in trying to win the local battle, means the war is lost. The fact of enrichment is no longer of normative significance. Other facts, misleadingly travelling under that label, are doing the work. As such, we have not improved upon 'quasi-contract' (indeed, it is worse, as nobody has taken that label seriously as dispositive of anything for at least a century).

If 'enrichment' is a normative rather than a factual matter, then the scope of the subject becomes unclear. Almost all claims can be asserted to be concerned with 'enrichment' in a normative sense. If I commit a civil wrong, whether a tort or a breach of contract, I have 'taken' a liberty with respect to you that I ought not to have had. I am, in a sense, normatively better off. Indeed, there are those who argue that there is an 'enrichment' in this sense when someone makes use of another's thing. The non-payment of a debt will lead to the debtor being better off. Is the action to recover usefully seen as an attempt to anticipate this enrichment?

The provision of services may in *some* contexts be legal, and not just factual, events. One example is the group of cases where one party's legal obligation is conditional upon an ongoing state of affairs, and another through his work removes that condition. If, for example, a public body is under a legal duty to provide a service (house the homeless, cure the sick, repair the roads) and another party does the necessary work, thereby removing the condition of the obligation and thereby

---

[19] But see Mitchell McInnes, Chapter 16 in this volume, n 87. *Sanderson v Campsall* 2000 BCSC 583; *Gould v Gould Estate (Trustee of)* 2009 BCSC 1528; and *Serbian League of Canada v Stojanovich* 2020 ONSC 105 do not involve strangers coming on to the defendant's property and improving it without the defendant's acceptance of the work. *Hertz Corp v McLaren Collision Centre* 2016 ONSC 1327, in allowing a claim against a party other than the one with whom the repairer had contracted, is wrong: see *Cahill v Hall* 161 Mass 512; 37 NE 573 (1894) (Holmes J); *Tappenden v Artus* [1964] 2 QB 185 (CA); *Brown & Davis Ltd v Galbraith* [1972] 1 WLR 997 (CA).

[20] Charles Mitchell, Paul Mitchell, and Stephen Watterson, *Goff & Jones: The Law of Unjust Enrichment* (9th edn, Sweet & Maxwell 2016) [4-03].

[21] James Edelman, 'The Meaning of Loss and Enrichment' in Robert Chambers, Charles Mitchell, and James Penner (eds), *Philosophical Foundations of the Law of Unjust Enrichment* (OUP 2009) 211, 223–41.

discharging it, if the intervener is not a volunteer (because, for example, mistaken as to whether they were the party properly so obliged or acting under moral compulsion in an emergency) they ought to have a claim to reimbursement. We are seeking to go forward to the world where the party properly subject to the legal obligation bears it. Such a claim is not, however, quantified by reference to the (fact) of enrichment. Hard-pressed public bodies, at least in the UK, rarely run a surplus. If, as a matter of fact, they are saved the expense of housing, curing, or repairing in one instance, the party who will, at the end of the day, be enriched is another person further down the priority queue who would not otherwise have been assisted. This is, however, irrelevant. It is the legal event (the discharge of a legal obligation properly borne by the defendant) rather than the factual state of affairs (an enrichment, the expense that would otherwise have been incurred) that is significant.

Closer to mistaken payment cases are services provided in discharge of an obligation owed to the defendant, where the obligation is subsequently set aside. An illustration is the classic, and still important, decision of *Whittington v Seale-Hayne*.[22] The plaintiff, who bred prize poultry, agreed to enter into a lease on the basis of an innocent misrepresentation by the defendant's agent that the premises were in a 'good sanitary condition'. As part of the agreement, the plaintiff covenanted to carry out such works as were required by the local authority. Unfortunately, the water supply was poisoned so that the tenant's manager became ill and most of the birds died. The defendant agreed to rescission, and to pay £20 for the rent and works carried out under the lease. The plaintiff claimed for the full loss they suffered as a result of entering into the deal, including the loss of stock, removal, and medical expenses, and the profits they would have made. These additional losses were denied. Farwell J did so on the basis that to award these additional sums would be to turn a claim for an indemnity into one for damages. An innocent misrepresentation was not, and where the defendant can show he had reasonable grounds for believing the statement to be true, still is not,[23] wrongful, and cannot support a claim for damages. However, the expenditure that the plaintiff had been *obliged* to incur was properly recoverable.

As the work was done in performance of a legal obligation, that the law itself now says should not have been required, this provides a good reason for the law to require its reversal.

Even more obviously legal in their subject matter are constructive and resulting trusts. For example:

---

[22] *Whittington v Seale-Hayne* (1900) 82 LT 49 (HC). See also *Newbigging v Adam* (1886) 34 ChD 582 (CA).
[23] Misrepresentation Act 1967 (UK), s 2(1).

As part of a joint venture agreement between P and D, P agrees to purchase title to land from X, title to be conveyed to D. After conveyance is completed, P rescinds the joint venture agreement because of innocent misrepresentations made by D.

The right to the land D has acquired is not one that was ever vested in P. It was acquired by D through P's performance. The right has been acquired from P without good reason, because the contract that justified it has now been avoided. D ought to be under a duty to P not to use the right so acquired for his own benefit.[24] A trust.

The subject matter of the resulting trust is the title to the land. The value of that right, if any, or the degree to which D is or is not better off as a result of the conveyance is irrelevant. As always with trusts, the subject matter of the duty of the trustee are rights vested in him.

In all of these examples, our concern is not with a factual event or state of affairs that operates as a free-standing source of a new legal obligation. In none of them is the subject matter of any claim the *fact* of the defendant's enrichment. Rather, the law is seeking correct a *legal* event that has occurred.

In each of these kinds of case, the restitutionary response is ancillary to, and created by, another legal event. These kinds of restitutionary claims are therefore quite different from contractual obligations, or the rights arising from taking possession of a tangible thing, which are independent of other legal rules.

C. Contractual Theories

1. Contractual claims for *quantum meruit*

Another thing 'property' theories get right is that they do not seek an overarching theory for all the material gathered together by the American Restatements or *Goff & Jones*. Clearly, where the claim is to the value of a service provided, 'property' theories provide no assistance. What can explain them, outside the narrow class of case represented by *Whittington v Seale-Hayne*?

One approach, again proposed by Stoljar, is that *all* claims for a *quantum meruit* are properly contractual.[25] Others, such as Professor Steve Hedley, have, at least in part, supported this idea, by claiming that it can do the heavy lifting if a more 'modern' expansive approach is taken to what constitutes a contract.[26]

Quantum meruit in English means 'as much as he deserves'. The label does not refer to any reason why the plaintiff may be deserving of anything. As a matter of

---

[24] cf *Dyer v Dyer* (1788) 2 Cox 92, 93; 30 ER 42, 43; *Sayre v Hughes* (1868) LR 5 Eq 376, 380.
[25] Stoljar (n 13) 187–90, 232–35. Compare Steve Hedley, *A Critical Introduction to Restitution* (Butterworths 2001) 30–54.
[26] See eg Hedley, ibid 49.

usage, it is incorrect therefore to refer to a claim in *quantum meruit*. Rather, a plaintiff claims for *quantum meruit*.

Undoubtedly, some claims for *quantum meruit* are based upon a contractual obligation to pay. Section 15(1) of the Supply of Goods and Services Act 1982 (UK) provides:[27]

> Where, under a relevant contract for the supply of a service, the consideration for the service is not determined by the contract, left to be determined in a manner agreed by the contract or determined by the course of dealing between the parties, there is an implied term that the party contracting with the supplier will pay a reasonable charge.

We find the same rule in the context of sale in s 8 of the Sale of Goods Act 1979 (UK):

> (1) The price in a contract of sale may be fixed by the contract, or may be left to be fixed in a manner agreed by the contract, or may be determined by the course of dealing between the parties.
> (2) Where the price is not determined as mentioned in sub-section (1) above the buyer must pay a reasonable price.

The action for the reasonable price or charge is one to enforce the (implied) primary obligation to pay, just as it would be if the amount owing were a liquidated sum expressly fixed by the parties. In the early cases, *some* implied contractual obligations to pay are clearly fictitious as there is no discernible agreement between the parties, but that does not mean that all are. These statutory provisions reflect the position at common law, the leading cases concerning agents' commissions.[28]

Illustrative of a contractual action is *Way v Latilla*.[29] Latilla asked Way to obtain for him information concerning gold-mining concessions in West Africa. The information enabled Latilla and his associates to acquire such concessions, which proved immensely valuable. There were long negotiations as to Way obtaining a share in the concessions, but these never reached a conclusion. Way brought a claim for remuneration calculated as a share of the concession.

Lord Atkin stated:

> But, while there is, therefore, no concluded contract as to the remuneration, it is plain that there existed between the parties a contract of employment under which Mr Way was engaged to do work for Mr Latilla in circumstances which clearly indicated that the work was not to be gratuitous.[30]

---

[27] See also Consumer Rights Act 2015 (UK), s 51 which seems to be identical, adding nothing.
[28] See eg *British Bank for Foreign Trade Ltd v Novinex Ltd* [1949] 1 KB 623 (CA).
[29] *Way v Latilla* [1937] 3 All ER 759 (HL).
[30] ibid 763.

Lord Wright stated:

> There was, I think, no justification for making for the parties ... a contract which they did not make themselves. It is, however, clear, on the evidence, that the work was done by the appellant and accepted by the respondent on the basis that some remuneration was to be paid to the appellant by the respondent. There was thus an implied promise by the respondent to pay on a *quantum meruit*, that is, to pay what the services were worth.[31]

The court therefore applied the rule now found in s 15 of the Supply of Goods and Services Act 1982 (UK).

The significance of the case is not that there was a (contractual) basis for recovery, which at the time was uncontroversial and not the issue in dispute, but rather the method of its quantification. The House of Lords rejected Latilla's argument that the calculation should be assessed on the basis of a fee for the work, a figure of 500 guineas, and which had been awarded by the Court of Appeal. The evidence of the parties themselves was that this was not what they had agreed. Rather, the parties had intended that Way would be paid on a participation basis, the calculation of which they had not settled. It was the parties' intention that he be reimbursed his expenses if the project was unsuccessful, but that if the concessions were obtained he would receive a proportion of their value as a reward. The court assessed this reasonable reward figure at £5,000.[32]

Both the result and reasoning of the court are only explicable in contractual terms. The court concluded that the agreement between the parties was not just that a fee would be paid for the work, but rather that, if successful, Way would be paid a reasonable sum based upon participation in the concession. It was this figure that the court then set, rather than the market value of the work done. That the agreement was enforceable would also have been important if either party had sought damages for breach.

Although *Way v Latilla* is sometimes claimed to be an action in 'unjust enrichment',[33] on any fair reading of the case, it was not. It is not a condition of an enforceable contract that the price has been reduced by the parties to a liquidated sum.[34]

2. Non-contractual claims for *quantum meruit*

To claim, however, as Stoljar did, that all claims for a *quantum meruit* are contractual is implausible. There are many cases where the value of work done under an agreement is recoverable, but where the agreement does not constitute an

---

[31] ibid 765.
[32] See also *Powell v Braun* [1954] 1 WLR 401 (CA).
[33] See eg Birks, *An Introduction to the Law of Restitution* (n 4) 272; Robert Goff and Gareth Jones, *Goff & Jones: The Law of Restitution* (7th edn, Sweet & Maxwell 2007) [23-002].
[34] Edwin Peel, *Treitel on the Law of Contract* (15th edn, Sweet & Maxwell 2020) [2-087].

enforceable contract. The reasons for want of enforceability are many, but perhaps the clearest examples are where legislation has expressly stipulated that no contractual claim of enforcement is possible. Today the formality requirements once contained in the Statute of Frauds 1677 are somewhat unfashionable, but the Act meant what it said, that for agreements within its scope, no action shall be brought upon such an agreement unless proved in writing.

In *James v Thomas H Kent & Co Ltd*, an agreement to employ the plaintiff as a director of the defendant company for a period of three years was entered into.[35] This agreement was never recorded in writing, and after a year of service the parties fell out and the plaintiff was dismissed. He claimed the balance of five months' salary that was still unpaid. As the agreement was not one 'to be performed within a space of one year', the Statute of Frauds required it to be proved by writing before it could be enforced. Denning LJ (with whom Romer J agreed) stated:

> If the servant had fully performed his part of the contract by serving his full time, or, what is the same thing, by serving his full time save when excused by sickness, he could sue for a reasonable remuneration which might be equal to his stipulated wages. Even if the servant has not served his full time, but is dismissed beforehand without good cause, then he can recover payment for any work he has done as upon a quantum meruit. It used to be said in the old days that in that case his action was on an implied contract ...; but that is not a correct way of approach because, in none of these cases can you have an implied contract covering the same ground as an existing special contract. The proper ground of the claim is not in contract at all, but in restitution. It is money which, in justice, ought to be paid for services rendered.[36]

That the claim is not the same as the contractual one to enforce payment may be apparent where the agreed rate is set above the market rate for the work (as in *Way v Latilla*). Although the agreement may be evidence of the appropriate market figure, it is not determinative, and where the agreed rate is higher, it cannot be claimed if there is no enforceable contract.

Denning LJ's approach was adopted by the Supreme Court of Canada in *Deglman v Guaranty Trust Co of Canada*, where the value of care work done by a nephew in exchange for an unenforceable promise to convey title to land by his aunt was recoverable;[37] and by the High Court of Australia in *Pavey & Matthews Pty Ltd v Paul*

---

[35] *James v Thomas H Kent & Co Ltd* [1951] 1 KB 551 (CA). See also *Scott v Pattison* [1923] 2 KB 723 (KB).

[36] *James v Thomas H Kent & Co Ltd* (n 35) 556 (citations omitted). For criticism of Denning LJ's approach, see Warren Swain, Chapter 1 in this volume, Section IV.

[37] *Deglman v Guaranty Trust Co of Canada* [1954] SCR 725. See also *Gray v Hill* (1826) Ry & M 420; 171 ER 1070.

by a builder whose agreement was unenforceable for failure to comply with state statutory formality requirements.[38]

Similar are cases where the parties have themselves agreed that their agreement is unenforceable, commonly by using the words 'subject to contract'. In *Cobbe v Yeoman's Row Management Ltd*, the defendant was the owner of land ripe for redevelopment, which they agreed in principle ('subject to contract') to sell to the claimant developer.[39] The developer was to prosecute the application for planning permission for residential redevelopment at his own expense. Once this permission was obtained, the defendant was to sell the land to the claimant for a fee. After the application was successful, the defendant refused to go ahead and sought to renegotiate the price, which the claimant refused to do. The House of Lords awarded the reasonable value of the service provided, to be subsequently assessed.

Finally, the UK Supreme Court's decision in *Benedetti v Sawiris* is (probably) an example where there was no contract because the agreement was insufficiently complete so as to be enforceable.[40] The failure to set a price is not necessarily fatal to the existence of a contract. As we have seen, if *A* agrees to buy goods from *B*, if no price is determined then a reasonable price must be paid, and the same is true for services. If, however, the parties agree that the price is to be agreed by them at some future point, this may be fatal to there being a contract.[41] The agreed obligation was not to pay a reasonable sum, which the court can itself fix, but an unknown sum that the parties never in fact agreed. This was the case in *Benedetti v Sawiris* itself, where the parties agreed to agree in the future a reward figure for the successful completion of the deal. A contractual *quantum meruit* was therefore unavailable. No figure could be placed upon what they would have agreed. Only a claim for restitution of the value of the performance rendered, which it had been agreed was conditional upon the agreement of a future reward, was therefore possible. Benedetti, dissatisfied with recovering only the market value of the work, attempted to recover a proportion of the huge profits made by the Sawiris group of companies as a result of the deal he had helped to broker going through. Such a 'reward' basis of remuneration was what had been expected, and indeed a level of reward higher that the market value of the work (€36 million) had been offered to him (€75 million) and declined. However, the court's inquiry was not to ascertain what reasonable parties would have agreed to pay, still less to strip the recipient of the incontrovertible gain consequent upon the success of the work, but rather to place a (market) value on the work done.

It may be speculated that a claim for contractual remuneration would have had more prospects in *Benedetti v Sawiris* for securing the greater sum, rather than

---

[38] *Pavey & Matthews Pty Ltd v Paul* (1987) 162 CLR 221.
[39] *Cobbe v Yeoman's Row Management Ltd* [2008] UKHL 55; [2008] 1 WLR 1752. For the recovery of a payment on similar facts, see *Chillingworth v Esche* [1924] 1 Ch 97 (CA).
[40] *Benedetti v Sawiris* [2013] UKSC 50; [2014] AC 938.
[41] *May and Butcher Ltd v R* [1934] 2 KB 17 (KB).

solely an attempt to claim by way of 'unjust enrichment' anything greater than the value of the work. The decision to abandon the contractual argument seems mistaken. If Mr Benedetti had not provided the agreed brokerage service, but had instead done work for other clients, so that the deal was lost, Sawiris ought to have had a claim for damages for breach of contract. It is not necessary for there to be an enforceable contract that all the details have been specified, including the price to be paid. Could it not be said that the parties had agreed that Benedetti be paid a reasonable reward, on a participation basis, as in *Way v Latilla*?

In any event, in *Benedetti v Sawiris* the plaintiff was limited to the market value of the service provided, whereas in *Way v Latilla* the plaintiff recovered several times the market value: the latter was brought on a contractual basis, while the former was not.

3. Claims where either approach is possible

If the agreement in *Way v Latilla* had been unenforceable (as it would have been if there had been a formality requirement as in *Pavey*), the plaintiff should have been restricted to claiming restitution of the value of the work (500 guineas). The work had been done on the agreed condition that it would be paid for on the basis of a reasonable level of participation in the concession. That sum not having been paid, the condition had failed.

Where the agreement amounts to an enforceable contract, such a claim should be available in the alternative. Either the condition under which the work was done (payment in exchange) has failed or the plaintiff is entitled under the contract to a reasonable sum for the work done. Where the contractual rate is higher, the restitutionary claim disappears from view as not worth pursuing.

In some cases, it will make no difference whether a contractual or restitutionary analysis is adopted because the appropriate sums will not differ. One possible example is the recent decision of the Court of Appeal in *Barton v Gwyn-Jones* (since overturned by the Supreme Court).[42]

The form of the agreement was the same as that in *Way v Latilla*. Barton was to be paid a fee for work (finding a buyer for a property), but to be paid a reward if a further condition was met. That condition was a sale at above £6.5 million. The differences between the cases were, first, that the figure payable as a reward had been specified and, secondly, that the condition for the reward had not been met.

It is, of course, possible for the parties to agree that the only sum ever payable is a reward if the condition is met. In a case such as *Barton*, however, this is a commercially improbable construction, as whether the condition is satisfied is under the control of the employer. The employer can prevent the condition from ever being

---

[42] *Barton v Gwyn-Jones* [2019] EWCA Civ 1999; [2020] 2 All ER (Comm) 652; *Barton v Morris* [2023] UKSC 3; [2023] 2 WLR 269. *William Lacey (Hounslow) Ltd v Davis* [1957] 1 WLR 932 (QB) is also equally explicable on a contractual or restitutionary basis.

satisfied by selling for slightly below the 'reward' figure, thereby preventing it from ever being triggered. In a sense, 'unjust enrichment' is relevant to the construction of the parties' agreement as it would be unrealistic to expect the agent to provide the valuable work, and for the seller to take the benefit of it and not pay for it. The Court of Appeal rightly rejected the 'if but only if' construction. This is therefore a case where the sum payable for the work in certain circumstances had been fixed, but not in others.

4. Importance

Seeing claims such as *Deglman v Guaranty Trust Co of Canada* or *Pavey & Matthews Pty Ltd v Paul* as contractual, in the teeth of the legislative words and judicial reasoning, is not a defensible position to adopt. Why then did the defendant have to pay for the service received?

The answer 'unjust enrichment' appears unsatisfactory. If I mistakenly make you better off, by failing to exercise a valuable contractual option before a deadline or by mistakenly repairing your car so as to save you the inevitable expense of doing so, there is not, without more, any claim and nor should there be. Providing a service in a way that is factually enriching, even by mistake, should not on its own give rise to a claim. What, then, was different in *Deglman* and *Pavey*?

Unjust enrichment theorists have been guilty of throwing the agreement baby out with the contractual bathwater. The agreement between the parties is normatively important even if it is not enforceable. *Pacta sunt servanda*.

That an agreement is not enforceable (ie it is not contractual) does not entail that it has no legal effects. The claim is restitutionary, it is neither a claim to compel performance of any primary duty of performance, nor is it a claim for damages for breach. Both proponents and opponents of 'unjust enrichment' have caused confusion by rejecting any intermediate position. Proponents have been so determined to establish the independence of their subject from contract and the quasi-contract label that any attempt to rely upon the importance of an agreement between the parties is dismissed as a version of the 'implied contract' heresy.

The recovery of payments of money made conditionally under agreements have traditionally been expressed as based upon a 'total failure of consideration' where that condition has failed. Enrichment theorists, in order to maintain continuity between the various 'unjust factors' have argued that such conditions are found in the mind of the payor, just as mistakes are also a state of mind. The former is described as based upon 'qualification' of consent, whilst the latter is said to be based upon its 'vitiation'. The correct position, however, is that the condition is found in an agreement objectively made between the parties, not in the state of mind of either of them, which may not correspond with what they have agreed at all. Such claims are dependent upon there being an agreement. Once the condition has failed, if recovery were denied the conditional performance would be treated as unconditional, contrary to the bargain. Such claims have a quite different justification, with consequently different rules, from claims based upon a lack of entitlement to a payment (or performance of other once-valid legal obligations). The latter require the contract to be set aside before recovery is permitted. The former not only do not require such setting aside, they are dependent upon the correct construction of the (extant) agreement itself, and the condition found within it.

Opponents, by contrast, have (implausibly) attempted to expand contract law to cover cases where the conditions for enforceability are not satisfied. This also distorts important differences between the different kinds of claim.

The truth is a score draw (or, perhaps more accurately, defeat for both teams). The agreement forms an essential part of what justifies the claim, but that does not entail that it is contractual. That it is not contractual does not entail that it has the same the same features or justification as claims to recover mistaken payments, nor does it follow that the agreement between the parties is a non-essential element of the justification for the duty to reimburse for the work received under the agreement.

D. Loss-Based Theories

1. The problem

A third move, related to but separate from the second, is to seek to explain some cases not in terms of the giving up of gains, but of compensation for loss. Again, Stoljar was an early proponent of this view, coining the label 'unjust sacrifice'. Beatson too adopted it, preferring the label 'injurious reliance'. Such accounts may gain support from claims generally thought of as outside 'unjust enrichment' travelling, confusingly, under the labels of proprietary or promissory 'estoppel' (sic), with the High Court of Australia taking the most expansive lead in *Waltons Stores (Interstate) Ltd v Maher*.[43] Similarly, claims in the law of torts for negligence following the decision in *Hedley Byrne & Co Ltd v Heller & Partners Ltd* are sometimes thought to be based upon 'reliance' and may be thought to be related.[44]

Materially identical to *Waltons Stores* was the earlier decision of the English Court of Appeal in *Brewer Street Investments Ltd v Barclays Woollen Co Ltd*.[45] The plaintiffs were landlords who entered into negotiations with the defendants to lease premises to them. Agreement was reached but expressed to be 'subject to contract'. The plaintiffs undertook to make certain alterations to the premises, with the cost to be borne by the defendants. Subsequent negotiations to conclude the leasehold contract broke down. Considerable work had gone into altering the premises by

---

[43] *Waltons Stores (Interstate) Ltd v Maher* (1988) 164 CLR 387.
[44] *Hedley Byrne & Co Ltd v Heller & Partners Ltd* [1964] AC 465 (HL).
[45] *Brewer Street Investments Ltd v Barclays Woollen Co Ltd* [1954] 1 QB 428 (CA). See also *Planché v Colburn* (1831) 5 C & P 58; 172 ER 876.

this point. As the defendants had never gone into possession, they were never in any meaningful sense enriched by what the plaintiffs did. A contractual action to enforce the payment obligation was unavailable as the condition precedent to such entitlement, the completion of the work, had not occurred. No action for damages for breach of contract was available, because the prospective tenants were not in breach. Denning LJ's view that the claim was restitutionary seems more defensible that that of Somervell LJ's preferred contractual analysis.

Most authors accept that the work did not benefit the prospective tenants, so that an 'unjust enrichment' analysis is unsatisfactory.[46] If the result is accepted, it is then common to accept the proposition of Stoljar and Beatson that a further 'loss'- or 'reliance'-based category of claim exists beyond the realm of unjust enrichment. If, however, this is so, it would render otiose most claims to services said to be based upon 'unjust enrichment' as the hitherto ignored 'reliance' claim would explain recovery without the need to identify any gain.

There are, however, reasons to doubt this 'reliance'- or 'loss'-based account.

First, and most fundamentally, no satisfactory reason for recovery is identified. The analysis goes little further than identifying a group of cases that are not explicable in terms of 'enrichment'.

In the common law, the *deliberate* infliction of loss is not, without more, actionable. It is *damnum sine iniuria*: loss absent the violation of any right. That the defendant has caused the plaintiff to be worse off in some sense cannot, alone, justify any duty of repair. It is mysterious why we should reach a different result where the mechanism for the causation of such loss takes the form of reliance upon something the defendant has done or said. Why should loss inflicted in this particular way be seen as a special case?

Secondly, this reliance-based analysis is not reflected in anything Denning LJ said.

Thirdly, such reliance- or loss-based analyses misidentify the gist of the action. If in *Deglman* the nephew would have done the work anyway, out of love for his aunt, regardless of the promise she made to leave him one of her properties in her will, this should make no difference to the result. What suffices is that the work was done conditionally under an agreement between the parties, and that condition has failed, regardless of whether, counterfactually, the work would have been done anyway. Loss does not have to be pleaded or proven.

2. Importance

As so often, the negative thesis is easier to defend than the positive. It is true that there are many claims for the recovery of the value of services where it is implausible to argue that the defendant is, as a matter of fact, better off as a result of its

---

[46] Birks is an isolated exception: Birks, *An Introduction to the Law of Restitution* (n 4) 283–85. He could see the implications.

provision. It is, however, an equal and opposite mistake to think that the explanation for recovery is to be found in any reliance loss suffered by the plaintiff.

The better view is that the defendant is liable in these cases for the market value of the service provided: regardless of whether the plaintiff has suffered any loss or the defendant made any gain. What the law seeks to reverse is the performance rendered under the agreement between the parties, not the consequential loss or gain for either of them.

III. Conclusion

One of the problems that has arisen because of the adoption of a uniform 'unjust enrichment' framework for thinking about this area of law is that the ordinary dialectic between those with different viewpoints in relation to it has been stifled. We have fallen into opposing camps who are not listening to one another.

In the preface to his final work, in discussing his abandonment of 'unjust factors', Peter Birks stated with characteristic verve:

> St Paul was relatively lucky. In one flash of blinding light he knew that he must change sides. In the university the awful sense of having been wrong comes on more slowly and with it the still more awful realization that one must befriend those whom one has persecuted and persecute those who are one's friends.[47]

In criticizing the work of the sceptics, it might be argued that I have chosen to persecute everyone.

The metaphor of religious belief that Birks employed is unhelpful in the university. No doubt I have made mistakes in my own account of the law, but the best response is both to criticize what is wrong, and to seek to salvage what truth there is. There is no place for camps or sides.

---

[47] Peter Birks, *Unjust Enrichment* (2nd edn, OUP 2005) xii.

8
Restitution, Corrective Justice, and Mistakes

James Penner[*]

I. Introduction

The interrelations between the concepts of 'corrective justice' and restitution, in particular in cases concerning mistakes, are subtle and various. Here I explore some of the landscape, rather than provide a definitive theory, of those interrelations.

II. Aristotle on Corrective Justice

In *The Nichomachean Ethics*, Aristotle famously distinguished between distributive and corrective justice.[1] He seemed to treat this division as comprehensive, as covering all matters of just interactions between individuals, but that is questionable. Before turning to that question, it is important to characterize the way in which Aristotle thought about justice.[2]

In the first place, Aristotle frames justice as a virtue, that is, a praiseworthy property or character trait of the 'just person'. Justice is therefore framed in terms of the acts of a person, which may be just or unjust. An injustice is an act that is both wrongful and harmful. For Aristotle, an unjust act is one that must be voluntary; it must reflect the character of the individual who more or less intentionally commits it. So, for example, mere carelessness (or negligence), whatever its effects might be, does not count as an act of injustice.[3] He divides 'voluntary' action into two types, confusingly called the 'voluntary' and the 'involuntary', but this refers to the person harmed by an injustice.[4] The former concerns voluntary transactions, contracts

---

[*] I am grateful for comments from and discussion with Robert Chambers, Hanoch Dagan, Duncan Horne, Sagi Peari, Robert Stevens, William Swadling, and Fred Wilmot-Smith.
[1] Aristotle, *The Nicomachean Ethics* (David Ross tr, OUP 2009) 82–88.
[2] The points that follow figure largely in Richard A Posner, 'The Concept of Corrective Justice in Recent Theories of Tort Law' (1981) 10 J Legal Studies 187; Bill Shaw and William Martin, 'Aristotle and Posner on Corrective Justice: The Tortoise and the Hare' (1999) 9 Business Ethics Quarterly 651 (hereafter Shaw and Martin, 'Tortoise and Hare').
[3] Aristotle, *The Nicomachean Ethics* (n 1) 93.
[4] ibid 84.

essentially, and the latter are what we would call torts. Finally, and perhaps most famously, for the purpose of corrective or rectificatory justice, the perpetrator is regarded as having a 'gain' which corresponds to the sufferer's 'loss', and justice is obtained by an award which reverses this. Thus, corrective justice responds 'arithmetically', correcting unjustly created pluses and minuses, as opposed to geometrically or proportionately, the latter being the formulation relevant to distributive justice. Aristotle is on unsteady ground here, for as Shaw and Martin point out:

> The notions of gain and loss do not seem to include wrongdoing [itself, as opposed to the *harmful effects* of the wrongdoing]. In fact, it would be a rather tricky business if it did because Aristotle conceives of justice as virtue, and therefore thinks that at some level the unjust man, in committing vice, injures himself.[5]

As Aristotle himself pointed out, 'justice' can be taken in a narrower or broader way, although his distinction here is not very precise, and can be framed in different ways.[6] Nevertheless, the basic idea is, I submit, correct. For some scholars, the concept of justice applies to all of our interpersonal interactions insofar as they morally concern us. The just man is the man who acts morally in relation to others.[7] This is the broad sense of 'justice'. The narrower sense is something like 'justice (or fairness) *in allocation*'; it concerns only those actions which cause losses or bestow gains, however loss or gain is to be conceived. It does not cover the whole field of morality. It does not concern, to use some of Aristotle's own examples, the virtues of courage (the coward who flees the field is not, without more, acting unjustly), temperance, liberality, humility, good temper, or friendliness.[8]

III. Types of Justice

Do corrective and distributive justice cover the field of justice as Aristotle seemed to think? Gardner doubts this, as do I. Gardner points out that justice in punishment, or 'retributive justice', does not easily fit within this division, nor does procedural justice.[9] I also doubt that what I have called private law penalties, for example the stripping of a fiduciary of an incidental profit, amount to a kind of corrective justice in any conventional sense.[10]

---

[5] Shaw and Martin, 'Tortoise and Hare' (n 2) 653 (footnotes omitted).
[6] Aristotle, *The Nicomachean Ethics* (n 1) 82–84.
[7] Finnis is one example: John Finnis, *Natural Law and Natural Rights* (Paul Craig ed, 2nd edn, OUP 2011) 165.
[8] For similar views endorsing the narrower version of justice, see John Gardner, 'What Is Tort Law For? Part 1. The Place of Corrective Justice' (2011) 30 L and Phil 1, 6–8.
[9] ibid 8–9.
[10] See James Penner, 'Punishments and Penalties in Private Law, with Particular Reference to the Law Governing Fiduciaries' in Elise Bant and others (eds), *Punishment and Private Law* (Hart Publishing 2021).

But for our purposes a different point must be straightened out. For Weinrib and others, corrective justice encompasses not only the remedial aspect of private law, but also the basic primary *moral* norms the breach of which gives rise to secondary remedial norms. I disagree.[11] In my view, the moral norms that govern (or ought to govern) our interpersonal relations are not a matter of corrective justice, because they are not norms of justice at all. They have nothing to do with justice or fairness in any kind of allocation. They exist because of our human nature,[12] or to put it in terms Kant liked, because of our membership in the Kingdom of Ends.[13] None of this is to deny that there may be grave disputes about what these moral norms are, and therefore what moral duties are themselves valid. The claim is rather that these disputes only make sense against an understanding of humans as valuing creatures who can pursue the realization of value rationally with others. This, as Gardner has put it, makes both rationality, and the particular aspect of rationality we call morality—that is, to be susceptible to moral appraisal of our actions—'inescapable' for creatures such as ourselves.[14]

Now in saying this I am talking in the first instance only about those moral norms that exist apart from the law. When we turn to legal norms which reflect these moral norms, which give shape to them and typically make them more certain and thus easier to apply, in particular in the settling of disputes,[15] questions of justice immediately arise. And they arise apart from whether the legal norm that governs some matter, say how the law of conversion reflects our duty not to interfere with the movable goods of others, *adequately* reflects the moral norms in question, which is not a matter of justice, but a matter of whether the law is worth obeying in the first place. The matter of justice that primarily arises here is one of distributive justice:[16] which moral norms should the law take up as part of its business, to enforce, remedy, and so on? This is partly a matter of state resources. How much should go to defence of the realm, how much to education, to healthcare, and so on, and how much to the administration of justice? But more importantly it reflects the state's attention to different classes of persons and different kinds of interactions. How much should go to commercial litigation? (Let them arbitrate, says Marie Antoinette.) How much to, for example, family law?[17]

---

[11] cf Gardner, 'What Is Tort Law For? (n 8) 23–24.
[12] John Gardner, 'Nearly Natural Law' (2007) 52 Am J Juris 1; John Gardner, 'The Negligence Standard: Political Not Metaphysical' (2017) 80 MLR 1; PMS Hacker, *The Moral Powers: A Study of Human Nature* (Wiley Blackwell 2021).
[13] Immanuel Kant, *The Moral Law: Kant's Groundwork of the Metaphysics of Morals* (HJ Paton tr, Routledge 1992) 101.
[14] Gardner, 'Nearly Natural Law' (n 12); Gardner, 'The Negligence Standard' (n 12).
[15] On a Razian, positivist account, which I endorse, morality *incorporates* those laws which properly reflect moral norms but make them more precise, etc. In this way, legal norms, norms which would not exist apart from the law, are moral norms.
[16] John Gardner, 'What is Tort Law For? Part 2. The Place of Distributive Justice' in John Oberdiek (ed), *Philosophical Foundations of the Law of Torts* (OUP 2014).
[17] For a detailed exploration of many of the difficult issues here, see Frederick Wilmot-Smith, *Equal Justice: Fair Legal Systems in an Unfair World* (Harvard UP 2019).

IV. All of Corrective Justice is Best Explained by the Principle of Unjust Enrichment

The heading of this section is facetious, but not entirely so. The point it encompasses was as far as I know first noticed by Lionel Smith.[18] If all of corrective justice is based on the principle of an arithmetical imbalance between the plaintiff and the defendant whereby the defendant has unjustly gained the precise amount that the plaintiff has unjustly lost, then all wrongs are reconfigured as unjust enrichments, whether breaches of contracts, or torts, or any other case in which private law will give a remedy. But if this is correct, then *this* principle of unjust enrichment just is the principle of corrective justice across the board. It does nothing to provide a particular principle of corrective or remedial justice in those cases which we conventionally regard as falling into the separate private law category of 'unjust enrichment' or 'restitution'.

A. Weinrib on Restitution of a Mistaken Payment as a Kind of Corrective Justice

Weinrib's explanation of restitution of a mistaken payment has two central elements: (1) the juridical significance of value and (2) the 'non-gratuitous transfer of value' principle, aka the 'something for nothing' principle.[19] I shall contend that these elements do not provide a sound moral or intellectual basis for understanding the law governing mistaken payments.

With respect to (1), the juridical significance of value, Weinrib, following Hegel, wishes to endorse the idea that value is a juridical rather than an economic concept. This is, in my view, mistaken. 'Right', 'duty', 'power', 'civil wrong', 'discharge', 'breach', 'waiver', and 'estoppel' are juridical concepts but 'value' is not; it is an economic concept and the value of any right is quite properly in law treated as *a matter of fact*, not of law,[20] even when the law sets a tariff, for example £30,000 for a severed foot; in this latter case, the legislature just picks a value based on general considerations, facts about human nature, emotional injury, the value of activities requiring the use of one's foot, and so on. And consider the economist's 'virtual pricing' of such

---

[18] Lionel Smith, 'Restitution: The Heart of Corrective Justice' (2001) 79 Tex L Rev 2115.
[19] Ernest J Weinrib, *Corrective Justice* (OUP 2012) 190–96.
[20] Though, of course, that valuation will reflect and rely upon legal concepts. Most obviously, courts typically value an award in the legal tender of their jurisdiction; they will also apply principles of forensic accounting. None of this is to deny, as Hanoch Dagan reminds me, that the law may heavily shape economic values in the marketplace. To take a fairly obvious example, the market value of any particular person's labour will reflect, eg, systematic bargaining power differentials between employees and employers, market prices for goods will reflect the stringency of competition law, and so on. I have previously discussed some of the issues in the text in James Penner, 'Value, Property, and Unjust Enrichment: Trusts of Traceable Proceeds' in Robert Chambers, Charles Mitchell, and James Penner (eds), *Philosophical Foundations of the Law of Unjust Enrichment* (OUP 2009) 306, 306–12.

things, for example 'how much would you take in money to give up your foot, your kidney, and so on'. This 'virtual pricing' model is economic through and through; no legal or juridical concepts are implicated.

Supporting Hegel's claim that value is a true juridical concept, Weinrib writes:

> Hegel regards value as an incident of property. One is entitled to the value of something by virtue of one's ownership of the thing that is the locus of the value. Hegel's description of value as an object of ownership reflects commonplace notions drawn from contract and tort law, respectively, that the owner of anything alienable is entitled to realize its value through exchange and to be compensated to the extent of its value in the event of wrongful injury or deprivation.[21]

We can pause there before proceeding. In the first place, it makes no sense to say that one is *entitled* to the value of what one owns, if 'entitled' means having a legal right or power that binds others. Against whom could such an entitlement lie? Whether we speak of use value or exchange value, value is something that the owner of that thing (or another, if the possession or title of it moves to that other, whether rightly or wrongly) may *realize*, either by use or exchange. The liberty to use or the power to enter into a contract of exchange are potentialities, obviously. Neither the juridical liberty to use nor the juridical contractual power to exchange make any reference to value, though of course their justification may do so, and our motivation in exercising them normally does. That is, it is not *analytic* of the liberty to use things or the power to enter into contracts in respect of them that any value whatsoever is thereby realized. Some uses are counterproductive and foolish, as are some exchanges. (Jack's magic beans, anyone?) As to the 'commonplace notions' drawing upon the law of damages for breach of contract or tort, the law uses market value *as a practical proxy*. Except in cases like the damages tariff for a lost limb, the law does not itself determine an 'objective' as opposed to a *determinate* money value, and no one as far as I know would claim that £30,000 for a severed foot is anything like 'objective' in a meaningful sense.[22] And the last point makes us remember that, for the law, our persons count just as much as our property for the violation of our rights. This is true in contract as well, when we frame our rights to our persons in terms of our liberty to provide a service to another. So if there is some kind of 'value theory' which is juridified, it cannot be restricted to the notion of *ownership of property*.[23]

---

[21] Weinrib, *Corrective Justice* (n 19) 190 (footnote omitted).
[22] Which is not to say that the tariff is arbitrary or capricious.
[23] Kantians regard our legal interests in our bodies as 'structured' in the same way as our right to our property. Our body rights just as much as our property rights are negative and relational. See Arthur Ripstein, 'Possession and Use' in James Penner and Henry E Smith (eds), *Philosophical Foundations of Property Law* (OUP 2013).

Weinrib would object to my thoughts about 'potentialities'. He carries on from the previous passage:

> The owner of the thing owns the value in the sense that ownership of the thing carries with it an entitlement to something equivalent when the thing is exchanged or injured. Value is thus the potentiality that is actualised through a set of legal operations—exchange and liability—with respect to things that one owns. Indeed, unless it were possible to conceive of this potentiality as an entitlement of the thing's owner, the transformation of an entitlement to what one owns into an entitlement to what is substituted for it through exchange or liability would make no sense. The entitlement to value thus marks the continuity through the process of exchange and the determination of liability of the owner's entitlement to the thing owned.[24]

Now I agree with Weinrib that exchange value is 'actualized' or realized in law through the legal mechanism of contract, but I deny that to make sense of this one has to juridify the concept of value itself, and the law does not do so. When I pay £50 for a jacket, the law regards this as an exchange of *rights*, not of value. Indeed, this fact partly explains why common law courts do not look into the adequacy of consideration. Moreover, even markets do not establish the 'objective' value of anything. What markets do, amongst other things, is aggregate the *subjective* preferences of those in the market; the market is not concerned with objective value, otherwise there would be many fewer things on the market which manifest execrable taste. (Chocolate martinis, anyone?) And likewise I would not say that any objective value is 'realized' when the law awards damages for interference with a property right. The law typically determines the quantum of damages on the basis of market value, which I have pointed out is not objective anyway, but more importantly the money received is not *for the plaintiff* any realization *by her* of the value of the damaged property. Indeed, Weinrib's picture seems quite distorted, as if a tort and the consequent damages award were to be regarded as an act or event unlocking the exchange value of an asset *for the plaintiff*. What she receives is a *substitute* asset, money, that she may then go on to realize the exchange value of as she pleases. In particular, the plaintiff is under no obligation to use the money to acquire the same type of thing that was damaged or destroyed.[25]

---

[24] Weinrib, *Corrective Justice* (n 19) 190.
[25] ibid 191–93 discusses further aspects of the concept of value, but I don't think they work to distinguish a juridical concept of value from an economic one.

B. Weinrib's 'Non-Gratuitous Transfer of Value' Principle of Unjust Enrichment

Succinctly put, Weinrib's theory of the legal principle of unjust enrichment turns on the idea that in a contractual exchange there is no 'transfer of value':

> [I]f the food is of equal value to the shoes, no value has been transferred. Exchange on such terms features the reciprocal transfer of things of value but not the transfer of value itself, since it keeps constant the value to which each party is entitled. Exchange demonstrates that value 'is distinct from the external things which change owners in the course of the transaction', because in an exchange external things are transferred but value is not.[26]

Gifts are different:

> Only to the extent that the transfer is gratuitous—that is, involves no receipt of equivalent value—does the transfer of a thing of value become a transfer of value as well. If I transfer shoes but receive in return nothing or food of less value ... then I have transferred not only the shoes as things of value but value itself. ... Through this gratuitous transfer the value of what is rightfully mine has been diminished and the value of what is rightfully the transferee's has been increased by the amount of value that has been transferred without reciprocation. In the language of unjust enrichment, the transferee has been enriched at my expense. This does not mean, of course, that the transferee is obligated to return the enrichment. That further consequence depends upon whether the retention of that enrichment is unjust—that is, whether the transfer occurred under conditions that generate an obligation to restore the transferred value.[27]

C. Weinrib's Theory of Unjust Enrichment and the Conditionality of Certain Payments

It is common ground amongst scholars and the courts that the justification for the return of a payment made on a conditional basis where the condition is not met is a simple case. If I transfer £2,000 to you, a builder, as an upfront payment under a contract that you do up my kitchen, and you perish the following day, *of course* I can demand the return of the money. The moral and legal justifications for this are perfectly obvious and not in dispute. Indeed, one may go so far as to say that the obligation to return the money is an implied term of the contract which any court

---

[26] ibid 194 (footnote omitted).
[27] ibid 194–95.

would find.[28] It is therefore tempting to try to establish that any payment for which a restitutionary claim will lie is subject to some kind of condition, however implicit and however far from the parties' minds. This seems to be Weinrib's strategy.[29]

The non-gratuitous transfer of value theory of unjust enrichment is that, outside gifts, transfers of value from P to D are reversible; the law imposes upon D a liability to make repayment out of his wealth. This is an *in personam* liability. It attaches to no specific right of D's. In Weinrib's terminology, this might also be referred to as the 'something for nothing' principle.[30] Where the transfer of a thing is intended by both parties as a gift, there is a transfer of value but this is fine as it is the joint will of both parties that it should occur.[31] In the case of non-gratuitous transfers, which appear to cover the entire field of transactions that are not gifts,[32] the underlying intentions of the parties is that there is *not* meant to be a gratuitous transfer of value, so where a transfer of value occurs, this does not reflect the will of the parties, and repayment must be made. This way of looking at things seems to be indistinguishable from the idea that in the non-gift context, every payment is *conditional* on there being a reciprocal transfer of value, so that no party acquires any enrichment of value; that is, is 'up in value' following the transaction. Where this condition is not met, the value received must be restored to the transferor. There are three particular features of this account that must be interrogated: (1) the juridical basis for the recipient's legal liability; (2) the claim that the parties' intentions here are objectively determined; and (3) Weinrib's treatment of services.

As to (1), Weinrib says:

> The law does not presume—and therefore those subject to the law are not entitled to presume—that someone has chosen to transfer value gratuitously, thereby surrendering the means for pursuing one's own ends. To be sure, a person may *on occasion* identify another's interest with one's own and therefore confer gratuitous benefits on the other. However, such donative intent must be established for each

---

[28] Robert Stevens, 'The Unjust Enrichment Disaster' (2018) 134 LQR 574, 585–86; Lionel Smith, 'Restitution: A New Start?' in Peter Devonshire and Rohan Havelock (eds), *The Impact of Equity and Restitution in Commerce* (Hart Publishing 2019) 112, 114–16. See also 107–08 for similar views on the case of a guarantor paying a debt.

[29] At one point Weinrib endorses the Canadian 'no juristic reason' justification for restitutionary recovery, but he does not, as far as I can tell, integrate that thought into the rest of his thesis: see Weinrib, *Corrective Justice* (n 19) 202.

[30] Weinrib uses this locution frequently: see ibid 196, 199, 203, 204, and elsewhere.

[31] Weinrib says a couple of things about gifts which are debatable. First, ibid 200, that property does not pass if there is a defect in the intentions of the parties—this may be true of gifts of chattels, but it need not be true in other cases, electronic transfers of money being an obvious example. Secondly, ibid 201, that a gift must be accepted to take effect. For a recent discussion of this point, which I think is immaterial to my arguments, see Alexander Georgiou, 'Mistaken Payments, Quasi-Contracts, and the "Justice" of Unjust Enrichment' (2022) 42 OJLS 606, 621–22.

[32] 'Unjust enrichment has aptly been called the law of non-gifts.' Abraham Drassinower, 'Unrequested Benefits in the Law of Unjust Enrichment' (1998) 48 UTLJ 459, 478; as cited in Weinrib, *Corrective Justice* (n 19) 218.

particular case, and not assumed to be *the general rule*. Except when the enrichment was intended and accepted as a gift, the defendant can be regarded as assuming that no benefit is given gratuitously, even if the defendant has not turned his mind to this issue.[33]

As far as I can tell, Weinrib nowhere justifies the law's taking this attitude, and making non-gratuitous transactions the baseline or default position as between persons.[34] And this is not an attitude which I think reflects morality generally. It would be silly to count up the number of gratuitous and non-gratuitous transactions into which I enter every week, but it is simply not true that people, or at least those who are not selfish, only *on occasion* identify another's interest with their own. And since selfishness is itself a moral deficiency, taking the perspective of the selfish person will not help us to understand the morality of personal interactions. And it is also not true as a matter of positive law that gifts are more difficult to establish—'in every particular case'—than are, say, contracts or other non-gratuitous transactions. In short, all Weinrib has done here is to assert a principle of *positive law*. It does not seem to me that he has effectively shown that this positive gift-restrictive presumption of law reflects moral sense. I think it doesn't, but since Weinrib has not, as far as I can see, really tried to justify the moral cogency of the positive legal principle he finds, I need make only a few brief comments. First, Weinrib may implicitly be assuming that his positive law principle is limited to relations between strangers, or something like that. One might regard the presumptions of resulting trust and advancement as one instance in the positive law which reflects this principle, though I would not myself. In any case, it seems not to be true that gifts to strangers are rare—think of generous tipping, crowdfunding, and gifts to charities, which are almost always gifts to strangers. These are common enough, I think, to suggest that a friend/family versus stranger dichotomy will not do the work Weinrib needs it to do if he adopted this refinement of his principle.

With a further refinement Weinrib would be on stronger ground. Consider the standard example of the mistaken liability payment: I pay my gas bill a second time, forgetting I paid earlier. The gas company and I are clearly in an ongoing arm's-length contractual relationship, and it would be extraordinary to regard my second payment as a gift to the gas company. So, applying Weinrib's logic, one might say that it is an implicit condition of any such payment that it actually discharges a liability to the gas company, a condition which the gas company would implicitly acknowledge, and explicitly acknowledge if queried about it. Of course, we would not call this a 'gas company-customer' principle. It would be wrong to slice our contexts that finely. So, one might say something like this: in all contexts, which

---

[33] Weinrib, *Corrective Justice* (n 19) 208 (emphasis added). See also 195.
[34] For a somewhat different criticism of this premise, see Frederick Wilmot-Smith, 'Should the Payee Pay?' (2017) 37 OJLS 844, 857–61.

are likely to be predominantly commercial, where a payment from A to B or from B to A can only be understood by both parties as intending to discharge a liability one owes to the other, unless that payment actually discharges a liability[35] (even if not the liability the payor intended to discharge[36]) then the payor will have a claim for its repayment. Fine. But, then, all this refinement has done is to provide *another context in which payments are held to be conditional*. It does nothing to establish a general principle of unjust enrichment which ties the differing cases together, unless the law of unjust enrichment just is the law of conditional payments and nothing else.

As to the parties' intentions, Weinrib insists that the parties' actual intentions, in particular the defendant's actual intentions, are irrelevant to the defendant's liability. The idea is that once the context of the paying transaction is identified, the parties' actual intentions regarding the payment are irrelevant, for the law imputes to them the objective basis of the payment context. The rationale for this seems to be to ensure that the defendant's will is implicated in the transaction, preserving bilaterality in the sense of the joining of the plaintiff's and defendant's wills in the transaction. More specifically, the defendant has to *accept* the payment in a way appropriate to the context of the payment transaction. Weinrib says:

> Acceptance is *imputed* when the law can reasonably regard the beneficial transfer as something that forwards or accords with the defendant's projects. The *imputation* of acceptance thereby connects the law's construction of the defendant's will both to the transferred value and to the terms on which it was transferred. In this context the will—the capacity to set and pursue one's own purposes—is a juridical, not a subjective or psychological notion: what matters is the purpose not as internally formed but as externally pertinent to the relationship of plaintiff and defendant. *Awareness of the benefit and acting with respect to it are sufficient but not necessary to indicate acceptance; a benefit can be consonant with the defendant's purposes even if these are lacking.* Acceptance goes, accordingly, not to the defendant's particular psychological state, but to what the law can reasonably impute to the defendant, given the defendant's purposes and the law's background assumptions about the significance of donative intent. Of course, any defendant might subjectively prefer to keep the transferred value rather than return it to the transferor. Nonetheless, by imputing acceptance of the enrichment as non-gratuitously given, the law indicates its view of how the defendant's will can reasonably be regarded as standing with respect to what was received, with

---

[35] This 'discharge of liability' principle would have to be suitably refined to cover cases where, say, I pay more to my credit company than the outstanding balance in order to ensure I don't exceed my credit limit whilst on holiday.
[36] *Steam Saw Mills Co Ltd v Baring Bros and Co Ltd* [1922] 1 Ch 244 (CA).

the implication that the defendant has no right to retain it for the service of his projects as if it had been given gratuitously.[37]

Two points about this passage. First, it cannot be the case that this imputed intention is not subject in some cases to the parties' genuine intentions concerning the transaction. Businesses do make gifts to each other and to their employees and customers, for example at Christmas time. So the imputation of intention cannot be bulletproof. Secondly, and more importantly, it is not clear to me that this reflects the positive law or what most scholars think of as part of the theory of private law; the law is generally *not* prone to imputing intentions where the parties' actual intentions are in evidence, as is clear, for example, in the construction of contracts and the issue of implied terms. Robert Stevens has also argued that the defendant recipient of a payment must accept it. In the case of payments into one's bank account, Stevens says:

> The bank's acceptance is attributed to its customer because that is what the bank has been authorised to do on its principal's behalf. The customer has accepted because its agent has accepted.[38]

I only point out that on Stevens's account no intention to accept is 'imputed' to the customer in Weinrib's sense of imputation. The customer's authorization of the bank to receive payments on their behalf is a genuine term of their contract with the bank. Lionel Smith also argues that the defendant must accept the mistaken payment but, again, this is a real acceptance on the defendant's part, not an imputed one.[39]

Let us now turn to point (3), Weinrib's treatment of services. It is a little surprising to me that Weinrib, as a Kantian, seems to juridify the provision of services as legally significant enrichments outside Kant's framework of acquired right, as 'free-standing' grounds for a possible legal claim.[40] As I think any Kantian would acknowledge, a person's mere actions, whatever their effect upon others, are legally insignificant unless and insofar as they (1) amount to a legal wrong; (2) amount to the exercise of a legal power; or (3) serve to discharge or fulfil an obligation, typically a contractual obligation. Outside these strictly defined boundaries, your actions are insignificant for the interpersonal morality of right,[41] and thus for private law. I have elsewhere argued that 'services' cases are not part of the law of unjust

---

[37] Weinrib, *Corrective Justice* (n 19) 208–09 (emphasis added).
[38] Stevens, 'The Unjust Enrichment Disaster' (n 28) 582.
[39] Smith, 'Restitution: A New Start?' (n 28) 112–13.
[40] Weinrib, *Corrective Justice* (n 19) 204–05, 210.
[41] This does not mean your actions are morally insignificant *tout court*. There is also the province of virtue, or the ethical. (I take them to be the same in this context.) Morality also judges whether, irrespective of right, your actions are kind, noble, generous, rewarding, aesthetically pleasing, or base, vicious, idiotic, intemperate, or careless.

enrichment, or the law of restitution for that matter,[42] so I shall address this issue briefly.

As I have just said, a person's actions, whether or not they benefit another and so might be regarded as providing a 'service' to that other, are not by themselves matters of legal cognizance. They only become legally cognized when they fall under one of (1) to (3) in the preceding paragraph.[43] So, take the case where a shoe-shiner shines my shoes without my permission. The only thing of legal relevance here is that he has committed a trespass to goods, albeit innocently. If I am so petty as to bring an action against him, I will get only nominal damages. That his 'service', his commission of the tort, happens on this occasion to be to my advantage, *maybe*,[44] is irrelevant to his liability, and I have no liability in respect of this 'enrichment'. With respect to services, all the action lies under (3), actions which fulfil or discharge an obligation. As we know, outside contract, persons may have claims for the value of their actions, their 'services' to others in a limited range of circumstances, based upon acquiescence, or an agreement which is not binding as a contract, and so on. As Stevens explains:

> Services that have no end product, and those that have not saved the defendant any necessary expense that would otherwise have been incurred, such as the painting of coal white, have long had to be paid for if freely accepted. But how can free acceptance establish that the defendant has been left better off by what the [plaintiff] had done? It cannot. The problem does not disappear by arguing that an 'enrichment' is established where benefits have been requested. Goods or services that I have requested do not necessarily leave me better off than I otherwise would have been either. Indeed, in some cases such as the painting of coal white, they may leave me worse off than I would have been had I never received them.[45]

What needs to be reversed is not the consequence of the performance from C to D, but the performance rendered by C and accepted by D. In the case of a service that needs reversal, the 'enrichment' is the service itself, not any realized gain that results from it. It does not matter that the balance sheet improvement of the defendant's position is vastly greater, or lower, than the market value of the service itself. The law takes as its starting point the market value of the service provided, not for arbitrary reasons but because that is what is being reversed.

---

[42] James E Penner, 'Basic Obligations' in Peter Birks (eds), *The Classification of Obligations* (OUP 1997) 102–19.

[43] This is arguably too narrow. As Rob Stevens pointed out to me, it wouldn't cover *Greenwood v Bennett* [1973] 1 QB 195 (CA), but it is fair to say that that case has not been easy to explain.

[44] This raises the issue of subjective devaluation for those who think it a working legal concept, but since I think it is legally inert, I shall not say more here.

[45] Stevens, 'The Unjust Enrichment Disaster' (n 28) 580 (footnote omitted).

In short, the notion of enrichment is spurious here, because whether the defendant is actually enriched or not is irrelevant to his liability. And since it is, the award is not gain-based. The payment rewards the plaintiff for his services, based on the market rate. So these are not cases of restitution either. The only quibble I have with this passage is the terminology of 'reversal' insofar as it suggests an analogy to the reversal of a transfer of rights. The performance of an action is not a transfer of anything, so it cannot be 'reversed' by being 'transferred back', even notionally. What happens in these cases is simply the law's recognition, outside the law of contract, of the defendant's obligation to compensate the plaintiff for his work. One might happily call this the law of quasi-contracts.[46]

So what verdict should we render on Weinrib's attempt to integrate the law of unjust enrichment into his version of corrective justice? Leaving aside the last issue concerning 'restitution' of the value of services—which should be excised from any account of unjust enrichment or restitution, and which Weinrib could excise as well without, I think, doing injury to the rest of his account—it seems that Weinrib's account is best framed as the law of non-gifts understood as conditional payments. This, I think, is a genuine advance, for which we should be grateful. But as I have insisted, this only works in very specifically defined circumstances, roughly between parties who deal with each other at arm's length under an existing commercial relationship. So we have also learned the lesson that we must examine different kinds of mistake and the contexts in which they occur and how one case might inform another.

V. Mistakes and the Law of Restitution

The beginning of wisdom here, I suggest, is to consider more broadly the law of mistake and see what aspects of it would give grounds for the restitution of a mistaken transfer or payment.

It seems to me that the most important distinction we should apply to distinguish mistake cases is the distinction between results and consequences, which von Wright famously observed.[47] It is a result of my killing you that you die. If you do not die, I haven't killed you. It may be a consequence of my killing you that I frustrate a contract of personal service you have with X. But this will obviously depend upon further facts—some such consequence, unlike the result, is not 'internal' to the concept of killing the way death is. Some mistakes are clearly about results. The very result intended was not achieved.

A clear example of such mistakes are what are sometimes called 'fundamental mistakes' in which title to goods does not pass to the recipient even though she has

---

[46] See Stevens, 'The Unjust Enrichment Disaster' (n 28) 585–86.
[47] Georg Henrik von Wright, *Norm and Action: A Logical Inquiry* (Routledge 1963) 39–41.

taken possession from the transferor. These mistakes are conventionally listed as mistakes as to the identity of the recipient, or as to the identity of the transferred goods, or as to the goods' quantity. In each case, the intended result was simply not achieved: the goods went to the wrong recipient, the wrong goods went to the recipient, or the wrong quantity of goods went to the recipient.[48]

Another clear example are the cases of *non est factum*, where a person signing a document did not intend its very result, as when, for example, a person signs what he believes to be a contract of sale which is in fact a deed of gift. Similar to this case is one in which an error in the written recording of a transaction gives rise to a claim for rectification.[49] The writing does not record the intended result. An example involving land is *Blacklocks v JB Developments (Godalming) Ltd*,[50] where a plan attached to the contract of sale of land included land which was not intended to be conveyed.

As to mistaken consequences, the law of trusts provides three examples. In *Ogilvie v Littleboy*, Mrs Ogilvie sought to have set aside appointments she made to charities.[51] She achieved the results of those appointments as intended, but several years later regretted the consequences of her decision on various grounds, principally having to do with the management and control of the charities. Her claim was rejected. In *Lady Hood of Avalon v Mackinnon*, Lady Hood made appointments of trust assets to each of her daughters of £8,600, and in doing so she achieved the very result she intended.[52] But her aim in doing so was to benefit the daughters equally, but she had forgotten about a previous appointment that she and her husband had made to one of the daughters some years before. Lady Hood sought to revoke the appointment of £8,600 to the daughter previously benefited on the ground of mistake. She succeeded. To my mind, the decision was justified because of the very close connection between the result she achieved and her intended consequences of that result. Finally, in *Pitt v Holt*, the settlor successfully had a trust set aside because the consequences of the settlement gave rise to extensive tax liabilities which could easily have been avoided if specific provisions relating to trusts for disabled beneficiaries been complied with.[53]

There is an important discussion in *Pitt* of the results/consequences distinction, framed in terms of 'effect' and 'consequences' by Millett J in *Gibbon v Mitchell*.[54] Lord Walker SCJ held that requiring that a mistake, to be reversible, had to be as

---

[48] The application of the rules is controversial, in particular where the mistake as to the identity of the recipient is fraudulently induced by the recipient: see *Shogun Finance Ltd v Hudson* [2003] UKHL 62; [2004] 1 AC 919.
[49] For the general principles governing rectification, see Robert Stevens, 'What is an Agreement?' (2020) 136 LQR 599.
[50] *Blacklocks v JB Developments (Godalming) Ltd* [1982] Ch 183 (Ch).
[51] *Ogilvie v Littleboy* (1897) 13 TLR 399 (CA); sub nom *Ogilvie v Allen* (1889) 15 TLR 294 (HL).
[52] *Lady Hood of Avalon v Mackinnon* [1909] 1 Ch 476 (Ch).
[53] *Pitt v Holt* [2013] UKSC 26; [2013] 2 AC 108.
[54] *Gibbon v Mitchell* [1990] 1 WLR 1304 (Ch), 1309.

to the effect of the transactions as opposed to its consequences, was too restrictive. He said:

> I would provisionally conclude that the true requirement is simply for there to be a causative mistake of sufficient gravity; and, as additional guidance to judges in finding and evaluating the facts of any particular case, that test will normally be satisfied only when there is a mistake *either as to the legal character or nature of a transaction, or as to some matter of fact or law which is basic to the transaction.*[55]

So one might say that Lord Walker SCJ accepts the results (or 'effects')/consequences distinction, but requires that the consequences be so closely related to the transaction as to be 'basic' to its execution.

We can now deal with mistaken payments cases. Cash, or rather coin, was the original payment system. Because payment made in coin or notes is made by delivery, it will attract the same 'fundamental mistake' rules as apply to goods. But assuming that payment is made such that those rules don't apply, we must not distinguish mistaken payment cases on the basis whether payment was made in cash, or made by way of another payment system,[56] by cheque or by credit card or by electronic 'transfer'.[57]

We should distinguish three kinds of mistaken payment cases.

(1) 'Weinrib cases': where two parties are in an ongoing arm's length commercial relationship there is an express or implied condition that a payment is made only to discharge a liability, and the mistaken payor is entitled to restitution. This brings us back to the standard example of the overpaid gas bill, as well as cases where, for example, X pays his credit card bill twice. There may well be actual contractual terms in such cases, such as that the recipient company will apply the overpayment to the payor's account to meet future indebtedness, with a provision for a refund if requested. But if so, these cases would lie entirely outside the law of restitution; everything would sound in contract.

(2) '*Pinkroccade*' cases:[58] where a payment is made to someone other than the person intended, for example where one simply ticks the bank account of X when one meant to tick the account of Y in making an electronic bank transfer. This would also cover those 'computer glitch' cases where a

---

[55] *Pitt v Holt* (n 53) [122] (emphasis added).

[56] On money and payment systems generally, see James Penner, 'Tracing and Payment Systems' in Sinéad Agnew and Marcus Smith (eds), *Law at the Cutting Edge: A Festschrift in Honour of Dame Sarah Worthington, DBE, KC (Hon)* (Hart forthcoming).

[57] In particular, we should not analyse mistaken payments as akin to compromised property transfers. For discussion, see JE Penner, 'We All Make Mistakes: A "Duty of Virtue" Theory of Restitutionary Liability for Mistaken Payments' (2018) 81 MLR 222, 239–42; Robert Stevens, Chapter 7 in this volume.

[58] After *Re Pinkroccade Educational Services Pte Ltd* [2002] SGHC 186; [2002] 4 SLR 867.

computer system goes haywire and starts making random payments. These cases are essentially on all fours with the mistaken identity 'fundamental mistake' case identified earlier. The wrong *result* is achieved. In *Pinkroccade* itself, the court held that the payment should be held on constructive trust, and this seems right to me, since that result is as near as possible to the result in fundamental mistake cases, where legal title does not pass at all. It is submitted that the same analysis should apply to payments of wrong amounts, say, where the payor mistakenly adds a zero to the amount in executing an electronic bank transfer, paying £1,000 when she meant to pay £100.

(3) 'Pure mistaken consequences cases': where the only reasons for giving restitution are that the payor's mistaken understanding of the consequences of the payment are the grounds for relief, *Ogilvie* et al discussed earlier being examples. These are the most difficult cases, since we should, as a matter of justice understood as a matter of *right*, live with the consequences of our mistakes. As Smith puts it:

> The common law's substantive duties are duties not to wrong others; in particular, duties not to wrong others by interfering with their person, property, liberty, or contractual promises made to them. Battering, trespassing, breaking contractual promises, carelessly injuring others, causing nuisances, and so forth are all non-consensual interferences of this kind. ... A substantive duty to correct an injustice, if it existed, would be very different from these duties. Failing to correct an injustice is not a wrong, or at least not a wrong in the sense that battery and so forth are wrongs. If I fail to return money that you paid me by mistake..., my failure is not an interference with your person, property, liberty, or a promise that I made to you. More generally, you cannot point to any right of yours that I am infringing by not making restitution or paying damages. All that I have done is fail to correct an injustice.[59]

This observation does not deny that correcting injustices is valuable. It is because correcting injustices is valuable that we are praised when we return mistaken payments and when we 'compensate' others whom we have harmed. But the fact that it is valuable (or 'virtuous',[60] 'commendable', 'useful', 'beneficial', and so forth) to do something is rarely a sufficient ground for the common law to recognize a substantive duty to do that thing.

We all have reason to address injustices, so why single out the defendant? The reason is that if I am materially implicated in an injustice it becomes part of my

---

[59] Stephen A Smith, *Rights, Wrongs, and Injustices: The Structure of Remedial Law* (OUP 2019) 232 (footnote omitted). See also 234–35, 246, 249.

[60] For my own claim that restitutionary liability for a mistaken payment is the legalization of a duty of virtue, see Penner, 'We All Make Mistakes' (n 57).

history, and so I stand in a special relationship to it. It is therefore reasonable, even if not required as a matter of right, to legalize an obligation upon me to do something about it. And, in a sense, this is for my own good. If I fail to address an injustice of which I am the beneficiary this would be a blot on my character.[61]

VI. Conclusion

The corrective justice strategy of explaining restitution of unjust enrichments only makes sense on the substantive duty-affirming basis—that is, that the right to restitution of a mistaken payment is a matter of right. And we have seen that, taking the hint from Weinrib, this works only by treating all mistaken payments as conditional, and relating other cases to the common law 'fundamental mistake' cases.

To the extent, then, that there remains a residue of cases in which restitutionary liability may arise, what I have called the pure mistaken consequences cases, then corrective justice does not explain every case of restitution.

[61] ibid 233–34.

9
Agreement and Restitutionary Liability for Mistaken Payments

Peter Chau and Lusina Ho[*]

I. Introduction

A perennial challenge in justifying a payee's liability to return mistaken payments lies in reconciling such liability with payee autonomy. Unlike a tortfeasor whose conduct causes harm to the claimant, the payee did nothing wrong, nor did the payee expressly undertake an obligation to repay. In the absence of an express undertaking and any wrongdoing on the payee's part, what is the justification for compelling them to give up their payment?[1]

In the broader literature on moral and political philosophy, we can find two general liberal strategies to justify obligations in the absence of wrongdoing and an express undertaking. Whilst both appeal to the agent's agreement, they rely on different types of agreement. The first strategy appeals to a *tacit* agreement: if an agent has voluntarily assumed an obligation, even if tacitly, there is no infringement on the agent's autonomy. John Locke's argument for an obligation to comply with the law based on voluntary residence is a well-known example of this approach.[2] The second strategy appeals not to an actual agreement, but to a *hypothetical* one. It considers an obligation reconcilable with an agent's rational autonomy if the obligation is grounded in a principle to which the agent would agree if they were reasonable. John Rawls's argument for our obligations towards fellow citizens exemplifies this approach: although we have not actually agreed to such obligations, we would *if* we were reasonable.[3]

Both strategies have recently been invoked to justify a payee's duty to return mistaken payments. Alexander Georgiou argues that when a payor pays a payee, there

---

[*] We would like to thank Tatiana Cutts, Alexander Georgiou, and participants at the conference for the present volume, in particular Elise Bant, Siyi Lin, and James Penner for their helpful comments.
[1] This concern has been raised by many. See eg Jennifer M Nadler, 'What Right Does Unjust Enrichment Protect?' (2008) 28 OJLS 245; Frederick Wilmot-Smith, 'Should the Payee Pay?' (2017) 37 OJLS 844, 855–61; JE Penner, 'We All Make Mistakes: A "Duty of Virtue" Theory of Restitutionary Liability for Mistaken Payments' (2018) 81 MLR 222, 224–25 (hereafter Penner, 'We All Make Mistakes').
[2] John Locke, *The Second Treatise on Civil Government* (Prometheus 1986) ch 8.
[3] John Rawls, *A Theory of Justice* (rev edn, OUP 1999) 12.

is 'almost always' a tacit agreement between them that the latter will return the payment if 'certain states of affairs' do not obtain, which is the case in mistaken payment situations.[4] Tatiana Cutts argues that a principle providing for restitutionary liability for mistaken payments would be accepted by all reasonable people.[5] The arguments offered by these two authors are promising. If they hold, the moral justification for restitutionary liability is compelling. This chapter maintains, however, that their analyses leave unresolved a number of important issues. Georgiou's approach of drawing multiple inferences from the act of payment, and the words accompanying it, raise doubts as to whether the conclusion of his chain of inferences is sufficiently probable. Further, it is questionable whether the idea of an actual agreement provides a suitable tool for shaping the law of unjust enrichment. Cutts does not explain why the restitutionary principle she proposes better addresses the concern she raises than alternative principles, and nor does her account accommodate certain axiomatic distinctions in the law of unjust enrichment (such as the distinction between mistakes and mispredictions). We conclude that it is too soon to jettison current theories of unjust enrichment in favour of an agreement-based explanation.

II. Actual Agreement

An obvious hurdle faced by implied contract theories of unjust enrichment is to demonstrate that notwithstanding the lack of any express undertakings, the payee of a mistaken payment has voluntarily assumed an obligation to repay. Georgiou seeks to overcome this hurdle by arguing that the payor and payee have 'almost always'[6] entered into a tacit agreement. He observes that the payor cannot just *pay* the payee; strictly speaking, the payor offers to pay, and the payment is completed only when the payee accepts the offer.[7] Drawing upon theories of intention and social convention, he argues that even though payors may not consciously intend to pay on the condition that the payee return the payment if certain states of affairs fail to obtain, they would, upon reflection, understand themselves to have intended so. Further, the payees almost always understand offers to pay as having been made on said condition. In accepting the payment, the payee accepts that condition.[8] Consequently, in cases of mistaken payment, when those states of affairs turn out to be untrue, the payee is bound by the agreement to return the payment. Georgiou

---

[4] Alexander Georgiou, 'Mistaken Payments, Quasi-Contracts, and the "Justice" of Unjust Enrichment' (2022) 42 OJLS 606, 611 (hereafter Georgiou, 'Mistaken Payments').
[5] Tatiana Cutts, 'Unjust Enrichment: What We Owe to Each Other' (2021) 41 OJLS 114, 128 (hereafter Cutts, 'Unjust Enrichment').
[6] Georgiou, 'Mistaken Payments' (n 4) 611.
[7] ibid 621–22. The same point was made in Robert Stevens, 'The Unjust Enrichment Disaster' (2018) 134 LQR 574, 581–82.
[8] Georgiou, 'Mistaken Payments' (n 4) 623.

also claims, conversely, that if the payee does not accept said condition, there is no agreement; if there is no agreement, there is no 'valid transfer'.[9] There being no justification for the payee to keep something that was never validly transferred to them, they should return it.[10]

Our discussion of Georgiou's thesis proceeds as follows. After challenging the claim that there is almost always an agreement of the kind he alleges in connection with payments, we query whether the concept of an agreement offers the best conceptual apparatus for shaping the law of unjust enrichment.

A. Finding an Agreement

In Georgiou's analysis, a payment involves a payor who offers to pay and a payee who accepts the payment. In Section II.A.1, we query whether a payor almost always intends to offer to pay on the condition Georgiou alleges. We turn to the payee's alleged acceptance in Section II.A.2 to examine whether it is almost always the case that, in receiving a payment, a payee accepts said condition.

1. Payor's intent

Georgiou devotes considerable space to discussing the philosophical literature on theories of action and intention to argue that because people rarely do things without a reason, the payor's intention to pay is always conditional on certain states of affairs being true, even if they are not consciously aware of it.[11] That discussion, whilst persuasive and illuminating, lends little support to his claim that offers to pay are almost always conditional in the relevant sense. The crucial term 'condition' needs clarification because it might bear at least two meanings: the *motivating cause* of the offer or the *terms* of the offer intended by the payor. A motivating cause states the reason that motivates the offer as a psychological matter and without which the offer would not have been made. Suppose that I offered X a job because I believed he was a law graduate. That belief is the motivating cause of my offer: I would not have offered X the job if I had believed him to be a graduate of another discipline. By contrast, a term of an offer is a provision in the offer that gives rise to a binding obligation once the offer is accepted. For example, it may be a term of an employment contract stipulating that employees should wear a uniform while on duty. The two types of condition are distinct. I have no recourse under the employment contract if X turns out not to be a law graduate, as it is not stipulated in the contract that he must be. By contrast, X would be in breach of contract if he refused

---

[9] ibid 621–22.
[10] ibid 622.
[11] ibid 611–20.

to wear a uniform while on duty, even though his doing so was not why I offered him the job.

The distinction makes clear that even if a payor's intention to pay is conditional, in the sense that they offer to pay only *because* they believe a certain state of affairs to be true, it does not follow that they *intend* to stipulate the term that the payee must return the payment if that state of affairs does not obtain. A common scenario serves to illustrate the point. Suppose that a payee supplies raw materials crucial to the payor-manufacturer's production process, and the parties maintain a good business relationship. On some occasions, the payor pays in advance of the payment due date for raw materials supplied. In the transaction that concerns us, the payor pays upon the mistaken belief that there is an outstanding debt with the supplier, and would not have paid otherwise. It does not follow that the payor intends to pay upon the term that the payment be returned if it transpires that there is no outstanding debt. In fact, given the parties' good business relationship, it is plausible that the payor would not intend to stipulate such a term.

A similar example can be found in relation to the mistaken transfer of property, with respect to which Georgiou claims that his analysis 'applies in almost identical terms'.[12] Suppose that the Economist Group sends us several issues of *The Economist* by mistake or a restaurant delivers an extra dessert by mistake. It is unclear why it would follow that the group or the restaurant intended to stipulate a requirement that we return the missent issues or the dessert; practicality and considerations of public relationship may counsel otherwise. Of course, we do not exclude the possibility that the sender may intend to stipulate such a requirement.[13] We merely doubt if senders generally do so.

Accordingly, even if Georgiou's theoretical foray supports his claim that almost all payors intend to pay because of the motivating cause that a certain state of affairs is true, it does not demonstrate that almost all payments are intended by the payor to be offered upon the term that the payment should be returned should such a state of affairs not obtain.

2. Communication and acceptance

Georgiou recognizes that payees are only bound by what payors 'outwardly express, not what [payors] privately think to [themselves]'.[14] Put simply, even if the payor privately intends to stipulate the return of the payment should a certain states of affairs fail to obtain, such a term does not bind the payee unless it has been communicated to and accepted by the payee.[15] This is the point when Georgiou makes the

---

[12] ibid 630.
[13] Such as in *Weatherby v Banham* (1832) 5 C & P 228; 172 ER 950. We are grateful to Georgiou for helpful discussion on this point.
[14] Georgiou, 'Mistaken Payments' (n 4) 623.
[15] Conversely, it seems that, on Georgiou's account, a term can bind the payee even if it does not form part of the payor's private intent in offering to pay, so long as the offer, objectively construed, includes the term.

next, even more controversial, move. He claims that communication and acceptance of such a term can almost always be inferred from the wording and context of the payment. His analysis pertains primarily to payments coupled with express wording on the payment purpose, although he contends that his account is also applicable to 'pure' payments that 'are not coupled with any express words' about the purpose of the payment.[16] As examples of pure payment, Georgiou cites 'bank transfers that are not accompanied by a "payment reference"' and the handing over of cash coupled with the utterance 'here you go'.[17]

Focusing first on payments coupled with express words about the purpose of the payment, suppose that a payor gives $100 cash to a payee, and says 'I am paying you because X'. Georgiou claims that the payee would understand the payor to mean 'If not X, then I want the money back'.[18] He reaches this conclusion through two steps of inference. First, the linguistic and philosophical literature on 'conditional perfection' suggests that unless the context indicates otherwise, the statement 'I am paying you because X' implies 'I am paying you only because X' (in other words, 'If not for X, then I wouldn't be paying you').[19] Secondly, the implied statement is most naturally understood as entailing 'If not X, then I want the money back'.[20]

This inferential argument is appealing, but is marred by Georgiou's failure to distinguish between a motivating cause and a term of the offer to pay, as in his previous claim about a payor's intent.[21] He assumes that the root statement 'I am paying you because X' must almost always be understood by the payee as stipulating *the terms on which* they are paid, not merely *why* they are being paid. As previously noted, this assumption is unjustified.[22] Without clarifying the root statement, the first inference— 'I am paying you *only* because X'—is ambiguous for the same reason. Given this ambiguity, there is scant justification for the payee to infer that the payor is stipulating the terms of the offer to pay, as opposed to merely observing the motivating cause of the offer.

In any event, even if the payee understands that in referring to X, the payor is stating the terms of the offer, it does not follow that the payee must also understand such terms to include an unqualified *remedial* duty to return the payment should X not obtain. Such a remedy is merely one of many possible forms of recourse. For example, it is plausible if not probable for customers who have received misdelivered goods to infer that the seller intended to reimburse them for the trouble of returning the goods or allow them to keep the goods at no charge or a discounted price. This particularly holds true if a customer's role in this sorry state

---

[16] Georgiou, 'Mistaken Payments' (n 4) 624.
[17] ibid.
[18] ibid 623–28.
[19] ibid 625–27.
[20] ibid 627–28.
[21] See text to nn 11–13.
[22] Georgiou, 'Mistaken Payments' (n 4) 627–28.

of affairs is entirely passive, and yet they are still saddled with the responsibility of dealing with the fallout.[23]

Georgiou's inferential argument rests on an even shakier foundation in pure payment cases. In the absence of express words specifying the purposes of such payments, the aforementioned concerns regarding the obscurity of payment terms apply even more forcefully.[24] Georgiou's contention that the payment context allows the payee to draw 'fairly reliable inferences' about the payment's purpose is overly optimistic.[25] Consider three common scenarios where the contexts are too thin. First, I left a $10 note on the counter after the barista served me a coffee that cost $7. The context is ambiguous as to whether I intended to leave a tip or overpaid by mistake. Secondly, an employer who was giving out discretionary year-end bonuses to employees mistakenly transferred the bonus meant for another employee to the defendant employee, who has not been awarded any bonus. It is not obvious from the context that the payment was a mistake. Thirdly, an art gallery advertised sales of a commemorative coin at $1,000. It invited interested customers to place their order (for any number of coins subject to availability) by sending a cheque for the requisite purchase price, with contact information on the back of the cheque. Shortly after the advertisement, a payor sent a $2,000 cheque with their contact information to the company. However, the payor did not know about the sale and paid upon the mistaken belief that they owed the company a debt pertaining to a completely unrelated business matter. In all three cases, the contexts do not allow the payee to draw 'fairly reliable inferences' about the purpose of the payment, let alone the existence of a condition that the payment must be returned if the purpose does not obtain. However, if these payments were made upon mistake, they are clearly recoverable.

Perhaps Georgiou can accommodate these cases by conceding that no tacit agreements can be inferred. Nonetheless, so he may say, the payees still need to return the payment because absent an agreement, there is no 'valid transfer', and 'the [payees have] no justification for keeping what was *ex hypothesi* never validly given to them'.[26] Such a move concedes that the explanation for these cases is no longer

---

[23] For a real-life example of how recipients of misdirected goods might respond, see Kevin Lynch, 'Sonos sent people too many speakers in order screw-up, then asked for them back' (TechRadar, 14 June 2022) <www.techradar.com/news/sonos-sent-people-too-many-speakers-in-order-screw-up-then-asked-for-them-back> accessed 11 January 2023.

[24] Georgiou's account is distinctive in seeing the payee's duty to make restitution as based on the commonality of the payor's conditional intent to pay and the communication of such intent to the payee. However, there are related accounts that focus on the 'acceptance' of the payment by the payee rather than the payee's mere enrichment: see Ernest J Weinrib, *Corrective Justice* (OUP 2012) ch 6; Lionel Smith, 'Restitution: A New Start?' in Peter Devonshire and Rohan Havelock (eds), *The Impact of Equity and Restitution in Commerce* (Hart Publishing 2019) 112–13; Stevens, 'The Unjust Enrichment Disaster' (n 7) 581–83. The oft-made critique of such accounts, a critique with which we broadly agree, is that payees often lack the relevant knowledge for their 'acceptance' to be morally significant: Cutts, 'Unjust Enrichment' (n 5) 127–28 (cited by Georgiou, 'Mistaken Payments' (n 4) without explicitly considering this critique); James Penner, Chapter 8 in this volume.

[25] Georgiou, 'Mistaken Payments' (n 4) 625.

[26] ibid 622 (emphasis in original).

agreement-based, and cannot draw on the normative significance of a voluntarily assumed duty to justify the duty to return. Furthermore, it is unclear why a transfer without a prior agreement is (morally) invalid and must be unwound, even though the payee has obtained rights under the rules of property regarding valid transfers. Perhaps Georgiou will also cast aside situations with no valid transfer as exceptional; but, if so, he owes us an explanation for why they are exceptional rather than the norm, as the three examples discussed earlier are plausible.

In the foregoing discussion, we register doubts about Georgiou's strategy for establishing the existence of a tacit agreement to return a mistaken payment through multiple inferences from the silent act of payment and elliptical statements accompanying it. We may grant these inferences up to a point: because people rarely pay without a reason, it is reasonable to infer that every offer to pay has a certain motivating cause. However, Georgiou's long chain of inferences continues: from the existence of a motivating cause of an offer to pay, to that of a term of the intended offer; from the intended term of paying only if a state of affairs is true, to that of returning the payment if that state does not obtain; and from the payor's intention to make an offer upon such a term, to the communication and acceptance of this term by the payee. This long series of inferences is remarkable. However, it is in the nature of non-deduction that the degree of probability diminishes at each step, and the conclusion weakens. One is thus left to wonder whether the final conclusion is sufficiently probable to justify a general duty in law to return mistaken payments.

B. Mismatch Between Agreement and Unjust Enrichment

Having established our doubts as to whether there is almost always a relevant tacit agreement in mistaken payment cases, here we make a more fundamental challenge; namely, that it is questionable whether the idea of a tacit agreement constitutes a suitable apparatus for determining the availability of restitution.

First, the idea of a tacit agreement is too broad to identify situations of unjust enrichment, as the agreement may specify the circumstances in which a payment needs to be returned, but those circumstances might not involve unjust enrichment. For example, the parties may tacitly agree that a payment be returned if made upon a misprediction, but it is axiomatic in the law of unjust enrichment that such a payment is not unjust.[27] To recover the payment, the payor would need to invoke

---

[27] *Kleinwort Benson Ltd v Lincoln CC* [1999] 2 AC 349 (HL) 399, 409; *Dextra Bank & Trust Co Ltd v Bank of Jamaica* [2001] UKPC 50; [2002] 1 All ER (Comm) 193 [29]; Charles Mitchell, Paul Mitchell, and Stephen Watterson, *Goff & Jones: The Law of Unjust Enrichment* (10th edn, Sweet & Maxwell 2022) [9-07]; Peter Birks and Charles Mitchell, 'Unjust Enrichment' in Peter Birks (ed), *English Private Law*, vol 2 (OUP 2000) 546; Weeliem Seah, 'Mispredictions, Mistakes and the Law of Unjust Enrichment' (2007) 15 RLR 93.

the law of contract, as the claim is not grounded in unjust enrichment. Georgiou's agreement-based account offers no basis for distinguishing between mistake and misprediction, as it views recovery in both situations as based solely on the idea of an agreement. Moreover, if, as he says, the recovery of mistaken payments is contractual, it remains to be seen why this species of agreement-based duty need not meet current requirements for imposing agreement-based liability such as those set out in contract law.

Secondly, the idea of a tacit agreement is also too narrow in that it excludes situations of unjust enrichment that do not permit any inference of a tacit agreement on the facts. For example, Georgiou's preoccupation with finding an agreement leads him to cast out duress, undue influence, and mental incapacity[28] from unjust enrichment's remit on the ground that no meaningful agreement can be made with a person suffering from duress or undue influence. This controversial claim prematurely excludes the possibility that a unifying principle of unjust enrichment runs through the recovery of payments made both by mistake and on the grounds cast out by Georgiou.

Thirdly, the idea of a tacit agreement is too vacuous. It lacks sufficient content to guide the development of detailed legal principles for resolving disputes in unjust enrichment. The idea directs the inquiry in such disputes towards examining the existence and terms of a tacit agreement with respect to their resolution. However, one might argue that the necessity for the law of unjust enrichment arises precisely because the parties are unable to reach such an agreement, let alone an agreement with details of the defences for and extent of the remedy. Consider the defence of a change of position, which is aimed at protecting the payee. It is difficult to imagine that, contrary to their own interests, payors would propose this defence as an implied term, and nor is it plausible to consider payees who merely receive payment as making a counter-offer that proposes the defence.[29] Accordingly, the idea of a tacit agreement has little to offer the law of unjust enrichment in developing detailed principles concerning when enrichment is unjust, what defences are available, and what remedy is just for both parties.

These three problems demonstrate the conceptual limitations of Georgiou's agreement-based account. As we have argued, an agreement to return a payment should certain states of affairs fail to obtain is neither necessary nor sufficient to establish a claim of unjust enrichment. The idea of a tacit agreement is also too vacuous to guide the development of detailed principles on liability, defences, and remedy. For decades, implied contract theory has blunted the development of the law of unjust enrichment. The theory's demise has unleashed efforts to search for

---

[28] Georgiou is silent about incapacity, but his emphasis on the payor's ability to enter into a meaningful agreement would exclude incapacitated payors from the law of unjust enrichment.
[29] Penner, 'We All Make Mistakes' (n 1) 245–46. See also Alexander YS Georgiou, 'What's "Unjust" About Unjust Enrichment: An Answer at Last?' [2021] LMCLQ 63 for a discussion of change of position.

the law's moral justification outside an actual agreement. These efforts have yet to succeed, but at least they are on the right path. By refocusing on an actual agreement, Georgiou's project risks unravelling the progress made so far.

III. Hypothetical Agreement

Unlike Georgiou, Cutts does not consider the idea of *actual* acceptance to be a relevant criterion for justifying the duty to return mistaken payments. Instead, she appeals to the contractualist idea of *reasonable* acceptance, arguing that reasonable people would accept only the following principle, which grounds the recovery of mistaken payments.

> *Principle R2*: 'a mistaken payee must repay ... to the extent that so doing will not cause her to be worse off than she was prior to payment.'[30]

In propounding this principle, Cutts modifies and applies Thomas Scanlon's moral theory of contractualism to the novel territory of mistaken payments. We begin with a brief summary of Cutts's modification of Scanlon's theory, and then lay out her argument that *Principle R2* follows from contractualist reasoning. Finally, we present a few objections to her analysis.

A. Cutts's Contractualism: Variation on a Scanlonian Theme

Scanlon derives the content of morality from the idea of reasonable agreement.[31] As his well-known formula states, 'an act is wrong if its performance under the circumstances would be disallowed by any set of principles for the general regulation of behaviour that no one could reasonably reject as a basis for informed, unforced general agreement.'[32] Whether a person can reasonably reject a principle depends on a 'pairwise comparison'[33] between the strength of that person's objection to the principle and the strength of other individuals' objection to the alternative. In other words, a person can reasonably reject a principle if their objection to it is stronger than anyone else's objection to the alternative, and vice versa.[34]

For Scanlon, the only permissible reasons for rejecting a principle are 'personal' reasons.[35] Personal reasons are reasons that a person can offer 'on his own

---

[30] Cutts, 'Unjust Enrichment' (n 5) 137. We adopt the label used by Cutts for the principle.
[31] Thomas Scanlon, *What We Owe to Each Other* (Harvard UP 1998) 153 (hereafter Scanlon, *What We Owe*).
[32] ibid, quoted in Cutts, 'Unjust Enrichment' (n 5) 129.
[33] Thomas Nagel, *Equality and Partiality* (OUP 1995) 67.
[34] Scanlon, *What We Owe* (n 31) 229–30.
[35] ibid 219.

behalf',[36] such as that the principle in question would reduce that person's well-being or is otherwise unfair *to that person*.[37] To use Scanlon's own example, consider a choice between (1) saving a person and (2) protecting a group of persons from minor harm.[38] A utilitarian would choose (2) if the group was sufficiently large, whereas a contractualist would choose (1) because one's personal reason to stay alive is much stronger than any other individual's personal reason to avoid minor harm.

Recent years have seen growing interest in developing contractualist accounts of private law. Scanlon himself has sought to justify contract law by reference to his contractualist moral framework,[39] and John Oberdiek has made a similar attempt with respect to tort law.[40] Cutts is the first scholar to extend the contractualist approach to mistaken payments. She embraces Scanlonian contractualism in its broad contours (as is obvious from the title of her article), but adopts two of Derek Parfit's modifications of Scanlon's account.

First, whilst Scanlon takes into account only 'information actually available to' a person in deciding the strength of the person's objection to a principle, Cutts agrees with Parfit that the relevant information should not be so restricted, and may include facts unavailable to the person.[41] Secondly, and more significantly, she sides with Parfit in claiming that both an individual's personal reasons and impartial reasons should be considered in determining the strength of their objection to a principle.[42] Impartial reasons are based on the goodness of an event 'from an impartial point of view', which takes into account others' interests.[43] Cutts adapts Parfit's lifeboat example to demonstrate the difference between the two kinds of reasons. Suppose that 'I am stranded on one rock, and five people are stranded on another'.[44] The rescuer can reach only one of the rocks. Cutts argues that under Scanlon's account I cannot reasonably *reject* a principle requiring the rescuer to save me instead of the five, as my rejection of a principle is reasonable only if my

---

[36] TM Scanlon, 'Reply to Gauthier and Gibbard' (2003) 66 PPR 176, 183.
[37] Scanlon, *What We Owe* (n 31) 216, 219.
[38] ibid 238.
[39] TM Scanlon, 'Promises and Contracts' in Peter Benson (ed), *The Theory of Contract Law* (CUP 2009) 100.
[40] John Oberdiek, 'Structure and Justification in Contractualist Tort Theory' in John Oberdiek (ed), *Philosophical Foundations of the Law of Torts* (OUP 2014) (hereafter Oberdiek, 'Structure and Justification'). See also Gregory C Keating, 'Rawlsian Fairness and Regime Choice in the Law of Accidents' (2004) 72 Fordham LR 1857; Emmanuel Voyiakis, *Private Law and the Value of Choice* (Hart Publishing 2017). For a critique of the utility of Rawlsian contractarianism in justifying private law (with particular reference to Keating's account), see Arthur Ripstein, 'The Division of Responsibility and the Law of Tort' (2004) 72 Fordham LR 1811 (hereafter Ripstein, 'The Division of Responsibility'). Our challenge to Cutts shares broad affinities with Ripstein's critique, although it is worthwhile mentioning that Ripstein's critique is particularly directed at contractualist accounts of private law that are 'consequentialist' in nature (1821–22), and it is unclear whether Cutts's account is consequentialist.
[41] Cutts, 'Unjust Enrichment' (n 5) 134.
[42] ibid 133–34.
[43] Derek Parfit, *On What Matters*, vol 1 (OUP 2011) 40.
[44] Cutts, 'Unjust Enrichment' (n 5) 133.

personal reason for rejecting the principle is stronger than anyone else's personal reason for rejecting the alternative. According to Cutts, Scanlon's account is, therefore, problematic because we should be allowed to appeal to the value of others' lives in deciding what to reject: a reasonable person can be altruistic.[45]

This chapter is not the occasion to question whether Cutts's modifications are justified, as neither her argument nor our objections hinge on the modifications. Nonetheless, we register two doubts about her modifications. Regarding the first modification to include facts unavailable to the agent, Scanlon has already made it clear that the goal of his contractualist theory is to guide deliberation as to the permissibility of acts, not to determine their permissibility from an omniscient God's eye view.[46] Given Scanlon's aim, it is only natural to exclude information that is unavailable to those deliberating.

Scanlon has also provided reasons against Cutts's second modification in his response to the same suggestion by Parfit. As Scanlon observes, the unconstrained admission of impartial reasons would permit the attainment of greater aggregate well-being at the expense of significant costs for a few.[47] Furthermore, Cutts's desired verdict in the lifeboat example can be accommodated within Scanlon's general contractualism framework through a minor modification without abandoning the personal reasons requirement wholesale. Drawing on Scanlon's discussion on 'tie-breakers',[48] a Scanlonian may hold that one can reasonably reject a principle *not only* if one's personal objection to it is stronger than another person's objection to the alternative, but also if another person's personal objection to the alternative is as strong as one's own objection to the principle *and* there are relevant 'tie-breakers'.[49] This is sufficient to reach Cutts's desired verdict in the lifeboat case: the number of people being rescued is a relevant tie-breaker, and my personal objection to not being saved is no stronger than any of those five persons' personal objections to not being saved.

B. The Argument

Cutts's defence of *Principle R2* proceeds in two steps. The first shows that a principle requiring payees to return mistaken payments is preferable to principles either denying relief completely or providing it via compulsory insurance (as opposed to

---

[45] ibid 134.
[46] TM Scanlon, *Moral Dimensions: Permissibility, Meaning, Blame* (Harvard UP 2010) 49–52.
[47] TM Scanlon, 'How I Am Not a Kantian' in Derek Parfit (ed), *On What Matters*, vol 2 (OUP 2011) 129, 135. But see also TM Scanlon, 'Contractualism and Justification' in Markus Stepanians and Michael Frauchiger (eds), *Reason, Justification, and Contractualism* (De Gruyter 2021). We thank Cutts for the reference.
[48] Scanlon, *What We Owe* (n 31) 230–41.
[49] For the idea of 'tie-breaking', see ibid 235, 240.

payee restitution), and the second qualifies the payee's duty by a change of position defence.

In detail, the first step compares *Principle R*, which requires payees to return the mistaken payment in full, to two other principles:[50]

> *Principle NR*: payees need not return the mistaken payment, and payors have no recourse.
> *Principle NR-S*: payees need not return the mistaken payment, and payors can claim compensation through a compulsory insurance scheme (a system analogous to New Zealand's Accident Compensation Scheme).

For the comparison between *Principle R* and *Principle NR*, Cutts claims that the costs imposed on a payee by *Principle R* are lower than those imposed on a payor by *Principle NR*.[51] The payor 'has shaped plans' around the sum paid but not the payee.[52] So, denying restitution would disrupt the payor's plans, whereas allowing it will have a lesser impact on the payee, who is only giving up 'an unplanned-for ("windfall") gain'.[53] Furthermore, requiring payees to shoulder the risk of payors' mistakes would also assure payors of the security of their payments and 'encourage [them] to pay [their] debts'.[54] Cutts concludes that contractualist reasoning explains why *Principle R* is favoured over *Principle NR*.

As between *Principle R* and *Principle NR-S*, Cutts offers three reasons why reasonable people would favour *Principle R* over *Principle NR-S*. First, *Principle NR-S* creates 'logistical problems'.[55] Secondly, the compulsory insurance premium payable under *Principle NR-S* may be 'intolerably ... burdensome' to people with limited means: it may 'remove their ability to afford basic necessities'.[56] Thirdly, burdens that are *unavoidable* (or cannot be reasonably avoided) are particularly hard to justify within a liberal framework. Unlike insurance premiums for drivers, which can be avoided by choosing not to drive, insurance premiums under *Principle NR-S* are compulsory and thus unavoidable. Modifying *Principle NR-S* in a way that requires only 'those who in fact make and receive payments' to pay the premium would not help, as making and receiving payments are inevitable facts of life.[57]

---

[50] Cutts, 'Unjust Enrichment' (n 5) 135. We have slightly modified the wording of the three principles without, we believe, affecting meaning.
[51] ibid 136.
[52] ibid 137.
[53] ibid 136, 137. For the importance of security in justifying private law, see eg Robert E Goodin, 'Compensation and Redistribution' (1991) 33 Nomos 143; John Gardner, *From Personal Life to Private Law* (OUP 2018) 181–89.
[54] In Cutts, 'Unjust Enrichment' (n 5) 135, Cutts cites and draws on Nicholas McBride, *The Humanity of Private Law*, vol 1 (Hart Publishing 2018) 191.
[55] Cutts, 'Unjust Enrichment' (n 5) 136. Presumably these are problems in collecting payments, assessing claims, and distributing payments.
[56] ibid 137.
[57] ibid.

Having tentatively established *Principle R*, Cutts then proceeds to the second step of her argument, which contends that a principle (*Principle R2*) that allows the recovery of mistaken payments subject to a defence along the lines of a change of position is preferable to *Principle R*.[58] She begins by observing that whilst it is important to avoid 'frustrating the plans' of payors, it is also important to avoid frustrating those of payees (in fact, her argument requires the assumption that the latter consideration is more important). Accordingly, payees should not be required to repay if they have 'built plans' on the money received.[59] For Cutts, it follows that payees should not be required to repay if repaying would make them worse off than they were prior to the impugned transaction.

C. Our Objections

Cutts's argument is interesting and thought-provoking, but ultimately unconvincing. First, the options she considers in her comparative exercise are unduly limited. In explaining why reasonable people would prefer a principle requiring the mistaken payee to return the payment, whether in full or subject to the change of position defence (*Principle R/R2*), she considers only two alternatives: *Principles NR* and *NR-S*. However, as we shall see, her reasons for choosing *Principle R/R2* actually does not forbid the choice of other plausible, if not better, alternatives. Secondly, the considerations Cutts takes into account in her contractualist reasoning, such as the security of plans, lack sufficient specificity to justify *Principle R/R2* as opposed to other principles that could accommodate those considerations. In what follows, we consider three objections stemming from this deficient comparative exercise.

1. Why is there a general duty to return mistaken payments?

Cutts appeals to the security of payors' plans in rejecting *Principle NR* in favour of *Principle R/R2*, which gives payors a general right to restitution. She is concerned that failure to recover an unplanned-for payment would disrupt payors' plans. According to Cutts, we make our spending choices based on the assumed amount of money at our disposal. If, for example, we are not allowed to recover a payment made upon the mistaken belief that the payee is our creditor, we will suffer a detriment that has not been planned for. For Cutts, 'the impact [of the disruption] on our lives may be severe'.[60] Requiring payees to give up an unexpected windfall, in contrast, exerts less of an impact. The security of a payor's plan therefore gives a

---

[58] Cutts claims that *Principle R2* 'encompasses change of position': ibid.
[59] ibid.
[60] ibid 136.

payor a reason to reject *Principle NR* that is stronger than the payee's reason to reject *Principle R/R2*.[61]

In response to Cutts's argument based on payor security, we should first bear in mind that it is an entirely contingent matter whether a payor's plan would suffer a disruption from a failure to recover the mistaken payment. Consider someone who mistakenly believes that a debt is due,[62] pays it, and then plans their life on the assumption that the money paid is no longer accessible. Denying such a payor recovery would not bring about any disruption of their plans; rather, allowing recovery might give them resources that they have not planned for in formulating their plans. Once we recognize the possibility of such a situation, it should be clear that we need not choose, as Cutts did, between two diametrically opposed principles that either allow or deny a *general* right to recovery. There are principles that, contrary to *Principle R/R2*, provide a more circumscribed right to restitution but, contrary to *Principle NR*, also protect the security of payors' plans. Consider, for example, the following principle, which affords payors only a qualified right to recover mistaken payments:

> *Principle X*: the payee must repay if and only if the payor has shaped plans around the amount paid, and non-recovery of the payment will disrupt those plans.

It is doubtful whether reasonable people would reject *Principle X* in favour of a principle that allows the payor to recover *regardless of* whether their plans would be disrupted by non-recovery (such as *Principle R/R2*). Comparison of *Principle X* and *Principle R* serves to illustrate the point.[63] Payors who suffer an adverse effect from the disruption of their payment-related plans have a right to recover mistaken payments regardless of whether *Principle X* or *Principle R* is adopted, so they have no reason to prefer one principle over the other. It is true that payors who have not made such plans have personal reasons to reject *Principle X* in favour of *Principle R*, as they can recover their payments under *Principle R* but not under *Principle X*. However, this reason is based not on the security of their plans but simply on the utility of money to them; if the utility of money is the determinative criterion, then payees have equally strong personal reasons to reject *Principle R* in favour of *Principle X*. Since the objection to *Principle X* by payors who have not made payment-related plans is *not stronger* than the objection to *Principle R*

---

[61] See text to nn 53–56. It is unclear to what extent Cutts's argument here—and elsewhere—is based on the idea of 'impartial' reasons, especially as she has little to say about how the impartial goodness of different outcomes should be judged, a problem she inherits from Parfit (Scanlon discusses this problem in Scanlon, 'How I Am Not a Kantian' (n 47)). Curiously, after introducing the need to include impartial reasons in comparing principles, Cutts makes no direct reference to such reasons in her argument.

[62] eg when payment is made upon a liability mistake.

[63] The result of the comparison also applies to *Principle R2*.

by payees who have received mistaken payments, such payors cannot *reasonably* reject *Principle X*.

If it is not already obvious, our objection is modelled on Cutts's argument for introducing the change of position defence, which is based on two main ideas: (1) whether the payee's plans will be disrupted by repaying is a contingent matter and (2) the payee's interest should be protected if and only if their plans will be disrupted by repaying.[64] In proffering *Principle X*, we are simply applying her logic to payors: if payees' interest should be protected only if they would otherwise be adversely affected by the disruption of their plans, then the same should apply to payors. However, it is not Cutts's aim to advocate for a significantly circumscribed right of recovery constructed upon the plans of individual payors, and nor does *Principle X* fit the existing law of unjust enrichment, which gives payors a general, prima facie right of recovery for mistaken payments regardless of their plans.

2. Why not socialize the loss?
We now turn to Cutts's discussion of *Principle NR-S*, which 'socialises' the loss; that is, spreads the payor's loss amongst a group of people who contribute to a public compensation fund.[65] As mentioned previously, she provides three justifications for why reasonable people would reject this principle. There may, indeed, be good reasons not to socialize payors' losses, but Cutts's justifications are unpersuasive.

We start with her second justification, namely, that the compulsory insurance premium under *Principle NR-S* may be 'intolerably ... burdensome' for people with limited means, as it 'would remove their ability to afford basic necessities'.[66] In the absence of empirical support, this claim is speculative. Further, even if we grant, for the sake of argument, that the insurance premiums under *Principle NR-S* would be unduly burdensome for the poor, and hence a poor person can reasonably reject that principle, this concern with the poor does not rule out other loss-socializing principles. Consider the following principle:

> *Principle Y*: the payee need not return the mistaken payment, and the payor is compensated by an insurance scheme funded by large business enterprises with a minimum annual turnover or balance sheet total.

Both *Principle Y* and *Principle NR-S* socialize the loss, but *Principle Y* spreads it amongst those who can afford it such that no person's basic needs will go unmet as a result of paying compulsory insurance premiums.

It is not clear that anyone could reasonably reject *Principle Y* in favour of *Principle R/R2*. As far as people with limited means are concerned, they are subject

---

[64] Cutts, 'Unjust Enrichment' (n 5) 137.
[65] ibid 136.
[66] ibid 137.

to a lighter burden under *Principle Y* than under *Principle R/R2*, as neither principle requires them to pay an insurance premium but the latter requires them to return the mistaken payment should they receive one. Whilst business enterprises shoulder an extra burden in the form of insurance premium under *Principle Y*, the premium is a business cost they can easily afford (and spread). In addition, under *Principle Y* business enterprises are relieved from the liability to return a mistaken payment should they receive one, and relatedly the cost of litigation should they wish to defend it. All things considered, it is unclear that the objection to *Principle Y* by business enterprises is stronger than the objection to *Principle R/R2* by people with limited means.

At first glance, *Principle Y* may appear vulnerable to Cutts's third objection to loss-socializing schemes, which focuses on the objectionability of unavoidable burdens. She might argue that business enterprises could reasonably reject *Principle Y* because it imposes on them a burden that is unavoidable, namely, insurance premiums. To this, we have two replies. First, we must not forget that under *Principle R/R2*, the mistaken payee owes an unavoidable duty to make restitution. As Cutts herself observes, such a mistaken payee 'does not and cannot choose whether to assume the burden of repayment'.[67] Given that both principles involve an unavoidable burden, the unavoidable burden concern gives us no reason to prefer *Principle R/R2* to *Principle Y*.

Secondly, even if the unavoidability of an insurance premium under *Principle Y* gives us a good reason to reject the principle, it does not give us a good reason to reject all loss-socializing principles, such as the following one:

Principle Z: the payee need not return the mistaken payment, and the payor obtains compensation from an insurance scheme funded by *voluntary subscription*, albeit only if the payor subscribes to the scheme.

Compared with *Principle R/R2*, *Principle Z* relieves payees of the burden of repaying a mistaken payment while giving payors a choice between paying an insurance premium and accepting the risk of not being able to recover a mistaken payment. As the insurance premium is avoidable under *Principle Z*,[68] and the burden imposed on individual payors is no heavier than that imposed on individual payees under *Principle R/R2*, it is unclear why *Principle Z* could be reasonably rejected.

What about Cutts's first objection based on the logistical problems of socializing the loss? No doubt, there are administrative costs in implementing loss-socializing principles, such as *Principle NR-S/Y/Z*. However, we should bear in mind that the status quo (represented by *Principle R/R2*) also comes with costs: for example,

---

[67] ibid 128.
[68] The payor, of course, has to choose between paying the insurance premium and accepting the risk, but the mere fact that both options have a cost does not mean that there is no real choice.

court time is precious, and payees have less confidence in the security of receipt.[69] Moreover, in denying recovery to mistaken payors who opt out of the insurance scheme, *Principle Z* provides incentives for them to take greater care in making payments. In any event, without empirical investigation into the scale of the logistical costs, a project Cutts has not undertaken, it remains an open question which principle (or a hybrid principle that socializes the loss for some but not all mistaken payments) will win out in the cost–benefit calculus. Drawing support from another branch of law, if the logistical problems involved in replacing (certain parts of) tort law by New Zealand's Accident Compensation Scheme are not prohibitive, then we must not jump too quickly to the conclusion that they are so decisive as to compel reasonable people to favour *Principle R/R2* over loss-socializing principles.

3. Why exclude mispredictions and certain gifts?

It is axiomatic in the law of unjust enrichment that not all causative mistakes give rise on their own to a right to restitution. For example, a mistake as to the future—more precisely, a prediction that subsequently turns out to be false—does not render the enrichment unjust. There was no incorrect belief at the time of the decision-making process to impair that process, and the payor is thus treated as having taken the risk of their assumption being incorrect.[70] As another example, if the enrichment is in the form of a gift, the causative mistake must be of 'sufficient gravity' to make it 'unjust' or 'unconscionable' to leave the mistake uncorrected.[71]

However, Cutts's contractualist reasoning, which appeals to the imprecise idea of the security of the payor's plans, does not distinguish mispredictions and mistaken gifts from other causative mistakes that give rise to a right to restitution. Payors who have paid upon a misprediction or made a gift upon a mistake may also suffer a disruption in their plans if denied restitution, but such a disruption is not a sufficient ground for liability. In *Dextra Bank & Trust Co Ltd v Bank of Jamaica*, Dextra considered the payment it had made to the Bank of Jamaica to be a loan, only to discover that both parties had been deceived by fraudsters who had appropriated the payment amount.[72] Even though Dextra's plans would be disrupted if it could not recover the sum paid, the Privy Council decided that the Bank of Jamaica had no liability—not even a prima facie one subject to the defence of change of position—to return the payment. For their Lordships, no liability can arise upon payments made upon a misprediction, as opposed to a 'relevant mistake of fact'.[73] In *Pitt v Holt*, the plaintiff (Mrs Pitt) would have been saddled with tax liabilities she had not planned for had she not been allowed to set aside the discretionary

---

[69] Cutts accepts that it is important to maintain payees' 'confidence in security of receipt' in Cutts, 'Unjust Enrichment' (n 5) 137.
[70] *Kleinwort Benson Ltd v Lincoln CC* (n 27) 399, 409; *Dextra v Bank of Jamaica* (n 27) [29].
[71] *Pitt v Holt* [2013] UKSC 26; [2013] 2 AC 108 [122].
[72] *Dextra v Bank of Jamaica* (n 27).
[73] ibid [33].

trust in question. It was nonetheless held that the mere fact that she made the gift under a mistaken belief was insufficient; the trust could only be set aside if the mistake were of 'sufficient gravity'.[74] Cutts's contractualist reasoning cannot account for these decisions. If, as Cutts asserts, one's interest in 'confidence in payment' is more important than one's interest in the 'possibility of [a] windfall',[75] then reasonable people would choose a principle under which Dextra would have been able to recover the payment (subject to a change of position defence by the Bank of Jamaica) and Mrs Pitt would not have needed to meet the additional requirement of sufficient gravity.

IV. Conclusion

In the foregoing discussion, we critically examine two recent agreement-based justifications for the duty to return mistaken payments. We express doubt about whether there is 'almost always' an actual agreement to return such payments, as alleged by Georgiou, and question the utility of the idea of actual agreement for shaping the law of unjust enrichment. Although we do not dispute the general, albeit arguably vacuous, contractualist idea that the permissibility of actions depends on reasonable agreement,[76] we argue that the considerations put forward by Cutts, such as the security of payors' plans, lack sufficient specificity to explain why reasonable people must favour restitution.

On a broader level, the limitations of these two authors' accounts demonstrate the constraints facing successful theories of unjust enrichment. Such theories must, first, explain why in the absence of any undertaking or wrongdoing on their part, recipients of mistaken payments must nonetheless make restitution against their will, and, secondly, pinpoint the underlying value that grounds claims in unjust enrichment. Although a few current accounts of restitution are well placed to satisfy these constraints, we highlight two by way of example.

First, consider the property-based accounts offered by Peter Jaffey and Charlie Webb.[77] In both authors' view, the law of unjust enrichment serves to protect the same interests as those recognized by property law. Their accounts fare better than those of Georgiou and Cutts, as it is widely accepted that property rights justify

---

[74] *Pitt v Holt* (n 71) [122].
[75] Cutts, 'Unjust Enrichment' (n 5) 137.
[76] See eg Scanlon, *What We Owe* (n 31) 214, 242–47; Ripstein, 'The Division of Responsibility' (n 40) 1823, 1829; HLA Hart, 'Rawls on Liberty and Its Priority' (1973) 40 U Chi L Rev 534; Oberdiek, 'Structure and Justification' (n 40) 113. For a discussion of whether this fact renders contractualism problematic as a moral theory, see eg Rahul Kumar, 'Reasonable Reasons in Contractualist Moral Argument' (2003) 114 Ethics 6. We thank James Penner for helpful comments on this point.
[77] See eg Peter Jaffey, *Private Law and Property Claims* (Hart Publishing 2007); Peter Jaffey, Chapter 11 in this volume; Charlie Webb, *Reason and Restitution: A Theory of Unjust Enrichment* (OUP 2016) chs 3, 4.

limiting others' freedom and the non-consensual usurpation of claimants' power to dispose of their assets better maps onto the law of unjust enrichment than the idea of an agreement or disruption of payors' plans. Secondly, James Penner recently argued that the legal imposition of a duty to return mistaken payments is justified by reference to the duty, not of right but of virtue, not to take advantage of others' mistakes even if it is within one's rights to do so.[78] This account is also more promising than those of Georgiou and Cutts. It is uncontroversial that duties of virtue can arise in the absence of any voluntary undertaking. Further, very few people would deny that a virtuous person would not obtain a benefit at the expense of another's mistake, regardless of whether doing so would disrupt the other's plans.

Nonetheless, to say that virtue- and property-based accounts offer better prospects is not to say that they are free from difficulties. The ultimate fate of a property-based account depends on the successful defence of the institution of private property, which is a daunting task. Penner himself admits that the duty-of-virtue account needs to explain exactly why the duty not to take advantage of others' mistakes is so important that, unlike many other duties of virtue, it can ground onerous legal duties.[79] Our aim is more modest: simply to show that Georgiou and Cutts have yet to present a convincing agreement-based justification for restitutionary liability, and therefore that it is too soon to jettison existing theoretical accounts of the basis for the law of mistaken payments.

---

[78] Penner, 'We All Make Mistakes' (n 1) 243–44.
[79] Penner's position as to whether such a legal duty can ultimately be justified is nuanced: see ibid, 233, 243–45.

10
Law of Unjust Enrichment or Law of Unjust De-Enrichment?

Lutz-Christian Wolff

I. Introduction

As the name suggests, the law of unjust enrichment focuses on the enrichment of defendants. The question is if this enrichment focus makes sense. Why should the law provide a remedy which focuses on the defendant's rather than on the claimant's position? A literature review reveals that this question has hardly ever been seriously considered. Peter Jaffey brought this to the fore when arguing that '[a] principle of unjust enrichment [has] never [*been*] satisfactorily identified'.[1] In contrast, the idea that unjust enrichments need to be given up for the benefit of a claimant seems to be generally accepted, apparently without much reflection.

This chapter argues that the enrichment focus of the current law lacks rhyme or reason, that the law of unjust enrichment should rather be understood as a law of unjust de-enrichment, and that such an approach has significant advantages. Most importantly, the focus on the claimant's de-enrichment would finally allow this whole area of law to be explainable as a coherent regime which offers practical and thus compelling solutions.

The discussion in this chapter is not jurisdiction-specific. However, the starting point is the English law of unjust enrichment which is benchmarked against features of other unjust enrichment regimes where this seems helpful. For these benchmarking purposes, jurisdictions have been selected which offer solutions which are different from the ones English law appears to provide.[2] Nonetheless, the arguments put forward and solutions proposed in this chapter are meant to apply everywhere. They do, of course, require contextualization to be in line with the specifics of particular jurisdictions.

Section II of the chapter discusses the enrichment focus of the law of unjust enrichment *de lege lata* and *de lege ferenda* (ie it asks if the status quo makes

---

[1] Peter Jaffey, Chapter 11 in this volume, text to nn 6–7.
[2] For the selection of jurisdictions for comparative purposes, cf Marieke Oderkerk, 'The Importance of Context: Selecting Legal Systems in Comparative Legal Research' (2001) 48 NILR 293; Lutz-Christian Wolff, 'Comparing Chinese Law ... But with Which Legal Systems?' (2018) 6 CJCL 151, 153–64.

sense). It concludes that remedial action is not required in the first place because of a defendant's enrichment, but rather to remedy the claimant's de-enrichment. Consequently, Section III suggests a reconstruction of the field towards a 'law of unjust de-enrichment'. It shows that such a reconstruction will lead to systemic consistency thus supporting convincing solutions for many of the currently disputed questions.

II. Enrichment or De-Enrichment?

A. Background

The law of unjust enrichment is based on the fundamental idea that nobody should enrich herself at the expense of another party and that any unjust enrichment should be given up for the benefit of anybody at the expense of whom the enrichment has occurred.[3] While this general idea appears easy to understand, the law of unjust enrichment is regarded as one of the most complicated areas of law in almost every jurisdiction. Terminology is not used in a uniform way,[4] very basic substantive aspects as well as details of the law of unjust enrichment are controversially discussed,[5] and some commentators even continue to question the very existence of a separate law of unjust enrichment.[6] But despite the ongoing debates, the law of unjust enrichment seems to be firmly established as an important part of most modern jurisdictions.[7]

B. The Enrichment Focus

Following the groundbreaking work of the late Professor Peter Birks, it is the prevailing opinion in today's common law world that unjust enrichment claims are neither based on consent (or quasi-consent[8]) nor on

---

[3] cf 'Developments in the Law: Unjust Enrichment—Introduction' (2020) 133 Harv L Rev 2062, 2062.
[4] Mitchell McInnes, 'The Measure of Restitution' (2002) 52 UTLJ 163, 163 ('semantic confusion'); David A Juentgen, 'Unjustified Enrichment in New Zealand and German Law' (2002) 8 Canta LR 505, 506.
[5] Steve Gallagher, Lin Siyi, and Lutz-Christian Wolff, 'The History of a Mystery: The Evolution of the Law of Unjust Enrichment in Germany, England and China' (2020) 3 ICPELR 337, 340; cf Steve Hedley, '"Unjust" at Common Law: So Many Concepts, So Little Clarity' (2006) 14 ERPL 399; Graham Virgo, *The Principles of the Law of Restitution* (3rd edn, OUP 2015) 51; Ernest J Weinrib, 'The Structure of Unjustness' (2012) 92 BU L Rev 1067, 1067, 1079.
[6] cf Robert Stevens, 'The Unjust Enrichment Disaster' (2018) 134 LQR 574; disagreeing Andrew Burrows, 'In Defence of Unjust Enrichment' (2019) 78 CLJ 521, 521–22, 525; Kit Barker, 'Unjust Enrichment in Australia: What Is(n't) It? Implications for Legal Reasoning and Practice' (2020) 43 MULR 903, 903, 906.
[7] For English law, cf Virgo (n 5) 61.
[8] For the revival of the notion of quasi-contracts in France, cf Pablo Letelier, Chapter 15 in this volume.

wrongs.⁹ The justification of remedies in this area of law is, rather, seen in the unjust enrichment of the defendant.¹⁰ As mentioned at the outset, this chapter challenges the enrichment focus of the law of unjust enrichment which will be discussed: (1) *de lege lata* and (2) *de lege ferenda*.

As for the *lex lata* (ie the current law of unjust enrichment), the focus on the enrichment of the defendant dominates almost everywhere. The enrichment of the defendant is regarded as the 'causal event' which triggers the restitutionary remedy.¹¹ And, the enrichment is also the object of that restitutionary remedy. More precisely, unjust enrichment law grants the claimant a right of restitution which under English law takes the form of a money claim.¹²

The focus of the law of unjust enrichment on the defendant's enrichment is embodied in many commentators' insistence that this area of law provides a 'gain-based remedy':

> When we speak of damages, we usually mean compensatory damages. It is a loss-based response. Restitution, in contrast operates to reverse or undo the defendant's enrichment. It is a gain-based response, and includes both 'giving back' and 'giving up'.¹³

But does the English law of unjust enrichment really always regard the defendant's enrichment as the causal effect that triggers the restitutionary remedy in all circumstances? One may doubt this for at least two reasons.

First, in cases where the defendant is no longer enriched, for example because the object of the enrichment was lost or destroyed, English law grants the defendant the change of position defence.¹⁴ Lord Goff famously explained the underlying idea in *Lipkin Gorman v Karpnale Ltd*:

---

⁹ Peter Birks, *Unjust Enrichment* (2nd edn, OUP 2005) 8, 13; Alvin WL See, 'An Introduction to the Law of Unjust Enrichment' (2013) 5 Malayan LJ i, text to fn 143.

¹⁰ cf Mitchell McInnes, '*BMP Global Distributions Inc v Bank of Nova Scotia*: The Unitary Action in Unjust Enrichment' (2009) 48 CBLJ 102, 103.

¹¹ cf Birks (n 9) 8, 11, 36; 'Developments in the Law' (n 3) 2062.

¹² Birks (n 9) 168; cf Burrows (n 6) 529, 541.

¹³ See, 'An Introduction to the Law of Unjust Enrichment' (n 9) text to fn 153; Birks (n 9) 3, 11; 'Developments in the Law' (n 3) 2062; also cf however, Stevens, 'The Unjust Enrichment Disaster' (n 6) 576; Mitchell McInnes, 'Unjust Enrichment: A Reply to Professor Weinrib' (2001) 9 RLR 29, 33.

¹⁴ cf *Lipkin Gorman v Karpnale Ltd* [1991] 2 AC 548 (HL) 579–80; *Globenet Droid Ltd v Hong Kong Hang Lung Electronic Co* [2016] HKCU 1559; [2016] 3 HKLRD 863; Birks (n 9) 8 ('horribly blunt hammer'); Mat Campbell, 'Change of Position: Retreating from *Barros Mattos*, then Rocking the Boat' (2014) 22 RLR 105, 105 ('over half a century later, its details are still being debated'); Tang Hang Wu, 'Taking Stock of the Change of Position Defence' (2015) 27 SAcLJ 148; Burrows (n 6) 535–36; Barker (n 6) 11; cf similar for German law, s 818 para 3 of the German Civil Code, the application of which has been narrowed down by German courts—Lutz-Christian Wolff, *Zuwendungsrisiko und Restitutionsinteresse: Struktur und Rückabwicklung von Zuwendungen Dargestellt am Beispiel von Synallagma und Leistungskondiktion* [*Property Rights' Transfer Risk and Restitutional Interest: Structure and Revocation of the Transfer of Property Rights Explained on the Basis of the Examples 'Synallagma' and 'Leistungskondiktion'*] (Duncker & Humblot 1998) 205–11 (hereafter Wolff, *Zuwendungsrisiko und Restitutionsinteresse* [*Transfer Risk and Restitutional Interest*]). For the fact that the general defence of de-enrichment is 'not fully recognized in English law', cf Birks (n 9) 208–09.

> [W]here an innocent defendant's position is so changed that he will suffer an injustice if called upon to repay or to repay in full, the injustice of requiring him so to repay outweighs the injustice of denying the plaintiff restitution. If the plaintiff pays money to the defendant under a mistake of fact, and the defendant then, acting in good faith, pays the money or part of it [away], it is unjust to require the defendant to make restitution to the extent that he has so changed his position.[15]

While this rationale is commonly accepted, it is simply not logical from the viewpoint of the enrichment focus of unjust enrichment law. If the claimant's restitutionary remedy is triggered by the unjust enrichment of the defendant, then the loss of the enrichment should mean that such trigger is gone and there should be neither a claim nor a need for a defence.[16] Robert Stevens has considered if this contradiction can be addressed by focusing on 'the time for the establishment of "enrichment"' while concluding that:

> The existence of any defence of change of position then poses a puzzle. The defence cannot be based upon any notion of 'disenrichment'. The 'enrichment' ... cannot be lost.[17]

In other words, if the defendant's enrichment is the basis of the unjust enrichment claim, then, if the enrichment no longer exists, there should simply be no claim and consequently also no need for a defence. In contrast, the change of position defence does make sense if the law's starting point was the de-enrichment of the claimant. If the restitutionary remedy was triggered by the claimant's de-enrichment, then—and only then—would there be a need to allow the defendant to 'indicate a reason why the defendant should not be liable or the liability should be reduced in some way'.[18] It would be for the defendant to raise the change of position defence and the defendant would have the burden of proof in that regard. But, again, this is not what the current English law of unjust enrichment seems to prescribe.

Secondly, it is one of the preconditions of unjust enrichment claims under English law that the enrichment was unjust. The question of what 'unjust' means in the law of unjust enrichment:

> ... has brought English law to the crossroads. There are broadly two different approaches taken by different legal systems to this question. The first is the Continental European approach to unjust enrichment which has also been adopted in Canada. It looks to the enrichment of the defendant and asks whether

---

[15] *Lipkin Gorman v Karpnale Ltd* (n 14) 579 (Lord Goff).
[16] cf Stevens, 'The Unjust Enrichment Disaster' (n 6) 586.
[17] ibid 587 (footnote omitted).
[18] cf Virgo (n 5) 60.

there is any juristic reason for the retention of that enrichment.... The second is the approach historically taken in many English decisions. This approach looks for an established legal ground which shows why the receipt of an enrichment by the defendant is unjust. It is described ... as the unjust factors approach ... [ie] an enquiry into whether there is any positive 'unjust factor' that entitles the claimant to restitution ...[19]

Again, one might question if the unjust factor approach is really in line with the understanding that unjust enrichment claims are gain-based remedies. If the unjust factor approach relates to circumstances that entitle the claimant to restitution, is the focus then not again on the position of the claimant rather than on the enrichment of the defendant? In fact, it appears that what the unjust factor approach really does is to ask if the de-enrichment of the claimant is unjust rather than inquiring if the enrichment of the defendant is unjust. Therefore, the unjust factor approach could also be understood as 'loss-based'[20] rather than 'gain-based'. A comparison with the continental European juristic reason approach to determine whether an enrichment is unjustified reinforces this conclusion. Under the continental European approach, an enrichment is unjustified if:

... there is no reason for the defendant to retain the enrichment[.] ... The unjust factors approach contrasts with the juristic reasons approach because it requires the claimant to show a reason why the enrichment is unjust rather than to show that there is no juristic reason for the defendant to retain the enrichment.[21]

To sum up, the two examples (ie the change of position defence and the unjust factor approach) may be seen as contradicting the common understanding that the law of unjust enrichment in England always insists on the gain-based approach. If this were, indeed, the case, then the potential for misunderstandings is rather obvious. If unjust enrichment claims are regarded as gain-based remedies while at least tacitly a loss-based approach is also (partly) adopted, then systemic coherence would be difficult to maintain. One could even speculate whether some of the significant uncertainties in the law of unjust enrichment are a result of this ambiguity.

One could, of course, also argue that the existing confusion is just a result of unfortunate language due to a lack of focus on the consequential differences between gain- and loss-based approaches. It is also important that the aforementioned observations can by no means be seen as argument to reinterpret the *lex lata*. Rather,

---

[19] James Edelman, 'The Meaning of "Unjust" in the English Law of Unjust Enrichment' (2006) 14 ERPL 309, 309, 311 (footnote omitted).
[20] The terminology adopted here has been developed by others: cf n 11. The term 'loss' must, of course, be understood figuratively as, eg, the provision of services or the grant of a right to use by the claimant would not lead to an actual loss on her part.
[21] Edelman (n 19) 311, 309.

they demonstrate that the current status is anything but clear and that there is a lack of awareness of what the enrichment focus of the current law of unjust enrichment really implies.

Finally, the fact that the loss-based approach of an unjust enrichment regime is not *a contradictio in adjecto* is demonstrated, for example, by the Dutch Civil Code[22] which reads in Book 6:212, paragraph 1:

> A person who has been unjustifiably enriched at the expense of another person, has the obligation towards that other person to repair the damage up to the amount of his enrichment, as far as this is reasonable.[23]

Ulrich Drobnig has pointedly concluded that Dutch law regards unjust enrichments as 'damage'.[24]

As mentioned earlier, the claim that the English law of unjust enrichment is a gain-based remedial system has hardly ever been seriously disputed. Consequently, it remains unexplained why the law's response in unjust enrichment scenarios should be gain-based and not loss-based. Steve Hedley has correctly observed that '[a]sserting that the defendant is unjustly enriched does not give a reason for the liability, indeed is not even the beginning of a valid explanation.'[25] Jerome E Bickenbach has sung the same tune: 'To say that the defendant must reimburse the plaintiff because otherwise he would be unjustly enriched is not to give a reason for the decision, it is to give the conclusion of an unstated argument.'[26]

Apart from these methodological shortcomings, and leaving the rather chaotic historical development of the law of unjust enrichment aside, it must indeed be asked if it is *de lege ferenda* justified to explain the cause of action in enrichment scenarios with the unjust enrichment of the defendant. If the law of unjust enrichment provides a remedy for the claimant at whose expense the enrichment has occurred, then why should the starting point be the position of the defendant? Except for the name of this area of law, are there any policy-based or even jurisprudential reasons which can justify the focus on the enrichment of the defendant rather than on what really needs to be remedied—that is, the de-enrichment of the claimant?

---

[22] An unofficial English version is available at Hendrik Goossens, 'Dutch Civil Code' (*Dutch Civil Law*) <www.dutchcivillaw.com/civilcodebook066.htm> accessed 20 May 2022; for background, cf Wouter Snijders, 'From Pomponius to Article 6:212 Dutch Civil Code—The Vicissitudes of a Tradition' (2006) 14 ERPL 391; Denis Tallon, 'The New Dutch Civil Code in a Comparative Perspective—A French View-Point' (1993) 1 ERPL 189; U Drobnig, 'Das neue niederländische bürgerliche Gesetzbuch aus vergleichender und deutscher Sicht' ['The New Dutch Civil Code from a Comparative and German View'] (1993) 1 ERPL 171.
[23] See also Drobnig, ibid 185.
[24] ibid.
[25] Steve Hedley, 'What is "Unjust Enrichment" For?' (2016) 16 OUCLJ 333, 334.
[26] Jerome E Bickenbach, 'Unsolicited Benefits' (1981) 19 UWO L Rev 203, 207; also cf Stevens, 'The Unjust Enrichment Disaster' (n 6) 576.

A remedy is conventionally regarded as 'a way of solving a problem'.[27] But what is the problem in unjust enrichment cases that requires the law's attention? If there was no de-enrichment of the claimant, why should the law be bothered with any enrichment at all?[28] Is it consequently not correct to say that only the interests of the de-enriched claimant necessitate a remedial tool?[29]

A 'remedy' can also be regarded as 'the means to achieve justice'.[30] Again, why should a restitutionary remedy be triggered by the defendant's enrichment when any injustice which ought to be corrected only stems from the loss of the claimant which is thus the only reason why a remedy is required? If it is the claimant's de-enrichment that needs to be remedied, then this should consequently be the starting point.

The reasons justifying the existence of the law of unjust enrichment as a whole are, of course, unsettled.[31] In the following, the most important of the related approaches will be briefly tested in regard to the question of whether they support the gain-based approach.

First, the law of unjust enrichment is often seen as being based on the notion of corrective justice:[32]

> [T]he idea of a duty to return all enrichment received out of another person's property ... stems from the theological doctrine of *restitutio*, and thus from the theological tradition of natural law.... [T]his theological doctrine of *restitutio* was turned into a natural law theory of corrective justice. Its purpose was primarily to explain moral duties of compensation for loss suffered by another person.[33]

As discussed in further detail later, the correlation between gain and loss is a core notion of corrective justice which in itself appears to defeat the idea that unjust enrichment law is (solely) gain-based.[34] Furthermore, if there were no 'loss suffered

---

[27] Cambridge University Press, 'remedy' (*Cambridge Dictionary*) <https://dictionary.cambridge.org/dictionary/english/remedy> accessed 20 May 2022.
[28] Hedley, 'What is "Unjust Enrichment" For?' (n 25) 333: '[E]nrichments sound like something that the law encourages, and usually *should* encourage rather than censure.'
[29] cf Stevens, 'The Unjust Enrichment Disaster' (n 6) 579–80.
[30] ALM Media Properties, 'remedy' (*Legal Dictionary*) <https://dictionary.law.com/Default.aspx?selected=1784> accessed 20 May 2022.
[31] Hedley, 'What is "Unjust Enrichment" For?' (n 25) 333.
[32] *Kingstreet Investments Ltd v New Brunswick (Finance)* 2007 SCC 1; [2007] 1 SCR 3 [32]; *Investment Trust Companies v Revenue and Customs Comrs* [2017] UKSC 29; [2018] AC 275 [43] (Lord Reed SCJ); Lionel Smith, 'Restitution: The Heart of Corrective Justice' (2001) 79 Tex L Rev 2115, 2115; McInnes, 'The Measure of Restitution' (n 4) 186; but see Dan Priel, 'The Justice in Unjust Enrichment' (2014) 51 Osgoode Hall LJ 813.
[33] Nils Jansen, 'Farewell to Unjustified Enrichment?' (2016) 20 Edin LR 123, 127–28; cf Frank L Schäfer, 'Ungerechtfertigte Bereicherung' ['Unjustified Enrichment'] in Mathias Schmoeckel and others (eds), *Historisch-Kritischer Kommentar Zum BGB Band III Schuldrecht: Besonderer Teil* [*Historical-Critical Commentary of the Civil Code, vol III Law of Obligations: Special Part*] (Mohr Siebeck 2013) 2584, 2592–604, 2679–80; 'Developments in the Law' (n 3) 2072; Virgo (n 5) 104.
[34] cf Section II.C entitled 'The Correlation Between Enrichment and De-Enrichment'.

by another person' then there would be no 'moral duties of compensation'.[35] Therefore, from the corrective justice point of view, it must also be the claimant's de-enrichment which triggers the need for a restitutionary remedy in the form of an unjust enrichment claim.

Secondly, similar considerations must apply in relation to attempts to consider unjust enrichment law as a tool to achieve fairness[36] or even to regard it as a 'supra law' which can be used to achieve equitable results when the application of black-letter law does not lead to satisfactory solutions.[37] Even if one were to accept this position, whether unfairness is regarded as triggering the need for a remedy in unjust enrichment cases or whether a need for corrections is seen on the basis of equity, from this point of view it is initially also the position of the claimant which is important rather than the defendant's enrichment.

Thirdly, some commentators have attempted to expound the law of unjust enrichment with proprietary arguments. According to this viewpoint, restitutionary claims are justified if and when the defendant holds the claimant's property[38] or when the enrichment 'belongs' to the claimant.[39] Apart from the fact that this approach cannot explain certain unjust enrichment scenarios, such as the unjust provision of services,[40] a proprietary approach would also have to start from the position of the plaintiff as the claim is about the restitution of her proprietary position.

Fourthly, according to Professor Birks, '[w]hether a particular right can be called a remedy depends entirely on whether its relation to its causative event triggers the metaphor of cure'.[41] Again, it is rather clear that what needs to be cured in unjust enrichment cases is not the enrichment of the defendant, but the de-enrichment of the claimant.

Finally, in the common law world the law of unjust enrichment is often seen as part of a law of restitution which is understood as the general law of gain-based recovery.[42] More precisely, the law of unjust enrichment is nowadays regarded as a separate subsection of the law of restitution.[43] For what it is worth, the term 'restitution' also relates to the claimant's position which needs to be restored.[44]

---

[35] Jansen (n 33) 128.
[36] Priel (n 32) 842–49; but see *Investment Trust Companies v Revenue and Customs Comrs* (n 32) [39] (Lord Reed SCJ).
[37] Priel (n 32) 849–52; also cf Emily Sherwin, 'Restitution and Equity: An Analysis of the Principle of Unjust Enrichment' (2001) 79 Tex L Rev 2083, 2093–101.
[38] SJ Stoljar, *The Law of Quasi-Contract* (2nd edn, Law Book Co 1989) 9–10, 250; cf Priel (n 32) 838.
[39] Samuel Stoljar, 'Unjust Enrichment and Unjust Sacrifice' (1987) 50 MLR 603, 604; cf the discussion in Robert Stevens, Chapter 7 in this volume.
[40] Virgo (n 5) 52.
[41] Birks (n 9) 165.
[42] ibid 3, 17. For the fact that there is no general concept of a law of restitution in modern continental Europe, cf Gallagher, Lin, and Wolff (n 5) 349.
[43] Birks (n 9) 4; 'Developments in the Law' (n 3) 2020.
[44] Tatiana Cutts, 'Unjust Enrichment: What We Owe to Each Other' (2021) 41 OJLS 114, 123; but see Birks (n 9) 167.

Is a different standpoint required because injustice is involved?[45] Is it even possible to argue that the claimant's de-enrichment is irrelevant because the enrichment was obtained by fulfilling the unjust factor requirement?[46] In this regard, reference should first be made to the previous discussion.[47] It appears to be unclear whether the unjust factor requirement is really in line with the gain-based approach. Secondly, it must be questioned if it is the task of private law to order anybody to give up whatever they are not entitled to. If private law is concerned with 'defin[ing], regulat[ing], enforc[ing] and administer[ing] relationships among individuals, associations, and corporations',[48] then the answer must be a firm 'no'. An enrichment alone which does not correspond with loss to another party would be a single-party matter and should not lead to any need for remedial action.[49] One could only reach a different conclusion if the law of unjust enrichment were to be regarded as a tool for sanctioning or even for punishing the enriched party.

But, sanctioning and punishing have never been seen as the goal of the law of unjust enrichment.[50] In fact, leaving the controversial issue of exemplary (punitive) damages[51] aside, private law as such should generally not be concerned with sanctioning and punishment.[52] In addition, the unjustness of an enrichment—be it because of a lack of justifying juristic reason, because of unjust factors,[53] or for other reasons—does not automatically imply that the debtor was at fault or that there is another reason for her to be sanctioned or punished.[54] In contrast, the fact that an enrichment qualifies as 'unjust' must ultimately stem from the fact that the enrichment belongs to the claimant. And, again, this shows that the starting point must be the claimant's de-enrichment rather than the defendant's enrichment. Samuel Stoljar has consequently concluded:

> ... we are not so much activating our sense of justice in response to an allegedly undue benefit (though we may do that too) as rather stating that [the defendant]

---

[45] *David Securities Pty Ltd v Commonwealth Bank of Australia* (1992) 175 CLR 353, 379 (Mason CJ, Deane, Toohey, Gaudron, and McHugh JJ); Barker (n 6) 28.
[46] cf See, 'An Introduction to the Law of Unjust Enrichment' (n 9) text to fns 146–47; Hedley, '"Unjust" at Common Law' (n 5) 402–03, 334; Juentgen (n 4) 512. For the civil law approach, cf Juentgen (n 4) 526; Hedley, '"Unjust" at Common Law' (n 5) 404–05.
[47] cf earlier in this section.
[48] Farlex, 'private law' (*The Free Dictionary*, 2008) <https://legal-dictionary.thefreedictionary.com/private+law> accessed 20 May 2022.
[49] cf potentially different McInnes, 'Unjust Enrichment: A Reply to Professor Weinrib' (n 13) 34.
[50] Birks (n 9) 25.
[51] cf Cedric Vanleenhove, *Punitive Damages in Private International Law* (Intersentia 2016) 1.
[52] For English contract law, cf *Ruxley Electronics and Construction Ltd v Forsyth* [1996] AC 344 (HL) 365.
[53] cf earlier in this section.
[54] Birks (n 9) 5.

is retaining money which, being non-consensually acquired, 'belongs' to [the claimant].[55]

While Stoljar's emphasis on the 'unjust sacrifice'[56] of the claimant is in line with the conclusions presented in this chapter, it is based on a proprietary theory which—as Stoljar himself admits—has 'serious limitations'.[57] More importantly, when seeing the unjustness 'in the retention of assets demonstrably belonging to somebody else',[58] Stoljar also does not seem to question the unjust enrichment idea as such.

C. The Correlation Between Enrichment and De-Enrichment

Many commentators have pointed out that enrichment and loss are correlative.[59] In particular, Ernest J Weinrib famously attempted to justify unjust enrichment law based on the Aristotelian notion of corrective justice,[60] arguing that 'what grounds liability is the correlation between gain and loss'.[61] This, of course, seems to defeat the conventional view that unjust enrichment law is a gain-based restitutionary tool, although Weinrib does not expressly acknowledge that.[62]

The scope of this chapter does not allow a discussion of Weinrib's intriguing theory which is in fact not limited to unjust enrichment, but also concerns *The Idea of Private Law*[63] as such.[64] Furthermore, the correlative relationship between enrichment and de-enrichment in unjust enrichment cases is rather self-evident. Current English law prescribes that the enrichment of a defendant has to come 'at the expense' of the claimant.[65] Unjust enrichment regimes of other countries,

---

[55] Stoljar, 'Unjust Enrichment and Unjust Sacrifice' (n 39) 603–04. See also J Beatson, 'Benefit, Reliance and the Structure of Unjust Enrichment' (1987) 40 CLP 71, 71–72; J Beatson, *The Use and Abuse of Unjust Enrichment: Essays on the Law of Restitution* (Clarendon Press 1991) 21–22.

[56] cf the title of the article Stoljar, 'Unjust Enrichment and Unjust Sacrifice' (n 39) 605; Robert Stevens, Chapter 7 in this volume, text to nn 12–13.

[57] Stoljar, 'Unjust Enrichment and Unjust Sacrifice' (n 39) 603; cf Virgo (n 5) 52.

[58] Stoljar, 'Unjust Enrichment and Unjust Sacrifice' (n 39) 604.

[59] cf ibid; Stevens, 'The Unjust Enrichment Disaster' (n 6) 582; Virgo (n 5) 104.

[60] Ernest J Weinrib, *The Idea of Private Law* (Harvard UP 1995) 140–42; Weinrib, 'The Structure of Unjustness' (n 5) 1068–70; Ernest J Weinrib, *Corrective Justice* (OUP 2012) 187.

[61] Prince Saprai, 'Weinrib on Unjust Enrichment' (2011) 24 CJLJ 183, 184; cf Smith (n 32) 2141; Virgo (n 5) 104.

[62] cf Saprai (n 61) 204.

[63] Weinrib, *The Idea of Private Law* (n 60).

[64] For criticism of Weinrib's approach, cf Saprai (n 61) 183–204; McInnes, 'Unjust Enrichment: A Reply to Professor Weinrib' (n 13) 29–51; Matthew Doyle, 'Corrective Justice and Unjust Enrichment' (2021) 62 UTLJ 229.

[65] Birks (n 9) 5; cf *Investment Trust Companies v Revenue and Customs Comrs* (n 32) [43] (Lord Reed SCJ). For the fact that according to prevailing opinion English law does not require a loss to the plaintiff corresponding to the enrichment of the defendant, see [45]; cf Tang Hang Wu, *Principles of the Law of Restitution in Singapore* (Academy Publishing 2019) 39, 40–41; Birks (n 9) 79–82, 168; Stevens, 'The Unjust Enrichment Disaster' (n 6) 578.

such as France[66] and Germany,[67] provide for similar requirements. And one may therefore ask if it really matters whether the focus is on the enrichment, on the de-enrichment, or—a third option—on both (ie the enrichment of the defendant and the de-enrichment of the claimant).[68] The answer is that the focus is tremendously important for the following reasons.

First, as outlined in the following sections in greater detail, the difference between the current law's focus on the enrichment of the defendant and the focus on the position of the claimant as suggested in this chapter has fundamental doctrinal and practical consequences.[69] At this point, it suffices to refer again[70] to the example of a lost enrichment. If the focus were on the position of the claimant, the loss of the enrichment should, as a matter of principle, be irrelevant as the claimant would still be de-enriched. It would be for the defendant to raise the loss as a defence.[71] In contrast, if the focus were—as current law pretends—on the defendant's enrichment, it would simply be illogical to grant a restitutionary remedy because such remedy would be based on a reason that is no longer valid. In other words, according to the current gain-based approach, there should be no basis for a claim if the enrichment does no longer exist. This doctrinal dilemma of the current law cannot be solved by arguing that it is only important that at one point there was an unjust enrichment because any later loss of the enrichment would in that case have to be ignored for the defendant's liability.[72]

Furthermore, also a shift from a gain-based approach to a correlative approach (ie an attempt to explain the liability of the defendant in unjust enrichment cases with reference to both the de-enrichment of the claimant and the enrichment of the defendant) is not tenable. Most importantly, this approach would deny that the goal of any restitutionary tool in related cases must be to remedy the claimant's loss in the first place (ie that any unjust enrichment claim is triggered by the claimant's loss). As demonstrated in the next section, this has practical implications, for example, for the scope of the unjust enrichment claim which must be determined by considering the position of the claimant rather

---

[66] cf art 1303 French Code Civil ('au detriment d'autrui doit'). An unofficial English translation is available at John Cartwright, Bénédicte Fauvarque-Cosson, and Simon Whittaker, 'French Civil Code 2016' (*Trans-Lex Law Research*, 10 February 2016) <www.trans-lex.org/601101> accessed 20 May 2022. For the French law of unjust enrichment, also cf Pablo Letelier, Chapter 15 in this volume.

[67] cf s 812(1) German Civil Code ('auf dessen Kosten'). An unofficial English translation is available at Langenscheidt Translation Service, 'German Civil Code' (*Federal Ministry of Justice*, 1 October 2013) <www.gesetze-im-internet.de/englisch_bgb/englisch_bgb.html> accessed 20 May 2022. Note, however, that according to the generally accepted doctrine this requirement does not apply to performance-based unjust enrichment claims.

[68] William Day, 'Against Necessity as a Ground for Restitution' (2016) 24 RLR 26, 31; also cf Stevens, 'The Unjust Enrichment Disaster' (n 6) 582.

[69] cf earlier in this section.

[70] ibid.

[71] cf Virgo (n 5) 61.

[72] Stevens, 'The Unjust Enrichment Disaster' (n 6) 587.

than the position of the defendant, or both.[73] If the claim were based on both (ie the enrichment as well as on the de-enrichment), a clear distinction between the positions of the claimant and the defendant would not be possible, resulting in a blurred picture of the involved interests and how they should be addressed. Again, the example of lost enrichments shows this clearly. If in unjust enrichment cases the liability were to be based on the loss of the claimant and also on the gain of the defendant, it would not be possible to justify any liability if the enrichment of the defendant did not exist even if that was as a result of action attributable to the defendant.

All of this does not mean that the position of the defendant should or can be ignored. Most importantly, the 'gain' has to be considered when identifying the defendant (ie when determining against whom the claim is to be directed). This and other aspects are discussed in the following sections with a focus on the differences between the current gain-based approach and the loss-based approach proposed in this chapter.

To sum up, the defendant's position is as important in unjust enrichment cases as in any other obligatory relationship. However, it must be the position of the claimant which has been adversely affected and which therefore triggers the unjust enrichment claim and is thus the basis of any liability under unjust enrichment law.

III. Towards a 'Law of Unjust De-Enrichment'

A. General

If, as outlined in the previous sections, the commonly accepted enrichment focus of the law of unjust enrichment is not tenable, then it must be considered whether the law of unjust enrichment needs to be reconstructed and turned into a 'law of unjust de-enrichment'.[74] This section highlights what this might mean.

---

[73] cf Section III.G entitled 'The Scope of Unjust De-Enrichment Claims'; cf in contrast with the Canadian law perspective, McInnes, 'Unjust Enrichment: A Reply to Professor Weinrib' (n 13) 33.

[74] During the online symposium 'Rethinking Unjust Enrichment—Part 1' (Online, 14 September 2022), Peter Jaffey had alternatively suggested that the need to give up the enrichment focus should result in enrichment scenarios being addressed by existing regimes such as contract law and tort law; also cf Peter Jaffey, Chapter 11 in this volume, Section IV.C: 'Most so-called unjust enrichment claims are in my view better understood as property-based or contract claims, or as "imputed contract" claims that operate in the shadow of contract.' This intriguing suggestion is not adopted here, as this chapter does not challenge the assumption of current unjust enrichment law that special remedy needs beyond contract law and tort law exist for certain case types.

B. The Role of a Law of Unjust De-Enrichment

For a 'law of unjust de-enrichment'[75] the de-enrichment of the claimant is the causal event that triggers the claimant's restitutionary claim. The goal to remedy the claimant's loss must consequently be the starting point of any consideration. Reversely mirroring the prevailing opinion regarding the role of the current unjust enrichment law,[76] a law of unjust de-enrichment would therefore aim to remedy unjust de-enrichments of claimants from which defendants have benefited and which are neither covered by contract (or quasi-contract) law nor by tort law.

C. Competition of Claims

The previous section implies that a law of unjust de-enrichment would de facto take a subsidiary role—that is, it would serve as a fallback remedy for cases of unjust de-enrichment of the claimant where contract law and tort law remedies are not available.[77] Also current common law unjust enrichment regimes seem to regard unjust enrichment law claims as fallback remedies. Some civil law jurisdictions, such as French law,[78] have taken a similar approach. However, one can also envisage a system where unjust de-enrichment claims compete with contract law or tort law claims on an equal footing. To prevent the claimant from double benefitting, the law would have to set priority rules or allow the claimant to select which of several available claims she wishes to pursue. For example, under German law unjust enrichment claims exist in addition and at the same level as other claims unless specifically stipulated otherwise by law.[79] Having said that, the subsidiary role of a law of unjust de-enrichment seems to make perfect practical sense. If contract law or tort law offer a remedy, there is no need for an additional loss-based claim which may, in any event, have to rely on value judgements made in other areas of law.

---

[75] cf for the related notion of 'impoverishment', Peter Linzer and Donna L Huffman, 'Unjust Impoverishment: Using Restitution Reasoning in Today's Mortgage Crisis' (2011) 68 Wash & Lee L Rev 949.
[76] Birks (n 9) 8–9; Beatson, *The Use and Abuse of Unjust Enrichment* (n 55) 2; cf Virgo (n 5) 51.
[77] For the possibility of overlaps between unjust enrichment claims and claims based on contract and tort law, cf 'Developments in the Law' (n 3) 2065–70; Gerrit E van Maanen, 'Subsidiarity of the Action for Unjustified Enrichment—French Law and Dutch Law: Different Solutions for the Same Problem' (2006) 14 ERPL 409, 414–16. 'In short, it can only fill gaps': at 412.
[78] cf van Maanen, ibid 412, 414.
[79] Hartwig Sprau, 'Titel 26. Ungerechtfertigte Bereicherung—Einführung' ['Title 26. Unjustified Enrichment—Introduction'] in *Palandt Bürgerliches Gesetzbuch Band 7* [*Palandt Civil Code, vol 7*] (77th edn, CH Beck 2018) side numbers 5–7; van Maanen (n 77) 409.

D. De-Enrichment

The shift towards the de-enrichment of the claimant proposed in this chapter stems from the acknowledgement that it is the claimant's position which is detrimentally affected in scenarios traditionally addressed by unjust enrichment law. It is therefore not the enrichment of the defendant, but the de-enrichment of the claimant, which must be remedied.[80] Any loss of the claimant—whether as a result of her own action or not—that has a money value[81] would qualify as de-enrichment.[82] It appears that the criteria and considerations which are currently applied to determine what qualifies as enrichment[83] can *mutatis mutandis* be used to decide if a claimant is de-enriched.

E. Identifying the Claimant–Defendant Relationship

Under current unjust enrichment law, the link between the defendant and a claimant is established through the requirement that any enrichment must be 'at the expense of the claimant'.[84] In contrast, for a law of unjust de-enrichment, the starting point has to be the claimant's position and the identification of the claimant–defendant relationship must follow the 'reverse direction' as compared with the current law. 'At the expense of the claimant' will consequently have to be replaced with 'for the benefit of the defendant'. This does not mean that the main argument of this chapter (ie that the focus should be on the position of the claimant) is abandoned. As mentioned earlier,[85] the correlation between enrichment and de-enrichment is the only way in which the obligation of the defendant towards the claimant can be established and by which the de-enrichment of the claimant becomes actionable. However, it is important that the reason for the liability of the defendant is the claimant's loss. It is this loss which triggers the restitutionary claim.

The identification of the defendant (ie the question of who has benefited from the claimant's loss) can be challenging, in particular when more than two parties are involved.[86] These scenarios will require decisions based on a comprehensive analysis of the interests and relationships of the parties concerned. It is, however, safe to say that the shift to de-enrichment does not increase the difficulties

---

[80] cf the Supreme Court of Canada's decision in *Kingstreet Investments Ltd v New Brunswick (Finance)* (n 32) [32].
[81] cf Virgo (n 5) 64.
[82] For the definitory difficulties, cf Beatson, *The Use and Abuse of Unjust Enrichment* (n 55) 74.
[83] Birks (n 9) 49–72.
[84] ibid 73–98; cf Orestis F Sherman, 'Counterfactual Arguments in Unjust Enrichment' (2019) 135 LQR 561, 566; Tang, *Principles of the Law of Restitution in Singapore* (n 65) 39 on the 'direct transfer' rule.
[85] cf Section II.C entitled 'The Correlation Between Enrichment and De-Enrichment'.
[86] cf Stevens, 'The Unjust Enrichment Disaster' (n 6) 581.

compared with current law. In contrast, such shift offers a coherent explanatory basis to resolve them by acknowledging the need to remedy the claimant's de-enrichment as the goal of any unjust enrichment claim.

F. Unjustness

Under current English law, it is one of the preconditions of any unjust enrichment claim that the defendant's enrichment is unjust. With the exception of Canada, common law jurisdictions have traditionally relied on the unjust factor test.[87] Mirroring this approach, a law of unjust de-enrichment could apply the same considerations based, however, on the acknowledgement that it is the unjustness of the claimant's de-enrichment rather than the defendant's enrichment which triggers the restitutionary claim.[88] As explained earlier,[89] one could even argue that the unjust factor approach of the current law of unjust enrichment has already adopted the de-enrichment focus.

G. The Scope of Unjust De-Enrichment Claims

Many issues regarding the scope of unjust enrichment claims under current English law remain unresolved. Interestingly, the situation is not much different in civil law jurisdictions despite their much longer history of operating unjust enrichment regimes. And, one could take this as an indicator that the unjust enrichment notion as such is not as straight forward as it sounds.[90] In contrast, a shift of focus to the de-enrichment of the claimant provides compelling answers to many of the open questions as summarized in the following.

If the de-enrichment of the claimant is the causal event that triggers the restitutionary remedy, then the detrimental impact on the claimant's position is key.[91] In other words, without a loss on the part of the claimant there should be no de-enrichment claim. While this notion seems to be supported by current Canadian,[92] but not by English[93] and

---

[87] cf Section II.B entitled 'The Enrichment Focus'; Birks (n 9) 105–08. A detailed analysis of the historical development is offered by Mitchell McInnes, Chapter 16 in this volume.
[88] cf Robert Stevens, Chapter 7 in this volume, Section II.D.1: 'In the common law, the *deliberate* infliction of loss is not, without more, actionable' (emphasis in original).
[89] cf Section II.B of this chapter, 'The Enrichment Focus'.
[90] cf Gallagher, Lin, and Wolff (n 5) 379.
[91] For the apparent focus of current English law on the defendant's gain, see McInnes, 'Unjust Enrichment: A Reply to Professor Weinrib' (n 13) 33 fn 23.
[92] *Pettkus v Becker* [1980] 2 SCR 834, 835; cf McInnes, 'The Measure of Restitution' (n 4) 172; Mitchell McInnes, '"At the Plaintiff's Expense": Quantifying Restitutionary Relief' (1998) 57 CLJ 472, 474.
[93] cf *Investment Trust Companies v Revenue and Customs Comrs* (n 32) [45] (Lord Reed SCJ); Birks (n 9) 79–82, 168; potentially different, however, from *BP Exploration Co (Libya) Ltd v Hunt (No 2)* [1979] 1 WLR 783 (QB).

German[94] unjust enrichment law, it makes perfect sense. Why should private law grant a remedy if the claimant was not aggrieved in some way?

Furthermore, with a focus on de-enrichment, the claim must as a matter of principle be object-oriented—that is, the claim must[95] in the first place be for exactly what the claimant has lost. It is at this point where this area of law 'takes its lead from property law or from ideas of property'.[96] There is no reason why the claimant should be restricted to or be allowed to opt for a money claim instead. A money claim can only come into play when the restoration of the parties' original position is impossible. This can be the case because of the (immaterial) nature of the object of a de-enrichment. Here the unjust de-enrichment claim must indeed be for compensation.[97] Scenarios of this kind include the unjust provision of services or the unjust grant of the right to use a thing.[98] In contrast, under current law with its focus on the enrichment of the defendant, any unjust enrichment claim appears to require some 'growth of wealth' on the part of the defendant.[99] This should mean that a claimant is only able to recover expenditure which the defendant has actually saved. If there is no such saving, for example because the defendant would not have bought a service because it would have been pure luxury for her to do so, then there would be no enrichment. As a result, it is not possible to justify any restitutionary claim.[100] The focus on the claimant's de-enrichment avoids this absurd outcome.[101] And this therefore appears to be the appropriate way forward because it stands to reason that the defendant had the benefit of the service. At the same time, the defendant's interests are not ignored. In contrast, they are to be considered by allowing the change of position defence and by baring unjust de-enrichment claims in cases which qualify as imposed enrichment as further discussed later.

Restitution in the form of a return of the original object of the claimant's de-enrichment may also not be possible if such object is lost or (fully or partly) destroyed. Here the claim against the defendant therefore also has to be for compensation. With a focus on the claimant's de-enrichment, the calculation of such compensation must be determined on the basis of the value of the loss for the claimant (ie the costs of purchasing a replacement at market price).[102] In contrast,

---

[94] Birks (n 9) 17, 168.
[95] For the similar approach under German law, cf ibid 168; cf Weinrib, *Corrective Justice* (n 60) 228; for the differing position of English law, see Birks (n 9) 168; also cf Hedley, 'What is "Unjust Enrichment" For?' (n 25) 340.
[96] Charlie Webb, *Reason and Restitution: A Theory of Unjust Enrichment* (OUP 2016) 86.
[97] cf Ross Grantham and Charles EF Rickett, *Enrichment and Restitution in New Zealand* (Hart Publishing 2000) 61.
[98] cf for the qualification of 'pure services' as enrichment, *BP Exploration Co (Libya) Ltd v Hunt (No 2)* (n 93).
[99] Juentgen (n 4) 516.
[100] See 'An Introduction to the Law of Unjust Enrichment' (n 9) text to fn 155.
[101] cf Stevens, 'The Unjust Enrichment Disaster' (n 6) 580.
[102] Wolff, *Zuwendungsrisiko und Restitutionsinteresse [Transfer Risk and Restitutional Interest]* (n 14) 207; cf Robert Stevens, Chapter 7 in this volume, Section II.D.

as already pointed out earlier,[103] if the focus were on the defendant's enrichment, it is difficult to justify any unjust enrichment claim in the first place.[104]

If the restitutionary claim is triggered by the claimant's de-enrichment, fruits, including interest, of the object of the de-enrichment should be owed to the claimant if she would have received them in the ordinary course of events.[105] In contrast, in situations where the fruits or other profits are 'outside the normal', the claimant should not be entitled to the 'extra' because this is not what she has lost.[106] Examples are gains as a result of the defendant's negotiating skills or her long-standing connection with another party.[107] With its focus on the defendant's enrichment, current law appears to draw very different conclusions.[108]

Does the defendant have to reimburse the claimant for the use of the object of the de-enrichment? Again, if the focus were on the claimant's de-enrichment, the answer must be negative because the use by the defendant does not de facto translate into any loss on the part of the claimant. A different conclusion may only be mandated if the claimant were prevented from using the object of the de-enrichment during the time when it was in the hands of the defendant.[109] In this case, however, the claim for reimbursement would derive from the fact that the claimant was deprived of the use of the de-enrichment object and not because of the defendant's use. Current law, with its focus on the defendant's enrichment, again requires a different assessment. Here, potentially even the mere possibility to use the object of the defendant's enrichment would qualify as enrichment on her part.

Finally, what is the situation in cases of an imposed enrichment (ie in situations where the claimant has actually forced unsolicited benefits upon the defendant)?[110] The common law position vis-à-vis cases of this kind is disputed.[111] It appears that an unjust enrichment claim is (only) available if the defendant had either freely accepted the unsolicited benefits or if the defendant's enrichment is incontrovertible.[112] While this approach may allow for practical solutions in particular cases, it is not logical. If it is the defendant's enrichment which triggers the unjust enrichment claim, then there is no reason why the acceptance or non-acceptance of the

---

[103] cf Section II.B entitled 'The Enrichment Focus'.
[104] Wolff, *Zuwendungsrisiko und Restitutionsinteresse* [*Transfer Risk and Restitutional Interest*] (n 14) 207.
[105] cf See, 'An Introduction to the Law of Unjust Enrichment' (n 9) text following fn 205.
[106] cf McInnes, '"At the Plaintiff's Expense": Quantifying Restitutionary Relief' (n 92) 474; Stevens, 'The Unjust Enrichment Disaster' (n 6) 580.
[107] Birks (n 9) 18.
[108] *Trustee of the Property of FC Jones & Sons v Jones* [1997] Ch 159 (CA); *Foskett v McKeown* [2001] 1 AC 102 (HL).
[109] cf in contrast eg s 818 para 1, first option, of the German Civil Code, which orders the defendant to reimburse the claimant for use of the object of the de-enrichment. An unofficial English translation is available at Langenscheidt Translation Service (n 67).
[110] cf Juentgen (n 4) 527.
[111] cf *Falcke v Scottish Imperial Insurance Co* (1886) 34 ChD 234 (CA) (Bowen LJ); Bickenbach (n 26) 203; Stoljar, 'Unjust Enrichment and Unjust Sacrifice' (n 39) 611.
[112] Birks (n 9) 55–62; Beatson, *The Use and Abuse of Unjust Enrichment* (n 55) 66–70.

benefit should make any difference. It is also unclear why an obligation to reject the benefit should be inflicted on the defendant. Finally, even if an enrichment were incontrovertible, the defendant may still not want the benefit, for example because it comes from a particular claimant whom she does not like.[113] In contrast, with the focus on the claimant's de-enrichment, cases of imposed enrichment are straightforward. The claimant's loss is a result of her own action and can therefore not be regarded as detrimentally affecting her position. In other words, in cases where the claimant imposes unsolicited benefits on the defendant the claimant cannot be regarded as being de-enriched because any claim to restore her original position would qualify as *venire contra factum proprium*.

IV. Conclusion and Final Remark

The notion of an unjust enrichment law implies—as the name suggests—a focus on the defendant's enrichment. This, however, does not adequately reflect the reason why a restitutionary remedy is needed (ie the de-enrichment of the claimant). In contrast, with a focus on the claimant's de-enrichment it is possible to develop compelling solutions in unjust enrichment cases on the basis of a clear definition of the remedial goal to be achieved. And, given the possibility to finally solve all the problems which have haunted unjust enrichment law for so long, a shift to the claimant's de-enrichment may not be as far-fetched as it appears at first sight.

---

[113] cf Bickenbach (n 26) 204 ('violation of the freedom to choose one's own benefits').

11
The Way Forward

Peter Jaffey[*]

I. The Theory of Unjust Enrichment

The theory of unjust enrichment is the theory that, as it was recently put, the claims identified in *Goff & Jones*,[1] which were historically treated as distinct, should be united in a single category of claim or cause of action in unjust enrichment governed by a common set of conditions. This takes the form of the three-stage framework for unjust enrichment: there must be: (1) a benefit or enrichment to D; (2) at C's expense; and (3) an 'unjust factor'. This I shall also refer to as the Birksian approach.[2] The claims taken to come within the category include all or most of the following: the claim to recover a mistaken payment, or an unauthorized payment, or a payment under duress or undue influence or legal compulsion; the equitable proprietary tracing claim; the claim for services mistakenly provided or mistaken improvements; the claim for payment for work done or to recover a payment under a terminated contract; the claim to recover taxes paid but not due; the claim for payment arising from 'necessitous intervention' such as maritime salvage; the claim for payment for the unauthorized use of property. There is no doubt that the theory has won recognition in English law.

A question commonly asked of proponents of the theory of unjust enrichment and in due course of its opponents was why it matters whether these various claims (or others) are treated together in a single doctrinal category. In fact, if the law always consisted of settled rules it would not matter in practice, since any dispute could be resolved merely by identifying the relevant rules and applying them. Classification of these settled rules would for practical purposes be just a matter of convenience, and the introduction of the new category of unjust enrichment would be simply a matter of the presentation of settled rules. Some commentators have regarded the controversy over the theory of unjust enrichment as misguided for this reason.

---

[*] I am grateful to Warren Swain and Sagi Peari for organizing the conference and this volume, and to the participants who commented on my paper, in particular Kit Barker.
[1] The latest edition is Charles Mitchell, Paul Mitchell, and Stephen Watterson, *Goff & Jones: The Law of Unjust Enrichment* (10th edn, Sweet & Maxwell 2022).
[2] Peter Birks, *An Introduction to the Law of Restitution* (rev edn, OUP 1989).

Of course, the law is often unsettled. Here the courts develop the law through analogical reasoning. They extend a rule by analogy or qualify a rule by disanalogy—that is, by distinguishing the case laying down the rule. This is how a body of rules develops out of a sequence of cases. Sometimes this process leads to the emergence of a new cause of action or claim, which governs how the law continues to develop. The introduction of the law of unjust enrichment through this ordinary process of legal reasoning would be justified if it brought together analogous claims. According to Birks,[3] and as Lord Burrows (Andrew Burrows) has recently insisted, they are analogous because they share the elements of an unjust enrichment claim identified in the framework, the claim to recover a mistaken payment being the standard example.[4]

However, even amongst proponents of the Birksian approach, there has been continuing controversy about which particular claims are included within the law of unjust enrichment as analogous claims. Some opponents (including myself) have argued that the category is entirely misconceived and should not be recognized at all, though they tend to suggest different alternative arrangements. Recently Lionel Smith and Robert Stevens, both originally supporters of the Birksian approach, have also concluded that it is misconceived.[5] They both think that there should be a new cause of action, which for Smith preserves the core of the Birksian approach, and for Stevens is a new type of claim (though their approaches seem very similar).[6] Although there are numerous views about how we should understand the subject matter, they are mostly united (I should imagine) in accepting that analogous claims should be treated together.

How do we decide which claims are really analogous? Analogical reasoning in the development of the common law is a matter of moral judgement, subject to the constraints of precedent. Analogy and distinguishing are the usual means by which moral judgement is introduced into the law in its development. When a cause of action emerges through the ordinary process of common law reasoning, it is because it reflects a certain moral principle or justification, which justifies the common treatment of cases where the principle applies. This process is not a mechanical process and involves the exercise of judgement. How, then, do we assess whether such a category is sound?

A sound category will help to guide development and solve problems in the law. Issues will fall into place and confusion will clear. The area of law will appear less

---

[3] See Peter Birks, *Unjust Enrichment* (2nd edn, OUP 2005) 3.
[4] Andrew Burrows, 'In Defence of Unjust Enrichment' (2019) 78 CLJ 521.
[5] Lionel Smith, 'Restitution: A New Start?' in Peter Devonshire and Rohan Havelock (eds), *The Impact of Equity and Restitution in Commerce* (Hart Publishing 2019); Robert Stevens, 'The Unjust Enrichment Disaster' (2018) 134 LQR 574. I do not discuss Robert Stevens, *The Laws of Restitution* (OUP 2023).
[6] As I understand, they are both influenced by the corrective justice school of thought and so have something in common in particular with, eg, Ernest J Weinrib, *Corrective Justice* (OUP 2012) ch 6; Jennifer M Nadler, 'What Right Does Unjust Enrichment Law Protect?' (2008) 28 OJLS 245.

frequently in the appeal courts as certainty and clarity prevail. If it is a misconceived development, difficulties will seem intractable. Controversy and confusion will persist. Obscurities and fictions will persist or emerge. One might point to certain advances resulting from the introduction of the law of unjust enrichment, for example the abandonment of the fiction of implied contract and the mistake of law bar. However, these two examples have nothing to do with the theory of unjust enrichment itself—no alternative theory favours these relics of the past. It is true that, as a result of the interest generated by the theory of unjust enrichment, useful academic writing has been done in obscure areas that might otherwise have been starved of it, for example tracing or subrogation or compulsory discharge, though again in my view the progress made in these areas owes nothing to the theory of unjust enrichment itself. My impression is that the law has not reached the broad, sunlit uplands and will not do so under the influence of the theory of unjust enrichment.

More fundamentally, to establish whether the theory of unjust enrichment is sound, we need to ask what the underlying principle or justification is. Is there a justificatory principle that can explain the three-stage framework and show how the conditions should be understood? The development of a new cause of action by analogical reasoning does not necessarily reveal an underlying principle. A principle of unjust enrichment was never satisfactorily identified and is not the same thing as the conditions for a claim. There are possible principles that might be thought of as principles of unjust enrichment: for example, the disgorgement of wrongful profits principle, the principle of benefit and burden, or the principle that one should not reap where one did not sow. These principles have a place in the law, but none of them accounts for the Birksian approach to unjust enrichment. It seems to be increasingly recognized that such a principle is called for and that it has not been forthcoming.[7] Recently some commentators have recognized that the mistaken payment claim is not adequately understood simply as a claim based on a principle of unjust enrichment and attention has been directed at possible rationales.[8] It is worth labouring this point because some commentators continue to deny that the Birksian approach presupposes a principle of unjust enrichment in this sense. Birks himself thought the introduction of a cause of action in unjust enrichment was in some sense a matter of rational development but did not depend on a principle of unjust enrichment.[9]

In rejecting the Birksian approach, Stevens and Smith have both recognized this justificatory difficulty with the theory of unjust enrichment. They focus on the problem of 'overgeneralization'. In the absence of a justificatory principle, the three conditions of the Birksian approach, applied literally, seem to imply that

---

[7] cf Lutz-Christian Wolff, Chapter 10 in this volume.
[8] See eg the discussion in Peter Chau and Lusina Ho, Chapter 9 in this volume.
[9] Birks, *An Introduction to the Law of Restitution* (n 2) 22–25.

there should be a claim where intuitively it seems clear that there should not. In particular, there is the problem of 'incidental benefits', where C's activity, such as heating his room, incidentally confers a benefit on his next-door neighbour D by heating D's room as well.[10] I agree that this is a sound objection, though it tends to be of particular concern to commentators who support the theory of unjust enrichment but are concerned about its limits. But it is not in my view the only or even the main problem with the theory of unjust enrichment.

The pillars of private law are contract, tort, and property. Much of what is understood as the law of unjust enrichment is really property and contract, and the rest is helpfully considered in relation to contract, property, and sometimes tort. Before the development of the theory of unjust enrichment, it was standard to approach restitution along these lines, for example in the work of Stoljar and Atiyah, whose influence has unfortunately been eclipsed by more recent developments.[11] The more important problem with the theory of unjust enrichment is that it has obscured and interfered with these areas of law and their development. It has wrongly conflated claims within these areas and it has also created false divisions within them.[12] In the next section, I summarize the approach I suggested some years ago,[13] which starts from this older position, before coming back to consider the recent proposals from Stevens and Smith.

II. A Better Framework

A. The Proprietary Approach to Mistaken and Unauthorized Payments

Where goods owned by C come into the hands of D, D can be liable for conversion or interference with goods. This is conventionally understood as a claim for compensation for D's wrong, but the way it is understood disguises a distinction, in principle, between a claim for compensation for a wrong and a claim for restitution of an invalid transfer. For example, where D has appropriated property belonging to C, or disposed of it, or consumed or destroyed it, the issue is whether D should compensate C for loss caused by a wrong. Such a claim should not in principle

---

[10] See Smith (n 5); Stevens (n 5).
[11] SJ Stoljar, *The Law of Quasi-Contract* (2nd edn, Law Book Co 1989); PS Atiyah, *The Rise and Fall of Freedom of Contract* (OUP 1979).
[12] False assimilation and false differentiation as I described them in Peter Jaffey, *Private Law and Property Claims* (Hart Publishing 2007) ch 8.
[13] Peter Jaffey, *The Nature and Scope of Restitution* (Hart Publishing 2000); Jaffey, *Private Law and Property Claims* (n 12).There are, of course, other well-known works critical of the theory of unjust enrichment, including Steve Hedley, *Restitution: Its Division and Ordering* (Sweet & Maxwell 2001); Steve Hedley, *A Critical Introduction to Restitution* (OUP 2001); Peter Watts, 'Restitution—A Property Principle and a Services Principle' (1995) 3 RLR 49; Peter G Watts, '"Unjust Enrichment"—The Potion that Induces Well-meaning Sloppiness of Thought' (2016) 69 CLP 289.

depend on whether D still has the property, and one would expect it to depend on whether D was at fault, or at least on D's conduct. By contrast, where D has simply received the property through an invalid transfer, that is to say where there was no valid exercise by C, as owner, of his power of transfer, the issue in principle is whether C should have a claim for restitution to recover the property, or its value in D's estate or general property. In principle, the claim should be a matter of strict liability; it should depend simply on whether D has received and still has the property or its value. It should not depend on whether D caused loss to C by acting wrongfully. D need not have caused the transfer at all. In principle, furthermore, the remedy should be proprietary rather than personal, whereas the claim for compensation should be personal. The claim for conversion has the form of a claim for compensation for a wrong, but it also of necessity does the work of the claim for restitution of an invalid transfer, without doing so adequately. It would be better if the two were distinguished, as various commentators have pointed out over the years.[14]

Consider the case of a transfer of C's money as cash from C to D with no authority, for example where it is lost and found, or stolen, or transferred by an agent without authority. How should the claim arising from the transfer be understood? It seems to be understood as a claim based on the infringement of a property right in the money, and so one might think that it is a claim for compensation for a wrong, like a claim in conversion, but it is also understood as a claim for restitution to reverse the transfer. For example, it is subject to the change of position defence. However, it is not understood as a claim to recover the property itself, because the recipient D acquires title to the cash. This is not because the transfer was valid, but because of a rule of law to protect third parties dealing with D with respect to cash, to ensure that the person in possession can deal with it as currency.[15] Nevertheless, since C has lost his property right, it would seem that the claim cannot be a claim to recover the money by enforcing a property right to it.

The current understanding of the law seems to be that, since it is not a claim in tort for compensation for a wrong of infringement, nor a claim to recover property invalidly transferred, it must be an unjust enrichment claim. This appears to be what was decided in *Lipkin Gorman v Karpnale Ltd*.[16] The unjust factor seems to be lack of authority or 'ignorance'. Some supporters of the Birksian approach deny that this is an unjust enrichment claim on the ground that the claim arises from an infringement of a property right, but since it is not a claim in tort for compensation for wrongful interference this does not seem to make it any clearer what sort of claim it is.

---

[14] See eg Tony Weir, *An Introduction to Tort Law* (2nd edn, OUP 2006) 166–67; Andrew Tettenborn, 'Conversion, Tort and Restitution' in Norman Palmer and Ewan McKendrick (eds), *Interests in Goods* (2nd edn, Routledge 1998).
[15] Or because the money is no longer identifiable.
[16] *Lipkin Gorman v Karpnale Ltd* [1991] 2 AC 548 (HL).

Now take mistaken payment of cash, generally understood as the classic case of unjust enrichment. Although the payment is mistaken, it is understood that the mistake does not affect the validity of the transfer of property. Thus there can be no basis in property for a claim, by way of either a continuing property right that might justify the recovery of the cash, or a wrongful infringement of a property right justifying compensation. What, then, is the basis of the claim? Again, it is the difficulty in accounting for the claim in terms of property or tort that has made the unjust enrichment approach seem so compelling, and this has become the orthodox position despite the fact that no principle of unjust enrichment has actually been advanced to explain it.

It is worth asking, first, whether the mistaken payment case is really any different from the unauthorized payment case. They seem to have been treated together in the past and in *Lipkin Gorman*. If C is mistaken, one might think that the reason for the claim is that the transfer was invalid because C's intention to transfer his property was vitiated. Again the passing of ownership is explicable on the basis of the need to protect third parties dealing with D despite the invalidity of the transfer. The conventional view is that there is a valid transfer of property, but if so, it is difficult to explain why the mistake operates to generate a claim at all: if the transfer of property is valid, why should there be a claim? The mistake is described as a 'vitiating factor', but what is vitiated if it is not the transfer of property or the owner's exercise of the power of transfer? It is more plausible to think that there was an invalid transfer of property, but again it seems to be the difficulty of explaining the claim in terms of the recovery of property or wrongful interference in tort that has made the unjust enrichment approach seem attractive.

In this light, it is helpful to consider the position where the cash is held by T on trust for C and it is transferred to D by T without authority under the trust. Legal title to the money passes to D, but C has a beneficial property right in the money by virtue of which (if D is not a bona fide purchaser) C has a proprietary claim to recover the money. This claim arises from a transfer of property that is invalid because of T's lack of authority, in consequence of which C's beneficial property right survives the transfer and binds D.

C's proprietary claim is made possible by the ability of equity to distinguish between a beneficial interest, which is a property right to some of all the benefit of the trust property, independent of control or possession, and legal title, which is the right to possession and control that is initially with T and then with D. This distinction enables equity to deal aptly with an invalid transfer of property. The distinction originated with the express trust and the protection of trust property with respect to unauthorized transfers by trustees (transfers in breach of trust). Because the trust itself involves a separation of the right to benefit from the right of possession and control, it is natural to extend the analysis to apply to a recipient of property invalidly transferred. But there is no reason, conceptually or in principle, why the same analysis cannot be used for all invalid transfers. Indeed it should be used, simply because it is the apt way to do justice with respect to invalid transfers of property.

The analysis is not available at common law because the common law does not recognize a beneficial property right distinct from the right of control or possession. A claim at common law can only be based on interference with a property right before title has passed, and so where this is unavailable the common law has resorted to a personal claim to reverse the transfer. The nature of the claim is obscure because it is actually a claim to reverse an invalid transfer of property but the common law has no means of recognizing it as such. A satisfactory law for the protection of money against invalid payments requires a distinction between a right to the benefit of the property and a right of control. This is what equity can supply, but unfortunately at common law the unjust enrichment approach has developed instead. It remains the case, however, that the justification for the claim is entirely a matter of property.

This analysis may be understood as an evasion: it fails to resolve the problem of the correct analysis of the common law claim, considered independently of equity. Surely we should provide this analysis before we decide whether to extend the equitable approach to the common law. This reflects a misunderstanding of the argument. The problem at common law is not that there is an alternative non-proprietary rationale awaiting discovery. The problem is that although the common law recognizes that a claim is required, it lacks the necessary tools to give proper effect to the true justification of the claim, which is the right to recover property invalidly transferred.

Most transfers do not, of course, involve cash as coin or notes. Say the payment is made from C's bank account. It is said that, in this sort of case, since C's relationship with his bank is purely a matter of contract, the payment from the account cannot be a transfer of property at all and so the claim cannot be a claim to recover an invalid transfer of property. Instead it is said that the payment is just a matter of the 'adjustment of contractual liabilities'.[17] This cannot be correct, in my view. It is true that, as between C and his bank, the position is purely contractual. But if this were a complete account of the position as against third parties such as D, there would be no justification for a claim against D at all. There would be no reason to say that a receipt by D from the bank was 'at C's expense'. C would be protected purely by contract against the bank, or by tortious interference with contract against a third party. In fact, C owns the right to payment from the bank (the account) as an object of property, and a payment from the account made by the bank is a transfer of C's property, which can be invalid if, for example, it was made by the bank with ostensible but not actual authority from C or by mistake on C's part.

---

[17] See eg Tatiana RS Cutts, 'Modern Money Had and Received' (2018) 38 OJLS 1; Charlie Webb, *Reason and Restitution: A Theory of Unjust Enrichment* (OUP 2016) 93–94.

Consider again a trust case, where money in an account in T's name is held on trust for C. If the money is paid without authority by T to D, C has a proprietary claim to recover the trust property from D. C has a beneficial property right in the account, which binds the money paid to D. However, it is not the existence of a trust that creates the property. Unless the account is an object of property, there cannot be a trust by virtue of which C has a beneficial property right in the account in T's name. If a payment from account to account is a transfer of trust property, then a payment from account to account must be a transfer of property, whether there is a trust or not.[18]

In cases of common law restitution of money payments, some judges seem to think intuitively in terms of a transfer of value or wealth.[19] Some commentators object that there is no such thing as a transfer of wealth or value, because a payment of money from account to account is not a transfer of property, or even because there is no such thing as intangible property.[20] However, this intuitive understanding of a money payment does make sense on the proprietary approach I have suggested.

The property approach does not merely supply a missing principle to explain the common law claim. It would also in my view be a step forward in the law. The traditional common law approach to property, in terms of a right against wrongful interference, is inadequate, particularly when we move beyond goods. With respect to money payments, the common law personal claim for restitution is inadequate to protect the property right in money. Where money is taken without authority from a bank account, or a payment is procured by fraud, and the money is immediately paid on through other accounts, only a proprietary account is adequate. Similarly, where C makes a mistaken payment to D who immediately goes bankrupt, in my view C ought to have a proprietary claim.[21]

---

[18] See further Peter Jaffey, 'Private Property and Intangibles' [2022] Conv 47.
[19] eg this seems to be the thinking in the cases discussed by Stevens: *Lipkin Gorman v Karpnale Ltd* (n 16); *Banque Financière de la Cité v Parc (Battersea) Ltd* [1999] 1 AC 221 (HL); *Sempra Metals Ltd v IRC* [2007] UKHL 34; [2008] 1 AC 561; *Investment Trust Companies v Revenue and Customs Comrs* [2017] UKSC 29; [2018] AC 275.
[20] The rules of tracing to determine what property D has are crucial.
[21] As in *Chase Manhattan Bank NA v Israel-British Bank (London) Ltd* [1981] Ch 105 (Ch). It appears to be accepted that in a case of theft or fraud from a bank account, traditionally purely a matter for the common law, an equitable proprietary claim is available: see *CMOC Sales & Marketing Ltd v Person Unknown* [2018] EWHC 2230 (Comm). One might object that the basis for the claim, if it is a matter of property, depends on the overall societal distribution of property and so directly on a matter of distributive justice which cannot realistically provide the basis for an interpersonal claim. Leaving aside the societal distribution, as between C and D the justification is that C invested to acquire property or received the property from someone who did so. See further Peter Jaffey, *Justice in Private Law* (Hart Publishing 2023).

B. Claims for Payment for Goods and Services

The discussion in the previous section was about protecting money as property with respect to invalid payments, including mistaken and unauthorized payments. Claims for payment for the provision of goods and services are quite different and should be treated differently (as, of course, they historically were by way of the *quantum valebat* and *quantum meruit*). The starting point is that a right to be paid for the goods or services normally requires a contractual agreement. Agreement is a way for people to make a mutually beneficial exchange of goods or services for payment. Agreement is apt because the value of goods or services to someone depends on that person's tastes, circumstances, and priorities, and an agreement, under which each party can decide what goods and services to acquire or supply and at what price, is the best way to ensure that so far as possible an exchange is mutually beneficial.

It follows from this that, if C simply confers a benefit on D with a view to being paid for it, but without first making a contract with D, he is a risk-taker—he bears the risk of not being paid. It is 'officious' to confer a benefit in such circumstances, to use the expression traditionally used in this context. This is what I understand by the famous dictum, in the form of a rhetorical question: 'One cleans another's shoes; what can the other do but put them on?'[22] C took the risk that D would not pay and D has no choice but to accept the benefit, unless he gives up his shoes, and has no liability for payment.

However, where C confers a benefit on D in circumstances where no contract was possible, for example because the benefit has to be conferred immediately in an emergency and so no negotiation is possible, it may be justified to require payment, if it is also quite clear that the effect is to secure a mutually beneficial exchange. This is the case for necessitous intervention, the standard example being maritime salvage. Because there is an emergency and D is saved from a serious loss, it is indisputable that there is a reasonable price at which there is a mutually beneficial exchange. Some would say that, even so, no claim should be allowed because D is made to pay despite never having agreed to pay, or having done anything else to incur liability. The liability, one might object, is an imposition and an infringement of D's liberty. On a law and economics or public policy approach, one might say that liability is justified because it promotes a policy of useful intervention, but this seems to disregard D's interests entirely.

If a claim is justified in such a case, as in my view it is, the rationale is what I have described as 'imputed contract'.[23] Despite the absence of agreement, it is not unfair to D if the conditions suggested are satisfied, that is to say if contracting is impossible, which means that D's right to determine the use of his resources is not

---

[22] *Taylor v Laird* (1856) 25 LJ Ex 329 (Exch) 332.
[23] Jaffey, *The Nature and Scope of Restitution* (n 13) ch 3.

subverted, and also if, at the price that D is required to pay, there is clearly a mutually beneficial exchange of goods or services for payment between C and D. The objective of the law is to secure a mutually beneficial exchange between C and D such as they would have agreed on if they had been able to. There is no contract, but the law has the same objective as contract law, in circumstances in which a contract is impossible.

The mistaken provision of services or mistaken improvements to property can be understood in the same way. By virtue of the mistake, C is not officious in conferring the benefit, in the expectation of payment but without a contract with D. Liability on the imputed contract basis is defensible if there is a price at which is it is clear that there is a mutually beneficial exchange. In this sort of case it may not be at all clear at what price, if at all, there is a mutually beneficial exchange. The extended debate over measurement of benefit, according to the 'incontrovertible benefit' test or other 'tests of benefit' should be interpreted accordingly.

Under the theory of unjust enrichment, in this sort of case, the issue is whether D has received a benefit, and the value of the benefit to D is taken to be the measure of recovery, as if there had been a transfer of a benefit of this value from C to D which should be reversed. But with respect to a liability to pay for goods or services, we should distinguish between the value of D's benefit to D, the cost to C of providing the benefit, and a fair price, which achieves a mutually beneficial exchange. The fair price may but need not be the market price. The market price merely reflects supply and demand across the marketplace. It is not an objective measure of the value of the benefit to D. 'Subjective devaluation',[24] which is used to justify reducing D's liability below the market price, is a concept that is required only because the unjust enrichment approach mischaracterizes payment in exchange for goods or services as the reversal of a transfer. The idea behind subjective devaluation, which is really that the fair price for a benefit varies according to the tastes and circumstances and priorities of the recipient, is intrinsic to contract law as a device for exchange.

A claim for payment for goods and services must be based either on contract or on imputed contract in this sense. An imputed contract cannot displace an actual contract. If there is a contract between the parties, the right to be paid for a benefit provided pursuant to the contract depends exclusively on the contract. By contrast, under the theory of unjust enrichment it is said that there can be a non-contractual claim for payment arising from the non-performance of a valid contract. Because the theory of unjust enrichment leaves open what the actual justification for the claim is, it leaves open the possibility that there is a distinct non-contractual basis for a claim. However, when we examine the 'unjust factor', which is 'failure of basis'

---

[24] Birks, *An Introduction to the Law of Restitution* (n 2) 109 ff.

or 'failure of condition', it becomes clear that in fact the justification for the claim is the contractual principle that agreements should be upheld, in a different guise. It is said that the contractual agreement was subject to an agreed basis that C's performance would be paid for, or included an agreed condition to that effect, by virtue of which a claim arises when the contract terminates. I do not think that it is right to say that contractual performance is made on this basis or is subject to such a condition. I doubt whether it even makes sense to say that services are provided conditionally since they cannot be returned or reversed in any literal sense, only paid for. In any case, if there is such a condition or such a basis it is part of the contract and the claim is contractual.

The problem in contract has been that, on the conventional view, expectation damages are the usual pecuniary remedy in contract, whereas these supposed unjust enrichment claims are for a *quantum meruit* for work performed under the contract or for restitution to recover a contractual prepayment, and these are understood not to be remedies available in contract. However, where there was a valid contract, whether these remedies should be available is a matter of contract. It is the function of contract law to determine what legal rights the contractual agreement creates and what remedies are appropriate to protect them. The unjust enrichment theory of failure of basis or failure of condition does not reveal any alternative non-contractual justification for a claim. If these remedies are justified, as I think they often are, the explanation must lie in a revised understanding of contract law.[25]

An unjust enrichment claim is also sometimes allowed in the absence of a contract, for example in the case of so-called 'precontractual claims', or where there was a request to provide a service. Again it is said that the basis for the claim is failure of basis or failure of condition, but again it eventually became clear that this always involves an agreement between the parties, though not, it is said, a contractual agreement. The agreement is not contractually binding because it does not meet all the conditions for a valid contract, for example consideration or certainty. Again, there is no justifying principle for such a claim other than the principle that agreements should be kept. If these agreements generate a claim for payment, it would be better to integrate them into contract law. One might argue that there are reasons to keep such claims outside contract law, even if the rationale is also the principle that agreements should be kept, but it remains the case that such claims cannot arise as non-contractual claims where there is a contractual agreement, and also that they are quite distinct from claims to recover invalid money payments.

---

[25] See further Peter Jaffey, 'Restitutionary Remedies in the Contractual Context' (2013) 76 MLR 429.

C. Particular Problems with Unjust Enrichment

The account I have outlined is, one might say, oriented towards property, tort, and contract. Not all so-called unjust enrichment claims are a matter of property or contract, but most of them are, and the rest should be understood in terms of their relation to these areas of law (eg in terms of imputed contract in the sense suggested). This would be a natural development of an older approach, predating the modern recognition of the theory of unjust enrichment. In the light of this, the more particular failings of the unjust enrichment approach are as follows:

(1) It fails to provide proprietary claims where they are appropriate, and it undermines the development of property law to apply to intangible things including money in a bank account.
(2) It interferes with and undermines contract law by creating, in effect, an alternative overlapping and inconsistent regime for payment for goods and services.
(3) It abandons the traditional approach of treating the recovery of invalid money payments separately from payment for the provision of goods and services, and so obscures their different bases in principle.

III. A New Cause of Action?

A. An Objection to Claims Arising From the Receipt of a Benefit

As I mentioned earlier, Robert Stevens and Lionel Smith both now accept that the Birksian approach went astray in combining different types of claim that should be treated separately. They both propose a new cause of action confined to the core of unjust enrichment on the Birksian approach. According to Stevens, this new cause of action is not a matter of unjust enrichment at all, but according to Smith it should be understood as a more restricted form of unjust enrichment claim (though the two approaches seem to me very similar). In the limited space available, I shall make some brief comments on their proposals.

Smith and Stevens share a concern that the theory of unjust enrichment is or may be inconsistent with the requirement of interpersonal justice as between the two parties C and D. They say (following Ernest Weinrib) that it would be unjust for C to have a claim against D that depends on a factor whose moral significance is relevant only to one party.[26] This I shall refer to as the 'bilateralism condition'. For example, it is said, under the unjust enrichment approach a claim based on

---

[26] Ernest J Weinrib, *The Idea of Private Law* (rev edn, OUP 2012) 54.

mistaken payment fails the bilateralism condition because the mistake is of moral significance only with respect to C, and not to D, and so there is no reason why D should have to bear the consequences of C's mistake. Stevens and Smith understand the bilateralism condition to mean that the claim must arise from something D has done, for example an acceptance or a request, amounting presumably to a voluntary undertaking of some sort or a wrong. If it does not arise from something D has done, the claim must be unjust to him, however much it may advance C's interests.

The idea that a claim can arise only from what D has done is inimical to the theory of unjust enrichment, which, on my understanding, holds that a claim arises from the receipt of a benefit, not directly from what D has done. It is also incompatible with the approach suggested earlier for the same reason. However, I do not think that my approach is at odds with the bilateralism condition.[27] In my view, the bilateralism condition does not require that the claim must arise from something that D has done. The claim to recover an invalid money payment arises from the fact that D has received C's money and still has it (or its value), and the claim to recover payment for goods or services on the 'imputed contract' basis arises from the receipt of the benefit in circumstances in which a mutually beneficial exchange is possible and liability is not inconsistent with D's liberty to contract. These claims meet the bilateralism condition, in the sense that they are justified as a matter of interpersonal justice, though they do not arise from anything that D has done. By contrast, I doubt whether the new approaches proposed by Stevens and Smith actually satisfy the bilateralism condition, though they do respect the condition that the claim arises from something D has done.

B. The 'Performance Claim'

According to Stevens, a claim arises where C has rendered a performance to D, and D has accepted it, knowing that there is no legal basis for the performance, for example because it was rendered by mistake. A performance is an action or doing, which encompasses both the payment of money and the provision of goods or services.[28]

Thus, with respect to mistaken payments, it is D's action of knowing acceptance of the mistaken payment from C, along with C's mistake, that generates liability. This is, first, at odds with the existing law. If D has no knowledge of the mistake when he receives it, he can still be liable. Normally he will find out about the mistake later, after acceptance, when C notifies him or takes or threatens proceedings. Liability does not arise from acceptance with knowledge, but from the receipt of

[27] Burrows (n 4) defends the theory of unjust enrichment.
[28] Stevens (n 5).

the money. In some cases, proceedings could be taken in D's absence when D remains in ignorance of the mistake, or even the receipt itself. If D goes bankrupt or dies before he has knowledge, liability has already accrued.[29]

For Stevens, if I understand correctly, knowledge ought to be a condition of the claim because D's action of knowing acceptance is the morally significant action that justifies liability. Without it the bilateralism condition is not met. But what exactly is the moral significance of D's knowledge? If the mistake vitiates the transfer of property, knowledge of it is not relevant to the claim for restitution because the claim in principle arises from the receipt of the property. The bilateralism condition is met because D receives C's property. On this understanding, knowledge is in principle relevant, not to the claim for restitution, but to the availability of change of position, or, if the claim is proprietary, to a claim for compensation for the loss of property received and wrongfully disposed of or consumed by D. Stevens's approach presupposes that the mistake is operative in some other way, not by vitiating the transfer, and that if the mistake operates in this other way D's knowledge of it is relevant to the claim. But it is not clear to me from Stevens's discussion how C's mistake, or D's knowledge of it, are relevant, because, so far as I can see, the underlying principle is not identified.[30]

On Stevens's approach, C's performance may also be the performance of an agreement subject to a condition and when the condition fails there should be restitution. This seems to be essentially the same as the idea of failure of condition as an 'unjust factor'. The relevant principle seems to be that C and D are bound by what they have agreed, including the condition.[31] Thus one might say that a claim arising from the acceptance of performance is actually a contract claim. Lord Burrows suggests this interpretation.[32] However, on Stevens's approach, the performance claim can arise out of an agreement or in the absence of an agreement, as in the case of mistaken payments and mistakenly provided goods or services. Although Stevens objects to the theory of unjust enrichment because it purports to encompass claims based on different underlying principles, the same difficulty seems to arise for his approach, since it is difficult to see what sort of principle could unite these cases. Stevens may have addressed his concern over 'incidental benefits' and the overreach of the theory of unjust enrichment, but it seems to me that he has not avoided the other pitfalls of the theory of unjust enrichment. Furthermore, one

---

[29] These issues have often been discussed in connection with liability for knowing receipt of trust property: see eg Peter Birks, *Restitution: The Future* (Federation Press 1992) 26 ff.

[30] According to Stevens, D either accepts the payment or rejects it. If he rejects it, the money does not become his, and the possibility of liability does not arise. If he accepts it, he becomes liable for restitution, but only if he does so knowingly. This leaves it unclear what the effect of acceptance itself is. This is surely that it signifies that property has been received. Acceptance may be apt as a condition of receipt for tangibles, but it is unrealistic to apply such a condition with respect to intangibles such as a payment into D's account, as Lord Burrows argues: Burrows (n 4).

[31] Stevens distinguishes between failure of basis which he equates with rescission or voidness and failure of condition.

[32] Burrows (n 4) 536. See also Steve Hedley, Chapter 14 in this volume.

cannot conclude that his approach satisfies the bilateralism condition, because, so far as I can see, it does not identify a satisfactory principle of interpersonal justice.

C. A Narrow Unjust Enrichment Claim

For Smith, the traditional Birksian approach should be replaced by a narrower category of unjust enrichment, covering the core of mistaken and compelled enrichments and failure of condition or basis.[33] This Smith understands to be concerned with a transfer in a loose sense (which seems rather like Stevens's concept of performance). The reason for narrowing the category is to ensure 'normative unity', but so far as I can see, like Stevens, Smith does not explain what the underlying principle is that supplies this normative unity. He says only that liability should respect the principle that people are responsible only for what they have done, and that the law should protect C's choices about how to use his resources whilst respecting D's as well. As I have argued, it is not necessary, in order to satisfy the bilateralism condition, that D's liability must arise from what D has done, and furthermore Smith's approach does not seem to identify a principle of interpersonal justice that could satisfy the bilateralism condition and provide a justification for a particular kind of claim.

Smith concludes that liability in unjust enrichment should depend on a request or acceptance with the opportunity to reject, which presumably requires that D knew or could have found out about the mistake or absence of basis for the transfer, so it seems to be similar to the knowing acceptance approach. With respect to the claim for mistaken payment, he suggests that the claim was conditional on a request in *Kelly v Solari*,[34] and on acceptance with an opportunity to reject in *Chase Manhattan Bank NA v Israel-British Bank (London) Ltd*.[35] In *Kelly v Solari*, there was a request for payment by D, who mistakenly thought an insurance payout was due from C. Such a request may justify denying D's change of position, if D ought to have known that C had no liability to make the payment, but again it is difficult to see why a request should be necessary for the claim to arise at all. This would seem to be a confusion of the claim to recover a mistaken payment with the claim for payment for requested goods or services, where a request is necessary because it gives rise to an agreement, on which the claim is based. In *Chase Manhattan*, the defendant presumably accepted the second, mistaken payment not knowing that it was mistaken, though it could presumably have found this out. The usual view, as I have said, is that D's knowledge and failure to act may be relevant, but the relevance is to change of position or liability for disposing of C's money, not to

---

[33] I am simplifying Smith's account, I hope not unfairly for present purposes: Smith (n 5).
[34] *Kelly v Solari* (1841) 9 M & W 54; 152 ER 24.
[35] *Chase Manhattan Bank NA v Israel-British Bank (London) Ltd* (n 21).

C's claim for restitution, and Smith does not, so far as I can see, provide an explanation, in the form of a justifying principle, of why they should be relevant to the claim for restitution.

IV. The Way Forward

A. Underlying Justification

Controversy over a doctrinal category or cause of action can only be resolved by considering its basis in a justifying principle. It is a weakness in the unjust enrichment literature that this issue has been largely avoided. The new sceptics Stevens and Smith acknowledge the significance of this issue but so far as I can see they do not really address it in their new approaches.

B. The Institutional Problem

There has always been opposition to and scepticism about the Birksian approach, certainly amongst contract, trusts, and property specialists, but over the last thirty years it has been rare to see any dissent from it in the pages of the leading English journals. In Peter Birks's time, the excitement was palpable at the Society of Legal Scholars' conference, and no doubt it was even more intense at the more exclusive events for the unjust enrichment elect. One can understand why the concerns of sceptics were not a focus of attention, but now that the excitement has somewhat subsided it may be worth drawing attention to the extraordinary concentration of influence in English legal academia that was behind the rapid acceptance of the Birksian approach. Even if the Birksian approach turns out to be right, as Lord Burrows and many others are convinced is the case, in my view it will be in better shape if it engages with its critics more thoroughly than it has done in the past.

C. Property and Contract

Most so-called unjust enrichment claims are in my view better understood as property-based or contract claims, or as 'imputed contract' claims that operate in the shadow of contract. This was broadly the approach of Stoljar and Atiyah, who were leading figures in this area before the Birksian approach became dominant. Of course, proponents of the Birksian approach, and others such as Stevens and Smith, do not accept this, but they do invariably have to make assumptions about contract and property because on any view the law of unjust enrichment or restitution has to operate on the basis of or in the context of contract and property. These are themselves very active areas of research, though with very limited engagement with the literature on restitution or unjust enrichment. A focus on property and contract provides the best promise of progress, even for proponents of the theory of unjust enrichment.

12
Doctrinal Design in Unjust Enrichment
On the Relation of Claims for Restitution and General Private Law

Nils Jansen

I. Introduction

Unjust enrichment is one of the most recent institutions in European private law. It did not become a separate category of liability until 1840 in Germany,[1] 1892 in France (in terms of an *actio de in rem verso*),[2] and 1991 in England.[3] During the twentieth century, it turned out to be one of the most dynamic institutions of private law and, in view of current discussions in Europe, it seems doubtful whether it has found a solid structure in any legal system. It is perhaps as a result of this uncertain state of national laws at present that the doctrinal discussion has remained remarkably international. This conference proves that doctrinal writers read, and respond to, foreign literature and comparative law treatises. They thereby assume that foreign experience may be helpful when it comes to delineating and defining

---

[1] Friedrich Carl von Savigny, *System des heutigen Römischen Rechts*, vol 5 (Veit 1841) 108 ff, 513 ff, 521 ff, 526: 'unjustified enrichment coming from the creditor's property'; cf Nils Jansen, 'Die Korrektur grundloser Vermögensverschiebungen als Restitution? Zur Lehre von der ungerechtfertigten Bereicherung bei Savigny' (2003) 120 Zeitschrift der Savigny-Stiftung für Rechtsgeschichte (Romanistische Abteilung) 106; Sagi Peari, Chapter 4 in this volume. For the Civil Code, see Gottlieb Planck, *Bürgerliches Gesetzbuch Nebst Einführungsgesetz: Recht Der Schuldverhältnisse*, vol 2 (1st and 2nd edn, Guttentag 1900), 'Vorbem. Ungerechtfertigte Bereicherung', at III. Important features of modern German law were, however, constructed only in the twentieth century through scholarly contributions, such as Walter Wilburg, *Die Lehre von der ungerechtfertigten Bereicherung nach österreichischem und deutschem Recht* (Leuschner & Lubensky 1934); Ernst von Caemmerer, 'Bereicherung und unerlaubte Handlung' in Hans Dölle and Max Rheinstein (eds), *Festschrift für Ernst Rabel*, vol 1 (JCB Mohr 1954) 333–401; Karl Larenz and Claus-Wilhelm Canaris, *Lehrbuch des Schuldrechts*, vol II/2 (13th edn, CH Beck 1994) 127–348.

[2] Recueil Sirey 1893, prem part, 281–83: principle of equity, *qui défend de s'enrichir au détriment d'autrui*; see Alfons Bürge, 'Der Arrêt Boudier von 1892 vor dem Hintergrund der Entwicklung des französischen Bereicherungsrechts im 19. Jahrhundert' in Michael Coester and Dieter Martiny (eds), *Privatrecht in Europa: Vielfalt, Kollision, Kooperation: Festschrift für Hans Jürgen Sonnenberger zum 70. Geburtstag* (CH Beck 2004) 3–21, 18 ff; Konrad Zweigert and Hein Kötz, *An Introduction to Comparative Law* (Tony Weir tr, 3rd edn, OUP 1998) 546 ff; Helmut Coing, *Europäisches Privatrecht*, vol 2 (CH Beck 1989) 500 f, all with further references. For the seventeenth- and eighteenth-century *actio de in rem verso*, see n 43.

[3] *Lipkin Gorman v Karpnale Ltd* [1991] 2 AC 548 (HL). The way had been paved for this decision by Robert Goff and Gareth Jones, *The Law of Restitution* (Sweet & Maxwell 1966); and Peter Birks, *An Introduction to the Law of Restitution* (OUP 1985).

doctrinal categories.[4] Comparative findings thus help us to gain distance from our national traditions and to establish a truly academic perspective on legal doctrine. They make it possible for scholars to think in alternative models and to deepen their understanding of the law's structures.[5]

Although the construction and development of doctrinal concepts and categories has always been part and parcel of the daily business of European jurists, they have rarely thought about how such concepts and categories should be designed appropriately.[6] Nevertheless, it is probably uncontroversial that concepts should be regarded as a means to rationalize the law. They should enable jurists to address legal issues in a comprehensible and transparent manner. Moreover, doctrinal concepts should be responsive to legal authorities (legislation or case law) and thus ideally be able to give expression to quite different values, rather than embody, and thus ossify, traditional ones.[7] Finally, as Jacques du Plessis has rightly remarked, sensitivity to practical application and simplicity should be valued more highly than doctrinal rigidity.[8] Nevertheless, there may be tensions between the elegance of abstraction and the practical values of functional responsiveness, contextual fairness, and explanatory power.[9] Abstract concepts may help to relate otherwise independent institutions and rules to each other, and may thus shed new light on the law. Where scholars and judges introduce such categories into a legal system, this may lead to fundamentally new insights and understanding; indeed, such categories can make visible salient features of the law, which formerly remained unnoticed or could not be appropriately articulated. There can be no doubt that in this way the notion of unjustified enrichment helped jurists 'detect', viz acknowledge, new claims which had formerly been rejected. At the same time, however, thinking in overly abstract concepts may lead us astray. It is trite knowledge that not all unjustified gains need to be restored; the fact that a gain was unjustified may explain a defendant's liability, but it never suffices to justify another person's corresponding claim. Thus, if the value of Anna's land increases as a consequence

---

[4] cf Helen Scott, 'South Africa' in Sarah Worthington, Andrew Robertson, and Graham Virgo (eds), *Revolution and Evolution in Private Law* (Hart Publishing 2018); Helen Scott, 'Change and Continuity in the Law of Unjust Enrichment' [2019] Acta Juridica 469.

[5] Nils Jansen, 'The Point of View of Legal Science' in Thilo Kuntz and Paul Miller, *Methodology in Private Law—International and Comparative Perspectives* (OUP 2023) (forthcoming).

[6] But see Friedrich Carl von Savigny, *Das Recht des Besitzes* (2nd edn, Giessen Heyer 1806) 4 ff; Gustav Rümelin, *Juristische Begriffsbildung* (Duncker & Humblot 1878); Paul Eltzbacher, *Über Rechtsbegriffe* (Halle-Wittenberg University 1899); Herbert Lionel Adolphus Hart, 'Definition and Theory in Jurisprudence' (University of Oxford, 30 May 1953); Gertrude Lübbe-Wolff, *Rechtsfolgen und Realfolgen* (Karl Alber 1981) 40 ff, 79 ff and *passim*; Rolf Wank, *Die juristische Begriffsbildung* (CH Beck 1985); Jaap C Hage and Dietmar von der Pfordten (eds), *Concepts in Law* (Springer 2009).

[7] Jansen, 'The Point of View of Legal Science' (n 5); Nils Jansen, 'Rechtsdogmatik, Rechtswissenschaft und juristische Praxis' (2018) 143 AöR 623, 650 f.

[8] Jacques du Plessis, 'Long Live the Law of Unjustified Enrichment—A Response to Jansen' [2019] Acta Juridica 371, 393 (hereafter du Plessis, 'Response').

[9] See already Nils Jansen, 'Farewell to Unjustified Enrichment?' (2016) 20 Edin LR 123, 124 f; cf also Steve Hedley, '"Farewell to Unjustified Enrichment?"—A Common Law Response' (2016) 20 Edin LR 326, 328.

of Benjamin's investment in his own land, Benjamin cannot bring a claim for unjustified enrichment in order to refinance his investment. Similarly, if Constantin and Dora contract, invalidly, for repair work to Constantin's violin, and the value of Constantin's violin increases as a result of that work by 5,000, but the value of Dora's work was only 3,000, Dora should not be allowed to claim more than 3,000. If claims for unjust enrichment were meant, or understood, to disgorge all unjustified gains, those observations might be difficult to justify.

It was in view of the state of international discussion, on the one hand, and my understanding of doctrinal design, on the other, that I presented a reflection on the history of claims for unjust enrichment in Germany at talks in Stellenbosch, Edinburgh, and Oxford.[10] Many common law jurists interpreted my presentation from the perspective of present debates in South Africa, Scotland, England, and other jurisdictions. As a result, the lecture provoked lively international debate. Reflecting on responses and criticisms raised by those scholars gives me a chance to clarify where I believe German experiences might be relevant for other legal systems. In what follows, I will therefore briefly restate the main aspects of that history in Section II, before turning to look at current international debates in Section III.

II. Unification and Disentanglement

The history of the German law of unjust enrichment could long be described as a development towards an apparently unified institution, and indeed a unified enrichment claim, culminating in ss 812–22 of the German Civil Code (Bürgerliches Gesetzbuch, BGB) in 1900. But this development was followed, in the words of Hector MacQueen, 'by a disintegrative process over the last 116 [now 123] years which was inevitable given that the unification was of ideas which were (and are) actually irreconcilable with each other'.[11]

One intellectual source of the twentieth-century general clause of unjust enrichment (s 812 (1) BGB)[12] was the Roman *condictio*: an action that allowed, inter alia, for the claiming back of mistaken transfers. Unlike modern enrichment laws, however, the *condictio* was never based on the principle against unjust enrichment, nor was it limited to value surviving. Instead, the action was strict, as it had been introduced for claims such as the repayment of a loan (*mutuum*). It

---

[10] Jansen, 'Farewell to Unjustified Enrichment?' (n 9).
[11] Hector L MacQueen, 'The Sophistication of Unjustified Enrichment: A Response to Nils Jansen' (2016) 20 Edin LR 312, 312–13; Hector L MacQueen, 'The Future of Unjustified Enrichment in Scotland' (2017) 25 RLR 14, 22. Further detail and references on what follows in Jansen, 'Farewell to Unjustified Enrichment?' (n 9).
[12] 'A person who obtains something as a result of the performance of another person or otherwise at the person's expense without legal grounds for doing so is under a duty to make restitution to him. ...' For simplicity's sake, I refer in this chapter only to German legislation; for the nearly identical state of Swiss and Austrian law, see Jansen, 'Farewell to Unjustified Enrichment?' (n 9).

was not originally used in some of the core case groups for s 812 (1) BGB, namely void or voidable contracts; infringements of rights (*Eingriffskondiktion*); discharges of others' debt (*Rückgriffskondiktion*); and expenditure on others' property (*Verwendungskondiktion*). Some of those claims had not yet been acknowledged in Roman times; others had been dealt with in other contexts, such as contract law, the *rei vindicatio*, or the *negotiorum gestio*.

The second source of modern law was entirely independent of the Roman sources. It was the early modern natural law doctrine of restitution (*restitutio*), which had been developed by sixteenth-century Catholic theologians to determine the duties in corrective justice with which sinners had to comply before claiming remittance of their sin.[13] One core idea of this doctrine was the principle that the sinner had to restore benefits resulting from their infringements of others' rights. This principle was independent of fault, but limited to value surviving; thus, the doctrine was an expression of the principle against unjust enrichment. It survived in the context of the natural law conceptions of property law of the seventeenth and eighteenth centuries.

Although the Roman *condictio* and the idea of the natural law *restitutio* do not square easily, nineteenth-century Pandectists relied on the basic idea of the natural law doctrine of restitution to explain the *condictiones* and transformed them into what was to become the BGB's general clause of unjust enrichment.[14] The assumption was that all *condictiones* were claims for restitution, in that they resulted from the shifting of some benefit from one person's property to another and were therefore limited to value surviving. At the end of the century, Pandectist doctrine thus presented the Roman *condictiones* as expressions of one single restitutionary claim based on an infringement upon another person's property. It therefore became increasingly self-evident that liability was limited to value surviving. As Hector MacQueen has pointed out, very similar developments can also be observed in other civilian legal systems,[15] though it seems that unjust enrichment is understood in systems such as South Africa or Scotland instead as a general principle, which encompasses a number of specific causes of action with different requirements.[16]

Now, the Pandectists' shifting-of-property formula had created no problems as long as it was understood not as an applicable rule, but rather as an abstract principle explaining quite different restitutionary claims. During the twentieth century, however, it became clear that the principle did not work well as a unified cause

---

[13] Nils Jansen, 'Restitution' in Harald Ernst Braun, Erik De Bom, and Paolo Astorri (eds), *A Companion to the Spanish Scholastics* (Brill 2021) 448.
[14] For the legislative process, see Horst Heinrich Jakobs and Werner Schubert (eds), *Die Beratung des Bürgerlichen Gesetzbuchs in systematischer Zusammenstellung der unveröffentlichten Quellen: Recht der Schuldverhältnisse*, vol III (De Gruyter 1983) 833 f; 'Motive' in Benno Mugdan (ed), *Die gesammten Materialien zum Bürgerlichen Gesetzbuch für das Deutsche Reich*, vol II (De Gruyter 1899) 463.
[15] MacQueen, 'The Sophistication of Unjustified Enrichment' (n 11) 313 ff.
[16] Du Plessis, 'Response' (n 8) 384: 'general requirements' which are not, though, applied in a uniform manner.

of action. Scholars such as Walter Wilburg, Ernst von Caemmerer, and Claus-Wilhelm Canaris, as well as the courts, split the unified principle into independent claims. The most important of these are enrichment by transfer; enrichment by infringement upon another person's rights; enrichment by expenditure on another's property; and enrichment by payment of another's debt (Wilburg/von Caemmerer typology).[17] Arguments explaining those claims have increasingly become independent from the provisions on unjust enrichment. Today, the requirement 'without legal basis' has assumed different meanings in different claims; and the enrichment is also determined in quite different ways.[18] Thus, in cases of infringement upon another person's property, loss of enrichment is no defence as far as the price paid by the debtor to acquire this property is concerned. Similarly, restitution in cases of failed contracts is normally reciprocal; the mutual claims are neither limited to value surviving, nor based on the defendant's 'unjustified enrichment'. And although s 812 (1) BGB is the legal basis for the recovery of transfers and other benefits in three-party situations, the rules governing such claims are explained with principles that do not at all derive from, and are unrelated to, the provisions on unjust enrichment.

III. Current Debates

All these propositions restate the orthodox position in Germany today; they give expression to what is standard knowledge expected from students in the first state exam.[19] Recent legislation, too, including the reform of the law of obligations in 2002, has been based on this modern conception of enrichment claims.[20] Interestingly, it mirrors the approach taken by the UNIDROIT Principles to unwinding failing contracts and to cases of undisclosed agency.[21] Clearly, central

---

[17] Wilburg, *Die Lehre von der ungerechtfertigten Bereicherung* (n 1) 5 ff, 7 ff, 27 ff; Von Caemmerer, 'Bereicherung und unerlaubte Handlung' (n 1).
[18] See also Sonja Meier, 'Enrichment "At the Expense of Another" and Incidental Benefits in German Law' [2019] Acta Juridica 453, 458 ff, 468.
[19] Hans Christoph Grigoleit, Marietta Auer, and Luca Kochendörfer, *Schuldrecht III. Bereicherungsrecht* (3rd edn, CH Beck 2022) [5] ff, [144] ff, *passim*. See also Meier, 'Enrichment "At the Expense of Another" and Incidental Benefits in German Law' (n 18) *passim*.
[20] Entwurf eines Gesetzes zur Modernisierung des Schuldrechts, *BT-Drucksache* 14/6040 (2001) 194; claims for enrichment by transfer as remedies in contract law. See also Art 38 Einführungsgesetz zum Bürgerlichen Gesetzbuch (1999), which provides for different rules for the different types of claims for restitution.
[21] Christiane Wendehorst, 'Die Leistungskondiktion und ihre Binnenstruktur in rechtsvergleichender Perspektive' in Reinhard Zimmermann (ed), *Grundstrukturen eines europäischen Bereicherungsrechts* (Mohr Siebeck 2005) 82 ff; Phillip Hellwege, *Die Rückabwicklung gegenseitiger Verträge als einheitliches Problem* (Mohr Siebeck 2004); Reinhard Zimmermann, '*Restitutio in Integrum*: The Unwinding of Failed Contracts under the Principles of European Contract Law, the UNIDROIT Principles and the Avant-projet d'un Code Européen des Contrats' (2005) 10 Unif L Rev 719; Nils Jansen, 'The Concept of Non-Contractual Obligations: Rethinking the Divisions of Tort, Unjustified Enrichment, and Contract Law' (2010) 1 JETL 16, 24 f.

notions in s 812 (1) BGB[22] have become highly ambiguous, in that they have assumed different meanings in different contexts and have ultimately broken apart.

It is important to understand that my analysis of the history and present state of German-speaking legal systems was not meant as a critique of the present state of legislation in Germany;[23] nor did I wish to suggest that Germany or any other legal system should abolish the idea of unjust enrichment altogether (thus the question mark in the title). Even less, and I made this quite clear,[24] does the article aim to support a traditional unjust-factors approach to restitution in the common law, or other 'pluralistic' approaches to unjust enrichment;[25] or to warn other legal systems against acknowledging a legal principle against unjust enrichment.[26] As Hector MacQueen has rightly observed, the idea that unjustified enrichments should be restored has been a 'powerful generalization of law' in many legal systems and should thus be regarded as an important doctrinal advance. It contributed to overcoming rather unsatisfactory categories, such as 'fictional' or 'quasi-contracts' and 'quasi-delicts', and it had remarkable 'creative effects'.[27] Likewise, Pablo Letelier has emphasized that the traditional French approach, with its pre-modern *ius commune* categories, was not to be preferred to the unitary German general clause.[28] But this does not mean that the law should, or even could, stand still or that the present dissolution of the general clause in Germany would invite judges to fall back on quasi-categories if they were confronted with new problems. Nothing like this has happened in Germany; nothing like this is to be expected. If the unification of enrichment law was a doctrinal advance, even more such progress has been made in its subsequent development into four independent groups of claims for restitution.

---

[22] See n 12.
[23] For such a critique ('Ungereimtheiten'), see Detlef König, 'Ungerechtfertigte Bereicherung' in Bundesminister der Justiz (ed), *Gutachten und Vorschläge zur Überarbeitung des Schuldrechts*, vol 2 (Bundesanzeiger 1981) 1520. Gerhard Dannemann seems to have misunderstood my intention in that respect; see Gerhard Dannemann, 'The Future of German Unjustified Enrichment Law' (2017) 25 RLR 44, 49 ff.
[24] Jansen, 'Farewell to Unjustified Enrichment?' (n 9) 124, 147 f.
[25] cf, in that sense, Siyi Lin, *The Law of Unjust Enrichment in China: Necessary or Not?* (Springer 2022) 257 f; Karmen Lutman, 'Change of Position as a Defence in Unjust(ified) Enrichment: Slovenian Law in Comparative Perspective' (2019) 67(1) Belgrade LR 49, 57; Steve Gallagher, Lin Siyi, and Lutz-Christian Wolff, 'The History of a Mystery: The Evolution of the Law of Unjust Enrichment in Germany, England and China' (2020) 3 ICPELR 337.
[26] But see Hedley, ' "Farewell to Unjustified Enrichment?"—A Common Law Response' (n 9) 330 ff; Robert Stevens, 'The Unjust Enrichment Disaster' (2018) 134 LQR 574, 601; Pablo Letelier, 'Another Civilian View of Unjust Enrichment's Structural Debate' (2020) 79 CLJ 527, 528, 534 ff. Other writers who refer to the paper in this context include: Andrew Burrows, 'In Defence of Unjust Enrichment' (2019) 78 CLJ 521, 522; Andrew Burrows, '"At the Expense of the Claimant": A Fresh Look' (2017) 25 RLR 167, 169; Helen Scott, 'Comparative Taxonomy: An Introduction' in Elise Bant, Kit Barker, and Simone Degeling (eds), *Research Handbook on Unjust Enrichment and Restitution* (Edward Elgar 2020) 163 ff; Birke Häcker, 'Unjust Factors versus Absence of Juristic Reason (*Causa*)' in ibid 306 ff.
[27] MacQueen, 'The Sophistication of Unjustified Enrichment' (n 11) 324.
[28] Letelier, 'Another Civilian View of Unjust Enrichment's Structural Debate' (n 26) 542.

A. Entanglements Between Unjust Enrichment and Other Parts of the Legal System

The purpose of my analysis of the German law of unjustified enrichment was thus, on the one hand, to contribute to the future development of German law and, on the other hand, to make it possible for jurists from other legal systems to learn from German experiences. In what follows, I will therefore formulate my main results in the form of three comparative observations. The first is, that the principle against unjust enrichment is often not necessary, or does not suffice, to explain claims which are usually included in a 'law of unjustified enrichment' viz restitution.

One example where the principle against unjust enrichment is unnecessary for legal analysis is failures of performance. Where performance is rendered to discharge an obligation that turns out to be void, or else non-existent, or which exists between different parties (eg where the debtor mistakenly believes that they themselves have caused some damage, which was in fact caused by a third person), the defendant is liable not because they are (still) enriched, but rather because the benefit they received was unjustified.[29] The basic reason for the claim is hence the fact that the purpose of the performance has failed. In many legal systems, such as Roman law, such claims will only exceptionally be limited to a resulting enrichment, viz value surviving. The principle against unjust enrichment is unnecessary to justify such claims;[30] Roman lawyers did not use it to explain the *condictio indebiti*.[31] Now, collecting such claims under the heading of unjust enrichment creates no problem, as long as it is clear that enrichment claims are not limited to an actual enrichment (ie value surviving). When the German legislator transformed the principle against unjust enrichment into a general claim, viz a cause of action, however, things got difficult, as enrichment claims were henceforth defined by their being limited to value surviving (s 818 (3) BGB).

1. Unwinding of failed contracts

However, even greater problems arise where performance has been rendered to discharge a contractual obligation. Problems here, and this is my second observation, result from the abstractness of enrichment claims and from the fact that

---

[29] See Scott, 'South Africa' (n 4) 216 ff.
[30] MacQueen, 'The Sophistication of Unjustified Enrichment' (n 11) 317 f.
[31] The issue is not disputed among Roman lawyers: 'The condictio ... was neither an action from nor for enrichment': Ulrich von Lübtow, *Beiträge zur Lehre von der Condictio nach römischem und geltendem Recht* (Duncker & Humblot 1952) 20. See further Berthold Kupisch, *Ungerechtfertigte Bereicherung: geschichtliche Entwicklungen* (Decker & Müller 1987) 1–27; Jansen, 'Die Korrektur grundloser Vermögensverschiebungen als Restitution?' (n 1) 110–23 with further references; Sebastian Lohsse, *Aequitas Martiniana* (Habilitationsschrift Bonn) (forthcoming), §§ 4–6, esp § 6 I. Du Plessis, 'Response' (n 8) 375 seems to misunderstand D 12,6,14, as Pomponius originally used the principle against unjust enrichment to justify an exception to the *condictio*, rather than the claim; cf also Jacques du Plessis, 'Equity, Fairness and Unjustified Enrichment: A Civil-Law Perspective' (2020) 83 THRHR 1, 5 f.

enrichment law long developed independently from other branches of the law. As far as the unwinding of failed contracts is concerned, the infelicitous result in many legal systems has been two sets of remedies, where restitution is sometimes based on contract and sometimes on unjust enrichment. Letelier and du Plessis seem to be in favour of such an approach,[32] and MacQueen has argued that the contractual relationship should not matter as far as a claim for unjust enrichment is concerned.[33] Yet, where a contract has failed, restitution clearly needs to be reciprocal, and it should not be limited to value surviving. Moreover, as it is often a matter of pure chance whether 'contractual' remedies for avoidance, termination, or withdrawal, or 'non-contractual' claims, such as a *condictio*, apply, German lawyers have long agreed that in such cases unjust enrichment and contract law need to be synchronized.[34] In effect, that meant aligning unjust enrichment with the contractual rules on revocation.[35] In a very detailed and clear comparative study, Sonja Meier has recently shown that this accords with an international trend, clearly visible in examples such as the UNIDROIT Principles,[36] towards a 'uniform restitutionary framework for all kind of failed contracts with room for different rules in detail where needed'.[37] Thus, it may be necessary to provide for special rules for long-term contracts,[38] but this does not depend on whether the contract has been frustrated, terminated, or avoided, or whether it was void from the beginning. The real problem is that it is often difficult and makes little sense retroactively to wind up contracts of employment or leases.[39] Enrichment claims for restitution of contracts thus need to respond to underlying rules and principles of contract law. Whether such a claim is ultimately 'classified' in contract law, unjustified enrichment, or in a separate, independent category, is of lesser significance. 'The point is' simply that, as Meier succinctly put it: 'it should not matter whether restitution is based on contract or unjustified enrichment.'[40]

---

[32] Letelier, 'Another Civilian View of Unjust Enrichment's Structural Debate' (n 26) 537 ff; Du Plessis, 'Equity, Fairness and Unjustified Enrichment' (n 31) 10.
[33] MacQueen, 'The Sophistication of Unjustified Enrichment' (n 11) 324. See however, for a different historical analysis of English law, Warren Swain, Chapter 1 in this volume.
[34] Sonja Meier, 'Unwinding Failed Contracts: New European Developments' (2017) 21 Edin LR 1, *passim*, esp 12. Letelier seems to misunderstand Meier and Zimmermann, whom he cites for his somewhat misleading picture of German law: Letelier, 'Another Civilian View of Unjust Enrichment's Structural Debate' (n 26) 539. There is certainly no disagreement between Meier, Zimmermann, and me on this issue; nor do German scholars dispute the assumption that the application of s 812 (1) 1 BGB should mirror contract law rules.
[35] Ulrich Büdenbender, 'Die Berücksichtigung der Gegenleistung bei der Rückabwicklung gegenseitiger Verträge' (2000) 200 AcP 627, 630 ff, 671 ff; Frank Bockholdt, 'Die Übertragbarkeit rücktrittsrechtlicher Wertungen auf die bereicherungsrechtliche Rückabwicklung gegenseitiger Verträge' (2006) 206 AcP 769. Meanwhile, the German legislator also assumes that the 'same principles should apply to reversal under the law of rescission and the law of enrichment': Entwurf eines Gesetzes zur Modernisierung des Schuldrechts (n 20) 194.
[36] See n 21.
[37] Meier, 'Unwinding Failed Contracts' (n 34) 28.
[38] Letelier, 'Another Civilian View of Unjust Enrichment's Structural Debate' (n 26) 538 f.
[39] Meier, 'Unwinding Failed Contracts' (n 34) 17 with references to French law, too.
[40] ibid 19.

2. Three-party cases

Similar problems are visible in three-party cases, such as cases of counter-mandated cheques. Where the third party was not informed about the countermand, du Plessis argues that the bank might have a claim for restitution against their client.[41] If there was indeed valid performance in favour of the third party, this might well be so. However, the decisive point is whether the client thereby lost any defence or right, such as a right of set-off. These may be tricky issues of contract law, which need to be accounted for when awarding a claim for restitution. Yet, the principle against unjust enrichment and the idea of a shifting of property clearly lead us astray if no performance was effected because the underlying contract was void. Property seems to be shifted directly from the bank to the third party, but that should not allow the bank to bypass their client, as the third party might have defences or counterclaims against their contract partner.

More difficult, at first sight, are cases where a garage brings a claim against the owner of a car, which it had repaired under the terms of a contract with a third person, a non-owner, who never paid for those repairs. Obviously, such a claim can be explained neither in contract law nor in tort law. According to du Plessis, the fact that South African courts have acknowledged such claims thus proves that such cases need to be analysed from an enrichment perspective.[42] Now, these cases seem indeed to be difficult, and there may be good reasons for a legal system to provide for a contractor's lien in the car. The garage may have relied on having the car as a security for its claim, and such a lien may appropriately protect contractors against the risk of their client's insolvency. Absent such a lien, however, du Plessis' argument ignores the fact that the third party is usually responsible—either in contract or tort—to the owner for having the car repaired. It is not obvious why the garage should be entitled to shift their risk of the contractor's insolvency to the owner of the car, who had only got what was due to them. The German legislator had good reasons to abolish the pre-modern *actio de in rem verso*,[43] which would reappear with such a claim.[44] In any event, the pivotal issue to decide such cases is the proper assignment of insolvency risks. German scholars agree that the answers to this issue cannot be gauged from the principle against unjust enrichment, but can instead from the rules and principles of insolvency and contract law, or—as far as a lien in the car is concerned—from the law of property.[45]

---

[41] Du Plessis, 'Response' (n 8) 389 f.
[42] ibid 389.
[43] On which, see Reinhard Zimmermann, *The Law of Obligations: Roman Foundations of the Civilian Tradition* (OUP 1990) 880 ff; Robert Feenstra, 'Grotius' Doctrine of Unjust Enrichment as a Source of Obligation: Its Origin and its Influence in Roman-Dutch Law' in Eltjo JH Schrage (ed), *Unjust Enrichment: The Comparative Legal History of the Law of Restitution* (2nd edn, Duncker & Humblot 1999) 227 ff, 233 ff; Berthold Kupisch, *Die Versionsklage* (Winter 1965) 17 ff, 40 ff, 70 ff.
[44] Nils Jansen, 'Gesetzliche Schuldverhältnisse: Eine historische Strukturanalyse' (2016) 216 AcP 112, 147 f; cf BGHZ 100, 95, 104 (1987).
[45] The standard authority in Germany is Larenz and Canaris, *Lehrbuch des Schuldrechts* (n 1) 199 ff, 246 f.

Outside Germany, this suggestion does not yet seem so uncontroversial. Letelier still defends the *actio de in rem verso* for situations such as that in the *Arrêt Boudier*,[46] in which the claimant had sold fertilizer to a farmer, who had applied it to a piece of land held in tenancy before later becoming insolvent.[47] According to Letelier, the Cour de cassation's decision to grant a claim against the landlord, to whom the land had been returned, was convincing, and such a claim could only be explained in terms of the landlord's unjustified enrichment. Now, this *arrêt* was in line with the predominant view in Europe during the eighteenth century;[48] today, too, there can be no doubt that the landlord should be liable to return any enrichment resulting from the application of fertilizer to his land. Yet, with all respect, I see no convincing reason to grant such a claim to the seller of the fertilizer, rather than to the farmer's insolvency estate. Like any other creditor, the claimant would then have to settle for their quota. In cases of farmers' insolvencies, there is simply no reason to privilege the suppliers of fertilizers vis-à-vis other creditors, such as (most likely) the landlords themselves, other suppliers of goods, and banks. It is exactly a policy against such 'leapfrogging' that led to the abolition of the *actio de in rem verso* in Germany. Indeed, it should be for parliaments, rather than for judges, to grant insolvency privileges; and the basis for such privileges should be economic and social policies, rather than judicial notions of equity. Thus, connecting enrichment law with the principles of insolvency, property, and contract law makes it possible to address the relevant normative issues in a transparent way, rather than in terms of judicial equity. This thus also keeps enrichment law responsive to the legislature's policies. In my eyes, such transparency is a clear example of doctrinal progress.

B. Classification and Explanation

Du Plessis has rightly observed that such observations on the relationship between unjust enrichment and other parts of the legal system may also become relevant insofar as the mapping of the law is concerned; one important issue in many legal systems being the question of whether unjust enrichment should be recognized as a 'distinct field of law'.[49] It would lead us astray here, of course, if such legal categories, viz 'fields of the law', were misunderstood in an essentialist way. Legal institutions, categories, or 'fields of the law' are practical devices; they may be designed in different ways in different legal systems. Arguments of legal coherence

---

[46] See n 2.
[47] Letelier, 'Another Civilian View of Unjust Enrichment's Structural Debate' (n 26) 535 ff.
[48] See n 43. In the eighteenth century, such cases were typical examples of the action.
[49] Du Plessis, 'Response' (n 8) 371 ff.

thus necessarily relate to a specific legal system;[50] no legal system can be an ideal 'model' for others, as different legal systems work with different categories and concepts. Weighing doctrinal elegance with functional responsiveness, contextual fairness, practical simplicity, and explanatory power[51] may lead to quite different, though equally appropriate, results in different legal settings.

Nevertheless, analogies may be drawn where legal systems are similar; hence, something may be learned from the German experience. This 'lesson' consists in the problems resulting from the extraordinary abstractness of unjust enrichment and rather young age of the institution, on the one hand, and the enormous rationalizing effects of connecting unjust enrichment law with other branches of the legal systems, on the other. This is my third comparative observation. According to du Plessis, the law of unjust enrichment is given its specific 'coherence of integration' by its 'purpose of promoting corrective justice'.[52] But this would not distinguish this 'field of law' from torts or contracts. And the idea that the purpose of unjust enrichment might be the 'skimming off' of undeserved benefits[53] can only be understood in a very loose sense,[54] which likewise fails to distinguish it from other fields of law. Where the metaphor is taken seriously, it leads us astray with regards both to cases involving expenses and those concerning infringements of rights. Those claims for restitution do not fully skim off the defendant's gains where such benefits exceed the claimant's expenses, viz loss.[55]

Where a new institution of such an exceptionally high abstractness is introduced into a private legal system alongside its traditional categories, such as contracts, torts, property, and equity, frictions and tensions are probably unavoidable. German law has experienced many such frictions and tensions. Of course, those problems are not a cogent reason not to acknowledge unjust enrichment as a new 'field of law'. Problems may also arise with more narrowly constructed groups of claims, and all those problems can be resolved. Thus, as far as the unwinding of failed contracts is concerned, the rules and remedies of contract law may be constructed as *leges speciales* with regard to more abstract claims in unjust enrichment (which would not, of course, mean dealing with overpayments on contracts in contract law rather than in the context of the *condictio indebiti*).[56] In the same way,

---

[50] I have made such arguments where I have suggested that certain rules 'belonged' to, ie were best placed within, a specific legal institution. Ibid 383 finds this difficult to understand, yet there is no essentialist implication connected with this *façon de parler*.
[51] See Section I.
[52] Du Plessis, 'Response' (n 8) 380 ff.
[53] ibid 381 f, referring to Larenz and Canaris, *Lehrbuch des Schuldrechts* (n 1) 128.
[54] Immediately afterwards, Canaris thus describes the German claims of unjust enrichment more specifically in terms of the 'unwinding of contracts' and 'protection of legal rights': Larenz and Canaris, *Lehrbuch des Schuldrechts* (n 1) 130.
[55] For detailed analysis, see Jansen, 'Gesetzliche Schuldverhältnisse' (n 44) 182 (expenses), 186 ff (infringements of rights).
[56] But see du Plessis, 'Response' (n 8) 386 f. The argument that the unwinding of contracts is most appropriately analysed from a contract law perspective does not, of course, entail that there would be 'duplicate sets of rules on overpayments'. Overpayments are simply a different matter.

marriages are usually dealt with in family law today, although nobody doubts that they come into existence through contracts.[57]

As far as unjust enrichment is concerned, German law has taken an alternative path, constructing claims for restitution to mirror rules and principles of other parts of the law, such as contract,[58] tort, performance, and insolvency; I have described this process in a number of previous articles[59] and with the two examples in Section III.A of this chapter. This was about more than specifying the general principle against unjust enrichment in a number of specific groups or categories.[60] Much more importantly, the principle against unjustified enrichment has been entangled, viz doctrinally connected, with other parts of the law and their specific rules. Here, the important lesson to draw from the German experience is that entangling claims for restitution with other branches of the legal system may be at least as important as the search for a unifying principle. Indeed, this connection of the law of unjust enrichment with rules stemming from other parts of the legal system is the very gist of the Wilburg/von Caemmerer typology.

IV. Conclusion

Whether the result of such an entangling of unjust enrichment with other parts of private law is best described as a 'disintegration' of unjust enrichment, and thus a re-mapping of the law, or else as a 'growing sophistication',[61] may be a matter of judgement, and it depends on many features of a legal system. In any event, it has been seen that mapping should not be confused with explaining: placing a claim for restitution in the 'field' of unjust enrichment does not mean that it has to be explained with the idea of a 'shifting of property', or with the 'skimming off' of undeserved benefit. Unjust enrichment claims always need to be connected with other branches of the law. Thus, my argument, that in cases of failing contracts the *condictio ob rem* and the *condictiones indebiti* should not be constructed as enrichment claims in a narrow sense, is not controversial in Germany and seems to be in agreement with an international trend.[62] Whether the unwinding of contracts

---

[57] Thus, the argument that marriages would have to be dealt with in contract law if the *condictio causa data non secuta* were analysed in its contractual context (du Plessis, 'Response' (n 8) 388) does not ultimately seem convincing.

[58] Jansen, 'Gesetzliche Schuldverhältnisse' (n 44) 157 f. See Section II.A.1.

[59] Jansen, 'Farewell to Unjustified Enrichment?' (n 9); Jansen 'Gesetzliche Schuldverhältnisse' (n 44) 132–228.

[60] cf MacQueen, 'The Sophistication of Unjustified Enrichment' (n 11) 318 ff; MacQueen, 'The Future of Unjustified Enrichment in Scotland' (n 11) 23 f.

[61] MacQueen, 'The Sophistication of Unjustified Enrichment' (n 11) 324; MacQueen, 'The Future of Unjustified Enrichment in Scotland' (n 11) 27 f; cf also Letelier, 'Another Civilian View of Unjust Enrichment's Structural Debate' (n 26) 544 f: 'nuanced approach' vs 'splitting up'.

[62] See n 58. For the *condictio ob rem*, see von Caemmerer, 'Bereicherung und unerlaubte Handlung' (n 1) 346 ff; Larenz and Canaris, *Lehrbuch des Schuldrechts* (n 1) 150 f; Wendehorst, 'Die

is placed in a law of unjust enrichment, in contract law, or in a separate category[63] will often be a matter of legal tradition and conventional expectations. While reconnecting the claim for restitution for infringements of rights with the rules of tort law makes much sense in a rights-oriented system of tort law, it may be less plausible where rights feature less prominently as grounds for action in a system of private law in general and in tort law in particular. And whether overpayments are dealt with in the context of performance or as an independent *condictio* is less important than understanding the intellectual connection between the rules on performance and restitution.

When I prepare German students for the *Staatsexamen* (which I regularly do), I do not tell them to forget unjust enrichment, nor that they simply have to split it into four causes of action. Instead, my lesson is that they have to understand the interconnections between unjust enrichment and the relevant rules in other parts of the legal system. Much more important than any debate about 'disintegration' and 'sophistication' could ever be is thus the underlying process of rationalization, viz making explicit the normative interconnections between claims for restitution and other branches of the legal system. The aim of my papers has not been to stop enrichment lawyers writing books on the law of unjust enrichment. Rather, it has been to invite them to look for such interconnections, which—I am sure—can be detected in every legal system; to translate them into an appropriate doctrinal framework; and thus to contribute to turning claims for restitution into transparent expressions of legal principle.

Leistungskondiktion und ihre Binnenstruktur in rechtsvergleichender Perspektive' (n 21) 75. For the non-legislative codifications, see n 21.

[63] See Meier, 'Unwinding Failed Contracts' (n 34) 17–19.

PART IV
DOCTRINE

13
Monism versus Pluralism in Unjust Enrichment

Mindy Chen-Wishart and Emma Hughes

I. Introduction

The primary test of a theory is one of fit—fit with the law *as it stands*, and not law that must be artificially forced into alignment with the preferred theory. The unjust factors of incapacity, mistake, duress, undue influence, and unconscionable bargains are traditionally theorized by sole reference to (1) the claimant's defective intention. But that theoretical shoe does not fit the legal foot; the pinch points are many and varied. The response of some has been to take refuge in another ill-fitting shoe—(2) the defendant's unconscientious inducement of the claimant's consent. Neither, singly or in combination, provides fulsome 360-degree accounts of the law in question.

In response, we advance a limited pluralism that acknowledges four additional factors that shape the details of these unjust factors beyond the two already mentioned, namely: (3) the claimant's responsibility to act reasonably in making the transfer; (4) the subject matter and fairness of the transaction; (5) public policy and community standards; and (6) the administration of justice (ie making workable rules). We call this the '2+4' limited pluralism.

Given the ambition of our thesis, the breadth of the doctrines covered, the wealth of literature on the unjust factors, and the claimant-sided versus the defendant-sided debates in all major texts on restitution and unjust enrichment, we content ourselves with a gallop on a horse's back through the vast territory covered by this subject. Our purpose is to show the inadequacy of a monistic analysis and to make the pluralism that inhabits the unjust factors overt. The separate question (doubtlessly more difficult) of the precise relationship between these factors must await further analysis.

II. Orthodoxy: Defective Consent

A. The Theory

The orthodox approach is that a defendant's enrichment at the claimant's expense is unjust when the claimant's consent is 'vitiated'.[1] This is the basis for restitution since it nullifies an otherwise voluntary (and hence valid) transfer. The claimant's consent may be defective because it is:

- *impaired*, as where a claimant lacks capacity, labours under a mistake, is subject to the undue influence or coercion of another, or when the contractual transfer is unconscionable;
- *qualified*, as where the transfer is conditional on a basis that fails; and
- *absent*, as where the claimant is ignorant of the defendant's enrichment at their expense.
- A supplementary category of 'policy-motivated' unjust factors accommodates a miscellaneous group of unjust factors that do not fit within this tripartite framework; namely, necessity, legal compulsion,[2] illegality, and the unlawful obtaining of a benefit by a public authority.

In addition to the five unjust factors conventionally regarded as concerned with impaired consent (incapacity, mistake, duress, undue influence, and unconscionable bargains), we will discuss the *Etridge* doctrine,[3] which sheds important light on the unjust factors as it is the only occasion in recent reported decisions in England[4] where a contract involving three parties has been avoided without the defendant's knowledge of the unjust factor.

---

[1] Peter Birks, *An Introduction to the Law of Restitution* (rev edn, OUP 1989) ch 6 (hereafter Birks, *Introduction*); Peter Birks, *Unjust Enrichment* (2nd edn, OUP 2005) 42, 105–06; Andrew Burrows, *The Law of Restitution* (3rd edn, OUP 2011) 86, 199 (hereafter Burrows, *Restitution*); James Edelman and Elise Bant, *Unjust Enrichment* (2nd edn, Hart Publishing 2016) 126; Andrew Burrows, *A Restatement of the English Law of Unjust Enrichment* (1st edn, OUP 2012) 32 (hereafter Burrows, *Restatement*).

[2] While Birks put legal compulsion alongside duress and undue influence in his vitiation of consent chapter (Birks, *Introduction* (n 1) 173), Burrows views this as misleading '[g]iven that the pressure on C cannot be regarded as illegitimate': Burrows, *Restitution* (n 1) 437.

[3] *Royal Bank of Scotland plc v Etridge (No 2)* [2001] UKHL 44; [2002] 2 AC 773 (hereafter *Etridge (No 2)*).

[4] In two non-contractual cases (*Bridgman v Green* (1755) 2 Ves Sen 627; 28 ER 399 and *Huguenin v Baseley* (1807) 14 Ves Jun 273; 33 ER 526), donees tainted by the undue influence of third parties over the claimants were strictly liable for their return: see text to n 106. But this rationale has not been followed and no recent English authorities have discussed these cases (cf the Singaporean decision in *BOM v BOK* [2018] SGCA 83; [2019] 1 SLR 349 [102]–[103] following *Bridgman v Green*). Notably, in *Barclays Bank plc v O'Brien* [1994] 1 AC 180 (HL) 195 (hereafter *O'Brien*), Lord Browne-Wilkinson described the liability of third parties as dependent on notice.

B. Defective Consent to Absence of Basis

Professor Birks, the chief architect of the vitiation of consent model,[5] famously recanted his taxonomy in favour of the civilian 'absence of basis' approach[6] for its 'surgical simplicity'.[7] Nevertheless, the unjust factors remain foundational within Birks's preferred analytical framework. Defective consent and policy-motivated unjust factors still operate at the base of Birks's pyramid as the *reasons* for the absence of basis higher up, which, in turn, explains the unjustness of the enrichment and the justness of restitution.[8]

Moreover, the precise nature of the unjust factor in play still frames the precise restitutionary response,[9] by dictating the rigour with which the bars to rescission are applied (eg fraud neutralizes the laches bars and dilutes the *restitutio in integrum* bar) and the applicability of the change of position defence (eg not where the unjust factor involves the defendant's bad faith[10] or the claimant's incapacity[11]). In any event, the courts[12] and commentators[13] remain firmly committed to the defective consent approach.

1. Attractions of the defective consent approach

These are the attractions:

(1) *Elegance*: the approach mirrors the structure and reasoning of civil law jurisdictions and avoids concessions to the messiness of common law methodology. It is a ready answer to the criticism that unjust enrichment lacks the unity of other private law subjects.[14]

---

[5] Birks, *Introduction* (n 1).
[6] Birks, *Unjust Enrichment* (n 1) ch 5.
[7] ibid ch 6, 129.
[8] ibid ch 5, 116.
[9] Mindy Chen-Wishart, 'Unjust Factors and the Restitutionary Response' (2000) 20 OJLS 557; Mindy Chen-Wishart, 'In Defence of Unjust Factors: A Study of Rescission for Duress, Fraud and Exploitation' in David Johnston and Reinhard Zimmerman (eds), *Unjustified Enrichment: Key Issues in Comparative Perspective* (CUP 2002). See also Edelman and Bant, *Unjust Enrichment* (n 1) 123–24.
[10] This defence is generally invisible in cases of induced mistake, duress, and undue influence: see eg *Royal Bank of Scotland plc v Etridge (No 2)* [1998] 4 All ER 705 (CA) 718, where the Court of Appeal saw 'difficulties in [the change of position] analysis, not least that there is no trace of it in *O'Brien*' (referring to *O'Brien* (n 4)). At most, a very limited change of position applies where the loss may be apportioned (as in *Cheese v Thomas* [1994] 1 WLR 129 (CA), see Mindy Chen-Wishart, 'Loss Sharing, Undue Influence and Manifest Disadvantage' (1994) 110 LQR 173).
[11] See *Williams v Williams* [2003] EWHC 742 (Ch).
[12] *Test Claimants in the FII Group Litigation v Revenue and Customs Comrs* [2012] UKSC 19; [2012] 2 AC 337 [162] (Lord Sumption SCJ); *Patel v Mirza* [2016] UKSC 42; [2017] AC 467 [246] (Lord Sumption SCJ); *Swynson Ltd v Lowick Rose LLP* [2017] UKSC 32; [2018] AC 313 [22] (Lord Sumption SCJ); *Dargamo Holdings Ltd v Avonwick Holdings Ltd* [2021] EWCA Civ 1149; [2022] 1 All ER (Comm) 1244 [58] (Carr LJ).
[13] Burrows, *Restitution* (n 1); Burrows, *Restatement* (n 1); Edelman and Bant, *Unjust Enrichment* (n 1) 20, 126, 195, 250.
[14] *Orakpo v Manson Investments Ltd* [1978] AC 95 (HL) 104 (Lord Diplock); *Patel v Mirza* (n 12) [246] (Lord Sumption SCJ).

(2) *Autonomy*: it is unsurprising that the defective consent account of the unjust factors is so firmly entrenched in the academic literature given the normative force of personal autonomy in liberal democratic societies; if the claimant's consent is impaired, the defendant's enrichment ought to be reversed. This justifies the state's coercion.

2. Problems with this approach
The problems are as follows:[15]

(1) *Lack of fit with the law*: for example: (a) transactions are voidable (ie valid unless and until the claimant chooses to rescind) and not void as the logic of vitiated consent would dictate; (b) it cannot explain why different things must be proved for the same vitiating factor depending on the nature of the transaction (contract, gift, or will);[16] (c) neither can it explain why the bars to rescission (and so restitution) and the change of position defence differ across the unjust factors; and (d) the logic of vitiated consent should allow restitution where third parties are responsible for the impaired consent, yet this has almost never been permitted.[17] Conceptual simplicity is desirable but the simplest explanation is not necessarily the *best* explanation and should not be preferred over a more complex but more accurate theory; Occam's razor does not require the adoption of the simplest theory *come what may*. According to Einstein, everything should be kept as simple as possible, but no simpler.[18] Hart cautioned that 'uniformity of pattern', although 'pleasing' may come at 'too high a price'.[19] There must be a proper trade-off between simplicity and adequacy of fit.

(2) *Conclusory not explanatory*: consent is a matter of degree and determining when it is 'defective' can only be done by reference to factors *external* to the claimant's state of mind in deciding whether the 'consent ... procured ought not fairly to be treated as an expression of a person's free will'.[20] Thus, references to defective consent are conclusory, not explanatory; it is merely shorthand for the variety of factors rendering a transaction defeasible. The real question is the identity of those external factors.

---

[15] Mindy Chen-Wishart, 'The Nature of Vitiating Factors in Contract Law' in Gregory Klass, George Letsas, and Prince Saprai (eds), *Philosophical Foundations of Contract Law* (OUP 2014).
[16] See eg text to n 80 and n 128 below.
[17] See n 4, there are no reported cases on restitution where a third party has coerced the claimant to pay the defendant: see Burrows, *Restatement* (n 1) s 11(7).
[18] See Albert Einstein, 'On the Method of Theoretical Physics' (1934) 1 Philos Sci 163, 165. Dubbed 'Einstein's razor', it counters appeals to Occam's razor that result in an oversimplified and false explanation.
[19] HLA Hart, *The Concept of Law* (3rd edn, OUP 2012) 38.
[20] Etridge (No 2) (n 3) [7] (Lord Nicholls).

(3) *Burden of proof*: on the defective consent model, the defendant should logically have the burden of proving the absence of any and all unjust factors to *validate* the transfer. Instead, it is the claimant who must prove the existence of an unjust factor to avoid the basis for a transfer that is, otherwise, presumptively valid.

(4) *Insulting characterization of claimants*: a troubling feature of claimant-sided accounts is the depiction of claimants who succumb to duress or undue influence as sub-normal or otherwise lacking in rationality,[21] when the reverse is strongly arguable.[22]

(5) *Normatively inadequate*: most legal systems allow a claimant to recover a benefit conferred by mistake where there is no contract between the parties, and the defendant may not have committed any wrong. The defective consent model does not explain why the *defendant* is obliged to make restitution.[23]

III. Unconscientious Conduct

A. The Theory

The principal rival to the claimant-oriented approach is a defendant-sided approach. The defendant's 'unconscionability' has been suggested as the common denominator of duress, undue influence, and unconscionable bargains[24] (incapacity and mistake remain claimant-sided), due to the defendant's 'abuse of the unequal position between the parties'.[25] For example, Rick Bigwood explains undue influence by reference to the defendant's failure to protect the claimant from transactional harm,[26] and Stephen Smith has argued that wrongdoing is a distinct principle underpinning duress.[27] On these accounts, it is the defendant's unconscientious conduct coupled with the maxim that one ought not profit from one's own wrong that justifies restitution.

---

[21] Peter Birks and Chin Nyuk Yin, 'On the Nature of Undue Influence' in Jack Beatson and Daniel Friedman (eds), *Good Faith and Fault in Contract Law* (OUP 1995). See text to nn 107–11.

[22] Mindy Chen-Wishart, 'Undue Influence: Vindicating Relationships of Influence' (2006) 59 CLP 231.

[23] Robert Stevens, 'The Unjust Enrichment Disaster' (2018) 134 LQR 574, 581–82; Frederick Wilmot-Smith, 'Should the Payee Pay?' (2017) 37 OJLS 844; Steve Hedley, 'Justice and Discretion in the Law of Unjust Enrichment' (2019) 48 CLWR 94, 98–104.

[24] David Capper, 'Undue Influence and Unconscionability: A Rationalisation' (1998) 114 LQR 479.

[25] John Cartwright, *Unequal Bargaining: A Study of Vitiating Factors in the Formation of Contracts* (OUP 1991).

[26] Rick Bigwood, 'Contracts by Unfair Advantage: From Exploitation to Transactional Neglect' (2005) 25 OJLS 65.

[27] Stephen A Smith, 'Contracting Under Pressure: A Theory of Duress' (1997) 56 CLJ 343.

B. Advantages of the Unconscientious Inducement Approach

(1) *Some fit*: this account explains cases of fraudulent and negligent misrepresentation, duress to the person and property, and some cases of actual undue influence, where the defendant's conduct is wrongful or at least unconscientious.
(2) *Explains voidability*: it explains why a contractual transfer is only rendered voidable: while the claimant's consent is not defective; the claimant can elect to avoid the transaction because of the defendant's bad conduct.
(3) *Explains ineffectiveness of third-party unconscientiousness*: it explains why unconscientious inducement by a third party is ineffective against a good faith defendant.
(4) *Explains change of position defence*: it explains why only bad faith defendants are shut out of the change of position defence.

C. Problems with the Unconscientious Inducement Approach

(1) *Lack of fit*: aside from those unjust factors listed earlier, the defendant's conduct in the remaining unjust factors may not constitute a 'wrong' or even be obviously untoward (ie innocent misrepresentation, some economic or lawful act duress, some actual and all presumed undue influence, and non-commercial guarantees). Certainly, no compensatory damages are available to claimants in these cases.[28] Indeed, wrongdoing on the defendant's part has been described as 'passive'[29] or 'constructive',[30] and on occasions admittedly absent.[31]
(2) *Variation dependent on transaction*: the defendant-sided approach cannot explain why the elements to be proved in cases of mistake[32] and undue influence[33] differ depending on whether the transaction is contractual, gratuitous, or testamentary.
(3) *Bars to rescission*: it also cannot explain the bars to rescission of third-party rights, lapse of time, and inability to effect mutual restitution.
(4) *Change of position defence*: this is not automatically disapplied for unconscientious defendants (eg infancy), and this points to the force of other factors.

---

[28] With the exception of s 2(1) of the Misrepresentation Act 1967, which creates a statutory right to reliance damages relying on the 'fiction of fraud', unless the defendant can meet the 'reasonable grounds' qualification.
[29] *Hart v O'Connor* [1985] AC 1000 (PC) 1024 (Lord Brightman).
[30] See discussion of *Etridge* non-commercial guarantees at text to n 140.
[31] See discussion of *Bridgman v Green* at text to n 106.
[32] See text to nn 79–84.
[33] See text to n 128.

IV. The '2 + 4' Approach

We have argued that defective consent and unconscientious conduct cannot, separately or together, satisfactorily explain the unjust factors covered in this chapter. They are relevant, but neither necessary nor sufficient. Our response is to supplement them with four factors in constructing a limited pluralistic model. In the rest of this chapter, we show how resort to these factors are necessary to account for the precise shape and size of each unjust factor covered.

Proponents of the monistic accounts do not deny that other factors are operating at the edges but the tendency, to date, has been one or more of:[34] (1) subsuming them within an artificially enlarged concept of claimant-consent or defendant-wrongdoing;[35] (2) rejecting their normative relevance and advocating for their removal; (3) downplaying their role as 'pragmatic restrictors' aimed at preventing 'too much restitution';[36] or (4) subject the master principle (defective consent or defendant unconscientiousness) to the standard *ceteris paribus* ('all-things-being-equal') get out.[37] It amounts to saying that *voluntariness rules*, unless it doesn't, other things being important. It is true, but only trivially so.

This '2+4' limited pluralism allows the law in each unjust factor to be fully accounted for, without suppression, artificiality, or embarrassment. Accordingly, the six factors in play are:[38]

(1) *The claimant's impaired consent* rooted in the value of autonomy.
(2) *The defendant's unconscientious inducement* based on the law's justified concern with fair dealing and preventing wrongdoers from being enriched by their own wrong.
(3) The expectation that *a claimant will act reasonably* in making the transfer is similarly justified by the concern with fair dealing as well as the need to protect the security of receipts.
(4) *The appropriateness/fairness of the transfer* is a controversial factor that can be rationalized as evidence of (1) or (2), in terms of a concern with the claimant's future autonomy (thus, the institution of bankruptcy preserves a social minimum), or as a response to significant inequality of bargaining power.

---

[34] Chen-Wishart, 'The Nature of Vitiating Factors in Contract Law' (n 15) 305–12.
[35] eg where avoidance of contracts for common mistake and frustration are explained as implied-in-fact terms based on the parties' intention: see C Slade, 'The Myth of Mistake in the English Law of Contract' (1954) 70 LQR 885; cf Chen-Wishart, 'The Nature of Vitiating Factors in Contract Law' (n 15) 305–09.
[36] Birks and Chin, 'On the Nature of Undue Influence' (n 21) 62, 82, 90.
[37] Chen-Wishart, 'The Nature of Vitiating Factors in Contract Law' (n 15) 310–12.
[38] See ibid.

(5) *Public policy and community standards* inform every area of law to give meaning to our actions. The law can legitimately prevent valuable social institutions from being undermined or abused.

(6) *Administration of justice* raises pragmatic restrictors because when specific purposes are translated into workable laws, some distortion is inevitable. For example, to avoid intractable problems of proof, the law may assist with evidential or legal presumptions; to avoid the difficulty of valuing or monetizing partial performance, the law lays down the bar to rescission of impossibility of precise restitution (*restitutio in integrum*),[39] and preconditions restitution of money paid on a *total* failure of consideration.[40]

There will be inevitable disagreement about the precise scope of each factor and where the balance should be struck between them. Discussion of this must be left to another day. The limited thesis of this chapter is that the '2+4' limited pluralism is normatively and descriptively justified, and provides a better account of the law on incapacity, mistake, duress, undue influence, unconscionability, and the *Etridge* doctrine in cases of non-commercial guarantees.

V. Incapacity

An infant (under 18)[41] or mentally incapacitated individual who confers a benefit may be entitled to restitution. On the defective consent model, incapacity should be the purest case for restitution since relief is granted because a 'claimant who lacks capacity does not truly intend to benefit the defendant'.[42] The strongest protective stance is shown to infants who can plead change of position even if fraudulent; the infant cannot be made to pay for the property received under the invalid contract, but only needs to return what is left.[43]

Yet, the conditions of relief evince the force of all the six factors identified earlier:

---

[39] *Valentini v Canali* (1889) 24 QBD 166 (QB). It is arguable that this concern has been taken too far and that monetized restitution should be permitted for what cannot be returned: see Chen-Wishart, 'Unjust Factors and the Restitutionary Response' (n 9).

[40] Strong arguments favour permitting restitution for partial failure of consideration: see Burrows, *Restitution* (n 1) 313–14.

[41] Family Law Reform Act 1969, s 1.

[42] Burrows, *Restitution* (n 1) 311.

[43] In *R Leslie Ltd v Sheill* [1914] 3 KB 607 (CA), a child fraudulently misrepresented his age to obtain a loan, which he used up. The Court of Appeal rejected the suggestion that the child should repay the amount but accepted that, in principle, equity could compel restitution of any remaining enrichment. See Chen-Wishart, 'Unjust Factors and the Restitutionary Response' (n 9) 561.

- A mentally incompetent adult (1) can only rescind[44] a contract where the defendant *knows* of their incapacity,[45] showing concern with the defendant's unconscientiousness (2); and the public policies (5) of protecting good faith transferees' security of receipts, and avoiding the infantilization of the elderly.[46] This knowledge requirement is dispensed with in gift cases, where reciprocity is absent (4), since concern with the defendant's security of receipts (5) is less compelling, and infantilization is less concerning for infants.
- The concern with the claimant's responsibility in making transfers (3) is logically disengaged where the claimant is incapacitated.
- The fairness/appropriateness of the transfer (4) clearly shapes the restitutionary response. Thus, for example, incapacitated parties must still pay a reasonable price for necessaries received.[47] Where the defendant is ignorant of the claimant adult's mentally incapacity, a contract is only voidable if it is unconscionable,[48] necessitating proof of an improvident bargain.[49] Moreover, contracts that are generally beneficial to the infant are valid unless set aside.[50] All other contracts are unenforceable against the infant unless the infant ratifies them on reaching adulthood.[51]
- The concern with the administration of justice (6) explains why infancy is determined by a bright-line rule of a fixed age. It is irrelevant that a claimant would still have made the contract had they been 18 and of full capacity; the infant is only given this choice to ratify upon reaching the age of adulthood.[52]

These deviations from the impaired intention approach have led some supporters of the approach to reclassify incapacity as a policy-motivated unjust factor.[53] But, this just makes 'policy' a black box into which anything non-consent-compliant is consigned. It begs the question rather than answers it.

---

[44] A contract will only be void where the affairs of the mental incompetent have been placed in the hands of the Court of Protection or in an extreme case where the claimant lacks capacity to understand the nature of the document he is signing (*non est factum*).
[45] *Imperial Loan Co Ltd v Stone* [1892] 1 QB 599 (CA) 601 (Lord Escher MR); *Hart v O'Connor* (n 29).
[46] Birks, *Unjust Enrichment* (n 1) ch 3, 42.
[47] Mental Capacity Act 2005, s 7 (adults); *Peters v Fleming* (1840) 6 M & W 42; 151 ER 314 (infants).
[48] *Hart v O'Connor* (n 29); *Imperial Loan Co Ltd v Stone* (n 45).
[49] See discussion in text to n 132.
[50] Charles Mitchell, Paul Mitchell, and Stephen Watterson, *Goff & Jones: The Law of Unjust Enrichment* (9th edn, Sweet & Maxwell 2016) [24-19].
[51] Ibid.
[52] Burrows, *Restatement* (n 1) s 14(1).
[53] Mitchell, Mitchell, and Watterson (n 50) [24-05]; Edelman and Bant, *Unjust Enrichment* (n 1) 312-13. The same is also true for 'legal compulsion': see (n 2).

VI. Mistake

Birks regards the mistaken payment of a non-existent debt as the 'core case' of impaired consent (1), with other unjust factors derived from it.[54] There is some support for this position. First, mistake renders contracts void rather than voidable. Secondly, the scope of mistake has been widened (liability mistakes[55] are unnecessary and the mistake of law bar has been abolished)[56] moving closer to the impaired consent rationale allowing restitution for *any* 'but for' mistake.[57] Thirdly, the claimant's carelessness does not bar relief.[58]

Nevertheless, many deviations from the strict logic of the impaired consent rationale point to the force of other factors:

- Reference to the defendant's unconscientious inducement (2) is necessary to explain:
  o why a lower test of causation applies if the defendant has induced the mistake by misrepresentation; the claimant need only prove that the mistake was *a* cause of the transaction,[59] and, post *Zurich Insurance Co plc v Hayward*,[60] the claimant may not even need to prove that they were mistaken (ie they believed the misrepresentation);
  o whether a proprietary remedy is available (Lord Browne-Wilkinson considered that a trust may arise over a mistaken payment where the payee knows of the payor's mistake);[61] and
  o why a defendant is barred from the change of position defence.[62]
- The *Kelly v Solari* principle that the claimant's carelessness in making the transfer (3) will not bar relief is now under pressure:[63]

---

[54] Birks, *Unjust Enrichment* (n 1) ch 1, 3.
[55] *Barclays Bank Ltd v WJ Simms Son & Cooke (Southern) Ltd* [1980] QB 677 (QB).
[56] *Kleinwort Benson Ltd v Lincoln CC* [1999] 2 AC 349 (HL).
[57] See eg *Lloyds Bank plc v Independent Insurance Co Ltd* [2000] QB 110 (CA); *Deutsche Morgan Grenfell Group plc v Inland Revenue Comrs* [2006] UKHL 49; [2007] 1 AC 558 (hereafter *Deutsche Morgan*).
[58] *Kelly v Solari* (1841) 9 M & W 54, 59; 152 ER 24, 26 (Parke B). For further cases affirming that negligence does not bar restitution, see *Imperial Bank of Canada v Bank of Hamilton* [1903] AC 49 (PC) 56 (Lord Lindley); *RE Jones Ltd v Waring and Gillow Ltd* [1926] AC 670 (HL) 689; *Pitt v Holt* [2013] UKSC 26; [2013] 2 AC 108 [114] where Lord Walker SCJ said that this proposition was 'uncontroversial'.
[59] *Edgington v Fitzmaurice* (1885) 29 Ch D 459 (CA).
[60] *Zurich Insurance Co plc v Hayward* [2016] UKSC 48; [2017] AC 142.
[61] *Westdeutsche Landesbank Girozentrale v Islington London BC* [1996] AC 669 (HL) 715 (Lord Browne-Wilkinson).
[62] *Lipkin Gorman v Karpnale Ltd* [1991] 2 AC 548 (HL) 579–80 (Lord Goff). For the definition of bad faith, see *Niru Battery Manufacturing Co v Milestone Trading Ltd* [2002] EWHC 1425 (Comm); [2002] 2 All ER (Comm) 705 [135] (Moore-Bick J); *Abou-Rahmah v Abacha* [2006] EWCA Civ 1492; [2007] 1 All ER (Comm) 827; *Jones v Churcher* [2009] EWHC 722 (QB).
[63] Graham Virgo, *The Principles of the Law of Restitution* (3rd edn, OUP 2015) 179; Tang Hang Wu, 'The Role of Negligence and Non-Financial Detriment in the Law of Unjust Enrichment' (2006) 14 RLR 55.

o in respect of contractual transfers, no restitution is available if the claimant enters a contract 'with minimal knowledge of the facts to which the mistake relates but is content that it is a good speculative risk'.[64] A plea of frustration (a future mistake) will fail if the alleged frustrating event is self-induced;[65]

o the line between someone who 'runs the risk' and so is barred from restitution, and a careless claimant who is not, is difficult to draw precisely because of the legitimate concern that claimants should act responsibly in transacting. Aside from the gift, contract, or wills context, claimants who render benefits with a high degree of doubt about the accuracy of a matter are barred from restitution because they have run the risk of being wrong.[66] Mistake requires that a claimant believed that it 'was more likely than not' that the true facts or true state of the law were otherwise than they actually were and a claimant may be denied relief on the basis that he 'responded unreasonably to his doubts, and so unreasonably ran the risk of error'.[67] For example, in *R (Rowe) v Vale of White Horse DC* the council was the 'author of its own discomfort'.[68] Its claim for restitution was denied because of its own 'administrative oversight' and 'extraordinary error of judgment'.[69] In *Pitt v Holt*, Lord Walker[70] approved Lloyd LJ's observation with respect to *Re Griffiths (decd)* that there 'would have been a strong argument for saying that, having declined to follow the recommendation that he should take out term insurance, Mr Griffiths was taking the risk that his health was, or would come to be, such that he did not survive';[71]

o increasingly, commentators have argued that claimants should be under a duty to act responsibly;[72]

o the rejection of mispredictions also points to the relevance of the claimant's responsibility. Birks's explanation is that where a claimant mis-predicts a future event, their belief is only falsified post-transaction.[73] Yet, the claimant's consent is vitiated whether their belief is falsifiable at the time

---

[64] *Associated Japanese Bank (International) Ltd v Crédit du Nord SA* [1989] 1 WLR 255 (QB) 268, approved in *Great Peace Shipping Ltd v Tsavliris Salvage (International) Ltd* [2002] EWCA Civ 1407; [2003] QB 679, 707 (Lord Phillips MR).
[65] *Monarch Steamship Co Ltd v Karlshamns Oljefabriker (A/B)* [1949] AC 196 (HL).
[66] *Marine Trade SA v Pioneer Freight Futures Co Ltd BVI* [2009] EWHC 2656 (Comm); [2010] 1 Lloyd's Rep 631 [76]–[77]; *Deutsche Morgan* (n 57) [27] (Lord Hoffmann), [65] (Lord Hope), [175] (Lord Brown). In *Pitt v Holt* (n 58) [114], Lord Walker said that restitution will be denied if 'the circumstances are such as to show that [the claimant] deliberately ran the risk, or must be taken to have run the risk, of being wrong'.
[67] *Tecnimont Arabia Ltd v National Westminster Bank plc* [2022] EWHC 1172 (Comm) [155]. See also *Capital Insurance Co Ltd v Samsoondar* [2020] UKPC 33; [2021] 2 All ER 1105 [24] (Lord Burrows).
[68] *R (Rowe) v Vale of White Horse DC* [2003] EWHC 388 (Admin) [15] (Lightman J).
[69] ibid [14] (Lightman J).
[70] *Pitt v Holt* (n 58) [113].
[71] *Pitt v Holt* [2011] EWCA Civ 197; [2012] Ch 132 [198] (Lloyd LJ).
[72] Mitchell, Mitchell, and Watterson (n 50) [9-30]–[9-34].
[73] Peter Birks, 'Mistakes of Law' (2000) 53 CLP 205, 226–27; Birks, *Introduction* (n 1) 147.

of the transaction or only thereafter.[74] Like failure of basis, the claimant did not intend to enrich the defendant *as things have turned out*. This is recognized in contract law, which treats the doctrines of frustration and mistake as dealing with essentially the same problem despite the temporal distinction: whether the parties' assumptions are, or turn out to be, radically different from those assumed by the parties *when they entered into the contract*. The law can avoid the contract irrespective of *when* the assumption is falsified.[75] The mistake/misprediction boundary is slippery and open to manipulation,[76] with different restitutionary outcomes.[77] So, why persist with it when it contradicts the impaired consent rationale? The answer lies in the concern to ensure claimant responsibility by mediating it through the language of 'risk-taking' and 'misprediction';

o in South Africa, the excusability of the claimant's mistake determines whether restitution should be permitted.[78]

- The law manifests concern with the substance of the transaction (4). In the contractual context, the mistaken assumption must be 'fundamental'[79] and the frustrating event must bring about a radical change in the obligations undertaken.[80] Even in *Pitt v Holt*, a gift case, Lord Walker required a 'causative mistake of sufficient gravity' with gravity 'to be assessed in terms of injustice—or ... unconscionableness'.[81] Lord Walker's ratio may be confined to the equitable remedy of rescission[82] or to gifts transferred by way of a deed.[83] But, many commentators support a stricter scope of qualifying mistakes in all gift cases to prevent the claimant from unwinding them too readily,[84] a policy concern (5).

- The defective consent model cannot explain why the demands of the mistake doctrine are heightened when the enrichment is conferred pursuant to a contract, but public policy (5) can. The concern to protect the defendant's security

---

[74] Further, 'mistakes' of law are really mispredictions that the law will not change going forward.

[75] In *Krell v Henry* [1903] 2 KB 740 (CA), the common assumption that the coronation would take place was falsified after formation (the contract was frustrated). In *Griffith v Brymer* (1903) 19 TLR 434 (KB), it was falsifiable at the time the contract was made (the contract was void for mistake).

[76] Sometimes it is possible to conjure up a mistake out of a misprediction as *Dextra Bank* sought to do in *Dextra Bank & Trust Co Ltd v Bank of Jamaica* [2001] UKPC 50; [2002] 1 All ER (Comm) 193.

[77] In *Re Griffiths (decd)* [2008] EWHC 118 (Ch); [2009] Ch 162, the result depended on the judge's 'hair's breadth finding': *Pitt v Holt* (n 58) [113] (Lord Walker).

[78] *Divisional Council of Aliwal North v De Wet* (1890) 7 SC 232.

[79] *Bell v Lever Bros Ltd* [1932] AC 161 (HL) 208.

[80] *Davis Contractors v Fareham UDC* [1956] AC 696 (HL) 729.

[81] *Pitt v Holt* (n 58) [122], [124].

[82] This is the interpretation favoured by Terence Etherton, 'The Role of Equity in Mistaken Transactions' (2013) 27 TLI 159.

[83] Paul S Davies and Graham Virgo, 'Relieving Trustees' Mistakes' (2013) 21 RLR 74, 83–84.

[84] Andrew Tettenborn, *The Law of Restitution in England and Ireland* (3rd edn, Taylor & Francis 2002) 76–77; Sonja Meier and Reinhard Zimmermann, 'Judicial Development of the Law Error *Iuris*,

- of receipt explains the high threshold for qualifying mistakes and the reluctance to allow mere ignorance (even if causative) to qualify.[85]
- The administration of justice concern (6) is manifest in the requirement in contractual transfers that the relevant mistake must be made by both parties, the commonality corroborating the existence of a mistake.

VII. Duress

Birks regarded duress as a claimant-sided unjust factor (1); the claimant's consent being impaired by the defendant's illegitimate threat.[86] In contrast, some commentators[87] and judges[88] have conceded that duress does not overbear the will. Several features of the law on duress also deviate from the claimant-sided analysis; for example:

- the claimant's consent is equally coerced whether the cause originates with the defendant or not, yet the duress by necessitous circumstances does not yield restitution;[89] and
- likewise, there are no reported cases of restitution for duress applied by a third party; a contract is only voidable if the defendant has actual knowledge of the third party's pressure, or was acting as the third party's agent.[90]

Much can be said in support of duress as a defendant-sided unjust factor (2):

---

and the Law of Unjustified Enrichment—A View from Germany' (1999) 115 LQR 556; Tang Hang Wu, 'Restitution for Mistaken Gifts' (2004) 20 JCL 1; Stephen Watterson, 'Reversing Mistaken Voluntary Dispositions' (2013) 72 CLJ 501, 504 who describes this interpretation of *Pitt v Holt* as the 'most plausible'; cf Birke Häcker, 'Mistaken Gifts after *Pitt v Holt*' (2014) 67 CLP 333. In *Deutsche Morgan* (n 57) [87], Lord Scott said that restitution in gift cases should only be allowed where the recipient induces the donee's mistake.

[85] *Pitt v Holt* (n 58) [108] (Lord Walker).
[86] Birks, *Introduction* (n 1) 140, 173–74; Birks and Chin, 'On the Nature of Undue Influence' (n 21) 88–89. See also *Pao On v Lau Yiu Long* [1980] AC 614 (PC) 635; *Occidental Worldwide Investment Corp v Skibs A/S Avanti (The Siboen and the Sibotre)* [1976] 1 Lloyd's Rep 293 (QB) 336 (Kerr J).
[87] PS Atiyah, 'Economic Duress and the "Overborne Will"' (1982) 98 LQR 197, 200; Burrows, *Restitution* (n 1) 269; Edelman and Bant, *Unjust Enrichment* (n 1) 198–99.
[88] *DPP for Northern Ireland v Lynch* [1975] AC 653 (HL) 695; *Crescendo Management Pty Ltd v Westpac Banking Corp* (1988) 19 NSWLR 40 (NSWCA) 45–46 (McHugh JA); *Dimskal Shipping Co SA v International Transport Workers Federation (The Evia Luck) (No 2)* [1992] 2 AC 152 (HL) 166 (Lord Goff); *Universe Tankships Inc of Monrovia v International Transport Workers Federation (The Universe Sentinel)* [1983] 1 AC 366 (HL) 384 (Lord Diplock), 400 (Lord Scarman); *Sapporo Breweries Ltd v Lupofresh Ltd* [2013] EWCA Civ 948; [2013] CN 1213 [29] (Tomlinson J); *Al Nehayan v Kent* [2018] EWHC 333 (Comm) [189]; [2018] 1 CLC 216 (Leggatt J).
[89] With the exception of the salvage doctrine (eg *The Port Caledonia and the Ann* [1903] P 184 (Prob).
[90] See n 17.

- Some cases refer to the 'wrong of duress',[91] or the prevention of 'unconscionability'.[92]
- Duress requires the defendant's threat to be illegitimate and judges have discussed this in terms of 'unconscionable conduct',[93] or 'highly reprehensible' behaviour.[94]
- The causation test decreases with the wrongfulness of the threat (lower for duress to the person than for the 'less serious' economic duress).[95]
- A defendant tainted with duress cannot appeal to change of position, and the court is keen to dismantle the *restitutio in integrum* bar to prevent an undeserving defendant from retaining the unjust enrichment.[96]

Nevertheless, the relevance of other factors is clear:

- The concern with the claimant's responsibility (3) explains the requirement that the claimant had 'no practicable alternative' but to submit to the defendant's demand.[97] Where the claimant *had* a practicable alternative course of action (such as resort to law), they must take full responsibility.[98]
- Substantive unfairness (4) also plays a role: whether the pressure applied by the defendant is illegitimate depends on the nature of the threat and the nature of the *demand*[99] (particularly in lawful act duress cases[100]) and, the extent of unfairness of the demand is evidence of causation (ie the threat must have induced the claimant to make the unfair transfer).[101]
- Community values and public policy (5) explain the existence of lawful act duress.[102] The policy of facilitating contractual renegotiation in limited

---

[91] *The Universe Sentinel* (n 88) 400 (Lord Scarman); *Attorney-General v R* [2003] UKPC 22; [2003] EMLR 24 [15] (Lord Hoffmann).

[92] *Huyton SA v Peter Cremer GmbH & Co* [1999] 1 Lloyd's Rep 620 (QB) 637–38 (Mance J) (hereafter *Huyton*).

[93] *Crescendo Management Pty Ltd v Westpac Banking Corp* (n 88) 46 (McHugh JA). This passage was referred to by Lord Goff in *The Evia Luck (No 2)* (n 88) 165–66. See also *Alf Vaughan & Co Ltd v Royscot Trust plc* [1999] 1 All ER (Comm) 856, 863 (Judge Rich QC); *Borrelli v Ting* [2010] UKPC 21; [2010] Bus LR 1718 [32] (Lord Saville).

[94] *Times Travel (UK) Ltd v Pakistan International Airlines Corp* [2021] UKSC 40; [2021] 3 WLR 727 [2]–[4], [17]–[25] (Lord Hodge SCJ) (hereafter *Times Travel*).

[95] *Huyton* (n 92) 636 (Mance J).

[96] See *Halpern v Halpern* [2007] EWCA Civ 291; [2008] QB 195 [76].

[97] *DSND Subsea Ltd v Petroleum Geo-Services ASA* [2000] BLR 530 (QB) [131] (Dyson J); *Kolmar Group AG v Traxpo Enterprises PVT Ltd* [2010] EWHC 113 (Comm); [2011] 1 All ER (Comm) 46 [92] (Christopher Clarke J). It can be presumed in cases of duress to the person or to property, see Hugh Beale (ed), *Chitty on Contracts* (34th edn, Sweet & Maxwell 2022) vol 1 [10-44].

[98] *Hennessy v Craigmyle & Co Ltd* [1986] ICR 461 (CA) 468–69; *Bank of India v Riat* [2014] EWHC 1775 (Ch) [65].

[99] *The Universe Sentinel* (n 88). See also *The Evia Luck (No 2)* (n 88); *Huyton* (n 92); *Attorney-General v R* (n 91); *Times Travel* (n 94).

[100] See *Times Travel* (n 94).

[101] *Barton v Armstrong* [1976] AC 104 (PC) 118.

[102] Birks, *Introduction* (n 1) 177 (cited by Lord Burrows SCJ in *Times Travel* (n 94) [82]).

circumstances explains why not all threats to breach a contract (hence to commit a wrong) amount to illegitimate pressure.
- The de facto presumption that threats of unlawful action are illegitimate, and that threats of lawful action are legitimate are aids to the administration of justice (6).

VIII. Undue Influence

A claimant can prove undue influence actually or with the help of an evidential presumption raised by proof of a 'relationship of trust and confidence' and a 'transaction calling for an explanation'.[103] The basis of undue influence is contentious. Some cases support an impaired consent approach (1).[104] Birks and Chin support this by highlighting what is required to rebut the presumption of undue influence, namely, proof that the claimant's consent was 'free, full and informed';[105] it is insufficient to show the absence of the defendant's wrongdoing. Birks and Burrows also note a single three-party case where a recipient of a gift procured by the undue influence of a third party on the claimant was liable to make restitution.[106]

However, claimant-sided characterizations of the undue influence claimant are unrealistic and insulting. Birks and Chin describe them as having 'excessive'[107] or 'morbid dependency',[108] as lacking 'the capacity for self-management';[109] and their judgement is described as 'markedly substandard'[110] or 'impaired to an exceptional degree'.[111] Claimants (like the former nun in *Allcard v Skinner*) may be naive, idealistic, trusting, or altruistic, but they should not be regarded as thereby 'subnormal' or 'morbid[ly] depend en[t]'. When the nun gave away her worldly possessions, she did not lack autonomy—she *exercised* it. Consistently, Lord Nicholls recognized in *Royal Bank of Scotland plc v Etridge (No 2)*, that the victim's consent is only *deemed* to be defective.[112]

Post *Etridge*, the dominant view in English law is that undue influence targets the defendant's reprehensible conduct in inducing the claimant's transfer (2).[113]

---

[103] *Etridge (No 2)* (n 3) [14] (Lord Nicolls).
[104] *Commercial Bank of Australia Ltd v Amadio* (1983) 151 CLR 447, 474 (Deane J); *Thorne v Kennedy* [2017] HCA 49; (2017) 263 CLR 85 [87] (Gordon J).
[105] *Inche Noriah v Shaik Allie Bin Omar* [1929] AC 127 (PC), as relied on in Birks and Chin, 'On the Nature of Undue Influence' (n 21) 75.
[106] *Bridgman v Green* (n 4); see Burrows, *Restitution* (n 1) 292, 426.
[107] Birks and Chin, 'On the Nature of Undue Influence' (n 21) 57.
[108] ibid 80.
[109] ibid 86.
[110] ibid 67.
[111] ibid 69.
[112] See n 20.
[113] *Etridge (No 2)* (n 3) [8], [106]–[107], [132], [142]. See also *National Commercial Bank (Jamaica) Ltd v Hew* [2003] UKPC 51; [2004] 2 LRC 396 [28].

Certainly unconscientious conduct is required where undue influence is actually proved.[114] However, English courts have repeatedly held that undue influence may be found even if the defendant's conduct is 'unimpeachable'.[115] Indeed, the overwhelming majority of undue influence cases rest on the evidential presumption, rendering proof of the defendant's unconscientiousness redundant. In many cases, it is impossible to identify any bad faith in the defendant's conduct, as in the seminal case of *Allcard v Skinner* itself.[116]

Again, a multi-factorial approach is necessary to provide a complete picture:

- Claimants are expected to act responsibly (3): they will fail if they have acted foolishly[117] or, if the receipt of independent advice has emancipated them from the defendant's influence, thereby rebutting any presumption.[118]
- Substantive unfairness to the claimant (4) is a vital element where undue influence is proved via an evidential presumption. A transaction that 'calls for an explanation'[119] (in the sense that its evident disadvantage to the claimant is not explicable by reference to the parties' relationship) strongly supports the inference that the claimant–defendant relationship was one of influence, that the defendant improperly procured the claimant's consent to the transaction,[120] or that the claimant was not sufficiently emancipated from the defendant's influence.[121]
- Despite the ruling in *CIBC Mortgages plc v Pitt* to the contrary,[122] it is submitted that a 'transaction calling for an explanation' must be critical even to proof of *actual* undue influence. Influence is all pervasive and the sorts of pressure involved in undue influence cases are relatively low level (they would not register on the radar of duress). The same influence may be exerted to get a friend to take his medication, as to transfer his house; it is the outcome that points to whether the pressure applied was 'due' or 'undue'. Moreover, an unfair outcome is evidence that the pressure, and not something else, induced

---

[114] This led Birks and Chin to reclassify these as duress cases to preserve the claimant-sidedness of undue influence: see Birks and Chin, 'On the Nature of Undue Influence' (n 21) 57, 63.

[115] *Cheese v Thomas* (n 10) 138; *Hammond v Osborn* [2002] EWCA Civ 885 (CA) [32]; *Jennings v Cairns* [2003] EWCA Civ 1935 [40]; *Niersmans v Pesticcio* [2004] EWCA Civ 372 [20]; *Macklin v Dowsett* [2004] EWCA Civ 904.

[116] *Allcard v Skinner* (1887) 36 Ch D 145 (CA) 170–72 (Cotton LJ), 190–91 (Bowen LJ).

[117] See eg *Clarke v Prus* [1995] NPC 41 (Ch).

[118] The severity of the defendant's influence over the claimant may be such that the claimant is rendered incapable of benefiting from independent advice. See *Bank of Montréal v Stuart* [1911] AC 120 (PC) 137. In *Crédit Lyonnais Bank Nederland NV v Burch* [1997] 1 All ER 144 (CA) 156–57 (hereafter *Crédit Lyonnais*), Millett LJ said that the claimant may not be emancipated *even if the employee had received advice*. See also Mindy Chen-Wishart, 'The *O'Brien* Principle and Substantive Unfairness' (1997) 56 CLJ 60.

[119] *Etridge (No 2)* (n 3) [29].

[120] See eg *Re Craig (decd)* [1971] Ch 95 (Ch); *Crédit Lyonnais* (n 118) 154–55.

[121] See eg *Hammond v Osborn* (n 115); *Bank of Montréal v Stuart* (n 118); *Crédit Lyonnais* (n 118).

[122] *CIBC Mortgages plc v Pitt* [1994] 1 AC 200 (HL) 208–09.

the claimant's transfer. Indeed, it can even raise an inference of improper pressure sufficient for a finding of actual undue influence in the absence of any direct evidence.[123]
- The public policy (5) of upholding valuable social relationships and protecting them from abuse lies at the heart of undue influence. Trusting relationships are constituted by social norms that entail the trusted party having regard for the trusting party's interest. The content of these norms depends on the particular society's values, customs, and expectations. For example, guaranteeing the debts of one's son does not call for an explanation,[124] but guaranteeing the debts of one's employer does.[125] The doctrine is communally calibrated. This explains why the application of the doctrine may differ radically between different jurisdictions.[126]
- Public policy (5) also underlies the law's especially protective attitude to certain parties where a trusting relationship is irrebuttably presumed.[127] It also explains why *actual* undue influence is necessary to avoid testamentary gifts.[128] The testator, on death, has no continuing need for their funds or assets, which must pass to someone; and it is natural for those in relationships of trust and confidence with the testator to appeal to the relationship in the hope of benefiting under the will. Moreover, wills are commonly made with legal advice, unlike most *inter vivos* transactions.
- The concern with the administration of justice (6), namely to overcome gaps in evidence, explains the acceptance of the *presumption* of undue influence. Further, the rare case of restitution for third-party undue influence has been rationalized[129] in terms of the pragmatism of preventing third parties from exerting undue influence to induce a gift to the third party's family or close associate.

IX. Unconscionable Bargains

This doctrine varies in scope across jurisdictions; Australia, New Zealand, and Canada recognize a greater role for the doctrine than English law.[130] It does not require the application of illegitimate pressure or a relationship of influence between

---

[123] See *Re Craig (decd)* (n 120) 409 (Ungoed-Thomas LJ).
[124] *Portman Building Society v Dusangh* [2000] 2 All ER (Comm) 221, 225.
[125] *Crédit Lyonnais* (n 118) 158.
[126] See Mindy Chen-Wishart, 'Legal Transplant and Undue Influence: Lost in Translation or a Working Misunderstanding?' (2013) 62 ICLQ 1.
[127] This irrebuttable presumption arises in class 2A relationships where the law takes a 'sternly protective attitude': see *Etridge (No 2)* (n 3) [18] (Lord Nicholls). Kim Lewison, 'Under the Influence' (2011) 19 RLR 1 argues that these should be a rebuttable presumption instead.
[128] *Re Edwards (decd)* [2007] EWHC 1119 (Ch) [47] (Lewison J); *Hubbard v Scott* [2011] EWHC 2750 (Ch); *Boyse v Rossborough* (1857) 6 HLC 2 (HL) 45, 47–49.
[129] Pauline Ridge, 'Third Party Volunteers and Undue Influence' (2014) 130 LQR 112, 115–16.
[130] See Beale, *Chitty on Contracts* (n 97) [10-165]–[10-166], [10-171]–[10-178].

the parties. It arises in cases where the poor, sick, mentally or physically infirm, illiterate, drunk, or uneducated enter into manifestly improvident transactions. The doctrine originated in the protection of an expectant heir from losing their prospective inheritance.[131] The modern doctrine has a broader application. The leading cases[132] set out four requirements for relief: (a) the claimant must be at a serious disadvantage to the defendant;[133] (b) the defendant must exploit this weakness in a morally reprehensible manner; (c) the resulting transaction must be overreaching and oppressive to the claimant; and (d) the claimant must lack adequate independent advice.

The older cases explained the doctrine in terms of the impaired consent (1) of the 'poor and ignorant'.[134] This rationale supports the requirements of (a) and (d), but not (b) and (c).

The prevailing view in more recent cases is that this unjust factor is defendant-sided (2), and this appears to explain (b) and (c). But, serious qualifications are needed:

- While the improvidence of the contract (4) is strong evidence of (a), (b),[135] and that the presumption of unconscionable conduct is not rebutted (c),[136] it is also an indispensable element,[137] even if (a), (b), and (c) were independently proved.
- What is unconscionable, in the substance of the contract and in the defendant's conduct, may be calibrated by reference to community norms (5), such as the claimant's other socially calibrated responsibilities.[138]
- Since active unconscionable conduct is rare, the use of a presumption is again deployed to make the doctrine more workable (6).[139]

---

[131] See eg *Earl of Aylesford v Morris* (1873) LR 8 Ch App 484.
[132] *Alec Lobb (Garages) v Total Oil* [1983] 1 WLR 87 (Ch); *Boustany v Piggott* (1995) 69 P & CR 298 (PC).
[133] *Times Travel* (n 94) [77] (Lord Burrows SCJ).
[134] *Fry v Lane* (1888) 40 Ch D 312 (Ch) 322 (Kay J); *Evans v Llewellin* (1787) 1 Cox 333, 340; 29 ER 1191, 1194 (Lord Kenyon MR); *Clark v Malpas* (1862) 31 Beav 80, 87; 54 ER 1067, 1070 (Sir John Romilly MR), on appeal from *Clark v Malpas* (1862) 4 De GF & J 401, 404; 45 ER 1238, 1240 (Knight Bruce LJ).
[135] *Boustany v Pigott* (1995) 69 P & CR 298 (PC) 301, 303.
[136] Mindy Chen-Wishart, *Contract Law* (7th edn, OUP 2022) 387–89.
[137] *Portman Building Society v Dusangh* (n 124) 229; *Multiservice Bookbinding Ltd v Marden* [1979] Ch 84 (Ch) 110.
[138] *Bridgewater v Leahy* (1998) 194 CLR 457, where a farmer's sale at significant undervalue to a favoured nephew substantially disinheriting his wife and four daughters; *Randall v Randall* [2004] EWHC 2258 (Ch), where the claimant's gifts effectively disinherited close relatives who lived on part of the land.
[139] *Earl of Aylesford v Morris* (n 131) 491 (Lord Selbourne); *O'Rorke v Bolingbroke* (1877) 2 App Cas 814 (HL) 833 (Lord Blackburn).

The unconscionability jurisdiction is not concerned with the claimant's carelessness in transacting (3) because of their bargaining impairment, unless they have been emancipated by adequate independent advice.

X. *Etridge* Non-Commercial Guarantees

This recently developed doctrine is unique in allowing a third-party unjust factor to operate in a very specific fact pattern in which the non-commercial claimant (typically a wife) has been induced to guarantee the debts (typically by offering the family home as security) of a primary debtor (typically her husband or his company) to a lender by the primary debtor's undue influence, misrepresentation, or other unjust factor. The factors engaged are delicately balanced. The claimant's consent to a disadvantageous transfer (4) can be said to be impaired (1). Although it is the primary debtor and not the lender who has behaved reprehensibly, the lender benefiting from the guarantee may suspect this from what it knows (2), and so is not entirely free of taint. Public policy (5) goes both ways: it is preferable to avoid the dire consequences of enforcing such guarantees (ie homelessness, with its attendant social problems for adults and especially children); but such lending is socially and economically useful by unlocking the wealth tied up in the family home for commercial purposes, and lenders will be reluctant to lend if they lack confidence in the enforceability of their securities.[140]

The law has mediated these factors by providing guidelines for lenders, which, if adhered to, will ensure the guarantee's enforceability (6).[141]

The law may appear to support an impaired consent approach (1) by allowing restitution even when the defendant is, strictly speaking, not tainted by the unjust factor. However, only public policy (5) explains the narrow application of this doctrine,[142] namely: tripartite guarantees involving a debtor, creditor, and guarantor; are one-sided since the guarantor receives no direct benefit; and the creditor is aware of this.[143]

Equally, the defendant unconscientiousness view (2) struggles to explain the sufficiency of such low-level 'knowledge' (imputed from the lender's knowledge of the non-commercial relationship between the primary debtor and the guarantor, and the guarantor obtaining no direct benefit from the loan). As Lord Nicholls recognized, talk of notice here is a misnomer.[144]

---

[140] In *Etridge (No 2)* (n 3) [34], Lord Nicholls noted that 95 per cent of all businesses in the UK are small businesses relying on bank loans raised by second mortgages on the domestic home.
[141] *O'Brien* (n 4).
[142] Burrows, *Restatement* (n 1) s 12(7).
[143] *Etridge (No 2)* (n 3) [43].
[144] ibid [44].

Moreover, the concern with claimant responsibility in transacting (3) is evident in the general position that a guarantor who receives independent advice cannot avoid the transaction. While it is not for a legal advisor to veto the claimant's decision,[145] the courts have acknowledged that in 'exceptional cases' (often characterized by extreme improvidence to the claimant) the presence of independent advice may not guarantee the enforceability of the security.[146] This concern with catastrophic outcomes for the claimant (4) is also obvious from the restriction of the doctrine to non-commercial guarantors who obtain no direct benefit from the guarantee.[147]

Finally, the concern with the administrability of justice (6) explains the clear rules[148] that lenders must follow to ensure the enforceability of the guarantee.

XI. Conclusion

To say that the law of incapacity, mistake, duress, undue influence, unconscionable bargains, and the *Etridge* doctrine is concerned with the claimant's defective consent, or the defendant's unconscientious conduct (separately or in combination) will only give the most approximate idea of when restitution is available. Four other factors need to be brought into play to provide a more precise, useful, and transparent account of the law, namely, responsibility in contract formation, protection of vulnerable parties from harsh outcomes, public policy, and the demands of administrability. Even when some or all of our four factors are acknowledged by defenders of the orthodox accounts, their roles are downgraded and not accorded the attention that they deserve as consistent determinants of the precise shape and size of these unjust factors. The failure to acknowledge these legitimate concerns can also lead to erroneous calls for significant change to align with the consent or unconscientiousness models.[149]

Undoubtedly, more work needs to be done to determine the precise relationship between the six factors. A few preliminary comments can be made at this stage.

---

[145] See ibid [61]–[62] (Lord Nicholls).
[146] See n 118.
[147] See eg *CIBC Mortgages plc v Pitt* (n 122); *Darjan Estate Co plc v Hurley* [2012] EWHC 189 (Ch); [2012] 1 WLR 1782, where the doctrine did not apply.
[148] *Etridge (No 2)* (n 3) [46] (Lord Nicholls), [100] (Lord Hobhouse).
[149] One example of an expansion favoured by some defective consent defenders is that ignorance should be recognized as an unjust factor since it follows inexorably from the logic of the vitiation of consent model because the paradigm case would be one where the claimant's consent is not just vitiated, but *wholly absent*: Burrows, *Restitution* (n 1) 403; Birks, *Introduction* (n 1) 140–46; Peter Birks, 'Misdirected Funds: Restitution from the Recipient' [1989] LMCLQ 26. Such recognition would require a re-examination of the defences to the tort of conversion (as the defence of change of position would apply to the unjust enrichment claim) and liability in knowing receipt (where the requirement of 'unconscionability' would unjustifiably distinguish between the protection afforded to a legal title as compared with the beneficial interest).

First, the exact combination of factors and the weight to be accorded to each factor will vary as between the unjust factors. Secondly, these factors (being legitimate concerns of the law) operate across all the unjust factors and, indeed, they are likely to apply across private law more generally. Thirdly, sometimes our four additional factors cut back the scope of restitution from the consent and unconscientiousness baselines and may therefore be seen as subsidiary in some sense. However, fourthly, they may take a leading role; for example, substantive unfairness (4) plays a key role in undue influence, unconscionable bargains, and non-commercial guarantees. Lastly, no algorithm or abstract formula can provide the answer as to how these six factors interact on the facts of each case. Conflict between these six factors is inevitable if each is taken to an extreme, for example if freedom and so consent is vitiated by *any* influences, if 'responsibility in making transfers' can be negated irrespective of impaired bargaining power, and if the fairness/appropriateness of the transfer ignores individual choice. However, conflict is avoidable if each factor is understood as an interpretive concept such that the scope of each factor draws upon and complements one another.[150]

The obsession with monistic bases for these unjust factors is unhelpful. All six factors play a role and draw on one another in generating defensible and meaningful limits to the scope of operation for each. This integrated, complementary, and limited pluralism is principled and generates a more complete fit with the law.

---

[150] See Ronald Dworkin, *Taking Rights Seriously* (Gerald Duckworth 1977).

14
Unjust Enrichment
Looking for a Role

Steve Hedley

I. Introduction

For most of the common law's history, the law of restitution (if it has existed at all) has been a jumble of dissimilar claims. The maxim *nemo locupletari debet cum aliena iactura* (nobody can be made rich at the expense of another) has long been known, but was of limited use in describing the legal remedies available. More recently, for a few brief decades it has been argued that restitution is more than the sum of its individual parts: that the apparent chaos conceals a deeper conceptual order, and that a law of unjust enrichment can be made both coherent and useful. The current author has never been convinced of this, and has watched the ups and downs of 'unjust enrichment' with some interest.

In Section II, I review the reasons why the law of restitution has traditionally been fragmented, heterogeneous, and entirely on the fringes of private law, arguing that this is no anomaly, but on the contrary is precisely what we should expect. The disunity and low status of restitution is the price we pay—and rightly pay—for the stability and importance of core subjects such as property and contract. In Section III, I recount Peter Birks's attempt to demonstrate the contrary, suggesting that there was a coherent and important principle of unjust enrichment, which should properly have comparable status to that of the core subjects; also the long retreat from that position in the literature, as subsequent scholarship and judicial decisions reasserted restitution's diversity and marginality. And in Section IV, I discuss ongoing attempts to redivide restitution into manageable chunks. I argue that the best ways of doing this will reflect the rationale of restitution, as the sweeper-up of the common law, providing rather limited assistance to those inconvenienced by the harsher rules in the core subjects, but quite deliberately posing no major challenges to those rules.

II. What Sort of a Subject is Restitution?

A. The Primacy of the *Ex Ante*

When we consider how private law acts in the wider community, we can immediately distinguish between the *ex ante* and the *ex post*. In the forward-looking perspective, the *ex ante* perspective, people are buying and selling, making commitments for the future, planning for possible gains and possible setbacks, and transferring property or arranging for its future transfer. Ideally at least, the role of the law is to help them in this, and (sometimes) to designate whose consent to the planning is necessary. In the backward-looking perspective, the *ex post* perspective, something has gone wrong. There is a dispute over who owns a particular asset, whether certain commitments actually bind legally or what they meant, or whose responsibility certain losses are. The law is then needed to resolve this.

Of course, it's the same law in both situations. But if the law is to serve the needs of the community, it must prioritize the *ex ante* case. It must be relatively easy and straightforward to make contracts, to transfer property and other assets, to insure, to marry: these things happen all the time, and indeed much of the time without lawyers necessarily being involved. The law's rules must make it relatively simple and uncontentious to carry through these everyday dealings. But *those rules must generally hold up if there is ever an* ex post *dispute*. Any subsequent litigation is likely to involve disputed facts, moral ambiguity, and conflicting memories and points of views. Practical certainty and security of transaction strongly urge that, *ex ante*, it must be relatively easy to transact, to minimize any risk that the transaction will subsequently be thought improper or unjust. The grounds for upsetting transactions must be relatively narrow.

This is what I am calling 'the primacy of the *ex ante*'. Stability of transaction requires that it be relatively easy to carry through standard legal transactions; as a practical matter, the relevant procedures should be simple and involve minimal—if any—inquiry into the justice or appropriateness of the transactions. *And there has to be a weighty presumption in favour of the validity of such transactions if,* ex post, *there is some dispute over them*. Any legal system will recognize *some* cases where a properly conducted transaction will not settle the parties' legal rights in quite the way it was meant to; but it will always insist that a strong case be made before the transaction is disrupted.

So even though *ex ante* the law largely goes by rather crude and external criteria—whether certain documents were made and formally assented to, whether certain words were spoken—that crudeness is not allowed to detract overmuch from the validity of properly executed transactions. And, if there is a subsequent dispute, there is a tendency towards binary thinking: either the transaction is valid or it isn't. *Ex post*, of course, it is all much more complicated: multiple reasons of justice can often be adduced to argue either that the transaction should not stand, or that other liabilities should achieve a different balance between the parties' entitlements from that which the transaction suggested; and sometimes the just solution subverts the binary approach, holding that the transaction should be treated as valid in some respects but not others. But the default solution to any dispute is to uphold the *ex ante* transaction: that contracts are fully enforceable, and that the owner of an asset reaps its benefits, and bears its loss if it is lost.

So to maintain the integrity of the core, fringe doctrines that can disrupt their impact tend to be kept on a very short leash, to maintain simplicity and certainty of transaction. The courts tend to be suspicious of arguments that certain contracts or transfers are unfair, or that good faith purchasers are affected by matters they were unaware of. A plea that a particular transaction is unjust can be, and often is, met with some variant of 'I do not understand by what standard it is said to be unjust when the parties have agreed that it should be so.'[1] To be clear: this chapter is not much concerned with whether the balance is fairly struck. The point is a more basic one, that there *is* a balance to be maintained, and that the courts will weight that balance heavily in favour of transactions having the effect that, *ex ante*, they were intended to have.

In summary, then, we can look on private law as having a 'core' and a 'fringe'. The core rules make ordinary everyday transactions possible, enabling parties *ex ante* to plan their affairs with a tolerable degree of certitude. Legal transactions or their effects may be questioned *ex post* on a variety of grounds, but the courts are rightly careful to make sure that these grounds are sufficiently narrow to facilitate *ex ante* planning. The character of the relevant legal rules flows from this, up to a point at least. Formalities rules are notoriously arbitrary; the point, *ex ante*, is to know what the law requires, and it really doesn't matter why the law uses one formality rather than another, so long as everyone knows where they stand. Arbitrariness and formalism are, however, less acceptable when devising solutions to *ex post* disputes: the relevant rules are looser, there are more appeals to fairness, to analogy, to treating like cases alike. So (for example) *ex ante* it must be very clear whether a particular transaction is a legal contract; *ex post*, it may be fair to argue that the parties' dealings were *like* a contract in all the respects that matter, that they deserve to be treated *quasi-contractually*. And the brute fact of doctrinal uncertainty, that the court cannot describe or enumerate *all* the circumstances in which it would be prepared to find a quasi-contract, is beside the point.[2]

---

[1] *International Energy Group Ltd v Zurich Insurance plc UK Branch* [2015] UKSC 33; [2016] AC 509 [183] (Lord Sumption SCJ).
[2] On the relative insignificance of doctrinal uncertainty in many of the more involved disputes (because the presence of other, more powerful sources of uncertainty), see *Guest v Guest* [2022] UKSC 27; [2022] 3 WLR 911 [82] (Lord Briggs SCJ).

B. Restitution as a Textbook Subject

Historically, core notions arose before fringe notions: the basic rules for transacting were established before the fringe rules for questioning those transactions. So the binding effects of deeds was only slowly eroded by limiting doctrines; the common law of property stood for some time before equity began to question those absolute entitlements; contracts were enforced long before quasi-contracts. And sometimes, over long periods of legal development, fringe doctrines rose to secure core status: so the trust grew, from a mere ad hoc appeal to a property owner's conscience, to a scheme of property in its own right, another mechanism for people to plan the future disposition and use of their entitlements.[3] Of 'unjust enrichment' there was little sign until relatively recently: 'It is sometimes tempting to assume that if there was ever a legal category without a history then unjust enrichment is it.'[4]

Yet, late in the common law's history, its scholars and practitioners adopted a rather particular scheme through which to view private law—we see private law today as a series of textbook titles, as property, contract, tort, equity, and so forth. Where do we see the division between the 'core' and the 'fringe' in that? Property and contract are clearly for the most part clearly core disciplines: the need for economic actors (whether business or consumer) to be clear which assets they own, how they can transfer them, and what their ongoing obligations are, is manifest; and while there are some fringe areas for *ex post* disputes (remedies, or questioning the fairness of the contract), those areas are kept under careful judicial control. Tort tends to be stated in rather messy 'fringe' terms—it is by definition concerned with losses which (from the claimant's point of view) are unforeseen and unprovided for, though in modern circumstances the wide deployment of insurance goes a long way towards allowing defendants to price and plan for its liabilities. Equity continues, much as it has for several centuries past, to live a double life, providing the core planning instrument of the trust, but also playing a major part in the fringe, with a number of doctrines addressing the plight of those who failed to secure the protection of core rules.

Restitution, a newcomer to the textbook tribe, is nearly all fringe: people claiming contract-like remedies where they failed to make a contract (or they had one, but it misfired); or property-like remedies where they have no property (or had it and transferred it way); or simply complaining that they paid a debt which they had paid already, or which should have been paid by someone else. Within the broad range of liabilities that have been considered restitutionary, there might

---

[3] So much so, indeed, that limits on its planning capabilities have been necessary: see eg Mark Bennett and Adam Hofri-Winogradow, 'The Use of Trusts to Subvert the Law: An Analysis and Critique' (2021) 41 OJLS 692.

[4] Warren Swain, 'Unjust Enrichment and the Role of Legal History in England and Australia' (2013) 36 UNSWLJ 1030, 1031.

perhaps be a few which raise *ex ante* issues. While of course nobody sets out to make or to receive mistaken payments, nonetheless large (public or private) organizations might find this occurring with sufficient regularity to merit planning, and against that background to demand rules governing that situation. (Of course, if such rules are to be fair, they will presumably provide that the organization take *ex ante* steps to minimize the risk of such mistakes, a task to which existing unjust enrichment law seems poorly suited.[5]) But relatively few restitutionary issues are of this type; the typical restitution dispute involves issues neither party planned for.

So if it is asked 'what sort of a subject restitution is', the answer is that, properly viewed, it is almost all fringe—rather like the messier parts of tort or equity. It exists in a world where contract and property rule the roost; restitution for the most part points to niche situations where those core rules lead to demonstrable injustice. Its role is corrective and supplementary. It is misleading to think of restitution as a subject like contract; rather, it is at least in part *generated* by contact, addressing injustices that contract law leaves in its wake.

Some confusion has been generated in this context, by the suggestion that unjust enrichment liability is 'subsidiary' to other areas of private law. In the sense in which proponents of this idea use it, it chimes with the argument here: restitution is a subject 'inherently one whose place in the ecology of the private law is defined by other doctrines'.[6] But 'subsidiarity' can be used in various senses; Mat Campbell finds none of them particularly relevant here,[7] and he questions how much sense it makes to say that a particular restitutionary claim is 'subsidiary' to other areas of law, when what we mean is that there is no such restitutionary claim.[8] Use of that term may therefore be counterproductive.

It will be obvious that the rationale I am proposing for unjust enrichment is very similar to rationales that have been suggested for equity. So, for example (following Irit Samet's account of equity), we can very well see restitution as an area of law built on top of bright-line common law rules, pointing to some particular situations where the holder of common law rights must in justice be instructed not to exercise them, lest the result be a too-open flouting of the need for morally defensible results.[9] And their common focus on transactions which are lawful yet

---

[5] For discussion, see Hanoch Dagan, *The Law and Ethics of Restitution* (CUP 2004) 60–63.
[6] Ross Grantham and Charles EF Rickett, *Enrichment and Restitution in New Zealand* (Hart Publishing 2000) ix. See also Ross Grantham and Charles Rickett, 'On the Subsidiarity of Unjust Enrichment' (2001) 117 LQR 273; Lionel Smith, 'Property, Subsidiarity and Unjust Enrichment' in David Johnston and Reinhard Zimmermann (eds), *Unjustified Enrichment: Key Issues in Comparative Perspective* (CUP 2002).
[7] Mat Campbell, 'Subsidiarity in Private Law?' (2020) 24 Edin LR 1.
[8] Mat Campbell, 'Doubting the Subsidiarity of Unjust Enrichment' [2021] LMCLQ 535; Mat Campbell, 'Against the Subsidiarity of Unjust Enrichment' (2022) 138 LQR 368.
[9] Samet calls this 'accountability correspondence': 'When legal rules impose liability it should ideally correspond to the pattern of moral duty in the circumstances to which the rules apply': Irit Samet, *Equity: Conscience Goes to Market* (OUP 2018) 28. See more generally ch 1; Irit Samet, 'Equity' in Hanoch Dagan and Benjamin C Zipursky (eds), *Research Handbook on Private Law Theory* (Edward Elgar 2020).

nonetheless unjust again suggests that they have much in common.[10] (And as Ben McFarlane notes, remedying abuses of core rules actually buttresses those rules, strengthening their justification rather than weakening it.[11]) How far the similarity between equity and restitution can be pushed is not something I wish to probe here,[12] given that there are long-running disputes over equity's organization,[13] and indeed over whether it deserves to survive as a distinct area of law.[14] My point is a more basic one, that crude core rules are bound to lead to injustice in *some* cases, and both equity and restitution can play a part in remedying this.

So restitutionary liability does not march in step with most other private law liabilities. It follows after them, deferring to them on most matters, trying to patch up the more serious injustices they leave in their wake. It does not *necessarily* follow, of course, that restitution will be patchy and sporadic in its application. But in the nature of things this seems likely: if there were something *systematically* wrong with the core liability, then reformers would have focused their attention there; restitution tackles the more random injustices, that do not merit correction in the core doctrine. So the disorder of restitution is the price we pay for order in the core doctrines. Restitution has, and was always likely to have, the character that Hanoch Dagan describes as a classic 'realist' pattern: a collection of categories that will be narrow, overlapping, and constantly changing.[15] Further, it is not *inevitable* that restitution will often proceed by borrowing concepts from core doctrines and applying them by analogy, such as by speaking of 'constructive' trust or 'implied' contract. But, again, it is what we should expect. This is often objected to by purists—surely there either is a trust (or a contract) or there isn't, away with these fictions!—but unless they mean to dispense with the use of analogies altogether (a bold move for common lawyers) it is hard to see what the objection is.

---

[10] See Nolan Sharkey, Chapter 6 in this volume.

[11] Ben McFarlane, 'Equity and the Justification of Private Rights' in Simone Degeling, Michael JR Crawford, and Nicholas A Tiverios (eds), *Justifying Private Rights* (Hart Publishing 2020). See also Ben McFarlane 'Unjust Enrichment, Rights and Value' in Donal Nolan and Andrew Robertson (eds), *Rights and Private Law* (Hart Publishing 2012).

[12] For some of the questions that arise, see Jacques du Plessis, 'Equity, Fairness and Unjustified Enrichment: A Civil-Law Perspective' (2020) 83 THRHR 1; Dan Priel, 'The Justice in Unjust Enrichment' (2014) 51 Osgoode Hall LJ 813, 849–52; Lusina Ho, 'Unjust Enrichment and Equity' in Elise Bant, Kit Barker, and Simone Degeling (eds), *Research Handbook on Unjust Enrichment and Restitution* (Edward Elgar 2020).

[13] See eg Samuel L Bray and Paul B Miller, 'Getting into Equity' (2022) 97 Notre Dame L Rev 1763.

[14] See eg Anna McLean, 'Fusion: Can It Encompass the Trust? An Assessment in Light of the Trusts Bill 2017' (2019) Victoria University of Wellington Legal Research Paper 25/2019 <http://ssrn.com/abstract=3477018> accessed 13 December 2022; Jennifer Nadler, 'What is Distinctive about the Law of Equity?' (2021) 41 OJLS 854; Andrew Burrows, 'We Do This at Common Law But That in Equity' (2002) 22 OJLS 1.

[15] Hanoch Dagan, 'Restitution's Realism' in Robert Chambers, Charles Mitchell, and James Penner (eds), *Philosophical Foundations of the Law of Unjust Enrichment* (OUP 2009).

If this is correct, what would we expect to find in the law of restitution? We would not expect to find a single cohesive doctrine, because there is not one single well-defined problem that core private law institutions fail to address. (If there were, the core institutions would have been remodelled to address it.) Rather, there are a variety of distinct problems, which core institutions are unable to address without unsettling consequences. So there is a litany of issues where the potential for unfairness is obvious, but the relevant core institution seems incapable of addressing it. Parties may fail to satisfy the *ex ante* rules for a valid transaction, but *ex post* it may become clear that it is unfair to count this against them; transactions may be entered into under mistake, and sometimes a good *ex post* case may be made that it should be unwound at least in some respects. In these and in several other cases, the dilemma for private law is obvious: the rules of the core institution are clearly productive of injustice in some instances, but the injustice is not one that can sensibly be addressed through the core institution itself. Something must be done; very often, restitution does it. This chapter considers these cases in detail.[16]

Of course, many difficulties would be avoided if, contrary to expectations, some sort of coherent principle implicit in 'unjust enrichment' could be stated, which could explain all these various liabilities as mere examples of its application. And with the beginnings of serious common law scholarship in this area in the early-to-middle twentieth century, many harboured a wish that such a principle could be developed—that the common law could do what the civil law had done in earlier centuries, namely, to extract a general principle from the apparently pattern-less instances that the law already recognized. Yet in the early years this was not achieved—both the *Restatement of Restitution* (1st edn) and *Goff and Jones* (1st edn) stated broad principles of unjust enrichment but then merely considered isolated examples of liability.[17] Lord Diplock's famous late-1970s description of the law of restitution—'specific remedies in particular cases of what might be classified as unjust enrichment in a legal system that is based upon the civil law'[18]—was entirely accurate as a matter of fact, even if it was a fact that some theorists were unhappy with. It was not until the 1980s that Peter Birks formulated a tolerably rigorous theory of the principle, which forms the backdrop to much restitutionary scholarship to this day. To this theory and its products I now turn.

---

[16] See Section IV entitled 'The Emerging (Lower Level) Categorization'.
[17] American Law Institute, *Restatement of Restitution* (1937); Robert Goff and Gareth H Jones, *The Law of Restitution* (Sweet & Maxwell 1966); Emily Sherwin, Chapter 5 in this volume. On what *Goff and Jones* (1st edn) owes to the first Restatement, see WR Cornish, 'Reviews: The Law of Restitution. By Robert Goff and Gareth Jones' (1966) 29 MLR 579.
[18] *Orakpo v Manson Investments* [1978] AC 95 (HL) 104.

III. The Birksian Interlude

A. Competing Prophets

In the wake of the development of common law unjust enrichment theory, two eminent jurists played prophet, both acknowledging that future scholarship would give a deeper understanding, and speculating on where that deeper understanding would take us. Peter Birks contended that restitution would further prove its value as time progressed: 'it is unlikely that Restitution will ever again be split up and hidden under the fringes of other better-known subjects'.[19] His colleague Patrick Atiyah, by contrast, thought 'unjust enrichment' a mere surface phenomenon; its growth was a clear indication of dissatisfaction with core private law doctrines, but in time those core doctrines would be reconfigured to fit modern circumstances; 'the law of restitution' was ultimately no more than the sum of its parts, and very diverse parts they were. 'The various cases show little signs of coming together to cohere into one new body of law, and this may be just as well.'[20] Observers at the turn of the century could have been forgiven for thinking Atiyah a poor prophet indeed, but subsequent developments tell a different story.

What is the issue? The trouble with 'unjust enrichment' is not that it is incomprehensible, but on the contrary that it can be used to describe an incredible range of liabilities. How to tame this radical conceptual promiscuity? The Birksian approach was to tame it without making it subordinate or subsidiary to other legal ideas. Rather, it was to be rigorously defined, and when so defined, was to be regarded as dominant within its own territory. 'Unjust enrichment' was to be as fundamental as contract and tort, and in no way subsidiary or subordinate to them; it was supreme within its own territory, which Birks and like-minded thinkers made it their business to define and map.

To be plausible, this Birksian approach had to satisfy two criteria: it had to be *conceptually pure*, so that we could say with a high degree of precision what it means for a claim to be one in 'unjust enrichment'; and it had to be *territorial*, so that a claim properly described as one in unjust enrichment could *not* properly be described in other terms. Of course, the traditional way of defining restitutionary claims, as based on quasi-contract, offended against both criteria: it left unclear *when* a claim was sufficiently analogous to a contract to be treated in the same way, and it seemed to blur the line between 'real' contracts and 'implied' contracts. So a new basis had to be found, and the Birksian approach was to look for it in precise

---

[19] Peter Birks, *An Introduction to the Law of Restitution* (rev edn, OUP 1989) 5 (hereafter Birks, *Introduction*).
[20] PS Atiyah, *The Rise and Fall of Freedom of Contract* (OUP 1979) 768; 'Contracts, Promises and the Law of Obligations' in PS Atiyah, *Essays on Contract* (OUP 1988) 49–56.

definitions of 'unjust', 'enrichment', 'at the expense of the claimant', and of relevant defences.

The *conceptual purity* requirement was stated as a demand for rationality[21] or a 'skeleton of principle':[22] that unjust enrichment was a 'causal event' capable of definition conceptually and consistently. For example, while there was room for argument over precisely how the enrichment represented by money and the enrichment represented by services were to be identified, yet once identified, the same rules applied to both enrichments. The possibility that the rules on the recovery of money and the rules on recovery for services were simply different, was either ignored or treated as blinkered and outdated thinking. This insistence on conceptual purity led to protracted (and ultimately unresolved) disagreements over how to discern a unity that was far from apparent: such as how to quantify the enrichment that services represented, or how an ordinary claim to recover a mistaken payment was governed by the same rules as a claim in subrogation. The assertion that claims which looked very different were in fact based on the same set of rules was experienced by many as invigorating and liberating; though, as appears later in this chapter, the slow realization that these different claims are indeed undeniably different is precisely what has slowly killed the Birksian approach.

As to *territoriality*, again, while sometimes the requirement was stated as being that there was a 'map' of private law in which unjust enrichment had a defined area or place, or that private law should be divided by 'species and genus',[23] the most persistent phrase was that there was a 'taxonomy' of all possible claims, defining and dividing them.[24] The point was that once unjust enrichment's territory was established, then within that territory it was sovereign. On this view using (say) contractual concepts to help in the definition of unjust enrichment claims is a mistake: claims are either based on unjust enrichment or they are not, just as a particular creature either is a dog or is not.

Unjust enrichment was therefore in the Birksian view a sort of *terra nullius* on which no other discipline has a proper claim. The problem is that it sneaks in a claim to *exclusivity* within unjust enrichment's territory, without justifying it. Other legal subjects aren't like this: legal subjects routinely overlap, and concepts useful in one context are often useful in others. Birks acknowledged this, conceding that most legal subjects are 'contextual' and only recognize borders based on what researchers are actually interested in.[25] But aren't *all* legal subjects 'contextual', and if not, how do we tell which are not? Is Birks's 'consent-based liabilities'

---

[21] Birks, *Introduction* (n 19) 38.
[22] ibid 1.
[23] ibid 75.
[24] See especially Peter Birks, 'This Heap of Good Learning: The Jurist in the Common Law Tradition' in Basil Markesinis (ed), *Law Making, Law Finding, and Law Shaping: The Diverse Influences* (OUP 1997).
[25] Birks, *Introduction* (n 19) 73–74.

contextual? At root, the distinction is based on simple assertion. So his description of the boundary between contract and restitution begins disarmingly—'[t]here is in a sense no boundary to be described'[26]—followed by an account of various reasons why jurists over the course of eighteen centuries did not see much of a problem;[27] then comes the abrupt announcement that failing to distinguish the two is a 'heresy', 'is muddled', is like confusing chalk with cheese, and 'serves to underline the need for a new start'.[28] The distinction is not reasoned; it is simple asserted as an axiom, which Birks himself described as 'dogmatic'.[29]

Birks's conceptual purity and territoriality came at a cost. One such cost was that they discouraged the use of basic common law technique—their application brutally restricted the use of analogy. Indeed, the most common analogies in this area—*quasi*-contracts, *constructive* trusts—were frequently the target of his derision. Birks was not, in his heart, a common lawyer; he did not think that any legal system worthy of the name would be founded on case law, but rather on some coherent conceptual scheme. And the common law's traditional strength—its vagueness, sufficient to adapt to novel circumstances—was to Birks not a strength at all.

His approach was also at the expense of *values*, of any sense of what the subject was *for*. He not only exaggerated the importance of unjust enrichment, but also simultaneously removed most of its point. His approach took the subject from a realm where it could (occasionally and rather randomly) help in struggles against injustice, and into a cold logical space of 'events and responses' where it could bask in its theoretical perfection while avoiding discussion of fairness and justice. And equity, which clearly addressed overlapping subject matter and was quite openly concerned with correcting apparent injustices, was regularly the target of Birks's scorn: arguments based on unconscionability were no better than those invoked by the Nazis,[30] and the division between law and equity was 'the work of the devil'.[31] Birks dealt with the legal system as if it were a final, finished, perfect product, and was never happy to see it as a work in progress—even though, invariably, it must be.

To be sure, the occasional throwaway reference by Birks hints at a wish to achieve just and defensible results. His taxonomy was intended as the 'common sense behind a subject's technical detail'.[32] Restitutionary liability 'rests ultimately on a policy or value-judgement', and each 'is the product of a decision which balances different goods and bads; and that is nothing if not policy'.[33] Yet he preferred

---

[26] ibid 29.
[27] ibid 29–38.
[28] ibid 38–39.
[29] ibid 44.
[30] Peter Birks, 'Equity in the Modern Law: An Exercise in Taxonomy' (1996) 26 UWALR 1, 16–17. See also Peter Birks, 'Equity, Conscience, and Unjust Enrichment' (1999) 23 MULR 1, 21–22.
[31] Peter Birks, 'Civil Wrongs: A New World' in *Butterworths Lectures 1990-91* (Butterworths 1992) 55.
[32] Birks, *Introduction* (n 19) 1.
[33] ibid 294.

to speak as if justice had little to do with the matter, and that he might have eliminated the use of such words if he could, preferring to talk merely of 'disapproved' or 'reversible' enrichment.[34] He once playfully proposed that we should speak of 'pink' enrichment (to make his disavowal of value judgements absolutely plain), holding back only because the 'weakly normative' concept of unjustness might 'encourage fine-tuning'.[35] Birks's scheme was therefore not guided by any sentiment as to which cases should in justice receive a remedy, but was simply seeking the most economical arrangement of those instances where court had been driven to provide a remedy. As to what considerations had actually driven the courts to grant a remedy in some cases rather than others, Birks did not inquire.

This leaves a problem: do the best taxonomies actually inform us about real and significant features of the disputes they cover (giving useful clues as to how they might be resolved), or are they simply arbitrary criteria with no particular moral or social significance? Are they reason-based or merely formal?[36] The problem does not seem to have particularly interested Birks. Yet a doctrinal theory is 'far more than an elaborate arrangement of pigeonholes into which the cases can be slotted';[37] can Birks help with the 'more', or must it come from elsewhere? The human sense of justice is multi-faceted and incapable of being summed up in any neat intellectual formula, yet is bound to affect judicial decisions; Birks's aim was not to take the decision for the judge, but to avoid the worst excesses of judicial discretion by confining it within a rigid and bloodless conceptual scheme.

Yet without some sort of moral or social vision to guide it, the subject is essentially rudderless. Birks's ideas about how unjust enrichment was to develop were a little vague, consisting mainly of expressions of faith that the collective understanding of it would steadily improve—and in this we see mostly clearly how he differed from Atiyah. Both were well aware that different generations of lawyers have seen the law very differently, but Birks tended to treat this simply as indicating lesser or greater awareness of timeless truths to which serious inquiry into legal concepts will lead any culture, at any time. Restitution, he said, 'knowable by reason' and 'does not change its shape from day to day'.[38]

Atiyah, by contrast, was more aware that legal concepts are by no means solid bedrock, and that in studying their malleability we often see the effects of fundamental shifts in values. So the rise of 'unjust enrichment' in contractual contexts was clear evidence of dissatisfaction with traditional notions of contract; but if this dissatisfaction was to be resolved, it would be by better understanding of contract

---

[34] ibid 19.
[35] Peter Birks, *Unjust Enrichment* (2nd edn, OUP 2005) 275 (hereafter Birks, *Unjust Enrichment 2nd*).
[36] Emily L Sherwin, 'Legal Taxonomy' (2006) Cornell Legal Studies Research Paper 06-020 <http://ssrn.com/abstract=925129> accessed 13 December 2022. On this debate today, see text to n 130.
[37] Robert Reed, 'Theory and Practice' in Andrew Dyson, James Goudkamp, and Frederick Wilmot-Smith (eds), *Defences in Unjust Enrichment* (Hart Publishing 2016) 314–15.
[38] Peter Birks, *Unjust Enrichment* (1st edn, OUP 2003) xiii (hereafter Birks, *Unjust Enrichment 1st*).

rather than by supplementing it with vague novelties. Birks saw the force of this in particular contexts, agreeing that some novel decisions which had been taken to exemplify 'unjust enrichment' were simply contract in a new guise,[39] even relabelling 'contract' on his taxonomic map to 'consent' to acknowledge this.[40] But as a general matter Birks refused to consider whether his taxonomic categories were simply temporary expedients; and his general failure to engage with Atiyah except where Atiyah *explicitly* mentioned unjust enrichment (so ignoring most of what Atiyah had to say) cut debate short. Indeed, the very phenomenon that Atiyah examined in such depth—the changing significance of 'contract' in the legal system and beyond—seems to have passed Birks by entirely.[41] To Atiyah, law changes because each generation asks different things of it; he would no doubt have endorsed his colleague Jeffrey Hackney's wish that we could be 'not shackled by ideas invented for different people, in different communities, a long time ago'.[42] To Birks, the law changed because different generation of jurists show different levels of ability in discerning the single underlying reality.

In summary, unjust enrichment as Birks left it seemed to its supporters to be a triumph for conceptualism: a logically coherent schema, abstract enough to have wide application, yet concrete enough to produce definite predictions as to how courts could act. The quagmires represented by differing views of morality and of social policy were avoided largely by failing to discuss them, beyond asserting that 'unjust enrichment' was concerned with the law as it is, not as it should be.[43] The remaining conceptual puzzles were meant to disappear soon, by a process of 'complex adjustments and refinements',[44] and the status of unjust enrichment would become unanswerable.

Of course, in a living legal system no heaven of pure concepts can ever last for long. While some academic theorists might be motivated solely by a wish to achieve and maintain logical consistency, that is not a very probable motivation for a judge. Sooner or later, choices will have to be made between the logic of unjust enrichment and societal demands for a fair law, and logic will not always win—nor should it. And the apparent avoidance of issues of fairness is only achieved by the high level of abstraction employed: the more detailed the discussion, the harder it is to avoid the intrusion of views on which results are just or serve good policy. It follows that more detailed scholarly consideration of legal doctrine (especially by

---

[39] Birks, *Introduction* (n 19) 47 and 292–93, commenting on *Crabb v Arun DC* [1976] Ch 179 (CA).
[40] Peter Birks, 'Misnomer' in WR Cornish and others (eds), *Restitution: Past, Present and Future—Essays in Honour of Gareth Jones* (Hart Publishing 1998) 19–21.
[41] For discussion of this change and its implications for restitution, see Warren Swain, Chapter 1 in this volume.
[42] Jeffrey Hackney, 'More than a Trace of the Old Philosophy' in Peter Birks (ed), *The Classification of Obligations* (Clarendon Press 1997) 155.
[43] "This book ... does not often say what the law "ought" to be. And when it does the appeal is to the humdrum values of intelligibility and consistency." Birks, *Introduction* (n 19) vii.
[44] ibid 1.

scholars who place a high value on conceptual purity) was bound to unearth issues on which policy can hardly be avoided. The course of further scholarship was never likely to shore up a conceptualist approach—the only question was, how quickly and how thoroughly it would be undermined.

B. The Long Retreat: The Theory

From the high point represented by the publication of Birks's *Introduction to Restitution*, decline set in, and unjust enrichment started to progress from a solution to novel problems, to being itself a problematic doctrine that must be kept under careful restraint. The detail is different in different common law jurisdictions, though the downward trend seems universal. Peak 'unjust enrichment' can be identified as the 1990s. It is in this decade that we see some of the most enthusiastic judicial pronouncements in its favour, as well as some of the more significant instances of a broadening of liability to fit theoretical orthodoxy. But the fragility of the alliance of judicial and academic interests that led to its emergence was apparent even then: academic writers found much to unsettle them in the terms in which judges supported the theory.

Birks declared in 1985 that his inquiry was aimed at 'finding the simplest structure on which the material in *Goff and Jones* can hang',[45] but each decade of inquiry has unearthed further examples where *Goff and Jones* had included materials that did not belong together, with a consequent narrowing of the range of liabilities that unjust enrichment was thought to explain.[46] So:

- Rewards for benefits rendered in an emergency, which in the *Goff and Jones* vision could happily be included in restitution,[47] were slowly abandoned by theorists, as closer analysis showed that the availability and measure of liability followed different rules. Maritime salvage in particular, the principles of which were already well established, did not fit the unjust enrichment mould. There is still some support for importing the civilian doctrine of *negotiorum gestio* (though all recognize that this would constitute a major step beyond the current case law[48]); views differ over whether that doctrine can truly be called

---

[45] ibid 3.
[46] This section, which is refers largely to English/Welsh law, compares the coverage of Robert Goff and Gareth Jones, *The Law of Restitution* (2nd edn, Sweet & Maxwell 1978) (hereafter Goff and Jones, *Restitution 2nd*) with subsequent developments. For another angle on this gradual retreat in coverage, see Nguyen Sinh Vuong, 'Lord Reed and Unjust Enrichment: A Correct(ive) Retreat from Expansionism' (2021) 51 HKLJ 203.
[47] Goff and Jones, *Restitution 2nd* (n 46) 235–43, chs 15–16.
[48] Charles Mitchell, Paul Mitchell, and Stephen Watterson, *Goff & Jones: The Law of Unjust Enrichment* (9th edn, Sweet & Maxwell 2016)ch 18.7 (hereafter Mitchell, Mitchell, and Watterson, *Goff & Jones 9th*); Tim W Dornis, 'The Doctrines of Contract and *Negotiorum Gestio* in European Private

'restitutionary'.[49]
- Special statutory regimes for restitution of benefits received, which *Goff and Jones* treated as statutory instantiations of the unjust enrichment principle,[50] have increasingly been acknowledged to have little in common with Birksian theory. The courts have rejected arguments that the common law of unjust enrichment can supplement statutory provisions on recovery of social security payments[51] or interest on damages.[52] Robert Goff J considered the special regime for frustrated contracts to bring in the whole gamut of contemporary restitutionary theory,[53] but the Court of Appeal disagreed,[54] upholding his judgment simply on the ground that his approach was a permissible exercise of his discretion.[55] Some (including Lord Goff himself[56]) have protested at this, but cases of frustration are rather rare and often complex, and a discretionary solution seems best.
- *Goff and Jones* made much of cases where a defendant wronged the claimant and made a profit thereby.[57] But this was always hard to reconcile with Birksian notions of territoriality, and in 1999 Birks declared that while recovery in these cases might be examples of *restitution*, they could not be said to be examples of *unjust enrichment*: rather, they derived from contract, tort, or whatever legal doctrine had determined that the defendant's action was wrongful.[58] This influential declaration has left the concept of 'restitutionary damages' in a strange limbo, though the current signs are that the courts are slowly reintegrating those liabilities into notions of recovery of loss, rather than recovery of benefits.[59]
- The *Goff and Jones* approach tended to fudge the distinction between a claim in unjust enrichment and a simple claim to recover property: tracing claims

Law: Quest for Structure in a No Man's Land of Legal Reasoning' (2015) 23 RLR 73 (hereafter Dornis, 'No Man's Land').

[49] Birks, *Introduction* (n 19) 308; Andrew Burrows, *The Law of Restitution* (3rd edn, OUP 2011) 485–86.
[50] See eg Goff and Jones, *Restitution* 2nd (n 46) 564–83.
[51] *R (Child Poverty Action Group) v Secretary of State for Work and Pensions* [2010] UKSC 54; [2011] 2 AC 15.
[52] *Prudential Assurance Co Ltd v Revenue and Customs Comrs* [2018] UKSC 39; [2019] AC 929.
[53] *BP Exploration Co (Libya) Ltd v Hunt (No 2)* [1979] 1 WLR 783 (QB).
[54] '[Counsel] submitted that the concept behind the Act was to prevent unjust enrichment. This is what the judge had thought. We get no help from the use of words which are not in the statute': *BP Exploration Co (Libya) Ltd v Hunt (No 2)* [1981] 1 WLR 232 (CA) 243 (Lawton LJ).
[55] ibid.
[56] Robert Goff, 'The Search for Principle' (1983) 69 Proceedings of the British Academy 169, 181–82.
[57] Goff and Jones, *Restitution* 2nd (n 46) chs 32–37.
[58] Birks, 'Misnomer' (n 40). Most, though not all, theorists have followed Birks's lead here; eg Mitchell, Mitchell, and Watterson, *Goff & Jones 9th* (n 48) does not cover these cases (see 1.04–1.05). For one dissenting voice, see Kit Barker, 'The Nature of Responsibility for Gain: Gain, Harm, and Keeping the Lid on Pandora's Box' in Robert Chambers, Charles Mitchell, and James Penner (eds), *Philosophical Foundations of the Law of Unjust Enrichment* (OUP 2009).
[59] See text to n 189.

were treated as examples of unjust enrichment, without much analysis of why that was,[60] and later theorists pursued the idea that some property rights were a 'response' to unjust enrichment, or simply a remedy which a court could use where a personal liability on the unjustly enriched defendant would be insufficient.[61] But while there is the occasional judicial dictum taking this line— '[a] proprietary remedy may arguably be justified because ... such a remedy, rather than a personal remedy, is the most appropriate response to the unjust enrichment found in this case'[62]—instances of the courts acting on this are few and far between.

- Recent UK Supreme Court rulings have reduced the scope of unjust enrichment claims considerably, by declaring that the relevant enrichment must usually be 'direct', that is, conferred by the claimant on the defendant and not merely incidentally arising from the facts and circumstances.[63] While a number of theorists have protested that this restriction seems too narrow,[64] the courts themselves show no sign of resisting this limit on the doctrine.

At a more abstract theoretical level, substantial obstacles remain to recognizing the systemicity and territoriality that Birks thought he saw; the differences between the various liabilities he sought to unite keep on reasserting themselves in awkward ways.

- A late change Birks made to his theory—stipulating that the law should be arranged not by listing the factors that made an enrichment *unjust*, but rather by listing the factors which *justified* the enrichment[65]—strongly appealed to those who prized theoretical neatness above all, but was rather less attractive to those with an eye on the cases.[66] Yet if (as seems to be the majority preference) we retain the 'unjust factors', this simply papers over the very different approaches for different liabilities without doing anything to unify them; 'The solution must be to admit that a range of other values are in play.'[67] Meanwhile

---

[60] Goff and Jones, *Restitution 2nd* (n 46) ch 2.
[61] For a range of views on whether unjust enrichment theory requires this, see Mitchell, Mitchell, and Watterson, *Goff & Jones 9th* (n 48) 37.07–37.26.
[62] *Menelaou v Bank of Cyprus UK Ltd* [2015] UKSC 66; [2016] AC 176 [109] (Lord Carnwath SCJ). Lord Carnwath SCJ, however, did not go on to apply that notion to the facts in front of him: 'that is not how the case has been argued, and ... it is not necessary for my decision on the appeal ...'.
[63] *Prudential Assurance Co Ltd v Revenue and Customs Comrs* (n 52).
[64] See eg Andrew Burrows, 'In Defence of Unjust Enrichment' (2019) 78 CLJ 521, 536–41.
[65] Birks, *Unjust Enrichment 1st* (n 38) ch 5.
[66] See eg Thomas Krebs, 'In Defence of Unjust Factors' in David Johnston and Reinhard Zimmermann (eds), *Unjustified Enrichment: Key Issues in Comparative Perspective* (CUP 2002); Birke Häcker, 'Unjust Factors versus Absence of Juristic Reason (*Causa*)' in Elise Bant, Kit Barker, and Simone Degeling (eds), *Research Handbook on Unjust Enrichment and Restitution* (Edward Elgar 2020).
[67] Mindy Chen-Wishart and Rory Gregson, 'Impaired Intention Unjust Factors?' in Elise Bant, Kit Barker, and Simone Degeling (eds), *Research Handbook on Unjust Enrichment and Restitution* (Edward Elgar 2020) 343. See also Mindy Chen-Wishart and Emma Hughes, Chapter 13 in this volume.

the most prominent of the unjust factors, mistake, is widely recognized as a confused area, both because of the difficulty of distinguishing 'mistakes' which ground liability and 'mispredictions' which do not, and because of the need to span both private law and public law cases.[68]

- The common law traditionally distinguished money from other benefits, providing significantly more generous remedies in money cases. Birks protested that this was irrational; yet the rest of the law clearly rejects this idea that all benefits are alike. Try telling a criminal lawyer that borrowing money and refusing to return it *must* be theft, because that is what we say for other chattels; try telling a property lawyer that whatever rules apply to land *must* apply to other sorts of property; try telling an employment lawyer that selling your time is only a minor variant on selling your house or your car. Benefits are not treated uniformly by the law, nor should they be. 'Wealth', 'benefit', and 'enrichment' are too abstract to yield much assistance in stating doctrine.

The academic writing therefore is relaxing some of the Birksian rigour: unjust enrichment is claiming less territory, and within that territory less is claimed for it. What of unjust enrichment in the courts?

C. The Long Retreat: The Courts

From one point of view, the adoption of the language of 'unjust enrichment' across the common law world was a success for that theory. But the key decisions were not much motivated by a wish for theoretical purity, even if the theory temporarily pointed in the direction the court wished to go. Very often the immediate cause of unjust enrichment's recognition in particular jurisdictions was in response to claims that in a more perfect legal system would have been contractual, but an over-broad bar on contractual claims left the claimant unfairly out of pocket. In Canada, the context was a cohabitation agreement;[69] in Australia, a contract for building work that failed to satisfy statutory formalities;[70] in England and Wales, an interest rate swap that one of the parties was not authorized to make.[71] In each of those cases, the theory of unjust enrichment achieved a just result that seemed unattainable without it, and the Birksian dogma that unjust enrichment is territorially distinct from contract was, in those precise contexts, very convenient.

---

[68] For recent discussions, see Andrew Trotter, 'Mistakes and Mispredictions' (2021) 137 LQR 212; Aidan Briggs and Jian Jun Liew, 'Mistake, Misprediction, and Risk-Taking in Tax-Avoidance' (2022) 28 Trusts & Trustees 285.
[69] *Deglman v Guaranty Trust Co of Canada* [1954] SCR 725.
[70] *Pavey & Matthews Pty Ltd v Paul* (1987) 162 CLR 221.
[71] *Kleinwort Benson Ltd v Lincoln City Council* [1999] 2 AC 349 (HL).

In fact, unjust enrichment has been used for a number of such corrective purposes. Two problems in particular stood out, though their precise relevance differed across jurisdictions. The first was the absence of a substantial remedy in cases of long-term cohabitation, where a couple had lived together over many years and had paid little attention to their mutual property entitlements, suddenly finding them relevant on break-up or the death of one of them. The second was a gap in public law remedies, typically cases of taxes wrongly demanded and paid, but also sometimes more complex transactions. Both sorts of cases have been influential in the development of unjust enrichment law.[72] Yet how many problems are there in the common law, that can be addressed in this way? There are a number of suggestions in the law journals: there is support for using unjust enrichment to address current inadequacies in the law in the areas of medical risk-taking,[73] privacy,[74] and climate justice.[75] Little of this can, however, be done within the Birksian framework, and most judges would feel uncomfortable invoking unjust enrichment without *something* solid to constrain it. Indeed, the impulse to systematize the law (which played such an important role in Birks's thought[76]) is always likely to be at odds with attempts to put the law to entirely new uses. Crudely, it is beginning to look as if we have run out of *new* things for unjust enrichment to do.

This leaves unjust enrichment as merely a tool for managing existing controversies in well-established doctrines—a much less inviting prospect, as most of those doctrines were established before the Birksian theory was developed. We immediately notice that the picture is rather different in each common law jurisdiction, so the use of a one-size-fits-all theory is almost inevitably going to be limited. There are significant differences in the sorts of disputes that unjust enrichment is considered relevant to: notably disputes between cohabitees, which some jurisdictions consider an important area for unjust enrichment, but others keep unjust enrichment away from. Use of unjust enrichment as private law's Swiss army knife, to tackle new problems that resist solution otherwise, is perhaps most pronounced in the US jurisdictions, no doubt because of the weak hold that unjust enrichment theory has there. Whether and to what extent unjust enrichment is seen as distinct from equity attracts very different views, with the United States[77] and Australia[78] keenest on grouping them together, and New Zealand not far

---

[72] See especially Peter Birks and Francis Rose (eds), *Lessons of the Swaps Litigation* (Informa 2000).
[73] Tsachi Keren-Paz, 'Injuries from Unforeseeable Risks which Advance Medical Knowledge: Restitution-Based Justification for Strict Liability' (2014) 5 JETL 275.
[74] Bernard Chao, 'Unjust Enrichment: Standing Up for Privacy Rights' (2023) 108(49) Iowa Law Review Online 49.
[75] Santiago Truccone-Borgogno, 'Climate Justice and the Duty of Restitution' (2022) 10 Moral Philosophy and Politics 203.
[76] See especially Sagi Peari, Chapter 4 in this volume.
[77] See 'The Intellectual History of Unjust Enrichment' (2020) 133 Harv L Rev 2077.
[78] See Rohan Havelock, 'Rivalry over Liability for Defective Transfers' in Peter Devonshire and Rohan Havelock (eds), *The Impact of Equity and Restitution in Commerce* (Hart Publishing 2019); Joachim Dietrich, 'Unjust Enrichment versus Equitable Principles in England and Australia' in Jamie Glister and Pauline Ridge (eds), *Fault Lines in Equity* (Hart Publishing 2012).

behind.[79] New Zealand has been largely happy to make relatively little use of unjust enrichment theory, with one Supreme Court Justice extrajudicially endorsing the description of unjust enrichment as a 'platypus', resisting unambiguous classification.[80] US state law is the stand-out example of this theory-avoidance, and while UK scholars have in the past suspected that this simply reflected lack of interest in the subject from US academics (or that they are simply more 'forgiving of conceptual impurity'[81]), the recent *Restatement (Third)*[82] has put paid to this: the neglect of Birksian theory is a reasoned choice, such precision being deemed 'specious'[83] and productive of 'serious errors'.[84]

Other jurisdictions by contrast have made extensive use of theory. England and Wales, Canada, and Australia are all examples; and some smaller jurisdictions (Ireland,[85] Hong Kong,[86] Singapore[87]) initially followed the English lead, though they have each since begun to develop distinct approaches. Each of the larger jurisdictions is a theoretical world on its own. Canada is distinctive in its toleration of remedial constructive trusts, its insistence that not merely must the defendant have

---

[79] On New Zealand's equity jurisprudence, see Andrew Butler and Tim Miller, 'Thoughts on Equity in New Zealand and New South Wales' in Jamie Glister and Pauline Ridge (eds), *Fault Lines in Equity* (Hart Publishing 2012).

[80] Susan Glazebrook, 'Unjust Enrichment: The Platypus of Private Law' (2018) 28 Commonwealth Lawyer 25. For argument, see Tessa Cooksley, 'The Role of Unjust Enrichment in New Zealand' (2019) Victoria University of Wellington Legal Research Paper 21/2019 <http://ssrn.com/abstract=3466517> accessed 13 December 2022.

[81] Frederick Wilmot-Smith, '§ 38 and the Lost Doctrine of Failure of Consideration' in Charles Mitchell and William Swadling (eds), *The Restatement Third: Restitution and Unjust Enrichment—Critical and Comparative Essays* (Hart Publishing 2013) 88. For other criticisms, see especially Andrew Burrows, 'Is There a Defence of Good Consideration?' in Charles Mitchell and William Swadling (eds), *The Restatement Third: Restitution and Unjust Enrichment—Critical and Comparative Essays* (Hart Publishing 2013).

[82] On the *Restatement (Third)*, see generally Andrew Kull, 'Three Restatements of Restitution' (2011) 68 Wash & Lee L Rev 867; Joachim Dietrich, 'The Third Restatement of Restitution, the Role of Unjust Enrichment and Australian Law' (2011) 35 Aust Bar Rev 160; Douglas Laycock, 'Restoring Restitution to the Canon' (2012) 110 Mich L Rev 929.

[83] American Law Institute, *Restatement (Third) of Restitution and Unjust Enrichment* (2011) vol 1, §1, comment d (hereafter American Law Institute, *Restatement (Third)*), quoted in Charles Mitchell and William Swadling (eds), *The Restatement Third: Restitution and Unjust Enrichment—Critical and Comparative Essays* (Hart Publishing 2013) (hereafter Mitchell and Swadling, *Restatement Third Essays*).

[84] American Law Institute, *Restatement (Third)* (n 83) 8, 14, quoted in Mitchell and Swadling, *Restatement Third Essays* (n 83) 166. On US 'imprecision' (or, more strictly, its un-Birksian priorities), see especially Andrew Kull, 'Restitution and Unjust Enrichment' in Elise Bant, Kit Barker, and Simone Degeling (eds), *Research Handbook on Unjust Enrichment and Restitution* (Edward Elgar 2020); Emily Sherwin, Chapter 5 in this volume.

[85] Niamh Connolly, 'The Future of Irish Restitution Law' (2017) 25 RLR 136; John Breslin and Bláthnaid Breslin, 'Restitution Renaissance' (2019) 26 Commercial Law Practitioner 199.

[86] Arthur R Lee and Joshua Yeung, 'Semblance and Separation: Comparing the Law of Unjust Enrichment in Hong Kong and England' (2021) 9 CJCL d; Connie HY Lee and Joshua Yeung, 'Reconsidering the "Conduit Pipe" Defence to Unjust Enrichment Claims for Intermediary Recipients' (2021) 9 CJCL 262.

[87] Hang Wu Tang, 'The Role of the Law of Unjust Enrichment in Singapore' (2021) 9 CJCL 1; Rachel Leow and Timothy Liau, 'Birksian Themes and Their Impact in England and Singapore: Three Points of Divergence' [2021] LMCLQ 350; Rachel Leow and Timothy Liau, 'A Pyrrhic Victory for Unjust Enrichment in Singapore? *Esben Finance Ltd v Wong Hou-Lianq Neil*' (2023) 86 MLR 518.

gained but the plaintiff must have lost, its acceptance of late Birks ('unjustified enrichment') rather than early Birks ('unjust enrichment'),[88] and its special regimes for cohabitation cases[89] and public law cases.[90] Australian unjust enrichment law, by contrast, has seen a number of very sharp theoretical twists and turns, the result of very different views held on the matter by leading judicial figures;[91] all of which makes the current position rather hard to state with any clarity.[92] India and China—both of which have long and unique histories of restitutionary claims—are now engaging with theory from abroad, with mixed results.[93]

The current approach in England and Wales might be described as loosely Birksian, in the sense that the Birksian four-stage test is routinely used but without Birks's characteristic rigour. In contrast to civil law systems, the theory does not really unify the different liabilities it relates to but 'allows a diverse series of restitutionary claims to be grouped together'.[94] The four requirements are seen as superior to 'an unstructured approach driven by perceptions of fairness ... [But a]t the same time, the questions are not themselves legal tests, but are signposts towards areas of inquiry involving a number of distinct legal requirements'.[95] 'Flexibility is embedded within the unjust factors scheme';[96] and there is an inevitable drift towards the normative, with judges not always asking whether there is an identifiable 'unjust factor' but simply whether the enrichment was actually unjust, without obvious reference to any particular theory.[97] As I have argued elsewhere, the judicial approach can fairly be described (despite judicial denials) as discretionary, not in the positive sense of their feeling free to extend the law as they choose, but in the

---

[88] On which, see especially Mitchell McInnes, Chapter 16 in this volume.

[89] Mitchell McInnes, *The Canadian Law of Unjust Enrichment and Restitution* (1st edn, LexisNexis Canada 2014) ch 28.

[90] ibid ch 24; Paul Daly, 'Restitution and Reasonableness Review: *Ontario Addiction Treatment Centres v. Canada (Attorney General)*, 2022 FC 393' (*Administrative Law Matters*, 14 April 2022) <www.tinyurl.com/f5kkx7px> accessed 13 December 2022. For reviews of the current Canadian unjust enrichment doctrine, see Mitchell McInnes, 'Life Insurance, Unjust Enrichment and Constructive Trusts in Canada' (2019) 135 LQR 358; Matthew P Harrington, 'Leapfrogging, Risk, and Unjust Enrichment in Canada after *Moore v Sweet*' (2020) 96 Supreme Court Law Review (2d Series) 191; John D McCamus, '*Moore v Sweet*: Four Lessons in Unjust Enrichment from the Supreme Court of Canada' (2020) 98 Can Bar Rev 109.

[91] For the history, see Elise Bant, 'The Evolution of Unjust Enrichment and Restitution Law in the High Court of Australia' (2017) 25 RLR 121.

[92] On the current position, see Frederick Wilmot-Smith, 'Contract and Unjust Enrichment in the High Court of Australia' (2020) 136 LQR 196; Samuel Walpole and Kit Barker, 'Unjust Enrichment in Australia' [2020] LMCLQ 311. For criticism, see Burrows, *The Law of Restitution* (n 49) 35–43.

[93] On India, see Arpita Gupta, Chapter 3 in this volume. On China, see Siyi Lin, Chapter 2 in this volume.

[94] Dário Moura Vicente, *Comparative Law of Obligations* (Edward Elgar 2021) 387.

[95] *Investment Trust Companies v Revenue and Customs Comrs* [2017] UKSC 29; [2018] AC 275 [41] (Lord Reed SCJ). This is a much-cited passage, most recently (at the time of writing) in *Tecnimont Arabia v National Westminster Bank* [2022] EWHC 1172 (Comm) [102] (Judge Bird).

[96] *Dargamo Holdings Ltd v Avonwick Holdings Ltd* [2021] EWCA Civ 1149; [2022] 1 All ER (Comm) 1244 [63] (Carr LJ).

[97] On judicial treatment of 'unjust', see Steve Hedley, 'Justice and Discretion in the Law of Unjust Enrichment' (2019) 48 CLWR 94, 108–09.

negative sense that they may *refuse* to extend the law in the directions that Birksian theory encourages them to do.[98] And they are well aware (as Birks himself was not, or at least gave no sign that he was) that Birksian theory has considerable potential to expand liability, a potential it is not always sensible to exploit: as the judiciary recognized in the belated overruling of the *Sempra* judgment on compound interest,[99] and the restrictive *Pitt* ruling on mistake.[100]

As to the approach of individual judges, the differences seem to be every bit as broad as within the Australian judiciary, if more decorously expressed. Lord Sumption provided textbook examples of soggy Birksian analysis, freely using the Birksian theory but also feeling free to throw in other considerations, in a way no true Birksian would tolerate.[101] Lord Burrows is (of course) precisely the sort of critic who might have objected to such imprecise thinking,[102] but his arrival in the Supreme Court is too recent for any conclusions as to how he will develop the law. Lord Reed, by contrast, was insistent on the limits of what any theory of Birks's sort could tell judges, and scathing about those who used it beyond its limits.[103] Future developments are hard to predict.

D. The Long Retreat: What is the Theory *For*?

Along with these disputes over the scope and details of the theory of unjust enrichment, more fundamental questions are being asked about it: what does the theory really do, what is it *for*? Whatever else the theory does, it does not actually *justify* the liabilities it describes. Even if it could be shown that the law complied precisely with the Birksian scheme, that would tell us nothing about whether the law was fair and just, or whether it deserved to be extended or reduced in scope. And we do not have any widely accepted theory which explains either why it would be a good thing for the law to reverse unjust enrichments, or which explains the merits of the liability Birks took to be the exemplar and model of the liability, the liability to return a mistaken payment. Indeed, some argue that the values implicit in the

---

[98] ibid.
[99] *Prudential Assurance Co Ltd v Revenue and Customs Comrs* (n 52), overruling *Sempra Metals Ltd v IRC* [2007] UKHL 34; [2008] 1 AC 561. For criticism, see Burrows, 'In Defence of Unjust Enrichment' (n 64) 538–41.
[100] *Pitt v Holt* [2013] UKSC 26; [2013] 2 AC 108. For discussion, see Birke Häcker, 'Mistaken Gifts after *Pitt v Holt*' (2014) 67 CLP 333; Imogen Dodds, 'Recovery for Mistaken Dispositions: Possible Effects of *Pitt v Holt*' (2016) 24 RLR 129; Adam Hofri-Winogradow and Gadi Weiss, 'Trust Parties' Uniquely Easy Access to Rescission: Analysis, Critique and Reform' (2019) 82 MLR 777; Thomas Watts and Hugh Gunson, 'An Honest Mistake: Two Cases of Mistaken Dispositions' (2020) 26 Trusts & Trustees 289.
[101] See Graham Virgo, 'Unjust Enrichment' in William Day and Sarah Worthington (eds), *Challenging Private Law: Lord Sumption on the Supreme Court* (Hart Publishing 2020).
[102] Burrows, 'In Defence of Unjust Enrichment' (n 64).
[103] Reed, 'Theory and Practice' (n 37).

theory are so out of line with those most of us hold, that it has become positively pernicious,[104] or that its emphasis on enrichment (as opposed to loss) is wrong in principle.[105]

It is easy to assert that the principle against unjust enrichment is a normative principle,[106] or that it 'explains' liabilities that would otherwise rest on fictions;[107] but actually stating such a principle in terms that an ethicist or moral philosopher would recognize is a great deal harder; too hard, indeed, for us. We do not lack for suggestions here, but so far none of them justify the law as it is, though some of them might justify a rather different law. In this brief review of theories which aim at justifying unjust enrichment in a moral or political sense, their weakness is apparent.

It is not, in fact, that these theories are weak or implausible (though some are). The point is that none of them justify the Birksian focus on *enrichment*—so whatever it is they justify, it is not the Birksian theory. Unjust enrichments no doubt call for a legal response, but so does *any* instance of injustice—'unjust φ calls for a remedy' is true for all values of φ. As Barker points out, the theoretical rigour that led to the shrinking of the theory—such as the denial that restitution for wrongs was an example of unjust enrichment—has come back to bite the theory itself, as the most obvious examples of what a moralist would take to be 'unjust enrichment' are in fact *not* included within the theory.[108] If the Birksian theory has a moral justification, what form can such a justification take?[109]

- Ernest Weinrib has long argued that much of unjust enrichment can be justified by the theory of corrective justice, which he expounds within a Kantian framework of ideas. The law responds to unjust transfers of value, compelling the defendant to correct the injustice by returning the value received.[110] So stated, this is rather limited idea, being effectively confined to cases of

---

[104] Peter G Watts, '"Unjust Enrichment"—the Potion that Induces Well-Meaning Sloppiness of Thought' (2016) 69 CLP 289 (hereafter Watts, 'Potion').
[105] Lutz-Christian Wolff, Chapter 10 in this volume.
[106] See eg Burrows, 'In Defence of Unjust Enrichment' (n 64) 529, though he immediately concedes that it is 'normatively disparate'.
[107] See eg Andrew Burrows, 'Form and Substance: Fictions and Judicial Power' in Andrew Robertson and James Goudkamp (eds), *Form and Substance in the Law of Obligations* (Hart Publishing 2019) 29–31.
[108] Kit Barker, 'Centripetal Force: The Law of Unjust Enrichment Restated in England and Wales' (2014) 34 OJLS 155, 164.
[109] For a general review of justificatory theories, see Dennis Klimchuk, 'Unjust Enrichment and the Forms of Justice' in Elise Bant, Kit Barker, and Simone Degeling (eds), *Research Handbook on Unjust Enrichment and Restitution* (Edward Elgar 2020).
[110] Ernest J Weinrib, 'The Structure of Unjustness' (2012) 92 BU L Rev 1067; Ernest J Weinrib, 'Correctively Unjust Enrichment' in Robert Chambers, Charles Mitchell, and James Penner (eds), *Philosophical Foundations of the Law of Unjust Enrichment* (OUP 2009); Ernest J Weinrib, 'The Corrective Justice of Liability for Unjust Enrichment' in Elise Bant, Kit Barker, and Simone Degeling (eds), *Research Handbook on Unjust Enrichment and Restitution* (Edward Elgar 2020)(hereafter Weinrib, 'Corrective Justice of Liability').

'direct' enrichment. Yet even so limited, it is unsatisfactory, because Weinrib's conception of injustice requires that the defendant be guilty of wrongdoing, whereas typically in these cases the defendant does nothing at all.[111] Talk of a *duty* to abstain from unjust enrichment does not make sense of what the law does.[112] Weinrib's reply—that defendant's acceptance of the transfer can be regarded as a positive act[113]—has not convinced many.[114]

- More generally, some justify these liabilities as protecting the claimant's autonomy: so (for example) allowing rights holders to correct mistaken transfers makes them that much more secure in the enjoyment of their rights. Protection of autonomy is, of course, not a single theoretical notion, but can be approached from many angles, whether Kantian,[115] contractualist,[116] or liberal.[117] There is clearly something in this, but it sounds like the *start* of a justification, not the whole thing. (The claimant's autonomy deserves respect, but so does the defendant's; how are those concerns reconciled? And why does the law respect autonomy in *this* way, and not others?[118]) But the main point is that 'autonomy' theories are meant to justify *the whole of* private law, and so are orthogonal to Birks's concern to establish unjust enrichment as a distinct area *within* private law. 'Autonomy' theories do not buttress Birksian theory; they pass like ships in the night. Indeed, Dagan is explicit in his preference for stating the law in narrow and perhaps overlapping categories (to better to connect to the human needs the law serves); 'the maxim of preventing unjust enrichment can harmlessly serve as a loose common theme'.[119]

- Again, economic rationales can be found for many of the liabilities treated within unjust enrichment, but these rationales give no support to a general

---

[111] See Prince Saprai, 'Weinrib on Unjust Enrichment' (2011) 24 CJLJ 183; Matthew Doyle, 'Corrective Justice and Unjust Enrichment' (2012) 62 UTLJ 229. See also James Penner, Chapter 8 in this volume.

[112] Stephen A Smith, 'Justifying the Law of Unjust Enrichment' (2001) 79 Tex L Rev 2177; Stephen A Smith, *Rights, Wrongs, and Injustices: The Structure of Remedial Law* (OUP 2019) 224–25, 237–49.

[113] Weinrib, 'Corrective Justice of Liability' (n 110) 177–79.

[114] However, some believe that an acceptable Kantian justification for the law can be found through appealing to *public* right (crudely, that while the defendant has committed no private wrong, the integrity of the property system requires that a remedy be available): see Andrew Botterell, 'Private Law, Public Right, and the Law of Unjust Enrichment' (2021) 12 Jurisprudence 537.

[115] Jennifer M Nadler, 'What Right Does Unjust Enrichment Law Protect?' (2008) 28 OJLS 245.

[116] Tatiana Cutts, 'Materially Identical to Mistaken Payment' (2020) 33 CJLJ 31. See also Tatiana Cutts, 'Unjust Enrichment: What We Owe to Each Other' (2021) 41 OJLS 114. For commentary, see Peter Chau and Lusina Ho, Chapter 9 in this volume.

[117] Hanoch Dagan, 'Just and Unjust Enrichments' in Andrew Robertson and Tang Hang Wu (eds), *The Goals of Private Law* (Hart Publishing 2009); Hanoch Dagan, 'Restitution and Relationships' (2012) 92 BU L Rev 1035; Hanoch Dagan, 'Autonomy, Relational Justice and the Law of Restitution' in Elise Bant, Kit Barker, and Simone Degeling (eds), *Research Handbook on Unjust Enrichment and Restitution* (Edward Elgar 2020).

[118] Ernest J Weinrib, 'Restoring Restitution' (2005) 91 Va L Rev 861.

[119] Dagan, 'Restitution's Realism' (n 15) 54, 80. Note also his earlier comment on the Birksian model that, properly understood, 'we ... end up with a loose framework that—while potentially useful—should always be applied with a grain of salt': Dagan, *The Law and Ethics of Restitution* (n 5) 33. For comment on Dagan's thesis, see Dennis Klimchuk, 'Restitution and Realism' (2007) 20 CJLJ 225.

theory; each narrow category of liability is a distinct problem.[120] Indeed, it would be rather extraordinary if it were otherwise—if a theory which is said to be fundamental to the economic stability of capitalist societies should make *enrichment* the core of what it objected to and remedied. On the contrary, the wish to achieve personal enrichment is taken to be the very motor of economic growth.[121]

We see a similar pattern when we look at the specific liability to return a mistaken payment, when the payer accidentally paid the same debt twice—which Birks took as the core case of unjust enrichment liability. Intuitively there should be a remedy here, at least if that remedy can be carefully applied so as not to leave the payee out of pocket. But what is the rationale? Is it about reversing a transaction that should never have occurred?[122] Is it about protecting rights in the money handed over?[123] Is it about minimizing economic costs?[124] Is it simply what virtue requires of the defendant?[125] We simply do not know.[126] And not knowing, we can hardly make use of this instance of liability as the basic pattern for a much wider area of law. We cannot extend it by analogy, if we cannot discern the *point* of the analogy.

E. The Long Retreat: A Lesser Role for the Taxonomy?

Yet if the justification of these liabilities cannot be stated in terms that link it to the Birksian taxonomy, then the credibility of that taxonomy is inevitably weakened. Unsurprisingly therefore, there is growing academic support for abandoning 'unjust enrichment' as a framework for discussing restitutionary liabilities. What would have been surprising is if all of those who have spent a career expounding the law within the Birksian framework were to suddenly abandon it; and this has not, of course, happened. But how has its continued use been justified?

Some are trying to bluff it out, ignoring justificatory questions entirely. This approach is particularly attractive to those who have not been convinced by all of the

---

[120] See eg Chris Wonnell, 'A Law and Economics Perspective on Restitution' in Elise Bant, Kit Barker, and Simone Degeling (eds), *Research Handbook on Unjust Enrichment and Restitution* (Edward Elgar 2020).
[121] For an attempt to state an economic criterion for 'unjust', see Maytal Gilboa and Yotam Kaplan, 'The *Other Hand* Formula' (2022) 26 LCLR 883.
[122] Cutts, 'Materially Identical to Mistaken Payment' (n 116).
[123] Charlie Webb, *Reason and Restitution: A Theory of Unjust Enrichment* (OUP 2016) ch 5.
[124] Maytal Gilboa and Yotam Kaplan, 'The Costs of Mistakes' (2022) 122 Colum L Rev 61; Dhammika Dharmapala and Nuno Garoupa, 'The Law of Restitution for Mistaken Payments: An Economic Analysis' (2022) University of Chicago Coase-Sandor Institute for Law & Economics Research Paper No 931, George Mason Law & Economics Research Paper No 21-18 <http://ssrn.com/abstract=3902607> accessed 13 December 2022.
[125] JE Penner, 'We All Make Mistakes: A "Duty of Virtue" Theory of Restitutionary Liability for Mistaken Payments' (2018) 81 MLR 222.
[126] Frederick Wilmot-Smith, 'Should the Payee Pay?' (2017) 37 OJLS 844.

attempts to retreat from Birksian theory, and so see unjust enrichment as a broad and diverse area, but nonetheless a coherent subject of study. As Charles Mitchell explains, there is no real consensus as to 'the degree of normative unity that one believes a body of rules must possess before it can count as a "category" of obligations law'.[127] A common argument is that while unjust enrichment's overall coherence may be minimal, the same may be said of the law of tort.[128] But that, of course, begs the question of how satisfactory the category of tort is (a question on which there is a massive literature). Yet those who support the taxonomy are for the most part reluctant to abandon all reference to fairness, though some insist that its role should merely be as an influence on when framing rules, not in applying them.[129] It is obvious *both* that our values must have some influence on the law *and* that it is rather difficult to state the values which the taxonomy represents.

What, then, is there still to say in favour of the taxonomy? I summarize three sorts of arguments made on this, in order of increasing plausibility.

First, it is said that *some* sort of taxonomy is a necessity for rational thought about law; either we have a taxonomy, or we have intellectual chaos. Therefore, the response to weaknesses in the Birksian scheme should not be to abandon it, but to modify it, being careful to retain the good while abandoning the bad.[130] This is a little hard to take seriously. It is a testament to the high profile Birks earned himself in common law thought, outside the United States at least, that 'taxonomy' is almost invariably taken to be a reference either to his theory or to those of the civil law theorists on whom he was drawing. But if we are to have a serious discussion of possible taxonomies, the term must be used more broadly. In particular, it must extend to the taxonomical scheme represented by the forms of action, which (as Maitland famously remarked) 'we have buried, but they still rule us from their graves'.[131] Ever since Birks enunciated his theory, the battle has not been between those who believe in taxonomies and those who do not, but rather as to the appropriate level of abstraction: as high as Birks claimed, or at a lower level?

---

[127] Charles Mitchell, 'Other Reasons for restitution' in Elise Bant, Kit Barker, and Simone Degeling (eds), *Research Handbook on Unjust Enrichment and Restitution* (Edward Elgar 2020) 380–81.

[128] See eg Burrows, 'In Defence of Unjust Enrichment' (n 64) 526–28; Barker, 'Centripetal Force' (n 108).

[129] See Birke Häcker, '"Substance over Form": Has the Pendulum Swung Too Far?' in Andrew Robertson and James Goudkamp (eds), *Form and Substance in the Law of Obligations* (Hart Publishing 2019) 64–67.

[130] For variations on this general theme, see Ewan McKendrick, 'Taxonomy: Does It Matter?' in David Johnston and Reinhard Zimmerman (eds), *Unjustified Enrichment: Key Issues in Comparative Perspective* (CUP 2002); Duncan Sheehan and TT Arvind, 'Private Law Theory and Taxonomy: Reframing the Debate' (2015) 35 LS 480; Kit Barker, 'Unjust Enrichment in Australia: What Is(n't) It? Implications for Legal Reasoning and Practice' (2020) 43 MULR 903.

[131] FW Maitland, *The Forms of Action at Common Law: A Course of Lectures* (first published 1909, CUP 1941) 2.

Secondly, it is said that we need to take the civil law origins of the Birksian taxonomy more seriously than we have done up to now. Birks did not assume that his taxonomy described the *reasons* for liability, nor that cases which his scheme classifies as materially identical will fall to be resolved by the same rule or the same set of values. In other words, it is *because* the Birksian scheme lacks a coherent moral basis that we should expect judges to bring justice to bear at the level of *actually applying* the law, rather than expecting the taxonomy to do this work for them. 'This does not mean that Birks' scheme was "banal" or "inert"'; rather, we can only reap its benefits if we bear in mind that its proper role is limited.[132] As a comment on the very different ways in which common lawyers and civil lawyers use general propositions of law, either generally[133] or specifically in relation to unjust enrichment,[134] there is a lot in this. And there is much for common lawyers to learn from civilian-informed debate over 'unjust factors',[135] and as to whether unjustified enrichment is better expounded as a unified category or as a set of distinct liabilities.[136] But is it really plausible to suggest that common lawyers will abandon their core methodology simply to make use of the Birksian scheme, that they will accept that doctrine actually *is* 'an elaborate arrangement of pigeonholes into which the cases may be slotted'?[137] Traditionally they have always demanded rather more, that the doctrine should state on its face what problems it is meant to solve and what we should look for in applying it. A doctrine which was not meant to be applied that way would not strike common lawyers as 'rational', but as quite deliberately *irrational*.

Thirdly, there is the argument from 'sophistication': that we should not see the decline in the use and significance of the taxonomy as a fragmentation of

---

[132] Pablo Letelier, 'A Wrong Turn? Reconsidering the Unified Approach to Unjust Enrichment Claims' (2020) 136 LQR 121, 130; Pablo Letelier, 'Another Civilian View of Unjust Enrichment's Structural Debate' (2020) 79 CLJ 527, 542.

[133] See eg René Brouwer, 'On the Meaning of "System" in the Common and Civil Law Traditions: Two Approaches to Legal Unity' (2018) 34 Utrecht J Int'l and European L 45; Lionel Smith, 'Civil and Common Law' in Andrew S Gold and others (eds), *The Oxford Handbook of the New Private Law* (OUP 2021) 227.

[134] For a variety of approaches, see Nikolaos A Davrados, 'Demystifying Enrichment Without Cause' (2018) 78 La L Rev 1223; James Gordley, 'Unjust Enrichment: A Comparative Perspective and a Critique' in Elise Bant, Kit Barker, and Simone Degeling (eds), *Research Handbook on Unjust Enrichment and Restitution* (Edward Elgar 2020); Pietro Sirena, 'Towards a European Law of Unjustified Enrichment' [2012] Osservatorio del Diritto Civile e Commerciale 113; Vicente (n 94) ch 6.

[135] Francesco Giglio, 'A Systematic Approach to "Unjust" and "Unjustified" Enrichment' (2003) 23 OJLS 455; Häcker, 'Unjust Factors versus Absence of Juristic Reason (*Causa*)' (n 66).

[136] Nils Jansen, 'Farewell to Unjustified Enrichment?' (2016) 20 Edin LR 123; Hector MacQueen, 'The Sophistication of Unjustified Enrichment: A Response to Nils Jansen' (2016) 20 Edin LR 312; Jacques du Plessis, 'Long Live the Law of Unjustified Enrichment—A Response to Jansen' [2019] Acta Juridica 371; Helen Scott, 'Comparative Taxonomy: An Introduction' in Elise Bant, Kit Barker, and Simone Degeling (eds), *Research Handbook on Unjust Enrichment and Restitution* (Edward Elgar 2020). See also Daniel Visser, 'Unjustified Enrichment in Comparative Perspective' in Mathias Reimann and Reinhard Zimmermann (eds), *The Oxford Handbook of Comparative Law* (2nd edn, OUP 2019).

[137] Reed, 'Theory and Practice' (n 37) 314–15.

that approach, but on the contrary as a sign that it has done its work, drawing connections and filling in gaps in the law. This view has been strongly urged by Hector MacQueen,[138] and while Andrew Burrows does not use quite that language, his *Restatement* can be read in that way, as a detailed account of the law which happens to use the taxonomy as an organizational tool but can readily be appreciated regardless of what one thinks of the taxonomy itself.[139] All very sophisticated; but that very sophistication looks to many like an abandonment of what would earlier have been the theory's principal selling point, that it is based on clear concepts that unite the whole area. This approach leads us back to the very world Birks led us away from, one where we do not seek out or prize broad principles, but on the contrary expect to consider the law in very small fragments indeed, the better to reach a fair solution to them[140]—what Birks called a 'contextual' subject,[141] or Frank Easterbrook popularized as 'the law of the horse'.[142] Ultimately, it seems to lead to the approach Nils Jansen now advocates,[143] where the emphasis is not on unjust enrichment's supposed unity but on close connection to, and integration with, *other* heads of the law. In civilian systems, it might still then make sense to assert that there is still a general principle of 'unjust enrichment' under all the detail; but in a common law system, having neither a tradition of this nor a consensus on what such a tradition entails, it is hard to see that it has a useful purpose.

As for whether this represents progress, views will differ. There is a famous fable of Aesop. An aging farmer wishes to provide for his lazy sons, but knows that they will never work the farm diligently merely because he asks them to. So on his deathbed he invents a story: that there is a fabulous treasure hidden on the farm, though he does not know the precise spot. So motivated, his sons turn over every foot of ground with their spades; they never find the treasure, but the farm prospers mightily from their efforts. In time, they come to realize that their father's advice had indeed led them to treasure, though not quite in the way they had expected. Similarly, academics have been lured by the promise of a shiny new theory, into doing the necessary spadework of describing significant areas of law. And perhaps there will always be a few who do not quite believe that the old man could have misled them, that the theory's secrets will be finally unlocked if only they look in the right place. Either way, the work has been done, with very useful results. What is the next task?

---

[138] MacQueen, 'The Sophistication of Unjustified Enrichment' (n 136).
[139] Andrew Burrows, *A Restatement of the English Law of Unjust Enrichment* (OUP 2012).
[140] Barker, 'Centripetal Force' (n 108).
[141] See text to n 25.
[142] See Frank H Easterbrook, 'Cyberspace and the Law of the Horse' [1996] U Chi Legal F 207.
[143] Nils Jansen, Chapter 12 in this volume.

IV. The Emerging (Lower Level) Categorization

A. Naming Problems, Not Solutions

So, after the long Birksian detour, we come back to the original problem. The core doctrines of private law—contract and property above all—are dominated by the need to avoid disputes, to provide easy and straightforward ways of allowing people to plan their lives. For this reason (perhaps also for others), many of their rules exhibit a strong willingness to facilitate those who allow themselves to be guided by the law, to play by its rules. Inevitably, in a few cases, those rules can lead to examples of unfairness *ex post*: for example, there are good *ex ante* reasons why property law usually insists on formalities, but not all of those who come to grief *ex post* through the neglect of those rules can be dismissed as meritless spongers. The courts have consistently shown not only that they value the integrity of the *ex ante* rules, but also that a sufficiently powerful case that the rules have resulted in injustice can be remedied.

We should therefore expect there to be a significant collection of legal liabilities that are *just* outside the core areas: that are very like contractual or proprietary claims, but for some reason do not qualify under the core rules. We would expect the moral force of these claims to be rather like those motivating the core case, indeed (to lay minds) in many cases virtually indistinguishable from them. We would not necessarily expect these claims to fall into any overall juristically satisfying pattern: they have little in common except that the core law does not recognize any of them. And we should not be surprised if we find that any patterns we can see involve indistinct, overlapping groupings of cases. There is likely no rigid intellectual order to be found. The intellectual disorder here is the price that must be paid for intellectual order elsewhere, in the core doctrines.

It is therefore unsurprising that for many centuries and in many jurisdictions these claims have been expressed through analogy. The mistaken payer protests, 'I want my money back!' To a strict property lawyer, it is a sufficient answer that it is no longer their money. To someone who cares about justice, that is at best a partial answer, and a closer look is needed before we can say whether the money should be recoverable. Or again, someone who has expended time and energy to another's profit may well protest that while they had no contract, they deserve to be paid as if they had—that a quasi-contractual claim lies. Again, a strict contract lawyer might reject such a claim, but to an attentive judge, further inquiry will often be appropriate. The precision of core private law's concepts serves a purpose, but the law has many purposes, some of which it implements in these restitution cases. As Henry Smith notes:

> [A]ll legal systems have to address different audiences, combine elements of formalism and contextualism, achieve some generality without exploitation and

unfairness, and keep things humming while being ready for the unexpected. Meta-law should be part of the toolkit for addressing these questions, and the fragments of equity can be reassembled to do the job.[144]

And so can the fragments of 'unjust enrichment'. In fact, collecting and naming the fragments has long been a task for those common lawyers who have been unconvinced by the unitary Birksian approach; while no two writers have divided the law in *precisely* the same way, there are clear family resemblances in the lists of liabilities discerned by Joachim Dietrich,[145] Margaret Halliwell,[146] Ian Jackman,[147] Peter Jaffey,[148] Dan Priel,[149] Lionel Smith,[150] Stephen Smith,[151] Robert Stevens,[152] Samuel Stoljar,[153] Peter Watts,[154] and myself.[155] Once the nature of the problem is grasped—that we are not trying to fit the various jigsaw pieces into a single puzzle, but rather into four or five puzzles only distantly related to one another[156]—theorists begin to think along similar lines.

But the nature of what is being offered might be misunderstood. To outline a situation where a bright-line core rule can lead to an unjust result does not always tell us immediately what a just result would look like. Quite possibly, there is no way of providing justice through bright-line rules, and so the law simply (and entirely appropriately) gives an explicit discretion to courts faced with it. In other words, the scheme here names problems, not solutions: it merely identifies where

---

[144] Henry E Smith, 'Equity as Meta-Law' (2021) 130 Yale LJ 1050, 1135.
[145] See especially Joachim Dietrich, *Restitution: A New Perspective* (Federation Press 1998).
[146] See especially Margaret Halliwell, 'Modern Equity' in Steve Hedley and Margaret Halliwell (eds), *The Law of Restitution* (Butterworths 2002).
[147] See especially Ian Jackman, *The Varieties of Restitution* (2nd edn, Federation Press 2017).
[148] See especially Peter Jaffey, *The Nature and Scope of Restitution* (Hart Publishing 2000); Peter Jaffey, *Private Law and Property Claims* (Hart Publishing 2007).
[149] See especially Priel, 'The Justice in Unjust Enrichment' (n 12); Dan Priel, 'In Defence of Quasi-Contract' (2012) 75 MLR 54.
[150] See especially Lionel Smith, 'Defences and the Disunity of Unjust Enrichment' in Andrew Dyson, James Goudkamp, and Frederick Wilmot-Smith (eds), *Defences in Unjust Enrichment* (Hart Publishing 2016); Lionel Smith, 'Restitution: A New Start?' in Peter Devonshire and Rohan Havelock (eds), *The Impact of Equity and Restitution in Commerce* (Hart Publishing 2019).
[151] See especially Stephen Smith, 'Unjust Enrichment: Nearer to Tort than Contract' in Robert Chambers, Charles Mitchell, and James Penner (eds), *Philosophical Foundations of the Law of Unjust Enrichment* (OUP 2009); Stephen A Smith, *Rights, Wrongs, and Injustices: The Structure of Remedial Law* (OUP 2019) ch 8.
[152] Robert Stevens, 'The Unjust Enrichment Disaster' (2018) 134 LQR 574; Robert Stevens, 'Private Law and the Form of Reasons' in Andrew Robertson and James Goudkamp (eds), *Form and Substance in the Law of Obligations* (Hart Publishing 2019).
[153] See especially SJ Stoljar, *The Law of Quasi-Contract* (2nd edn, Law Book Co 1989).
[154] See especially Peter Watts, 'Taxonomy in Private Law—Furor in Text and Subtext' [2014] NZ L Rev 107; Watts, 'Potion' (n 104).
[155] See especially Steve Hedley, *Restitution: Its Division and Ordering* (Sweet & Maxwell 2001); Steve Hedley, *A Critical Introduction to Restitution* (Butterworths 2001); Steve Hedley, 'Implied Contract and Restitution' (2004) 63 CLJ 435.
[156] 'What has remained is, however, still four or five different jigsaw puzzles in one box. They are not even different parts of the same overall picture, unless that picture is private law itself': Stevens, 'The Unjust Enrichment Disaster' (n 152) 574.

application of core rules has frequently led to injustices. The Birksian approach assumed that all of these problems had but a single solution, which could be summed up in a sufficiently precise conceptualization of 'unjust enrichment'. If we realize that this is fallacious, it still leaves the need to find solutions, though each one of them can be rather different and so (hopefully) more attuned to the realities of each individual case.

Talk of quasi-property or quasi-contract in the abstract is indeed vague[157] (as, in the abstract, is talk of unjust enrichment), and it may indeed be that there is no single normative principle that will resolve all the cases this approach might lead us to group together;[158] but the same could be said of many justice problems, and the problems that restitution addresses might have been specially selected precisely because there is no very obvious rule to separate the just from the unjust. It is, of course, true that one would get nowhere before a judge merely by observing that your client's claim was rather like a contractual claim;[159] but who has suggested that the claimant would say no more than that?

The starting point has to be that the legal concepts of 'contract' and 'property' are imperfect, both in sense that they do not perfectly capture what our intuitions tell us those concepts should cover, and in that straightforward application of those legal concepts *without more* can often lead to unacceptable results. One of the things restitution does is to address those imperfections. This is why the repeated criticism that the quasi-contractual approach is fictitious[160] misses the point. The same could equally be said of many of the core contract rules (how may parties actually *intend* the courts to give the contract the legal effect that they do?). The point is that while a strict interpretation of core contract would reject such claims, nonetheless they are considered sufficiently analogous to merit a legal remedy. In fact, the line between 'real' and 'fictitious' contracts is frequently rather hard to draw with any precision, even though there are some cases that we can firmly put one side of the line or other, and the traditional common law blurring of the line (by talking of 'implied contracts') simply reflects reality. In these cases, the courts have found the analogy with contract useful, and the Birksian model betrays its respect for party intention (talking of 'the contract ceiling' or 'subjective devaluation') while unconvincingly insisting that any resemblance to contract law is entirely coincidental. Contract law does not lose effect sharply the moment an offer and an acceptance cannot be discerned; it tapers off, and restitutionary cases often focus on that tapering.

---

[157] Tariq Baloch, *Unjust Enrichment and Contract* (Hart Publishing 2009) 61–62.
[158] Duncan Sheehan, 'Implied Contract and the Taxonomy of Unjust Enrichment' in Paula Giliker (ed), *Re-Examining Contract and Unjust Enrichment: Anglo-Canadian Perspectives* (Martinus Nijhoff 2007) 201.
[159] Baloch (n 157) 63–64.
[160] See eg Sheehan, 'Implied Contract and the Taxonomy of Unjust Enrichment' (n 158) 200–11.

Here, if you like, is the fundamental difference between the Birksian approach and mine: we both know that the rules cannot make the decision for the judge, that after a certain point in the analysis the paper rules can help no further, and the values which guide the decision must come from elsewhere—where we differ is in *how quickly* we get to that point when considering the law of restitution. Of course, there are other ways of handling the ultimate decision on the merits, which avoid the need to rely on the law for something it cannot give us: we can explicitly make the solution depend on a judicial discretion, or (as Lord Mansfield would have done) we can leave it to a jury. But Birks's solution—to torture the law itself for a precise answer—has been tried, and found wanting.

What, then, is the best way to divide up the problems restitution addresses? The scheme I use here is chosen to emphasize the key point, that each of these liabilities needs consideration as part of restitution precisely because the problem it addresses is *not* dealt with as part of the core of private law.

B. Property

From an *ex ante* point of view, the important point is ease of transfer and clarity of expectations. The possibility of future disputes is always to mind, but can be minimized by proper attention to formalities and routine inquiries into possibly conflicting rights. While all property lawyers know that property is as much about human relations as it is about things, nonetheless inevitably the focus is on the thing (the *res*) and who can be said to own it. This focus ensures that security of title is emphasized, and certain other problems are pushed to the sidelines. Five such problems often regarded as 'restitutionary' are:

(1) In some cases, property dealings deserve respect even though there is a blatant failure to comply with statutory formalities. When is this so?
(2) In some cases, a couple might live together for a considerable period, yet never marry. On breakdown of the relationship, or the death of one of them, can any of the remedies usually associated with marriage be claimed?[161]
(3) In some cases, one party does valuable work which improves the value of another's property, either in ignorance of the precise legal position or in the belief that the property was theirs. Can the improver claim any recompense?
(4) In some cases, the point of the dispute is missed if we focus on the thing, the *res*. Take the thief who steals an artwork, then sells it for cash, then invests the proceeds in shares, which increase greatly in value. If the victim of the

---

[161] For some of the literature on how rights of cohabitees could be fitted into private law, see Albertina Antognini, 'Nonmarital Contracts' (2021) 73 Stan L Rev 67; E Gary Spitko, 'Integrated Nonmarital Property Rights' (2022) 75 SMU L Rev 151.

theft contemplates an action for those shares (and sometimes the law does indeed allow this), then we have clearly stepped outside normal property regimes. When does a claim lie?
(5) Property might be transferred in a way that satisfies ordinary rules as to formalities, but nonetheless defeats the transferor's legitimate expectations—they were coerced into making the transfer, or were under some false impression about it. Can it be corrected?

These problems clearly call for solutions. Some protest at the invocation of 'property' in these contexts—but while those arguments are not uninteresting, the aim here is to identify problems rather than to dictate solutions, and the scheme here proposed is not invalidated by doubts as to how far 'property law' might extend. If the law protects property, it is unsurprising that it grants a remedy where property is lost to its owner, whether by destruction or by unjust transfer, and for present purposes such a remedy can be regarded as related to property. And we can agree with Sarah Worthington that, so understood, analysis of property entitlements must be considered first in private law analysis: 'property questions must be answered before liability questions'.[162]

In the pre-Birksian conception of unjust enrichment, it seemed obvious that many of the defendants in these cases were unjustly enriched, and so the law's remedy was treated as part of restitution. But more rigorous Birsksian analysis pointed to a number of problems—most having to do with the ineptness of the remedy as an assessment of defendant's enrichment—and so these cases have for the most part been kept away from the mainstream of unjust enrichment theory.

- Case 1—*informal dealings*: in a number of contexts, such as those involving either neighbours or close family, it would be outrageous if the generally applicable formalities were always applied. This is reflected in various doctrines, including proprietary estoppel, secret trusts, and *donationes mortis causa*, all of which are heavy with discretionary considerations. But the appropriate remedy is usually either to enforce the transaction as initially intended, or to recompense the claimant for expenditure in the belief that it would be carried through; either may, accidentally, happen to correspond to a measure of the other party's enrichment, but overall 'unjust enrichment' is a misleading focus.
- Case 2—*cohabitation*: as noted previously, some common law jurisdictions have found unjust enrichment a useful tool in providing a remedy to reflect contributions to the joint household over the course of a long cohabitation. Unsurprisingly, however, this has drawn away from the core of the

---

[162] Sarah Worthington, 'The Commercial Triple Helix: Contract, Property and Unjust Enrichment' in Peter Devonshire and Rohan Havelock (eds), *The Impact of Equity and Restitution in Commerce* (Hart Publishing 2019) 35–38, 63–64.

subject—neither the injustice nor the enrichment really fall to be judged by commercial standards—and so there is little to be gained by pretending that the law here is part of the same unitary entity as the mainstream.[163]

- *Case 3—improvers*: the primary question here is a classic property law question—does title to the improved property remain with its original owner, or can the improver claim to have some sort of shared ownership in it? Occasionally, there are cases where the strict property issue has gone against the improver, who nonetheless makes a personal claim against the owner to reflect their work. These cases are very rare, and successful claims reflect a number of different ideas, few of which are easy to fit into the straight-jacket of 'unjust enrichment'.[164]

- *Case 4—tracing*: this is a puzzle for mainstream property lawyers, because the process of tracing potentially leads through property of all different sorts, even though common law has little else to say about 'property' in general—there are very few propositions that can be taken as safely established as to realty *and* as to personal chattels *and* as to intellectual property *and* as to money (in all its many forms). This made it attractive to assert that the 'value' that tracing tracks is the same thing as the 'enrichment' in unjust enrichment. But this turns out to be illusory: the rules identifying when an asset is traceable owe nothing to the rules defining an 'enrichment'. For those already committed to a Birksian theory of unjust enrichment, it can be slotted into that theory,[165] but tells nothing about the relevant rules.[166]

This leaves the central case, of the simple transfer of property, which the transferor subsequently asserts that they did not *really* consent to, whether as a result of cognitive impairment, unfair pressure, or mistake. To which assertion the law has essentially three possible responses, if it responds at all: that title to the property at common law does not pass at all; that it passes at law but not in equity, and so can be recovered back subject to the rights of certain types of good faith recipients; or that title passes for all purposes, but a personal claim lies against the transferee. It

---

[163] For a general review of common law approaches, see Matthew Harding, 'The Limits of Equity in Disputes over Family Assets' in Jamie Glister and Pauline Ridge (eds), *Fault Lines in Equity* (Hart Publishing 2012). For the Scottish position, see Hector MacQueen, 'Cohabitants, Unjustified Enrichment and Law Reform (Part 1)' (2019) 160 Greens Family Law Bulletin 1; Hector MacQueen 'Cohabitants, Unjustified Enrichment and Law Reform (Part 2)' (2019) 161 Greens Family Law Bulletin 1.

[164] English and Welsh discussion tends to focus on *Greenwood v Bennett* [1973] QB 195 (CA): see Burrows, 'In Defence of Unjust Enrichment' (n 64) 534–35; Duncan Sheehan, 'The Property Principle and the Structure of Unjust Enrichment' (2011) 19 RLR 138, 158; Stevens, 'The Unjust Enrichment Disaster' (n 152) 584.

[165] See eg Birks, *Unjust Enrichment 2nd* (n 35) 198–201.

[166] See eg Peter Jaffey, 'Proprietary Claims to Recover Mistaken or Unauthorised Payments' in Peter Devonshire and Rohan Havelock (eds), *The Impact of Equity and Restitution in Commerce* (Hart Publishing 2019) 66–77; Jonathan Silver, 'Tracing Delusions' (2021) <http://ssrn.com/abstract=3848966> accessed 13 December 2022.

will be observed that these responses are strongly similar, differing principally as to *which* recipients of the asset in question are liable to make restitution. It seems reasonable, therefore, to treat them together.

This is the 'proprietary' theory of restitution, most fully elaborated (in different ways) by Peter Jaffey[167] and by Charlie Webb.[168] It certainly has the merit of being simple in conception—the root reason why a claimant might succeed is simply because they were recovering their property. As Webb notes, the core case is not that of the debt wrongly paid, but the (much less controversial) case of recovering stolen money from the thief who took it.[169] This opens the way to rational consideration of which recipients of the asset in question can fairly plead that the original payer's misfortune should not be remedied at their expense.

The 'unjust enrichment' solution, by contrast, awkwardly bifurcates the area by assuming that personal claims are justified by an entirely different theory from those justifying a proprietary claim, and then elaborately theorizes about when a personal claim might be upgraded to a proprietary claim ('when does unjust enrichment lead to a proprietary response?'[170]). The principal objection to treating the personal claim as strongly analogous to the proprietary claim appears to be the argument that if title has passed to the transferee, it makes no sense for the transferor to base their claim on property principles: the thing claimed is not their property, though it once was. With Webb,[171] I do not consider this a serious point. The claimant's argument is that, in a just world, it still would be the claimant's property; there are reasons why strict property law does not agree, but those reasons are insufficient to deny the moral force of the claim now being made. Just as equity sometimes recognizes x as owner because x *ought* to be owner, so a claimant in money had and received can argue for the recovery of money to which they should never have lost title; the claimant has 'moral title'.[172]

A major advantage of the 'proprietary' approach is that it makes it obvious from the first that the law may apply very different rules depending on the type of asset in question. The rules on mistaken transfer of land are not much like those for mistaken transfers of money,[173] and there is no a priori reason for anyone to think that

---

[167] Jaffey, *The Nature and Scope of Restitution* (n 148) chs 9–10.
[168] Webb, *Reason and Restitution* (n 123) ch 4.
[169] ibid 122.
[170] On the supposed 'proprietary response to unjust enrichment', see Birks, *Unjust Enrichment* 2nd (n 35) ch 8; Burrows, *The Law of Restitution* (n 49) ch 8; Aisha Shah, 'Unjust Enrichment and Proprietary Restitution' [2021] Conveyancer and Property Lawyer 352; Timothy Liau and Rachel Leow, 'Proprietary Restitution' in Elise Bant, Kit Barker, and Simone Degeling (eds), *Research Handbook on Unjust Enrichment and Restitution* (Edward Elgar 2020).
[171] Webb, *Reason and Restitution* (n 123) 70–73.
[172] Priel, 'The Justice in Unjust Enrichment' (n 12) 838–42; and compare equity's conflation of property we *actually* own with property we *ought* to own ('Equity Looks On That As Done Which Ought To Have Been Done'): Larissa Katz, 'Equitable Remedies: Protecting "What We Have Coming to Us"' (2021) 96 Notre Dame L Rev 1115.
[173] See eg Mark Diggle, 'Altering the Land Register on Grounds of Mistake' (*Ropewalk Chambers*, November 2019) <tinyurl.com/3x5k3dx3> accessed 13 December 2022.

they are. And the traditional approach of common law in allowing broad actions for money had and received and for money paid, yet providing no analogous actions for other assets, makes a great deal of sense in the light of the (practical and legal) ease with which strict legal title to money may be lost. 'Unjust enrichment', by contrast, treats these differences as indefensible anomalies, to be dissolved away by developing enrichment rules which explain (so far, to few people's satisfaction) what sum of money a given enrichment will be taken to represent, and even (to the satisfaction of even fewer) how services are to be valued. On this, the traditional common law is right and Birks is wrong: money *is* different from other assets, and the law should reflect this.[174]

Neither theory, of course, does a very good job of explaining when the personal claim is available; though since we are by definition concerned with a problem which (at least one of) the parties did not anticipate, certainty in the law is less important than it might otherwise be. Nonetheless, the uncertainty seems extreme. There is not yet consensus on whether we should be trying identify cases where the law should intervene ('unjust factors') or cases where it shouldn't ('just factors'), or both. It is unpredictable when a court will regard a particular misconception on a transferor's part as a 'mistake' (which may lead to liability) or a 'misprediction' (which will not). It is far from clear how much difference—if any—it makes that one of the parties was a public body rather than a private one.[175] And when the defence of 'change of position' should be available is a largely unanswered question. The truth is that in many cases there is very little to say in favour of either side's position—the claimant is asking to be relieved from the consequences of their own stupidity, the defendant is asking to keep a windfall they did nothing to deserve—and so it is no surprise that the court finds it hard to choose between them. And in one context at least, the law is beginning to look extremely un-rule-like, much more like a discretion, the test to be applied being whether the mistake was 'of so serious a character as to render it unjust on the part of the donee to retain the property given to him'.[176]

C. Contract

From an *ex ante* point of view, contract law is about deliberately planning future liabilities. It is a legal tool by which free and sovereign individuals (of age, entirely

---

[174] On the special position of money, see Hamish Dempster, 'A Closer Look at Account and Money Had and Received' (2016) 24 RLR 47.
[175] For comparative discussion, see Steven Elliott, Birke Häcker, and Charles Mitchell (eds), *Restitution of Overpaid Tax* (Hart Publishing 2013).
[176] This is the test as expressed in *Ogilvie v Littleboy* (1897) 13 TLR 399 (CA) 400 (Lindley LJ), upheld on appeal as *Ogilvie v Allen* (1899) 15 TLR 294 (HL), which was substantially reaffirmed in *Pitt v Holt* (n 100).

capable of managing their affairs, and no more influenced by others than they choose to be) mutually agree what each is to do and what legal consequences will follow if they do not. And respect for party intention operates both positively and negatively: the law imposes obligations where the parties agreed that there should be obligations, it declines to impose obligations where agreement was absent.

All well and good. But:

(1) In some cases, an actual agreement is impossible to discern, but it is nonetheless reasonable to assume that an agreement would have been made had the parties taken more time to spell out their intentions (as with services supplied on request) or if a sudden crisis had not rendered negotiations impossible (emergency salvage, 'agency of necessity', or *negotiorum gestio* cases). In a few of these cases, it is just to impose obligations *as if* the parties had agreed them.

(2) Rules on unfair pressure and cognitive impairment are blunt tools. In some cases, the impairment of one party's consent is sufficiently extreme that they can deny they made a contract, but in fact the apparent terms were justifiable and the other party has complied with them. An example would be an apparent agreement for necessary medical services, with the patient subsequently revealed as too mentally ill to make any such agreement. Very often, the fairest solution turns out to be to remunerate the service provider under the terms of the 'contract'.

(3) It may be that the contract was at some level illegal—should not have been made, or should not have been performed in the way that it was—and so is not fully enforceable. It does not always follow, however, that it must be ignored when analysing the mutual rights and entitlements of the parties.

(4) Subsequent events—whether a breach, or a frustrating event—may entitle one party to declare that the contract does not bind. Nonetheless, remuneration for work (whether done before or after the event that killed the contract) may still fairly depend on what the contract provided, and to that extent it is still treated as binding.[177]

Some writers reject this approach out of hand, arguing that either there is a contract or there isn't, and there is no scope for 'implying' a contract the parties themselves did not make.[178] In its cruder forms, this is a hopeless argument. Contract law is always having to provide details of agreements which parties did not see fit

---

[177] Other liabilities can also be suggested to be 'quasi-contractual'; for present purposes nothing turns on this, though the simile is not infinitely adaptable. See eg Jaffey, *The Nature and Scope of Restitution* (n 148) chs 2–4; Alexander Georgiou, 'Mistaken Payments, Quasi-Contracts, and the "Justice" of Unjust Enrichment' (2022) 42 OJLS 606.

[178] See Sheehan, 'Implied Contract and the Taxonomy of Unjust Enrichment' (n 158); Baloch (n 157).

to spell out for themselves; spelling out an obligation to pay (in a case where services were evidently being supplied on a commercial basis) is well within the range of obligations contract lawyers typically imply. More sophisticated versions of the objection complain rather that we should not talk of 'contract' where there was neither any kind of shared expectation nor any prospect of one. But analogy is a routine common law tool, and it is unclear why its use is being disclaimed here. In market sectors where the services in question are almost invariably supplied as a contractual matter, it is unsurprising that we might consider the analogy of contract when, exceptionally, they are supplied non-contractually but in an obviously reasonable (or even praiseworthy) manner. No doubt a court will look closely at the reason why no formal contract was made, but that reason will not always suggest a denial of liability. It would indeed be outrageous for a court to imply a contract without explanation (just as, indeed, it would be outrageous to assert that there had been 'unjust enrichment' without explanation); but no one has suggested that this should happen.

The first three cases can be dealt with relatively briefly:

- *Case 1: parties had capacity to contract, but didn't do so*: as a number of writers have observed, the bulk of the cases here are simply informal contracts: the service provider was always clear that they were acting on a commercial basis, and the service recipient knew this. It is entirely beside the point whether a binding commitment could have been inferred *before* the services were rendered. Analysing these cases as being concerned with 'unjust enrichment' merely complicates them, to no one's advantage: the law is not much interested in whether the recipient was actually enriched, as distinct from what the going market rate for the services was. In a tiny number of cases, no agreement can realistically be inferred, perhaps because the services were rendered in an emergency precluding any communication between the parties.[179] There seems to be a consensus that a few of these will merit being treated as contractual, where either the parties' prior relationship envisaged this, or the service provider's intervention was evidently meritorious and of a type deserving encouragement. Normative assessment usually suggest that this category of liability should be narrow, but not non-existent.[180]
- *Case 2: one of the parties lacked capacity, but both acted as if they were contracting*: in cases of personal incapacity (such as lack of age), the common law rule is simple: if the benefits supplied are necessary and reasonably priced,

---

[179] Priel, 'In Defence of Quasi-Contract' (n 149) 68–71.
[180] For discussion, see Dornis, 'No Man's Land' (n 48); William Day, 'Against Necessity as a Ground for Restitution' (2016) 24 RLR 26; Hanoch Dagan, 'In Defense of the Good Samaritan' (1999) 97 Mich L Rev 1152; Elliot S Rosenwald, 'Rethinking the Emergency-Room Surprise Billing Crisis: Why Are Patients Liable for Emergency Care They Do Not Seek?' (2021) 64 Wash U J L & Pol'y 253.

the recipient will be treated as having contracted despite their lack of capacity; otherwise, no contract. Again, an unjust enrichment analysis adds nothing: either the arrangement is contractual or it creates no liability at all, with no intermediate case where it makes the recipient return the enrichment.
- *Case 3: a contract was in fact made, but it was illegal*: it has long been settled that the illegality of a contract does not necessarily doom all claims made under it or in respect of it. In the current English approach, we need to consider the effect of the illegality on each such claim—would denial of the claim be proportionate to any wrongdoing? What was the purpose of the prohibition breached? What policy considerations were relevant?[181] This certainly does not suggest that making a restitutionary claim on these facts takes us outside the realm of contract; on the contrary, it leaves us well within it, considering what modifications need to be made to ordinary contract remedies in the light of the illegality. Treating the claim as somehow extra-contractual does nothing to aid the analysis.

The final case—where the contract was perfectly valid, but performance somehow misfired—is the one that has given rise to most debate. On the Birksian view, if the contract has failed—whether through breach or frustrating change of circumstances—then a distinct principle of unjust enrichment steps in to provide remedies. On the opposing view, any claims made are still entirely dependent on contract—either a money claim for payment on a failed consideration (a label which persists, despite Birks-inspired protestations that it is 'unfortunate'[182]), or a *quantum valebat* or *quantum meruit* claim (effectively, an argument that the parties made a fresh contract to replace the failed one). So on one view, unjust enrichment corrects an injustice arising from contract; on the other, any injustice is a *contractual* injustice.[183]

Fortunately, this difference of view makes little difference most of the time. Awkwardly for the Birksian view (though not fatally so), all acknowledge the priority of contract law here: anyone seeking a remedy not explicitly granted by the contract will have to establish a 'gap' in the contractual allocation of remedies, and any claim for remuneration for benefits conferred on a failure of consideration can be defeated by a demonstration that the claimant's contract allocated the risk of non-remuneration to the claimant. Still more awkward, the English courts

---

[181] *Patel v Mirza* [2016] UKSC 42; [2017] AC 467 [120] (Lord Toulson SCJ).
[182] Mitchell, Mitchell, and Watterson, *Goff & Jones 9th* (n 48) ch 3.38, which unconvincingly asserts that 'consideration' has a contractual meaning and an unjust enrichment meaning. In fact, both meanings (which are closely related, and rarely give rise to any confusion) are common currency in contract law.
[183] Peter Jaffey, 'The Unjust Enrichment Fallacy and Private Law' (2013) 26 CJLJ 115, 123–26.

have insisted that the failure (of the contract or of a severable part of to) be must total[184]—a restriction which makes a great deal of sense if priority of contract is an important principle here, not so much if contract and unjust enrichment are co-equal territories. But, mostly, it doesn't matter: contract lawyers assume this is part of contract law, unjust enrichment lawyers assume it is part of unjust enrichment law, but the two pictures are not so different.

The important question, however, is whether thinking of these issues as 'unjust enrichment' adds value. It is very hard to see that it does. Civil lawyers who doubt the utility of a highly abstract 'unjust enrichment' regard this area as a powerful example to buttress their case.[185] If the unjust enrichment theory is to bear any resemblance to the actual case law, the 'enrichment' would have to be equated with the going market rate at the time the enrichment is conferred; yet not only is this *not* how enrichment is measured in other contexts, but also it has proved necessary to introduce the notion of 'subjective devaluation', that if I did not desire the enriching item then its value is taken to be zero. But this is simply wrong as a theory of value. There would be many items I do not want (such as sports memorabilia for sports I have no interest in), but it would be highly contentious to say that *therefore* I regard them as valueless. This is simply a roundabout way of saying that I don't have to pay for a consignment of them unless I asked for that consignment, in circumstances where the supplier obviously meant to charge. And that is contractual reasoning.

A relatively recent suggestion for these (and other) liabilities is that a claimant can recover if their conferment of benefits can be styled a *performance*. Robert Stevens has recently suggested that many of the direct-enrichment cases can be summed up in a doctrine of restitution for 'performance', which consists of the reversal of something: (1) done by the claimant; (2) intended to have been done for the defendant; and (3) accepted by the defendant.[186] Yet 'performance' does not sound like a very promising doctrine in common law—it is 'a very odd use of the English language'[187] in many of the cases to which Stevens wishes to apply it—and is a very inadequate translation of the German *leistung* (though no better one is very obvious).[188] For present purposes, I need only say that if the acceptance

---

[184] This has been laid down many times, most recently (at the time of writing) in *London Trocadero (2015) LLP v Picturehouse Cinemas Ltd* [2021] EWHC 2591 (Ch). The position in Australia may be a little different: see *Mann v Paterson Constructions Pty Ltd* [2019] HCA 32; (2019) 267 CLR 560 on which see Wilmot-Smith, 'Contract and Unjust Enrichment in the High Court of Australia' (n 92).

[185] For various views, see Jansen, 'Farewell to Unjustified Enrichment?' (n 136) 141–42; MacQueen, 'The Sophistication of Unjustified Enrichment' (n 136) 322–24; Sonja Meier, 'Unwinding Failed Contracts: New European Developments' (2017) 21 Edin LR 1; Christiane Wendehorst, 'Restitution in the Proposal for a Common European Sales Law' (2012 PE 462.465, Directorate General for Internal Policies Policy Department C: Citizens' Rights and Constitutional Affairs).

[186] Stevens, 'The Unjust Enrichment Disaster' (n 152) 581; Stevens, 'Private Law and the Form of Reasons' (n 152) 13–133; Robert Stevens, Chapter 7 in this volume.

[187] Burrows, 'In Defence of Unjust Enrichment' (n 64) 531, and see more generally 531–36. For different criticisms, see Smith, 'Defences and the Disunity of Unjust Enrichment' (n 150) 48–51.

[188] For other criticisms, see Peter Jaffey, Chapter 11 in this volume.

by the defendant is clear, and the claimant was acting on a non-gratuitous basis, there seems to be no reason why such cases should not be regarded as implied contracts: both parties knew that payment was expected and went ahead on that basis.

D. Wrongs

The standard common law remedy for wrongdoing—whether tortious, contractual, equitable, or other—is compensation for the victim, a sum of money calculated to represent what the claimant has lost. Exceptionally, other remedies are made available, whether consisting of a different measure of money, or perhaps a different sort of judicial order entirely. One suggestion often made in this context is that there should be a money award, measured not by reference to the claimant's loss from the wrong but by reference to the defendant's gain. This is immediately controversial, because it looks rather similar to *punishing* the defendant for their wrongdoing, which only some commentators think is a legitimate thing for private law to be doing.

Argument over when the law can really be said to be departing from the compensatory measure is bedevilled by terminology. Some would consider a remedy for feelings injured or outraged by defendant's conduct to have departed from purely compensatory norms, whereas others feel that such 'aggravated' damages can still legitimately be described as compensation. Again, there is regular controversy over the 'licence fee' cases, where a defendant took liberties with the claimant's proprietary or other rights, liberties which the claimant might well have consented to if paid an appropriate fee, but which the defendant took for nothing. If a court remedies this breach of rights by ordering payment of the fee at current market rates, is it: (1) compensating the claimant for loss of a market opportunity; or (2) forcing the defendant to disgorge a benefit wrongly acquired; or (3) imputing a contract between the parties—the contract they should have made? Views differ, and no one point of view seems to have a killer argument.[189]

The difficulty in basing all or most of this on unjust enrichment is, of course, that it is entirely inflexible, as it ties the law to the proposition that the remedy will consist of (some measure of) the defendant's enrichment, no more and no less.

---

[189] For various views, see Jaffey, *The Nature and Scope of Restitution* (n 148) ch 4; Andrew Burrows, 'Negotiating Damages' in Charles Mitchell and Stephen Watterson (eds), *The World of Maritime and Commercial Law—Essays in Honour of Francis Rose* (Hart Publishing 2020); Katy Barnett, 'Gain-Based Damages' in Roger Halson and David Campbell (eds), *Research Handbook on Remedies in Private Law* (Edward Elgar 2019) 319–26; Charles Mitchell and Luke Rostill, 'Making Sense of Mesne Profits: Causes of Action' (2021) 80 CLJ 130; Charles Mitchell and Luke Rostill, 'Making Sense of Mesne Profits: Remedies' (2021) 80 CLJ 552; Matthew J Forrest, 'Understanding Loss of (Right To) Use Damages: Defining Fair and Reasonable Compensation for Loss of Use in Light of Historical Origins and Practical Considerations' (2022) 42 Pace L Rev 247.

Yet if (as most commentators seem to assume) the object is to deter wrongdoing, it is only by accident that this will be the appropriate measure; on many occasions the award should be higher, on many other occasions lower. Statements that such-and-such a remedy may act as an appropriate deterrent are easy to make, but hard to demonstrate with any rigour (as is the related contention that the remedy is appropriately 'expressive'[190]); and if this talk of 'deterrence' is seriously meant, then perhaps more attention should be paid to what law-and-economics scholars have to say on the matter, as this is their focus.[191] As it is, the law here is 'in a state of confusion and flux',[192] and without clearer thought on what the law is trying to achieve, it seems likely to remain so.

E. Multiple Liabilities

Private law is not overall very well integrated: the same set of facts may give an injured claimant a number of different avenues of recourse against different individuals, without establishing any particular priority between them. So a claimant may exercise whichever right of action is most convenient. If two defendants are severally liable for the same tort, the claimant may sue either or both; if one defendant guaranteed a loan made to another, the creditor may sue either or both. Crucially, claimants need not concern themselves with the justice of this: they may employ whichever right of action yields the quickest and most efficacious results. Yet *as between the two defendants* it may be more just that one should pay rather than the other.

This, then, is the final problem routinely encountered in restitution cases: one party has paid a debt which, as between themselves and another, ought to have been paid by that other. Unfortunately, the law here developed over the centuries under a number of different headings, which have only been very imperfectly united into a single conception. First, the law began to recognize that debts could be assigned, so if the payer could seek reimbursement if they were not so much 'paying another's debt' as purchasing the benefit of that debt from the creditor. Secondly, in some contexts it was recognized that a payer could recover in cases of 'contribution' (= fully paying a debt which the two of them were equally liable for) or 'compulsion' (= being forced to pay another's debt). Thirdly, the rather amorphous doctrine of 'subrogation' arose—a more general idea that one who paid another's debt could 'step into the shoes' of the creditor. This increased not only the range of situations where

---

[190] See eg Sigurd Lindstad, 'Benefiting from Wrongdoing and Moral Protest' (2021) 24 Ethical Theory and Moral Practice 753.

[191] See eg Antony W Dnes and Nuno Garoupa, 'Efficient Breach and Ex-Post Disgorgement of the Defendant's Gain: A Comparative Contract Law and Economics Perspective' (2022) 18 European Review of Contract Law 32.

[192] Barnett (n 189) 330.

liability could be found, but also the scope of the remedy—if the original debt was secured, the payer might be subrogated to the creditor's securities. Finally, statute introduced a number of discretions, under which the payer might ask the court to apportion the debt fairly as between all who could have been found liable.[193]

Unfortunately, very little has been done to bring all of these threads together, and the law is still generally discussed under different heads such as 'recoupment' and 'subrogation' as distinct entities. Vital theoretical questions are not answered: bluntly, we have no good common law theory on what happens when a debt is paid. And the policy of the law is obscure. All can see the justice of allowing recovery where one is *forced* to pay another's debt (though determining that the debt is truly 'another's', rather than one's own, is still pretty seat-of-the-pants stuff)—but what if the decision to pay that debt was not forced on the payer, but was entirely voluntary? The law is confused, with some cases saying compulsion is necessary, others denying it, and yet others allowing for a 'compulsion' that is evidently bogus (because the 'compelled' party could easily have escaped the compulsion if they had wished to). There is clearly a problem here meriting a solution.

Can the doctrine of unjust enrichment supply that solution? It is not obvious what it adds. Demonstrating that there is an 'enrichment' in these cases requires considerable theoretical work; and the 'unjust factors' certainly do not map neatly onto the instances where liability has been found. 'Unjust' and 'enrichment' would have to be given rather different meanings from those they bear in other contexts—which from a Birksian point of view defeats the purpose of the explanation. As Leeming notes, the question is not whether the law *can* be described in terms of unjust enrichment, but rather: 'Would the resultant reasoning be less opaque, and would the law be more coherent or more predictable? It seems likely that the reverse would ordinarily be the case.'[194] An insistence that it is nonetheless an example of unjust enrichment appears to be a mere theoretical exercise rather than an aid in deciding these cases; 'labelling something as a remedy for unjust enrichment seems to be an expository classification and not a dispositive one'.[195]

V. Conclusion

The thesis that 'unjust enrichment' is an integrated unit in private law has had a good run in common law scholarship, over half a century. Its implications have been thoroughly explored. And the overwhelming conclusion is that its supposed coherence has, at best, been considerably overstated. Unjust enrichment is not an

---

[193] See Hedley, *Restitution: Its Division and Ordering* (n 155) ch 5.
[194] Mark Leeming, 'Subrogation, Equity and Unjust Enrichment' in Jamie Glister and Pauline Ridge (eds), *Fault Lines in Equity* (Hart Publishing 2012) 40. See also Rob Merkin and Jenny Steele, *Insurance and the Law of Obligations* (OUP 2013) 100–02.
[195] Rory Gregson, 'Is Subrogation a Remedy for Unjust Enrichment?' (2020) 136 LQR 481, 505.

island, entire of itself. It is at best an archipelago, most likely it is a mere collection of offshore islets; and the interesting and significant thing about these islets is not any connection they have with each other, but the connection each has with some portion of the main body of the law. No doubt we learn *something* by considering these islets together, though (lacking any solid theory to pull them together) such studies will likely be miles wide yet inches deep. A fuller understanding seems more attainable by exploring the connections to the wider law.

15
Embracing Private Law's Miscellany?
Unjustified Enrichment and the Civilian Category of Quasi-Contracts

Pablo Letelier[*]

I. Introduction

Despite relentless criticism from generations of French lawyers, the notion of quasi-contract still plays a role in the division and ordering of the French law of obligations. This role was confirmed by the recent reform of the French Civil Code, which undertook the most significant revamp of the rules applicable to obligations beyond contracts and delicts since 1804. Departing from the approach adopted by other major European legal systems, the reform persisted in recognizing quasi-contracts as one of the main sources of obligations in contemporary French private law.

This may come as a surprise in common law jurisdictions, where the notion of quasi-contracts has been decried as a form of heresy.[1] After attaining some prominence during the nineteenth century, this long-standing category was replaced by an entirely different approach to non-contractual obligations, which focused on the alleged common principles governing the restitution of unjust enrichment. While this approach would eventually become the dominant position, its far-fetched ambitions swung the pendulum back to earlier times. Today, the conclusion that beyond contracts and wrongs there is only a miscellany of obligations seems to be gaining traction once again.

In this context, the chapter explores the recent evolution of the notion of quasi-contract in French law, focusing on the reasons behind its inclusion in the latest reform of the French Civil Code. The chapter argues that, unlike what first impressions may suggest, modern French law does not conceive the quasi-contract category as a mere collection of situations giving rise to entirely different

---

[*] I would like to thank Lionel Smith, James Penner, and Hanoch Dagan for their insightful comments on an earlier version of this chapter. I would also like to thank Adrián Schopf, Francesco Cámpora, and the other participants of the 'Seminario de Investigación' hosted by the Universidad de Chile Department of Private Law, which helped me to further refine this chapter's arguments. All remaining errors are mine alone.

[1] Peter Birks, *Unjust Enrichment* (2nd edn, OUP 2005) 268 (hereafter Birks, *Unjust Enrichment 2nd*).

non-contractual obligations. In fact, the reform seems to have chosen to preserve this category out of a belief that some coherence would exist among the rules governing such obligations. The way in which this idea became accepted by French lawyers and its consequences in the decision of cases involving obligations arising outside contracts or delicts may help to evaluate the convenience of abandoning the 'restitution of unjust enrichment' approach in common law jurisdictions.

The chapter is divided as follows. Section II describes the place of quasi-contracts in contemporary English law, as an example of the role played by this notion in some common law jurisdictions. Section III explains the recent evolution of the quasi-contract category in French law and details the place this category found in the latest reform of the Civil Code. Section IV explores some of the difficulties following from the persistence of the quasi-contract category in contemporary French law. Section V summarizes the main conclusions and identifies some outstanding questions.

II. A New Appeal for Quasi-Contracts

While it may seem all but forgotten today, the notion of quasi-contract was once widely accepted in common law jurisdictions. Following one of the most dramatic changes experienced by private law research and teaching in the last century, that notion was replaced by an entirely different approach to obligations arising beyond contracts and wrongs. According to this approach, the kind of situations where quasi-contracts were relevant ought to be analysed as spawning a right to reverse the defendant's unjust enrichment.

The 'restitution of unjust enrichment' approach has recently been subject to serious objections. Some of them seem to suggest that common law jurisdictions would be better off by restoring the notion of quasi-contract and accepting the inherent diversity which distinguished situations where the notion was relevant. This section explains the seeming revival of a doctrine which until recently appeared to be banished from modern private law.

A. Quasi-Contracts and Implied Contracts

By the beginning of the nineteenth century, the orthodox analysis of obligations outside contracts and wrongs looked very different than it does today. In the case of English law, the complex history of the action of assumpsit had led common law lawyers to assume that claims for the recovery of mistaken payments or contribution between co-sureties, for example, were recognized because an implied promise by the defendant to pay the claimant was deemed to have taken place between them. The basis of liability in these cases was hardly comparable to the basis of liability in claims governed by the law of contracts. Yet an 'orgy of fictions' enabled the courts to treat the rules applicable to these unusual situations as a branch of contractual liability. Borrowing a term from civilian legal systems, the situations in which these claims were available came to be known as 'quasi-contracts'.[2]

Much of the blame for the adoption of this approach was laid at the door of the influential William Blackstone, who endorsed the doctrine that quasi-contractual obligations rested on actual promises and belonged to the law of contracts.[3] Importantly, Blackstone did not explain this doctrine as an unintended result of the kind of pragmatic and piecemeal developments which characterized much of the history of the common law.[4] Instead, he saw the implied contract theory as providing an appropriate solution to the puzzle of why all legal systems recognize obligations arising involuntarily which are not premised upon wrongdoing.[5]

Yet the range of situations covered by the law of quasi-contracts raised issues which tended to be obscured by Blackstone's implied contract theory. For example, in *Sinclair v Brougham*, the House of Lords infamously held that money paid under *ultra vires* contracts was not recoverable through an action in quasi-contract, because the law could not imply promises repayment in situations where an actual promise would be indisputably void.[6] And in *Cowern v Nield*, it was held that no action in quasi-contract could lie to recover from a minor against whom no real contract could be enforced.[7] In both cases, the court's analysis about the plausibility of an implied contract disregarded the key question of whether the law should recognize a non-contractual claim to recover money paid under a contract which was subsequently avoided.

These types of decision ultimately resulted in a consensus emerging which concluded that the implied contract theory must be wrong.[8] After all, it was a fictional approach which did not provide any positive criteria to establish in which situations an obligation should be recognized. On the contrary, it concealed the similarities existing between different claims to recover benefits in situations where no contract and no wrongful conduct could be identified.[9] A new approach focusing on these similarities was needed to bring coherence and clarity to the law outside contracts and wrongs. This approach renamed the law of quasi-contract as the law of restitution of unjust enrichment.

---

[2] DJ Ibbetson, *A Historical Introduction to the Law of Obligations* (OUP 1999) 276.
[3] 3 Bl Comm 158–66.
[4] On which, see Warren Swain, Chapter 1 in this volume.
[5] Blackstone offered the notion of quasi-contracts as proof that a 'social contract' explained all legal consequences imposed on people by operation of the law. See Peter Birks and Grant McLeod, 'The Implied Contract Theory of Quasi-Contract: Civilian Opinion Current in the Century Before Blackstone' (1986) 6 OJLS 46, 51; Peter Birks, *An Introduction to the Law of Restitution* (rev edn, OUP 1989) 36–37.
[6] *Sinclair v Brougham* [1914] AC 398 (HL) 452 (Lord Sumner).
[7] *Cowern v Nield* [1912] 2 KB 419 (KB) 313–15.
[8] Robert Goff and Gareth H Jones, *The Law of Restitution* (Sweet & Maxwell 1966) 10.
[9] Andrew Burrows, *The Law of Restitution* (3rd edn, OUP 2011) 28.

B. Making Sense of a Residual Miscellany

Under the new approach, the law of obligations recognized a 'third pillar' beyond contracts and wrongs, where liability originated as an instantiation of the principle against unjust enrichment. This principle explained why a right to recover a benefit obtained by the defendant was recognized in all various situations previously examined as quasi-contracts. Significant consequences followed. Earlier decisions were explained from a new perspective,[10] and established rules—such as the rule preventing recovery of money paid under a mistake of law—were overturned.[11] By the end of the twentieth century, common law lawyers had become used to the language of restitution of unjust enrichment, and the notion of quasi-contracts was almost entirely removed from textbooks on private law.[12]

An important concern of this new approach was mapping the structure of the law of obligations. This concern is particularly apparent in the work of Peter Birks, who persistently remarked on the merits of a classificatory scheme such as that adopted by civilian legal systems.[13] In his view, one of the main advantages of the restitution of unjust enrichment approach was that it promoted a clearer understanding of the boundaries existing between obligations arising from contracts, wrongs, and the miscellany of other events existing beyond these two main categories. Obligations—and the rights corresponding to their positive end—originated either from manifestations of consent (including contracts and declarations of trust); wrongs (including torts, equitable wrongs, and breaches of statutory duties); unjust enrichment (including most situations formerly examined as giving rise to quasi-contracts, as well as other situations covered by discrete equitable doctrines); or from a residual miscellany of various other events.[14]

Birks frequently noted that recognizing the category of 'miscellaneous other events' was a sort of cheat, because it only served the purpose of ensuring the veracity of the classification, without saying anything useful about the other assorted events.[15] These events included, for example, an uninvited intervention in the affairs of another (or *negotiorum gestio*), and the liability to pay taxes. While the restitution of unjust enrichment approach did not claim to provide a single explanation for all these events, it played a key role in reducing the size of the residual miscellany, which needed to be restrained if the common law were to attain rationality and avoid haphazard and incoherent decisions. In Birks's view, such an approach was necessary to save quasi-contractual obligations from being unintelligible.[16]

---

[10] See eg *Unjust Enrichment 2nd* (n 1), reinterpreting *Kelly v Solari* (1841) 9 M & W 54; 152 ER 24.
[11] See eg *Kleinwort Benson Ltd v Lincoln CC* [1999] 2 AC 349 (HL) 385 (Lord Goff).
[12] Ibbetson (n 2) 288.
[13] See eg Peter Birks, 'Equity in the Modern Law: An Exercise in Taxonomy' (1996) 26 UWAL Rev 1 (hereafter Birks, 'Equity in the Modern Law'); Peter Birks, 'Definition and Division: A Meditation on *Institutes* 3.13' in Peter Birks (ed), *The Classification of Obligations* (OUP 1997) 3–4.
[14] Birks, *Unjust Enrichment 2nd* (n 1) 21–22.
[15] Birks, 'Equity in the Modern Law' (n 13) 9–10.
[16] Birks, *Unjust Enrichment 2nd* (n 1) 22.

C. A Dustbin Category?

While the restitution of unjust enrichment approach has proven to be controversial,[17] it is difficult to deny its massive influence in common law legal systems. In the case of English law, for example, it seems to have completely replaced the implied contract theory of quasi-contractual obligations.[18] Several decisions delivered by the UK Supreme Court over the last few years have confirm the acceptance of unjust enrichment as a distinct area of the law of obligations.[19]

Yet the case has been made that this approach may result in more harm than good to the common law. Two forms of criticism seem particularly relevant to illustrate the point. According to a first, this approach assumes that all cases covered by the unjust enrichment category should be subject to the same conditions of liability, when in fact in many of them the defendant's liability might be—and, indeed, has historically been—subject to quite different rules.[20] According to the second form of criticism, the restitution of unjust enrichment approach may lead both courts and commentators to extend liability beyond recognized causes of action, under circumstances where it seems evident as a matter of authority and even common sense that no liability should arise.[21]

Underlying these objections lies a fundamental doubt about the feasibility of the unjust enrichment taxonomic project. Unlike contracts and wrongs, the area of the law this approach endeavours to explain comprises different types of claim which can be hardly justified by the same reasoning. For all its inconveniences, the previously abandoned category of quasi-contracts did at least enable the identification of a distinct group of claims from those originating in contracts or wrongs, without disregarding their inherent diversity. Now that the fictional implied contract theory has been decisively abandoned, a 'dustbin category' of quasi-contracts may serve the common law better than a unified category of restitution of unjust

---

[17] See eg Steve Hedley, *Restitution: Its Division and Ordering* (Sweet & Maxwell 2001) ch 9; Peter Jaffey, *Private Law and Property Claims* (Hart Publishing 2007) ch 8; Peter G Watts, '"Unjust Enrichment"—The Potion that Induces Well-Meaning Sloppiness of Thought' (2016) 69 CLP 289.

[18] See eg *Westdeutsche Landesbank Girozentrale v Islington London BC* [1996] AC 669 (HL) 710 (Lord Browne-Wilkinson): 'The common law restitutionary claim is based not on implied contract but on unjust enrichment: in the circumstances the law imposes an obligation to repay rather than implying an entirely fictitious agreement to repay.'

[19] See *Investment Trust Companies v Revenue and Customs Comrs* [2017] UKSC 29; [2018] AC 275 [39]–[40]; *Swynson Ltd v Lowick Rose LLP* [2017] UKSC 32; [2018] AC 313 [22]; *Prudential Assurance Co Ltd v Revenue and Customs Comrs* [2018] UKSC 39; [2019] AC 929 [36], [40], [72].

[20] See eg Robert Stevens, 'The Unjust Enrichment Disaster' (2018) 134 LQR 574, 577; Lionel Smith, 'Restitution: A New Start?' in Peter Devonshire and Rohan Havelock (eds), *The Impact of Equity and Restitution in Commerce* (Hart Publishing 2019) 90.

[21] Consider the case of an upper floor tenant who is benefited by the heat rising from the claimant's flat, the lower floor neighbour. The unjust enrichment analysis may lead us to the conclusion that the defendant is enriched at the expense of the claimant, and thus a restitutionary claim for value should be recognized. Yet courts and commentators have long acknowledged that no liability should arise in this kind of scenario. See eg Stevens, 'The Unjust Enrichment Disaster' (n 20) 578; Smith, 'Restitution: A New Start?' (n 20) 92–93.

enrichment, as it does not threaten to distort the particular rules governing the miscellany of claims beyond contracts and wrongs.[22]

III. The Resilience of Quasi-Contracts in French Law

Considered from a comparative perspective, French private law stands out for preserving the Roman division of the law of obligations into four key categories: contracts, delicts, quasi-contracts, and quasi-delicts. While the notion of quasi-delict has lost its importance due to the expansive development of the law of civil wrongs (or extra-contractual liability), rights and obligations organized under the quasi-contract category remain clearly distinct. Unlike other civilian systems, and particularly the German system, French law has chosen not to recognize a unified unjustified enrichment law as a 'third pillar' of the law of obligations, opting instead to maintain a number of discrete quasi-contracts governed by different sets of rules.

This remarkable feature may indicate that French law provides an appropriate illustration of how a 'dustbin category' helps to arrange claims which do not fit well within other better known branches of the law of obligations. Indeed, the lack of a unified regime applicable to quasi-contracts suggests that French lawyers are happy with the conclusion that beyond contracts and delicts lies only a miscellany of events which are better left undisturbed. This section reviews the recent evolution of the quasi-contract category in French law to show that unification projects are not entirely alien to French private law.

A. Roman Roots and Nineteenth-Century Developments

Quasi-contracts have a long history in the French legal system. In Roman law, the notion of a contract was initially used to indicate lawful acts generating obligations, even where those acts did not reflect genuine consent between the parties. Understood in this way, a dichotomy between contracts and delicts or unlawful acts exhausted the division of obligations. Eventually, the notion of a contract evolved to indicate acts expressing consent of the persons bound by them. This evolved notion of contract, however, left unexplained a number of lawful but non-consensual acts, including, most notably, the receipt of undue payments, which gave rise to consequences similar to those following from the contract of loan or *mutuum*, and the unsolicited intervention in the affairs of another, which gave rise to consequences such as those following from the contract of mandate or *mandatum*.

---

[22] Hedley, *Restitution: Its Division and Ordering* (n 17) 228; Smith, 'Restitution: A New Start?' (n 20) 99–100, 105–106; Robert Stevens, *The Laws of Restitution* (OUP 2023) 28–30.

Thus, later commentators adopted the notion of *quasi ex contractu* to emphasize that obligations following from these lawful but non-consensual acts originated 'as though upon a contract', when in reality there was none.[23]

Pothier preserved the Roman category of quasi-contracts, renouncing any ambition of identifying a theme unifying obligations beyond contracts and delicts.[24] In traditional fashion, he conceived quasi-contracts as acts permitted by the law which created an obligation between two persons even if no contract existed between them.[25] This notion was consistent with the entirely negative approach adopted by Roman law, which emphasized that obligations arising *quasi ex contractu* did not originate in a contract or a delict. Pothier noted that these obligations were underpinned by natural justice,[26] and went on to explain the rules governing the Roman actions of *negotiorum gestio* and *condictio indebiti*, among other quasi-contracts recognized by Roman law.[27]

The drafters of the French Civil Code of 1804 followed these ideas closely, as they did with most of Pothier's work on the law of obligations. Thus, original art 1371 of the French Civil Code did not provide any positive criterion to distinguish quasi-contracts, stating only that they were voluntary actions from which resulted commitments to third parties, and sometimes reciprocal commitments between two parties.[28] No unifying theme was acknowledged. Instead, the rules ascribed by Pothier to the Roman *negotiorum gestio* and *condictio indebiti* were organized under two separate headings, dealing respectively with the quasi-contract of *gestion d'affaires* and *répétition de l'indu*.[29]

In line with these definitions, the French Civil Code did not include a general clause on unjustified enrichment, or any explicit reference to a common principle underpinning obligations arising from quasi-contracts.[30] Soon after the enactment of the Code, however, it became apparent that the specific rules provided

---

[23] Peter Birks, *The Roman Law of Obligations* (Eric Descheemaeker ed, OUP 2014) 249. For a detailed account, see Eric Descheemaeker, *The Division of Wrongs: A Historical Comparative Study* (OUP 2009) 65.

[24] This sober approach led some commentators to pour scorn on Pothier. See eg John P Dawson, *Unjust Enrichment: A Comparative Analysis* (Little, Brown 1951) 95, describing Pothier as 'a man of quite inferior talent, with a gift for simplification'.

[25] '[L]e fait d'une personne permis par la loi, qui l'oblige envers une autre, ou oblige une autre personne envers elle, sans qu'il intervienne aucune convention entre elles': Robert Joseph Pothier, *Traité des obligations* (Dalloz 2011) 52.

[26] '[C]'est la loi seule ou l'équité naturelle qui produit l'obligation': ibid 53.

[27] JM Augustin, 'Les Classifications des Sources des Obligations de Domat au Code Civil' in Vincenzo Mannino and Claude Ophèle (eds), *L'Enrichissement sans Cause: La classification des sources des obligations* (LGDJ 2007) 126–27. Interestingly, Pothier did not adopt the implied contract theory of quasi-contract promoted by some of his civilian contemporaries, most notably Grotius. See Birks and McLeod (n 5) 58.

[28] '[L]es faits purement volontaires de l'homme, dont il résulte un engagement quelconque envers un tiers, et quelque fois un engagement réciproque des deux parties.'

[29] See old arts 1372 and 1376 of the French Civil Code.

[30] EJH Schrage and B Nicholas, 'Unjust Enrichment and the Law of Restitution: A Comparison' in Eltjo JH Schrage (ed), *Unjust Enrichment: The Comparative Legal History of the Law of Restitution* (2nd edn, Duncker & Humblot 1999) 22.

for the two recognized quasi-contracts were insufficient to deal with a number of situations where obligations seemed to arise despite no contract or civil wrong existing. For example, if outside a contractual setting a claimant mistakenly rendered a service to the defendant, no form of recovery could be pursued, because the quasi-contract of *répétition de l'indu* only covered cases where the claimant transferred a sum of money or other form of property.[31] To deal with this and other resulting inadequacies, the courts were pushed to reconsider the French Civil Code's laconism on quasi-contracts by adopting two different doctrines.

On the one hand, the scope of the quasi-contract of *gestion d'affaires* was expanded to enable a claimant to recover in cases where a defendant obtained a benefit from the claimant's unrequested services, even if those services were not intended to benefit the defendant, as required by the French Civil Code. This doctrine, known as *gestion d'affaires anormale*, found support in the work of Pothier, who concluded that a person who benefited another as a consequence of mistakenly intervening in their affairs should always have a claim based on the principle that no person should be enriched at the expense of another.[32]

On the other hand, a general action in unjustified enrichment, known as *enrichissement sans cause*, was recognized by the Cour de cassation in 1892 as a claim provided by French private law to cover every situation not addressed by the established quasi-contracts where a defendant obtained an undeserved benefit at the expense of a claimant.[33]

Both doctrines would prove instrumental in persuading French lawyers that the same logic may lie behind all quasi-contractual obligations.

B. An Underlying Coherence

At the turn of the twentieth century, French lawyers did not recognize any common rationale binding quasi-contracts together. In fact, the very idea of a quasi-contract was considered to be an inconvenient anachronism which needed to be ousted from French private law. According to widely accepted opinion, the drafters of the Civil Code had misunderstood the relevance of quasi-contracts in Roman law, where the notion was never used to describe an independent source of obligations.[34] Perhaps the most prominent exponent of this opinion was Henry Vizioz, who criticized the notion of quasi-contracts as being useless, as they did not reveal

---

[31] François Terré and others, *Droit civil: Les obligations* (12th edn, Dalloz 2018) para 1362.
[32] Christian P Filios, *L'enrichissement sans cause en droit privé français: analyse interne et vues comparatives* (Emile Bruylant 1999) 81.
[33] Jacques Flour, Jean-Luc Aubert, and Éric Savaux, *Droit civil: Les obligations, vol II: Le fait juridique* (14th edn, Sirey 2011) 41.
[34] See eg G Ripert and M Teisseire, 'Essai d'une théorie de l'enrichissement sans cause en droit civil français' (1904) Revue Trimestrielle de Droit Civil 741.

anything relevant about the rules governing the situations recognized as quasi-contracts; this was dangerous as it led to the conclusion that the rules governing contracts may also apply to quasi-contracts; and was also false, as it suggested that there was some unity among obligations that had nothing in common.[35]

In that context, French lawyers had no reason to bring the recently recognized general unjustified enrichment action into the fold of the quasi-contract category. While some authors saw a vague relation between the quasi-contracts established in the Civil Code and *enrichissement sans cause*, most commentators believed that the obligation explained by the doctrine found its source directly in law.[36] In fact, many believed that French law had to reject the quasi-contract category altogether and adopt a position where the only sources of obligations beyond contracts and delicts would be *negotiorum gestio* and unjustified enrichment.[37] It is thus unsurprising that the French courts did not recognize any explicit connection between quasi-contracts and unjustified enrichment until at least 1960.[38]

During the 1960s, however, the situation radically changed. The catalyst seems to have been the work of the influential Jean Carbonnier, who revisited earlier accounts of the law of obligations to conclude that there was, in fact, a deep connection between quasi-contracts and unjustified enrichment.[39] This connection was particularly evident in the rules governing the quasi-contract of *répétition de l'indu*, the French version of the Roman *condictio indebiti*, as had been noted time and again since the time of Grotius. In addition, it was also apparent in the rules applicable to the quasi-contract of *gestion d'affaires*, as demonstrated by the doctrine of *gestion d'affaires anormale*. Both quasi-contracts were specific instances of the same principle underpinning the doctrine of *enrichissement sans cause*; that is, the Roman maxim according to which no one should be enriched at the expense of another. Thus, the sources of obligations recognized by French law beyond contracts could be conveniently divided into two types: delicts, or acts resulting in harm, and quasi-contracts, or acts resulting in profit.[40]

Carbonnier's elegant scheme did not take long to become accepted and further developed by many French commentators.[41] Despite the uncontested criticism

---

[35] Henry Vizioz, *La Notion de Quasi-contrat, Étude Historique et Critique* (Cadoret 1912) para 75.
[36] See eg François Goré, *L'enrichissement aux dépens d'autrui, Source autonome et générale d'obligations en droit privé français* (Dalloz 1949).
[37] A Colin and H Capitant, *Cours élémentaire de droit civil français*, vol 2 (7th edn, Dalloz 1932) paras 6–7; L Josserand, *Cours de droit civil positif français*, vol 2 (3rd edn, Sirey 1939) para 10; G Marty and P Raynaud, *Droit civil: Les obligations*, vol 1 (2nd edn, Paris: Sirey 1988) para 378; Boris Starck, Henri Roland, and Laurent Boyer, *Droit civil: Les obligations, vol II: Contrat* (6th edn, Litec 1998) para 2126.
[38] Mélodie Combot, *Quasi-contrat et enrichissement injustifié* (LGDJ 2023) para 229.
[39] See eg Charles Toullier, *Le droit civil français suivant l'ordre du Code*, vol 11 (Warée & Warée 1824) para 112; Marcel Planiol, *Traité élémentaire de droit civil*, vol 2 (LGDJ 2018) paras 807, 811.
[40] J Carbonnier, *Droit civil, vol II: Les biens, les obligations* (PUF 2004) para 1114.
[41] See eg M Douchy, *La notion de quasi-contrat en droit positif français* (Economica 1997); Flour, Aubert, and Savaux (n 33) para 1; Yvaine Buffelan-Lanore and Virginie Larribau-Terneyre, *Droit civil: Les obligations* (15th edn, Sirey 2016) para 1972; Terré and others (n 31) para 1263; Bertrand Fages, *Droit des obligations* (10th edn, LGDJ 2020) para 457.

directed against the notion of quasi-contract since the enactment of the French Civil Code in 1804, the idea that the different quasi-contracts were inspired by a common rationale became the dominant position. On the eve of the Code's reform in 2016, it seemed that the notion of a quasi-contract had finally found a meaningful purpose in French law.[42]

C. Quasi-Contracts After the Reform

The new art 1300 of the French Civil Code provides that quasi-contracts are events giving rise to 'a duty in a person who benefits from them without having a right to do so'.[43] This formulation echoes the conclusion that all quasi-contracts reflect the principle against unjustified enrichment and can be distinguished from other non-contractual sources of obligations, because they involve 'profitable' conduct as opposed to 'harmful' conduct.[44]

At least two other innovations confirm that the reform was inspired by the unifying ideas popularized by Carbonnier.

First, the new arts 1303 to 1303-4 establish *enrichissement injustifié*, or unjustified enrichment, as a third quasi-contract alongside the traditional *gestion d'affaires* and *répétition de l'indu*. This 'new' quasi-contract is no different from the action of *enrichissement sans cause* recognized by French case law since the end of the nineteenth century, and the reform merely codified the rules already developed by the courts and commentators to limit the scope of such a claim. In doing so, however, the reform seems to have confirmed that unjustified enrichment was the quasi-contract of general application, and that *negotiorum gestio* and *répétition de l'indu* were only specific instances of the principle underpinning the whole quasi-contract category—that is, the principle against unjustified enrichment.[45]

Secondly, art 1300 of the French Civil Code deliberately left the door open for recognition of additional quasi-contracts.[46] This is confirmed by the preamble to the reform, which clarifies that the list of quasi-contracts is not exhaustive and that innominate quasi-contracts may be recognized in situations not covered by the rules provided for in the Code.[47] Considering that the reform does not adopt a

---

[42] François Chénedé, *Le nouveau droit des obligations et des contrats* (2nd edn, Dalloz 2018) para 131.
[43] Article 1300 of the French Civil Code provides: 'Quasi-contracts are purely voluntary actions which result in a duty in a person who benefits from them without having a right to do so, and sometimes a duty in the person performing them towards another person...'
[44] This solution was proposed in Pierre Catala, *Avant-projet de Réforme du Droit des Obligations et de la Prescription* (Ministère de la Justice, 22 September 2005) 75.
[45] Eric Descheemaeker, 'The New French Law of Unjustified Enrichment' (2017) 25 RLR 77, 79.
[46] Chénedé (n 42) 130–31; Olivier Deshayes, Thomas Génicon, and Yves-Marie Laithier, *Réforme du droit des contrats, du régime général et de la preuve des obligations* (2nd edn, LexisNexis 2018) 536.
[47] Ministère de la Justice, *Rapport au Président de la République relatif à l'ordonnance no 2016-131 du 10 février 2016 portant réforme du droit des contrats, du régime général et de la preuve des obligations* (Journal Officiel de la République Française, 11 February 2016) para 25: 'l'énumération non exhaustive

common regime applicable to nominate quasi-contracts, the preamble seems to imply that the courts are free to determine the rules applicable to the new quasi-contracts they might discover by relying on the rationale underlying those foreseen situations; this is the principle against unjustified enrichment.[48]

The conclusion that French law recognizes an entirely miscellaneous category of obligations beyond contracts and delicts is therefore only partly true. There is no doubt that the French Civil Code does not recognize a 'third pillar' of the law of obligations, and that the category of quasi-contract emerged and has traditionally been understood as a collection of situations giving rise to obligations subject to quite distinct rules. However, the definition of quasi-contracts provided by the new art 1300, the general scope recognized of the quasi-contract of unjustified enrichment, and the power granted to the courts to identify new quasi-contracts and establish their rules suggest that the quasi-contract category is not conceived of as a mere collection of entirely different claims. As the next section explains, this feature is key to understanding some of the main difficulties posed by obligations organized in such a category.

IV. A Doubtful Legacy

While obligations beyond contracts and delicts do not seem to raise much interest among French lawyers, recent works show a growing concern for the approach to quasi-contracts adopted by the reform of the French Civil Code. In particular, it has been argued that the approach rests on ideas that lead to poor legal reasoning and unpredictable decisions. This section explores some of the main concerns raised by the role assigned to quasi-contracts by contemporary French law.

A. Fundamental Differences

As explained earlier, one accepted opinion holds that the principle against unjustified enrichment helps us to understand the defining feature of every quasi-contract. Thus, the new art 1300 of the French Civil Code provides that every quasi-contract arises from conduct which benefits a person who is not entitled to retain such benefit. Considered carefully, however, the specific rules governing quasi-contracts established in the French Civil Code—*gestion d'affaires, répétition*

---

des quasicontrats dans le second alinéa implique qu'il puisse exister des quasi-contrats innommés, dont le régime juridique n'est pas prévu par le Code civil'.

[48] Gaël Chantepie and Mathias Latina, *Le nouveau droit des obligations* (2nd edn, Dalloz 2018) para 248.

de l'indu, and *enrichissement injustifié*—demonstrate that most obligations originating from quasi-contracts are not concerned with the reversal of benefits and cannot be generalized into the definition included in art 1300.

Take *gestion d'affaires*. According to arts 1301 to 1301-5 of the French Civil Code, such quasi-contract is relevant where a person voluntarily acts to the benefit of another person without being requested to do so. In such situations, the law imposes duties on both parties: the principal shall reimburse the expenses incurred for the provision of the benefit, and the intervener shall account for their actions, remaining liable for any loss caused by a failure to exercise care and diligence. Leaving aside the duty of the intervener to compensate damages, which seems to fit squarely into the rules on extra-contractual liability, art 1301-2 clearly shows that the intervener's claim for reimbursement does not seek restitution of the principal's enrichment but, rather, making the principal bear the costs incurred and to indemnify any loss suffered.[49] Thus, if the intervener does not incur any expense or suffer any loss, no action in *gestion d'affaires* will be available, even if the principal was enriched as a consequence of the intervener's actions.[50]

Something similar occurs with the newly recognized *enrichissement injustifié*. According to arts 1303 to 1303-4 of the French Civil Code, this quasi-contract is relevant in every situation not covered by the other quasi-contracts where the defendant benefits from an unjustified enrichment at the expense of the claimant. Despite its name, however, this general action is not really aimed at reversing the defendant's enrichment, but at compensating the claimant's loss. This feature is apparent in art 1303, which provides that the claimant may seek an indemnity equivalent to the lesser of the two sums represented by their impoverishment and the defendant's surviving enrichment at the time the action is brought.[51] Thus, if the claimant does not incur any expense or suffer any loss, no action in *enrichissement injustifié* will be available, even if it can be argued that the defendant was enriched.[52]

Of course, these considerations do not prevent the quasi-contract category finding a common foundation on the principle against unjustified enrichment, which is sufficiently broad to accommodate claims subject to different requirements and aimed at obtaining different forms of relief. At this point, however, it seems clear that the perceived unity between different types of quasi-contracts has nothing to do with unity predicated on contracts or wrongs as distinct sources of

---

[49] Article 1301-2 of the French Civil Code provides: 'A person whose affairs have been managed usefully must fulfil any undertakings which the person intervening contracted in his interest. He must reimburse the person intervening for expenses incurred in his interest and compensate him for harm which he has suffered as a result of the management...'
[50] Combot (n 38) paras 265–66.
[51] Article 1303 of the French Civil Code provides: 'Apart from the situation of management of another's affairs and undue payment, a person who benefits from an unjustified enrichment to the detriment of another person must indemnify the person who is thereby made the poorer to an amount equal to the lesser of the two values of the enrichment and the impoverishment.'
[52] Combot (n 38) para 241.

the French law of obligations. A category whose limits are defined in such broad terms seems difficult to distinguish from a category comprising the whole of private law.[53]

B. Poor Legal Reasoning

A general action in unjustified enrichment was recognized to cover situations where a defendant benefits from an unjustified enrichment at the expense of a claimant, there not being any other quasi-contract available to redress such a situation. This action was originally subject to extremely loose requirements, but a number of important restrictions were developed to make sure that it was applied only in rather exceptional cases.[54] However, the seemingly technical nature of these restrictions has not prevented the courts from relying on general considerations of fairness in order to determine the situations in which a quasi-contract of *enrichissement injustifié* should apply.

A useful illustration is provided by cases where the general action in unjustified enrichment has been brought by cohabitants following the dissolution of their relationship. In deciding these cases, the courts seem to focus first and foremost on the situation of the claimant, without considering in any detail the extent of the enrichment obtained by the defendant. For example, in a case where the claimant bore all the costs of obtaining credit intended to build a house on the defendant's land, the general action in unjustified enrichment was rejected because the earnings of the claimant, a dental surgeon, were significantly higher than those of the defendant, his dental assistant. As the home was used by both cohabitants, it was considered fair to allocate to the claimant the full cost of building the common home, even though it was beyond dispute that the defendant remained enriched at the claimant's expense after the dissolution of the relationship.[55]

These and other cases have led commentators to argue that the scope of a general unjustified enrichment action is not really determined by the application of the restrictions adopted by arts 1303 to 1303-4 of the French Civil Code. Instead, the action seems to succeed in the exceptional cases where, in the absence of a contract or delict, judges are persuaded that they lack any other legal remedy to strike a fair balance between the loss and the gain between the parties. While the restraint shown by judges in granting this action prevents the overall result from

---

[53] The point is confirmed by the list of provisions in the French Civil Code which have been traditionally explained as instances of the principle against unjustified enrichment. See eg René Demogue, *Traité des obligations en général, I, Sources des obligations*, vol 3 (Librairie Arthur Rousseau 1923) 122; and more recently, François Chénedé, *Les commutations en droit privé. Contribution à la théorie générale des obligations* (Economica 2008) paras 351–55.
[54] These restrictions were adopted by the reform in arts 1303 to 1303-4 of the French Civil Code. On these restrictions, see Descheemaeker, 'The New French Law of Unjustified Enrichment' (n 45) 86.
[55] Cour d'Appel de Colmar, 18 March 2016, no 14/03014.

appearing to be entirely chaotic, the case law on general actions in unjustified enrichment demonstrate that judicial *équité* or fairness certainly plays the role of a direct source of obligations in modern French law.[56]

C. Unpredictable Decisions

In French law, the notion of an 'innominate contract' describes a contract agreed by the parties which does not fit into any of the contracts expressly regulated by law. This notion is useful because it helps us to understand the situations where there are no specific provisions governing particular kinds of contract, and thus where the general principles of the law of contracts should apply.[57] Similarly, the notion of 'innominate quasi-contracts' describes the possibility of 'discovering' quasi-contracts not expressly recognized by the French Civil Code.[58] As explained earlier, the reform left the door open for the recognition of 'innominate quasi-contracts' on the basis of the common elements set forth in art 1300. Yet the few innominate quasi-contracts which have been recognized by the French courts do not seem to rest on any common rationale.

Consider the quasi-contract of *loteries publicitaires*. This notion was used by the Cour de cassation to justify recognition of a claim against a company which, for publicity purposes, led clients to believe that they had won a lottery.[59] In the court's view, the company's false promise of a gain originated in a voluntary but non-consensual obligation to deliver on the gain, so the idea of an innominate quasi-contract came in handy for explaining liability in the absence of a contract or any harmful behaviour.[60] Yet this situation had little in common with the quasi-contracts recognized by the French Civil Code, and even the broadest formulation of the principle against unjustified enrichment seemed inappropriate for explaining the existence of an obligation in that situation.[61]

It could be argued that the decisions recognizing *loteries publicitaires* as innominate quasi-contracts are wrong, because they fail to acknowledge that art 1300 of

---

[56] Combot (n 38) para 261.
[57] Terré and others (n 31) para 95.
[58] In the absence of a common regime applicable to all quasi-contracts, it is hard to understand how this procedure works and why it would be relevant. Nonetheless, French authors have traditionally recognized the existence of innominate quasi-contracts. See Toullier (n 39) 135.
[59] The trick worked as follows. A company sent letters identifying potential clients as winners of a sum of money, the receipt of which required the clients to provide certain specified information. After proceeding as required, the clients eventually discovered that the letters also said in the fine print that the award of the money was conditional on the results of an additional lottery. See eg Terré and others (n 31) para 1327.
[60] Rémy Libchaber, 'Un faux pas de plus dans la construction du régime des loteries publicitaires' (2015) 1 RDC 861.
[61] A complete analysis of the quasi-contract of *loteries publicitaires* and its implications for a unified theory of quasi-contracts are provided in Cyril Grimaldi, *Quasi-engagement et engagement de droit privé: Recherches sur les sources de l'obligation* (Defrénois 2007) para 106.

the French Civil Code requires every quasi-contract to result in obligations intended to reverse the defendant's enrichment, and not just to deter the defendant's unconscionable behaviour. But the fact remains that the principle against unjustified enrichment provides little guidance when it comes to deciding when an innominate quasi-contract must be recognized. In that context, French courts retain an alarming leeway for identifying new quasi-contracts under circumstances which simply cannot be anticipated.[62]

V. Conclusion

It is tempting to assume that the French law of quasi-contract remains a tranquil haven where a number of miscellaneous claims harking back to Roman times are preserved impervious to the debates that shape contemporary private law.[63] This conclusion is reaffirmed by the lack of interest shown by French lawyers on the topic.[64] Unlike many other legal systems, French law seems to have been somehow spared from the enduring puzzles posed in other jurisdictions by obligations arising involuntarily which are not premised upon wrongdoing.

When we consider the rules governing quasi-contracts adopted by the recent reform of the French Civil Code, however, it appears that this seemingly unproblematic area is riddled with difficulties. Unfortunately, no single explanation for these difficulties is available. Under one view, many of them would disappear if French law renounced the quasi-contractual anachronism and followed the example of other jurisdictions in developing a sophisticated law of unjustified enrichment as the third pillar of the law of obligations.[65] Under another view, the quasi-contract would not cause any harm if French law embraced the conclusion that the different types of quasi-contract are just a rag-bag collection of situations governed by specific rules and no overarching principle.[66]

Be that as it may, the recent evolution of quasi-contracts in French law shows that residual miscellanies are difficult to handle. As noted by Birks, nobody will be happy for long with admitting the existence of an unruly residue of 'other' sources of obligations. Attempts will be made to find overarching principles, even if that implies running the risk of simplifying the analysis to attain the appearance of

---

[62] Eric Descheemaeker, 'Quasi-contrats et enrichissement injustifié en droit français' (2013) 112 Revue Trimestrielle de Droit Civil 1 (hereafter Descheemaeker, 'Quasi-contrats') notes that allowing courts to recognize non-consensual obligations not premised upon wrongdoing in situations which cannot be anticipated in any way comes close to destroying legal certainty in interpersonal relations.
[63] See eg Denis Mazeaud, 'D'une source, l'autre ...' (2002) Recueil Dalloz 2963, describing quasi-contracts in French law as a *paisible ruisseau*.
[64] Rémy Libchaber, 'Le malheur des quasi-contrats' (2016) 258 Droit & Patrimoine 73.
[65] Descheemaeker, 'Quasi-contrats' (n 62) 26; Combot (n 38) paras 571–73.
[66] Stevens, *The Laws of Restitution* (n 22) 28.

order.[67] By purporting to unify the regime applicable to quasi-contracts with a vague maxim of justice, the reform of the French Civil Code seems to have fallen into that trap. Common lawyers should ask themselves whether replacing the restitution of unjust enrichment approach with a 'dustbin category' of obligations beyond contracts and wrongs will reduce the risk of suffering a similar fate.

---

[67] Birks, *The Roman Law of Obligations* (n 23) 248–49.

16
Challenges for Canadian Unjust Enrichment

Mitchell McInnes

I. Introduction

The Canadian law of unjust enrichment has changed dramatically over the last fifty years. Some of those changes mirror developments that have occurred throughout the Commonwealth. For instance, as the subject matured, it became clear that a robust notion of unjust enrichment requires a change of position defence[1] and generally has no need to distinguish between mistakes of fact and mistakes of law.[2] In other respects, however, Canadian courts have gone off on their own. For better or worse, the Canadian regime governing restitutionary liability now looks very different than its counterparts in other common law jurisdictions. As would be expected, challenges have arisen. Some involve isolated issues, others pertain to basic structural matters. Some have been overcome, others remain outstanding.

Examples are plentiful. The peculiarly Canadian belief that the whole of unjust enrichment is 'equitable' in both origin and nature frequently creates problems.[3] Contrary to their counterparts in other jurisdictions,[4] Canadian courts frequently impose liability on indirect recipients,[5] but have not yet fully realized the implications of doing so. More worryingly, an extended conception of interceptive

---

[1] *Rural Municipality of Storthoaks v Mobil Oil Canada Ltd* [1976] 2 SCR 147; *Lipkin Gorman v Karpnale Ltd* [1991] 2 AC 548 (HL) (hereafter *Lipkin Gorman*); *David Securities Pty Ltd v Commonwealth Bank of Australia* (1992) 175 CLR 353 (hereafter *David Securities*).

[2] *Air Canada v British Columbia* [1989] 1 SCR 1161 (hereafter *Air Canada*); *Canadian Pacific Air Lines Ltd v British Columbia* [1989] 1 SCR 1133 (hereafter *Canadian Pacific*); *Kleinwort Benson Ltd v Lincoln City Council* [1999] 2 AC 349 (HL), 373; *David Securities* (n 1).

[3] Even if a restitutionary claim historically sounded in law, a Canadian judge may, eg, subject it to the equitable 'clean hands' doctrine (*Chao Yin Canada Group Inc v Xenova Property Development Ltd* 2021 BCSC 1445 [116]; *Patel v Chief Medical Supplies Ltd* 2019 ABQB 620 [78]) or dismiss it on the ground that the court does not have jurisdiction over 'equitable' matters: *Pearce v 4 Pillars Consulting Group Inc* 2021 BCCA 198 [242].

[4] *Prudential Assurance Co Ltd v Revenue and Customs Comrs* [2018] UKSC 39; [2019] AC 929 [68].

[5] *Moore v Sweet* 2018 SCC 52; [2018] 3 SCR 303 [45]; *Pro-Sys Consultants Ltd v Microsoft Corp* 2013 SCC 57; [2013] 3 SCR 477 [50] (hereafter *Pro-Sys*); *Alberta v Elder Advocates of Alberta Society* 2011 SCC 24; [2011] 2 SCR 261 (hereafter *Alberta v Elder Advocates*); *Cannon v Funds for Canada Foundation* 2012 ONSC 399 [266].

subtraction threatens to capture cases well beyond restitution's usual remit.[6] Perhaps because it has yet to deal with a truly difficult case—that is, one involving an insolvent defendant with many creditors—the Supreme Court of Canada has set an unusually low bar for remedial constructive trusts.[7] While the recently formulated doctrine of 'joint family venture'[8] may eventually provide a principled basis for such relief, Canadian courts dealing with claims between former cohabitees have long used the language of 'unjust enrichment' to award non-restitutionary remedies that fulfil expectations rather than reverse transfers.[9]

Canadian judges have created difficulties for themselves on those issues but, on other matters, they have enjoyed greater success. The Supreme Court of Canada's decision in *Atlantic Lottery Corp Inc v Babstock*[10] resolved a fundamental challenge that had long confounded judges. The problem largely originated with the *Restatement of the Law of Restitution: Quasi Contracts and Constructive Trusts*[11] in 1937. The American work profoundly influenced the development of the modern law of unjust enrichment, particularly during the middle of the twentieth century.[12] It was a magnificent achievement, but unsurprisingly, as the first attempt

---

[6] *Moore v Sweet* (n 5) [43]–[53]; *Citadel General Assurance Co v Lloyds Bank Canada* [1997] 3 SCR 805 [30] (hereafter *Citadel v Lloyds*); *Lac Minerals Ltd v International Corona Resources Ltd* [1989] 2 SCR 574, 669–70 (hereafter *Lac Minerals*).

[7] *Moore v Sweet* (n 5) [91] (a court must be satisfied that: (1) the impugned enrichment is 'linked or causally connected' to the target asset; and (2) a personal remedy would be inadequate or *inconvenient*). See also *Professional Institute of the Public Service of Canada v Attorney General of Canada* 2012 SCC 71; [2012] 3 SCR 660 [149] (hereafter *PIPSC*); *Kerr v Baranow* 2011 SCC 10; [2011] 1 SCR 269 [50]–[51]; *Peter v Beblow* [1993] 1 SCR 980, 988.

[8] *Kerr v Baranow* (n 7) [80]–[100].

[9] *Pettkus v Becker* [1980] 2 SCR 834; *Sorochan v Sorochan* [1986] 2 SCR 38; *Rawluk v Rawluk* [1990] 1 SCR 70; *Peter v Beblow* (n 7); *Kerr v Baranow* (n 7). The cohabitational cases contrast sharply with the decision that introduced the unjust enrichment principle into Canadian law: *Deglman v Guaranty Trust Co of Canada* [1954] SCR 725 (hereafter *Deglman*). A young man provided beneficial services to his aunt in exchange for her promise to leave her house to him, but was disappointed when her will did not contain the expected devise. While the oral agreement was unenforceable under the Statute of Frauds, a restitutionary claim succeeded. The remedy was properly confined to the value of the nephew's services—not the value of his aunt's house. Canadian courts have understandably refused to similarly treat former cohabitees as hired help, but they cannot explain how unjust enrichment supports expectation relief.

[10] *Atlantic Lottery Corp Inc v Babstock* 2020 SCC 19 (hereafter *Atlantic Lottery*).

[11] American Law Institute, *Restatement of Restitution* (1937). See now American Law Institute, *Restatement (Third) of Restitution and Unjust Enrichment* (2011).

[12] The most recent editions of *Goff & Jones* advocate more limited views of 'unjust enrichment' and 'restitution', but early editions reflected the *Restatement*'s understanding of those terms: Robert Goff and Gareth H Jones, *The Law of Restitution* (Sweet & Maxwell 1966); cf Charles Mitchell, Paul Mitchell, and Stephen Watterson, *Goff & Jones: The Law of Unjust Enrichment* (9th edn, Sweet & Maxwell 2016) (hereafter Mitchell, Mitchell, and Watterson, *Goff & Jones 9th*). Between 1985 and 2005, Peter Birks abandoned the ambiguous use of 'unjust enrichment', but somewhat surprisingly, given his commitment to taxonomic clarity, maintained the broad view of 'restitution': Peter Birks, *An Introduction to the Law of Restitution* (rev edn, OUP 1989); Peter Birks, *Unjust Enrichment* (2nd edn, OUP 2005) (hereafter Birks, *Unjust Enrichment 2nd*). Going one step further, John McCamus, the dean of Canadian 'restitution', remains steadfast in his allegiance to the *Restatement*'s position regarding both of the key terms. Only a few months separated Brown J's decision in *Atlantic Lottery* and McCamus's latest work, which presents an extended defence of the American model: John D McCamus, *An Introduction to the Canadian Law of Restitution and Unjust Enrichment* (Thomson Reuters 2020) (hereafter McCamus,

at drawing together previously scattered doctrines and organizing them into a coherent principle, the *Restatement* was flawed. Most significantly, its broad definitions of 'unjust enrichment' and 'restitution' were dangerously ambiguous. 'Unjust enrichment' was said to encompass both: (1) a benefit that unjustifiably moved from the plaintiff to the defendant regardless of any wrongdoing; and (2) a benefit that the defendant obtained, usually from a third party, by virtue of breaching an obligation owed to the plaintiff. 'Restitution' was said to be either: (1) a remedy that reversed a transfer that occurred between the parties; or (2) a remedy that stripped away wrongful gains. Those ambiguities predictably led to error and injustice. Even if scholars working in the area were up to the challenge, lawyers and judges, who only occasionally encountered 'restitutionary' claims, tended to conflate or confuse the concepts. Rules and requirements appropriate in one context were imported into another;[13] misconceived pleadings deprived claimants of any chance of success.[14] In *Atlantic Lottery*, Brown J finally set the matter straight by firmly distinguishing two sets of ideas.[15] 'Unjust enrichment' is a 'causative event'[16] consisting of the defendant's enrichment, the plaintiff's corresponding deprivation, and the absence of any juristic reason for the transfer between the parties. '[R]estitution

Introduction). See also Peter D Maddaugh and John D McCamus, *The Law of Restitution* (looseleaf edn, Canada Law Book) (hereafter Maddaugh and McCamus, *Restitution*).

[13] *Lac Minerals* (n 6) (disgorgement confused with restitution—plaintiff wrongly required to satisfy elements of unjust enrichment); *Pro-Sys* (n 5) (reversal of unjustified transfers conflated with stripping of wrongful gains).
[14] *Rosenfeldt v Olson* (1986) 25 DLR (4th) 472 (BCCA), reversing *Rosenfeldt v Olson* (1984) 16 DLR (4th) 103 (BCSC) (lawyer mistakenly seeking restitution for unjust enrichment instead of disgorgement of wrongful gain).
[15] *Atlantic Lottery* also sounded the death knell for 'waiver of tort' in Canada. Though long dormant in England, that doctrine enjoyed a remarkable revival in Canada following the liberalization of class action rules. Lawyers became keen to identify causes of action that large numbers of claimants could pursue against wealthy defendants. The tort of negligence offered some hope insofar as it is often possible to allege a duty of care and a breach of the standard of care in connection with some disappointing product or service, but proving actual loss on a class-wide basis is frequently impossible. To overcome that obstacle, lawyers habitually argued, in line with an academic proposal, that the tort of negligence can be 'waived' by replacing proof of the plaintiff's loss with proof of the defendant's gain (eg by proving that the defendant profited by carelessly cutting costs during the manufacturing process): John D McCamus, 'Waiver of Tort: Is There a Limiting Principle?' (2014) 55 CBLJ 333. On that view, 'waiver of tort' can reorient the tort of negligence from wrongful injuries to wrongful enrichments. Lower courts never actually upheld that argument, but unsure what to make of the ancient doctrine, they also refused to summarily strike such claims. Confronted with certified class actions, and deterred by the prospect of costly litigation, risk-averse defendants commonly settled for substantial sums. As Brown J eventually explained, however, the argument was premised on a fundamental error. 'Waiver of tort' was simply the language through which courts historically recognized that some wrongs support 'a choice between possible remedies'—ie compensation and disgorgement: *Atlantic Lottery* (n 10) [29], quoting *United Australia Ltd v Barclays Bank Ltd* [1941] AC 1 (HL) 13. The remedial option consequently required complete proof of an existing cause of action. And since the plaintiffs in *Atlantic Lottery* could not establish loss on a class-wide basis, their disgorgement claim necessarily failed as well. Finally, to avoid confusion in the future, Brown J directed Canadian lawyers to abandon the language of 'waiver of tort' and to speak instead of disgorgement of wrongful gains: *Atlantic Lottery* (n 10) [23]. He refrained from deciding whether a fully proven claim for negligence is capable of supporting gain-based relief: [35].
[16] *Atlantic Lottery* (n 10) [23]–[24].

is the law's remedial ... response to th[at] causative event.'[17] By reversing an unjustified transfer, it equally remedies the 'the defendant's gain and the plaintiff's deprivation'.[18] In contrast, a remedy that is 'calculated exclusively by reference to the defendant's wrongful gain, irrespective of whether it corresponds to damage suffered by the plaintiff and, indeed, irrespective of whether the plaintiff suffered damage at all' is not 'restitution' but 'disgorgement'.[19] And rather than being triggered by 'unjust enrichment', disgorgement is simply 'an alternative remedy for certain forms of wrongful conduct'.[20]

Now that the Supreme Court of Canada has restricted unjust enrichment to the reversal of unjustified transfers, the most significant challenges pertain to the precise nature and scope of concept.

II. The Canadian Model of Unjust Enrichment

The primary difference between unjust enrichment in Canada and its counterparts elsewhere lies in its test of injustice. Canadian courts historically followed the common law model by requiring the plaintiff to prove, in addition to a transfer between the parties, an *unjust factor*—that is, a reason for *reversing* the transfer. By 1980, however, the Supreme Court of Canada was speaking the civilian language of *juristic reason*—that is, a reason for *retaining* a transfer. In effect, the two tests work in opposite directions. A test of unjust factors says, 'No restitution unless ...'; a test of juristic reasons says, 'Restitution unless ...' It would have been astonishing for the Court—without argument, explanation, or even recognition—to abandon centuries of common law analysis in favour of the civilian approach. The shift, however, was merely semantic and not substantive.[21] In *Pettkus v Becker* itself, liability was imposed only because the plaintiff had established the unjust factor of free acceptance.[22] Similarly, while the civilian terminology was occasionally taken at

---

[17] ibid.
[18] ibid [24].
[19] ibid [23].
[20] ibid [27].
[21] Why, then, did the Supreme Court of Canada begin using civilian terminology in common law cases? The answer will probably never be known for certain, but it seems that the semantic shift was an accident of Canadian bijuridicalism. In 1976, a case on appeal from Quebec required the Supreme Court of Canada to state the elements of the civilian claim for *de in rem verso* or 'unjustified enrichment'. Adhering to civilian tradition, Beetz J explained that restitution was premised upon proof of, inter alia, an 'absence of justification': *Cie Immobilière Viger Ltée v Lauréat Giguère Inc* [1977] 2 SCR 67, 77. Dickson J concurred in that judgment. Two years later, in a dispute on appeal from Ontario, he similarly framed the common law action in terms of 'an absence of any juristic reason': *Rathwell v Rathwell* [1978] 2 SCR 436, 455. And two years after that, he won majority support for his formulation of unjust enrichment in *Pettkus v Becker* (n 9). The civilian phrase, it seems, simply stuck in Dickson J's mind when it came time to deal with the common law claim.
[22] *Pettkus v Becker* (n 9) 849. See also *Sorochan v Sorochan* (n 9) [14].

face value,[23] Canadian courts overwhelmingly continued to demand proof of unjust factors.[24]

Canadian courts limped along in that way—saying one thing, doing another—for more than two decades before the matter came to a head. In *Garland v Consumers' Gas Co Ltd*, the Supreme Court of Canada held that an unjust enrichment requires proof of an absence of juristic reason.[25] It did not, however, simply import a test from civil law. It adopted the essential idea, but concerned that it may be 'nearly impossible' 'to prove a negative, namely the *absence* of juristic reason',[26] it devised a unique two-stage test. First, having shown an enrichment and a corresponding deprivation, the plaintiff must negate the 'established categories' of juristic reason—that is, contract, disposition of law, donative intent, and 'other valid common law, equitable or statutory obligations'.[27] If that burden is satisfied, then the plaintiff is prima facie entitled to restitution. At the second stage, however, the defendant can adduce evidence of some 'residual'[28] type of juristic reason, typically by drawing on 'two factors: the reasonable expectations of the parties, and public policy considerations'.[29]

While it is not clear *why* the Court chose to do so,[30] *Garland* undoubtedly introduced a civilian-inspired test of injustice into Canadian law. In contrast to the earlier occasion, the Court acknowledged the issue and expressly implemented the juristic reason model. And with the exception of a single cryptic anomaly,[31] it has consistently followed that approach since 2004.[32]

---

[23] *Reference Re: Goods and Services Tax* [1992] 2 SCR 445, 476–77 (hereafter *Re GST*); *Peter v Beblow* (n 7) 991–95; *Attorney General of Nova Scotia v Walsh* 2002 SCC 83; [2002] 4 SCR 325 [165].

[24] Mistake: *Nepean (Township) Hydro Electric Commission v Ontario Hydro* [1982] 1 SCR 347 (hereafter *Nepean*); *Air Canada v British Columbia* [1989] 2 SCR 1067; *Air Canada* (n 2). Compulsion: *Re Eurig Estate* [1998] 2 SCR 565 [47]; cf *Regional Municipality of Peel v Canada* [1992] 3 SCR 762, 790–92 (hereafter *Peel*). Failure of consideration: *Palachik v Kiss* [1983] 1 SCR 623, 633. Knowing receipt: *Citadel v Lloyds* (n 6); *Gold v Rosenberg* [1997] 3 SCR 767.

[25] *Garland v Consumers' Gas Co Ltd* 2004 SCC 25; [2004] 1 SCR 629 (hereafter *Garland*).

[26] ibid [42] (emphasis added), citing Lionel Smith, '"The Mystery of "Juristic Reason"'' (2000) 12 SCLR (2d) 211 (hereafter Smith, 'Mystery').

[27] *Garland* (n 25) [44].

[28] ibid [45].

[29] ibid [46]. Both considerations are worrisome: Mitchell McInnes, *The Canadian Law of Unjust Enrichment and Restitution* (2nd edn, LexisNexis 2022) §4.03[3][b] (hereafter McInnes, *Unjust Enrichment*). Public policy, a 'very unruly horse', is apt to run into difficulties if it is not kept under a tight rein: *Richardson v Mellish* (1824) 2 Bing 229, 252; 130 ER 294, 303. Reasonable expectations occasionally have a role to play within unjust enrichment, but they also have a tendency to draw judges into contract-like, forward-looking relief: *Robinson v Saskatoon (City)* 2010 SKQB 98.

[30] Neither party asked the Court to address the point, let alone opt for the civilian approach. In England, Peter Birks had dramatically announced a preference for that model in Peter Birks, *Unjust Enrichment* (OUP 2003) 98, but Canadian commentary was wary of any move away from unjust factors: Smith, 'Mystery' (n 26); Mitchell McInnes, 'Unjust Enrichment—Restitution—Absence of Juristic Reason: *Campbell v Campbell*' (2000) 79 Can Bar Rev 459, 464. More importantly, Canadian judges had been faithfully adhering to the common law tradition notwithstanding introduction of the civilian terminology in the 1970s. It may be telling, however, that the Court in *Garland* viewed its judgment as merely a matter of 'some redefinition and reformulation': *Garland* (n 25) [44]. The Court arguably did not fully comprehend the scale of the change that it introduced. It may have mistakenly believed that it was simply clarifying the test that judges were already employing.

[31] *BMP Global Distribution Inc v Bank of Nova Scotia* 2009 SCC 15; [2009] 1 SCR 504 (hereafter *BMP*).

[32] *Pacific National Investments Ltd v Victoria (City)* 2004 SCC 75 (hereafter *Pacific National Investments*); [2004] 3 SCR 575; *Attorney General of Canada v Gladstone* 2005 SCC 21; [2005] 1 SCR 325 (hereafter *Gladstone*); *Jedfro Investments (USA) Ltd v Jacyk* 2007 SCC 55; [2007] 3 SCR 679 (hereafter

III. *Garland*'s Challenges

Given the difficulties inherent in replacing a common law doctrine with a civilian doctrine, Canadian judges have adjusted remarkably well. The vast majority of cases are decided in accordance with precedent and principle. Perhaps the quarter century between *Pettkus v Becker* and *Garland* provided a test drive of sorts, allowing lawyers to become comfortable with the language of 'juristic reasons' without having to actually implement that model. Post-*Garland* decisions further suggest that the civilian model is surprisingly[33] accessible insofar as there is, in one respect at least, only ever one reason for restitution—that is, an absence of juristic reason. Finally, the task was made easier by the fact that, as discussed later,[34] juristic reasons and unjust factors coexist. Though decisions are now expressed in different terms, much of the underlying reasoning remains the same. *Garland* did not saddle judges with a *tabula rasa*. The shift from unjust factors to juristic reasons did, however, create challenges.

Some of those challenges arise from the specific manner in which the *Garland* test was formulated. The contents of the 'established categories' of juristic reason are not entirely clear.[35] Nor did the Supreme Court of Canada adequately distinguish between the various parts of its test. Why is the plaintiff responsible for negating some juristic reasons while the defendant bears responsibility for proving others? Are the categories closed, or can a judge, having repeatedly recognized a particular type of 'residual' juristic reason, reclassify it as a new 'established category', so as to place the burden on the plaintiff rather than the defendant? What is the relationship between 'residual' juristic reasons and defences? Canadian courts

---

Jedfro); *Ermineskin Indian Band v Canada* 2009 SCC 9; [2009] 1 SCR 222 (hereafter *Ermineskin Indian Band*); *Kerr v Baranow* (n 7); *Alberta v Elder Advocates* (n 5); *i Trade Finance Inc v Bank of Montreal* 2011 SCC 26; [2011] 2 SCR 360; *PIPSC* (n 7); *Pro-Sys* (n 5); *Sun-Rype Products Ltd v Archer Daniels Midland Co* 2013 SCC 58; [2013] 3 SCR 545; *Moore v Sweet* (n 5); *Atlantic Lottery* (n 10); cf *Kingstreet Investments Ltd v New Brunswick (Finance)* 2007 SCC 1; [2007] 1 SCR 3 (hereafter *Kingstreet*).

[33] Peter Birks believed that while the civilian model enjoys the benefit of elegance, insofar as there is only ever one reason for restitution, it is relatively inaccessible to laypersons because that one reason consists of a nullity—ie an *absence* of legal basis: Peter Birks, 'Mistakes of Law' (2000) 53 CLP 205, 230–32. There is no evidence as to how laypersons view *Garland*, but lawyers and judges quickly adjusted to the civilian model of injustice.
[34] See text to n 81.
[35] 'Disposition of law' obviously requires definition, but even the seemingly simple category of 'contract' occasionally demands careful elucidation as well. It must be determined, eg, whether a contract continues to constitute a juristic reason even after it has been discharged for breach. Historical cases allowing recovery (eg *Boomer v Muir* 24 P 2d 570 (Cal App 1933)) have been roundly criticized (*Taylor v Motability Finance Ltd* [2004] EWHC 2619 (Comm) [24]), but the High Court of Australia recently held that there is room for restitution after all: *Mann v Paterson Constructions Pty Ltd* [2019] HCA 32; (2019) 267 CLR 560. Does contract trump unjust enrichment as long as the aggrieved claimant has a right to sue for expectation damages or does a contract constitute a juristic reason only if the agreement's primary obligations are in play? See Mitchell McInnes, 'Contracts Discharged for Breach and Unjust Enrichment: A Matter of Principle' (2022) 52 Adv Q 481.

have not yet wrestled with those issues, but *Garland* could easily be improved. In practice, there is never any question of requiring a claimant to negate every imaginable juristic reason. At most, two or three possibilities are in play.[36] As a result, there is no reason why the usual rules of civil litigation cannot be used. The plaintiff should be required to satisfy the elements of unjust enrichment by demonstrating either that a transfer was non-purposive[37] or that it failed to satisfy its intended purpose. The defendant would then be entitled to defeat or reduce liability by either rebutting the plaintiff's proof or invoking a defence.

A second set of challenges arises from the fact that Canada's common law courts have little experience with juristic reasons. The lack of familiarity will naturally diminish over time, but the lack of substance is currently a problem. A test of restitutionary injustice never operates in isolation. It exists within an integrated set of rules. Consequently, while different legal systems built on the same fundamental propositions—for example, personal autonomy, private property—typically generate similar results, they may do so by different means. Consider a variation on the facts of *Ulmer v Farnsworth*.[38] The parties owned adjacent quarries that became flooded. With the defendant away on vacation, the plaintiffs decided to proceed alone and seek remuneration later. The plaintiffs drained their own quarry, and as anticipated given the lie of the land, necessarily drained the defendant's quarry as well. The defendant enjoyed a benefit, but was he unjustly enriched?

Under a traditional common law analysis, liability is impossible because the plaintiffs cannot point to an unjust factor. The plaintiffs' intention was not impaired and the defendant did nothing to expose himself to liability. Before 2004, a Canadian court would have easily dismissed the claim. Civilian systems reach the same result by different means.[39] The result must be the same in Canada today, but it is no longer easily achieved. Since none of the 'established categories' of juristic reason apply, the plaintiffs are prima facie entitled to restitution, and *Garland*'s second stage is not very helpful. The plaintiffs may have had a reasonable expectation of being paid, but the defendant had no expectation at all. And to ask whether

---

[36] While it is not unreasonable to ask a claimant to negate a handful of potential juristic reasons, problems may arise when several possibilities are in play. Canadian courts have occasionally imposed liability after being satisfied by dis-proof of a *single* juristic reason, without requiring the negation of others: *Low v Pfizer Canada Inc* 2015 BCCA 506, reversing *Low v Pfizer Canada Inc* 2014 BCSC 1469. That arguably was true in *Garland* (n 25). See also *Pacific National Investments* (n 32); McInnes, *Unjust Enrichment* (n 29) §4.03[1][c][ii]. Perhaps the common law mind, accustomed to acting upon proof of one unjust factor, instinctively stops with the negation of one juristic reason.

[37] That is true if the plaintiff either: (1) played no active role in a transfer, as in cases of theft and finding; or (2) knowingly created a benefit but did not intend to transfer it to the defendant, as in cases of mistaken improvements to property: McInnes, *Unjust Enrichment* (n 29) chs 5, 6.

[38] *Ulmer v Farnsworth* 15 A 65 (Me SC 1888).

[39] Quebec's Civil Code states that an enrichment is 'justified where it results ... from an act performed by the [plaintiff] for his personal and exclusive interest or at his own risk and peril, or with a constant liberal intention': SQ 1991, c 64, Art 1494. Germany's Civil Code would deny liability because of the lack of a 'purposive' and 'direct' transfer: German Civil Code (BGB) s 812(1); Konrad Zweigert and Hein Kötz, *Introduction to Comparative Law* (3rd edn, Clarendon Press 1998) 540–41.

a reasonable person in the defendant's position would have expected to pay is to confuse the objectivity of contract law with the subjectivity of unjust enrichment. At the same time, to baldly ask if 'policy' justifies the defendant's enrichment is to pose a hopelessly open-ended question. Most likely, a Canadian judge would cast the inquiry in terms of 'incidental benefit', but on that point, the common law mind is under-developed.[40] Because incidental benefits are apt to occur in the absence of unjust factors, Canadian courts previously had little reason to explore the concept.[41] Under the common law model, bars and defences become relevant only after the claimant has fully proven the cause of action. That gap must now be overcome. The same is true of other doctrines as well.[42]

IV. A Cause of Action

Unjust enrichment has been accepted throughout the common law world, but its precise role varies from place to place. Despite earlier optimism,[43] Anglo-Australian courts have grown cautious. The UK Supreme Court has said that unjust enrichment's elements are 'signposts towards areas of inquiry' but 'not themselves legal tests'.[44] The High Court of Australia believes that while unjust enrichment

---

[40] The failure to examine the issue of incidental benefits has improperly led courts to award restitution: *MacLellan v Morash* 2006 NSSC 101; cf *Catalyst Capital Group Inc v Dundee Kilmer Developments Limited Partnership* 2020 ONCA 272 [86].

[41] *Peel* is the leading Canadian authority, but on that occasion, the Court merely said that 'While not much discussed by common law authorities to date', a restitutionary enrichment 'must ... be more than an incidental blow-by. A secondary collateral benefit will not suffice': *Peel* (n 24) 797.

[42] *Officiousness*, like an incidental benefit, tends to occur in situations involving neither unjust factors nor juristic reasons. The difference, of course, is that whereas an absence of unjust factors obviates the need for the bar, an absence of juristic reason leads to liability unless the bar is invoked. As a result, Canadian courts must now develop the concept: *Binichakis v Smitherman* 2009 BCPC 131.
The doctrine of natural obligations similarly requires attention. Assume that the plaintiff lost a bet to the defendant and paid only because of the mistaken belief that wagers are legally enforceable. In fact, the law will neither compel payment of a wager nor compel repayment if a wager is honoured. Traditionally, restitution would have been denied on the ground that the operative error was a mistake of law, rather than fact, and hence not actionable: *Bilbie v Lumley* (1802) 2 East 469; 102 ER 448. The result must be the same in Canada today, but the explanation does not easily come to hand. The key undoubtedly lies in the concept of a 'natural' obligation—ie an obligation that, while not *positively* enforceable, may justify a transfer that does occur. The losing gambler's payment is irrecoverable because it was binding 'in conscience' or, more accurately, it fulfilled its intended purpose (notwithstanding the mistake). Lord Mansfield noted that possibility in *Moses v Macferlan*, but because of the mistake of law doctrine, common law judges rarely explored it: *Moses v Macferlan* (1760) 2 Burr 1005, 1012-13; 97 ER 676 (KB) 680-81. In contrast, the doctrine is well known in civilian systems. It must now be worked into Canadian law. Under *Garland*, however, an additional challenge exists: where does the doctrine fit? Because it is not positively enforceable, a natural obligation does not appear to fall within the miscellaneous fourth 'established category' of juristic reason—ie 'valid common law, equitable or statutory obligations'. See McInnes, *Unjust Enrichment* (n 29) ch 27.

[43] *Lipkin Gorman* (n 1); *Banque Financière de la Cité v Parc (Battersea) Ltd* [1999] 1 AC 221 (HL) 227 (hereafter *Banque Financière*); *Benedetti v Sawiris* [2013] UKSC 50; [2014] AC 938 [10]; *Menelaou v Bank of Cyprus UK Ltd* [2015] UKSC 66; [2016] AC 176 [18]; *Skandinaviska Enskilda Banken AB (Publ) v Conway* [2019] UKPC 36; [2020] AC 1111 [79]-[80]; *Pavey & Matthews Pty Ltd v Paul* (1987) 162 CLR 221, 256-57.

[44] *Investment Trust Companies v Revenue and Customs Comrs* [2017] UKSC 29; [2018] AC 275 [41]. See also *Swynson Ltd v Lowick Rose LLP* [2017] UKSC 32; [2018] AC 313 [22], [112].

may assist in the recognition of new categories of recovery and, by guiding the analysis, ensure that the subject does not 'degenerat[e] into an exercise in idiosyncratic discretion', restitution is 'not necessarily available whenever ... a defendant is enriched at the plaintiff's expense in circumstances that render the enrichment unjust'.[45] Unjust enrichment, in other words, is not a free-standing cause of action in those jurisdictions.[46]

In Canada, unjust enrichment undoubtedly does constitute a cause of action.[47] While acknowledging that the traditional categories of recovery remain relevant as manifestations of the principle, the Supreme Court of Canada has held that unjust enrichment 'permits recovery whenever the plaintiff can establish three elements: an enrichment of ... the defendant, a corresponding deprivation of the plaintiff, and the absence of a juristic reason for the enrichment'.[48] Restitutionary claims are routinely resolved entirely on the basis of the three-part action and, significantly, often without any mention of the more discrete heads of liability.[49] Several issues have arisen in connection with that practice.

A. 'Novel' Claims and Beyond

A judgment's impact cannot truly be known until it has been interpreted by later courts. On arrival, *Garland* raised a number of questions. Most importantly, was the Court serious about juristic reasons or, as happened two decades earlier in *Pettkus v Becker*,[50] was the civilian turn merely semantic? If *Garland* itself left any room for doubt, subsequent decisions made it clear that the law had substantively changed.[51] Nevertheless, Professor McCamus somewhat surprisingly insisted that the juristic reason analysis was restricted to 'novel' claims and that the common law's traditional unjust factors otherwise continue to govern.[52] He continues to hold that view.[53] That proposal has been examined at length elsewhere.[54] For now it is enough to observe that it is unsupported by principle or precedent.

---

[45] *Mann v Paterson Constructions Pty Ltd* (n 35) [213].
[46] That view enjoys some academic support: see text to n 87.
[47] *Canada (Attorney General) v Geophysical Services Inc* 2022 NSCA 41 [91], [95].
[48] *Kerr v Baranow* (n 7) [32]. See also *Moore v Sweet* (n 5) [37].
[49] *Atlantic Lottery* (n 10) [69]-[71]; *Ermineskin Indian Band* (n 32) [182]-[184]; *Jedfro* (n 32) [30]-[36]; *Gladstone* (n 32) [16]-[22].
[50] *Pettkus v Becker* (n 9).
[51] *Pacific National Investments* (n 32); *Gladstone* (n 32).
[52] Maddaugh and McCamus, *Restitution* (n 12) §3:200; John D McCamus, 'Mistake, Forged Cheques and Unjust Enrichment: Three Cheers for *BMP Global*' (2009) 48 CBLJ 76 (hereafter McCamus, 'Mistake'); John D McCamus, 'Unjust Enrichment, "Existing Categories" and *Kerr v Baranow*: A Reply to Professor McInnes' (2012) 52 CBLJ 390.
[53] McCamus, *Introduction* (n 12) 199.
[54] Mitchell McInnes, '*Garland*'s Unitary Test of Unjust Enrichment: A Response to Professor McCamus' (2011) 38 Adv Q 165; Mitchell McInnes, 'Revising the Reason for Restitution: *Garland* Ten Years After' (2015) 57 CBLJ 1; McInnes, *Unjust Enrichment* (n 29) §4.03[1][b]; Chris DL Hunt, 'The Civilian Orientation of Canadian Unjust Enrichment Law: A Reply to Professor McCamus' (2010) 48 CBLJ 498.

1. Principle

McCamus's proposal is based largely on the belief that the juristic reason test would 'wip[e] out all prior law' and require Canadian judges to work from a 'blank slate'.[55] If that was true, it might be a good reason for minimizing *Garland*'s reach.[56] The premise, however, is false. Older authorities remain relevant. That obviously is so for issues other than injustice, but even on that point, the pre-*Garland* precedents continue to inform the analysis. Juristic reasons and unjust factors operate at different levels of abstraction.[57] A transfer is reversible if it is *unjust*. It is unjust because it occurred without *juristic reason*. And in the vast majority of cases,[58] there is a lack of juristic reason because the plaintiff undertook the transfer for a purpose that was defeated by some concept that traditionally served as an *unjust factor*. A contract may be negated by duress,[59] an apparent gift may be undermined by unconscionability,[60] and so on.

2. Precedent

In addition to the problems in principle, McCamus's proposal is incorrect as a matter of precedent. Despite the passage of nearly two decades, there is *no* judicial support for the belief that the juristic reason analysis is confined to 'novel' cases. *Garland* itself said nothing of the kind. In *Kerr v Baranow*, the Supreme Court of Canada heard an appeal arising from the dissolution of a cohabitational relationship.[61] On the issue of injustice, it was a routine case. Cromwell J nevertheless explained that while 'the early cases of domestic unjust enrichment claims'[62] had consistently turned on the unjust factor of free acceptance, that approach was no longer appropriate. 'The need to

---

[55] McCamus, 'Mistake' (n 52) 98.
[56] Even in that situation, McCamus's proposal would create considerable difficulties. What is a 'novel' case? If a 'novel' situation arises for a second time, does it become 'not novel' and thereby attract a different test of injustice? In one sense, of course, *every* case is novel (*Overseas Tankship (UK) Ltd v Morts Dock & Engineering Co Ltd (The Wagon Mound)* [1961] AC 388 (PC); *Overseas Tankship (UK) Ltd v The Miller Steamship Co Pty (The Wagon Mound (No 2))* [1967] AC 617 (PC)), but in a system that evolves incrementally and by analogy, very few cases truly warrant that label. Moreover, even if 'novel' cases could be consistently identified, Canadian unjust enrichment would forever be split in two, some cases decided by the common law's unjust factors and others by juristic reasons, purely on the basis of whether the categories of claim were first recognized before or after 22 April 2004. And significantly, as Birks observed, 'absence of basis is not another unjust factor'—ie the two tests, proceeding from opposite perspectives, cannot be integrated: Birks, *Unjust Enrichment 2nd* (n 12) 114.
[57] In Birks's memorable phrase, unjust factors and juristic reasons occupy different positions within a 'pyramid of limited reconciliation': Birks, *Unjust Enrichment 2nd* (n 12) 116.
[58] Canadian courts have recognized that just as restitution is available if a transfer was undertaken for a purpose that failed, so too, it is available if, from the plaintiff's perspective, the transfer was non-purposive: discussed in n 37. That most obviously is true when the defendant finds or steals the plaintiff's property: *Manning v Algard Estate* 2008 BCSC 1129; *Pershad v Lachan* 2015 ONSC 5290 [44]; *Steele Industrial Supplies Inc v Elliott* 2019 ONSC 3904 [51] (hereafter *Steele*).
[59] *Intermarket Cam Ltd v Weiss* 2021 ONSC 4445 [53].
[60] *Smith (Litigation Guardian of) v Croft* [2015] OJ No 517 (ONSC) [230].
[61] *Kerr v Baranow* (n 7).
[62] ibid [118]. See also *Kingstreet* (n 32) [36].

engage in this analysis of the claimant's reasonable expectations and the defendant's knowledge' had, he explained, been 'overtaken by' *Garland*, which 'mandated a two-step approach to the juristic reason analysis'.[63] Lower courts have expressly rejected the suggestion that juristic reasons are confined to 'novel' cases.[64]

In resisting that conclusion, McCamus places great weight on *BMP Global Distribution Inc v Bank of Nova Scotia*,[65] but that decision offers no support at all. A rogue induced a $900,000 payment between the parties. Writing for the Supreme Court of Canada, Deschamps J resolved the dispute entirely on the basis of the 'doctrine of mistake'. It is true that she made no mention of *Garland* or 'juristic reason', but nor did she mention 'unjust factors'. Remarkably, the phrase 'unjust enrichment' is missing as well. It is, on any reckoning, a strange judgment. It reads like a document from a much earlier era, written some time before Canada's adoption of the unjust enrichment principle in 1954.[66] It is probably best explained as an anomaly, a common law decision written by one of the Court's civil law judges.

B. Duplication

BMP leads into to another challenge for Canadian courts. The Supreme Court of Canada has established that unjust enrichment is a cause of action that invariably requires an absence of juristic reasons. They are not in a position to deny that fact, but lower court judges, especially in British Columbia, occasionally act as if unjust enrichment sits alongside more traditional grounds for restitutionary liability, such as money had and received,[67] *quantum meruit*,[68] and mistake of fact.[69]

That makes little sense. Granted, a claimant is generally entitled to pursue distinct causes of action in the alternative. A single set of facts may simultaneously

---

[63] *Kerr v Baranow* (n 7) [121].
[64] *Annapolis (County) v Kings Transit Authority* 2012 NSSC 401 [6], [56]; *Alberta Union of Provincial Employees v Alberta (Boulter Grievance)* (2016) LAC (4th) 149 [64].
[65] *BMP* (n 31).
[66] *Deglman* (n 9).
[67] *International Longshore & Warehouse Union, Local 502 v Ford* 2016 BCCA 226 [23]–[25] (hereafter *International Longshore*); *Newman v Beta Maritime Ltd* 2018 BCSC 1442 [173] (hereafter *Newman*); *Sivia v British Columbia (Superintendent of Motor Vehicles)* 2016 BCCA 245 [34]; *Barafield Realty Ltd v Just Energy (BC) Limited Partnership* 2015 BCCA 421 (hereafter *Barafield*); *Wong v Jang* 2015 BCSC 1540 [77]; cf *Samji (Trustee of) v Whitmore* 2017 BCSC 1917 [113] ('Although "money had and received" has arguably been subsumed in the law of unjust enrichment, the courts have continued to treat it as a distinct cause of action').
[68] *Shamrock Fencing (1992) Ltd v Walker* 2016 BCPC 244 [9]; *Consulate Ventures Inc v Amico Contracting & Engineering (1992) Inc* 2011 ONCA 418; *Maver v Greenheat Energy Corp* 2012 BCSC 1139; *Gregory N Harney Law Corp (cob Shields Harney) v Angleland Holdings Inc* 2016 BCCA 262 [73]; *Levesque v New Brunswick* 2010 NBQB 150.
[69] *Newman* (n 67); *Canadian Imperial Bank of Commerce v Bloomforex Corp* 2020 ONSC 69 [9]; *Huang v Li* 2020 BCSC 1727 [439]; *1242311 Alberta Ltd v Tricon Developments Inc* 2020 ABQB 411 [190]–[195]; *Radio 1540 Ltd v Muhammad* 2018 ONSC 1377 [73]; cf *Bank of Montreal v Asia Pacific International Inc* 2018 ONSC 4215 [37] (mistake of fact 'originate[d] from the doctrine of unjust enrichment'); *CropConnect Conference Inc v Bank of Montreal* 2020 MBQB 186 [44], [46].

support pleadings for, say, negligence and breach of contract.[70] If successful on both counts, the plaintiff elects between the two. That option exists because negligence and breach of contract constitute distinct grounds of liability. One consists of a careless act that inflicts a loss upon a neighbour; the other arises from the failure to fulfil an enforceable promise. In contrast, unjust enrichment covers the same ground as the traditional restitutionary pleas. The three-part claim, devised in *Pettkus v Becker* and revised in *Garland*, has been applied in all of the circumstances that were historically addressed under various discrete heads. Unjust enrichment is the genus that encompasses the historic species.

As discussed later, some commentators believe that it was an error to adopt a generalized action in unjust enrichment, and argue that restitution should, to some extent, continue to be governed by traditional forms of liability. That is an arguable proposition, at least in theory. It is a preference for the narrow species over the broad genus. In contrast, it is difficult to understand why Canadian law, having embraced a generalized action for unjust enrichment, should allow a claimant to argue *both* genus and species.

There is nothing to be gained by allowing the plaintiff to assert a single proposition in a variety of voices. More importantly, that practice carries risks. Confusion is inevitable as lawyers perceive a multiplicity of actions where only one actually exists. In relying on traditional grounds of recovery—and consequently traditional precedents[71]—courts apply concepts or criteria that are no longer good law.[72] Reliance on the 'mistake doctrine' may, for instance, entail a demand for proof of a 'liability mistake' or a mistake 'between the parties'.[73] One of the benefits of the generalized concept of unjust enrichment is that it has allowed judges to rise above the traditional precedents in order to identify and eliminate inappropriate elements.[74]

---

[70] *Central Trust Co v Rafuse* [1986] 2 SCR 147; *British Columbia Hydro and Power Authority v BG Checo International Ltd* [1993] 1 SCR 12.

[71] *Royal Bank v The King* [1931] 2 DLR 685 (MBKB), 689 is commonly cited for criteria that are no longer good law; *Pinnacle Bank NA v 1317414 Ontario Inc (cob Jay-B Conversions)* [2002] OJ No 281 (ONCA) [10]; *Ontario (Pension Board) v Hosack* [2004] OJ No 1105 (ONSC) [21]; *Walsh v Quoddy Holdings Ltd* 2006 NBQB 356 [38] (hereafter *Walsh*); *Alterna Savings and Credit Union Ltd v Norman* [2006] OJ No 485 (ONSC) [38]; *Perfect Auto Lease & Sales Inc (cob Pals Auto Wholesale) v Gagnier Trucking (Fingal) Ltd (cob Beaudry Bros)* [2007] OJ No 5471 (ONSC) [22]; *Bank of Nova Scotia v Jorgensen* [2008] OJ No 1490 (ONSC) [27] (hereafter *Jorgensen*); *Pattison Outdoor Advertising Ltd v Winchester Real Estate Investment Trust Ltd* 2018 ONSC 4277 [23] (hereafter *Pattison*); *Chevallier Estate v Chevallier Geo-Con Ltd* 2019 ABQB 190 [37]; cf *BMP* (n 31) [21].

[72] Duplication may also lead judges to perceive differences where none exist: *Barafield* (n 67) [54], [63]–[64] (believing that 'damages' for money had and received is measured by the transfer between the parties whereas 'damages' for unjust enrichment extends to profits).

[73] *Balmoral Holdings Inc v Rogers Communications Inc* 2021 BCSC 2330; *Pattison* (n 71) [23]; *Jorgensen* (n 71) [28]; *Walsh* (n 71) [38]–[39]; *CIBC Trust Corp v Bayly* 2005 BCSC 133 [53]; *Dyson Estate v Moser* 2003 BCSC 1720 [43].

[74] *Air Canada* (n 2) 1199; *Canadian Pacific* (n 2) 1157; *Nepean* (n 24) 364 (no justification for distinguishing mistakes of fact and mistakes of law); *Air Canada v Liquor Control Board of Ontario* [1997] 2 SCR 581 [80]; *Central Guaranty Trust Co v Dixdale Mortgage Investment Corp* [1994] OJ No 2949 (ONCA) (no reason for requiring proof of recipient's knowledge of mistaken payment); *Barclays Bank Ltd v WJ Simms Son & Cooke (Southern) Ltd* [1980] 1 QB 677 (QB), 697.

It is counterproductive to abolish unprincipled requirements for the purposes of the action in unjust enrichment but retain them for, say, the action for 'money had and received' or 'mistake of fact'.[75] Failing to decide like cases alike violates the rule of law. Allowing the *same* case to come to different results under different variations of the *same* theory of liability is simply inexcusable.

While that problem persists, there are signs for hope. Several intermediate-level courts have expressly held that the traditional heads of liability have been 'assimilated',[76] 'subsumed',[77] or 'encompassed'[78] in the cause of action in unjust enrichment.[79] At the highest level, *Garland* itself treated the action for unjust enrichment as the sole basis for restitutionary relief.[80]

Unfortunately, even if *BMP* is recognized to be an anomaly, the Supreme Court of Canada has occasionally clouded the issue by suggesting that 'the principled unjust framework and the [traditional] categories co-exist'.[81] Those comments are invariably cited to *Regional Municipality of Peel v Canada*,[82] which predated *Garland* by a decade. In the course of tracing the evolution of restitutionary liability and proposing ways forward, McLachlin J referred repeatedly to both the 'traditional categories' and the 'general principle'. The 'cause of action for unjust enrichment,' she explained, has 'grown out of the traditional categories of recovery[,] is informed by them[, and] is capable ... of going beyond them'. Significantly, however, she stressed that 'the traditional categories of recovery, while instructive, are *not the final determinants* of whether a claim lies'.[83] In most instances, the two approaches are reconcilable, but if a case does 'not fit into an established category of recovery', liability may still be imposed 'on the basis of the general rule'.[84] It necessarily follows that elements included in historical claims, but absent from unjust

---

[75] *Newman* (n 67) [177] ('liability mistake' required for money had and received).
[76] *Chevron Canada Resources v Canada (Attorney General)* 2022 ABCA 108 [43]. See also *Van Camp v Chrome Horse Motorcycle Inc* 2015 ABCA 83 [40]–[41].
[77] *BNSF Railway Co v Teck Metals Ltd* 2016 BCCA 350 [10].
[78] *Best v Hendry* 2021 NLCA 43 [124].
[79] *Ileman v Rogers Communications Inc* 2014 BCSC 1002 [117] ('While the Plaintiff alleges separate causes of action in unjust enrichment and money had and received, the latter is merely a special case of the former'), affirmed by *Ileman v Rogers Communications Inc* 2015 BCCA 260 [21]. See also *Nicholson v Brown Estate* 2018 BCSC 141 [87] (no 'authority for the proposition that there is a restitutionary remedy called "*quantum meruit*" that is independent of the concept of unjust enrichment'); *Canadian Imperial Bank of Commerce v Desrochers* 2020 ONSC 7629 [34] ('mistake in fact is rooted in the principles of unjust enrichment' and requires proof of an enrichment, a corresponding deprivation, and an absence of juristic reason).
[80] *Garland* (n 25) [30]. In most instances, the Court applies the action in unjust enrichment without any discussion of traditional categories of recovery.
[81] *Moore v Sweet* (n 5) [37]. See also *Bhasin v Hrynew* 2014 SCC 71; [2014] 3 SCR 494 [68] (the law has been developed 'through application of an organizing principle without displacing the existing specific doctrines').
[82] *Peel* (n 24).
[83] ibid 789 (emphasis added).
[84] ibid 789.

enrichment, must be abandoned. The traditional categories remain helpful only insofar as they manifest the general action for unjust enrichment.

Cromwell J more recently echoed that view in *Kerr v Baranow*.[85] After referring to traditional 'categories' and 'unjust enrichment', he held 'that there is and should be no separate line[s] of authority for' different contexts. While 'they must be applied in the particular factual and social context out of which the claim arises', 'the legal principles remain constant across subject areas'. '[C]oncern for clarity and doctrinal integrity mandate that "the basic principles governing the rights and remedies for unjust enrichment remain the same for all cases".'[86] There is ultimately only one road to restitution.

C. 'Disaster'

In Canada, restitution is invariably triggered by unjust enrichment. Causes of action that historically generated such relief are now subsumed within the generalized three-part claim. Domestically, the challenges that remain are primarily products of the Supreme Court of Canada's decision to shift from unjust factors to juristic reasons. A different set of challenges—far more profound—has largely arisen outside Canada. A number of academics have rejected the unjust enrichment enterprise, in whole or in part.[87] Restitution, they argue, arises in response to a variety of distinct claims that serve different goals, protect different interests,

---

[85] *Kerr v Baranow* (n 7) [32]–[34].
[86] ibid [33], quoting in part *Peter v Beblow* (n 7) 997.
[87] Robert Stevens, 'The Unjust Enrichment Disaster' (2018) 134 LQR 574 (hereafter Stevens, 'Disaster'); Robert Stevens, *The Law of Restitution* (OUP 2023); Lionel Smith, 'Restitution: A New Start?' in Peter Devonshire and Rohan Havelock (eds), *The Impact of Equity and Restitution in Commerce* (Hart Publishing 2019) 91 (hereafter Smith, 'New Start'); Steve Hedley, '"Farewell to Unjustified Enrichment?"—A Common Law Response' (2016) 20 Edin LR 326. See also Peter G Watts, '"Unjust Enrichment"—The Potion that Induces Well-Meaning Sloppiness of Thought' (2016) 69 CLP 289.

Many of the same critics insist that the grounds for liability must involve both parties. That requirement takes several forms—eg the reason for restitution must be 'bilateral', the defendant must 'accept' the plaintiff's 'performance', liability is impossible unless and until the defendant enjoys a 'genuine opportunity to reject' a proffered benefit: Ernest J Weinrib, *The Idea of Private Law* (Harvard UP 1995) 133–42 (hereafter Weinrib, *Private Law*); Ernest J Weinrib, 'The Gains and Losses of Corrective Justice' (1994) 44 Duke LJ 277; Stevens, 'Disaster' (n 87) 581; Smith, 'New Start' (n 87) 111–13. However it is expressed, the essential idea is that the defendant must be morally implicated in the events that lead to liability.

Given the depth and sophistication of those arguments, a full response must await another day: Andrew Burrows, 'In Defence of Unjust Enrichment' (2019) 78 CLJ 521, 533; Mitchell McInnes, 'Unjust Enrichment: A Reply to Professor Weinrib' (2001) 9 RLR 29; Lionel Smith, 'Restitution: The Heart of Corrective Justice' (2001) 79 Tex L Rev 2115; cf Smith, 'New Start' (n 87) 102. A few comments can nevertheless be offered.

The most contentious cases involve services. Unlike money, services have no inherent value; unlike money and unconsumed goods, they cannot be returned *in specie*. In his contribution to this collection, Robert Stevens additionally observes that whereas a payment is a recognized 'legal event' that necessarily brings the parties together, that is not true with respect to the provision of a pure service. And that difference, he says, is crucial to the question of liability. Whereas a legal event that occurs 'without justification provides the law itself with a good reason for its correction', in a case of mistaken services, '[n]othing, legally, has happened that requires justification': Robert Stevens, Chapter 7 in this volume, Section II.B.2. More broadly, in the absence of an agreement, he states that there should be

and require proof of different elements. It is not a question of historical claims running alongside a generalized action for unjust enrichment. Unjust enrichment, the critics say, is either a cause of action of very limited scope or no cause of action at all. From that perspective, the project that has consumed so much energy over

no liability if, eg, the plaintiff 'mistakenly repair[s the defendant's] car so as to save [the defendant] the inevitable expense of doing so': Section II.B.4. Penner similarly denies the possibility of liability for unrequested benefits: James Penner, Chapter 8 in this volume, text to nn 40–46. See also Stevens, 'Disaster' (n 87) 584; Weinrib, *Private Law* (n 87) 116. As a matter of precedent, however, Canadian law undoubtedly imposes liability for unrequested services as long as the defendant was incontrovertibly benefited: *Sanderson v Campsall* 2000 BCSC 583; *Serbian League of Canada v Stojanovich* 2020 ONSC 105; *Hertz Corp v McLaren Collision Centre* 2016 ONSC 1327; *Gould v Gould Estate (Trustee of)* 2009 BCSC 1528. Stevens's analysis accounts for cases in which the parties had a non-contractual agreement (*Deglman* (n 9)) or the plaintiff removed a condition that would have subjected the defendant to a legal obligation (*County of Carleton v City of Ottawa* [1965] SCR 663), but Canadian law goes well beyond those concepts. It is easy to understand why. As a result of a clerical error, the plaintiff mistakenly replaces the roof on the defendants' house. Upon returning home at the end of the day, the defendants are delighted with the service, especially because they had intended to hire a third party to replace the badly damaged roof. Regardless of any request or acceptance, the Canadian conception of unjust enrichment would reverse the parties corresponding loss and gain.
    There is, however, one aspect of Canadian law that may give pause for thought. Though they come at the point from different directions, many of unjust enrichment's critics insist that the grounds of liability must look to both parties. For the most part, Canadian courts have rejected that proposition. The reason for restitution may be entirely plaintiff-sided: *Air Canada v Liquor Control Board of Ontario* (n 74); *Steele* (n 58) [51]; *International Longshore* (n 67) [25]; *Barafield* (n 67) [66]. Unfortunately, the issue is not entirely settled. When an unjustified transfer occurs within the context of a trust, LaForest J held that 'one must necessarily focus on the defendant's state of mind': *Citadel v Lloyds* (n 6) [51]. It may be possible to explain that rule as an error or an anomaly unique to the principles at play under the equitable form of unjust enrichment known as knowing receipt. *Moore v Sweet* (n 5) presents a more serious puzzle. The Canadian test of injustice is routinely phrased in terms of an 'absence of any juristic reason for the [defendant's] enrichment': *Pettkus v Becker* (n 9) 848; *Peel* (n 24) 784, 789; *Garland* (n 25) [30]; *Pro-Sys* (n 5) [85]; *Kerr v Baranow* (n 7) [32]. In *Moore v Sweet*, however, Côté J said that each of the 'established categories' of juristic reason 'points to a relationship between the plaintiff and the defendant that justifies the fact that a benefit passed from the former to the latter. To focus exclusively on the reason why the defendant was enriched,' she said, 'is to ignore this key aspect of the law of unjust enrichment': *Moore v Sweet* (n 5) [62]; see also *Kerr v Baranow* (n 7) [40] ('The third element of an unjust enrichment claim is that the benefit *and corresponding detriment* must have occurred without a juristic reason') (emphasis added).
    At first glance, Côté J's reasoning appears to accurately reflect the subject's persistent binary nature. The event necessarily joins the defendant and the plaintiff together in a transfer; the remedy simultaneously takes from one and gives back to the other. Moreover, in most instances, juristic reasons do pertain to both the defendant's enrichment and the plaintiff's corresponding deprivation. A gift entails both an intention to give and an intention to receive: *Nishi v Rascal Trucking Ltd* 2013 SCC 33; [2013] 2 SCR 438 [35]. A validly enacted tax explains both the government's gain and the taxpayer's loss: *Re GST* (n 23) 477. A judgment debt requires the defendant to pay and entitles the plaintiff to receive: *Capilano Mobile Home Park v Squamish Indian Band* 2016 BCCA 437. A simple contract involves a give and take of consideration: *Jedfro* (n 32). And so on. As the dissentients in *Moore v Sweet* observed, however, 'it will be near impossible to find an explanation that can simultaneously capture both' the defendant's enrichment and the plaintiff's deprivation 'where multiple parties are involved and wealth is not transferred directly from one to another': *Moore v Sweet* (n 5) [119]. Consider, eg, a case in which a property owner receives a subcontractor's services, but the general contractor becomes insolvent and the subcontract is invalid. The general contract justifies the enrichment even though it involved the defendant owner but not the plaintiff subcontractor: *NR Excavating & Services Ltd v Mand* 2013 BCSC 723 [79]. Contrary to the dissentients, however, a juristic reason does not invariably pertain to the defendant. Assume that a third party hires the plaintiff to confer a benefit on the defendant. When the third party becomes insolvent without paying, the plaintiff looks to the defendant. Restitution will be denied even though the contract that constitutes the juristic reason involves the plaintiff but not the defendant: *Dantzer v CP Loewen Enterprises Ltd (cob Loewen Windows)* 2004 ABQB 5, affd *Dantzer v CP Loewen Enterprises Ltd (cob Loewen Windows)* 2005 ABCA 159. It is not exactly clear what Côté J had in mind when she said that a juristic reason must focus on both the plaintiff and the defendant, and Canadian courts have not otherwise considered the matter. That issue remains to be resolved.

the last eighty years—that is, the effort to explain all instances of restitutionary liability in terms of the three- (or four-)[88] part principle of unjust enrichment—has been nothing short of a 'disaster'.[89] The problem, it is said, is not merely that unjust enrichment fails to fulfil its intended role. Far worse, by forcing all restitutionary claims into a single framework, it frequently imposes liability without justification.

1. General and specific

Those arguments cannot be adequately addressed in this space, but two points can be noted. First, the critics understate unjust enrichment's subtlety and sophistication. It has been said that a simple test of enrichment, deprivation, and injustice cannot sensitively respond to the variety of circumstances that give rise to restitutionary claims.[90] Rules appropriate for a simple mistaken payment are purportedly ill-suited to demands arising from, say, necessitous intervention, compulsory discharge of another's liability, or unauthorized use of property.[91] That argument, however, does unjust enrichment an injustice.[92] As Andrew Burrows explained shortly before his appointment to the UK Supreme Court, unjust enrichment is

---

[88] Whereas Canadian law conceives of unjust enrichment in terms of: (1) an enrichment; (2) a corresponding deprivation; and (3) a reason to reverse the transfer, other systems; add (4) an absence of a defence: *Banque Financière* (n 43) 227.

[89] To quote Robert Stevens' provocative description: Stevens, 'Disaster' (n 87).

[90] In *Kingstreet* (n 32), the Supreme Court of Canada controversially formulated an independent *public* law action for the recovery of constitutionally invalid taxes. Despite acknowledging that 'the retention of improperly collected taxes' might be said, '[i]n a colloquial sense', to 'unjustly enrich[] governments', the Court rejected use of the *private* law action on the grounds that its 'technical interpretation of "benefit" and "loss" is hard to apply in tax recovery cases' and 'the unjust enrichment framework adds an unnecessary layer of complexity to the real legal issues': at [35]. Bastarache J worried that '[s]ome of the components of the modern doctrine ... are rather liable to confuse the proper application of the key principles of constitutional law at issue': at [35]. It is difficult to know what to make of that view. The receipt and payment of money constitutes an incontrovertible benefit and a corresponding deprivation, and constitutional invalidity negates a purported tax as a juristic reason. *Garland* makes for a simple claim in such circumstances. In any event, the important point for present purposes is the Court's recognition that the action for unjust enrichment is capable of accommodating diverse and complex private law claims.

[91] Smith, 'New Start' (n 87) 93. There undoubtedly are claims that *should* be resolved outside unjust enrichment. As Smith says, that is true of most disputes between former cohabitees: at 108. Canadian courts have long used the language of 'unjust enrichment' (and 'constructive trust') to effectively redistribute assets and fulfil expectations engendered by cohabitational relationships: *Pettkus v Becker* (n 9); *Peter v Beblow* (n 7). In truth, however, because it looks forward to what the plaintiff anticipated enjoying, rather than backward to what she transferred to the defendant, such relief is non-restitutionary and hence not a function of unjust enrichment. Fortunately, despite continued references to 'unjust enrichment' and 'restitution', the Supreme Court of Canada recently moved closer to a coherent explanation for such relief when it adopted a doctrine of 'shared family venture' that operates on a partnership model: *Kerr v Baranow* (n 7) [81].

[92] Consider the 'Case of the Destroyed Stamp' in Smith, 'New Start' (n 87) 99–100; Stevens, 'Disaster' (n 87) 578. There were only two existing copies of a rare stamp. The plaintiff owned one, the defendant owned the other. After the plaintiff mistakenly destroyed his stamp, the value of the defendant's stamp doubled. According to Smith, the generalized conception of unjust enrichment appears to demand restitution. The plaintiff's loss was causally connected to the defendant's gain and there was no legal basis for that enrichment. While it would be absurd to find for the plaintiff, Smith says that '[t]here is nothing in the three questions' posed by unjust enrichment 'that explains why there is no liability': Smith, 'New

capable of operating at different levels.[93] While complex claims cannot be resolved on the basis of a broadly stated test, the action's constituent elements run as deep as the circumstances require. The 'single normative principle of unjust enrichment' contains a large number of 'specific normative manifestations'.[94] And while the more specific manifestations may have traditionally existed within more discrete causes of action, the overarching three-part concept has helped to identify unprincipled errors and anomalies within historical claims and ensures that judicial minds are consistently drawn to relevant issues.

In that sense, unjust enrichment can be most accurately compared not with the law of contracts or torts,[95] but rather with the tort of negligence. As with unjust enrichment, negligence's basic elements—that is, duty of care, breach of standard of care, causation of compensable loss—might appear to be too vague to sensitively address difficult cases. When pressed, however, those three elements open up to reveal a wide range of analytical tools. As a result, the same cause of action governs a remarkable variety of claims. The tort of negligence can accommodate acts and omissions,[96] deeds and words,[97] private citizens and public authorities,[98] physical damage and pure economic losses.[99] The same three elements are capable of handling not only simple events like traffic accidents and slip-and-fall cases, but also situations that raise complex scientific, social, or political problems, like psychiatric conditions[100] and injuries suffered *in utero*.[101] Moreover, given its breadth

---

Start' (n 87) 100. But that is true only if the three-part test is given a wide interpretation and applied without regard to principle or precedent. The Canadian model of unjust enrichment requires proof of the defendant's enrichment and the plaintiff's 'corresponding deprivation'. As between the philatelists, there undoubtedly was a 'correspondence' between the gain and loss insofar as they were both caused by the same event. As a term of art, however, 'correspondence' must be defined in context. And whatever meaning the word may bear in other situations, Canadian courts have consistently subjected the action's first two elements to a 'straightforward economic analysis': *Peter v Beblow* (n 7) 990. Since 'the purpose of the doctrine is to reverse unjust transfers, it must first be determined whether wealth has moved from the plaintiff to the defendant', such that 'enrichment and detriment ... are the same thing from different perspectives': *PIPSC* (n 7) [151]–[152]. See also *100193 PEI Inc v Canada* 2016 FCA 280 [21].

[93] Burrows, 'In Defence of Unjust Enrichment' (n 87). The current authors of *Goff & Jones* similarly maintain that work's allegiance to unjust enrichment: Mitchell, Mitchell, and Watterson, *Goff & Jones 9th* (n 12) §1-09.
[94] Burrows, 'In Defence of Unjust Enrichment' (n 87) 529.
[95] ibid 530; Mitchell, Mitchell, and Watterson, *Goff & Jones 9th* (n 12) §11–13; cf Stevens, 'Disaster' (n 87) 575–76. In contrast to unjust enrichment (and contract), torts is a grab bag. There is almost no end to the wrongs that parties may inflict on each other. Different torts are committed in a variety of ways, they infringe a variety of interests, and they are addressed by a variety of claims.
[96] *Horsley v MacLaren* [1972] SCR 441.
[97] *Hercules Managements Ltd v Ernst & Young* [1997] 2 SCR 165; *R v Imperial Tobacco Canada Ltd* 2011 SCC 42; [2011] 3 SCR 45.
[98] *Just v British Columbia* [1989] 2 SCR 1228; *Odhavji Estate v Woodhouse* 2003 SCC 69; [2003] 3 SCR 263.
[99] *R v Martel Building Ltd* 2000 SCC 60; [2000] 2 SCR 860.
[100] *Mustapha v Culligan of Canada Ltd* 2008 SCC 27; [2008] 2 SCR 114; *Saadati v Moorhead* 2017 SCC 28; [2017] 1 SCR 543.
[101] *Montreal Tramways Co v Léveillé* [1933] SCR 456 (duty of care generally owed to unborn child); *Dobson v Dobson (Litigation Guardian of)* [1999] 2 SCR 753 (no duty of care owed by mother).

and accessibility, negligence frequently applies in contexts that were traditionally resolved by more discrete actions.[102]

2. Practical limitations

Given that unjust enrichment is capable of sensitively addressing a wide range of disputes, it is doubtful that litigants would be better served if the generalized claim were unpacked and distinct causes of action were developed for restitution's many sub-categories. But even if a disaggregated approach were thought to be preferable in theory, a different conclusion would be required in practice.

Law is a pragmatic exercise.[103] Granted, scholars have profoundly influenced unjust enrichment's evolution during the last fifty years and there is every reason to believe that they will continue to play a prominent role. On common law (ie judge-made) subjects, however, courts have the final say. From that perspective, scholarship is important insofar as it helps judges to consistently decide disputes in accordance with prevailing precedents, principles, and policies. Theory must be integrated within practice. And in that respect, it is worth noting that unjust enrichment occupies a small part of the judicial calendar. The Supreme Court of Canada is quite active, hearing approximately one restitution case a year, but a lower court judge might expect to deal with unjust enrichment every three years.[104] Moreover, in comparison with tort or contract, unjust enrichment is not well known within the profession. Canadian law schools seldom offer courses on the subject; publications rarely appear. Most lawyers may be able to state the three-part principle, but knowledge of the area does not run deep.

The unified action in unjust enrichment addresses those shortcomings by providing easy access to the many instances of restitutionary liability. Lawyers know that any type of unjustified transfer may be reversed under the three-part test and the principles embedded within its constituent elements. In contrast, split up and scattered amongst a variety of claims, the same principles would frequently escape notice. Errors would occur; claims sounding in one restitutionary sub-category would be framed in another. Similarities between different heads of liability would be obscured; reasoning by analogy would be more difficult. The

---

[102] *Reibl v Hughes* [1980] 2 SCR 880; *Hopp v Lepp* [1980] 2 SCR 192 (informed consent to medical treatment now generally governed by negligence rather than battery); Law Reform Act 1993 (SNB), ch L-1.2, s 2 (replacing traditional occupiers' liability rules with the tort of negligence).

[103] See Lord Burrows, 'Judges and Academics, and the Endless Road to Unattainable Perfection' (2022) 55 Israel L Rev 50.

[104] A *very* rough estimate. In 2021, Canada had approximately 1,200 federally appointed judges and Quicklaw revealed around 400 reported decisions that substantively discussed 'unjust enrichment' or 'restitution'. That number should, however, be viewed in historical context. Between 1954 and 1980 (from *Deglman* (n 9) to *Pettkus v Becker* (n 9)), Canadian courts heard approximately sixteen unjust enrichment cases per year. Between 1980 and 2004 (from *Pettkus v Becker* to *Garland* (n 25)), that number rose to 147 cases per year. And between 2004 and 2021 (from *Garland* to present), the annual average stood at 242.

world of unwarranted transfers would begin to look like it did in the days before the *Restatement* and *Goff & Jones*. Lawyers and judges, unaccustomed to working in the area of restitution, would find it difficult to see the forest for the trees.

A fundamental reorganization of the grounds of restitutionary liability would be particularly difficult to achieve in Canada. Prior to 2004, Canadian law employed a unified conception of unjust enrichment that required proof of unjust factors. *Garland* replaced the traditional common law approach with a civilian-inspired test of injustice that supports recovery in the absence of juristic reasons. Canadian courts managed that transition well enough, but there is no denying that it created significant challenges, some of which persist two decades later. Those problems would be multiplied if the Supreme Court of Canada or the legislatures were to announce that unjust enrichment's critics were right and that the rules governing restitution must be broken up and redistributed amongst a host of independent causes of action. Even before the dust had settled from the last upheaval, lawyers and judges would be expected to remake the law of restitution yet again. It is very difficult to imagine that happening.

V. Conclusion

Eighty years ago, Lord Wright said that 'any civilized system of law is bound to provide remedies for cases of what has been called unjust enrichment'.[105] The reference to 'civilized' systems of law is apt to raise eyebrows today, but the proposition stands. It does not, however, mean that unjust enrichment must be the same everywhere. Some similarities are to be expected among systems that share fundamental values (eg commitments to private property and personal autonomy), especially if they evolved from a common ancestor (eg English common law), but that still leaves room for substantial differences. And in the past fifty years, Canadian courts have increasingly cut their own path. It cannot plausibly be argued that the current Canadian model of unjust enrichment is the product of a grand design. On the contrary, some of its essential features arose by accident. The doctrine of juristic reasons is, in one sense, an inadvertent function of the country's bijuridical nature.[106] Nor can it be denied that the subject continues to face significant challenges. Nevertheless, the situation has much improved in recent decades and there is reason to believe that that trend will continue. Now is the time to redouble the effort to eliminate errors and inconsistencies within unjust enrichment.

---

[105] *Fibrosa Spolka Akcyjna v Fairbairn Lawson Combe Barbour Ltd* [1943] AC 32 (HL) 61.
[106] See n 21.

Conclusion

Sagi Peari and Warren Swain

History, sociology, doctrine, and theory play an important role in thinking and rethinking a phenomenon called 'unjust enrichment'. *Rethinking Unjust Enrichment* traces the historical roots, tackles the societal forces, and contemplates the conceptual grounds and maps as well as the doctrinal fluctuation of unjust enrichment. The four perspectives are also pivotal for placing unjust enrichment within a broader context of such themes as legal history, the relationship between academia and practice, the universality of legal ideas, and the nature and soundness of law reform.

The four perspectives of *Rethinking Unjust Enrichment* are deeply interconnected. The division of the volume into four parts is by no means a rigid one. Thus, the contributors to the 'History' section (Professors Swain, Gupta, and Lin) frequently engage with the doctrinal, sociological, and conceptual dimensions of the field. In significant parts, the works of the contributors to the 'Sociology' section (Professors Sherwin, Sharkey, and Peari) go beyond the sociological context of unjust enrichment. A similar point applies to the contributions to the 'Theory' (Professors Stevens, Penner, Chau and Ho, Wolff, Jaffey, and Jansen) and 'Doctrine' (Professors Chen-Wishart and Ms Hughes, Hedley, McInnes, and Dr Letelier) section of the collection. This fundamental interconnectedness underlies the significance of the multi-layered approach for fully grasping the true nature of unjust enrichment.

As mentioned in the Introduction, we hope that *Rethinking Unjust Enrichment* will facilitate a meaningful dialogue between the supporters of unjust enrichment and its sceptics. Without aiming to reach a consensus, the sceptics have provided in this volume a joint manifesto which discusses such topics as the role of unjust enrichment in society; what we can learn from its historical development; its current doctrinal status; and the way to move forward. Although these are all important considerations, *Rethinking Unjust Enrichment* intends to do more than bundle the voices of sceptics together in a comprehensive, multidisciplinary way. Rather, the collection primarily aims to initiate a constructive dialogue between supporters and sceptics of unjust enrichment. It is hoped that the supporters of unjust enrichment, who may profoundly disagree with much of what is said in this volume, will at least be interested in some of the points made. These chapters are offered in the spirit of genuine academic inquiry and debate.

The sceptics have set the ball rolling. It is time for the supporters to join the call and respond to the concerns, hesitations, observations, and suggestions made in *Rethinking Unjust Enrichment*. Supporters and sceptics both share good motives. Everyone wants to help to shape the law into the best it can be. As a relatively new and evolving body of legal doctrine, it might even be easier to bring about meritorious change than is possible in some long-established areas of private law. This can only be a good thing that benefits the community as a whole. When legal doctrine is securely grounded in sound historical, societal, and conceptual foundations it is more likely to be secure, lasting, and efficacious.

Index

For the benefit of digital users, indexed terms that span two pages (e.g., 52–53) may, on occasion, appear on only one of those pages.

absence of basis approach 43–44, 46, 51–52
   defective consent 255–57
absence of juristic reason 6, 337, 342
academics 4–5
   see also Birks, Peter; von Savigny, Friedrich Carl
   absence of 79–81
   autonomy of law 82–85
      deep research 81
      judicial and legal role of 80–81
      legal change and 77–99
      legal scholars as agents of change 85–87
      nature of law 82–85
      social reality 82–85
      socio-legal theory 85–87
acceptance
   imputation of 172–73
   knowing acceptance approach 233–34
account 11–12, 14–15
act of the court, definition of 66–67
actio de in rem verso 237–38, 245–46
action of debt 89
acts and omissions 349–50
actual contracts 26–27
administration of justice 253, 260, 261, 265, 269, 272
administrative law 4–5, 84
agency of necessity 309
aggravated damages 313
agreement 3
   business relationships 184
   concepts of 14
   motivating cause 183–84
   tacit 181–82, 186–88
American Law Institute (ALI)
   origins 101–2
   Restatement 71
apprenticeship 17–18
Aquinas, St. Thomas 4–5
Aristotle 4–5
   on corrective justice 163–64
Ashhurst, Justice 24
assumpsit 11–12, 22–23
   contractual nature of 14–17
      damages 19–20

      implied 62
   implied promises 25
Atiyah, Patrick 222, 234–35, 282, 285–86
Atkin, Lord 154
Australia 160, 269–70, 290, 291–93, 294, 340–41
   deliberate trusts 119
   social rules 123–24
   unjustified enrichment 5
Austria 145
autonomy theory 296
   autonomy of law 82–85

bad faith 255, 267–68
bargain model of contract 3, 13–14, 19–20
Barr Ames, James 2
Bathurst, Henry 22–23
benefit, tests of 228
   see also inconvertible benefits test
Bigwood, Rick 257
bilateralism condition 230–31, 232
Birks, Peter 2–3, 4–5, 12–13, 64, 77–78, 84–85, 87–93, 97–98, 99, 114–15, 117–18, 143–44, 145–46, 162, 202–3, 208, 219, 220, 221–22, 223, 233, 234–35, 255, 267, 275, 281, 282–300, 302, 320, 331–32
   coherency 87–90
   competing prophets 282–87
   conceptual purity 282–83, 284
   courts 290–94
   duress 265
   exclusivity 283–84
      lesser role for the taxonomy 297–300
   Formula 1 11, 91–93
   legal academics 87–90
   mistake 262
   Roman law 87–90
   technical terminology 92
   terra nullius 283–84
   territoriality 282–84
   theory 287–90
   use value of the theory 294–97
Blackburn, Justice 13–14, 21
Blackstone, William 319
bona fide 33, 35, 44–45, 47, 51–52, 145n.5, 224

bound by law, definition of 60–61
breach of contract 12–13, 22–23, 160–61, 343–44
Buckley, Lord Justice 19
building contracts 290
burden of proof 42–43, 257
Burrows, Andrew 80, 145–46, 220, 232–33, 267, 294, 299–300, 348–49
business networks 124

Campbell, Mat 279
Canada 215–16, 269–70, 290, 292–93, 333–51
  absence of juristic reason 6
  cause of action 340–51
  common law 339–40
  disaster 346–51
  general 348–50
  practical limitations 350–51
    specific 348–50
  duplication 343–46
    Garland's challenges 338–40
    legal context 333–36, 351
    model of unjust enrichment 336–37
    novel claims and beyond 341–43
    precedent 342–43
    principles of unjust enrichment 342
    Supreme Court 342–43, 350, 351
Canaris, Claus-Wilhelm 240–41
Carbonnier, Jean 325–26
carelessness 262–63
Casey, Justice 136–37
causative reason of obligations 47
cause of action 230–34
  Canada 340–51
  narrow unjust enrichment claim 233–34
  objection to claims arising from the receipt of a benefit 230–31
  performance claim 231–33
  for unjust enrichment 340–51
ceteris paribus (all-things-being-equal) 259
change of position defence 149
Chau, Peter 6, 353
Chen-Wishart, Mindy 6–7, 353
child maintenance 16–17, 20–21
children 124
  see also family law
Chin, Nyuk Yin 267
China 3–4, 29–54, 292–93
  absence of basis 46
  academics, role of 84
  ancient China 30–31
  Annotation of Tang Code 30–31
  anti-Rightist Movement 38
  Canon of Laws 30–31

Civil Code 29–30, 36–49, 51–53
civil law, concepts of 38
concept of unjust enrichment 29–30
constituent elements of claims 44–47
criminal punishment 31
defences 46–47
doctrinal uncertainty 51–52
Draft civil codes
  1925 34–35
  1950s 37–38
  1960s 37–38
  1970s 38–39
  1980s 38–39
  1990s 39–43
economic reform 38
enrichment 45
ethical customs 31, 53–54
evaluation of Chinese law of unjust enrichment 49–53
General Principles of Civil Law of the People's Republic of China (GPCL) 39–43
Great Leap Forward 38
historical developments 29–54
Kuomintang era 34–36, 49–50
loss 45
lost property, return of 30–31
Ming dynasty 30–31
nature of law 47–49
open door policies 38
overview 43–44
People's Republic of China (PRC) 36–43
piecemeal approach 39
political impact 49–50
political instability and change 34, 36–37
Qing dynasty 29–31, 40, 52
  late period 31–34
Qing's Draft Civil Code 31–36, 41–42, 43–44, 49–50
remedies 47
Republican Civil Code 34–36
Revolution (1911) 34
self-development, lack of 52–53
shifts of nature 49–50
social rules 123–24
Tang dynasty 30–31
uncertainty in the function of the law of 50–51
Chinese Communist Party (CCP) 36–37
civil law tradition 1–2, 84
civilized systems of law 351
Clark, Charles E. 107
'clean hands' doctrine 118–19
codification theory 70
coercion, state 256

cohabitation agreements 290, 305–6, 329
coherence
  Birksian approach 87–90
  coherent whole 94
    constituent parts, of 94
    of integration 247
Coke, Chief Justice 15
common law 65–66
  claims for money 64
  English law 57, 58, 62, 70
  equity and 117–20
  pragmatism of 4–5
communism 36–37
community standards 6–7
community values 266–67
Conaglen, Matthew 128–32, 133
condictio ob rem 248–49
  see also Roman law
condictiones indebiti 3, 247–48, 323, 325
conditional perfection 185
conflict of laws doctrine 95
Confucianism 122
Coningsby, Justice 15
conscience, objectivity of 138–39, 140
consent 259
  see also defective consent; vitiation
    claimant-consent, concept of 259
    enrichment theory 202–3
    impaired 254, 267
    infancy 19
    qualification of 159–60
    victims' 267
consideration doctrine 19–20
constructive trusts 280, 284, 333–34
  Birksian approach 91
  history of 109
  mistaken payments 177–78
  US approaches 102–3, 104
contract law 1–2, 6, 108–9, 248
  agreement, notion of 3
  capacity to contract 310
  categorization 308–13
    classical model of contract 2–3, 12–13, 16, 26
    cognitive impairment 309
    concept of contract 303
    crises 309
    failed contracts 22–25, 311
    formal contract law, reliance on 124–27
    formalities 20–22
    illegal contracts 309, 311
    injustice 311
    lack of capacity to contract 310–11
    nature of contracts 12–14

    subsequent events 309
  theories 153–60
    claims where either approach is possible 158–59
    importance 159–60
    quantum meruit 153–58
    unenforceable contracts 22–25
contractual liabilities 60–61
  adjustment of 225
  incapacity 17–20
contractual reasoning 22
contractualism theory 189–91
contradictio in adjecto 206
contribution, suits of 60
corrective justice 163–79, 207, 247
  Aristotle on 163–64
  justice, types of 164–65
  legal context 179
  mistake, interrelationship of concept with 163
  mistaken payments 5
  mistakes and the law of restitution 175–79
    principle of unjust enrichment and 166–75
    restitution, interrelationship of concept with 163
  Weinrib's approach to 166–75
    conditionality of certain payments 169–75
    mistaken payments 166–68
    non-gratuitous transfer of value principle 169
    theory of unjust enrichment 169–75
Cotterell, Roger 130
Cotton, Lord Justice 19
counter-restitution 92
covenants, medieval 13–14
Cozens-Hardy MR 19
criminal law 84
critical discourse analysis (CDA) 139–40
  see also linguistics
Cromwell, Justice 346
culture 123, 131–32
customs 122–23
Cutts, Tatiana 181–82, 189, 190–92, 193–94, 195, 197–99
  contractualism 189–91

Dagan, Hanoch 87, 280, 296
damages
  assumpsit 19–20
  physical 349–50
damnum sine iniuria 161
Dannemann, Gerhard 78
Dawson, John P. 105, 116
de lege ferenda 201–3, 206

de lege lata 201–3
de-enrichment 6–7, 201–18
  claimant-defendant relationship, identification of 214–15
  competition of claims 213
  enrichment compared 202–12
    background 202
    correlations 210–12
    enrichment focus 202–10
    general 212
  law of unjust de-enrichment, towards a 212–18
  legal context 201–2, 218
  role of 213
  scope of 214
  unjust de-enrichment claims, scope of 215–18
  unjustness 215
dealing, mode of 125
debt 11–12, 14–15
  deed, absence of 19–20
  discharge of 239–40
  paying others' 314–15
  repayment of 59
  time-barred 32–33
deeds and words 349–50
defective consent 6–7, 254–57, 259
  absence of basis 255–57
  absent consent 254
  attractions of the approach 255–56
  autonomy of approach 256
  burden of proof 257
  conclusory not explanatory approach 256
  elegance of approach 255
  impaired consent 254
  insulting characterization of claimants 257
  lack of fit with the law 256
  normative inadequacy 257
  policy-motivated unjust factors 254
  problems with the approach 255–56
  qualified consent 254
  theory 254
delicts 322
Denning, Lord Justice 156–57, 160–61
Deschamps, Justice 343
deterrence 313–14
Dietrich, Joachim 302
Diplock, Lord 281
disaster 346–51
  general 348–50
  practical limitations 350–51
  specific 348–50
disenrichment 47, 92
  see also de-enrichment

disgorgement 334–36
distributive justice, concept of 72
doctrinal design 237–49
  classification 246–48
  current debates 241–48
  disentanglement 239–41
  explanation 246–48
  failed contracts, unwinding of 243–44
  legal context 237–39, 248–49
  three-party cases 245–46
  unification 239–41
  unjust enrichment and 243–46
doctrine, irreducible indeterminacy of 86–87
donationes mortis causa 305
Drobnig, Ulrich 206
Du Plessis, Jacques 78, 243–44, 245, 246–47
duress 188, 254, 257–58, 260, 272
  unconscientious conduct 265–67
  wrong of 266

East India Company 56
Easterbrook, Frank 299–300
economic justice, concept of 71
economics 108, 144, 166–67, 227
Edelman, James 145–46
education
  see also academics
  expenses 59
    legal/judicial 79–81, 82, 108–9
    programmes 80
    state resources 165
Ehrlich, Eugen 86
Einstein, Albert 256
emergency salvage 309
employment contracts 21–22
English law 215–16, 219, 237–38, 239, 269–70, 290, 292–94, 318–19, 321, 351
  see also United Kingdom (UK)
Enlightenment era 120–21
enrichissement sans cause 324, 325, 326
enrichment theory 150–52, 295, 296–97, 315
  see also de-enrichment
  concept of enrichment 174–75
  de-enrichment compared 202–12
    background 202
    correlations 210–12
    enrichment focus 202–10
entitlement 167, 168
equal freedom, concept of 95
equity 5
  see also palm tree justice
  cases 102–3
  conscionability and 122–23
  critique of 117–20

principles of 60, 65–66, 117
  rational basis of 117
  secular critique of 121
  social duties and 127–40
  Brunninghausen v Glavanics 134–37
  Coleman v Myers 134–37
  enforceable family duties 137–40
  evidence of support 132–33
  family duty 134–37
  fiduciary loyalty 127–29
  fiduciary relationships 130–32
  morality 130–32
error of judgment 263
estoppel 108–9
  promissory 160
  proprietary 305
ethics 122–23, 131–32, 295
Etridge doctrine 254, 260, 272
  non-commercial guarantees 271–72
Evans, William 26–27
executed contracts 20–21
execution proceedings 65–66
express contracts 22, 24–25
  fallacy 13–14

failed contracts 22–25
  unwinding of 243–44
failure of basis 1–2, 228–29
failure of condition 228–29, 232–33
fair play principle 65–66
fairness principle 42, 118, 119, 165, 208, 277, 297–98, 329–30
family duty 134–37
  enforceable 137–40
family law 165, 247–48
  see also marriage
  correct interests 137–38
  family company, definition of 137–38
  technically close relationship, definition of 135
  tightly held family company, definition of 137
fictious contracts 21
fictitious contracts 303
fiduciary duties 119, 125–26
  loyalty 127–29
  relationships 130–32
fields of the law 246–48
Finn, Paul D. 128, 130, 133
Fitzgibbon, Scott 130
Fitzjames Stephen, James 15, 56–57
Flannigan, Robert 128
formality requirements 20
France 210–11, 213, 237–38, 246, 317–32
  see also quasi-contracts

coherence 324–26
enrichissement injustifié 327–28, 329
enrichissement sans cause 324, 325, 326
French Civil Code, reform of 6, 317–18, 323–32
  gestion d'affaires doctrine 323, 324, 325, 326, 327–28
  innominate contracts 330–31
  legal context 317–18, 331–32
  legal system 144
  loteries publicitaires 330–31
  nineteenth-century developments 322–24
  post-reform 326–27
  quasi-contracts, resilience of 322–27
  répétition de l'indu doctrine 323, 326, 327–28
  Roman law compared 322–24
fraud 149, 255, 258
free acceptance 92, 150–51
free will 256
freedom, concept of 95–96
frustration 22–23, 263–64

gain-based remedies 203, 205, 206, 211–12
Gaius 88–89
Gardner, John 164–65
gas companies 171–72
'generated by contract' 12–13
Georgiou, Alexander 181–89, 198–99
Germany 34–35, 116, 210–11, 213, 215–16, 237–38, 239, 243–44, 245, 246, 247–49, 322
  absence of basis approach 43–44, 92–93
  Bürgerliches Gesetzbuch (BGB) 145, 239–42
  Civil Code 29–30, 32–34, 43–44, 49–50
  debt, discharge of 239–40
  expenditure on others' property 239–40
  legal system 144
  natural law tradition 90
  rights infringement 239–40
  void/voidable contracts 239–40
gifts 169, 170, 171, 176, 197–98
Goff, Robert 2–3, 64, 112–14, 143–44, 145, 153, 203, 204, 219, 281, 287–89, 350–51
good faith 105, 204, 261, 277, 306–7
Green, Leon 107
Gupta, Arpita 6, 353

Halliwell, Margaret 302
Handley, Justice 134
Hart, H. L. A. 256
hearings, delayed 65–66
Hedley, Steve 3, 4–5, 13–14, 153, 353
Hegel, George W. F. 167
heresy 317

Ho, Lusina 6, 353
Hong Kong 292–93
Hughes, 353
Hughes, Emma 6–7
Hungary 38

Ibbetson, David 26
ignorance 223
implied contract 2–3, 62, 280, 303, 309–10, 319
   India 69–70
   liability 6
   quasi-contract and 11–12, 69–70, 318–19
   unenforceable 21–22
implied promises 25
improvers 306
imputed contract 6, 231, 234–35
in personam liability 170
in utero injuries 349–50
incapacity 16–17, 254, 255, 260
   contractual liability 17–20
   unconscientious conduct 260–61
   see also mental incapacity
incidental benefits 221–22, 232–33
inconvertible benefit test 92, 145, 228
indebitatus 15, 22–23
India 55–73, 292–93
   see also Indian Contract Act 1872
      British colonial rule 56–57
      case pendency rates 67–68
      Code of Civil Procedure 65–68
      common law jurisdictions, divergence/
         convergence with 70–71
      delaying tactics 67–68
      historical background 56–57
      post-codification 57
      pre-codification 57
      injunctions 67–68
      interlocutory orders 67–68
      judicial delays 67–68
      legal background 55–56
      protracted litigation 65–68
      public authorities/officials 68, 73
      public law, application to 71–72
      public trust, breach of 68
      quasi-contract 58
      vs implied contract 69–70
      salient features of the law 69–72
      scope of the law 65–68
      stays of execution 67–68
Indian Contract Act 1872 6
   codification 55–56
   restitution 58–65
      payment/delivery made under mistake or
         coercion 64–65

      payment due by another 59–61
      performance of non-gratuitous acts 61–63
      providing necessaries 58–59
infancy 17–18
   consent to contracts 19
   enforceable contracts 19
   liability for debt in rent 19
   voidable contracts 19
Infants Relief Act 1874 18
inferences 186
informal dealing 305
inheritance 269–70
injurious reliance 146–47, 160
innominate contracts 330–31
insolvency 245–46, 248
instrumentalism 132
insurance 192, 195–97, 263, 278
intention theory 182–83
inter vivos transactions 269
interceptive subtraction 92, 145
interest rates
   compound vs simple 67
   swaps 290
'interested', scope of the term 59–60
interpretation of contract 126
   objective interpretation 126
   subjective interpretation 126
Ireland 292–93
ius commune 242

Jackman, Ian 302
Jaffey, Peter 6, 198–99, 201, 302, 307, 353
Jansen, Nils 7, 299–300, 353
Japan 34–35, 43–44
joint family venture doctrine 333–34
joint ventures 125, 153
Jones, Gareth 2–3, 64, 112–14, 143–44, 145, 153, 219, 281, 287–89, 350–51
judges and jurists, relationship between 4
judicial delay 67–68
juries 13–14, 16
   discretion of 19–20
juristic reason 341–42
   absence of 6, 337, 342
   approach 205
      doctrine of 351
      established categories of 337
      residual 338–39
just persons 163–64
justice
   see also corrective justice; distributive justice;
      economic justice; palm tree justice
   inherent 118
   interpersonal 232–33

principles of 65–66
remedies, requirement for 207
theory of 72
types of 164–65
justification 97
Justinian 3, 88–89

Kant, Immanuel 82–83, 94–96, 165, 173–74, 296
Keener, William 2
Kenyon, Lord 23–24
Kull, Andrew 102–3, 104, 111, 114

land acquisition cases 68
lawful action 267
lawfully, definition of 62–63
leases 21, 152
Leeming, Mark 315
legal change *see* academics
legal duties 127, 128–29
legal positivism 84–85
legal realism 86–87, 107–8, 112, 115, 280
leges speciales 247–48
legitimate basis, without 42–43
Letelier, Pablo 6, 242, 243–44, 246, 353
lex lata 205–6
liability
  bona fide vs *mala fide* 33, 35, 44–45, 51
  damages, for 38, 39
  exemption of 33
  implied contract 6
  loss-based explanations 6
  multiple 43
  scope of 6–7
  torts, for 38, 39
  types of 12–13
Lin, Siyi 3–4, 353
Lindley, Lord Justice 19
linguistics 139–40
Littleton JCP 18
loans
  contracts (*mutuum*) 322–23
  of money 17
  with infants 17–18
Locke, John 181
loss-based theories 160–62, 205, 206
  claimants 6–7
  deliberate infliction of loss 161
  importance 161–62
  problem 160–61
Lush JJ 21

Macaulay, Thomas 56–57
MacCormick, D. N. 130

MacQueen, Hector 239, 240, 242, 243–44, 299–300
Maine, Henry 11, 12, 26–27, 70
Maitland, F. W. 132–33, 298
Mansfield, Lord 23–24, 102–3, 111, 304
marriage 247–48, 304
  see also family law
Martin, William 163–64
Marxism 36–37
Mason, Justice 133
Matsuoka, Yoshimasa 31–32
McCamus, John D. 341–43
McFarlane, Ben 279–80
McInnes, Mitchell 6, 353
Meier, Sonja 243–44
mental incapacity 188, 260, 261
  see also psychiatric conditions
mercantile customs 16
misprediction 263–64, 289–90
mistake 254, 260, 272
  see also mistaken payments
  corrective justice, interrelationship of concept with 163
  doctrine of 344–45
    of fact 343, 344–45
    fundamental 175–76, 177–78, 179
    law of restitution and 175–79
    liability 344–45
    non est factum 176
    results/consequences distinction 176–77
    unconscientious conduct 262–65
mistaken payments 5
  actual agreement 182–89
  agreement and unjust enrichment, mismatch between 187–89
  agreements and restitutionary liability for 181–99
  argument 191–93
  communication and acceptance 184–87
  Cutt's contractualism 189–91
  finding an agreement 183–87
  general duty to return 193–95
  gifts 197–98
  hypothetical agreement 189–98
  legal context 181–82, 198–99
  objections 193–98
  mispredications 197–98
    payment systems 177
    payor's intent 183–84
    Pinkroccade cases 177–78
    proprietary approach to 222–26
    pure mistaken consequences cases 178
    Scanlonian themes 189–91
    socialization of loss 195–97
    Weinrib cases 166–68, 177

Mitchell, Charles 297–98
monism *see* defective consent; pluralism
moral duties of compensation 207–8
moral norms 165
moral philosophy 295
morality 11, 122–23, 128, 131–32, 140, 164, 173–74, 189
  fiduciary relationships and 130–32
motivation 1–2
Moulton, Fletcher LJ 19
multi-factorial approach 268–69
multiple liabilities 43
multiple stays 65–66
mutatis mutandis 214

natural law 90, 99, 207, 240
natural rights 94–95
nature of law 82–85
Nazism 284
necessaries, exceptions for 18–19
  damages claims 19–20
  debt repayment 59
  education expenses 59
  executory contracts 19
  house repairs 59
  legal expenses 59
  reasonable sums 19–20
  revenue arrears, payment of 59
necessitous intervention 219
necessity 62
negligence 2–3, 37–38, 160, 343–44, 349–50
negligent misrepresentation 258
negotiorum gestio 3, 31–32, 44–45, 48, 239–40, 309, 320, 323, 325, 326
nemo locupletari debet cum aliena iactura 275
Netherlands 206
New Zealand 134, 269–70, 291–92
  accident compensation 192, 196–97
  social rules 123–24
Nicholls, Lord 267, 271
Nisi Prius decision 23–24
non-contractual liabilities 13–14
non-gratuitous transfer of value principle 166, 169
normative unity 233
norms 131–32
North, Douglass 123, 132

Oberdiek, John 190
Oliphant, Herman 107–8
organic unity 94

pacta sunt servanda 159
palm tree justice 117–40
  see also equity; family duty; fiduciary duties; morality; social duties
  historical context 117
  legal context 140
  rationalism, rise of 120–22
  reliance on formal contract law 124–27
  social institutions 122–24
Palmer, George 105
Parfit, Derek 191, 193–91
Parke, Baron 58–59
partnerships 125, 127–28
payment in exchange 158
Peari, Sagi 4–5, 353
Penner, James 5, 198–99, 353
performance, concept of 233, 248, 312–13
  performance claim 231–33
personal liability 58–59, 288–89
  direct 60–61
philosophical theory 82–83
pluralism
  see also defective consent
  2+4 limited 253
  monism vs 253–57
  pluralistic approaches 242
Posner, Richard A. 79–80, 82, 88
Pother, Robert J. 26–27, 323, 324
Pound, Roscoe 86
practical legal scholarship 4
practitioners 4–5
  see also academics
pragmatic restrictors 259
precontractual claims 229
Priel, Dan 302
private citizens 349–50
private law
  see also doctrinal design; quasi-contracts
  academic research 144
  autonomy theories 296
  Birksian approach 78, 89–90, 91–92, 282
  Canada 348n.90
  China 29–30, 50, 52–53
  coherency of 92
  conflict of laws and 95–96
  contractualist accounts of 190
  core rules 277, 278, 281, 301, 304
  corrective justice and 165
  de-enrichment and 209, 210–11
  doctrines of 301
  historical context 11–12, 56, 57, 71, 88–89
  impact on community 276, 354
  India 55
  judge-made approach to 94
  multiple liabilities 314
  organic growth of 94
    penalties 164
    pillars of 222
    property questions 305
    remedies 215–16

Restatement of Restitution and 108
restitution as a distinct category of 106, 110–11, 166, 315–16
restitutionary liability 280
subsidiarity 279
territoriality 283
theory of 5, 173, 272–73, 275
von Savigny's approach 98
Weinrib's approach 82–83, 165
procedural justice 164
property law 1–2, 6, 108–9
  concept of property 303
    definition of 147–48
    estate management 63
    future prospects 234–35
    ownership of property 167
    property-based accounts 199
    renovation works 21
    repairs to property 63
    scope of 305
    theories 147–53
      importance 150–53
      problems 147–50
prophylactic duties 128, 130–31, 132
proprietary base 145, 208
proprietary estoppel 305
proprietary theory of restitution 307–8
psychiatric conditions 349–50
  see also mental incapacity
public authorities 349–50
public policy approach 6–7, 227, 253, 260, 261, 266–67, 269, 271, 272
public trust, breach of 68
punishment 209
pure economic loss 349–50
pure payment 184–85

quantum meruit (for work done) 15, 16–17, 21–25, 62, 227, 229, 311, 343
  contractual claims for 153–55
  non-contractual claims for 155–58
  pleading 26–27
  substance 26–27
quantum valebant (for goods sold and delivered) 15, 24–25, 227, 311
quasi ex contractu 322–23
quasi-contracts 2–3, 11, 51–52, 102–3, 104, 175, 277, 284, 303, 317–32
  appeal for 318–22
    dustbin category 321–22, 331–32
    implied contracts 318–19
    residual miscellany 320
    Birksian approach 91
    definition of 48
    doubtful legacy 327–31
    fundamental differences 327–29

  poor legal reasoning 329–30
  unpredictable decisions 330–31
  enrichissement injustifié 327–28, 329
  French law and the resilience of 322–27
    coherence 324–26
    nineteenth-century developments 322–24
    post-reform 326–27
    Roman law 322–24
  gestion d'affaires doctrine 323, 324, 325, 326, 327–28
  history of 109
  implied contract 11–12
  India 58, 69–70
  legal context 317–18, 331–32
  loteries publicitaires 330–31
  répétition de l'indu doctrine 323, 326, 327–28
  Roman law and 3

rationalism, rise of 120–22
rationality 165, 257, 283
Rawls, John 181
realism see legal realism
reasonable agreement, concept of 189, 198
reciprocity 19–20
recission 256
recoupment 315
recovery of benefits 288
recovery of loss 288
Reed, Lord 294
regulation, prominence of 12–13
rei vindicatio 239–40
relational contracting 12–13
reliance claims 160–61
religion 140
  Medieval institutions 17
  rationalism, impact on 120–22
remedial duties to return payment 185–86
requests 16–17, 62
rescinded contracts 43
restitutio in integrum 207, 255, 260, 266
  origins of the concept 240
restitution
  see also proprietary theory of restitution; unjust enrichment
  big tent approach 2
  concept of 64
  corrective justice, interrelationship of concept with 163
  definitions 208, 334–36
    subject definition 276–81
  doctrine of 62
  equitable conception of 111
  ex ante, primacy of 276–77
  Indian Contract Act 58–65

restitution (*cont.*)
  payment/delivery made under mistake or coercion 64–65
  payment due by another 59–61
  performance of non-gratuitous acts 61–63
  providing necessaries 58–59
  liability 6, 12–13
  liability 32–33
  loss or injury 64–65
  mistake and the law of 175–79
  mistaken payments 5
  power of 65–66
  principle of 65–66
  textbook subject, as a 278–81
    unjust enrichment compared 288
    US origins 103
    wrongdoing vs unjust enrichment 73
    wrongs, for 145
restitutionary claims 153
  damages, concept of 288
  liability 47
  principle 67–68
retributive justice 164
risk-taking 263–64
Robinson, Edward 107
Roman law 3–5, 62, 92, 93, 94, 95, 96, 102, 117, 239–40, 331
  Birksian approach 87–90
    categorization of law 322
    Condictio 89, 96–98, 239–40, 243–44, 248–49
    quasi-contract 322–24
Romer, Justice 156
Rotman, Leonard Ian 130, 131–32
rule of law 87, 118, 120, 139–40, 223, 344–45

Sale of Goods Act 1893 18, 20–21
  see also *quantum meruit*
Scanlon, Thomas 189–91
Scott, Austin 102–3, 110, 128
Scottish law 239, 240
Seavey, Warren 102–3, 110
secret trusts 305
services/service economy 174–75
set-off, right of 245
Sharkey, Nolan 353
Shaw, Bill 163–64
Sherwin, Emily 2, 353
shifting-of-property formula 240–41
Siems, Mathias M. 81–82, 83
Singapore 292–93
'slip-and-fall' cases 349–50
Smith, Henry 301–2
Smith, Lionel 166, 173, 178, 220, 222, 230–31, 233–35, 302

Smith, Stephen 257, 302
social arrangements 124–27
social convention theory 182–83
social duties 123, 132–33
social institutions 122–24
social reality 82–85
socialist market economy 41
socio-legal studies 86
  theory 85–87
sociology 86, 140, 353
Somervell, Lord Justice 160–61
'something for nothing' principle 166, 170
South Africa 239, 240, 245, 264
Soviet Union 37, 49–50
  confiscation requirement 40
  Fundamental Principles of Civil Legislation 1962 38
special contracts 24–25
  see also express contract
'spirit' 85, 87
standard terms 12–13
state sovereignty 95
Statute of Frauds 1677 20, 155–56
statutory control 125
Stevens, Robert 1, 6, 204, 220, 222, 230–31, 232–33, 234–35, 302, 312–13, 353
Stoljar, Samuel 147, 209–10, 222, 234–35, 302
Story, Justice 102–3
subject to contract 157, 160–61
subjective devaluation 92, 145, 228
subjective intention 127
  see also interpretation of contract
subrogation principle 60, 315
subsidiarity 279, 282
substantive rights 89
supply of goods 17
Swain, Warren 3, 302, 353
Switzerland 34–35, 145
systematicity 90, 94

taxation
  indirect 71
  refunds 64, 71, 73
taxonomical approach 4–5, 298
three-party cases 245–46
Tindal, Chief Justice 25
tort law 29–30, 108–9, 248, 297–98
total failure of consideration 22–23, 159–60, 260
totality of sources 94
tracing 306
traffic accidents 349–50
transfer
  appropriateness of 261

INDEX

of benefits 40–41
  fairness of 6–7, 261
  gratuitous *see* non-gratuitous transfer of value principle
  non-purposive 339
  normatively defective 64
  property 146–47
  responsibility to act reasonably 6–7
  subject matter 6–7
  valid 182–83, 186–87, 224–25, 257
  of value 91–92, 169
true contracts 11
trust and confidence, relationships of 267
trusts 125, 127–28
  intention to create 125
Twining, William 80–81

unconscientious conduct 6–7, 257–73
  '2+4' approach 259–60
  administration of justice 260
  appropriateness/fairness of the transfer 259
  bars to rescission 258
  change of position defence 258
  claimant will act reasonably 259
  claimant's impaired consent 259
  community standards 260
  defendant's unconscientious inducement 259
  duress 265–67
    Etridge non-commercial guarantees 271–72
  explains change of position defence 258
  explains ineffectiveness of third-party unconscientiousness 258
  explains voidability 258
  incapacity 260–61
  lack of fit 258
  legal context 272–73
  mistake 262–65
  public policy 260
  some fit 258
  theory 257
  unconscientious inducement 258
    advantages of 258
    problems with unconscientious inducement approach 258
  unconscionable bargains 269–71
  undue influence 267–69
  variation dependent on transaction 258
unconscionability 5, 107–8, 197, 257, 260, 266
unconscionable bargaining 72, 254, 257, 269–71, 272
undue influence 188, 219, 254, 257, 258, 260, 272–73
  presumption of 269

unconscientious conduct 267–69
undue payments 322–23
unenforceability of contracts 20–25
unfairness 72–73
UNIDROIT Principles 241–42, 243–44
United Kingdom (UK)
  see also English law; Scottish law
  Commonwealth countries 112–14
    social rules 123–24
    Supreme Court decisions 157, 289, 348–49
    US, impact on 112–14
United States (US) 291–92, 298
  American legal realism 86–87, 107–8, 115
  'big tent' approach 104, 115–16
  First Restatement of Restitution 101–5
  post-First Restatement events 105–9
  global impact 112–16
    Commonwealth countries 112–14
    England 112–14
    tripartite approach 114–16
  historical developments 2
  legal context 101
  modern American restitution 109–12
  Restatement on the Law of Restitution 71, 143–44, 145, 350–51
  Restatement (Third) 109–12
  restitution in 101–16
unjust, definition of 204–5
unjust enrichment
  see also restitution
  agreement and, mismatch with 187–89
  alternatives to 6–7, 143–62
    contractual theories 153–60
    legal context 143–46, 162
    loss-based theories 160–62
    options 146–47
    property theories 147–53
  causative event, as a 334–36
  cause of action for 230–34, 340–51
  claims for payment for goods and services 227–29
  concept of 5–6, 102–3, 302–3, 344–45
  concurrent versus subsidiary claims 46
  critiques of 144–46
  definition 104, 334–36
  disintegration of 248–49
  distinct field of law, recognition as a 246–47
  doctrinal design 243–46
  doctrine of 72, 315
  emerging (lower level) categorization 301–15
    cohabitation 305–6
    contract 308–13
    improvers 306

unjust enrichment (*cont.*)
  informal dealings 305
  multiple liabilities 314–15
  problems 301–4
  property 304–8
  solutions 301–4
  tracing 306
  wrongs 313–14
  final determinants 345–46
  future prospects for 219–35
  general principles of 171–72
  history of 2–4, 11–27
  improved framework 222–30
  institutional problem 234
  narrow claims 233–34
  path forward 234–35
  problems with 230
  property and contract 234–35
  restitution compared 288
  role of 275–316
  sceptics of 1–2
  scope of 6
  specific normative manifestations 348–49
  successfulness of 143–44
  theory of 169–75, 219–22
  tort, distinguished from 37–38
  underlying justification 234
  unhistorical, as 5
  unified law, arguments against 12
  universal concept of 5–6
  unjust de-enrichment *see* de-enrichment
  unjustified enrichment compared 111–12, 115–16
unjust factors 1–2, 6–7, 70, 144, 145, 159–60, 162, 204–5, 228–29, 254, 255, 256, 258, 261, 272–73, 289–90, 293–94, 299, 308, 315, 336–37, 342, 343
unjust sacrifice 146–47, 160, 210
unjustified enrichment 5, 240–41
utilitarian ideology 122

value
  juridical significance of 166–67
  monetary 214
  theory 167, 312
  value-free society 122
values 123, 131–32, 284
Vavasour, Serjeant 18

venire contra factum proprium 217–18
virtual pricing model 166–67
virtue-based accounts 199
vitiation 159–60, 224, 254, 255, 256
Vizioz, Henry 324–25
void/voidable contracts 20–21, 43, 239–40, 256, 258, 262
voluntariness rules 259
voluntary payments 61
voluntary/involuntary action 163–64
voluntary/participatory enrichment 92
von Caemmerer, Ernst 240–41, 248
von Savigny, Friedrich Carl 4–5, 77–78, 84–85, 93–99
  Formula 2 96–98
  mixed foundations of scholarship 93–96
  technical terminology 94
vulnerable parties, protection of 272

Walker, Lord 264
Watts, Peter 302
Webb, Charlie 147, 150, 198–99, 307
Weinrib, Ernest J. 5, 82–83, 128, 165, 166–75, 210, 230–31, 295–96
  conditionality of certain payments 169–75
  mistaken payments 166–68
  non-gratuitous transfer of value principle 169
  theory of unjust enrichment 169–75
West Africa 154
Wilburg, Walter 145, 240–41, 248
will theory 3, 11
wills 269
windfall gains 192, 197–98, 308
'without legal basis' requirement 240–41
Wolff, Lutz-Christian 6–7, 353
Wood, Thomas 4–5
Woodward, Frederic 2
World War II 105–6
Wright, Lord 155, 351
written contracts 20
wrongdoing 73
  constructive 258
  defendant 259
  harmful effects of 164
  passive 258
  wrongful conduct 130

Zimmermann, Reinhard 78